Starkman
2011
EAP 500

Fourth Canadian Edition

English Skills WITH READINGS

EXAMINING PARAGRAPHS

John Langan
Atlantic Community College

Sharon Winstanley
Seneca College

Claire Jewell
Acadia University

McGraw-Hill Ryerson

Toronto Montréal Boston Burr Ridge, IL Dubuque, IA Madison, WI New York
San Francisco St. Louis Bangkok Bogotá Caracas Kuala Lumpur Lisbon London
Madrid Mexico City Milan New Delhi Santiago Seoul Singapore Sydney Taipei

English Skills With Readings: Examining Paragraphs
Fourth Canadian Edition

ISBN-13: 978-0-07-095787-9
ISBN-10: 0-07-095787-8

1 2 3 4 5 6 7 8 9 10 TCP 0 9

Printed and bound in Canada

Care has been taken to trace ownership of copyright material contained in this text; however, the publisher will welcome any information that enables them to rectify any reference or credit for subsequent editions.

Vice President, Editor-in-Chief: Joanna Cotton
Sponsoring Editor: Lisa Rahn
Marketing Manager: Michele Peach
Developmental Editor: Sarah Braithwaite/Jennifer Oliver
Editorial Associate: Marina Sequin
Supervising Editor: Graeme Powell
Copy Editor: Evan Turner
Production Coordinator: Sharon Stefanowitz
Cover Design: Michelle Losier
Cover Image: © Masterfile
Interior Design: Michelle Losier
Page Layout: Aptara®, Inc.
Printer: Transcontinental Gagne

Library and Archives Canada Cataloguing in Publication

Langan, John, 1942-
    English skills with readings : examining paragraphs edition / John Langan, Sharon Winstanley, Claire Jewell. — 4th Canadian ed.
      Includes index.
      ISBN 978-0-07-095787-9

    1. English language—Paragraphs. 2. English language—Rhetoric. I. Winstanley, Sharon II. Jewell, Claire
PE1439.L35 2009
808'.042   C2009-901425-4

www.mhhe.com

Contents

Punctuation

Word Use

SECTION FIVE

Twelve Reading Selections 451

Knowing Ourselves and Our Values 457

Education and Self-Improvement 480

Human Groups and Society 504

Preface

The *English Skills with Readings* Approach

English Skills with Readings, Fourth Canadian Edition, helps students understand, learn, and apply the basic principles of effective writing and reading comprehension. Focusing on challenges faced by first-year Canadian students, this text relies on a direct, prescriptive, and supportive approach that gives confidence to emerging writers.

English Skills with Readings bases its approach on four essential principles that are keys to effective writing for any medium: **unity, support, coherence, and sentence skills.** This time-tested philosophy aims to de-complicate writing.

In addition to the four bases, other significant factors are involved in writing effectively. First, in order to ensure that writers master the fundamentals, paragraph writing precedes essay writing. This text teaches composition principles using paragraph models and assignments to develop the student's ability to support ideas within a variety of paragraph forms. Writing an effective paragraph is then applied to essay composition later in the text.

Second, writing skills are developed and worked through in stages to create a more manageable learning experience. This edition devotes continued attention to each stage of the writing process, with enhanced focus on prewriting and revising as essential activities.

Third, writing is presented as a learnable process that includes self-expression and critical reflection. The text's presentation of good writing as an attainable goal that requires genuine effort offers realistic advice to students willing to participate in the process of learning to communicate effectively.

Fourth, this edition of *English Skills with Readings* acknowledges that writing from personal experience is a good way for "under-prepared" or unwilling students to begin writing. After students master the skill of presenting a point and providing support from personal experience, they are ready to write from a more objective stance. Promoting writing in the third-person voice where appropriate, the text requires students to extrapolate from their own reasoning or externally derived sources of information.

Fifth, reading and writing are inextricably connected, and pratising one helps the other. Accordingly, this edition presents twelve professional essays that prompt students to see how professional writers use composition principles, and demonstrates their application in writing assignments for both paragraphs and essays.

Text Organization

- Section One, "Basic Principles of Effective Writing," focuses on the first three bases while introducing the fourth base.
- Section Two employs the four bases to paragraph development.

- Section Three applies the four bases to multiple-paragraph and research essays.
- Section Four serves as a concise handbook of sentence skills.
- Section Five contains twelve reading selections.

Features

- **Focus on paragraph mastery:** Devoting six chapters to paragraph development, students learn how to create a well-crafted paragraph prior to extending their skills to essay writing.
- **Emphasis on academic writing:** Requiring the use of the third-person voice and viewpoint where appropriate, students learn to meet the expectations of writing in a post-secondary environment.
- **The importance of writing as a process:** The text underscores that one of the most important factors in writing effectively is recognizing that writing is a process with distinct steps.
- **Prewriting as an iterative activity:** Repeatedly advising readers to spend significant time on prewriting in order to discover and clarify ideas, examples demonstrate students doing at least two stages of prewriting.
- **Visual rhetoric:** Using photos and illustrations as writing prompts to stimulate creativity and to explain the various rhetorical modes makes the material engaging not just for visual learners, but for all students.
- **Practise, practise, practise:** Activities, writing assignments, and review tests provide students with ample opportunities to practise what they learn.
- **Engaging professional essays:** Twelve readings, five of which are new, reinforce the concepts and rhetorical modes taught in this text.
- **Connection between reading and writing:** Subscribing to the philosophy that reading and writing are linked, the twelve professional essays enable students to practise their critical thinking, advance their reading skills, and ultimately improve their writing.
- **Accessible for all learners:** Clear explanations, frequent examples, and *Further Insight* boxes that feature language tips, make the material accessible for all students, particularly those who are second-language acquisition learners.

Pedagogy

- **Learning Outcomes** open each chapter to help students preview chapter content and study effectively.
- **Checklist of Learning Outcomes** end each chapter so students can review key concepts.
- **Activities** appear after each concept so students can immediately apply the material, which reinforces learning.
- New! *Challenge* boxes give students an opportunity to stretch their abilities with more depth.
- New! *Further Insight* boxes provide basic language instruction for students who may need quick referral for difficult issues.
- **Writing assignments** guide students step-by-step through a writing task from prewriting through revising in an effort to demonstrate that the initial stages are not difficult.

What's New in the Fourth Canadian Edition

Colour interior design: Focus groups with faculty and students uncovered the desire for a colour textbook . . . we listened!

Created for visual learners: Since students respond readily to visuals and must learn to evaluate images critically, photos and images appear throughout the text to enhance the understanding of rhetorical techniques, and to prompt writing.

Academic examples: Throughout the text, new third-person exemplars have been added, replacing many written in the first-person.

More academic writing assignments: Added to the end-of-chapter material, new writing assignments, which require the use of the third-person voice and viewpoint, acquaint students with writing at the post-secondary level. They also expose students to a greater range of career-related possibilities for using various modes in their writing.

Increased emphasis on prewriting and revising: A stronger focus on prewriting and revising, the text provides additional techniques for each.

New chapters on research skills and research writing: Two new chapters have been added to respond to academic and professional expectations for student accuracy when writing research essays.

Five new professional essays: Chosen for their appeal and relevance, these high-interest selections will engage students.

Major structural and content changes in the Fourth Canadian edition are outlined below.

Section One: Basic Principles of Effective Writing

- The content in the six chapters of Section One has been rearranged so that discussion and activities regarding basic writing principles and structures are presented in a more logical order. Chapter 1 now provides foundation material and activities, while Chapter 2 includes all elements of the writing process, including more prewriting and revising techniques.
- Chapter 1, "An Introduction to Writing," launches the concept of the "rhetorical triangle" or "writer's triangle" of subject, purpose, and audience, so that new writers will be able to incorporate this understanding from the beginning of their writing.
- Chapter 1 encourages students to become familiar with objective writing from the onset, which is reinforced throughout Sections One, Two, and Three, as well as in the writing assignments in Section Five.
- Chapter 2, "The Writing Process," in its exploration of prewriting, presents a new technique, cubing, as a *Challenge* activity for students who are able to undertake topics with a more analytic approach.
- Chapter 2 presents outlining as an essential step, and this edition presents a modified outlining template.
- Chapter 2 presents a new paragraph model written in the third person, "Becoming Canadian," which provides an example of objective writing.
- Chapter 3, "The First and Second Steps in Writing," has been reorganized so that the first step, "Make a Point," is immediately followed by in-depth direction and

practice in that skill set. Thus, the important instruction that helps students to determine if a topic sentence is an announcement, and if it is too narrow or too broad, is presented so that it is immediately useful. Similarly, the second step, "Support the Point with Specific Evidence" is presented more clearly by allowing the pedagogical elements immediately preceding the extensive practice exercises.

- Chapter 3 provides instruction on the types of transitions that should be used in various circumstances, which are then supported through ample practice activities.

Section Two: Paragraph Development

- Each chapter provides models and examples of objective writing, and many offer additional instruction in specific skills to assist students to master a particular style. For example, in Chapter 7, "Narrating an Event," readers see examples that demonstrate when an objective narrative might be required—such as in professional reports—followed by tips to help them achieve the required objectivity.
- Chapter 7, "Narrating an Event," discusses a greater variety of narrative writing types and emphasizes the relevance of narrative writing both in the post-secondary environment and in the real world.
- Chapter 9, "Providing Examples," explains how to use extended examples, such as anecdotes and analogies, to organize a paragraph.
- Chapter 11, "Examining Cause and Effect," clarifies the relationship between the two techniques, and cautions against the misinterpretation of that relationship. Graphic organizers that illustrate cause and effect have been added.
- The section on logic and logical fallacies in Chapter 15, "Arguing a Position," has been completely rewritten to improve clarity. This chapter also includes a discussion and illustration of the relationship between fact and opinion.

Section Three: Essay Development

- Chapter 17, "Research Skills," provides instruction regarding the process, goals, and techniques writers need in order to undertake research with the sophistication required at the post-secondary level. Presented in five distinct steps that take readers through the research process using library and Internet sources, this chapter reinforces the need to evaluate and use sources effectively. Students follow these steps by performing their own research tasks, which not only gives them concrete practice, supports an essay task in the next chapter.
- Chapter 18, "Preparing a Research Essay," guides readers through six writing steps specific to the research paper while reinforcing the writing process concepts presented earlier. This chapter offers crucial instruction to avoid plagiarism by covering paraphrasing, summarizing, quoting, and documenting material. It addresses both MLA and APA documentation styles, making it relevant for a wide range of writing projects.

Section Four: Sentence Skills (Grammar, Mechanics, Punctuation, Word Use, and Practice)

- Self-testing and self-review chapters ("Sentence Skills Diagnostic Tests," "Combined Mastery Tests," "Editing Tests," and "Sentence Skills Achievement Tests") are now available on the text's Online Learning Centre (www.mcgrawhill.ca/olc/langan). Streamlined and re-designed for an online environment, students can diagnose their strengths and weaknesses as well as review material from Section Four with the benefit of receiving automatic feedback. Professors can use these tests for assessment if desired.

- In response to reviewer feedback, the following chapters have been removed from the text and are now located on the Online Learning Centre:
  - "Manuscript Form"
  - "Improving Spelling"
  - "Vocabulary Development"
- "ESL Pointers" content has been dispersed throughout the text where appropriate instead of relegating the material to one chapter.

Section Five: Readings

- Five new reading selections have been included in the Fourth Canadian Edition, all of them Canadian. The new selections provide a wide range of contexts, styles, tones, and lengths. The readings offer a range of reading levels to allow instructors to accommodate the diverse nature of English classes. These readings model the skillful writing accomplishment outlined in the various rhetorical modes presented in *English Skills with Readings,* and present emerging writers with thoughtful insight relevant to Canada in the twenty-first century.
- In "The Unexpected Mazto," the author reflects upon the role charity played in reaffirming the place of community that helped her survive as a Jew in Eastern Europe during World War II.
- Another reflection, given as a keynote speech in a conference for specialists in youth issues, looks at the role of adults when children run into conflict with society, in "Surviving the Journey."
- Columnist Joe Fiorito returns to discuss food, and this time with commentary on the need for more attention to Canada's food production, in "Our Home and Native Land."
- The concept of literacy is addressed as "Many Forms of Literacy" by an avid sailor who marvels at the value of various accomplishments.
- Responding to dominance of the Internet in modern life, a guide to designing internet pages, "Website Design: Keep Your Audience in Mind" draws a parallel between a designer's approach to website design with the basic concepts of writing that are presented in this text.

Supplements

Superior Service

Primis Online Primis Online gives you access to our resources in the best medium for your students: printed textbooks or electronic e-books. There are over 350,000 pages of content available from which you can create customized learning tools from our online database at www.mhhe.com/primis.

CourseSmart CourseSmart brings together thousands of textbooks across hundreds of courses in an eTextbook format providing unique benefits to students and faculty. By purchasing an eTextbook, students can save up to 50 percent off the cost of a print textbook, reduce their impact on the environment, and gain access to powerful Web tools for learning including full text search, notes and highlighting, and email tools for sharing notes between classmates. For faculty, CourseSmart provides instant access to review and compare textbooks and course materials in their discipline area without the time, cost, and environmental impact of mailing print examination copies. For further details, contact your *i*Learning Sales Specialist or go to www.coursesmart.com.

Instructor Resources

Online Learning Centre at **www.mcgrawhill.ca/olc/langan** The Online Learning Centre for *English Skills with Readings* features learning and study tools, as well as a password-protected Instructor's Site with downloadable supplements, including the complete Instructor's Manual and Microsoft PowerPoint presentations for Sections One through Four.

- The **Instructor's Manual** contains hints and tips for approaching the course, a model syllabus, and supplementary activities and tests.
- **PowerPoint® Presentations** summarize text content and outline main concepts and themes for each chapter.

Student Resources

Online Learning Centre at **www.mcgrawhill. ca/olc/langan** The Online Learning Centre for *English Skills with Readings* features learning and study tools such as learning outcomes, self-quizzes, internet-based questions, web resources, and bonus material on spelling, formatting, and vocabulary development.

Catalyst at **www.mcgrawhill.ca/olc/catalyst** With *Catalyst,* students can go beyond the book to practise and sharpen their writing skills in a fun and interactive online environment. For 40 grammatical skill areas, this resource provides instruction and examples through its streaming audio and video, and 4000 practice exercises. *Catalyst* also offers 12 writing tutors that teach students the patterns of organization step-by-step, includes guidelines on how to avoid plagiarism, introduces Bibliomaker to help create a works cited page quickly, and much more.

Acknowledgements

I offer my heartfelt gratitude to the editors at McGraw-Hill, Higher Education, who have encouraged me through every step of this worthy endeavour. It is only through their dedicated expertise, delivered through their wisdom, wit, and warmth that I could have seen my way through. I thank especially Sponsoring Editor Lisa Rahn, Developmental Editors Sara Braithwaite and Jennifer Oliver, as well as so many who have helped through every stage of production. Thanks also go to my personal supporters, including my mother, Jean Jewell, and my partner, Ted Longley, and to my marvelous students in English 1306 at Acadia University.

Finally, I would like to thank the reviewers who provided helpful ideas and feedback for the Fourth Canadian Edition:

Marsha Hodgson, *Algonquin College*
Dina Chipouline, *Seneca College*
Janet Allwork, *Douglas College*
Joanne Bakker, *Niagara College*
Barry Fox, *Acadia University*
Ingrid Hutchinson-Young, *Fanshawe College*
Rhonda Sandberg, *George Brown College*
Rodica Vasiliu, *St. Clair College*
Sylvia Vrh-Zoldos, *Centennial College*
Danny Wrench, *Kwantlen University College*
Deanna Gilholm, *Nova Scotia Community College*
Wendy Struthers, *Centennial College*
Jennifer Jianghai Mei, *Centennial College*
Prita G. Sethuram, *Centennial College*
Wendy Morgan, *Fleming College*
Linda Bamber, *George Brown College*
Donna Fairholm, *Humber College*
Veronica Abbass, *Seneca College*

Claire Jewell
Acadia University

Readings Listed by Rhetorical Mode

Note: Some selections are listed more than once because they illustrate more than one rhetorical* mode of development.

Narration

Description

Examples

Process

Cause and Effect

Comparison or Contrast

---

*The word "rhetorical" refers to a particular structuring method or format chosen by a writer for its effectiveness in communicating the selection's message to an audience. Many of these selections, and most writers, make use of more than one rhetorical mode or format in any one piece of writing; for example, an essay may be *narrative* in basic style, but may also *contrast* two different ideas.

Section 1

Basic Principles of Effective Writing

Preview

Section One begins by introducing you to the book and to paragraph form. As you work through the brief activities in "An Introduction to Writing," you will gain a quick understanding of the book's purpose, how it is organized, and how it will help you develop your writing skills. After presenting a series of important general factors that will help you create good paragraphs, Section One describes four basic steps that can make you an effective writer. The four steps are:

1) Make a point.

2) Support the point with specific evidence.

3) Organize and connect the specific evidence.

4) Write clear, error-free sentences.

Explanations, examples, and activities are provided to help you master the steps. (You will also be referred to Section Four of the book for more detailed treatment of the fourth step.) After seeing how these steps can help you write effective paragraphs and essays, you will learn how they lead to four standards, or "bases," of effective writing: unity, support, coherence, and sentence skills. You will then practise evaluating a number of paragraphs in terms of these four bases.

Chapter 1

An Introduction to Writing

After reading this chapter and completing its activities, you will

- recognize writing as a learnable skill and a process of discovery;
- discover the benefits of paragraph and essay writing;
- identify the basics of effective writing;

- understand the roles of purpose, audience, and point of view in writing; and
- apply those basics in writing a simple paragraph.

First-semester students in Canadian colleges face multiple challenges, many of which relate to the need to communicate effectively. Although you and your fellow students arrive in the classroom from diverse backgrounds and educational experiences, you share the desire to build a future for yourselves. This future and your career in the twenty-first century will depend on your ability to communicate clearly in English. This book's general aim is to help you to do so.

Many students reveal a feeling of *communication anxiety* about the writing demands they face in college. This anxiety is nearly always what keeps these students from expressing their ideas clearly, whether it is rooted in past school experiences or in the difficulties associated with writing in a second or third language. The specific aim of *English Skills with Readings* is to encourage students to feel confident about college writing by providing a realistic, experience-based, and step-by-step approach to writing tasks.

Consider that writing is simply communicating in a set of characters or symbols to express some meaning. Writing is just one significant part of your lifelong process of communicating with others. No one is a "born writer"; in fact, all writers must learn the same lessons if they are to reach an *audience* for whatever *purpose* they may have. The lessons and rules for effective writing developed gradually from the success or failure of those who tried to write in various ways. Patterns and rules grew from seeing "what worked." Writing is mainly a matter of practice, perseverance, and gradually increasing skill. Becoming an effective writer involves no mysteries and no impossible tasks.

English Skills with Readings, fourth Canadian edition, explains the basic process and principles of writing so that you can master writing skills one step at a time, and then practise them as you review each skill, Ultimately, you will be able to face your college writing assignments with confidence, rather than anxiety.

APPROACHING WRITING

As you work through the text, keep in mind the guiding principles outlined here:

- Writing is a skill; anxiety and confusion decrease as writers learn to follow clearly set out and workable methods and practices.

- Writing often depends on the attitude of the writer. Because writing is self-expression, it is closely tied to feelings of self-worth, so its quality will increase as the writer feels competent. Working on writing in stages and being determined to write well are keys to a good attitude about writing.

- Writing is a process of discovering, arranging, and revising thoughts, and clear expression of ideas results from understanding and following this process.

- Writing the traditional paragraph or essay, whose main point is logically supported, is the best preparation for effective communication in most media.

Begin by considering each of these themes in turn, knowing that they can help you approach writing with more confidence and stronger motivation.

Writing is a Skill

Most people, if they are honest, feel discomfort about putting thoughts on paper. Writing exposes the writer: to himself or herself, and to others. When thoughts and feelings are on paper and language difficulties are manifested, many writers feel vulnerable. Perhaps nowhere is anyone more vulnerable than in the classroom, where judgments have mark values. Students feel *they*, not their writing skills, are being judged.

Students may then jump to two wrong conclusions: first, that only they find writing difficult; and, second, that they lack the talent to write well. Attitudes such as these lead to avoidance behaviours so that some students delay trying to improve and may even shun writing altogether. This can create a self-fulfilling prophecy where, as trying results in failing, there seems to be no reason to even try. From this comes a cycle of self-defeat and hopelessness. Such a situation calls for a more positive attitude about writing.

To avoid hopelessness, approach writing with a sense of reality: begin with the idea that *writing is a skill*. All skills are acquired and mastered in stages. Like learning to cook, drive, or design websites, learning to write is a step-by-step process. Writing requires the willingness to learn, the patience to revise and correct, and the determination to work through each step.

Writing well consists mainly of a conscientious approach to a series of tasks; it is not a gift or mystery, nor does it result from a flash of inspiration. Clear writing requires intense thinking and analytic skills—challenges for anyone. It can be demanding to find words and phrases that accurately translate ideas to paper, or difficult to decide what is worth keeping, out of hours of writing. It can be frustrating to discover that an apparently simple topic has become complex. Yet, it can also be rewarding. *Writing well is hard work,* but learning any skill requires work. There is significant achievement in owning the skill of effective communication. Once acquired, the ability to write can continue to develop and serve you throughout your future in any way that you need. Writing well will reward you by replacing anxiety with confidence.

Now, think about some attitudes about writing that may help you see the writing process realistically.

Writing is Affected by Attitude

Consider how you may have developed any attitudes you may have about writing. Have your experiences been mainly positive, or have there been negative associations with former writing activities?

- *How do you feel when you face beginning a writing task?* Many people feel *vulnerable.* They feel their shortcomings will be exposed on paper, either in their ideas or in the way they express them, or both. A good way to manage this feeling is to write *only for yourself* when you are working on the first stages of the writing process; visualize yourself as *your only audience* as you begin. The more often you do this, the less exposed you will feel.

- *Do you worry about your instructor's evaluation of your first assignments?* Every student does. You do not know your instructor—your audience—the first few times you submit an assignment in a new course. You may worry that your instructor will see you as less than intelligent or "bad at writing" when he or she marks your first submissions. In reality, your college English or communications instructor is an ally and is *the audience you need,* not your enemy. Your instructor is willing to see your work positively and to share his or her knowledge with you. Start by feeling comfortable about asking for help and not expecting immediate perfection of yourself.

Writing is a Process of Discovery

Believing that writing is a natural gift leads students to the false assumption that writing flows in a single straight line from the writer's mind to the page. Good writing is never a simple one-draft trip to a flawless final text.

Writing is a process of discovery and occurs in a series of steps. The process loops and zigzags in many directions as the writer finds new ideas and connections between thoughts and associated feelings and mental images. Most writers do not know what they want to say or what their focus will be until they follow the paths of their thoughts in writing. Look at the following illustrations of the writing process:

Seldom the Case
Starting point ⟶ Finished paragraph

Usually the Case
Starting point ⟶ Finished paragraph

As you write, you will find new avenues of thought, change direction, or even reverse your thinking. Writers reflect upon these discoveries throughout the process, and in turn develop even more insight into new thoughts, feelings, and images. An example would be Farida, the writer of this chapter's sample paragraph. She was asked to write about some aspect of college life. Only after freewriting on a wild assortment of college-related topics did she realize that most of her details concerned using the computer and her college's server. She only discovered her subject in the course of preliminary writing.

Allow your ideas to emerge by keeping an open mind. You may work out an opening sentence and realize suddenly that this is your conclusion. Or you may find yourself caught up in explaining some detail, only to find it could be the main point of your paragraph. Do not feel that you must proceed in a linear fashion when you write. What is important now, as you begin to write, is to know that writers usually do not know their precise destination when they start out. Be relaxed and patient with yourself and understand that the directional shifts in thoughts and directions are not mistakes. In doing so, you are using a writing process—discussed in Chapter 2—and discovering what you want to say as well as the shape and direction of your paper.

Do whatever is easiest and remain flexible. As you form words on the page, it will make what you have left to do a bit easier. Sometimes as you work on one section, a new focal point for your paragraph will emerge. If your writing tells you that it wants to be something else, then revise or start over as needed to take advantage of that discovery. Do not be rigid or critical of yourself as this discovery stage of the writing process is not a time for "by the rules" thinking. Your goal is to wind up with a paragraph that solidly makes and supports a point. Be ready and open to make whatever adjustments are needed to reach your goal.

Writing Paragraphs and Essays Offers Many Benefits

Now you know some reassuring facts about writing in general. As you move to the paragraph as a specific form, consider the benefits of writing paragraphs and essays—benefits that may surprise and motivate you.

Mastering the structural requirements of paragraphs and essays gives you the foundation for all college writing assignments. In other courses, you will be assigned a variety of writing forms that will be variations on paragraph and essay forms: exam answers, short reports, analyses, business or technical documents, response papers, and even website text. You begin with paragraphs because these serve as the basic building blocks of essays, the most common form of writing in college.

Paragraph writing also readies you for the requirements of electronic communication. During your career, you may write online as often as on paper. Stating a point and backing it up concisely are the essentials of efficient e-mail correspondence and website content. Even the *subject line* in an e-mail requires the writer to state a point so that the reader will immediately be able to determine what the e-mail content will be. Screen readers impatiently scan a document's opening for its point and spend only seconds to check for evidence of support and explanation. Writing for these purposes will also depend upon the patterns and skills you learn from writing effective and efficient paragraphs.

Disciplines you acquire in paragraph and essay writing strengthen the other essential communication skills of reading and listening. During college and your career, you will be evaluated on how well you absorb, use, and transmit information. Learning to manage ideas in paragraphs makes you a more perceptive reader. As you clarify your own ideas and learn to support them, your awareness of how other writers handle ideas and proof grows stronger. You become more critically aware of other writers' and speakers' ideas and the evidence they provide.

The most important advantage of developing effective writing abilities is that paragraph and essay writing makes you a stronger thinker. Writing a clearly reasoned paragraph or essay requires mental discipline and close attention to a set of logical rules. Each time you meet the challenge of writing a topic sentence or thesis statement supported by well-reasoned, convincing evidence, your ability to express, order, and defend ideas grows stronger. Your message will be strong and your ideas taken seriously.

An Introduction to the Basic Principles of Effective Writing

These are the four steps to follow each time you begin a paragraph or essay writing assignment:

1) Discover and start with a clearly stated point.
2) Provide logically ordered, detailed support for your point.
3) Organize and connect your supporting material.
4) Revise and edit so that your content is concise and well stated and your sentences error-free.

Section One of this book explains each of these steps in detail and provides many practice materials to help you master them. We will begin by examining two basic elements of effective college writing: point and support.

Point and Support: An Important Difference between Writing and Talking

Every act of communication has a point. Humans are rarely aimless creatures; even when we wave to a friend in the hall, we have a reason to do so. Speech is even more purposeful, as, in everyday conversation, we make all kinds of points. We may say, "I love my job," "Sherifa's a really generous person," or "That exam was unfair." The points may concern personal matters or larger issues such as, "A lot of doctors are arrogant" or "Rises in tuition fees make students suffer."

Points raised in conversation often lack support, for two reasons. First, most conversations are brief and generally casual, unless we intend to argue or pursue a point more thoroughly. Second, the people with whom we speak do not always challenge us to support our statements. They may be aware of the context and therefore know why we feel as we do, or they may already agree with us, or they simply may not want to put us on the spot. Thus, they do not always ask "Why?" But the people who *read* what we write may not know us, agree with us, or feel in any way obliged to us.

Points made in print need support. First, we rarely write as briefly as we speak. We can supplement speaking with visual cues, exclamations, and other effects which cannot be done in written forms. Readers' knowledge of you and of the context for your ideas is usually limited to the words you have written. You are not there to interrupt your text and explain what you mean so you must give detailed support for your points. Of more importance, print allows readers to consider our views at their leisure and form their own responses. Reading even a paragraph asks readers for their time and some concentration. Readers do not like wasting time and energy so they want to know immediately what you are writing about and why you are writing.

Therefore, communicating effectively means making a point understood by the audience. To communicate effectively with readers, a skilled writer provides solid evidence for any point he or she makes. An important difference between writing and talking is that *in writing, any idea advanced must be supported with specific reasons and details.*

Readers are generally reasonable people. They will not take our views on faith, but they *are* willing to consider what we say *as long as we support it.* Therefore, we must remember to support any statements that we make with specific evidence.

Point and Support in a Paragraph

You read print in blocks of sentences, or paragraphs. The look of a group of sentences placed together and surrounded by white space suggests a paragraph's purpose: it is a container for a series of thoughts tied to one idea. A paragraph is a basic unit of writing, ideally of 150 words or more. It usually consists of an opening point called a *topic sentence* followed by a *series of specifics,* in the form of sentences, that support the point. Much of the writing featured in this book will be of paragraphs.

A Sample Paragraph: Following is a paragraph on why Farida, a student writer, finds her college's Internet server annoying.

Net Eats Student's Time!

Using my college's server can be a terrible waste of time. Yesterday evening was typical of how irritating "collegenet" can be. First of all, the server itself was down for two hours. This happened on the evening when I wanted to check the college library site for an article my marketing professor mentioned. I was determined to find the article, so I kept trying my connection, and I was too restless to concentrate on my accounting assignment. Once the server started up again at 10:30 p.m., I found the article, printed it, and then decided to check my e-mail. The second stage in my growing irritation began with the twenty-three pointless messages I found. A lot of mail that the college sends out means nothing to me, like postings about parking charges at other campuses and announcements from student groups I've never heard of, so scrolling through these e-mails just to delete and trash them is a time-waster. The final stage in my annoyance was still waiting for me. Unlike the college notices, these were mysterious posts that took forever to download. As I sat there at midnight, yawning and drumming my fingers on the desk, the mystery mails finally revealed themselves as chain letters with huge address lists on them. These were the names and e-mail addresses of dozens of students—everyone the sender knew. Students who send these chain letters, complete with the usual threats about "breaking the chain," obviously have more time on their hands than I do.

Notice what the details in this paragraph do. They provide you, the reader, with a basis for understanding why the writer feels as she does. Through specific evidence, the writer has explained and communicated her point successfully. The evidence that supports the point in a paragraph often consists of a series of reasons or subtopics introduced by signal words (*first of all, second,* and the like) and followed by details and examples that support the reasons or expand on the subtopics. That is true of the sample paragraph above: three reasons are provided, followed by details and examples that back up those reasons.

● ● ● ● ● **Activity 1**
_____

Complete the following outline of the sample paragraph. Summarize *in a few words* the details that develop each reason, rather than writing the details out in full.

Point: _____

_____

Reason 1: _____

   Details that develop reason 1: _____

   _____

   Example: _____

Reason 2: _____

   Details that develop reason 2: _____

   _____

   Example: _____

Reason 3: _____

   Details that develop reason 3: _____

   _____

   Example: _____

Conclusion: _____

Writing a Paragraph: An excellent way to get a feel for the paragraph is to write one. Your instructor may ask you to do that now. The only guidelines you need to follow are the ones described here and on the previous pages. Some advantages to writing a paragraph immediately are that it will provide you with a writing benchmark and reveal your areas of need as a writer. Keep this sample to refer to over the semester as your writing progresses to help you analyze your areas of strengths and potential improvements.

Writing Your First Paragraph

● ● ● ● **Activity 2**

Write a paragraph on the best or worst meal you have ever had. Provide three reasons why that meal was the best or the worst, and give plenty of details and specific examples to develop each of your three reasons. Note that the sample paragraph, "Net Eats Student's Time," has the same format your paragraph should have. The author:

1. states a point in her first sentence,
2. gives three reasons to support the point,
3. introduces each reason clearly with signal words (*first of all, second,* and *finally*), and then
4. provides details and specific examples that develop each of the three reasons.

Write your paragraph in a new file. Be sure to give it a clear and unique name.

Challenge—Write an objective paragraph

Most college writing is intended to provide information to an educated audience, and is not *subjective,* or merely about personal experiences. College writing should be *objective* so that the audience learns about the concept rather than the writer's own personal life. To achieve this, writers develop an idea or opinion about a subject that is removed from their own personalities, and is therefore more informative than reflective.

Such writing is effective when written in the third-person point of view so that personal considerations do not manipulate the information. Often, the information used is factual or verifiable. For example, instead of writing about the best or worst meal *you* have experienced, it would be more informative to write about the qualities of a meal that a food services *professional* would suggest for an excellent dining experience (or conversely, would warn to avoid for a substandard experience) based upon professional expertise.

Challenge: Write a paragraph that describes qualities of a meal that make it particularly satisfactory (or unsatisfactory). Start by defining which kind of meal will be discussed; for example, your topic sentence may be something such as, "The most impressive Thanksgiving dinners represent the bounty of the season through all the senses."

Try to write this paragraph without referring to "I," or yourself. Instead, refer to "it"—the meal—and the details and examples you present as support for your main point. Some examples to consider:

- a meal hall or college cafeteria
- a child's lunch
- your own choice
- a wedding
- a cultural meal
- an awards banquet
- a house party

For an example of a third-person paragraph, see the paragraph, "Becoming Canadian," in Chapter 2.

A NOTE ABOUT PARAGRAPH LENGTH

Paragraph length depends on three main considerations:

- the purpose of the paragraph,
- the reading audience's needs, and
- the medium and format in which the paragraph appears.

Paragraphs in popular media—the kinds you probably see most often—vary significantly from those required for college purposes. Popular media generally aims to make a sharp impact upon its audience, rather than to engage readers in a thoughtful exposition. Their purposes are often commercial as well as informative, so the articles are designed for rapid and easy consumption, allowing the reader to move on to other content. Newspapers often use paragraphs of single sentences fit into narrow columns, yet single sentence paragraphs are never used in college writing. Similarly, popular media make use of various devices, from colour to other sensory elements, to supplement their print or online pages, maintain reader interest, and often divert readers to other material.

College paragraphs, by contrast, are intended to take the audience through a carefully structured, thoughtful, and complete exposition that presents an idea it supports through its text. While a college paper will indeed present its main point at the beginning, the important information is distributed so that each element can be stated and considered methodically. The standard college paragraph is written with the expectation that the reader will thoroughly digest the content. The paragraph outline form on page 33 shows that a college paragraph should be at least ten full sentences, and certainly no fewer than 150 words. That is a mere guideline, as it is the complete meaning, rather than a word count, that matters in college writing.

IMPORTANT CONSIDERATIONS AS YOU BEGIN TO WRITE

Whether or not you have found writing difficult in the past, and even if you are writing in your second (or third) language, you are now making a fresh start in college. If you approach each writing task in any subject by considering the three important ideas that follow, you may find writing less confusing.

If you know or can find out something about your subject, you will be able to concentrate on how to express what you know. If you know what your purpose is—whether it is to report objectively on some matter or to give your personal views on a situation—then you can judge how to shape your information and details. Finally, once you have determined who your audience is, you will find it easier to choose the right words and tone to carry your message effectively. As with any activity, when you narrow the field and focus on one thing at a time, you will find writing less intimidating.

Look at the "writer's triangle" below. Each time you receive a writing assignment, draw yourself a triangle like this one. Before you even begin to brainstorm or do another form of prewriting, ask yourself the questions you see here. Your answers will make your prewriting easier in two ways: you will begin to focus on your subject area and feel less confusion, and you will see immediately whether you should do a bit of research before prewriting.

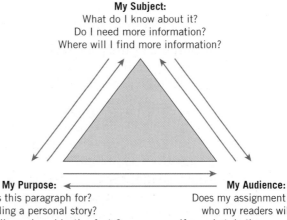

My Subject:
What do I know about it?
Do I need more information?
Where will I find more information?

My Purpose:
What is this paragraph for?
Am I telling a personal story?
Am I mainly discussing objective facts?
How much do I need to say to make my point?

My Audience:
Does my assignment tell me
who my readers will be?
If so, what do they need to know?
How casual or formal should I be?

Most of the writing you will do at college prepares you for career writing tasks. Most career writing is aimed at definite groups of readers and has definite purposes. You will always need to know enough about your subject to satisfy those readers' needs. Each point of this triangle relates to the others, as the arrows demonstrate. So begin now to consider "what" (subject knowledge), "why" (purpose), and "for whom" (audience) each time you write. Every time you do so, you will refine your writing skills and become a more effective writer.

WHAT?—KNOWING YOUR SUBJECT

Knowing your subject is not the impossible task it may seem. Here are three simple strategies for approaching a list of subjects or coming up with one of your own.

1 Follow Your Interests

Whenever possible, try to write about a subject that interests you. Your interest will give you energy and enthusiasm that come through in your writing. You will also find it easier to put more time into your work.

2 Discover What You Already Know

Try to write on a subject that you already know something about. You may know some things because you have direct personal experience with them. Sometimes your knowledge may come from prior indirect experience; you may have read, thought, or talked about subjects. Either direct or indirect knowledge may be enough, but that depends on the aim of your paper and how deeply you wish to pursue your subject.

3 Do Some Basic Research

The word *research* tends to make people anxious, but learning more about a subject could be as straightforward and easy as talking to someone who knows about it. Never hesitate to discuss a subject in which you're interested with a few people; it may help you to generate ideas of your own or stimulate you to do some book or Internet research.

In college writing, you may be asked to write about a topic that requires more than casual research or a topic about which you have no experience or knowledge, so you will want to set aside some time to spend online or at the library. Chapter 17 will show you how to look up relevant information and use it effectively.

Direct or indirect experience and research provide you with the specific evidence you need to develop the point you wish to make. Knowing your subject is an essential part of writing effectively.

WHY?—KNOWING YOUR PURPOSE

Generally, the main purpose for writing is to entertain, to inform, or to persuade. These are broad headings that sometimes confuse students who are simply trying to write a paragraph or essay. Try seeing each one in a different way by thinking about the explanations below. Remember as well that your writing will probably have a main purpose and a secondary purpose. Each time you start writing, think of your audience as you consider your purpose or purposes.

1 Writing to Entertain

Although entertaining your readers (or your professor) will rarely be your main purpose, you may be naturally humorous or entertaining. College writing will rarely ask you to entertain, so use your judgment and knowledge of your subject and your audience—mainly your instructor—to guide you when entertaining readers is your secondary purpose.

2 Writing to Inform

Writing to inform actually means writing to explain what you mean in some detail to readers. "Writing to clarify" might be another way of expressing this idea; in business or technical communication, the phrase might mean "writing to transmit information" or "writing to report on something." Even a paragraph relating a personal story informs readers about the writer and his or her life and thoughts. What "writing to inform" does *not* mean is simply restating research; writing must always make a point and show your own ideas or response to others' ideas. Much of your college writing will have this general purpose. In fact, whenever you make a point and explain its validity with specific proof, you are writing to inform.

3 Writing to Persuade

Most paragraphs that present a point and proof for that point seek to persuade readers to varying degrees. The best type of persuasion is the clear and convincing presentation of factual details. Paragraphs that mainly use description or other methods of development to make their point may be quite persuasive, in fact. If you intend to put across a strong point of view, then your main purpose is usually persuasion. In Chapter 15, you will learn some techniques specific to stating an argument.

Three Models

Each of the following passages introduces student writing about the general subject of "movies." What is the purpose of each of these introductions?

1) Hello everyone, and welcome to *Mailing's Movies*, the cool site where I can tell you about my favourite movies of the season!

2) From the jerky and often melodramatic movies of the Silent Era, to the computer-enhanced blockbusters of today, movies have been made with

The purposes of writing: entertainment, information, and persuasion.

the dual goals of entertaining the public, and of making a lot of money for the studios.

3) Many movie reviewers focus strictly on the amount of money in box-office receipts a new movie makes in its first weekend of release, rather than on the dramatic, social, and artistic merit of the production, with the result that moviegoers frequently find themselves with only noisy, gaudy, and meaningless pulp for presumed "entertainment."

Line 1 is casual, uses the first person, slang, and an exclamation mark. These are all features of writing to entertain.

Line 2 uses standard college English in the third person and introduces material to inform, meanwhile expressing a point.

Line 3 also uses standard college English, and sets up a comparison and contrast which will in turn be used to persuade the audience to agree with the author. The elements of persuasion are evident through the use of language that expresses a firm opinion. Note, though, that the opinion is expressed without using "I believe...."

WHO?—KNOWING YOUR AUDIENCE

You already know something about writing for different audiences. When you e-mail a friend, you use a way of speaking that is familiar to both parties, and you know roughly what you want to say. If you have written to your college or applied for a job, you wrote a bit more formally and were concerned about what to put in those letters. In other words, you are probably aware of the need to change your tone, content, and wording to suit your reader.

When you submit writing assignments in college, your audiences are mainly your instructors and sometimes other students. These people represent a generalized peer group, a typical educated adult audience. They expect you to present your ideas in a clear, direct, organized way. If you learn to write to persuade or inform such a general audience, you should feel confident that you have accomplished a great deal.

As you work through the chapters that follow, you will learn techniques to help you break your writing into manageable steps. You will also write some papers for more specific audiences. By doing so, you will develop a skill that you will refine throughout your life: the ability to choose words and adopt a tone of "writing voice" that is just right for a given purpose and a given group of people.

1   What Do Readers Need to Know?

Begin by putting yourself "in the shoes" of your reader. How much does this person know about your subject? How much background information does he or she need to be able to follow your point through its proof to its conclusion? Your reader cannot see into your thoughts and experiences and does not know why you hold the views you do.

2   What Kind of Language Will Readers Expect?

General readers want one thing: to understand easily what you have to say. Therefore, your language in college writing should always aim for clarity, for a neutral middle ground of language. Slang or overly casual, conversational word use carries the risk of losing readers who may not know you. Too formal or too grand words with many syllables may lose readers; people may not see your points clearly or easily if the points are hidden behind a forest of words. Aim for accuracy when you choose your words, and always follow the main principle requiring clear and error-free sentences.

3   What Tone or Degree of Formality Is Best?

A sense of tone develops with time and with frequent writing practice. Your own experience can guide you in the beginning. Begin by visualizing your reader and assessing how well he or she knows you. Then consider the circumstances of your writing task; you will generally write more formally to someone in a college, organization, or business situation than you would to your peers.

Choose an appropriate point of view:

A) The *first person:* Use the first person (*I* and *we*) *only* for informal work with a familiar audience, unless otherwise directed. The first person is most suitable for storytelling—narration—or creative description. It is usually considered too subjective for college or expository writing.

B) The *third person:* Use the third person (*she, he, they,* or equivalent terms such as *student, people, experts,* and so on) for most college writing assignments. The third person is controlled, intended to be fair, and therefore objective. This allows authors to analyze and synthesize material without imposing their own views into the supporting material (or seeming to accept all information without qualification). The third person also flows more naturally with the specific language required in college writing.

Note: Instructional writing, such as this text, often uses the *second person,* in the form of the rhetorical *you* (such as in the instructions for Activity 3, below). It is generally not used for college assignments.

The exercise below will help you to see the connection between subject, purpose, and audience more concretely, and will give you opportunities to compare the first- and third-person points of view.

Activity 3

This activity will stimulate your awareness of the relationship between subject, purpose, and audience. You may work on this activity alone or as part of a group; if you do this assignment as a group, compare all groups' results in class.

Imagine yourself as your English instructor; you are trying to devise a set of new writing assignments. Develop five subjects; then consider what you would want readers to know, and why, and for whom you would logically write. One example each of subject, purpose, audience, and in first and third points of view, is supplied for you below.

Subject	*Purpose*	*Audience*	*Point of view*	
Example			**1st-person**	**3rd-person**
everyday fashion	how to shop for great cheap clothes	readers of college paper	I like to find great deals when I go shopping....	Students appreciate bargains when they shop....
1.				
2.				
3.				
4.				
5.				

Discovering Your Topic and Your Focus

Sometimes you will not know your subject before you start writing. At other times you will be given a broad subject area and will need to find a definite topic within it. You will often discover your topic at one point or another during the writing process. When a student named Paul was given the general subject "learning from experience" (page 41) *experience* acted as a keyword for him and triggered some thoughts about working out. At first, his prewriting showed a focus on all the reasons why he had started going to the gym. When he tried asking himself questions, however, he found that his topic was really the benefits he had gained from maintaining his workout schedule. Paul *thought* he knew where his focus lay when he finished his freewriting. In fact, he *discovered* his true focused topic *during the process of writing*.

Another student, Alexa, started with a broad assigned subject: part-time jobs. She immediately thought that because she had quit high school and worked at several jobs, her topic might be how boring such jobs were. But as she accumulated details, she realized that she was really more challenged and sometimes even upset at work—*bored* did not, in fact, describe her true feelings. She sensed that the strongest source of her real feelings was the memory of her nightly routine as a telemarketer. "That was it," Alexa explained. "I had a picture in my head of every step I went through five nights a week. I knew I had something to turn into a paragraph." Then it was just a matter of detailing exactly how her work routine felt each evening. Her paragraph, "Torture by Telephone," is on page 80. Alexa changed her topic focus again when she turned her paragraph into the essay that appears on pages 270–271.

Sometimes you must write a bit in order to find out just what you want to write. Writing can help you think about and explore your topic and decide just what direction your work will finally take. The techniques presented in "Prewriting"—the section starting on page 41—will suggest specific ways to discover and develop a subject.

REVIEWING THE LEARNING OUTCOMES FOR CHAPTER 1

To assure yourself that you have understood and met the learning outcomes for this chapter, answer the following questions.

- ✔ What does the idea of "writing as a learnable skill" mean to you, based on your own experiences?
- ✔ How will writing paragraphs and essays specifically benefit you during your college years and your career?
- ✔ What level of formality, tone, and point of view are required for most college writing assignments?
- ✔ What are the four basic steps in effective writing?
- ✔ How were you able to put some of this chapter's ideas to specific use in writing your first paragraph?

Visit the *English Skills with Readings: Examining Paragraphs* Online Learning Centre at www.mcgrawhill.ca/olc/langan to access self-quizzes, internet-based questions, web resources, and other learning and study tools.

Chapter 2

The Writing Process

After reading this chapter and completing its activities, you will

- recall the four steps to writing an effective paragraph or essay;

- understand the main purposes for writing and the importance of writing for a specific purpose;

- identify the expectations of your audience;

- choose a topic and discover information about your topic;

- recognize why prewriting is important and demonstrate four different ways to discover ideas;

- understand the importance of outlining and how to create an effective outline; and

- know what revising is, why it is essential, how to revise, and how revising differs from editing and proofreading.

Chapter 1 introduced you to the paragraph form and some basics about writing. The chapters that follow in Section One will explain the steps in writing a paragraph and standards for evaluating a paragraph. This chapter sets you on the road to effective writing by introducing you to *writing as a process with a purpose.* The focus will be on prewriting, outlining, and revising: strategies that help you create solid paragraphs every time you use them.

Four steps for creating effective paragraphs are set out below. Internalizing these steps and making them constant habits will guide you every time you approach a writing task.

Four Steps to Effective Writing
• Discover your point—often through prewriting.
• Develop logical, detailed support for your point—through more prewriting and appropriate research.
• Organize your point and supporting material into an outline.
• Write a first draft, then revise and edit in further drafts.

Each of these steps uses different parts of your mind and different ways of thinking. Learning how the writing process works at each step will help you to focus your mind for that step and lessen your confusion about writing effectively. The chapters that follow cover the steps in detail, allowing you to practise them and absorb the sequence thoroughly.

Before you "test drive" the writing process, you may face common first-semester challenges: discovering your purpose and audience and choosing a topic. Here is some advice to help you with these preliminary tasks.

AN OVERVIEW OF THE WRITING PROCESS

A blank page or screen can intimidate anyone. As you sit wondering how to develop a paragraph, you may develop a mental block instead. The blank, confused feeling is usually the result of "mental clutter," trying to think of too many things at once.

Beginning to write is difficult, but these two strategies will help you immediately:

1) Review the four steps to effective writing in the box below, and see how these steps mesh with and lead to the four clear-cut goals for an effective paragraph. Doing so will give you a structure and path to follow.

2) Focus on *one* writing task at a time. No one can come up with a point before knowing what his or her thoughts are; no one writes a final draft in one sitting. Begin at the beginning—this chapter will show you where and how to begin to write good paragraphs.

Four Steps to Effective Writing	Four Goals for Effective Writing
1) **Discover** a point.	1) **Unity:** The point guides and controls all details.
2) **Develop** solid support for the point.	2) **Support:** There are sufficient supporting details and each is clearly explained.
3) **Organize and connect** supporting details by outlining and drafting.	3) **Coherence:** Supporting details are in an appropriate order; transitions connect ideas.
4) **Write and revise** to develop your point most clearly through supporting details and to ensure that language or mechanical errors do not interfere with your message.	4) **Effective Sentence Skills:** Sentences, spelling, and punctuation are free of errors; readers will see your point without interference.

When you start to write a paragraph, you begin a process that is not straight-forward. Your mind is not blank, as it is full of ideas and connections. Writing, like drawing, speaking, or making music, is a way of finding out what your ideas are, then giving them a shape.

The writing process has four general stages, and each calls for a different approach. The "discovery" stage, or *prewriting,* requires more openness in mental processes, than the "shaping" stages of *outlining, which* requires decision making. *Drafting,* is a stage of actual writing, and finally the *revising* stage requires attention to detail.

In the following pages, you will learn how to best use your abilities during the different stages of writing, and you will explore tested strategies to help you over blocks and problems—skills you can practise in writing situations for the rest of your life.

STAGE 1: PREWRITING

Prewriting describes the first stage of the writing process, the creative discovery period. During prewriting, you free your mind to discover the directions in which your ideas flow most freely. This is not a time to use "ordering" or "cor-recting" functions in your mind—those work against the relaxed, open mental state you need for exploratory prewriting. Do not censor or inhibit yourself dur-ing prewriting: this stage is entirely for yourself and need never be shared, so you do not have to worry about explaining your thought processes to others.

Various techniques of prewriting—often called "brainstorming"—have been found useful by many writers. Some of the most common are described in the following pages.

1) Freewriting
2) Questioning
3) List making
4) Clustering

1   Freewriting

Freewriting is particularly helpful in opening your mind to ideas or unblocking it when you are unsure of the subject. In freewriting, you write on your topic for ten minutes, but without worrying about spelling or punctuating correctly, about erasing mistakes, or about finding exact words. Simply write without stop-ping. If you get stuck for words, write a note to yourself, repeat words, or even make a mark until you review your work.

Freewriting will limber up your writing muscles and make you familiar with the act of writing. It is a way to break through mental blocks about writing and overcome the fear of making errors. It is vital to actually write your first thoughts, as your initial ideas and impressions will often become clearer once they are visible. Through continued practice in freewriting, you will develop the habit of thinking as you write.

Freewriting to Generate Ideas: A Student Model

Terry was assigned a paragraph on the general topic of a change that had affected him. He began with some freewriting about any changes he could think of. His spelling and grammar errors have been corrected for readability in the text below; but in freewriting, do not worry about such things. Concentrate on chasing your thoughts and feelings.

> There've been so many changes in the last while I can't think where to start here. Coming to Toronto was one of them. Funny, I used to dream about living in Toronto and now it doesn't seem that much better than home. It's just more expensive and bigger. College is another change, and I think it's a good one. At least I hope I end up with a job at the end so I don't have to worry about moving home and not getting work. There's not much left to my town any more, and I don't think some people in my class who grew up in a city could understand what it's like to watch the place you live die out. It felt so deserted, like a ghost town, when I went home for Thanksgiving. I didn't even want to walk down Queen Street because it was even emptier than what I remembered—you feel more attached to streets and places maybe than you would in a city.

Focused Freewriting: Narrowing a Topic

That evening, Terry read over his notes and realized he had a few potential topics. He asked himself what he had felt strongest about, and which point he could make that could be covered in a paragraph. Terry saw that his freewriting was mainly concerned with how his hometown was suffering. He *narrowed his topic* down to the changes in his town and then he did some focused freewriting to explore the topic he had discovered.

> Two years ago, the town where I grew up on the shore of Lake Erie started to dry up and disappear. The biggest employer, the car-parts factory, had just closed down for its third strike in five years, and the labour problems were getting worse and worse. More workers were being laid off as more and more parts were being made in Mexico or in Asia. Last night's paper said the U.S. parent company is going to close the factory for good. There isn't anywhere near here for all those hundreds of people to work. Will all those families still be able to live here? One of the two big chain stores just outside of town closed in the last year, and the other one became part of an American chain. Wal-Mart took over the big discount store, but they brought in their own management and people from some of their other stores, so a third of the original store's employees didn't end up working at the new store. The saddest sight of all is Queen Street, the town's old main street. Everybody used to walk along Queen Street; it always looked like it would never change and it was the real heart of town. A year ago, a big new mall was built just outside of London, only a half-hour's drive away. People drive there to do all their shopping, and even to do

> their banking, or go to the movies. Half the stores on Queen Street are closed and empty today, and two of the bank branches have shut down. No one has any reason to "go downtown" any more. Right now, it feels like my hometown is on the way to becoming a ghost town.

Notice how Terry was able to write a more focused topic sentence when he reassessed his freewrtiting. Terry's next step was to use the freewriting as the basis for a list and an outline for a paragraph about the causes of the changes in his hometown. (An effective paragraph that eventually resulted from freewriting, an outline, and a good deal of rewriting appears on page 47.)

Tips and Comments

- Freewriting is *for you*; you are the audience and no one is checking over your shoulder.
- The whole point of freewriting is to go with the flow of your ideas; don't stop as you discover what's in your mind—get ideas down just as they come to you.
- Correcting problems is a different mental process from exploring; shifting mental gears or trying to "get it right" can slow or stop the discovery stage of the writing process.

Writing Practice 1 To get a sense of freewriting, use a sheet of paper or a blank document on a computer to freewrite about your chosen field of study. See how many ideas and details you can accumulate in ten minutes. Title this as Writing Practice Freewriting. Keep this in a hard or word-processed folder titled *Writing Practice: Chapter 2.*

2   Questioning

Questioning as a technique works in a different way than freewriting. If you are an order-oriented, methodical person who enjoys linear thinking, questioning may offer a comfortable framework to use. Freewriting bypasses the ordering parts of your mind; questioning requires you to confront yourself with a set of specific demands. Questioning's structured approach gives a sense of direction to prewriting. Ask yourself as many questions as you can think of about your subject; your answers will be a series of different takes or focuses on it. Such questions include "Why?" "When?" "Where?" "Who?" and "How?", and are widely known as the *journalists' questions*.

To begin, divide your document into two columns: "Questions" and "Answers," as you see on the next page. Leave enough space in the "Answers" column so that you can return to a particular response if more details come to you later. Next, ask yourself this preliminary question: "What's my subject?" Write your answer as a reference point for the rest of your question and answer series. If one question stops you, just go on to another.

Here is an example of how one student, Mark, used questioning to generate material for a paragraph. Mark felt that he could write about a painful moment he had experienced, but he was having trouble getting started after doing some freewriting. So he asked himself a series of questions about the experience. As a result, he accumulated a series of details that provided the basis for the paragraph he finally wrote.

Here are the questions Mark asked and the answers he wrote.

Questions	Answers
<u>Where</u> did the experience happen?	In my younger brother's residence room at the University of Alberta
<u>When</u> did it happen?	A week before his first-year spring break
<u>Who</u> was involved?	My brother Josh, his roommate, and I
<u>What</u> happened?	I found out my brother was failing every course but one, and wasn't even planning to tell our parents. His marks in December weren't good, and his bulletin board was covered with tests with big red Fs on them. He'd even changed the address for his spring transcripts by claiming his main residence was his roommate's mother's house.
<u>Why</u> was the experience so painful?	My brother always did better than I did in school, and my parents were paying for his tuition and residence fees. They really wanted him to succeed at university. I worked for five years before I started putting myself through college for the last two years. The trip from Winnipeg cost me a lot of money, and I was really looking forward to it.
<u>How</u> did my brother react?	He tried to lie to me at first, pretending that nothing was wrong when I asked how his marks were. Then he got tense and defensive, saying he wasn't sure what he was doing yet anyway and that he needed time off to travel.

How did I react?	I was in a rage. I couldn't believe how dishonest he was and how he could let down our parents this way. I wanted to get out of there and call home, then I thought better of it. I was jealous of all the advantages he was ready to waste. Then I decided to wait and see if he would admit what he was doing to the family.

After discovering all these details from his questioning, Mark's next step was to prepare an outline. He then worked his way through several drafts of the paper, focusing on revealing his own responses to his disappointment with his brother.

Tips and Comments

Questioning works well as a second stage for your prewriting, too. If you have done some general freewriting but are still not sure of a focus for your paper, then try questioning, using your freewriting as a reference.

- Questioning may reveal your focus quickly when one answer in particular is more detailed than others.
- Questioning can yield answers that may be rich sources of *connected* details—making some of your organizing and outlining a little easier.
- Questioning can show you directions for paragraphs; if you have many answers to "Why?" your mind may want to explore the causes of a subject.
- These questions are often referred to as *journalists' questions, or W5,* (even though there is a sixth question, *"How?"*). They should also be revisited later in your writing process, to assure yourself that you have included enough specific details. If, after reading a paragraph, your audience asks one of those questions, there is a good chance that not enough details have been supplied.

Writing Practice 2 To get a sense of questioning, use a sheet of paper or a blank document on a computer to ask yourself a series of questions about your expectations of your program of study or future career. See how many details you can accumulate about that place in ten minutes. Save this in a file titled *Writing Practice: Questioning.*

3   List Making

Making a list is another way to get your ideas flowing. Simply list as many different items as you can think of about your topic. Do not worry about repeating yourself, and do not allow yourself to be sidetracked into the ordering stage of sorting out major ideas from lesser ones or supporting details. Spelling and punctuation are not concerns here; you are the only audience. A list's lack of structure works for you—there are no sentences to be concerned about; write in point form. Your goal is to accumulate as much raw material related to your topic as possible.

Jennifer, a first-semester student in a digital media program, was assigned a paragraph on the general subject of "an important decision." First she made a list to focus her topic. She listed all the decisions she could think of that she had made within the past six months and noticed that she was adding points to one item in particular.

Here is Jennifer's first try at list making, when she was narrowing her topic for her paragraph. Notice that the list is structured in a vertical column.

<u>Decisions</u> (my topic)

1. renting an apartment
   —finding roommates—rent
2. cutting my hair ?
3. applying to Sheridan
   —not going to university
4. taking digital media
   —want to design video games, I love to play them
   —really interested in digital graphics and how games work
   —jobs in the gaming industry?
   —never thought I could work at something that's fun
5. buying my own computer

Making this list clearly showed Jennifer one good topic focus for a paragraph: her decision to enter a digital media program.

Next Jennifer prepared a second list, to generate ideas for her paragraph. She felt more confident now, because making the first list had revealed to her that she had lots of thoughts about why she had registered in her program. Following is the list she made to accumulate all her ideas and details on the topic she had discovered with her first list.

<u>Decision</u>—to take digital media

1. it will let me take courses in game design
2. love working with graphics (spend hours with Photoshop—thought I was wasting my time)
3. playing v.g. almost an obsession (want to know how to make them myself)
4. making up stories about characters for games
5. orientation for program—talked about jobs in the gaming industry
6. I could work at something I really love
7. kinds of games—first person

Notice that with this list, Jennifer is starting to expand on her items. She puts parentheses around some notes to herself of ideas and details that relate to, explain, and expand on the items she thinks of. Very often, as you make a list, you will discover ways to develop your writing. Jot down any ideas that connect to your list items.

Tips and Comments

List making works as a first or second stage of prewriting. As a first stage, listing is a quick, easy method that you are already familiar with from making everyday to-do lists.

- List making frees you of concerns about your sentences in prewriting; simply list your ideas as phrases.
- List making works if you like to make notes to yourself as you work; just include something like "good first idea" in parentheses after an item.

List making is an effective second stage of prewriting. You may find it useful to make a list by referring to your page of freewriting.

- List making after freewriting can stimulate your mind so you think of more points and details.
- Listing your ideas after freewriting, questioning, or clustering displays your thoughts in simple uncluttered form, so you can proceed to evaluate them.
- Listing is an excellent sorting method; number your points and ideas in your preferred order before outlining, or sort out points and their related supporting details from your list.
- Listing is useful for writers who like to connect ideas graphically with lines and circles—you can quickly sketch in relationships between ideas and note anything special.
- Listing is helpful for writing that should be done objectively and in the third person; as listing deals with the essential details of a thought, it is easy to replace "I" with "it" as you review your information.

Writing Practice 3 To get a sense of making a list, use a sheet of paper or new document to list the specific goals you have through the program you are taking. List as many ideas and details as you can in ten minutes. Save this as *Writing Practice: Listing.*

4   Clustering

Clustering, also known as *mapping* or *diagramming,* is another prewriting activity that can help you generate ideas and details about a topic. In clustering, you use lines, boxes, arrows, and circles to show relationships among the ideas and details that come to you.

Clustering is helpful to people who like to think visually.

Whether you use a diagram, and just how you proceed with it, is up to you.

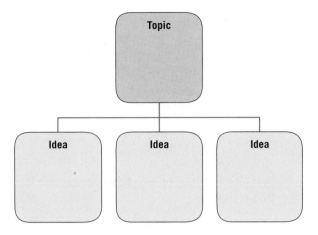

To use clustering to generate ideas, or as a first stage in prewriting, state your subject in a few words in the centre of a blank sheet of paper or as the main box in a word-processed diagram. Then, as ideas and details come to you, write them inside circles or boxes. When you discover connections between ideas and between groups of ideas, draw lines to connect them to one another and to your central idea.

There is no right or wrong way to diagram or cluster; it is a way to think on paper about how various ideas relate to one another. Below are the beginnings of some first-stage clustering done by a student named Devon, as he began to prepare for a paragraph on his job as a police officer.

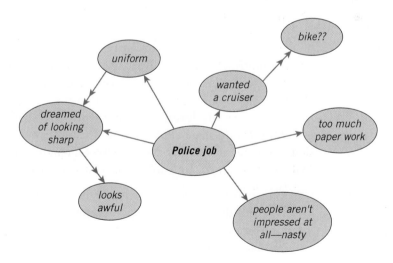

On page 28, the second stage of Devon's diagramming for that paragraph. He now knew he could write about the differences between his job as he imagined it and as it turned out to be. The cluster diagram, with its clear picture of relationships, was especially helpful for the comparison–contrast paragraph that Devon was doing. His final draft appears on page 217.

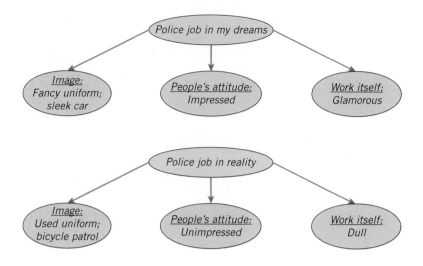

Tips and Comments

Clustering excels as a prewriting tool for the visually minded writer, for both the first and the second stages of prewriting. As a primary method of generating ideas, clustering frees you from the linearity of the page or screen.

- Clustering prevents "sentence block"; you note points and details in words and phrases.
- Clustering instantly shows you connections between ideas as you use lines and arrows to link one thing with another. If one idea seems to branch off from another, try using double arrows to show that connection, as in Devon's first-stage cluster diagram.

Clustering's only disadvantage is that your page may become too messy to follow. Avoid this by starting a second page where you distinguish visually between possible subtopics and details. Refer to both of Devon's diagrams for techniques to help you clarify levels of support, possible structures, and connections.

As a second stage of prewriting, clustering demonstrates relationships between ideas and details, as it has done for Devon. Clustering can also "preview" your paragraph's content and focus.

- Cluster diagrams reveal clearly both a paragraph's focus and the possible levels of details within a paragraph.
- Clustering as a second stage, if you show levels of links between points and details, prepares you for outlining and drafting.

Writing Practice 4 To get a sense of diagramming, use a sheet of paper or a new document to make a diagram of factors to consider as you become a professional in your field. See how many ideas and details you can accumulate in ten minutes. Then, draw a second diagram that would group those ideas as "positive" or "challenging" as you encounter them. Save each of these separately in your Writing Practice folder.

Challenge—Cubing

Another prewriting technique, commonly known as *cubing*, is very useful when dealing with complex topics or issues. Draw the topic as a three-dimensional cube with six sides. Each side represents a different form of analysis of the topic for you to assess, asking you to

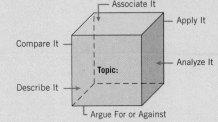

- describe it,
- compare it,
- apply it,
- associate it,
- analyze it, and
- argue for or against it.

    Once you have finished the process, you should have a more complex grasp of your topic. How would you apply this to your previous writing activity?

Source: Adapted from FOR-PD's Reading Strategy of the Month, July 2004. Accessed at http://forpd.ucf.edu/strategies/stratCubing.html

Using Four Techniques

Prewriting techniques are designed to open up your mind, to allow you to discover ideas and the connections between those ideas. No rules govern your use of prewriting techniques; go with what works for you. You may use several techniques almost simultaneously when writing. You may, for example, ask questions while making a list; you may diagram and perhaps sort through a list as you write it; you may ask yourself questions and then freewrite answers to them. And keep in mind that if you try one technique and are not satisfied, you can simply go on to another one. All the techniques are at your disposal. Choose those that work best for you.

Activity 1

Freewrite about these prewriting techniques, or discuss them with a partner. Each prewriting technique that you used in the previous activities was about the general theme of *your program of study*. Consider your prewriting experiences through those activities as you respond to these questions and ideas:

1. Which prewriting technique have you used previously?
2. Which prewriting technique did you think worked best for you, this time? Why?
3. Use a combination of any two or more of the prewriting techniques that you have just tried, to plan a piece of writing about your "Professional Career" (real or imaginary)?

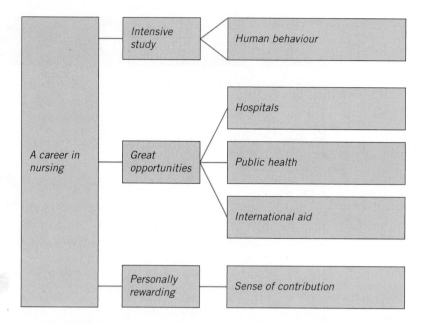

Challenge—A real-world application

Write a plan for a brochure that promotes the area of study you are in. Your plan would require more objectivity than a personal piece and would require writing in the third person to a specific audience (others who are interested in the same educational program). How would you adjust your prewriting to meet that goal? An example of prewriting through diagramming is shown, above.

STAGE 2: OUTLINING

Outlining is the essential second stage in the writing process. You may first have to do a fair amount of prewriting to discover your topic and focus on the point you want to make; many writers spend over 60 percent of their time on this first, prewriting, stage. Generally, you will create an outline from your prewriting, followed by a first draft: this is the sequence this book demonstrates. Outlining and sometimes re-outlining are needed to untangle and clarify your prewriting.

The quality of your outline can determine the success or failure of your paragraph. A paragraph is effective when its content is logically arranged and sufficiently detailed to make a point and to support it thoroughly. Such a paragraph does not result from patching together random pieces of prewriting into a final draft. Paragraphs written without good outlines are as ramshackle as buildings constructed without blueprints.

- Creating a formal outline requires three thought processes: sorting, ordering, and evaluating. These are decision-making activities: you will consider your point and supporting details. The quality and the arrangement of your raw material are what add up to a solid paragraph.

- Sorting, ordering, and evaluating are organizational skills that develop your ability to think clearly and logically. Outlining lets you work on the bare bones of your paragraph without the distracting clutter of phrases and sentences. You will see both your ideas and the connections between them.
- Use a hierarchical structure, specifically the Paragraph Outline Form on page 33, to ensure that your topics and subtopics are clearly defined.
- A good outline allows you to relax and write your first draft without worrying about what you will say next—you have your "blueprint" at hand.

Before you become intimidated by the prospect of outlining, know that with your prewriting done, you already have most of your content. There are some sorting techniques you can use to bridge the gap between rough notes, lists, or clusters and a finished outline.

Creating an Outline for an Effective Paragraph

The outlining process may not proceed in exactly the order set out below. You may find it easier to note your main subtopics before you are able to write a suitable topic sentence. Discovering the structure within your prewriting is one of the values of making an outline.

Students sometimes avoid making outlines, or they make quick and often odd-looking outlines *after* writing paragraphs. Outlining takes work, but it exposes repeated or similar ideas and weak connections between ideas, and makes writing a good paper much easier. Do not avoid outlining; instead use it to map your thoughts and keep your intentions for your paragraph clear.

A good time to make an outline is after you have done some prewriting. Pause for a while so that you see your ideas with fresh eyes. Remember that outlines tend to change as you work on them, so try not to judge yourself harshly while you work.

There are many ways to start an outline, but the following method works if you allow yourself the time to go through it a step at a time.

1) Copy the outline form on page 33. Leave spaces to fill in, and save it as a blank document, or template, that you can copy for repeated use.

2) Start or open a new document and name it appropriately. Ask yourself two questions: "What is my point?" and "Why do I believe my point is true?" Write out your point in one sentence—now you have a topic sentence, a trial statement of your point. Be prepared to change the sentence if you find your point changing. Now list any words or phrases that bring to mind facts or situations that back up your point; these are your subtopics.

3) Next, look at your prewriting as well as at the page or screen document where you just noted your point and reasons for that point. Try to rank your reasons in order of importance, in order of time, or in another order that seems appropriate to you. Look back at your trial topic sentence to see if it is general enough to cover your subtopics or, revise it as necessary.

4) For each subtopic, list *in point form* the related details from your prewriting or any new details that occur to you. To ensure balance in your paragraph, it is desirable to have approximately the same number of details to support each subtopic.

5) You are ready to start your outline. Don't worry if you change or eliminate examples or think of a new way to explain a detail. If you are stalled at some point, fill in another section of the outline—you do not have to work from top to bottom in a straight line. The point of outlining is to see and shape your thoughts; you can always rearrange parts of your outline. A messy outline is usually a good outline.

Hint: Remember to keep your supporting reasons and details in point form, at this stage: full sentences can be hard to review when you are drafting or

Challenge—Writing effective topic sentences

An effective topic sentence is vital for a strong paragraph, so you must construct the topic sentence carefully. As you review your prewriting, consider each idea and what it means. Develop a topic that can add to discussion of your general subject by promoting an idea that is sensible, but also unique. A good topic sentence includes a sense of action or attitude so that it does not merely make a statement about a "thing," but declares a point that a reader would find worth considering.

One way to discover how to phrase your topic sentence is to ask yourself a question about the topic and then phrase your response as the topic sentence. Remember, though, that college writing *tells* rather than *asks*, so be sure to word your topic sentence as a strong statement, and never as the question, itself. You may wish to play with the ideas in the question in order to find the exact statement you need to make. Chapter 3 gives more guidance in writing effective topic sentences.

Practise writing topic sentences as answers to specific questions. Choose two of the following questions and answer them in topic-sentence form. Provide the governing idea for a potential paragraph, but do not give the supporting reasons in the topic sentence:

Example: Question: *What are the features of a good webpage?*
Answer: *The most important feature of an effective webpage is that it reflects the audience it is intended to serve.*

Choose from these questions:

1) What must a student consider when applying for entrance to college?
2) How can new drivers learn defensive driving?
3) Who serves as a positive role model for adolescents?
4) Where is the best place to look for a new computer?
5) Who should be responsible for creating a positive workplace?

revising. Additionally, writing long passages at this stage may take some of your mental energy so that you may feel depleted by the time you actually start writing a draft.

The exercises following this section will help you to discern the difference between more general subtopics and the specific details that clarify, explain, or illustrate those subtopics.

Paragraph Outline Form

To write an effective paragraph, first prepare an outline. Save this outline form as a template to reuse it each time you write.

Point

    Topic Sentence: _____

    _____

Support

    Subtopic 1: _____

    _____

    Supporting Details (explanations, examples):

        a. _____

        b. _____

        c. _____

    Subtopic 2: _____

    _____

    Supporting Details (explanations, examples):

        a. _____

        b. _____

        c. _____

    Subtopic 3: _____

    _____

    Supporting Details (explanations, examples):

        a. _____

        b. _____

        c. _____

    Conclusion: _____

The following series of exercises will help develop the outlining skills that are so important to writing an effective paper.

• • • • **Activity 2**

___

One key to effective outlining is the ability to distinguish between general ideas and specific ideas. Read each group of ideas below, then determine which is the appropriate general or specific idea. Note that the general idea should not be too broad or too narrow. Begin by trying the example items, and then reading the explanations that follow.

Example   *Specific ideas:* egg salad; tuna salad; bacon, lettuce, and tomato; peanut butter and jelly
The general idea is:
a. foods.
b. sandwich fillings.
c. salads used as sandwich fillings.

Explanation: It is true that the specific ideas are all food, but they have in common something even more specific—they are all sandwich fillings. Therefore, answer *a* is too broad; the correct answer is *b*. Answer *c* is too narrow because it doesn't cover all of the specific ideas: two of the sandwich fillings are not salads.

Example   *General idea:*   Breakfast choices
             Specific ideas: muffins
                          bacon and eggs
                          cereal
                          pancakes

Explanation: Here, the food items listed are all specific examples of the general idea "Breakfast choices."

1. *Specific ideas:* Easter, Thanksgiving, Valentine's Day, New Year's Day
    The general idea is:
    a. days.
    b. holidays.
    c. religious holidays.

2. *Specific ideas:* skating, ice hockey, skiing, snowboarding
    The general idea is:
    a. sports.
    b. toys.
    c. winter sports.

3. *Specific ideas:* pineapple, guava, mango, lychee
    The general idea is:
    a. tropical fruit.
    b. produce.
    c. fruit.

4. *General idea:* _____
   Specific ideas: birthday
                     anniversary
                     get well
                     graduation

5. *General idea:* _____
   Specific ideas magazines
                    radio
                    television
                    podcasts

6. *General idea:* _____
   Specific ideas: student
                     intern
                     volunteer
                     co-op participant

● ● ● ● **Activity 3**

Major and minor ideas, or subtopics and details, are mixed together in the paragraph outlined below. Place subtopics in the numbered spaces. Place each appropriate detail or minor idea under each subtopic in the spaces labelled *a* and *b*.

A. *Topic sentence:* People can be classified by how they treat their cars.
   Seldom wax or vacuum car
   Keep every mechanical item in top shape
   Protective owners
   Deliberately ignore needed maintenance
   Indifferent owners
   Wash and polish car every week
   Accelerate too quickly and brake too hard
   Abusive owners
   Inspect and service car only when required by provincial law

   1. _____

      a. _____

      b. _____

   2. _____

      a. _____

      b. _____

   3. _____

      a. _____

      b. _____

Challenge—General to specific

A very important writing skill to develop is an awareness of whether details are general (broad) or specific (narrow), and then to present them in the most effective order. General information helps to orient the audience to the overall subject that you will be discussing. As you progressively develop more specific details, you illustrate your point, show how the details relate to each other, and focus on the particular aspects that support your idea.

Think, for example, of a discussion of a favourite Canadian subject—the weather. By following a logical progression of the material, this seemingly banal subject could become an informative topic *about* a particular weather event.

- A general idea about Canada's weather could be that distant weather systems can affect what happens here
- This may depend largely upon the season
- Canadian autumns are usually comfortable
- Autumn weather may be affected by tropical storms
- Some tropical storms develop into hurricanes
- In 2003, Hurricane Juan struck directly into Halifax, Nova Scotia
- Coastal areas were swamped due to a combination of high winds of up to or more than 140 km/hr; the high tides that occur in September; an additional storm surge that raised the tide up to 2.9 metres above normal; and recorded waves of 9 to 20 metres
- Hurricane Juan was responsible for at least eight deaths and caused approximately $200 million in damage across a swath of the Maritimes
- Because of the scope of the disaster it caused, the name *Juan* was officially retired from the list of hurricane names in 2004

Note how this list of information travels from a general observation about Canadian weather to specific data about Hurricane Juan. What could be the point you would make to write a paragraph using this information?

Here are some other broad subjects where a discussion might provide more specific information. Choose two or three of the suggestions. Then, supply progressive details for each to develop the idea from a general thought to specific details.

- A business plan
- Biofuels
- Computer maintenance
- Healthy lifestyles
- Globalization
- Your choice

Activity 4

Read the following informative paragraph; then, outline it in the space provided. Write out the topic sentence and summarize the subtopics in a few words. Then note the supporting details that fit under each subtopic. Note that, in order to be informative, this paragraph is written in an objective and third-person point of view. The author's point is clear, and strengthened as it avoids the word "I."

Becoming Canadian

Young second-generation Canadians frequently report severe stress as they straddle a fine line between being accepted by their peers and approved of by their parents. Often, children whose parents were not born in Canada may have better English- or French-language abilities than either of their parents. This means that they can be relied upon too much, at times—and while they are still very young—to provide complex translations between their families and their communities. It is not unusual to see children in constant attendance to their parents, doing adult tasks such as banking, dealing with civic authorities, and even going to doctors, strictly to serve as translators. These children are often very proud of their abilities, and devoted to their elders, but these demands can also curtail the children's own social development. When children must give the time that they should otherwise use for school, extracurricular activities, or simple play, they are denied opportunities to attend to their own needs. If a child cannot attend soccer games or play activities with friends, that child may have trouble fitting in with neighbourhood children, making social adjustment even more difficult than is to be expected. But probably the most stressful part of growing up within two cultures, is finding a workable balance between "new-world" permissiveness and "old-world" traditional expectations. Generally, second-generation children want as desperately to be seen as "natural" in Canada as they wish to respect their parents, which can cause upset between the generations. Clothing is a frequent source of anguish when young new Canadians wish to dress as their school peers, but with styles that transgress their families' standards. At times there are open conflicts, but, generally, problems resolve over time as families sort out their own expectations. Of course, while this pattern is obvious in the modern context, Canadians should not forget that this type of adjustment has been happening in various forms for over three hundred years.

Topic sentence: _____

_____

Subtopic 1: _____

    a. _____

    b. _____

Subtopic 2: _____

    a. _____

    b. _____

Subtopic 3: _____

    a. _____

    b. _____

Conclusion: _____

Writing Practice 5 Return to the prewriting you did earlier in Chapter 2. Select the ideas that seem to work for a single paragraph. Use the outline form on page 33 to construct your own paragraph outline using those ideas. Title this *Writing Practice: Outline.*

STAGE 3: WRITING FIRST DRAFTS

Writing an effective paragraph is never done all at once. First, prewrite until you feel confident about your topic, subtopics, and supporting details. Then work with your prewriting until you are satisfied that you can create a complete and logical paragraph outline. Now you are ready for the third stage of the writing process: creating a first draft. (Chapters 3 and 4 will give you more details about this stage.)

All your work on the first two stages will now pay off. If possible, allow some time between outlining and writing a draft. A day or even a few hours will let you approach your material with a fresh outlook and a new perspective on what you want to say. Here are some tips on creating a first draft.

- Never try to make a first draft a *final* draft. That would defeat the purpose of working on writing as a process. A first draft is only one part—*the third stage after prewriting and outlining*—in creating your effective paragraph. It represents your first try at putting your ideas and structure into sentence and paragraph form. Second, you will inhibit yourself by trying to make each sentence "perfect." Saying exactly what you mean in the way you want to say it takes time. In your first draft, concentrate on getting the points and details on your outline down as sentences. Trying to write a finished piece of work in one draft forces your mind to do too many things at once: creating, choosing the right words, spelling correctly, and all the other tasks you perform as you write. Do one thing at a time. *Concentrate on your content.*
- Write on every other line, or set the format in your word processor to double spacing Doing so enables you to make changes and to add and subtract ideas, words, and phrases in your revision drafts. The *white space* around your working draft will prevent the text from being too dense and will help you to see sections that need revision when you reread it.
- Do not worry about spelling errors or sentence problems. Correcting these belongs to the final stage of the writing process: *revising, editing, and proofreading.* Focus on getting your ideas down in sentences. Any other concern will only distract you.
- Do not worry if you leave out an idea or detail in your outline or add some new point or detail. The writing process is never straightforward. Do not sacrifice a potentially good idea or vivid example for the sake of sticking rigidly to your outline. You can always revise your outline, and you will be revising your draft.

Your instructor may want you to include your first draft with the draft you submit, so be sure to save it. Alternatively, you may participate in peer evaluations of your first draft with your classmates. In such evaluations, focus is always on *content:* how clear is your point, and how well is it supported?

Writing Practice 6 Use the outline that you constructed to write a first draft of your paragraph about your program of study or intended career. Follow the guidelines above, concentrating on expressing your ideas and organizing them effectively. Title this *Writing Practice: First Draft.*

STAGE 4: REVISING, EDITING, AND PROOFREADING

Revising Content

Revising is the first part of the fourth stage of the writing process. Revising means literally "re-seeing" material; *it focuses on content* and how accurately or fully that content is expressed. Working with your first draft, you shape, add to, and perhaps subtract from your raw material as you take your paragraph through two or more drafts.

To revise the content of your paper, recall the four goals for effective writing from page 19, and ask the following questions.

1) Is my paper **unified?**
   - Do I have a main idea that is clearly stated at the beginning of my paragraph?
   - Do all my supporting points truly support and back up my main idea?
2) Is my paper **supported?**
   - Are there separate subtopics for the main idea?
   - Do I have *specific* evidence for each subtopic?
   - Is there *enough* specific evidence for the subtopics?
   - Is the audience fully informed of all necessary details?
   - Are there specific examples for each supporting point?
3) Is my paper **coherent?**
   - Do I have a clear method of organizing my paragraph?
   - Do I use transitions and other connecting words?
   - Is the point of view consistent, using the first or third person as directed?

Your goal in revising is to *make clear the single point* of your paragraph. Achieving this goal involves working on two activities: development of evidence and organization of evidence.

Writing Practice 7 Return to your file *Writing Practice: First Draft* that you just completed. Revise your draft by assessing it against the goals listed above. Do not become bogged down in many details; remember that revising is a specialized "art," in itself, and your abilities will improve with continued practice. Simply look for the main features that identify your draft as a complete paragraph.

Peer Revision

As a student, you are responsible for the content and quality of your own work; however, under certain circumstances you may be able to call upon a peer—a classmate or friend. Do not feel that you must struggle through every decision without any help. A *peer reviewer* may help you see beyond the written debris that could be blocking your way. The term "reviewer" is more appropriate at this stage than "editor," as you will be asking for help with ideas and support, not grammar and punctuation.

However, if you are going to ask a peer for help, you must consider the reviewer's role carefully. Always be sure that your instructor has approved the use of a peer; some may give specific instructions regarding the type of assistance that is acceptable, and others may prefer that peers not help each other too much. Often, instructors do not want students to touch each other's work, but may allow peers to ask questions or make suggestions. Never ask a peer to "fix" or alter your work, in any way. A peer's most useful role is to help *you* determine the strengths and weaknesses of the piece you are working on. Ask a peer to serve as a second set of eyes, and to review your work using the same questions, stated on page 39, that you have just asked yourself. Looking for adequate support and evidence in a piece of writing is not much different from looking for lost items in a jumbled room: with a little help, the extra and unnecessary items can be sorted and cleared and the desired ones discovered. Of course, in the spirit of *teamwork,* you can reciprocate and offer your insight into another's writing, as well.

The next two chapters will give you more detailed information and more practice in achieving **unity, support,** and **coherence** in your writing.

Revising Sentences: Editing and Proofreading

Editing and proofreading are the final activities in this fourth stage of the writing process.

You *edit* the next-to-final draft; that is, you check it carefully for sentence skills—grammar, mechanics, punctuation, and usage. Run the spell checker on your final draft, but also use a Canadian dictionary to look up any words you are likely to have misspelled.

To revise individual sentences in your paragraph, ask the following questions.

1) Do I use *parallelism* to balance my words and ideas?
2) Do I have a *consistent point of view?*
3) Do I use *specific words?*
4) Do I use words effectively by avoiding *slang, clichés, pretentious language,* and *wordiness?*
5) Do I *vary my sentences* in length and structure?

Chapter 5 will give you practice in revising your sentences, and page references for all sentence-skills issues appear on the inside front cover.

Finally, you *proofread* the final copy of the paragraph for any mistakes in keying or handwriting.

Editing and proofreading are important steps that some people avoid, often because they have worked so hard (or so little) on the previous stages.

Ideally, you should have enough time to set your writing aside for a while, so that you can check it later from a fresh point of view. Remember that locating and correcting sentence-skills mistakes can turn an average essay into a better one and a good essay into an excellent one. A series of editing tests, available on the Online Learning Centre, will give you practice in editing and proofreading.

PRACTICE IN SEEING THE ENTIRE WRITING PROCESS

This section will show you the stages, as covered in this chapter, in writing an effective paragraph. You will see what one student, Paul, did in preparing a paragraph about learning from experience.

There is no single sequence that all people follow in writing a composition. However, the different stages in composing that Paul went through in writing his paragraph should give you some idea of what to expect. Paul did not just sit down and proceed neatly from start to middle to finish. Writing seldom works like that.

Stage 1: Prewriting

Paul's assignment was to write a paragraph on learning unexpected things from experience. His first step was to do some freewriting on his topic.

I've learned a lot from experience, for sure. Things I didn't expect were usually bad things, but sometimes I think I learn only by experiencing things. Starting to work out taught me a lot. Nothing bad there. Except being really stiff and not wanting to go sometimes. But I've changed a lot from when I started going to the gym. I've stopped avoiding stuff as much as I used to. I feel a lot better and I'm more confident about myself. I guess this is one of the best things I've ever done. Just feeling better kept me going back a lot of the time, even when I didn't feel like it. My self-esteem is a lot better than it was, even at school, in classes. I feel like I can face challenges better than I used to—I don't put things off as much. I've got more energy, too. And then when the gym offered me a job as a trainer, I knew I didn't just learn to do my routines well and build up my strength. All of a sudden, someone thought I was good enough at something to get paid for it. I like helping people to learn how to train. Some of them remind me of myself.

Note: To keep Paul's work as readable as possible, his spelling and sentence-skills mistakes have been corrected throughout this section. Ordinarily, a number of such mistakes might be present, and editing his work to remove them would be the final part of the writing process.

At this point, Paul has found a specific focus for his topic: some unexpected benefits he realized from working out. He then decided to move on to another prewriting technique—making up a list of details about what he learned from going to the gym consistently. Here is Paul's list.

How working out worked for me

went because I felt out of shape
clothes didn't fit and I felt bad all the time
(What did I learn though?)
learned to go even when I didn't feel like it
learned to follow routines, even when I thought I could jump past something
saw other people there in worse shape than me
it hurt a lot at first, but I started to get stronger and have more endurance
could run up the stairs at school without panting
feel like I can do all kinds of things now
stopped procrastinating so much
my jeans fit better—I bought a smaller size—like shopping for clothes
learned some discipline and patience
stuck with routines the way the trainer said to
got a job, get paid to go to the gym

Stage 2: More Prewriting and Creating an Outline

Freewriting and list making helped Paul to accumulate material for his paragraph. He *thought* he was ready to start lining up his details about things he hadn't expected to learn from working out. As he looked over his list, something occurred to him. Did he really want to discuss why he went to the gym in the first place? Did that really relate to learning unexpected things? He decided it did not, and he opted to omit those items. Paul also thought he could fill out some of the list items with more details to explain how important each of those benefits was to him.

Before trying to order the list items he thought were of value and risking frustration or forgetting which items he wished to add to, Paul decided to "step backwards." He tried another type of prewriting: asking himself questions. He thought of asking himself what were the *things he had learned* at the gym. Then he asked himself what were the *most unexpected benefits* he had gained. When he tried this, he found he had many details to add about what benefits he had gained and which of these were most important to him.

I learned a lot of unexpected things by going to the gym. What were they?

1. I could stick at something
   —hated doing the exercises at first
   —but I had paid for it
   —went when I didn't feel like it
   —used to give up on things easily
2. learned to follow instructions
   —did what the trainer told me to
   —hated it sometimes—felt like I was just repeating stuff for no reason
3. I felt better
   —stopped panting on stairs
   —lost weight
4. got good enough at working out to get a job
5. self-esteem—really didn't expect this

Paul felt, at this point, that he was not coming up with anything new, and he worried that he might lose track of some of the details he wanted to add to his list. As well, as he wrote the final two items on the list above, he realized he wanted to discuss the most important things he had learned from fitness training. He decided to move on to ranking what he had learned by asking himself what were the *most unexpected things* he had learned.

What was most unexpected?

1. Learning to stick with something
   —used to just give up on games when I didn't do well
   —gave up on schoolwork when it was too hard
   —would get impatient at following rules and instructions, and give up before I finished—learning drafting
2. Felt better because I kept going—self-esteem improved
   —compliments on looking better
   —buying smaller jeans
   —got more patient—stopped giving up on hard assignments
   —felt like I was actually changing in a lot of ways
3. Being offered a job at the gym
   —total surprise
   —never had a job I cared about
   —never had jobs where I was rewarded for being good at something
   —I'm responsible for showing people what I can do and what I learned—big thing to me

Looking at the two steps he had worked through, Paul now knew he had some organization for his points, and he could create a reasonable outline. He started to fill in the copy of the paragraph outline form he had saved on his disk. As he did so, he found new details to add.

Point

Topic Sentence: The experience of working out at the gym taught me some unexpected lessons.

Support

Subtopic 1: I learned to stick with something I started.

Supporting Details (examples, explanations):

a. bought a gym membership

b. after a few times, I was ready to stop

c. so out of shape that the exercises left me stiff and in pain at first

d. but my jeans fit better, so I pushed myself to go back—vanity

e. first time I didn't quit something—I was surprised when I realized this

f. same thing as schoolwork?

Subtopic 2: I learned discipline and patience.

Supporting Details (examples, explanations):

a. impatient with repetitions and learning routines—thought I knew better

b. didn't listen to the trainer at first—breathing improved—could run on stairs

c. made a chart, started to track myself

d. started building up routines—trainer knew what she was talking about

e. felt like I was "relaxing"—got more patient—same thing happened with a couple of assignments—I actually kept at them, didn't avoid doing them

Subtopic 3: My self-esteem really improved and I'm more responsible.

Supporting Details (examples, explanations):

a. six months later, I'm not just working out, I do endurance running

b. gym offered me part-time job as training assistant

c. stopped procrastinating with school and chores—feel good about myself

Conclusion: The best part—responsible for showing people what I learned.

Notice that Paul changed his subtopics. He decided that he wanted to focus on three things he had learned, so he worked these into his outline.

Stage 3: Writing a Full Draft

Paul now moved on to a first full draft.

> Sticking with my workout program has taught me some unexpected lessons. I used to be ashamed of being a quitter. When I bought a gym membership, I wanted to stop after two weeks. But I had paid for it, so I felt worse about quitting. Besides, the exercises made me stiff and sore. I think I went back only because my clothes started to fit better. It turned out that this was probably the first time I didn't quit something I started. I learned a lot about discipline and patience from working with my trainer. She made me keep doing repetitions ~~of the same things~~. Then I started to relax and enjoy following my routines. Having discipline made me work better at college, too. I stopped avoiding things so much. I have a lot more self-esteem ~~because of this~~. Now I do endurance running and, best of all, the gym gave me a part-time job as a training assistant. I do more now and I stopped procrastinating so much with schoolwork. For the first time, I feel good about myself. I know I can count on myself, and now I am responsible for showing people what I have learned.

Notice that Paul, after writing his first draft, was still trying to make his details more specific. He struck out vague phrases.

Stage 4A: Revising

Paul put his work aside for a day and began to revise his paragraph the next morning. Revising is as important a part of the writing process as prewriting and writing the first draft. *Revising* means that you rewrite a draft, building on what has been done to make it stronger and better. One writer has said about revision, "It's like cleaning house—getting rid of all the junk and putting things in the right order." A typical revision means *writing at least one or two more drafts.*

Shown below is Paul's revised second draft. He copied and pasted his first draft into a new document titled "Gym Draft 2." Notice that he double spaced this draft, so that he could make changes easily. He made his changes in red, so that he could see them clearly. Phrases and sentences that Paul removed are shown as struck out, although he would simply have deleted them in his second draft.

> [1]Starting and sticking with my workout program have taught me some unexpected lessons. [2]First, I have learned not to give up so easily. [3]~~I used to be ashamed of being a quitter.~~ [4]When I bought a gym membership, I wanted to stop after two weeks. [5]But I had paid for it, ~~so I felt worse about quitting~~ so I kept going, even though [6]~~Besides,~~ the exercises made me stiff and sore. [7]~~I think~~

I only went back at first because my clothes started to fit better, so maybe vanity inspired me. [8]~~It turned out that~~ This was probably the first time I didn't quit something I started. [9]The next thing I learned ~~a lot about~~ was discipline and patience ~~from working with my trainer.~~ [10]~~She~~ My trainer made me slow down, keep doing repetitions, and work on the way I performed my exercises, so ~~of the same things.~~ [11]~~Then~~ I started to relax and enjoy following my routines. [12]I worked at getting better, not just at getting things over with. [13]Learning to be ~~Having~~ disciplined made me work better at college, too. [14]I stopped avoiding things so much. [15]I have a lot more self-esteem because my marks are better and I feel better physically. ~~because of this.~~ [16]Now I do endurance running and, best of all, the gym gave me a part-time job as a training assistant. [17]~~I do more now and I stopped procrastinating so much with schoolwork.~~ [18]For the first time, ~~I feel good about myself.~~ [19]I know I can count on myself, and now I am responsible for showing people what I have learned.

* * * * **Activity**

Fill in the missing words or sentence numbers, and underline the correct goal in the parentheses.

1. To clarify the organization or coherence of his paragraph, Paul added at the beginning of the first supporting point the transitional word _____, and he set off the second supporting point with the phrase _____.

2. In the interest of (*unity, support, coherence*), he crossed out sentence number _____. Paul realized that this sentence was not a relevant detail to support the idea of learning not to give up.

3. To eliminate wordiness, he removed the words _____ in sentence 7 of his revision.

4. To add more (*unity, support, coherence*), Paul added the phrases _____ _____ and _____ to sentence 10.

5. For greater sentence variety, he combined sentences 10 and 11 with the word _____.

Stage 4B: Editing and Proofreading

Paul now printed a next-to-final draft of his paragraph. He marked in pen any areas where he was unsure of his sentence skills and circled words to look up in his dictionary. When you reach the editing and proofreading stage, you, like Paul, will have finished revising the content and organization of your draft. Print a double-spaced copy of your paragraph, leaving room for grammar and spelling corrections.

Editing and proofreading, the final activities in the writing process, mean checking the work carefully for spelling, grammar, punctuation, and other errors. You are ready for this stage when you are satisfied with your content: your choice of subtopics and supporting details; the order in which they are presented; and the way they and your topic sentence are worded.

Using the hints in the box that follows, read through your paragraph carefully. Check for typing errors, spelling errors, omitted words, and any other errors you may have missed so far. Refer to Section Four of this book for help with grammar and sentence-skills questions. Use your dictionary to be certain of any choices you made with the spell checker and to check spellings of any words of which you are still uncertain. At this stage such close and attentive work is often hard to do—students have spent so much time on their writing, or so little, that they want to avoid any more work. But if it is done carefully, this important final stage will ensure that an essay looks as good as possible.

Hints for Editing and Proofreading

- One helpful technique is to read your writing out loud. You will probably hear awkward wordings and become aware of spots where the punctuation needs to be improved. Make the changes needed for your sentences to read smoothly and clearly.

- Another technique is to use a sheet of paper to cover your paragraph so that you can expose and check carefully just one line at a time.

- A third strategy is to read your paragraph backward, from the last sentence to the first. Doing so helps keep you from getting caught up in the flow of the paragraph and missing small mistakes—which is easy to do, since you are so familiar with what you meant to say.

After editing and proofreading, Paul wrote the final draft of his paragraph.

Lessons from the Gym

Starting and sticking with my workout program have taught me some unexpected lessons. First, I have learned not to give up so easily. When I bought a gym membership, I wanted to stop after two weeks. But I had paid for it, so I kept going, even though the exercises made me stiff and sore. At first, I probably went back because my clothes started to fit better. Maybe vanity inspired me, but this was the first time I didn't quit something I started. The next things I learned were discipline and patience. My trainer made me slow down, keep doing repetitions, and work on the way I performed my exercises, so I started to relax and enjoy following my routines. I worked at getting better, not just at getting things over with. Learning to be more disciplined made me work more carefully on assignments at college, too. I faced challenges, instead of avoiding them. My self-esteem has increased because my marks are higher and I feel better physically. Best of all, the gym gave me a part-time job as a training assistant. For the first time, I know I can count on myself, and now I am responsible for showing people what I have learned.

Writing Practice 8 By now you have reviewed the principles of the writing process, seen it applied in writing models, and followed it in your own Writing Practice Activities. All that is left is for you to revise, edit, and proofread your own work, and then you will have a complete writing sample of your own. Finish your practice, now, and save it as *Writing Practice: Final Draft*. Keep this, along with the other steps you have done in the writing process, as a reminder and a guide for the remainder of this writing course. In time you may wish to revisit it and perhaps practise some of the writing techniques that will be introduced later. For now, though, enjoy your accomplishment, and take pride in the manner in which you accomplished your first whole piece in such little time.

REVIEWING THE LEARNING OUTCOMES FOR CHAPTER 2

To assure yourself that you have understood and met the learning outcomes for this chapter, answer the following questions.

✓ What are the four steps involved in writing an effective paragraph or essay?

✓ What are the three main purposes for writing? Which will you encounter most often in college? Why?

✓ Who is your main reading audience? What is your audience looking for in a paragraph or essay that you write? How will you express your point of view?

✓ What should be your guide as you choose a subject to write about? Why? How will you acquire information about a subject of which you have no experience or knowledge?

✓ What is the goal of all prewriting techniques? Why do several different techniques exist?

✓ At what point in the writing process will you create an outline? What are the two main sections of a paragraph outline? What are the purposes of outlining?

✓ What is revising? Why and how is revising different from editing? What is the role of a peer reviewer? What restrictions are there on a peer editor's role? What is proofreading?

Visit the *English Skills with Readings: Examining Paragraphs* Online Learning Centre at www.mcgrawhill.ca/olc/langan to access self-quizzes, internet-based questions, web resources, and other learning and study tools.

Chapter 3

The First and Second Steps in Writing

LEARNING OUTCOMES

After reading this chapter and completing its activities you will

- be prepared to begin a paragraph by making a single, clear point;

- know the relationship between a paragraph's topic sentence and the rest of the paragraph;

- understand the difference between a subtopic and supporting details;

- know the two main functions of specific supporting details; and

- know why writers must provide enough supporting details.

Chapter 2 emphasized the ways in which prewriting and revising can help you become an effective writer. This chapter will focus on the first two steps in writing an effective paragraph:

1) Begin with a point.
2) Support the point with specific evidence.
   Chapters 4 and 5 will then look at the third and fourth steps in writing:
3) Organize and connect the specific evidence.
4) Write clear, error-free sentences.

STEP 1: MAKE A POINT—OVERVIEW

Your first step in writing is to think about your subject, decide what point you want to make about that subject, and write that point in a single sentence. The point is commonly known as a *topic sentence*. As a guide to yourself and to the reader, put that point in the first sentence of your paragraph. Everything else in the paragraph should then develop and support in specific ways the single point given in the first sentence.

● ● ● ● **Activity 1**

Your goal is to develop your awareness of two things: a clear, single point and focused, specific support for that point.

Read the two paragraphs below, written by students on the topic "cheating in everyday life." Which paragraph clearly supports a single point? Which paragraph fails to start with a clear point and rambles on in many directions, introducing a number of ideas but developing none of them?

Paragraph A

Cheating

Cheating has always been a part of life, and it will be so in the future. An obvious situation is that students have many ways of cheating in school. This habit can continue after school is over and become part of their daily lives. There are steps that can be taken to prevent cheating, but many teachers do not seem to care. Maybe they are so burned out by their jobs that they do not want to bother. The honest student is often the one hurt by the cheating of others. Cheating at work also occurs. This cheating may be more dangerous, because employers watch out for it more. Businesses have had to close down because cheating by employees took away a good deal of their profits. A news story recently concerned a server who was fired for taking a steak home from the restaurant where he worked, but his taking the steak may have been justified. Cheating in the sense of being unfaithful to a loved one is a different story because emotions are involved. People will probably never stop cheating unless there is a heavy penalty to be paid.

Paragraph B

Everyday Cheating

Cheating is common in everyday life. For one thing, cheating at school is common. Many students will borrow a friend's homework and copy it in their own handwriting. Other students take or buy essays from Internet sites and claim them as their own. People also cheat on the job. They use the postage meter at work for personal mail, spend hours of company time sending personal e-mails, or take home office supplies such as tape, paper, or pens. Some people who are not closely supervised or who are out on the road may cheat an employer by taking dozens of breaks or using work time for personal chores. Finally, many people cheat when they deal with large businesses. For instance, few customers will report an incorrect bill in their favour. Visitors in a hotel may take home towels, and restaurant patrons may take home silverware. A customer in a store may change price tags because "this is how much the shirt cost last month." For many people, daily cheating is an acceptable way to behave.

Complete the following statement: Paragraph _____ is effective because it makes a clear, single point in the first sentence and goes on in the remaining sentences to support that single point.

Paragraph B starts with a *single idea,* that people cheat in everyday life, and then supports that idea with several different examples. But paragraph A does not begin by making a definite point. Instead, we get two broad, obvious statements: that cheating "has always been a part of life" and "will be so in the future." Because the author has not focused on a clear, single point, what happens in this paragraph is inevitable.

The line of thought in paragraph A swerves about in various directions. In the second sentence, we read that "students have many ways of cheating in school," and we think for a moment that this will be the author's point: he or she will give us supporting details about different ways students cheat in school. But the next sentence makes another point: that after school is over, students may continue to cheat as "part of their daily lives." We therefore expect the author to give us details backing up the idea that students who cheat continue to cheat after they leave or finish school. However, the next sentence makes two additional points: "There are steps that can be taken to prevent cheating, but many teachers do not seem to care." These are two more ideas that could be, but are not, the focus of the paragraph. By now we are not really surprised at what happens in the following sentences. Several more points are made: "The honest student is often the one hurt by the cheating of others," cheating at work "may be more dangerous," an employee who stole a steak "may have been justified," and cheating by being unfaithful is different "because emotions are involved." *No single idea is developed; the result is confusion.*

In summary, paragraph B is unified, but paragraph A shows a complete lack of unity.

PRACTICE IN MAKING AND SUPPORTING A POINT

The first important step in competent writing is to make a point. This section will expand and strengthen your understanding of how to make a strong point in a topic sentence.

You will first work through a series of activities on *making* a point:

1) Identifying Common Errors in Topic Sentences
2) Understanding the Two Parts of a Topic Sentence
3) Selecting a Topic Sentence
4) Writing a Topic Sentence: I
5) Writing a Topic Sentence: II

1   Identifying Common Errors in Topic Sentences

When writing the main point in a topic sentence, people sometimes make mistakes that undermine their chances of producing an effective paper. One mistake is to substitute an *announcement of the topic* for a true topic sentence. Other mistakes include *writing statements that are too broad or too narrow*. Here are examples of all three errors, along with contrasting examples of effective topic sentences.

Announcement

The purpose of this paragraph is to discuss why people move to cities.

The statement above is a simple announcement of a subject, rather than a topic sentence in which an idea is expressed about the subject. Announcing the purpose is both clumsy and redundant as an announcemtent adds unnecessary phrases, and the audience is already aware that they are reading a paragraph.

Statement That Is Too Broad

Many people move to cities.

The statement above is too broad to be supported adequately with specific details in a single paragraph.

Statement That Is Too Narrow or Does Not Take a Position

Regina is a city.

The statement above is too narrow to be expanded into a paragraph. Such a narrow statement is sometimes called a *dead-end statement* because there is no place to go with it. "Regina is a city" is a simple fact; it does not take a position on the city and therefore does not call for any support.

Effective Topic Sentence

The advantages of urban living have encouraged more Canadians to move to cities than at any other time.

The statement above expresses an opinion that could be supported in a paragraph. The writer could offer a series of specific supporting reasons, examples, and details to make it clear why he or she hates the car.
Here are additional examples.

Announcements

The subject of this paper will be my apartment.
I am writing this letter to protest the proposed tax increase.

Statements That Are Too Broad

The places where people live have definite effects on their lives.
Everybody pays taxes.

Statements That Are Too Narrow or Do Not Take a Position

I have no hot water in my apartment at night.

The proposed tax-rate increase has advantages and disadvantages.

Effective Topic Sentences

My apartment is a terrible place to live.

The proposed tax-rate increase is not appropriate at this time.

• • • • Activity 2

Identify the stronger topic sentences in each of the following pairs:

A. For each pair of sentences below, write *A* beside the sentence that only *announces* a topic. Write *OK* beside the sentence that *advances an idea* about the topic.

1. _____ a. I am going to write about my job as a gas station attendant.

   _____ b. Working as a gas station attendant was the most demanding job I ever had.

2. _____ a. Telemarketing is the subject of this paragraph.

   _____ b. People should know what to do when they receive a telemarketing phone call.

3. _____ a. In several ways, my college library is very easy to use.

   _____ b. This paragraph will deal with the college library.

B. For each pair of sentences below, write *TN* beside the statement that does not take a position or is *too narrow* to be developed into a paragraph. (Such a narrow statement is also known as a *dead-end sentence*.) Write *OK* beside the statement in each pair that calls for support or development of some kind.

1. _____ a. Farid works nine hours a day and then goes to school three hours a night.

   _____ b. Farid is an ambitious man.

2. _____ a. I started college after being away from school for seven years.

   _____ b. Several of my fears about returning to school have proved to be groundless.

3. _____ a. Parts of the NFB film *Get a Job* are interesting to college students.

   _____ b. Our class watched the NFB film *Get a Job* yesterday.

C. For each pair of sentences below, write *TB* beside the statement that is *too broad* to be supported adequately in a short paper. Write *OK* beside the statement that makes a limited point.

1. _____ a. Professional hockey is a dangerous sport.

   _____ b. Professional sports are violent.

2. _____   a. Married life is the best way of living.

   _____   b. Teenage marriages often end in divorce for several reasons.

3. _____   a. Computers are changing our society.

   _____   b. Using computers to teach children is having excellent results.

2   Understanding the Two Parts of a Topic Sentence

The point that opens and controls the content of a paragraph is expressed in a *topic sentence*. When you look closely at a topic sentence, you can see that it is made up of two parts:

1) The topic
2) The writer's *attitude* about the topic

The writer's attitude, position, or idea is usually expressed in one or more *keywords*. All the details in a paragraph should support the idea expressed in the keywords. In each of the topic sentences below, a single line appears under the topic and a double line under the idea or attitude about the topic (expressed in a keyword or keywords).

Highway accidents are often caused by absent-mindedness.

Voting should be required by law in Canada.

Students must learn effective study habits.

In the first sentence, the topic is *highway accidents,* and the keyword that determines the focus of the paragraph is that such accidents are often caused by *absent-mindedness.* Notice each topic and keyword or keywords in the other two sentences as well.

● ● ● ● ●   **Activity 3**

For each point below, draw a single line under the topic and a double line under the idea about the topic.

1. Billboards should be abolished.
2. My boss is an ambitious woman.
3. Politicians may be self-serving.
4. The apartment must be repaired.
5. Television commercials may be misleading.
6. My parents should not have such rigid racial attitudes.
7. The middle child is often a neglected member of the family.
8. The language in many movies today is offensive.
9. Doctors do not need to be insensitive.
10. Homeowners today must be more energy-conscious than ever before.

Further Insight—Modals

Modals are auxiliary verbs that express a variety of ideas including ability, possibility, certainty, strong advice, permission, expectation, criticism, and opinion.

Examples include (they may also be negatives):

to be able to	can	could	have to	may	might
must	need to	ought to	should	will	would

Modals are always followed by the simple version of the main verb, but are not, themselves, conjugated. Ideas expressed in college writing often require modal forms. When an author expresses an opinion in a topic sentence (as elsewhere) such as *Billboards should be abolished,* he or she is expressing an opinion and using the modal form.

Be alert to modal forms when you read and write. Modals are effective for their distinct expression of thought, but take care to choose the correct modal verb in its proper construction. Which of the topic sentences in Activity 3 used modals?

3 Selecting a Topic Sentence

Remember that a paragraph is made up of a topic sentence and a group of related sentences that develop and support the topic sentence. It is also helpful to remember that the topic sentence is a somewhat *general* statement. The other sentences provide specific support for the general statement. Supporting sentences include *subtopics,* which are subsections or categories of the topic presented. Each subtopic requires *specific supporting details* or examples to make it clear.

Activity 4

Each group of sentences that follow could be written as a short paragraph. Circle the letter of the topic sentence in each case. To find the topic sentence, ask yourself, "Which is a general statement supported by the specific details in the other three statements?"

Begin by trying the example item below. First circle the letter of the sentence you think expresses the main idea. Then read the explanation.

Example   a. Substitute water for coffee or pop at least once a day.
                b. Park farther away from the mall or the college, so you walk more.
                c. By changing a few habits, you can live a healthier life.
                d. Change one "empty calorie" snacking pattern a month.

Explanation: Sentence *a* describes one healthy habit. Sentences *b* and *d* also offer definite healthful behaviour choices. In sentence *c*, however, no one specific habit is mentioned. The words "changing a few habits" refer only generally to such habits. Therefore, sentence *c* is the topic sentence; it expresses the author's main idea. The other sentences support that idea by providing examples.

1. a. Its brakes are badly worn.
    b. My old car is ready for the junk pile.
    c. Its floor has rusted through, and water splashes on my feet when the highway is wet.
    d. My mechanic says its engine is too old to be repaired, and the car isn't worth the cost of a new engine.

2. a. It helps the body to produce the 'feel-good' hormones, endorphins.
    b. It gets air circulating through the lungs.
    c. Laughter is the best medicine.
    d. It helps people forget the troubles of the world.

3. a. Tobacco is one of the most addictive of all drugs.
    b. Selling cigarettes ought to be against the law.
    c. Non-smokers are put in danger by breathing the smoke from other people's cigarettes.
    d. Cigarette smoking kills many more people than all illegal drugs combined.

4. a. Contract workers are valuable commodities for employment agencies and for employers with specific needs.
    b. Contract workers are self-employed, for tax purposes, so they can write off many expenses such as gas used during the drive to work and back.
    c. Contract workers earn slightly less than permanent employees but may have the same net income because of fewer company deductions.
    d. Contract workers have distinct advantages in the workplace of the twenty-first century.

4   Writing A Topic Sentence: I

● ● ● ● **Activity 5**

The following activity will give you practice in writing an accurate topic sentence—one that is neither too broad nor too narrow for the supporting material in a paragraph. Sometimes you will construct your topic sentence after you have decided what details you want to discuss. This activity will show you how to write a topic sentence that will exactly match the subtopics or supporting details you have developed.

1. *Topic sentence:* _____

_____

    a. The bistro owner greeted us with a smile and seated us at a window table as soon as we arrived.
    b. Our appetizers and main courses were delicious.
    c. Our server brought us extra bread and more water.
    d. The desserts were homemade and garnished with whipped cream.

2. *Topic sentence:* _____

_____

   a. Some are caused by careless people tossing matches out of car windows.
   b. A few are started when lightning strikes a tree.
   c. Some result when campers fail to douse cooking fires.
   d. The majority of forest fires are deliberately set by arsonists.

3. *Topic sentence:* _____

_____

   a. The crowd scenes were crudely spliced from another film.
   b. Mountains and other background scenery were just poorly done computer graphics.
   c. The "sync" was off, so that the audience heard voices even when the actors' lips were not moving.
   d. The so-called monster was just a spider that had been filmed through a magnifying lens.

5   Writing a Topic Sentence: II

Often you will start with a general topic or a general idea of what you want to write about. You may, for example, want to write a paragraph about some aspect of school life. To come up with a point about school life, begin by narrowing your topic. One way to do this is to make a list of all the subtopics you can think of that fit under the general topic.

Activity 6

On the following pages are three general topics and a series of subtopics that fit under them. Make a point out of *one* of the subtopics in each group.

Hint: To create a topic sentence, ask yourself, "What point do I want to make about (*my subtopic*)?"

Example   Recreation
- Movies
- Dancing
- TV shows
- Reading
- Sports parks

Your point: *Sports parks today have some truly exciting games.*

1. Your college
- Instructor
- Cafeteria
- Specific class
- Particular room or building

- Particular policy (attendance, marking, etc.)
- Classmate

Your point: _____

2. Job
   - Pay
   - Boss
   - Working conditions
   - Duties
   - Co-workers
   - Customers or clients

Your point: _____

3. Money
   - Budgets
   - Credit cards
   - Dealing with a bank
   - School expenses
   - Ways to get it
   - Ways to save it

Your point: _____

STEP 2: SUPPORT THE POINT WITH SPECIFIC EVIDENCE—OVERVIEW

The first essential element in writing effectively, to *start with a clearly stated point*, was discussed in the first five sections of this chapter. The second basic step is to *support that point with specific evidence:*

6) Recognizing Specific Details: I
7) Recognizing Specific Details: II
8) Providing Specific Supporting Evidence
9) Identifying Adequate Supporting Evidence
10) Adding Details to Complete a Paragraph
11) Writing a Simple Paragraph

Following are the two examples of supported points that you have already read, on page 8 and on pages 50–51.

Example A

Point

Using the college's server can be a waste of time.

Subtopics

1. The server can go down for hours.

2. The college sends out a lot of e-mail I do not need.
3. Students clog up e-mail with chain letters.

Further Insight—General and specific and abstract and concrete

Topic sentences are often general statements that suggest abstract concepts—or concepts that can be understood, but not touched. It is only with the addition of adequate details that the topic becomes tangible. Consider the following quote by Canadian artist, Emily Carr:

"Cedars are terribly sensitive to change of time and light—sometimes they are bluish cold-green, then they turn yellow warm-green—sometimes their boughs flop heavy and sometimes float, then they are fairy as ferns and then they droop, heavy as heartaches."

The general topic, "cedars," and abstract concept, "sensitive to time and light," become more concrete and *specific* (albeit poetically) through the descriptions of colour that add fullness and life to the details of the whole image.

Example B

Point

Cheating is common in everyday life.

Subtopics and Supporting Details

1. At school
   a. Copying homework
   b. Cheating on essays
2. At work
   a. Using postage meter and company server for personal purposes
   b. Stealing office supplies
   c. Taking breaks and doing errands on company time
3. With large businesses
   a. Not reporting error on bill
   b. Stealing towels and silverware
   c. Switching price tags

The subtopics and supporting details are needed so that we can see and understand for ourselves that each writer's point is sound. By providing us with particulars about her experiences with the college server, the first writer shows why she believes it can be a waste of time. We can see that she has made a sound point. Likewise, the author of "Everyday Cheating" has supplied specific supporting examples of how cheating is common in everyday life. That paragraph, too, has provided the evidence (in the form of subtopics and details to support each) that is needed for us to understand and agree with the writer's point.

● ● ● ● ●   **Activity 7**

Your goal for this activity is to develop a sense of the varied and specific details that let a reader "see" the writer's point.

Both of the paragraphs that follow resulted from this assignment: "Write a paper that details your reasons for being in college." Both writers make the point that they have various reasons for attending college.

- Which paragraph then goes on to provide plenty of specific evidence to back up its point?
- Which paragraph is vague and repetitive and lacks the concrete details needed to show us exactly why the author decided to attend college?

Hint: Imagine that you've been asked to make a short film based on each paragraph. Which one suggests specific pictures, locations, words, and scenes you could shoot? Adequate and vivid details illustrate your writing, providing concrete images for your audience to see.

Paragraph A

Reasons for Going to College

I decided to attend college for various reasons. One reason is self-respect. For a long time now, I have felt little self-respect. I spent a lot of time doing nothing, just hanging around or getting into trouble, and eventually I began to feel bad about it. Going to college is a way to start feeling better about myself. By accomplishing things, I will improve my self-image. Another reason for going to college is that things happened in my life that made me think about a change. For one thing, I lost the part-time job I had. When I lost the job, I realized I would have to do something in life, so I thought about school. I was in a rut and needed to get out of it but did not know how. But when something happens that is out of your control, then you have to make some kind of decision. The most important reason for college, though, is to fulfill my dream. I know I need an education, and I want to take the courses I need to reach the position that I think I can handle. Only by gaining confidence and experience can I get what I want. Going to college will help me fulfill this goal. These are the main reasons why I am attending college.

Paragraph B

Why I'm in School

There are several reasons I'm in school. First of all my father's attitude made me want to succeed in school. One night last year, after I had come in at 3 a.m., my father said, "Sean, you're losing all respect for yourself. When I look at my son, all I see is a young man who doesn't care about himself." I was angry, but I knew my father was right in a way. I had spent the last two years working at odd jobs delivering pizza and repairing bikes, then spending all night at raves with my friends. That night, though, I decided I would prove my father wrong. I would go to college and be a success. Another reason I'm in college is my girlfriend's encouragement. Marie has already been in school for a year, and she is doing well in her computer technology courses. Marie helped me fill out my application and register for courses. She even lent me a hundred dollars for textbooks. On her day off, she lets me use her car so I don't have to take the bus. The main reason I am in college is to fulfill a personal goal: I want to finish something, for the first time in my life. For example, I quit high school at the end of grade eleven. Then I enrolled in a provincial job-training program, but I dropped out after six months. I tried to get my grade twelve certificate, but I started missing classes and eventually gave up. Now I am registered as a mature student in a special program where I will make up my missing high-school credits at night as part of first-semester work. I am determined to accomplish this goal and to then go on and work for a diploma in broadcast technology.

Complete the following statement: Paragraph _____ provides clear, vividly detailed reasons why the writer decided to attend college.

Paragraph B is the one that solidly backs up its point. The writer gives us specific reasons why he is in school. On the basis of such evidence, we can clearly understand his opening point. The writer of paragraph A offers only vague, general reasons for being in school. We do not get specific examples of how the writer was "getting into trouble," what events occurred that forced the decision, or even what kind of job he or she wants to qualify for. We sense that the feeling expressed is sincere; but without particular examples we cannot really see why the writer decided to attend college.

● ● ● ● **Activity 8**

As noted above, Paragraph B is the better of the model paragraphs. The author's point is that he is in school for several reasons. Analyze the paragraph and summarize in the spaces below the three reasons he gives to support his point.

1. _____

2. _____

3. _____

Notice what the supporting details in this paragraph do. They provide the reader with the basis for understanding why the writer feels the way he does. The writer has explained and communicated his position successfully through specific evidence.

Also notice how the writer has linked his reasons (subtopics) by using appropriate *transition words*. In the paragraph at the beginning of this chapter, *Everyday Cheating*, the writer effectively uses the transitions "For one thing," "also," and "Finally" to show that a new subtopic is being introduced. Identify three transition words or phrases that the writer uses in the paragraph, "Why I'm in School":

1. _____

2. _____

3. _____

The Importance of Specific Details

As you read in Chapter 2 (page 33), a paragraph's content moves from a somewhat general opening position to more specific statements.

The point that opens a paper is a general statement. The evidence that supports a point is generally made up of subtopics and their specific details, reasons, examples, and facts.

Specific details have two key functions:

- Details and specific ideas *excite the reader's interest.* They make writing a pleasure to read, for we all enjoy learning particulars about other people— what they do and think and feel.
- Details *support and explain a writer's point;* they give the evidence needed for us to see and understand a general idea.

For example, the writer of "Net Eats Student's Time!" in Chapter 1 provides details that make vividly clear why she feels using the college's server wastes her time. She specifies a precise occasion when she had to wait while the server was down (and how long she had to wait—two hours) and describes how restless and distracted she was while waiting for service to resume. She mentions checking her e-mail and finding many messages from the college to scroll through, then goes on to specify exactly why these posts were a waste of time (they were irrelevant to her and she had to read them to discover this and then delete them). She then tells us two specific details of her final reason for frustration with spending time on the Net: (1) she finds a number of messages so heavily weighted with addresses that they take a long time to load, and (2) the messages turn out to be student "chain letters."

The writer of "Why I'm in School" provides equally vivid details. He gives clear reasons for being in school (his father's attitude, his girlfriend's encouragement, and his wish to fulfill a personal goal) and backs up each reason with specific details. His details give us many sharp pictures. For instance, we hear the exact words his father spoke: "Sean, you're losing all respect for yourself." He tells us exactly how he was spending his time ("delivering pizza and repairing bikes, then spending all night at raves with my friends"). He describes how his girlfriend helped him (filling out the college application, lending money and her car). Finally, instead of stating generally that "you have to make some kind of decision," as the writer of "Reasons for Going to College" does, he specifies that he has a strong desire to finish college because he dropped out of schools and programs in the past: high school, a job-training program, and another try at high school.

In both "Net Eats Student's Time!" and "Why I'm in School," the vivid, exact details capture our interest and enable us to share in the writer's experience. We see people's actions and hear their words; the details provide pictures that make each of us feel "I am there." The particulars also allow us to understand each writer's point clearly. We are *shown* exactly why the first writer finds the college server a time-waster and exactly why the second writer is attending college.

• • • • •   **Activity 9**

In this activity, you will continue to sharpen your sense of what makes good specific support. Each of the five points below is followed by two attempts at support (*a* and *b*). Write *S* (for *specific*) in the space next to the one that succeeds in providing specific support for the point. Write *X* in the space next to the one that lacks supporting details.

1. My two-year-old son was in a stubborn mood today.

   _____   a. When I asked him to do something, he gave me nothing but trouble. He seemed determined to make things difficult for me, for he had his mind made up.

   _____   b. When I asked him to stop playing in the yard and come indoors, he looked me square in the eye and shouted "No!" and then spelled it out, "N . . . O!"

2. Students should ask advisors to help them decide which courses to take.

   _____   a. Some courses may seem interesting, but don't meet the program requirements.

   _____   b. A computer student may not realize that a math course in algorithms is a prerequisite for the Computer Architecture course.

3. Keeping healthy requires regular exercise.

   _____   a. Medical professionals recommend weekly activities such as walking or cycling that promote endurance, stretching or dancing for flexibility, and tennis or swimming for strength.

   _____   b. It is important that everybody who is able gets up and moves now and then.

4. The key to success in college is organization.

   _____   a. Knowing what they are doing, when they have to do it, and so on is a big help for a student. A system is crucial in achieving an ordered approach to study. Otherwise, things become very disorganized, and it is not long before a student's grades begin to drop.

   _____   b. Organized students never forget paper or exam dates, which are marked on a calendar above their desks. Instead of having to cram for exams, they study their clear, neat classroom and textbook notes on a daily basis.

Comments: The specific support for point 1 is answer *b*. The writer does not just tell us that the little boy was stubborn but provides an example that shows us. In particular, the detail of the son's spelling out "N . . . O!" makes his stubbornness vividly real for the reader. For point 2, answer *b* gives a specific course, Computer Architecture, along with a specific mathematical skill, algorithm. For point 3, answer *a* backs up the idea that specific types of physical activity are recommended for specific purposes. Point 4 is supported by answer *b*, which identifies two specific strategies of organized students: they mark important dates on calendars above their desks, and they take careful notes and study them daily.

In each of the four cases, the specific evidence enables us to see for ourselves that the writer's point is valid.

The Importance of Adequate Details

One of the most common and most serious problems in students' writing is inadequate development. You must provide *enough* specific details to support fully the point you are making. You could not, for example, submit a paragraph about how your brother-in-law is accident-prone and provide only a single short example. You would have to add several other examples or provide an extended example of your brother-in-law's accident-proneness. Without such additional support, your paragraph would be underdeveloped.

At times, students try to disguise an undersupported point by using repetition and wordy generalities. You saw this, for example, in paragraph A ("Reasons for Going to College") on page 60. Be prepared to do the plain hard work needed to ensure that each of your paragraphs has full and solid support.

● ● ● ● ● **Activity 10**

Your goal in this activity is to develop a sense of when support is sufficient to make a point clear. The following paragraphs were written on the same topic, and each has a clear opening point.

- Which one is adequately developed?
- Which one has few particulars and uses mostly vague, general, wordy sentences to conceal the fact that it is starved for specific details?

Paragraph A

New Uses for Public Parks

Canadians are finding new ways to use city parks. Instead of visiting large parks for playgrounds or for walks among the trees, people may go to the park to exercise in groups. People of every age do Tai Chi stretches every morning, while others band together for organized walks each evening. Each park has its joggers, runners, and cyclists, while others bring their weights to do workouts in the park's fresh air and quiet. Canadian city parks also host concerts, art shows, and plays. Suburban and waterfront parks offer children's festivals every summer; musicians return to parks for annual folk and world music events, and Shakespeare comes to stages in Toronto parks every July. Perhaps the most interesting "new" use of parks is really an old one: public rental gardens. Large parks rent "allotment gardens" where apartment dwellers plant and cultivate gardens each year. These park-gardeners fence off their spaces, plant flowers, fruits, and vegetables, and faithfully tend their plots every day. Allotment gardens began in the Depression when families on tight budgets tried to supplement their diets, and recently a group of U of T students started growing fruit and vegetables for the university's food bank, to help feed hungry people in today's economy. Some gardeners are from cultures used to growing their own produce, and still others simply enjoy the contact with nature and the seasons. Parks are made for people, and today, people are finding new ways to use and enjoy the peace, space, and land that parks offer.

Paragraph B

Uses for Public Parks

People use parks for many hobbies and activities. Exercising in the open air is healthy, and many people choose to take advantage of this in a variety of ways. Different types of people can be seen every day getting different forms of exercise in various parks. In fact, every season is suitable for some form of exercise in the park. But working at fitness in the fresh air is not the only reason people go to parks. Parks offer entertainment of every kind these days, which benefits the cultural life of the cities where the parks are located and draws many visitors. Many of these people might not otherwise visit a public park. Today, parks are full of children and their parents, people working at fitness, people admiring the trees and flowers, and people walking their pets. It is certainly obvious that parks have many attractions for people in today's cities.

Complete the following statement: Paragraph _____ provides an adequate number of specific details to support its point.

Paragraph A offers a series of detailed examples of new ways in which people are using public parks. Paragraph B, on the other hand, is underdeveloped. Paragraph B mentions only "different types of people . . . getting different forms of exercise," while paragraph A refers specifically to people who "do Tai Chi stretches . . . joggers, runners, and cyclists," and weightlifters and groups of walkers. Paragraph B talks generally of "entertainment of every kind" in parks, while paragraph A specifies "concerts, art shows, and plays," as well as children's festivals, music events, and Shakespeare in outdoor park theatres. Moreover, there is no parallel in paragraph B for paragraph A's point and details about allotment gardens and the people who cultivate them. In summary, paragraph B lacks the full, specifically detailed support needed to develop its opening point convincingly.

● ● ● ● **Review Activity**

To check your understanding of the chapter so far, see if you can answer the following questions.

1. Someone has observed: "To write well, the first thing that you must do is decide what nail you want to drive home." What is meant by *nail?*

_____

2. How do you *drive home the nail* in a paper?

_____

3. What are the two reasons for using specific details in your writing?

 a. _____

 b. _____

6   Recognizing Specific Details: I

Specific details are examples, reasons, particulars, and facts. Such details are needed to support and explain a topic sentence effectively. Each subtopic sentence needs specific details to clarify and explain it, as well. Specific details provide the evidence needed for readers to understand, as well as to feel and experience, a writer's point. Specific details allow readers to *see* your point clearly.

Here is a topic sentence followed by two sets of supporting sentences. Which set provides sharp, specific details?

Topic Sentence

Some poor people must struggle to make meals for themselves.

Set A

They gather up whatever free food they can find in fast-food restaurants and take it home to use however they can. Unless they have access to food banks, they base their diet on anything they can buy that is cheap and filling.

Set B

Some add hot water to the free packets of ketchup they get at fast-food places to make tomato soup. Others buy cheap canned dog food and fry it like hamburger.

Set B provides specific details: instead of a general statement about "free food they can find in fast-food restaurants and take . . . home to use however they can," we get a vivid detail we can see and picture clearly: "free packets of ketchup they get at fast-food places to make tomato soup." Instead of a general statement about how the poor will "base their diet on anything they can buy that is cheap and filling," we get exact and vivid details: "Others buy cans of cheap canned dog food and fry it like hamburger."

Specific details are often like the information we might find in a movie script, as we mentioned on pages 59–60. They provide us with such clear pictures that we could make a film of them if we wanted to. You would know just how to film the information given in set B. You would show a poor person breaking open a packet of ketchup from some fast-food place and mixing it with water to make a kind of tomato soup. You would show someone opening a can of dog food and frying its contents like hamburger.

In contrast, the writer of set A fails to provide the specific information needed. If you were asked to make a film based on set A, you would have to figure out for yourself just what particulars you were going to show.

When you are working to provide specific supporting information in a paper, it might help to ask yourself, "Could someone easily film this information?" If the answer is yes, you probably have good details. Your specific details help you to *show*, not *tell*.

● ● ● ● ● **Activity 11**

Your aim in this activity is to strengthen your "eye" for specific details. Each topic sentence below is followed by two sets of supporting details (*a* and *b*). Write S (for *specific*) in the space next to the set that provides specific support for the point. Write G (for *general*) next to the set that offers only vague, general support.

1. *Topic sentence:* My roommate is messy.

    _____ a. He doesn't seem to mind that he can't find any clean clothes or dishes. He never puts anything back in its proper place; he just drops it wherever he happens to be. His side of the room looks as if a hurricane has gone through.

    _____ b. His coffee cup is covered inside with a thick layer of green mould. I can't tell you what colour his easy chair is; it has disappeared under a pile of dirty laundry. When he turns over in bed, I can hear the crunch of cracker crumbs beneath his body.

2. *Topic sentence:* Antonetta is very assertive.

    _____ a. Her assertiveness is apparent in both her personal and her professional life. She is never shy about extending social invitations. And while some people are turned off by her assertiveness, others are impressed by it and enjoy doing business with her.

    _____ b. When she meets a man she likes, she is quick to say, "Let's go out for coffee sometime." In her job as a furniture salesperson, she will call potential customers to let them know when new stock is coming in.

3. *Topic sentence:* Cell phones may be hazardous to people's health and safety.

    _____ a. Talking on a cell phone while driving has been found to diminish a person's ability to react as much as driving drunk. Electromagnetic radiation from both the phones and towers have been implicated in an increase in cancers and other disorders. It has even been suggested that cell phones have contributed to youth crime when they are used to invite others to participate in group violence.

_____ b. They interfere with driving. There's a chance that they can even make you sick. And now, people use cell phones to commit crimes.

Further Insight—W5, the journalists' questions

While college writing differs in structure and content from popular journalistic writing, both are intended to explain and give full information. Journalists are expected to cover their "stories" by assessing that in every case they have answered all journalists' questions, commonly referred to as W5. There are actually six questions that must be covered in order to provide full and adequate detail. They are:

Who?	What?	When?
Where?	Why?	How?

Journalists' questions can help you discover a topic, as described in Chapter 2. You can also use them to be sure you have provided a full explanation of each point you make by checking that each of the questions is answered. Identify the answers to each of the journalists' questions in the following passage:

Although the Canadian Constitution was repatriated from the United Kingdom to Ottawa in 1981, and officially signed in 1982, many leaders of the First Nations did not consider that the document adequately recognized their right to self-government. This was partly because the term "aboriginal" was not clearly defined, so Native leaders feared that people without sufficient claims to aboriginal status would nevertheless try to claim any benefits the Constitution would offer.

Ask questions specific to your point by anticipating what your *audience* will want to know. Check that your writing has completely covered all details by identifying the answers for each of the W5 questions.

---

7   Recognizing Specific Details: II

• • • •   **Activity 12**

At several points in the following paragraphs you are given a choice of two sets of supporting details. Write *S* (for *specific*) in the space next to the set that provides specific support for that point. Write *G* (for *general*) next to the set that offers only vague, general support.

Paragraph A

The Caribana festival in Toronto may look and sound like a big party, but there is more to it than just a good time. For one thing, Caribbean carnivals have more history than people realize.

_____ a. Caribana began in the Caribbean islands with various carnivals. On these islands, slaves could not get together socially or celebrate their heritage or African history. When they were freed, they began to hold parades for which they created songs and dances that mixed old and new ideas. They made fancy costumes and masks, and people wearing these misbehaved sometimes. Carnivals or masquerades could be quite wild events where people could speak their minds in songs and act out their thoughts in exciting dances. Caribbean festivals are now organized competitions.

_____ b. Caribana's beats and costumes began with carnivals on Trinidad and Tobago. When slavery ended on "T&T" in the 1830s, islanders celebrated the start of Lent with African drumming and dancing. They made their own versions of European gowns and fancy jackets in silks and satins to make fun of their former masters. Some costumes turned into full masquerade disguises like bats, clowns, and Indian rajahs. People could criticize bosses and politicians from behind their masks, and the parades grew longer, louder, and more organized. In the twentieth century, calypso singers spoke their minds in songs, and steel drums gave more new sounds to the carnivals. Soon people of all races were dressing up and "playing mas."

In Toronto, Caribana has an interesting story behind it as well.

_____ c. Over thirty-five years ago, it began as a community project for Canada's centennial. The people who started Caribana intended to show off Caribbean culture and how it belonged in Canada. Their first small parade started near Bloor and St. George and continued down Yonge Street for only a few blocks. At this one-day affair, participants simply went home after the parade or ended up at family parties. Now that one-day festival is a two-week event with nearly 300,000 visitors from New York, Ohio, Michigan, Pennsylvania, and Illinois. Caribana is now North America's largest Caribbean festival.

_____ d. Caribana was a little get-together for islanders when it started out. Most cultural groups had events they wanted to contribute to Canada's centennial celebrations, and West Indians were no exception. From a short parade with some lively music and dancers, the festival has turned into a marathon cultural show with picnics and parties. This major event lasts a couple of weeks and brings many visitors and tourist dollars to Toronto.

Finally, the best thing about Caribana might be the way it brings all kinds of people together.

_____ e. Caribana today isn't only for West Indians. Everyone can come and enjoy the party. People like to try different foods, and after listening to the mas bands, they want to try various ways of dancing along with the paraders, too. Now Spanish culture is starting to become part of the festival, with its Latin rhythms and spicy foods. Everyone loves a party, it seems.

_____ f. The first Caribana welcomed other West Indian countries, including Jamaica, the Bahamas, Antigua, and Barbados. Everyone brought his or her island's music, food, and costumes—from Jamaican ska to Trinidadian roti. Today floats from Brazilian entrants pulse with samba beats, and festival visitors try out their Spanish to order a *café* or sandwich *Cubano*. As the festival grows, more faces and sounds from Toronto's cultures appear at Caribana's functions.

Paragraph B

Many adult children move back in with their parents for some period of time. Although living with Mom and Dad again has some advantages, there are certain problems that are likely to arise. One common problem is that children may expect their parents to do all the household chores.

_____ a. They never think that they should take on their share of work around the house. Not only do they not help with their parents' chores, they don't even take responsibility for the extra work that their presence creates. Like babies, they go through the house making a mess that they expect their parents to clean up. It's as if they think their parents are their servants.

_____ b. They expect meals to appear on the table as if by magic. After they've eaten, they go off to work or play, never thinking about who's going to do the dishes. They drop their dirty laundry beside the washing machine, assuming that Mom will attend to it and return clean, folded clothes to their bedroom door. And speaking of their bedroom: every day they await the arrival of Mom's Maid Service to make the bed, pick up the floor, and dust the furniture.

Another problem that frequently arises is that parents forget their children are no longer adolescents.

_____ c. Parents with kids living at home want to know everything about their adult children's lives. They don't think their kids, even though they are adults, should have any privacy. Whenever they see their children doing anything, they want to know all the details. It's as though their children are still teenagers who are expected to report all their activities. Naturally, adult children get irritated when they are treated as if they were teenagers.

_____ d. They may insist upon knowing far more about their children's comings and goings than the children want to share. For example, if such parents see their adult son heading out the door, they demand to know: Where is he going? Who will he be with? What will he be doing? What time will he be back? In addition, they may not let their adult child have any privacy. If their daughter and a date are sitting in the living room, for instance, they may join them there and start asking the young man questions about his family and his job, as if they were interviewing him for the position of son-in-law.

Finally, there may be financial problems when an adult child returns to live at home.

_____ e. Having an extra adult in the household creates extra expenses. But many adult children don't offer to help deal with those extra costs. Adult children often eat at home, causing the grocery bill to climb. They may stay in a formerly unused room, which now needs to be heated and lit. They produce extra laundry to be washed. They use the telephone, adding to the long-distance bill. For all these reasons, adult children should expect to pay a reasonable amount to their parents for room and board.

_____ f. It's expensive to have another adult living in the household. Adult children would be paying a lot of bills on their own if they weren't staying with their parents. It's only fair that they share the expenses at their parents' house. They should consider all the ways that their living at home is increasing their parents' expenses. Then they should insist upon covering their share of the costs.

8 Providing Specific Supporting Evidence

This activity can be done by students individually or in groups.

Individual Activity Provide three details that logically support the points made in each of the following topic sentences. Your details can be drawn from your own experience, or they can be invented. In each case, the details should show in a specific way what the point expresses in only a general way. State your details briefly in phrases rather than in complete sentences.

Group Activity   In each group of five students, have each person select one of the following topic sentences. Each student will provide three details to specifically support and illustrate his or her point. Students may then exchange papers within the group and evaluate the quality of one another's supporting evidence, or groups may compare responses.

Example   The student had several ways of passing time during the dull lecture.

a.   *Shielded his eyes with his hand and dozed for a while*

b.   *Read the sports magazine he had brought to class*

c.   *Made an elaborate drawing on a page of his notebook*

1. I could tell I was coming down with the flu.

   a. _____

   b. _____

   c. _____

2. Canadians should vacation in their own country.

   a. _____

   b. _____

   c. _____

3. There are practical steps that can be taken to guard against identity theft.

   a. _____

   b. _____

   c. _____

4. Students often find clever ways to economize.

   a. _____

   b. _____

   c. _____

5. Exciting innovations are being developed that will help with energy conservation.

   a. _____

   b. _____

   c. _____

9 Identifying Adequate Supporting Evidence

● ● ● ● ● **Activity 13**

Two of the following paragraphs provide clear subtopics and sufficient details to support their topic sentences convincingly. Write *AD*, for *adequate development*, beside those paragraphs. There are also three paragraphs that, for the most part, use vague, general, or wordy sentences as a substitute for clear subtopics and concrete details. Write *U*, for *underdeveloped*, beside those paragraphs.

_____1.   **Street Hockey: Tradition or Torture?**

Street hockey has always been popular with boys and girls in Red Deer, Alberta, so we feel we have a tradition to keep up, but it is becoming an increasingly dangerous pastime. Games are constantly interrupted by cars and trucks. This fall, one of the new girl players, who was captain of her school's field hockey team, believed she had to prove herself to us. Unaware of the amount of traffic on seemingly quiet streets, she plowed forward, head down, eyes focused on the ball, and nearly wound up as the hood ornament on a minivan. Late-night drinking drivers make street hockey even more hazardous. Bottles thrown out the windows shatter on the pavement, and large chunks of glass get picked up by hockey sticks as we chase the ball. Two players ended up in Emergency: one with a dangerous cut over his eye, the other with six stitches in his forearm; both injuries were caused by flying glass. The most dangerous incident, though, had nothing to do with traffic; it was a combination of ordinary carelessness and modern lawn care. A wild shot sent the ball onto someone's newly treated front yard. Our forward sprinted to retrieve the ball, tripped over the "dangerous chemical" sign, and fell face forward into damp grass, freshly soaked in weed killer. He turned out to be violently allergic to the ingredients and went into something like an asthma attack. We had to call 911 for paramedics with inhalers and oxygen. So a traditional teenage prairie sport has lost some of its appeal these days and, in fact, has become more of a hazard than a tradition for its players.

_____2.   **Attitudes about Food**

Attitudes that we form as children about food are not easily changed. In some families, food is love. Not all families are like this, but some children grow up with this attitude. Some families think of food as something precious and not to be wasted. The attitudes children pick up about food are hard to change in adulthood. Some families celebrate with food. If a child learns an attitude, it is hard to break this later. Someone once said: "As the twig is bent, so grows the tree." Children are very impressionable, and they can't really think for themselves when they are small. Children learn from the parent figures in their lives and later from their peers. Some families have healthy attitudes about food. It is important for adults to teach their children these healthy attitudes. Otherwise, the children may have weight problems when they are adults.

_____3.   **Qualities in a Friend**

There are several qualities I look for in a friend. A friend should give support and security. A friend should also be fun to be around. Friends can have faults, like anyone else, and sometimes it is hard to overlook them. But a friend can't be dropped because he or she has faults. A friend should stick by a friend, even in bad times. There is a saying that "a friend in need is a friend indeed." I believe this means that there are good friends and fair-weather friends. The second type is not a true friend. He or she is the kind of person who runs when there's trouble. Friends don't always last a lifetime. Someone believed to be a best friend may lose contact if a person moves to a different area or goes around with a different group of people. A friend should be generous and understanding. A friend does not have to be exactly like you. Sometimes friends are opposites, but they still like each other and get along. Since I am a very quiet person, I can't say that I have many friends. But these are the qualities I believe a friend should have.

_____4.   **Schoolyard Card Sharks**

There is something odd about the evenings-only men's club in the nearby school playground. As dusk gathers over Halifax, under the arc lights provided for the children's protection, a group of gentlemen like to get together. The members of this society have a uniform: ball caps worn back to front, XXL-size shirts, and unlaced athletic shoes. Sheltering behind the wooden climbing castle, they arrange their chosen furniture, worn folding chairs stolen from the neighbourhood's front porches. Next, raised ritual handgrips are exchanged, and the fraternal greetings are heard: "How the h__ are ya?" "So where were ya last night?" As a rough circle is formed by the players' chairs, packs of Export A emerge from pockets and sleeves, and the sacramental beverages of Molson Ex and Gatorade are readied for the tense action to follow. Finally, the stakes are agreed upon, and the equipment is carefully placed on a pilfered card table: two dog-eared decks of playing cards. Is their game five-card stud or blackjack, deuces wild? No, it's euchre—the same game their grandparents play in their retirement homes. Youth and age meet in odd ways, in odd locations.

10   Adding Details to Complete a Paragraph

Each of the following paragraphs needs specific details to back up its supporting points. In the spaces provided, add a sentence or two of realistic details for each supporting point. The more specific you are, the more convincing your details are likely to be.

1.   **An Inspiring Instructor**

After only a class or two, it was clear that the new computer graphics instructor was very good at her job. First of all, she made personal contact with every student in the class. _____

_____

_____

_____

In addition, she gave out extremely clear course requirements. _____

_____

_____

_____

Finally, she encouraged all the students to ask questions. _____

_____

_____

_____

2.   **Helping a Parent in College**

There are several ways a family can help a parent who is attending college. First, family members can take over some of the household chores that the parent usually does. _____

_____

_____

Also, family members can make sure that the student has some quiet study time. _____

_____

_____

_____

Last, families can take an interest in the student's problems and accomplishments.

_____

_____

_____

11   Writing a Simple Paragraph

You know now that an effective paragraph does two essential things: (1) it makes a point, and (2) it provides specific details to support that point. You have considered a number of paragraphs that are effective because they follow these two basic steps or are ineffective because they fail to follow them.

You are ready, then, to write a simple paragraph of your own. Choose one of the three assignments below, and follow carefully the guidelines provided.

● ● ● ● **Assignment 1**

Turn back to the activities in Section 8 and, if you did the individual activity, select the point for which you have the best supporting details. Otherwise, choose a point for which you could develop strong support. Develop that point into a paragraph by following these steps.

   a. If necessary, rewrite the point so that the first sentence is more specific or suits your purpose more exactly. For example, you might want to rewrite the second point so that it includes a specific place: "Taking a vacation in and around Vancouver has many attractive possibilities."

   b. Use one or two methods of prewriting to generate details about your topic. When you are satisfied with what you have accumulated, see if the details can be grouped under more general or subtopic headings. You are looking for three subtopics for your topic. For example, a student writing about vacationing near Vancouver might find that he or she has details that fit under three headings: city attractions like Stanley Park, Whistler and ski resorts, and Victoria and the coastal islands. You may find it useful to reread Paul's experience with the writing process on pages 41–47.

   c. Using a copy or template of the Paragraph Outline Form on page 33, provide several details to develop fully each of your three subtopics. Make sure that all the information in your outline truly supports your point.

   d. Write your first draft based on your outline. Conclude your paragraph with a sentence that refers to your opening point. This last sentence "rounds off" the paragraph and lets the reader know that your discussion is complete. For example, the second paragraph about cheating on pages 50–51 begins

with "Cheating is common in everyday life." It closes with a statement that refers to and echoes the opening point: "For many people, daily cheating is an acceptable way to behave."

e. Revise your first draft. Does each sentence truly support your topic? Is the order in which you stated your ideas reasonable? Check to make sure that you use transition words like *first of all, second* or *next,* and *finally, most,* or *last* to introduce your three supporting details. It might be useful to call on a peer to check through your paragraph to check that you have provided adequate details and effective transitions.

f. Supply a title based on the point. For instance, point 4 page 72 might have the title "Ways to Economize."

g. Read your paragraph aloud, if possible, or to yourself. If any sentences do not sound right, correct them; refer to Section Four of this book where needed. If you have been drafting on the computer, run the spell checker and double-check your spelling choices with the dictionary. If you are handwriting your draft, use a dictionary to check any words of which you are not certain.

Use the following list to check your paragraph for each of the above items.

YES	NO	
————	————	Do you begin with a point?
————	————	Do you provide relevant, specific details that support the point?
————	————	Do you use the words *first of all, second,* and *finally* to introduce your three supporting details?
————	————	Do you have a closing sentence that refers back to your opening point?
————	————	Do you have a title based on the point?
————	————	Are your sentences clear and free from obvious errors?

• • • • • Assignment 2

In this chapter you have read two paragraphs (pages 60–61) on reasons for being in college. For this assignment, write a paragraph that would advise a young person how to assess their reasons for going to college. You might want to look first at the following list of common reasons students give for going to school. Your experience may offer other reasons that you think would be useful for a potential student to know about. Select three of the most important reasons for going to college as subtopics, and generate specific supporting details for each reason.

Before starting, reread paragraph B on pages 60–61. *You must provide comparable specific details.* Make your paragraph truly specific and helpful; do not fall back on vague generalities like those in paragraph A on page 60. Use the checklist for Assignment 1 as a guideline as you work on the paragraph.

APPLY IN MY CASE   *Reasons Students Go to College*

————   • To acquire employment-related skills

————   • To prepare for a specific career

_____   • To please their families

_____   • To educate and enrich themselves

_____   • To be with friends

_____   • To take advantage of an opportunity they didn't have before

_____   • To see if college has anything to offer them

_____   • To do more with their lives than they've done so far

_____   • To take advantage of provincial or federal assistance programs or other special funding

_____   • To earn the status that they feel comes with a college diploma

_____   • To get a new start in life

• • • • Assignment 3

Write a paragraph about conserving energy. Choose three of the following areas where energy is used and provide specific examples and details to develop each area.

Energy use at school
Energy use at work
Energy use at home
Energy use and transportation.

Use the checklist for Assignment 1 as a guideline while working on the paragraph.

REVIEWING THE LEARNING OUTCOMES FOR CHAPTER 3

To assure yourself that you have understood and met the learning outcomes for this chapter, answer the following questions.

✓ What is the first sentence in an effective paragraph called? What does that first sentence do?

✓ How do the rest of the sentences in an effective paragraph relate to this sentence?

✓ How does a subtopic differ from a supporting detail?

✓ What are three reasons why specific supporting details are necessary for an effective paragraph?

✓ Why must there be adequate supporting details for each subtopic?

Visit the *English Skills with Readings: Examining Paragraphs* Online Learning Centre at <u>www.mcgrawhill.ca/olc/langan</u> to access self-quizzes, internet-based questions and research skills, web resources, and other learning and study tools.

Chapter 4

The Third Step in Writing

LEARNING OUTCOMES

After reading this chapter and completing its activities, you will

- know how to achieve coherence by organizing your paragraph's support with an appropriate ordering method;

- be ready to create coherence by using transitions to organize and connect supporting material;

- know six types of transitional signal words and phrases;

- know three methods of indicating transition or connection between ideas; and

- know why reading audiences require transitional words and phrases.

Chapter 3 introduced two vital goals for effective writing.

- First, it emphasized the necessity to make a point to establish **unity.**
- Next, it explained the necessity to provide sufficient details, to provide **support.**

In this chapter, you will be instructed how to maintain **coherence** by ensuring:

- that your details are presented in a *logical order,* and
- that your paragraph includes appropriate *transitions* to connect your ideas.

You will learn and practise the main ways to organize and connect the supporting information in a paragraph or essay.

Chapter 5 will then focus on the fourth step in writing: revising and editing for clear, **error-free sentences.**

STEP 3: ORGANIZE AND CONNECT THE SPECIFIC EVIDENCE

At the same time that you are generating the specific details needed to support a point, you should be thinking about ways to organize and connect those details. It is also vital to check for these as you revise your paragraph. All the details in your paper must **cohere,** or **stick together;** when they do, your reader is able to move smoothly and clearly from one bit of supporting information to the next. This chapter will discuss the following ways to organize and connect supporting details: (1) common methods of organization, (2) transitions, and (3) other connecting words.

Common Methods of Organization: Time Order, Thematic Order, and Emphatic Order

Time order, thematic order, and emphatic order are common methods used to organize the supporting material in a paper. You will learn more specialized methods of development in Section Two of the book.

Time order simply means that details are listed as they occur in time: *first* this is done; *next* this; *then* this; *after* that, this; and so on. Here is a paragraph that organizes its details through time order.

Torture by Telephone

When I left high school in grade eleven, I turned into an expert in the field of depressing short-term jobs. Every one of these jobs involved a routine, but none could compare to my nightly ritual as a telemarketer. First, my shift started every evening at five, just when everyone else was leaving work. The elevators kept letting out all these relaxed people, and there I was, waiting to go up to the twelfth floor and start work. After that, I walked down empty hallways and entered my torture chamber, where the fluorescent lights glared and computers hummed twenty-four hours a day. I started each shift by trying to adjust my chair, but it never worked, so I hunched over and turned on my computer terminal. I reached for my headset and silently prayed that it was clean. Then, when I turned on the set, I waited for the crackling sound that would rustle through every call all night long. I was never disappointed. The next step before actually starting to call people involved some suspense—would the right program open up on my terminal? I had to follow a script that appeared on the screen, and even if I had the right program, sometimes it ran so slowly that I ran out of things to say to the poor person on the other end of the line. The final treats every night were the supervisor's visits, when she always told me to do the impossible: "Smile and dial."

Fill in the missing words: "Torture by Telephone" uses the following words to help show time order: _____, _____, _____, _____, and _____.

Thematic order allows the author to make distinctions by dividing the topic into distinct classifications based on specific attributes. The advantage of using a thematic approach is that an author can discuss important issues in detail, while not attributing more importance to one over the other. In order to determine which order to present the points, divide the topic into three parts, and present them in an order that would draw the audience along to follow your understanding. The following paragraph follows a thematic approach.

Have Sense, Will Travel

As the need to conserve energy becomes more critical, people must rethink their attitudes about how they manage their daily travel. The family car is still an important tool to most Canadians, yet they must consider the types of vehicles that are sound environmental and economic purchases. Manufacturers are developing hybrid cars that run on a combination of electricity and gasoline. They may eventually offer alternatives to the energy-intensive internal-combustion engine that cars use now. Even choosing smaller, lighter, and more energy-efficient cars instead of large and heavy SUVs can result in significant savings. Of course, drivers should also assess how they drive, and how often, so they do not use resources unnecessarily. Experts advise that gas efficiency increases significantly when drivers travel below 100 kilometres an hour. This may be a "hard sell" to those who feel time pressured throughout their busy working lives, but such a small lifestyle adjustment may at least help to alleviate some stress by allowing drivers to stay away from gas stations a bit more often. Of course, another way to conserve energy is simply to use a car less frequently. Trips should be planned for efficiency, combining tasks such as driving children to their activities with necessary household shopping. Or, Canadians could adapt more to alternate transportation options, such as carpooling, cycling, and, of course, becoming regular users of public transit. Canadians may fear that increasing fuel costs may keep them from enjoying their accustomed manner of mobility, but perhaps while they undertake energy-saving measures, they may find that there are more options than they had realized.

Fill in the blanks: "Have Sense, Will Travel" offers the three main subtopics: _____, _____, and _____. How was the *thematic order* determined?_____

Emphatic order is a form of *thematic order, but is* sometimes described as "save-the-best-'til-last" order. It means that the most interesting or important detail is placed in the last part of a paper. (In cases where all the details seem equal in importance, the writer should impose a personal order that seems logical or appropriate to the details in question.) The last position in a paper is the most emphatic position because the reader is most likely to remember the last thing read. *Finally, last of all,* and *most important* are typical words showing emphasis. The following paragraph organizes its details through emphatic order.

Riding the Cranky Turtle

Who doesn't enjoy taking the car to school? Public transportation is not necessarily "the better way" for everyone. Many people do not enjoy using buses and subways, for a variety of reasons. First of all, at morning and evening rush hours, when most students are going to or leaving college, packs of people throng the bus stops and subway platforms. Riders lose their manners while fighting for a way through the narrow vehicle doorways. Rush-hour crowds can also mean standing during the ride, while carrying heavy bookbags or equipment. This discomfort should be multiplied by the number of people who push, shove, act rudely, or, worse, smell nasty. Additionally, there is the "turtle factor." Buses are often behind schedule and drivers seem to schedule coffee stops just when students are worrying about getting to nine o'clock classes. Subway trains have their mysterious dark pauses, usually inside tunnels, leaving riders unable even to read their watches. But most awful of all are the prices charged for all this inconvenience. Those who suffer most are students who live far from school and need to use several different bus systems that cost double or triple fares. Generally, fares are over two dollars for a one-way ride, and service barely exists. Drivers can be unpleasant or short-tempered from overwork, so asking even a simple question about a stop could result in a snarled answer or no answer at all. The four or five dollars spent on two tickets could pay for a day's parking and maybe even enough gas for the trip. If college students look tired or sour, perhaps it's the result of riding on a very cranky and expensive turtle.

Fill in the missing words: The paragraph lists a total of _____ different reasons why students dislike public transportation. The writer of the paragraph feels that the most important reason is _____. He or she signals this reason by using the emphasis words _____.

Some paragraphs use a *combination of time order, thematic order, and emphatic order*. For example, "Net Eats Student's Time!" on page 8 includes time order: it moves from the time the writer tried to access the server to the end of the evening. In addition, the writer uses emphatic order, ending with her greatest source of irritation, signalled by the words "the final stage in my annoyance."

1 Organizing Through Time Order

● ● ● ● Activity 1

Use time order to organize the scrambled list of sentences below. First choose the point that all the other sentences support, and write the number *1* next to it. Then choose one of three methods for completing the exercise:

1. Read all the items through, and write a number for each supporting sentence as it occurs in time sequence in the spaces provided.

2. Type each supporting item and use the cut and paste functions on your computer to move the sentences around until they are in the correct time sequence.

3. Number the sentences, and then print your document. [Or, if you are using paper, copy the sentences on one side of the sheet, leaving spaces between them so you can cut them into strips to rearrange.]

_____ The table is right near the garbage pail.

_____ So you reluctantly select a glue-like tuna-fish sandwich, a crushed-in apple pie, and watery, lukewarm coffee.

_____ You sit at the edge of the table, away from the garbage pail, and gulp down your meal.

_____ Trying to eat in the cafeteria is an unpleasant experience.

_____ Suddenly you spot a free table in the corner.

_____ With a last swallow of the lukewarm coffee, you get up and leave the cafeteria as rapidly as possible.

_____ Flies are flitting in and out of the pail.

_____ By the time it is your turn, the few things that are almost good are gone.

_____ There does not seem to be a free table anywhere.

_____ Unfortunately, there is a line in the cafeteria.

_____ The submarine sandwiches, doughnuts, and iced tea have all disappeared.

_____ You hold your tray and look for a place to sit down.

_____ You have a class in a few minutes, and so you run in to grab something to eat quickly.

2   Organizing Through Thematic Order

• • • • Activity 2

Use thematic order to organize the following scrambled list of sentences using one of the methods from Activity 1.

First, identify the three main themes that are discussed and number them *1, 2, 3*. Then identify the details that complete each of the subtopics.

Note: When using thematic order, arrange the subtopics in a sequence that suits you best, as there is no specific "correct" response.

_____ They will only investigate a site thoroughly if the information can be expected to be complete and credible.

_____ As an example, a site user trying to find a florist near her aunt in Moose Jaw is not going to tolerate a whirl of images from virtually every other city in Canada.

_____ The people who use Internet sites expect to be able to use them with ease.

_____ When creating web pages, it is important to consider the users who will access the site.

_____ If a person needs information about taxes or immigration services, as examples, that person will be willing to read more detail to gain all the necessary information.

_____ Internet users dislike distracting elements.

_____ They want to be able to see the print and understand the message without effort.

_____ A good designer will always keep these practical tips in mind.

_____ For this reason, website designers should avoid inappropriate computer graphics or flash introductions that may annoy a busy user.

_____ Users scan for information, rather than read intensely.

_____ If, for example, the font is too fussy to be clearly understood, or the writing so poor that the message is unclear, a user will not make an effort to return to that site.

3   Organizing Through Emphatic Order

● ● ● ●   Activity 3

Use emphatic order (order of importance) to arrange the following scrambled list of sentences. Write the number *1* beside the point that all the other sentences support. Then, using one of the methods suggested in the preceding activities number each supporting sentence, starting with what seems to be the least important detail and ending with the most important detail.

_____ The people in my area of Swift Current are all around my age and seem to be genuinely friendly and interested in me.

_____ The place where I live has several important advantages.

_____ The schools in this neighbourhood have a good reputation, so I feel that my daughter is getting a good education.

_____ The best thing of all about this area, though, is the school system.

_____ Therefore, I don't have to put up with public transportation or worry about how much it's going to cost to park each day.

_____ The school also has an extended daycare program, so I know my daughter is in good hands until I come home from work.

_____ First of all, I like the people who live in the other apartments near mine.

_____ Another positive aspect of this area is that it's close to where I work.

_____ That's more than I can say for the last place I lived, where people never seemed to say hello.

_____ The office where I'm a receptionist is only a six-block walk from my house.

_____ In addition, I save a lot of wear and tear on my car.

4 Organizing Through a Combination of Time Order, Thematic Order, and/or Emphatic Order

● ● ● ● **Activity 4**

Use a *combination* of time order, thematic order, and emphatic order to arrange the scrambled list of sentences below. Write the number *1* beside the point that all the other sentences support. Then, using one of the three methods suggested in the two preceding activities, number each supporting sentence. Paying close attention to transitional words and phrases will help you organize and connect the supporting sentences.

_____ I did not see the snake but visited my friend in the Gravenhurst hospital, where he suffered for days because of the snakebite venom.

_____ We were taking our time, dawdling along side roads, when we decided to eat lunch in the woods by the roadside.

_____ As I walked back to the car, I saw a long dark shape on the path in front of me.

_____ After my two experiences, I suspect that my fear of snakes will be with me for life.

_____ The first experience occurred when my best friend received a bite from a massasauga rattler.

_____ I looked down at my feet, but it was shady and dark in the woods and my legs were shaking.

_____ I had two experiences when I was eighteen that are the cause of my herpetophobia, or terrible and uncontrollable fear of snakes.

_____ We stopped the car at the side of the road and took out our lunches, and then I decided to walk into the woods a little farther.

_____ When I got back in the car, I felt sick to my stomach, light-headed, and faint.

_____ I saw the huge bandage on his calf and the discoloured, puffy swelling when the bandage was removed.

_____ Then it curved its horrible slinky body off sideways out of my way and slithered into the dark bushes nearby.

_____ I sat in the car for an hour afterward, shaking and sweating, trying to reassure myself that snakes could not open car doors.

_____ But my more direct experience with snakes happened one day when another friend and I were driving south to Barrie to buy concert tickets.

_____ Nearly touching the toe of my running shoe was a long, fat, grey snake, with a huge diamond-shaped head, looking straight at me.

_____ Most of all, I saw the ugly red scabs on his leg where the snake's fangs had ripped the flesh of his calf.

_____ I imagined the evil, muscular-looking snake lunging at me, opening its mouth wide, and attaching itself to my ankle.

_____ At the same time I cried out "Arghh!" and ran toward the car, and I never looked back.

_____ For a long, horrible second, the snake raised its head and eyed me coldly, as if it were thinking about how I would taste.

An important point about logic and order: Regardless of the method you choose to order your paragraph, always remember that the order you give to a piece—along with its supporting evidence—determines its overall *meaning*. The next section will deal with specific words and phrases used to connect information, and the next chapter with the sentence level of college writing; however, words and sentences can only be polished once the idea is developed, supported, and organized. Before you edit for word or sentence correction, review your work to check that it is supported, organized, and logical.

Transitions

Transitions are *signal words and phrases* that help readers *follow the direction of the writer's thought.* They show the relationship between ideas, connecting one thought with the next. They can be compared to road signs that guide travellers.

    To see the value of transitions, look at the following pairs of examples. Put a check beside the example in each pair that is easier and clearer to read and understand.

1. _____ a. Our building manager recently repainted our apartment. He replaced our faulty air conditioner.

    _____ b. Our building manager recently repainted our apartment. Also, he replaced our faulty air conditioner.

2. _____ a. I carefully inserted a disk into the computer. I turned on the power button.

_____ b. I carefully inserted a disk into the computer. Then I turned on the power button.

3. _____ a. Moviegoers usually dislike film monsters. Filmgoers loved Chucky and could not wait for him to return and take a bride.

_____ b. Moviegoers usually dislike film monsters. However, filmgoers loved Chucky and could not wait for him to return and take a bride.

You should have checked the second example in each pair. The transitional words in those sentences—*also, then,* and *however*—make the relationship between the sentences clear. Like all effective transitions, they help connect the writer's thoughts.

Transitions and other phrases of coherence serve as bridges, connecting each statement to the one previous so that the original thought makes a smooth and unbroken "journey" from the beginning of the paragraph in the topic sentence to the conclusion.

Transition words and phrases provide important links in any paragraph's coherence. They are also called "signal words" as they signal that more information is coming. As you write each sentence, always check that it is adding more detail and explanation; be careful that you do not simply restate information that has already been given.

In the following box are common transitional words and phrases, grouped according to the kind of signal they give readers.

Transitions

Addition signals: first of all, for one thing, second, the third reason, also, next, another, and, in addition, moreover, furthermore, finally, last of all

Time signals: first, then, next, after, as, before, while, meanwhile, now, during, finally

Space signals: next to, across, on the opposite side, to the left, to the right, in front, in back, above, below, behind, nearby

Change-of-direction signals: but, however, yet, in contrast, otherwise, still, on the contrary, on the other hand

Illustration signals: for example, for instance, specifically, as an illustration, once, such as

Conclusion signals: therefore, consequently, thus, then, as a result, in summary, to conclude, last of all, finally

---

Note: Certain words provide more than one kind of signal. In the paragraphs you write, you will often use addition signals: words like *first of all,* *also, another,* and *finally* will help you move from one supporting reason or detail to the next.

Consider the following passage:

> The industrialism of the last two centuries has occurred at heavy social and ecological costs. For example, over two hundred years or so, societies everywhere have changed. As a result, so has the environment. Meanwhile, industry has expanded, but not everyone has benefited. Many are suffering, consequently, and have been for decades and decades.

The above paragraph starts with an idea, but then it stalls. The remaining sentences merely repeat the same information, but add no more. The passage includes a number of transitions, but they are false transitions as they are used as fillers and not as proper signals for more detail. This is a common problem with student writing, especially when students focus too much on finding specific words and crafting correct sentences, but forget to assess for meaning.

As you complete the following activities, take note of the way each passage develops its meaning by providing more material. In a good paragraph, each sentence depends upon the previous one, but then takes the whole structure further. Understanding how to use the transitions and connecting words that follow will help you to develop your own writing, as long as you are sure to build upon your idea, rather than stall on a single thought.

● ● ● ● Activity 5

1. Underline the three *addition* signals in the following paragraph.

    I am opposed to provincial lotteries for a number of reasons. First of all, by supporting lotteries, provinces are supporting gambling. I don't see anything morally wrong with gambling, but it is a known cause of suffering for many people who do it to excess. Provinces should be concerned with improving people's lives, not causing more misery. Another objection I have to the provincial lotteries is the kind of advertising they do on television. The commercials promote the lotteries as an easy way to get rich. In fact, the odds against getting rich are astronomical. Last, the lotteries take advantage of the people who can least afford them. Studies have shown that people with lower incomes are more likely to buy lottery tickets than people with higher incomes. This is the harshest reality of the lotteries: provinces are encouraging people of limited means not to save their money but to throw it away on a provincial pipe dream.

2. Underline the four *time* signals in the following paragraph.

    A few things make it easy for a Canadian to know that he or she is home when crossing the border. First is always seeing the word "Douanes" underneath the word "Customs." Of course, unless someone is entering Quebec, it is unlikely that the traveller will actually hear any French, but there is something comforting and familiar about two languages on all the signs. Then, back on the highway, another signal tips off the Canadian that he or she is home: no more trying to figure out how far 276 miles might be. Road signs are in kilometres again. Next, if a glance at the gas gauge shows the needle pointing to *E*, the driver returns to the joy of buying gas in little litres, not in large U.S. gallons. And finally, desperate for a few minutes' rest and a snack, the returning Canadian stops at a doughnut shop named for a hockey player and is again able to order the one thing never seen south of the border: a butter tart.

3. Underline the three *space* signals in the following paragraph.

Standing in the burned-out shell of my living room was a shocking experience. Above my head were charred beams; all that remained of our ceiling. In front of me, where our television and stereo had once stood, were twisted pieces of metal and chunks of blackened glass. Strangely, some items seemed little damaged by the fire. For example, I could see the TV tuner knob and a dusty CD under the rubble. I walked through the gritty ashes until I came to what was left of our couch. Behind the couch had been a wall of family photographs. Now, the wall and the pictures were gone. I found only a waterlogged scrap of my wedding picture.

4. Underline the four *change-of-direction* signals in the following paragraph.

In some ways, train travel is superior to air travel. People always marvel at the speed with which airplanes can zip from one end of the country to another. Trains, on the other hand, definitely take longer. But sometimes longer can be better. Travelling across Canada by train allows people to experience the trip more completely. They get to see the cities and towns, the Rockies, and the prairies that too often pass by unnoticed when they fly. Another advantage of train travel is comfort. Travelling by plane means wedging into a narrow seat with knees bent and bumping the back of the seat in front and being handed a "snack" consisting of a bag of ten roasted peanuts. In contrast, the seats on most trains are spacious and comfortable, permitting even the longest-legged traveller to stretch out and watch the scenery just outside the window. And when train travellers grow hungry, they can get up and stroll to the dining car, where they can order anything from a simple snack to a complete meal. There's no question that train travel is definitely slow and old-fashioned compared with air travel. However, in many ways it is much more civilized.

5. Underline the three *illustration* signals in the following selection.

At the start of the twenty-first century, the most desirable status symbols are the smallest ones, and they are all powered by microchips. The home computer everyone secretly craves, for instance, is not the powerful-looking model with external drives, modems, and speaker boxes hanging off its side. No, the status computer is probably one of those cute little flip-up screen models or a titanium laptop that weighs less then some magazines. Or it might be a nearly invisible model, with a tiny console that fits in a drawer and an elegant flat screen mounted on a collapsible arm. But there is an even trendier example of tiny technology, something for the person who really wants to look organized: the BlackBerry. With the arrival of the millennium, the big leatherbound daybook went out of style. Instead, the busy person lists all of his or her appointments, phone numbers, and vital information on a little piece of equipment that looks like a grown-up GameBoy. And when this busy individual wants to make a call, he or she uses the tiniest piece of status technology of all: specifically, one of the itty-bitty new cellphones. These wee marvels are smaller than a deck of cards, fit into a pocket or purse, and let their owners "reach out and touch someone," play a video game, or even access their email. Status symbols are shrinking all the time. Perhaps one day they will be built right into their owners.

6. Underline the *conclu*sion signal in the following paragraph.

A hundred years ago, miners used to bring caged canaries down into the mines with them to act as warning signals. If the bird died, the miner knew that the oxygen was running out. The smaller animal would be affected much more quickly than the miners. In the same way, animals are acting as warning signals to us today. Baby birds die before they can hatch because pesticides in the environment cause the adults to lay eggs with paper-thin shells. Fish die because the Great Lakes are contaminated with acid rain or poisonous mercury. The dangers in the environment will eventually affect all life on earth, including humans. Therefore, people must pay attention to these early warning signals. If they do not, they will be as foolish as a miner who ignored a dead canary—and all people will die.

Other Connecting Words and Transitional Methods

In addition to transitions, there are three other kinds of connecting words that help tie together the specific evidence in a paper: repeated words, pronouns, and synonyms. Each will be discussed in turn.

Repeated Words

Many of us have been taught not to repeat ourselves in our writing. On the other hand, repeating keywords can help tie a flow of thought together. In the paragraph that follows, the word *retirement* is repeated to remind readers of the key idea on which the discussion is centred. Underline the word the five times it appears.

Oddly enough, retirement can pose more problems for the spouse than for the retired person. For a person who has been accustomed to a demanding job, retirement can mean frustration and a feeling of uselessness. This feeling will put pressure on the spouse to provide challenges at home equal to those of the workplace. Often, these tasks will disrupt the spouse's well-established routine. Another problem arising from retirement is filling up all those empty hours. The spouse may find himself or herself in the role of social director or tour guide, expected to come up with a new form of amusement every day. Without sufficient challenges or leisure activities, a person can become irritable and take out the resulting boredom and frustration of retirement on the marriage partner. It is no wonder that many of these partners wish their spouses would come out of retirement and do something—anything—just to get out of the house.

Pronouns

Pronouns (*he, she, it, you, they, this, that,* and others) are another way to connect ideas as you develop a paper. Using pronouns to take the place of other words or ideas can help you avoid needless repetition. Be careful, though, to use pronouns with care in order to *avoid unclear or inconsistent pronoun reference,* as described on page 102 and pages 383–384 of this book. Underline the seven pronouns in the passage below, noting at the same time the words to which the pronouns refer.

> A professor of nutrition at a major university recently advised his students that they could do better on examinations by eating lots of sweets. He told them that the sugar in cakes and candy would stimulate their brains to work more efficiently, and that if the sugar was eaten for only a month or two, it would not do them any harm.

Synonyms

Using synonyms (words that are alike in meaning) can also help move the reader clearly from one thought to the next. In addition, the use of synonyms increases variety and reader interest by avoiding needless repetition of the same words. Underline the three phrases used as synonyms for *ATMs* in the following passage.

> ATMs make it too tempting for the average Canadian to overspend. Because bank machines run "twenty-four/seven," we can take out another forty dollars any time of day or night instead of waiting for the bank to open and perhaps reconsidering how much we really need that extra money. Automated cash windows are temptingly placed nearly everywhere just for our spending convenience. "Instant tellers" sit in convenience stores, at gas stations, and all over malls, waiting to catch us when we are weakest. ATMs look so bright, friendly, and appealing that somehow we feel less guilty about withdrawing money from them than we might after filling out a withdrawal slip, waiting in line, and facing a teller. Perhaps it is just easier to face a screen that reads "Insufficient funds" than it is to hear a live bank teller say, "I'm sorry, but your account is overdrawn."

∘ ∘ ∘ ● **Activity 6**

To sharpen your sense of how *coherence,* or a sense of connection, is maintained throughout a paper, read the selection below and then answer the questions that follow.

The Worst Experience of My Week

[1]The registration process at McKenzie College was a nightmare. [2]The night before registration for my course officially began, I went to bed anxious about the whole thing, and nothing that happened the next day eased any of my tension. [3]First, even though I had paid my registration fee early last spring, the staff in the registration office had no record of my payment. [4]For some bizarre reason, they wouldn't accept the receipt I had. [5]Consequently, I had to stand in a special numbered line for two hours, waiting for someone to give me a paper that stated that I had, in fact, paid my registration fee. [6]The need for this new receipt seemed ridiculous to me, since, all along, I had proof that I had paid. [7]Next, I was told that I had to see my program coordinator in the International Business Faculty and that this faculty was in Section C, Phase 2, of the Champlain Building. [8]I had no idea what or where the Champlain Building was. [9]Finally, I found the ugly cinder-block structure. Then I began looking for Section C and Phase 2. [10]When I found these, everyone there was a member of the Communications Department. [11]No one seemed to know where International Business had gone. [12]Finally, one instructor said she thought International Business was in Section A. [13]"And where is Section A?" I asked. [14]"I don't know," the teacher answered. "I'm new here." [15]She saw the bewildered look on my face and said sympathetically, "You're not the only one who's confused." [16]I nodded and walked numbly away. [17]I felt as if I were fated to spend the rest of the semester trying to complete the registration process, and I wondered if I would ever become an official college student.

Questions

1. How many times is the key idea *registration* repeated? _____ ;

2. Write here the pronoun that is used for *staff in the registration office* (sentence 4): _____ ; for *Section C, Phase 2* (sentence 10): _____ ; for *instructor* (sentence 15): _____ .

3. Write here the words that are used as a synonym for *receipt* (sentence 5):

   _____ ;

   the words that are used as a synonym for *Champlain Building* (sentence 9):

   _____ ;

   the word that is used as a synonym for *instructor* (sentence 14):

   _____ .

PRACTICE IN CONNECTING SPECIFIC EVIDENCE

As you have learned to make a point and then support it with evidence, be aware that the placement of each sentence in your subtopics is also vital to the coherence of your paragraph. Each sentence must not only be related to your point and each subtopic, but must add significant information to them. You could imagine your sentences as parts of a construction set. Your point is the foundation upon which the rest of the paragraph depends. As you construct your paragraph, you must be sure to place your sentences so that each leads to the next, but is also dependent upon the last.

5 Identifying Transitions

The following three activities will increase your awareness of various transitional methods and your competence in using them. In meeting this learning outcome, you will achieve two necessities for effective writing: (1) you will connect your supporting ideas and details in ways that reflect your intention as a writer, and (2) you will make your point and the sequence of your supporting material easier to follow for your readers.

• • • • Activity 7

Locate the major transitions used in the following selection. Then write the transitions in the spaces provided.

Avoidance Tactics

Getting down to studying for an exam or writing a paper is hard, and so it is tempting for students to use one of the following five avoidance tactics in order to put the work aside. For one thing, students may say to themselves, "I can't do it." They adopt a defeatist attitude at the start and give up without a struggle. They could get help with their work by using such college services as tutoring programs and access and learning resources. However, they refuse even to try. A second avoidance technique is to say, "I'm too busy." Students may take on an extra job, become heavily involved in social activities, or allow family problems to become so time-consuming that they cannot concentrate on their studies. Yet if college really matters to a student, he or she will make sure that there is enough time to do the required work. Another avoidance technique is expressed by the phrase "I'm too tired." Typically, sleepiness occurs when it is time to study or go to class and then vanishes when the school pressure is off. This sleepiness is a sign of work avoidance. A fourth excuse is to say, "I'll do it later." Putting things off until the last minute is practically a guarantee of poor grades on tests and papers. When everything else seems more urgent than studying—watching TV, calling a friend, or even cleaning the oven—a student may simply be escaping academic work. Last, some students avoid work by saying to themselves, "I'm here and that's what counts." Such students live under the dangerous delusion that, since they possess a student card, a parking sticker, and textbooks, the coursework will somehow take care of itself. But once a student has a student card, he or she has only just begun. Doing the necessary studying, writing, and reading will bring real results: good grades, genuine learning, and a sense of accomplishment.

a. _____

b. _____

c. _____

d. _____

e. _____

f. _____

g. _____

h. _____

6   Providing Transitions

● ● ● ● **Activity 8**

In the spaces provided, add logical transitions to tie together the sentences and ideas in the following paragraphs. Use the words in the boxes that precede the paragraphs.

1.

however	a second	last of all
for one thing	also	on the other hand

Why School May Frighten a Young Child

Schools may be frightening to young children for a number of reasons. _____, the regimented environment may be a new and disturbing experience. At home children may have been able to do what they wanted when they wanted to do it. In school, _____, they are given a set time for talking, working, playing, eating, and even going to the toilet. _____ source of anxiety may be the public method of discipline that some teachers use. Whereas at home children are scolded in private, in school they may be held up to embarrassment and ridicule in front of their peers. "Fatima," the teacher may say, "why are you the only one in the class who didn't do your homework?" Or "David, why are you the only one who can't work quietly at your seat?" Children may _____ be frightened by the loss of personal attention. Their little discomforts or mishaps, such as tripping on the stairs, may bring instant sympathy from a parent; in school, there is often no one to notice, or the teacher is frequently too busy to care and just says, "Go do your work. You'll be all right." _____, a child may be scared by the competitive environment of the school. At home, one hopes, such competition for attention is minimal. In school, _____, children may vie for the teacher's approving glance or tone of voice, or for stars on a paper, or for favoured seats in the front row. For these and other reasons, it is not surprising that children may have difficulty adjusting to school.

2.

as a result	once	finally
second	when	first of all
	but	

Joining a Multicultural Club

Canadians are proud of the "diversity" of our population, but I learned first-hand about diversity when I joined a multicultural club. _____, the club has helped me become friends with a diverse group of people. At any time in my apartment, I can have someone from Pakistan chatting about music to someone from Portugal, or someone from Russia talking about politics to someone from Uganda. _____ I watched an Israeli student give falafels to three students from China. They had never eaten such things, but they liked them. A _____ benefit of the club is that it's helped me realize how similar people are. _____ the whole club first assembled, we wound up having a conversation about dating and sex that included the perspectives of fifteen countries and six continents! It was clear we all shared the feeling that sex was fascinating. The talk lasted for hours, with many different persons describing the wildest or funniest experience they had had with the opposite sex. Only a few students, particularly those from Canada and Japan, seemed bashful. _____, the club has reminded me about the dangers of stereotyping. Before I joined the club, most of my experience with Chinese Canadians was limited to some shy fellow high-school students. _____, I believed that most Chinese people worked in the computer or food service industries. _____ in the club, I met Chinese people who were soccer players, English majors, and graphic designers. I've also seen Jewish and Muslim students, people who I thought would never get along, drop their preconceived notions and become friends. Even more than my classes, the club has been an eye-opener for me.

REVIEWING THE LEARNING OUTCOMES FOR CHAPTER 4

To assure yourself that you have understood and met the learning outcomes for this chapter, answer the following questions.

✓ What is the first way to achieve coherence in a paragraph? What are the three main methods of ordering support?

✓ What are transitions?

✓ What are six types of transitional signals? Name two examples of each type.

✓ What are three other methods of indicating transition or connection between ideas?

✓ What are the main purposes for providing transitional words and phrases?

Visit the *English Skills with Readings: Examining Paragraphs* Online Learning Centre at www.mcgrawhill.ca/olc/langan to access self-quizzes, internet-based questions and research skills, web resources, and other learning and study tools.

Chapter 5

The Fourth Step in Writing

After completing the activities, you will

- know five strategies to help you revise your sentences so that they are clear and effective;

- know two aspects of sentence structure where a consistent point of view is essential;

- use specific words to capture readers' interest and make your meanings clear;

- use concise words to convey your meaning economically;

- revise your sentences to create variety and interest in your paragraphs by using four different methods; and

- know how to edit and proofread your sentences for correct use of sentence skills.

So far this book has emphasized the first three bases for writing an effective paragraph: **unity, support,** and **coherence.** These bases cover the essential meaning and organization of a paragraph. Those bases are often considered *higher-order* skills, as they require complex thinking that include connecting ideas and proving a stated point. Those are often the most challenging aspects of writing, but also the most gratifying. Your ability to manipulate your ideas while maintaining unity, support, and coherence is the essence of your individual success as a writer.

However, even the most brilliant ideas will not impress an audience if the sentences, themselves, are awkward or confusing. You must now proceed to revise at the sentence level. This chapter will focus on that, the fourth base for writing effectively: sentence skills. You will learn how to revise a paragraph so that your sentences flow smoothly and clearly to present the meaning you intend. Next, you will concentrate on how to edit a paragraph's sentences for errors in grammar, punctuation, and spelling.

Further Insight—Cognition and writing

One learning theory, first established by Benjamin Bloom, in 1956, divided the process students use to learn into a *taxonomy,* or hierarchy. This revised version of Bloom's Taxonomy, shows the cognitive process from its simplest at the bottom, *remembering,* to its most complex—or highest order—*creating,* at the top.

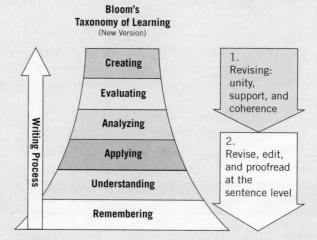

Adapted from Bloom B. S. (1956). *Taxonomy of Educational Objectives, Handbook I: The Cognitive Domain.* New York: David McKay Co. Inc.

The process you use to write scholastically follows a similar process. The *remembering* level refers to your prior knowledge (and attitudes) as you first encounter a task or assignment. You then work your way up the hierarchy using the *writing process,* to achieve the level of *creating*—or your drafted piece of writing. At this level, you have found and connected the unity, support, and coherence of a high-order task.

As with a math problem, the next step is to check for accuracy by reviewing the process backwards. As you would discover errors or omissions in a formula or experiment, you now look for them in your writing. You can work back down the hierarchy to revise and edit, starting from the concepts that you have created to return to the sentence skills that you can now remember to check.

STEP 4: REVISE TO WRITE CLEAR, ERROR-FREE SENTENCES

The work of revising your sentences means two things: first, reading your sentences with fresh eyes to discover what you wish to change; and, second, rewriting your sentences so that they say clearly just what you mean. Always leave some time between writing a draft and revising to give you distance from what you have written, so that you can view your work as objectively as possible. When revising, try to see your paragraph as your readers will—ask yourself where meanings are not clear, where sentences do not flow easily from one to the next, and where a group of sentences sound repetitive.

This chapter will sharpen your awareness of possible sentence problems and show you these strategies for writing sentences that express your meaning in a way that readers will follow easily:

- Use Parallel Structures
- Use Consistent Verb Tenses and Pronouns
- Use Specific Words
- Use Concise Wording
- Vary Your Sentence Types

USE PARALLEL STRUCTURES

Words in a pair or a series should have a parallel structure. By balancing the items in a pair or a series so that they have the same kind of structure, you will make a sentence clearer and easier to read. Notice how the parallel sentences that follow read more smoothly than the non-parallel ones.

Non-Parallel (Not Balanced)	*Parallel (Balanced)*
I made resolutions to lose weight, to study more, and *watching* less TV.	I made resolutions to lose weight, to study more, and to watch less TV. (A balanced series of *to* verbs: *to lose, to study, to watch*)
A consumer group rates my car as noisy, expensive, and *not having much safety.*	A consumer group rates my car as noisy, expensive, and unsafe. (A balanced series of descriptive words: *noisy, expensive, unsafe*)
Pei-Ti likes wearing soft sweaters, eating exotic foods, and *to bathe* in scented bath oil.	Pei-Ti likes wearing soft sweaters, eating exotic foods, and bathing in scented bath oil. (A balanced series of *-ing* words: *wearing, eating, bathing*)
Single life offers more freedom of choice; *more security is offered by marriage.*	Single life offers more freedom of choice; marriage offers more security. (Balanced verbs and word order: *single life offers . . . ; marriage offers . . .*)

You need not worry about balanced sentences when writing first drafts. But when you revise, you should try to put matching words and ideas into matching structures.

Errors in parallel structure show up most often in lists of items within sentences, as the activity below demonstrates. When you write college essays, your thesis statement frequently contains just this kind of list; when you set out your three supporting ideas in a thesis, try to make your ideas match grammatically. Mastering parallelism will improve and smooth your writing style.

● ● ● ● **Activity 1**

The unbalanced part of each of the following sentences is *italicized*. Rewrite the unbalanced part so that it matches the rest of the sentence. The first one is done for you as an example.

1. Mike Myers's films are clever, well-acted, and *have a lot of humour.* _humorous_

2. Filling out an income tax form is worse than wrestling a bear or *to walk on hot coals.* _____

3. The study-skills course taught me how to take more effective notes, read a textbook chapter, and *preparing* for exams. _____

4. Nadine plans to become a model, a lawyer, or *to go into nursing.* _____

5. Commercial graphic artists require talent, patience, and *have to get along with many people.* _____

6. Filled with talent and *ambitious,* Eduardo plugged away at his sales job. _____

7. Global warming has been identified as the cause of the melting of polar ice caps, rising sea levels, and *many species are extinct.* _____

8. While Canada's health care is intended to be free and universal, the health care in other countries *costs people a lot and only some of them can access it.* _____

USE CONSISTENT VERB TENSES AND PRONOUNS

See if you can find and underline the two mistakes in verb tense in the following passage.

> Kyle's eyes burned and itched all day long. When he looked at them in a mirror, he also discovers there were red blotches on his neck. He spoke to his mother about the symptoms, and she said that maybe he was allergic to something. Then he remembers he had been cuddling the kitten that Sarah had just bought the day before. "Good grief. I must be allergic to cats," he said to himself.

If you underlined *discovers* and *remembers,* you are correct. *Discovers* and *remembers* are present-tense verbs, and the paragraph is written in the past tense. The tense shifts are errors and disruptive for readers.

Consistency of Verb Tenses

Do not shift verb tenses unnecessarily. If you begin writing a paper in the present tense, don't shift suddenly to the past. If you begin in the past, don't shift without reason to the present. Notice the inconsistent verb tenses in the follow-ing example. You may wish to review Chapter 23, "Irregular Verbs," to check regular and irregular verb tenses.

> The shoplifter *walked* quickly toward the front of the store. When a clerk *shouts* at him, he *started* to run.

The verbs must be consistently in the present tense:

> The shoplifter *walks* quickly toward the front of the store. When a clerk *shouts* at him, he *starts* to run.

Or the verbs must be consistently in the past tense:

> The shoplifter *walked* quickly toward the front of the store. When a clerk *shouted* at him, he *started* to run.

Activity 2

In each item, one verb must be changed so that it agrees in tense with the other verbs. Cross out the incorrect verb and write the correct form in the space provided.

Example   ___carried___   Kareem wanted to be someplace else when the dentist ~~carries~~ in a long needle.

1. I played my CDs and watched television before I decide to do some home-work. _____

2. Some students attend all their classes in school. They listen carefully during lectures but they don't take notes. As a result, they often failed tests. _____

3. After waking up each morning, Neil stays in bed for a while. First he stretches and yawned loudly, and then he plans his day. _____

4. Several months a year, monarch butterflies come to live on Point Pelee along the Lake Erie shore. Thousands and thousands of them hang from the trees and fluttered through the air in large groups.
_____

5. The salespeople at Biggs's Department Store are very helpful. When people asked for a product the store doesn't carry or is out of, the salesperson recommends another store. _____

6. Students at the college science camp learn about crime scene forensics. They even examined DNA. _____

7. Part-time workers at the company are the first to be laid off. They are also paid less, and they received no union representation. _____

8. Smashed cars, ambulances, and police cars blocked traffic on one side of the highway. On the other side, traffic slows down as drivers looked to see what happened. _____

Consistency of Pronouns

Pronouns should not shift their point of view unnecessarily. When you write a paper, be consistent in your use of first-, second-, or third-person pronouns.

Type of Pronoun	Singular	Plural
First-person pronouns	I (my, mine, me)	we (our, ours, us)
Second-person pronouns	you (your, yours)	you (your, yours)
Third-person pronouns	he (his, him)	they (theirs, theirs, them)
	she (her, hers)	
	it (its)	

Note: Any person, place, or thing, as well as any indefinite pronoun like *one, anyone, someone,* and so on (page 381), takes a pronoun in the third person.

For instance, if you start writing in the third-person singular, using *she,* don't jump suddenly to the second person, *you,* or to the plural, *they.* Or if you are writing in the first person, using *I,* don't shift unexpectedly to *one.* Look at the examples.

Inconsistent	*Consistent*
I enjoy movies like *The Ring* that frighten *you.* (The most common mistake people make is to let *you* slip into their writing after they start with another pronoun.)	I enjoy movies like *The Ring* that frighten *me.*
When someone reaches a certain stage in learning a new skill, they can't believe they ever lived without it. (*They* is a shift in point of view and number from "someone.")	When someone reaches a certain stage in learning a new skill, *he or she* can't believe that *he or she* ever lived without it. (See also the note on *pronoun agreement* on page 383.)

● ● ● ● ● **Activity 3**

Cross out incorrect pronouns in the following sentences, and write the correct form of the pronoun above each crossed-out word.

Example   My dreams are always the kind that haunt ~~you~~ the next day.
(me written above crossed-out "you")

1. In our society, we often need a diploma before you are hired for a job.

2. A worker can take a break only after a relief person comes to take your place.

3. If a student organizes time carefully, you can accomplish a great deal of work.

4. If someone wants to go ashore to see local culture, make sure you check ahead.

5. Nobody agrees to have their shifts changed.

6. The doctor advised the patients that she must leave.

7. Insert the tab into the slot, but make sure they are facing inward.

8. You waste a lot of energy when each person takes their own car.

USE SPECIFIC WORDS

To be an effective writer, you must use specific, rather than general, words. Specific words create pictures in the reader's mind. They help capture the reader's interest and make your meaning clear. You may also wish to refer to Chapter 37, "Effective Word Choice," as you complete the following activities.

General	*Specific*
The boy came down the street.	Voytek ran down Woodlawn Avenue.
A bird appeared on the grass.	A blue jay swooped down onto the frost-covered lawn.
Some clouds mean rain.	Thick, grey, and flattening nimbostratus clouds threaten heavy rain.

The specific sentences create clear pictures in your reader's mind. The details *show* readers exactly what has happened.

Here are four ways to make your words and sentences specific.

1) Use exact names.
She loves her motorbike.
Kellie loves her *Honda.*

2) Use lively verbs.
The garbage truck went down Front Street.
The garbage truck *rumbled* down Front Street.

3) Use descriptive words (modifiers) before nouns.
A girl peeked out the window.
A *chubby, six-year-old* girl peeked out the *dirty kitchen* window.

4) Use words that relate to the five senses: sight, hearing, taste, smell, and touch.
That woman is a karate expert.
That *tiny, silver-haired* woman is a karate expert. (*Sight*)
When the dryer stopped, a signal sounded.
When the *whooshing* dryer stopped, a *loud buzzer* sounded. (*Hearing*)

Natasha offered me an orange slice.

Natasha offered me a *sweet, juicy* orange slice. (*Taste*)

The real estate agent opened the door of the closet.

The real estate agent opened the door of the *cedar-scented* closet. (*Smell*)

I pulled the blanket around me to fight off the wind.

I pulled the *scratchy* blanket around me to fight off the *chilling* wind. (*Touch*)

Activity 4

This activity will give you practice in replacing vague, indefinite words with sharp, specific words. Add three or more specific words to replace the general word or words underlined in each sentence. Make changes in the wording of a sentence as necessary.

Example   My bathroom cabinet contains many drugs.

My bathroom cabinet contains Aspirin, antibiotics, an herbal sedative,

and cough medicine.

1. Jeff looked it up on the Internet.

_____

_____

2. Hoi Yee enjoys various activities in her spare time.

_____

_____

3. Students have too much to do.

_____

_____

4. There are many ways to cut costs.

_____

_____

Activity 5

Again, practise changing vague, general, and indefinite words into lively, image-filled writing that captures your reader's interest and makes your meaning clear.

Using the methods described in the preceding activity, add specific details to the ten sentences that follow on a separate sheet of paper. Review the examples below.

Examples   The person got out of the car.

The elderly man painfully lifted himself out of the white station wagon.

The fans enjoyed the victory.

Many of the fifty thousand fans stood, waved Leafs sweaters, and cheered

wildly when Tretiak scored the winning goal.

1. An accident occurred.
2. The instructor came into the room.
3. The machine did not work.
4. The scientist discovered a cure.
5. The politician's statement changed.
6. Technology is improving people's lives.
7. They should do something about people using machines on the trails.
8. The climate is changing.

USE CONCISE WORDING

Wordiness—using more words than necessary to express a meaning—is often a sign of lazy or careless writing. Your readers may resent the extra time and energy they must spend when you have not done the work needed to make your writing direct and concise.

Here are examples of wordy sentences.

Anna is of the opinion that the death penalty should be allowed.
I am writing this paper to discuss the possibility that any more cuts to the financial assistance the government gives to programs such as soccer, hockey, and other sports that children enjoy, will result in many social problems among the children of our communities.

Omitting needless words improves the sentences.

Anna supports the death penalty.
Further cuts to government funding of children's activities may result in social discord.

The following box lists some wordy expressions that could be reduced to single words.

Wordy Form	Short Form	Wordy Form	Short Form
a large number of	many	in every instance	always
a period of a week	a week	in my own opinion	I think
arrive at an agreement	agree	in the event that	if
at an earlier point in time	before	in the near future	soon
at the present time	now	in this day and age	today
owing to the fact that	because	large in size	large
during the time that	while	plan ahead for the future	plan
for the reason that	because	postponed until later	postponed

Further Insight—Using a thesaurus

A thesaurus is as valuable a writing tool as a dictionary, and college writers should familiarize themselves with both. A thesaurus is particularly important when it is time to revise sentences for style and meaning; however, there are some things to keep in mind:

- There are two types of thesaurus. In one kind, words are listed by categories. In the other, probably the most familiar to college students, words are listed alphabetically.
- In general, words are listed so the closest in meaning are at the head of the list.
- Do not assume that a given word is an exact synonym.
- Do not use a word that you do not know, or cannot find out the meaning of to a level where you feel comfortable. Sometimes seemingly small differences in meaning can actually change the whole sense.
- Avoid electronic translators if you are trying to find a word from a different language in English. The choices offered in such translators are often archaic, colloquial, or meaningless except in very limited contexts.
- Do become familiar with a good-quality thesaurus and consult it often.

VARY YOUR SENTENCE TYPES

Varied types of sentences add interest to your writing. If every sentence follows the same pattern, writing becomes monotonous to read. This section explains four ways to create variety in your writing style. Coordination and subordination are important techniques for achieving different kinds of emphasis in writing.

Here are four methods you can use when revising to make your sentences more varied and more sophisticated:

1) Add a Second Complete Thought (coordination)
2) Add a Dependent Thought (subordination)
3) Begin with a Special Opening Word or Phrase
4) Place Adjectives or Verbs in a Series

Each method will be discussed in turn.

Add a Second Complete Thought

When you add a second complete thought to a simple sentence, the result is a compound (or double) sentence. The two complete statements in a compound sentence are usually connected by a comma plus a joining, or coordinating, word *(and, but, for, or, nor, so, yet)*.

Use a compound sentence when you want to give equal weight to two closely related ideas. The technique of showing that ideas have equal importance is called *coordination.*

Following are some compound sentences. Each contains two ideas that the writer regards as equal in importance.

I repeatedly failed the math quizzes, so I decided to drop the course.

Stan turned all the lights off, and then he locked the office door.

Activity 6

Combine the following pairs of simple sentences into compound sentences. Use a comma and a logical joining word *(and, but, for, so)* to connect each pair.

Note: If you are not sure what *and, but, for,* and *so* mean, see pages 361–362.

Example
- The car crept along slowly.
- Visibility was poor in the heavy fog.

The car crept along slowly, for visibility was poor in the heavy fog.

1. • The line at the deli counter was long.
   • Jake took a numbered ticket anyway.

   _____

2. • During a northern summer, the sun never sets.
   • The North is sometimes called "The Land of the Midnight Sun."

   _____

3. • Some of the most interesting photographs are of spontaneous moments.
   • A good photographer is ready for anything.

   _____

4. • Students often gain weight in their first term at college.
   • Studying requires a change in eating habits and lifestyle.

   _____

Add a Dependent Thought

When you add a dependent thought to a simple sentence, the result is a complex sentence. A dependent thought begins with a word or phrase like those in the box below. If you want more instruction about adding dependent thoughts, see the section in Chapter 21, "Fragments."

Note: The two parts of a complex sentence are sometimes called an *independent clause* and a *dependent clause.* A *clause* is simply a word group that contains a subject and a verb. An independent clause expresses a complete thought and can stand alone. A dependent clause does not express a complete thought in itself and "depends on" the independent clause to complete its meaning. Dependent clauses always begin with a dependent, or subordinating, word.

Dependent Words

after	if, even if	when, whenever
although, though	in order that	where, wherever
as	since	whether
because	that, so that	which, whichever
before	unless	while
even though	until	who, whoever
how	what, whatever	whose

A complex sentence is used when you want to emphasize one idea over another within a sentence. Look at the following complex sentence:

Although I lowered the thermostat, my heating bill remained high.

The idea that the writer wants to emphasize here—*my heating bill remained high*—is expressed as a complete thought. The less important idea—*Although I lowered my thermostat*—is subordinated to this complete thought. The technique of giving one idea less emphasis than another is called *subordination*.

Following are other examples of complex sentences. In each case, the part starting with the dependent word is the less emphasized part of the sentence.

Even though I was tired, I stayed up to watch the horror movie.

Products claiming to be environmentally sustainable must be carefully labelled, so that consumers are not misled.

Activity 7

Use logical subordinating words to combine the following pairs of simple sentences into sentences that contain a dependent thought. Place a comma after a dependent statement when it starts the sentence.

Example
- Our team lost.
- We were not invited to the tournament.

Because our team lost, we were not invited to the tournament.

1.
- I receive my diploma in June.
- I will begin applying for jobs.

_____

_____

2.
- Summer ends in Churchill.
- Polar bears wait impatiently for the ice to form.

_____

_____

3. • It may take several drafts to complete a paper.
   • The results will be worthwhile.

_____

_____

4. • The final exam covered sixteen chapters.
   • The students complained.

_____

_____

Begin with a Special Opening Word or Phrase

Among the special openers that can be used to start sentences are (1) -*ed* words, (2) -*ing* words, (3) -*ly* words, (4) *to* word groups, and (5) prepositional phrases. Here are examples of all five kinds of openers.

-*ed* **word**	Tired from a long day of work, Sharon fell asleep on the sofa.
-*ing* **word**	Using a thick towel, Chan dried his hair quickly.
-*ly* **word**	Fortunately, the damage was only minor.
to **word group**	To live comfortably, people must keep track of all of their expenses.
Prepositional phrase	With Mark's help, Samantha planted the evergreen shrubs.

● ● ● ● **Activity 8**

Combine the simple sentences into one sentence by using the opener shown in the margin and omitting repeated words. Use a comma to set off the opener from the rest of the sentence.

Example

-*ing* **word**   • The toaster refused to pop up.
                   • It buzzed like an angry hornet.

                   Buzzing like an angry hornet, the toaster refused to pop up.

-*ed* **word**

1. • Dimitri was annoyed by the poor TV reception.
   • He decided to get a satellite dish.

_____

_____

-*ing* **word**

2. • The star player glided down the court.
   • He dribbled the basketball like a pro.

_____

_____

-ly **word**

3. • Food will run short on our crowded planet.
   • It is inevitable.

   _____

   _____

to **word group**

4. • Measure twice and cut once.
   • Make sure the table is perfect.

   _____

   _____

prepositional phrase

5. • Suddenly the sun appeared.
   • It shone across the retreating clouds.

   _____

   _____

-ed **word**

6. • The flames skipped to the nearby rooftop.
   • They were fuelled by the gusty winds.

   _____

   _____

-ing **word**

7. • The people pressed against the doors of the theatre.
   • They pushed and shoved each other.

   _____

   _____

-ly **word**

8. • The actors waited for the curtain to open.
   • They were nervous.

   _____

   _____

to **word group**

9. • The little boy likes to annoy his parents.
   • He pretends he can't hear them.

   _____

   _____

prepositional phrase

10. • People must wear white-soled shoes.
    • They must do this in the gym.

    _____

    _____

Place Adjectives or Verbs in a Series

Various parts of a sentence may be placed in a series. Among these parts are adjectives (descriptive words) and verbs. Here are examples of both in a series.

Adjectives The *black, smeary* newsprint rubbed off on my *new butcherblock* table.

Verbs The quarterback *fumbled* the ball, *recovered* it, and *sighed* with relief.

• • • • **Activity 9**

Combine the simple sentences in each group into one sentence by using adjectives or verbs in a series and by omitting repeated words. If you are not sure whether to use a comma between the adjectives or verbs in a series, see page 427.

Example
- Before Christmas, I made fruitcakes.
- I decorated the house.
- I wrapped dozens of toys.

  Before Christmas, I made fruitcakes, decorated the house, and

  wrapped dozens of toys.

1. • My lumpy mattress was giving me a cramp in my neck.
   • It was causing pains in my back.
   • It was making me lose sleep.

   _____

   _____

2. • Lights appeared in the fog.
   • The lights were flashing.
   • The lights were red.
   • The fog was grey.
   • The fog was soupy.

   _____

   _____

3. • Joanna picked sweater hairs off her coat.
   • The hairs were fuzzy.
   • The hairs were white.
   • The coat was brown.
   • The coat was suede.

   _____

   _____

4. • The contact lens fell onto the floor.
   • The contact lens was thin.
   • The contact lens was slippery.
   • The floor was dirty.
   • The floor was tiled.

_____

_____

EDITING SENTENCES

Once you have revised sentences in a paragraph so that it has some variety and so that your sentences flow smoothly and clearly reflect your meaning, you need to *edit* the sentences for mistakes in grammar, punctuation, mechanics, usage, and spelling.

This looks like a long list of requirements, but even if your paragraph is otherwise well written, it will make an unfavourable impression on your reading audience if it contains such mistakes. Mechanical errors are sometimes called "noise," a term that vividly describes the effect of errors on readers' ability to understand or be persuaded by your point.

To edit a paragraph, do not rely greatly on the grammar checker in your word-processing program. These "editing applications," which may insert wiggly green lines under words or phrases on your screen, rely on pre-programmed "acceptable" word strings or patterns. Grammar checkers do not take into account the meanings of words and phrases; they simply recognize patterns. As a result, they may offer incorrect or bizarre substitutions for something they analyze as incorrect. Instead, check your paragraph against the agreed-upon rules and conventions of written English called *sentence skills* in this book.

Section Four of this text provides detailed explanations of these sentence skills, and related activities. The online diagnostic test will help you identify skills you may need to review. Your instructor will also identify such skills in marking your papers and may use the correction symbols shown on the inside back cover.

Note: The correction symbols, as well as the checklist of sentence skills on the inside front cover, include page references for easy referral.

Hints for Editing

Here are hints that can help you edit the next-to-final draft of a paper for sentence-skills mistakes. If you ask a peer to help, suggest that the peer look for specific areas that may need revision, rather than have the peer proofread for minor errors.

1) Have at hand two essential tools: a good dictionary and a grammar or sentence-skills handbook (you can use the one in this book in Section Four). A thesaurus is also a vital tool.

2) Use a sheet of paper to cover your paragraph, or scroll through a document on your computer, as you read so that you expose only one sentence at a time. Look for errors in grammar, spelling, and typing. It may help

to read each sentence out loud. If a sentence does not read clearly and smoothly, chances are that something is wrong.

3) Pay special attention to the kinds of errors you tend to make. For example, if you tend to write run-ons or fragments, be especially on the lookout for those errors. A peer may help you recognize these errors.

4) Try to work on a word-processed draft, where you'll be able to see your writing more objectively than you can on a handwritten page; freely use fonts and colour highlighting, or insert comments to indicate changes you should make. If you work from a hard copy, use a pen with coloured ink so that your corrections will stand out. If you make too many corrections, retype the page or enter corrections into your document file. File this draft under a new file name.

PRACTICE IN REVISING SENTENCES

You now know the basics of the fourth step in effective writing: revising and editing sentences. You also know that practice in *editing* sentences is best undertaken after you have worked through the sentence skills in Section Four.

Here you will practise *revising* sentences: using a variety of methods to ensure that your sentences flow smoothly and are clear and interesting. Your sentences and therefore your paragraphs will more clearly reflect your ideas and feelings, and readers will see your points more readily.

Work through these review tests to consolidate your understanding of sentence revision:

1) Using Parallel Structures
2) Using Consistent Verb Tenses and Pronouns
3) Using Specific Words
4) Using Concise Wording
5) Varying Your Sentence Types

Using Parallel Structures

● ● ● ● **Review Test 1**

Cross out the unbalanced part of each sentence. Then revise the unbalanced part so that it matches the other item or items in the sentence. The first one is done for you as an example.

1. Our professor warned us that he would give surprise tests, ~~the assignment of term papers~~, and allow no makeup exams.

   assign term papers

2. Pesky mosquitoes, humidity that is high, and sweltering heat make summer an unpleasant time for me.

3. My teenage daughter enjoys shopping for new clothes, to try different cosmetics, and reading teen magazines.

---

4. My car needed the brakes replaced, the front wheels aligned, and recharging of the battery.

---

5. Always check written assignments for fragments, misplaced modifiers, and if there are apostrophe mistakes.

---

6. The neighbourhood group asked the town council to repair the potholes and that a traffic light be installed.

---

7. Looking professional, being on time, and a good set of people skills will help new employees in their careers.

---

8. Senior Link is an organization that not only aids older citizens but also providing information for their families.

● ● ● ● **Review Test 2**

Cross out the unbalanced part of each sentence. In the space provided, revise the unbalanced part so that it matches the other item or items in the sentence.

1. While you're downtown, please pick up the dry cleaning, return the library books, and the car needs washing, too.

---

2. Making dinner is a lot more fun than to clean up after it.

---

3. Canada Post brought advertisements that were unwanted, bills I couldn't pay, and catalogues I didn't like.

---

4. Our house has a dented garage door, shutters that are peeling, and a crumbling chimney.

---

5. Fantastic special effects are part of the *Star Wars* movies, but dialogue that is believable is not.

---

6. Stumbling out of bed, a cup of coffee that he drinks, and listening to the weather report make up Todd's early-morning routine.

   _____

7. Ron's wide smile, clear blue eyes, and expressing himself earnestly all make him seem honest, even though he is not.

   _____

8. This position requires efficiency, have a good driving abstract, and dedication to the needs of clients.

   _____

Using Consistent Verb Tenses and Pronouns

● ● ● ● ● **Review Test 1**

Change verb tenses as needed in the following passage so that they are consistently in the past tense. Cross out each incorrect verb and write the correct form above it, as shown in the example below. You will need to make nine corrections.

> Late one rainy night, Mei Ling woke to the sound of steady dripping. When she got out of bed to investigate, a drop of cold water ~~splashes~~ *splashed* onto her arm. She looks up just in time to see another drop form on the ceiling, hang suspended for a moment, and fall to the carpet. Stumbling to the kitchen, Mei Ling reaches deep into one of the cabinets and lifts out a large roasting pan. As she did so, pot lids and baking tins clattered out and crash onto the counter. Mei Ling ignored them, stumbled back to the bedroom, and places the pan on the floor under the drip. But a minute after sliding her icy feet under the covers, Mei Ling realized she is in trouble. The sound of each drop hitting the metal pan echoed like a cannon in the quiet room. Mei Ling feels like crying, but she finally thought of a solution. She got out of bed and returns a minute later with a thick bath towel. She lined the pan with the towel and crawls back into bed.

● ● ● ● ● **Review Test 2**

Cross out the incorrect pronouns in the following sentences and revise by writing the correct form of the pronoun above each crossed-out word.

Example   I dislike working as a server, for ~~you~~ ^I^ can never count on a fair tip.

1. My kitchen is so narrow that one can't open the refrigerator without turning sideways first.

   _____

2. Wanting relief from her headaches, Carla asked her doctor if acupuncture could really do you any good.

   _____

3. As we entered the house, you could hear someone giggling in the hallway.

   _____

4. I hate going to the supermarket because you always have trouble finding a parking space there.

   _____

5. In this company, a worker can take a break only after a relief person comes to take your place.

   _____

6. Sometimes the Bradleys take the express highway, but it costs you five dollars in tolls.

   _____

7. As we sat in class waiting for the test results, you could feel the tension.

   _____

8. Sustainable agriculture is creating specialized production that you can do in smaller quantities.

   _____

Using Specific Words

● ● ● ● **Review Test 1**

Revise the following sentences, replacing the vague, indefinite words in italics with sharp, specific ones.

1. When I woke up this morning, I had *several signs of a cold.*

   _____

   _____

2. Lin brought *lots of reading materials* to keep her occupied in the dentist's waiting room.

   _____

   _____

3. To succeed in college, a student must possess *certain qualities*.

_____

_____

4. The cases were long and boring.

_____

_____

● ● ● ● ● **Review Test 2**

With the help of the methods described on page 103, add specific details to the sentences that follow.

1. The crowd grew restless.

_____

_____

2. I relaxed.

_____

_____

3. The room was cluttered.

_____

_____

4. The experiment was faulty.

_____

_____

Use Concise Wording

● ● ● ● ● **Review Test 1**

Rewrite the following sentences, omitting needless words.

1. There was this one girl in my class who rarely if ever did her assignments.

_____

_____

2. Seeing as how the refrigerator is totally empty of food, I will go to the supermarket in the very near future.

_____

_____

3. In this day and age it is almost a certainty that someone you know will be an innocent victim of criminal activity.

_____

_____

4. This paper will discuss the idea that it is in all likelihood a done deal that civilian patrols will be established in large urban cities.

_____

_____

• • • • Review Test 2

Rewrite the following sentences, omitting needless words.

1. Workers who are on a part-time basis are attractive to a business because they do not have to be paid as much as full-time workers for a business.

_____

_____

2. The game, which was scheduled for later today, has been cancelled by the officials because of the rainy weather.

_____

_____

3. At this point in time, I am quite undecided and unsure about just which classes I will take during this coming semester.

_____

_____

4. In and of itself, the winding path to successful achievement is not as tried and true as student learners might expect.

_____

_____

Varying Your Sentence Types

• • • • Review Test 1

Using coordination, subordination, or both, combine each of the following groups of simple sentences into one longer sentence. Omit repeated words. Various combinations are possible, so for each group, try to find the combination that flows most smoothly and clearly.

1. • His name was called.
   • Luis walked into the examining room.
   • He was nervous.
   • He was determined to ask the doctor for a straight answer.

2. • They left twenty minutes early for class.
   • They were late anyway.
   • The car overheated.

3. • Jake failed the midterm exam.
   • He studied harder for the final.
   • He passed it.

4. • A volcano erupts.
   • It sends tonnes of ash into the air.
   • This creates flaming orange sunsets.

5. • The boys waited for the bus.
   • The wind shook the flimsy shelter.
   • They shivered with cold.
   • They were wearing thin jackets.

6. • The graphics are impressive.
   • They are bright.
   • They are creative.
   • They are effective.

7. • Horticulture is fascinating.
   • It requires knowledge of plant species.
   • It requires understanding of soils.
   • It is a specialty.
   • It is rewarding.

8. • Children learn in many ways.
   • They learn through play.
   • They also learn through imitation.
   • Children learn as their bodies develop.
   • Their minds grow with each experience.

● ● ● ● **Review Test 2**

Part A Combine the simple sentences into one sentence by using the opener shown in the margin and omitting repeated words. Use a comma to set off the opener from the rest of the sentence.

-ed **word**

1. • We were exhausted from four hours of hiking.
   • We decided to stop for the day.

   _____

   _____

-ing **word**

2. • Enoch was staring out the window.
   • He did not hear the instructor call on him.

   _____

   _____

-ly word

3. • Measure the ingredients as directed.
    • Be careful.

_____

_____

to word group

4. • Always keep anti-virus programs updated.
    • This will help you to avoid worms and trojans.

_____

_____

Prepositional phrase

5. • Students can keep track of their progress.
    • They can do so by making appointments with their instructors.

_____

_____

Part B Combine the simple sentences into one sentence by using adjectives or verbs in a series and by omitting repeated words.

6. • The photographer waved a teddy bear at the baby.
    • She made a funny face.
    • She quacked like a duck.

_____

_____

7. • The bucket held a bunch of daisies.
    • The bucket was shiny.
    • The bucket was aluminum.
    • The daisies were fresh.
    • The daisies were white.

_____

_____

8. • The box in the dresser drawer was stuffed with letters.
    • The box was cardboard.
    • The dresser drawer was locked.
    • The letters were faded.
    • The letters were about love.

_____

_____

REVIEWING THE LEARNING OUTCOMES FOR CHAPTER 5

To assure yourself that you have understood and met the learning outcomes for this chapter, answer the following questions.

✓ What are the five strategies that will help you revise your sentences for clarity and effectiveness?

✓ What are two aspects of sentence skills in which maintaining consistency is important, and why?

✓ How exactly does using specific words help your readers?

✓ Why are concise word choices more appealing to readers than wordy phrases?

✓ What are four different methods for revising sentences to create variety and interest?

✓ What is the difference between revising your sentences and editing and proofreading your sentences?

Online LearningCentre   Visit the *English Skills with Readings: Examining Paragraphs* Online Learning Centre at www.mcgrawhill.ca/olc/langan to access self-quizzes, internet-based questions and research skills, web resources, and other learning and study tools.

Chapter 6

Four Bases for Evaluating Writing

BUT FATHER, I DON'T WANT TO STUDY
SPACE TIME TEMPORAL THEORIES IN
RELATION TO COLLAPSING PULSARS,
I WANT TO DO MY OWN THING!

L E A R N I N G   O U T C O M E S

After completing the activities in this chapter, you will

- know two guidelines for revising a paragraph for *unity;*
- revise for effective *support* by asking three questions;
- know how to revise for *coherence* with the use of an appropriate ordering method and transitional devices;
- be ready to identify and correct errors to meet the goal of *effective sentence skills;* and
- understand why and how to evaluate a paragraph for each base of effective writing.

Previous chapters in this section introduced the process of writing a college paragraph by developing **unity, support, coherence,** and **clear and error-free sentences.** This chapter will help you assess writing samples to identify the presence or absence of each of these four bases. You will have an opportunity to analyze a number of student models, first for unity, support, coherence, or clear and error-free sentences; then you will be given models to assess for all bases as they work together.

As you complete these activities based on the four bases of effective writing, you may find that you are more able in one base than another. Therefore, when you revise your writing, review it for one of the four bases at a time so that you will not be distracted by other details. For example, as you check for unity, ignore more complex sentence-skills errors until the end. This will allow you to concentrate on one base at a time and will prepare you for the writing, revising, and editing stages of writing tasks in the chapters that follow. You will eventually become able to do each with increasing ease and your confidence in your ability to write effectively will increase.

The box below shows how these steps lead to four bases, or standards, you can use in evaluating your work.

BASE 1: UNITY

Reviewing Unity

When you review your own paragraph, review first for unity. Remember that unity means that all of the information will be related to the main idea. To give you an idea, read the two paragraphs on pages 123–124, which were written by students on the topic "why students drop out of college." Then, decide which one makes its point more clearly and effectively, and why.

Four Steps ⟶	*Four Bases* ⟶	*Four Goals Defined*
1) If you make a point and stick to that point,	your writing will have *unity*.	**Unity:** a single main idea pursued and supported by the points and details of your writing
2) If you back up the point with specific evidence,	your writing will have *support*.	**Support:** for each supporting point, specific and definite details
3) If you organize and connect the specific evidence,	your writing will have *coherence*.	**Coherence:** supporting points and details organized and connected clearly
4) If you write clear, error-free sentences,	your writing will reflect effective *sentence skills*.	**Effective Sentence Skills:** sentence structure, grammar, spelling, and punctuation free of errors

Paragraph A

Why Students Drop Out

Students drop out of college for many reasons. First of all, some students are bored in school. These students may enter college expecting non-stop fun or a series of undemanding courses. When they find out that college is often routine, they quickly lose interest. They do not want to take dull required courses or spend their nights studying, and so they drop out. Students also drop out of college because the work is harder than they thought it would be. These students may have gotten decent marks in high school simply by showing up for class. In college, however, they may have to prepare for two-hour exams, write lengthy reports, or make detailed presentations to a class. The hard work comes as a shock, and students give up. Perhaps the most common reason students drop out is that they are having personal or emotional problems. Younger students, especially, may be attending college at an age when they are also feeling confused, lonely, or depressed. These students may have problems with roommates, family, boyfriends, or girlfriends. They become too unhappy to deal with both hard academic work and emotional troubles. For many types of students, dropping out seems to be the only solution they can imagine.

Paragraph B

Student Dropouts

There are three main reasons students drop out of college. Some students, for one thing, are not really sure they want to be in school and lack the desire to do the work. When exams come up, or when a course requires a difficult project or demanding essay, these students will not do the required studying or research. Eventually, they may drop out because their grades are so poor they are about to fail anyway. Such students sometimes come back to school later with a completely different attitude about school. Other students drop out for financial reasons. The pressures of paying tuition, buying textbooks, and possibly having to support themselves can be overwhelming. These students can often be helped by the school or the province because financial aid is available, and some schools offer work-study programs. Finally, students drop out because they have personal problems. They cannot concentrate on their courses because they are unhappy at home, they are lonely, or they are having trouble with boyfriends or girlfriends. Instructors should suggest that such troubled students see counsellors or join support groups. If instructors would take a more personal interest in their students, more students would make it through troubled times.

Fill in the blanks: Paragraph _____ makes its point more clearly and effectively because _____

Comment: Paragraph A is more effective because it is *unified.* All the details in paragraph A are *on target.* They support and develop the single point expressed in the first sentence: that there are many reasons students drop out of college. On the other hand, paragraph B contains some details irrelevant to the opening point: that there are three main reasons students drop out. These details should be omitted in the interest of paragraph unity. Go back to paragraph B and cross out the sentences that are off target—the sentences that do not support the opening idea.

The sentences to be crossed out are: "Such students sometimes . . . attitude about school"; "These students can often . . . work-study programs"; and "Instructors should suggest . . . through troubled times."

The difference between these two paragraphs leads to the first base of effective writing: *unity*. To achieve unity is to have all the details in your paper *related to the single point* expressed in the topic sentence, the first sentence. Each time you consider an idea, ask yourself if it relates to your main point. If it does not, leave it out. For example, if you were writing about a certain job as the worst job you ever had, do not spend a couple of sentences talking about the interesting people that you met there.

Checking for Unity

To check a paper for unity, ask yourself these questions:

1) Is there a clear opening statement of the point of the paper?

2) Is all the material on target in support of the opening point?

BASE 2: SUPPORT

Reviewing Support

Next, review your paragraph to check that it provides adequate support. Remember that a paragraph shows support through specific details. Read the following student paragraphs, which were written on the topic "a quality of some person or animal you know." Both are unified, but one communicates more clearly and effectively. Which one, and why?

Paragraph A

Laziness Defined

Cats may be the laziest creatures on earth, but they are also the smartest. Every day is divided up according to their pleasures and needs. They always find time to eat, without ever having to cook or prepare a meal. Enough complaining will make sure that their dishes are filled on time. Cats know they need exercise, too, so they take care of that by climbing the furniture and suddenly running up and down the stairs, usually at night. If they need someone to play with, they know enough not to strain themselves. Their radar can usually locate an owner who is busy at the computer or snoozing in front of the television, all ready for an eager furry playmate to nudge him or her into cooperating. Cats know their greatest need is for many hours of deep soothing sleep. Any time is the right time to sleep, and any place where humans are busy or where a fuzzy patch of cat fur will be appreciated is the right spot. Meeting all three needs keeps a cat healthy and occupied and shows humans just how smart a lazy creature can be.

Paragraph B

> ### My Generous Grandfather
>
> My grandfather is the most generous person I know. He has given up a life of his own in order to give his grandchildren everything they want. Not only has he given up many years of his life to raise his children properly, but he is now sacrificing many more years to his grandchildren. His generosity is also evident in his relationship with his neighbours, his friends, and the members of his church. He has been responsible for many good deeds and has always been there to help all the people around him in times of trouble. Everyone knows that he will gladly lend a helping hand. He is so generous that I almost have to feel sorry for him. If one day he suddenly became selfish, it would be earthshaking. That's my grandfather.

Fill in the blanks: Paragraph _____ makes its point more clearly and effectively because _____

_____

Comment: Paragraph A is more effective, for it offers *specific examples that show* us the laziness of cats in action. We see for ourselves why the writer describes cats as extremely lazy but clever. Paragraph B, on the other hand, gives us no specific evidence. The writer of paragraph B *tells us repeatedly* that the grandfather is generous *but never shows us* examples of that generosity. Just how, for instance, did the grandfather sacrifice his life for his children and grandchildren? Did he hold two jobs so that his son could go to college or so that his daughter could have her own car? Does he give up time with his wife and friends to travel every day to his daughter's house to babysit? Does he wear threadbare suits and coats and eat inexpensive meals (with no desserts) so that he can give money to his children and toys to his grandchildren? We want to see and judge for ourselves whether the writer is making a valid point about the grandfather, but without specific details we cannot do so. In fact, we have almost no picture of him at all. The best writing *shows*; it does not *tell*.

Consideration of these two paragraphs leads us to the second base of effective writing: *support*. After realizing the importance of specific supporting details, one student writer revised an essay she had done on a restaurant job as the worst job she ever had. In the revised essay, instead of talking about "unsanitary conditions in the kitchen," she referred to such specifics as "green mould on the bacon" and "ants in the potato salad." All your writing should include many vivid details.

Checking for Support

To check a paragraph for support, ask yourself these questions:

1) Are there *specific subtopics* to support the opening point?
2) Is there enough specific evidence?
3) Are specific details included?

BASE 3: COHERENCE

Reviewing Coherence

Review your paragraph a third time to check for coherence. Remember that to be coherent, a paragraph must be clearly and logically organized. The following two paragraphs were written on the topic "the best or worst job you ever had." Both are unified and both are supported. However, one communicates more clearly and effectively. Which one, and why?

Paragraph A

Pantry Helper

My worst job was as a pantry helper in one of Vancouver's well-known restaurants. I had an assistant from three to six in the afternoon who did little but stand around and eat the whole time she was there. She kept an ear open for the sound of the back door opening, which was a sure sign the boss was coming in. The boss would testily say to me, "You've got a lot of things to do here, Lina. Try to get a move on." I would come in at two o'clock to relieve the woman on the morning shift. If her day was busy, that meant I would have to prepare salads, prepare soup stocks, and so on. Orders for appetizers and cold plates would come in and have to be prepared. The worst thing about the job was that the heat in the kitchen, combined with my nerves, would give me an upset stomach by seven o'clock almost every night. I might be going to the storeroom to get some supplies, and one of the servers would tell me she wanted an order of fried calamari. I would put the fryer basket on and head for the supply room, and a waitress would holler out that her customer was in a hurry. Flies would come in through the torn screen in the kitchen window and sting me. I was getting paid only $6.50 an hour. At five o'clock, when the dinner rush began, I would be dead tired. Roaches scurried in all directions whenever I moved a box or picked up a head of lettuce to cut.

Paragraph B

My Worst Job

The worst job I ever had was as a server at the Westside Inn. First of all, many of the people I waited on were rude. When a baked potato was hard inside or a salad was limp or their steak wasn't just the way they wanted it, they blamed me, rather than the kitchen. Or they would ask me to pick up their cutlery from the floor, or bring them different wineglasses, or even take their children to the bathroom. Also, I had to contend not only with the customers but with the kitchen staff as well. The cooks and bussers were often undependable and surly. If I didn't treat them just right, I would wind up having to apologize to customers because their meals came late or their water glasses weren't filled. Another reason I didn't like the job was that I was always moving. Because of the constant line at the door, as soon as one group left, another would take its place. I usually had only a twenty-minute lunch break and a ten-minute break in almost nine hours of work. I think I could have put up with the job if I had been able to pause and rest more often. The last and most important reason I hated the job was my boss. She played favourites, giving some of the servers the best-tipping repeat customers and preferences on holidays. She would hover around during my break to make sure I didn't take a second more than the allotted time. And even when I helped out by working through a break, she never had an appreciative word but would just tell me not to be late for work the next day.

Fill in the blanks: Paragraph _____ makes its point more clearly and

effectively because _____

_____

Comment: Paragraph B is more effective *because the material is organized clearly and logically.* Using emphatic order, the writer gives us a list of four reasons why the job was so bad: rude customers, unreliable kitchen staff, constant motion, and—most of all—an unfair boss. Further, the writer includes transitional words that act as signposts, making movement from one idea to the next easy to follow. The major transitions are *first of all, also, another reason,* and *the last and most important reason.*

Although paragraph A is unified and supported, the writer does not have any clear and consistent way of organizing the material. Partly, emphatic order is used, but this is not made clear by transitions or by saving the most important reason for last. Partly, a time order is used, but it moves inconsistently from two to seven to five o'clock.

These two paragraphs lead us to the third base of effective writing: *coherence.* The supporting ideas and sentences in a composition must be organized so that they cohere or "stick together." As has already been mentioned, key techniques for tying material together are:

- a clear method of organization (such as time order or emphatic order),
- transitions, and
- other transitional phrases and connecting words.

Checking for Coherence

To check a paper for coherence, ask yourself these questions:

1) Does the paper have a clear method of organization?
2) Are transitions and other connecting words used to tie the material together?

BASE 4: SENTENCE SKILLS

Reviewing Sentence Skills

Finally, review your paragraph to check that it has clear and error-free sentences. Two versions of a paragraph are given below. Both are *unified*, *supported*, and *organized*, but one version communicates more clearly and effectively. Which one, and why?

Paragraph A

> ### Falling Asleep Anywhere
>
> [1]There are times when people are so tired that they fall asleep almost anywhere. [2]For example, there is a lot of sleeping on the bus or subway on the way home from work in the evenings. [3]A man will be reading the newspaper, and seconds later it appears as if he is trying to eat it. [4]Or he will fall asleep on the shoulder of the stranger sitting next to him. [5]Another place where unplanned naps go on is the classroom. [6]In some classes, a student will start snoring so loudly that the professor has to ask another student to shake the sleeper awake. [7]A more embarrassing situation occurs when a student leans on one elbow and starts drifting off to sleep. [8]The weight of the head pushes the elbow off the desk, and this momentum carries the rest of the body along. [9]The student wakes up on the floor with no memory of getting there. [10]The worst time to fall asleep is when driving a car. [11]Police reports are full of accidents that occur when people lose consciousness and go off the road. [12]If the drivers are lucky, they are not seriously hurt. [13]One woman's car, for instance, went into the river. [14]She woke up in a metre of water and thought it was raining. [15]When people are really tired, nothing will stop them from falling asleep—no matter where they are.

Paragraph B

> ### "Falling Asleep Anywhere"
>
> [1]There are times when people are so tired that they fall asleep almost anywhere. [2]For example, on the bus or subway on the way home from work. [3]A man will be reading the newspaper, seconds later it appears as if he is trying to eat it. [4]Or he will fall asleep on the shoulder of the stranger sitting next to him. [5]Another place where unplanned naps go on are in the classroom. [6]In some classes, a student will start snoring so loudly that the professor has to ask another student to shake the sleeper awake. [7]A more embarrassing situation occurs when a student leans on one elbow and starting to drift off to sleep. [8]The weight of the head push the elbow off the desk, and this momentum carries the rest of the body along. [9]The student wakes up on the floor with no

memory of getting there. [10]The worst time to fall asleep is when driving a car. [11]Police reports are full of accidents that occur when people conk out and go off the road. [12]If the drivers are lucky they are not seriously hurt. [13]One womans car, for instance, went into the river. [14]She woke up in a metre of water. [15]And thought it was raining. [16]When people are really tired, nothing will stop them from falling asleep—no matter where they are.

Fill in the blanks: Paragraph _____ makes its point more clearly and effectively because _____

_____

• • • • **Activity**

Paragraph A is more effective because it incorporates *sentence skills*, the fourth base of competent writing. See if you can identify the ten sentence-skills mistakes in paragraph B. Do this, first of all, by going back and underlining the ten spots in paragraph B that differ in wording or punctuation from paragraph A. Comparing paragraph B with the correct version may help you identify the differences between clear and error-free sentences and faulty sentences. Then try to identify these ten sentence-skills mistakes by giving the sentence number that applies to each of these errors.

Where are there unnecessary quotation marks? _____

Underline four sentence fragments.

Which word group is incorrect because contains a comma splice? _____

Which word group has a faulty subject and verb agreement? _____

Which word group contains an incorrect possessive? _____

Section Four of this book explains these and other sentence skills. You should review all the skills carefully. Doing so will ensure that you know the most important rules of grammar, punctuation, and usage—rules needed to write clear, error-free sentences.

PRACTICE IN USING THE FOUR BASES

By now you are becoming familiar with four bases or goals of effective writing: unity, support, coherence, and sentence skills. In this closing section, you will expand and strengthen your understanding of the four bases as you work through the following activities:

1) Evaluating Outlines for Unity
2) Evaluating Paragraphs for Unity
3) Evaluating Paragraphs for Support
4) Evaluating Paragraphs for Coherence

5) Revising Paragraphs for Coherence

6) Evaluating Paragraphs for All Four Bases: Unity, Support, Coherence, and Sentence Skills

1   Evaluating Outlines for Unity

The best time to check a paragraph for unity is when it is in outline form. An outline, as explained on pages 30–31, is one of the best techniques for getting started with a paragraph.

Look at the rough beginning of an outline that one student prepared and then corrected for unity:

I had a depressing weekend.

1.   Hay fever bothered me
2.   Had to pay seventy-seven-dollar car bill
3.   ~~Felt bad~~
4.   Boyfriend and I had a fight
5.   ~~Did poorly on my math test today as a result~~
6.   My mother yelled at me unfairly

Four reasons support the opening statement that the writer was depressed over the weekend. The writer crossed out "Felt bad" because it was not a reason for her depression. Saying that she felt bad is only another way of saying that she was depressed. She also crossed out the item about the day's math test because the point she is supporting is that she was depressed over the weekend.

● ● ● ●   **Activity**

In each outline, cross out items that do not support the opening point. These items must be omitted in order to achieve paragraph unity.

1.   The cost of raising a child keeps increasing.
     a. Education taxes get higher every year.
     b. A pair of children's running shoes now costs over a hundred dollars.
     c. Overpopulation is a worldwide problem.
     d. Providing nutritious food is more costly because of inflated prices.
     e. Children should work at age sixteen.

2.   College life can be very complicated.
     a. The registration process can be long and involved.
     b. A college offers many student resources.
     c. Students must keep careful track of their finances.
     d. It can be challenging to meet the work requirements in all courses.
     e. Lifelong friendships can be made.

3.   There are several ways to get better mileage in your car.
     a. Check air pressure in tires regularly.
     b. Drive at no more than ninety kilometres per hour.

  c. Orange and yellow cars are the most visible.
  d. Avoid jackrabbit starts at stop signs and traffic lights.
  e. Always have duplicate ignition and trunk keys.

2   Evaluating Paragraphs for Unity

• • • • Activity

Each of the following three paragraphs contains *sentences that are off target*— sentences that do not support the opening point—and so the paragraphs are *not unified*. In the interest of paragraph unity, such sentences must be omitted.

Cross out the irrelevant sentences and write the numbers of those sentences in the spaces provided. The number of spaces will tell you the number of irrelevant sentences in each paragraph.

Paragraph A

> ### A Kindergarten Failure
>
> [1]In kindergarten I experienced the fear of failure that haunts many schoolchildren. [2]My moment of panic occurred on my last day in kindergarten at Laurier Public School in Dauphin, Manitoba. [3]My family lived in Manitoba for three years before we moved to Toronto, where my father was a human resources manager for the Co-operators Insurance Company. [4]Our teacher began reading a list of names of all those students who were to line up at the door in order to visit the grade one classroom. [5]Our teacher was a pleasant-faced woman who had resumed her career after raising her own children. [6]She called every name but mine, and I was left sitting alone in the class while everyone left, the teacher included. [7]I sat there in absolute horror. [8]I imagined that I was the first kid in human history who had flunked things like crayons, sandbox, and swings. [9]Without getting the teacher's permission, I got up and walked to the bathroom and threw up into a sink. [10]Only when I ran home in tears to my mother did I get an explanation of what had happened. [11]Since I was to go to a separate school in the fall, I had not been taken with the other children to meet the grade one teacher at the public school. [12]My moment of terror and shame had been only a misunderstanding.

The numbers of the irrelevant sentences: _____ _____

Paragraph B

> ### How to Prevent Cheating
>
> [1]Instructors should take steps to prevent students from cheating on exams. [2]To begin with, instructors should stop reusing old tests. [3]A test that has been

used even once is soon known via the student grapevine. [4]Students will check with their friends to find out, for example, what was on Dr. Thompson's marketing final last term. [5]They may even manage to find a copy of the test itself, "accidentally" not turned in by a former student of Dr. Thompson's. [6]Instructors should also take some common sense precautions at test time. [7]They should make students separate themselves, by at least one seat, during an exam, and they should watch the class closely. [8]The best place for the instructor to sit is in the rear of the room, so that a student is never sure if the instructor is looking at him or her. [9]Last of all, instructors must make it clear to students that there will be stiff penalties for cheating. [10]One of the problems with our educational systems is a lack of discipline. [11]Instructors never used to give in to students' demands or put up with bad behaviour, as they do today. [12]Anyone caught cheating should immediately receive a zero for the exam. [13]A person even suspected of cheating should be forced to take an alternative exam in the instructor's office. [14]Because cheating is unfair to honest students, it should not be tolerated.

The numbers of the irrelevant sentences: _____ _____

Paragraph C

Other Uses for Cars

[1]Many people who own a car manage to turn the vehicle into a garbage can, a clothes closet, or a storage room. [2]People who use their cars as garbage cans are easily recognized. [3]Empty snack bags, hamburger wrappers, pizza cartons, pop cans, and doughnut boxes litter the floor. [4]On the seats are old CDs, blackened fruit skins, crumpled receipts, crushed candy boxes, and used tissues. [5]At least the garbage stays in the car, instead of adding to the litter on our highways. [6]Other people use a car as a clothes closet. [7]The car contains several pairs of shoes, pants, or shorts, along with a suit or dress that's been hanging on the car's clothes hanger for over a year. [8]Sweaty, smelly gym clothes will also find a place in the car, a fact passengers quickly discover. [9]The world would be better off if people showed more consideration of others. [10]Finally, some people use a car as a spare garage or basement. [11]In the back seats or trunks of these cars are bags of fertilizer, beach chairs, old textbooks, chainsaws, or window screens that have been there for months. [12]The trunk may also contain an extra spare tire, a dented hub cap, a four-litre container of window washer fluid, and old stereo equipment. [13]If apartments offered more storage space, probably fewer people would resort to using their cars for such storage purposes. [14]All in all, people get a lot more use out of their cars than simply the kilometres they travel on the road.

The numbers of the irrelevant sentences: _____ _____

3   Evaluating Paragraphs for Support

● ● ● ● **Activity**

The three paragraphs that follow lack sufficient supporting details. In each paragraph, identify the spot or spots where more specific details are needed.

Paragraph A

Chicken: Our Best Friend

[1]Chicken is the best-selling meat today for a number of good reasons. [2]First of all, its reasonable cost puts it within everyone's reach. [3]Chicken is popular, too, because it can be prepared in so many different ways. [4]It can, for example, be cooked by itself, in spaghetti sauce, or with noodles and gravy. [5]It can be baked, boiled, broiled, or fried. [6]Chicken is also convenient. [7]Last and most important, chicken has a high nutritional value. [8]Two hundred and fifty grams of chicken contains twenty-eight grams of protein, which is almost half the recommended daily dietary allowance.

Fill in the blanks: The first spot where supporting details are needed is after sentence number _____. The second spot is after sentence number

_____.

Paragraph B

Tips on Bringing Up Children

[1]In some ways, children should be treated as mature people. [2]For one thing, adults should not use baby talk with children. [3]Using real words with children helps them develop language skills more quickly. [4]Baby talk makes children feel patronized, frustrated, and confused, for they want to understand and communicate with adults by learning their speech. [5]So animals should be called cows and dogs, not "moo-moos" and "bow-wows." [6]Second, parents should be consistent when disciplining children. [7]For example, if a parent tells a child, "You cannot have dessert unless you put away your toys," it is important that the parent follow through on the warning. [8]By being consistent, parents will teach children responsibility and give them a stable centre around which to grow. [9]Finally, and most important, children should be allowed and encouraged to make simple decisions. [10]Parents will thus be helping their children prepare for the complex decisions that they will have to deal with in later life.

Fill in the blank: The spot where supporting details are needed is after sentence number _____.

Paragraph C

> ### Culture Conflict
>
> [1]I am in a constant tug-of-war with my parents over conflicts between their Vietnamese culture and Canadian society. [2]To begin with, my parents do not like me to have so many friends from Canada. [3]They think that I should spend all my time with other Vietnamese people and speak English only when necessary. [4]I get into an argument whenever I want to go to a fast-food restaurant or a movie at night with my friends from school. [5]The conflict with my parents is even worse when it comes to plans for a career. [6]My parents want me to get a degree in science and then go on to medical school. [7]On the other hand, I think I want to become a teacher. [8]So far I have been taking science courses, but soon I will have to apply for Carleton's education program. [9]The other night my father made his attitude about what I should do very clear. [10]The most difficult aspect of our cultural differences is the way our family is structured. [11]My father is the centre of our family, and he expects that I will always listen to him. [12]Although I am twenty-one years old, I still have a nightly curfew at an hour which I consider insulting. [13]Also, I am expected to help my mother perform certain household chores that I've really come to hate. [14]My father expects me to live at home until I am married to a Vietnamese man. [15]When that happens, he assumes I will obey my husband just as I obey him. [16]I do not want to be a bad daughter, but I want to live like my Canadian female friends.

Fill in the blanks: The first spot where a supporting detail or details are needed is after sentence number _____. The second spot is after sentence number _____. The third spot is after sentence number _____.

4   Evaluating Paragraphs for Coherence

● ● ● ● **Activity**

Answer the questions about coherence that follow each of the two paragraphs below.

Paragraph A

> ### Living Just Enough for the City
>
> [1]There are so many good reasons to live in the city that it is hard to know why suburbs even exist. [2]Most important, there is no reason ever to sit inside, become a TV-bound vegetable, trapped in a maze of courts, crescents, and curving streets going nowhere. [3]Any day or evening, the city and its attractions

are only a walk or subway ride away. [4]There is no need to rely on a car and add to the general pollution by driving to a movie, a concert, a museum, or an interesting stretch of stores or clubs. [5]Anything new listed in the paper or discussed in class is easily accessible to the city dweller and never involves a carefully planned or lengthy expedition "downtown." [6]Walking the streets is one secret pleasure of city folks; they can walk everywhere. [7]And city streets are fascinating and full of life. [8]These streets may not be as well manicured or as spacious as suburban residential areas, but they are "people-sized" and meant for walking and looking. [9]Each store window has its stories to tell, and every old house is unique. [10]There are no vast empty parking lots or stretches of closed business strip malls; every block is cluttered with people, dogs, storefronts, and sidewalk displays. [11]Every metre of city streets grabs the attention; the walker's eye is never starved for something interesting. [12]Walking only a block or so to shop every day at small stores where the owners say hello makes shopping a pleasure, not a chore. [13]The fruits and vegetables are fresh and not sealed under plastic so cleverly that the bruises don't show. [14]And the friendly human contact makes the city person's shopping a social activity as much as a consumer activity. [15]Somehow, living in the city makes it easier to be alert, alive, and human.

a. The paragraph should use emphatic order. Write *1* before the reason that seems slightly less important than the other two, *2* before the second-most-important reason, and *3* before the most important reason.

_____ Closeness to attractions

_____ Ability to shop near home

_____ The pleasures of walking

b. Before which of the three reasons could the transitional words *first of all* be added? _____

c. Before which of the three reasons could the transition *in addition* be added? _____

d. What words show emphasis in sentence 2? _____

e. How many times are the keywords *city, city folks,* and *city dwellers* repeated in the paragraph? _____

Paragraph B

Apartment Hunting

[1]Apartment hunting is a several-step process. [2]Visit and carefully inspect the most promising apartments. [3]Check each place for signs of unwanted guests such as roaches or mice. [4]Make sure that light switches and appliances work and that there are enough electrical outlets. [5]Turn faucets and flush the toilet to be sure that the plumbing works smoothly. [6]Talk to the building manager for a bit

to get a sense of him or her as a person. ⁷If a problem develops after you move in, you want to know that a capable person will be there to handle the matter. ⁸Find out what stores and services that match your interests are available in the neighbourhood. ⁹Your local newspaper and real estate offices can provide you with a list of apartments for rent. ¹⁰Family and friends may be able to give you leads. ¹¹And your college may have a housing office that keeps a list of apartments for rent. ¹²Decide just what you need. ¹³If you can afford no more than six hundred dollars a month, you need to find a place that will cost no more than that. ¹⁴If you want a location that's close to work or school, you must take that factor into account. ¹⁵If you plan to cook, you want a place with a workable kitchen. ¹⁶By taking these steps, you should be ready to select the apartment that is best for you.

a. The paragraph should use time order. Write *1* before the step that should come first, *2* before the intermediate step, and *3* before the final step.

_____ Visit and carefully inspect the most promising apartments.

_____ Decide just what you need.

_____ Find out what's available that matches your interests.

b. Before which of the three steps could the transitional words *the first step is to* be added? _____

c. Before which step could the transitional words *after you have decided what you are looking for, the next step is to* be added? _____

d. Before which step could the transitional words *the final step* be added?

_____

e. To whom does the pronoun *him or her* in sentence 6 refer? _____

f. What is a synonym for *building manager* in sentence 7? _____

g. What is a synonym for *apartment* in sentence 13? _____

5 Revising Paragraphs for Coherence

The two paragraphs in this section begin with a clear point, but in each case the supporting material that follows the point is not coherent. Read each paragraph and the comments that follow it on how to organize and connect the supporting material. Then do the activity for the paragraph.

Paragraph A

A Difficult Period

Since I arrived on the West Coast in midsummer, I have had the most difficult period of my life. I had to look for an apartment. I found only one place that I could afford, but the owner said I could not move in until it was painted. When I first arrived in Vancouver, my thoughts were to stay with my father and stepmother. I had to set out looking for a job so that I could afford my own place, for I soon realized that my stepmother was not at all happy about having me live with them. A three-week search led to a job shampooing rugs for a house-cleaning company. I painted the apartment myself, and at least that problem was solved. I was in a hurry to get settled because I was starting school at Simon Fraser in September. A transportation problem developed because my stepmother insisted that I return my father's bike, which I was using at first to get to school. I had to rely on a bus that often arrived late, with the result that I missed some classes and was late for others. I had already had a problem with registration in early September. My counsellor had made a mistake with my classes, and I had to register all over again. This meant that I was one week late for class. Now I'm riding to school with a classmate and no longer have to depend on the bus. My life is starting to order itself, but I must admit that at first I thought it was hopeless to stay here.

Comments: The writer of this paragraph has provided a good deal of specific evidence to support the opening point. The evidence, however, needs to be organized. Before starting the paragraph, the writer should have decided to arrange the details by using time order. He or she could then have listed in an outline the exact sequence of events that made for such a difficult period.

● ● ● ● **Activity 1**

Here is a list of the various events described by the writer of paragraph A. Number the events in the correct time sequence by writing *1* in front of the first event that occurred, *2* in front of the second event, and so on.

Since I arrived on the West Coast in midsummer, I have had the most difficult period of my life.

_____ I had to search for an apartment I could afford.

_____ I had to find a job so that I could afford my own place.

_____ My stepmother objected to my living with her and my father.

_____ I had to paint the apartment before I could move in.

_____ I had to find an alternative to unreliable bus transportation.

_____ I had to reregister for my courses because of a counsellor's mistake.

Your instructor may now have you rewrite the paragraph on a separate sheet of paper. If so, be sure to use time signals such as *first, next, then, during, when, after,* and *now* to help guide your reader from one event to the next.

Paragraph B

Sometimes Dreams Pay Off

When I was in elementary school, there was one boy my friends and I called "David the Dreamer," and we thought there were lots of good reasons for that nickname. Most of the time in class, David looked half asleep. In fact, he had long floppy bangs and rather droopy eyelids that seemed to cover his light blue eyes, and we usually knew he was drifting away at his desk because teachers would startle him from his snoozy posture each time they called his name during classes. Every year, we heard some teacher ask, "David, are you awake, or does none of this interest you?" Instead of looking sheepish or guilty, David always smiled, dreamily. He never showed any concern, he just went back to whatever he was thinking about as he slumped with his head on his elbows. We knew from talking to him in the schoolyard that he loved comic books. He had a huge collection and knew every character and all the artists who drew the characters. Those comics characters seemed more real to him than we were, so we decided that *they* were what he was dreaming about in class. At recess, he loved to make up stories of his own about the characters and to give them whole new adventures. When he was spinning his "X-Men" stories, he did not look sleepy at all, and his blue eyes were wide open and fixed on his listeners. Even in gym class, he leaned sleepily against a tree or the gym wall, unfazed by the loud insults of the gym teacher, who called him "Mr. Relaxation" and never chose him for a single team. David had his own world that he was happy enough to share, but he just never worried much about anyone else's world. A year ago, I was reading the arts section of the newspaper, and I realized how busy David had been during all that dreaming. There was a picture of David, floppy bangs, sleepy blue eyes and all, winning an award at the Toronto International Film Festival for best independent film. Apparently, he made the winning team, after all.

Comments: The writer of this paragraph provides a number of specifics that support the opening point. However, the supporting material has not been organized clearly. Before writing this paragraph, the author should have (1) decided to arrange the supporting evidence by using emphatic order and (2) listed in an outline the reasons why David's dreaminess was so intriguing and all-consuming, and the supporting details for each reason. The writer could also have determined which reason to use in the emphatic final position of the paper.

● ● ● ●   **Activity 2**

Create a clear outline for paragraph B by filling in the scheme below. The outline is partially completed.

When I was in elementary school, there was one boy my friends and I called "David the Dreamer," and we thought . . .

SUBTOPIC   1. *David's appearance* _____

SUPPORTING DETAILS   a. _____

                                                   b. _____

SUBTOPIC   2. _____

SUPPORTING DETAILS   a. _____

                                                   b. *Dozing at desk* _____

                                                   c. _____

                                                   d. _____

SUBTOPIC   3. *His fascination with comic books* _____

SUPPORTING DETAILS   a. _____

                                                   b. _____

                                                   c. _____

Your instructor may have you rewrite the paragraph on a separate sheet of paper. If so, be sure to introduce each of the subtopics or reasons with transitions such as *first, second, another reason,* and *finally.* You may also want to use repeated words, pronouns, and synonyms to help tie your sentences together.

6   Evaluating Paragraphs for All Four Bases: Unity, Support, Coherence, And Sentence Skills

● ● ● ●   Activity

In this activity, you will evaluate paragraphs in terms of all four bases: *unity, support, coherence,* and *sentence skills.* Evaluative comments follow each paragraph below. Circle the letter of the statement that best applies in each case.

Paragraph A

Drunk Drivers

People caught driving while drunk, even first offenders, should be jailed. Drunk driving, first of all, is more dangerous than carrying a loaded gun. In addition, a jail term would show drivers that society will no longer tolerate such careless and dangerous behaviour. Finally, severe penalties might encourage solutions to the problem of drinking and driving. People who go out for a good time and intend to have several drinks should follow media advice and always designate one person, who would stay completely sober, as the driver.

---

a. The paragraph is not unified.
b. The paragraph is not adequately supported.
c. The paragraph is not well organized.
d. The paragraph does not show a command of sentence skills.
e. The paragraph is well written in terms of the four bases.

Paragraph B

> ### A Frustrating Moment
>
> A frustrating moment happened to me several days ago. When I was shopping. I had picked up a tube of toothpaste and a jar of skin cream. After the cashier rang up the purchases, which came to $4.15. I handed her $10. Then got back my change, which was only $0.85. I told the cashier that she had made a mistake. Giving me change for $5 instead of $10. But she insist that I had only gave her $5, I became very upset and insist that she return the rest of my change. She refused to do so instead she asked me to step aside so she could wait on the next customer. I stood very rigid, trying not to lose my temper. I simply said to her, I'm not going to leave here without my change for $10. Giving in at this point a bell was rung and the manager was summoned. After the situation was explain to him, he ask the cashier to ring off her register to check for the change. After doing so, the cashier was $5 over her sale receipts. Only then did the manager return my change and apologize for the cashier mistake.

a. The paragraph is not unified.
b. The paragraph is not adequately supported.
c. The paragraph is not well organized.
d. The paragraph does not show a command of sentence skills.
e. The paragraph is well written in terms of the four bases.

Paragraph C

> ### A Change in My Writing
>
> A technique in my present English class has corrected a writing problem that I've always had. In past English courses, I had major problems with commas in the wrong places, bad spelling, capitalizing the wrong words, sentence fragments, and run-on sentences. I never had any big problems with unity, support, or coherence, but the sentence skills were another matter. They were like little bugs that always appeared to infest my writing. My present instructor asked me to rewrite papers, concentrating just on sentence skills. I thought that the instructor was crazy because I didn't feel that rewriting would do any good. I soon became certain that my instructor was out of his mind, for he made me rewrite my first paper four times. It was very frustrating, for I became tired of doing the same paper over and over. I wanted to curse at my instructor when I'd show him each new draft and he'd find skills mistakes and say, "Rewrite." Finally,

my papers began to improve and the sentence skills began to fall into place. I was able to see them and correct them before turning in a paper, whereas I couldn't before. Why or how this happened I don't know, but I think that rewriting helped a lot. It took me most of the semester, but I stuck it out and the work paid off.

a. The paragraph is not unified.
b. The paragraph is not adequately supported.
c. The paragraph is not well organized.
d. The paragraph does not show a command of sentence skills.
e. The paragraph is well written in terms of the four bases.

REVIEWING THE LEARNING OUTCOMES FOR CHAPTER 6

To assure yourself that you have understood and met the learning outcomes for this chapter, answer the following questions.

✓ What are two characteristics that must be present in order for a paragraph to be *unified?*

✓ What three elements must the body of paragraph have for it to be well *supported?*

✓ What activities are involved in creating a paper that is *coherent?* How do these two writing and revising activities lead to this standard?

✓ Where in this book will you find help with revising for effective *sentence skills?* At which stage of the writing process is identifying and correcting sentence-skills and grammatical errors appropriate, and why?

✓ Why are evaluating activities needed at different stages of the writing process?

Visit the *English Skills with Readings: Examining Paragraphs* Online Learning Centre at www.mcgrawhill.ca/olc/langan to access self-quizzes, internet-based questions and research skills, web resources, and other learning and study tools.

Section 2

Paragraph Development

Preview

Section Two introduces you to paragraph development and gives you practice in the following common types of paragraph development:

- Narrating an Event
- Describing a Scene or Person
- Providing Examples
- Explaining a Process
- Examining Cause and Effect
- Comparing or Contrasting
- Defining a Term
- Dividing and Classifying
- Arguing a Position

After a brief explanation of each type of paragraph development, student paragraphs illustrating each type are presented, followed by questions about those paragraphs. The questions relate to the bases for effective writing described in Section One. You are then asked to write your own paragraph. In each case, writing assignments progress from personal-experience topics to more formal and objective topics; some topics require simple research, and the last assignment in each section asks you to write with a specific purpose and audience in mind. At times, points or topic sentences for development are suggested, so that you can concentrate on (1) making sure your evidence is on target in support of your opening idea, (2) providing plenty of specific supporting details to back up your point, and (3) organizing your supporting material clearly.

Chapter 7

Narrating an Event

By working through the activities and writing tasks in this chapter you will create a narrative paragraph that

- displays the point of internal or external conflict within an experience: i.e., the focus of your narrative;
- shows careful selection of details related to your point;
- organizes and sequences your supporting material in time order to create an accurate and coherent narrative paragraph;
- is revised to include vivid and important factual details to "show" readers your point and re-create your events as accurately as possible; and
- concludes by returning to its point, rather than ending with its last event.

Narrative paragraphs and essays work toward the same purpose as the forms of exposition: such papers seek *to explain*. Narrative-based writing uses a storyline to explain and deepen the meaning of its point. Unlike a made-up story or fictional narrative where the meaning may reveal itself slowly as the story unrolls, a narrative announces its meaning in its topic sentence. Expository narrative, then, (1) makes a point *clear* by relating a detailed storyline about something that has happened and (2) presents its details *in the order in which they happened*. In an expository narrative, the events may be from a personal (subjective) or impersonal (objective) point of view, but as with other college writing, it will be nonfiction. The skill is in selecting which details support the opening point.

Here is a typical narrative illustrating the point "I was embarrassed yesterday."

> I was hurrying across campus to get to a class. It had rained heavily all morning, so I was hopscotching my way around puddles in the pathway. I called to two friends ahead to wait for me, and right before I caught up to them, I came to a large puddle that covered the entire path. I had to make a quick choice of either stepping into the puddle or trying to jump over it. I jumped, wanting to seem cool, since my friends were watching, but didn't clear the puddle. Water splashed everywhere, drenching my shoes, socks, and pants cuffs, and spraying the pants of my friends as well. I felt the more embarrassed because I had tried to look so casual.

This narrative or linked sequence of details is a vivid and real explanation of the writer's embarrassment: we see and understand just why he felt as he did.

Narrative's uses in college and career writing are numerous. Child care and social services workers write narrative-based case studies and reports; course writing and career writing in business and technology require reports of situations and procedures written as accurate recountings of events. Law enforcement officers must record every situation with which they are involved.

In this section, you will be asked to write narratives that illustrate a specific point. The paragraphs below both present narrative experiences that support a particular point. Read them, and then answer the questions that follow.

PARAGRAPHS TO CONSIDER

A Loss of Faith

[1]My younger brother Josh was always the "star" of the family, so six months ago our parents rewarded his good marks by paying for university tuition and residence fees. [2]A week before reading week in February, I used my own break from college to fly out to see him at the University of Alberta. [3]When I knocked on the door of his room, he looked surprised, but not in a pleasant way. [4]He introduced me to his roommate, who looked uncomfortable and quickly left. [5]I asked Josh how classes were going, and because Josh's jumpiness was making me nervous, I started to look around the room; the first thing I noticed was the big bulletin board above the desk. [6]As I focused my eyes on the board, dozens of papers tacked up there caught my eye. [7]Most of the papers were tests and lab reports, each one marked with either a big red F or an 0, but the largest paper up there was an official document from the university—an official notice of change of address for Josh McKenna. [8]"What's going on?" I said. [9]I stood there stunned and then felt my anger start

to grow. [10]"Who lives at 488 West 3rd Street in Calgary?" I asked. [11]Josh just shrugged and said, "What's it to you? Are you supposed to report back on me?" [12]I don't really remember all that he told me, except that he tried to lie at first, to pretend his marks were all right, before he admitted the truth: he was failing nearly every course and had stopped going to classes—he had even arranged to send his next transcripts to his roommate's mother's house, the Calgary address. [13]I felt a sharp pain in the pit of my stomach, and I wanted to be anywhere but in that residence room. [14]I wanted to hit him or tear down the papers and run out to call our parents, but I did nothing. [15]Clumsily I pulled on my jacket. [16]My stomach felt sick, and I worried that my rage would take control of my body. [17]I opened the room door, and suddenly more than anything I wanted to slam the door on my brother and his lies. [18]Instead, I managed to close the door quietly. [19]I walked away understanding what is meant by a loss of faith.

A Childhood Disappointment

[1]The time I almost won a car when I was ten years old was probably the most disappointing moment of my childhood. [2]One hot summer afternoon I was wandering around a local Bay store, waiting for my mother to finish shopping. [3]Near the toy department, I was attracted to a crowd of people gathered around a bright blue car that was on display in the main aisle. [4]A sign indicated that the car was the first prize in a sweepstakes celebrating the store's tenth anniversary. [5]The sign caught my attention because of the tiny lights embedded in the words "win" and "car." [6]White entry cards and shiny yellow pencils were scattered on a card table nearby, and the table was just low enough for me to write on, so I filled out a card. [7]Then, feeling very much like an adult, I slipped my card into the slot of a heavy blue wooden box that rested on another table nearby. [8]I then proceeded to the toy department, completely forgetting about the car. [9]However, about a month later, just as I was walking into the house from my first day back at school, the telephone rang. [10]When my mother answered it, a man asked to speak to a Jeff Wellesley. [11]My mother said, "There's a Jeff Castaldo here, but not a Jeff Wellesley." [12]He asked, "Is this 862-9715 at 29 Castaldo Street?" [13]My mother said, "That's the right number, but this is 29 Wellesley Street." [14]She then asked him, "What is this all about?" and he explained to her about the sweepstakes contest. [15]My mother then called me to ask if I had ever filled out an application for a sweepstakes drawing. [16]I said that I had, and she told me to get on the phone. [17]The man by this time had realized that I had filled in my first name and street name on the line where my full name was to be. [18]He told me I could not qualify for the prize because I had filled out the application incorrectly. [19]For the rest of the day, I cried whenever I thought of how close I had come to winning the car. [20]I am probably fated for the rest of my life to think of the "almost" prize whenever I fill out any kind of contest form.

Questions

About Unity

1. Which paragraph lacks a topic sentence?

    _____

    Write a topic sentence for the paragraph:

    _____

    _____

    _____

2. Which sentence in "A Childhood Disappointment" should be omitted in the interest of paragraph unity? (*Write the sentence number here.*) _____

About Support

3. What is for you the best (most real and vivid) detail or image in the paragraph "A Loss of Faith"?

    _____

    _____

    What is the best detail or image in "A Childhood Disappointment"?

    _____

    _____

    What is the most effective detail in "A Loss of Faith"?

    _____

    _____

4. Which paragraph or paragraphs provide details in the form of the actual words used by the participants?

    _____

    _____

About Coherence

5. Do the two paragraphs use time order or emphatic order to organize details?

    _____

6. List the transition words used in one of the two paragraphs:
    a. _____
    b. _____
    c. _____
    d. _____

FORMS OF NARRATIVE WRITING

All narratives relate a time-ordered series of events, but not all narrative writing is personal or deeply emotional. When we think of narratives, we often think of types of literature that include dialogue, personal stories, and the "great" narratives of myth and legend. Expository narratives, however, maintain the structure of standard essays, stating a point at the beginning, giving supporting reasons and details in time order, and returning to the initial point. An expository narrative will *not* use creative storytelling techniques such as mixing the beginning, middle, and end of the storyline; using imaginary details; or ending as a "cliffhanger" or otherwise without resolution.

Personal Narratives

- This chapter includes personal narrative paragraphs which show *why* people feel the way they do or *how* they learned some lesson in life. Narratives often point to a moral or teach a lesson.
- Personal narratives are often effective because of their intimate connection between reader and writer. The use of "I," the first-person singular point of view, offers this immediacy when the writer's purpose is to to share his or her experience.

Other Forms of Narrative

- This chapter will also offer you opportunities to write objective narratives, using the third-person point of view. Many narratives, including some personal stories, may be less personal in focus or tone. Writing a narrative in the third-person point of view places the reader's focus on the events or experience itself, rather than on the writer. There is no "I" to distract the reader. Such narratives allow readers more "distance" between themselves and the subject matter; their tone is cooler, less intimate.
- More objective third-person narratives may relate the "story" of a marketing campaign, the stages in a technical process, or the events occurring as part of an accident. Such narrative reports may be found as:
  - Applications for admittance
  - Proposals for grants
  - Reports by officials and inspectors
  - Status reports for committees
  - Medical or therapeutic reports
  - Reports used in criminal justice, social services, and a variety of public offices
- Narrative reports often supplement other information-gathering formats such as official forms or surveys.
- Narrative reports must naturally be more impersonal, but their general purpose is the same as that of all narratives: the vivid and accurate recreation of some experience or events.

Writers must decide whether their purpose is to focus on the events they narrate or on their connection to these events. The writer's decision dictates both the point of view used and the ultimate tone of the narrative.

Further Insight—Writing objectively

In some cases of narrative writing, the narrative will be subjective and is intended to lead readers to view an incident with the same attitude as the author. In other cases, and especially in reports and other official documents, the narrative must be stated objectively. A police officer must record the details of an incident in a way that does not unfairly prejudice the legal system, for example. In such cases, the tone must be accurate and dispassionate in order to maintain objectivity.

Some hints for maintaining objectivity are:

- Use a consistent third-person point of view. Do not refer to yourself as "I"; instead, identify the official role or capacity you hold ["the officer"; "the instructor"]. Check that all verbs and pronouns agree in number and tense.
- Use field-specific, but inclusive, terminology. Never use phrases such as, "One of the girls from the lab spotted something weird." Write, instead, "A technician in the histology laboratory identified an anomaly in the tissue sample."
- Be specific. Use the most appropriate nouns and verbs with appropriate descriptors to identify the details. Don't just say, "Bad food will make you sick." Try, "People can become infected by food-born diseases such as salmonella."
- Be accurate but fair by avoiding superlatives (*the greatest*) and other "hyped" language. Objective reports tell, not sell. Remember that opinions are not objective, so use terms that offer evidence. Rather than saying that, "a hybrid car is the best vehicle on the market," state that "a hybrid car is the most fuel efficient on the market." It is often advisable to provide evidence, either by elaborating further, or by citing a source (see Chapters 17 and 18).

DEVELOPING A NARRATIVE PARAGRAPH

Development through Prewriting

Mark's instructor was helping her students think of topics for their narrative paragraphs. "A narrative is just a story that illustrates a point," she said. "That point is often about a strong emotion you felt. Looking at a list of emotions may help you think of a topic. Ask yourself what incident in your life has led you to feel any of these emotions."

The instructor then jotted these feelings on the board:

Anger
Embarrassment
Jealousy
Amusement
Confusion
Thankfulness
Loneliness
Sadness
Terror
Relief

As Mark looked over the list, he remembered several experiences in his life. "The word *anger* made me think about the time when my kid brother took my skateboard without telling me, and he left it in the park, where it got stolen. *Amusement* made me think of a school trip to Quebec City, when Terry Levesque, who claimed he spoke French, tried to bargain with a street vendor but ended up paying more than the vendor asked for. When I got to *sadness*, though, I thought about my brother again and hit on something that still bothers me now. I visited my brother only a few months ago, and I still feel angry and sad about that. *Sad* isn't really a strong enough word, though—I felt angry and deceived. So I decided to write about losing my faith in someone."

Mark's first step was to do some freewriting. Without worrying about spelling or grammar, he just sat down at the computer and let fly all the thoughts and emotions he'd been worrying over since his visit to his brother. Here is what he came up with.

I was really looking forward to seeing Josh last spring. He went off to University of Alberta six months ago. I saved up enough for a discount plane fare from working at the garage part-time, and I was excited about going out west on my own. Travelling alone was a major thing for me. But from the moment I got to his residence room, I think I knew something was wrong. He looked so surprised when he saw me at the door and I didn't know why—he knew I was coming. His roommate left as soon as I got there and Josh was nervous and jumpy. And not just full-of-energy jumpy, either. All over his bulletin board were these failed assignments, like he was proud of them. There were cartons of beer bottles all over the floor, and garbage everywhere. I didn't know what to do. I didn't know what to say either, so I asked him about the address I saw on a university letter—it wasn't his address. Making me feel kind of sick. Even before he admitted anything I kept thinking about our parents. He was lying to them and hiding things. Josh was always the favourite, the guy who couldn't do anything wrong, and he was lying to everybody now. I wanted to hit him or yell at him or something. Instead I shut my mouth and realized I felt lied to, too. I couldn't believe anything he was saying, and I just wanted to go home.

Development through Revising

Mark knew that his first free writing needed work, but he also knew he had something to work with. After he reread it the following day, he said, "Although my point is supposed to be that my visit to my brother taught me about losing faith in someone, I didn't really get that across. I needed to say more about how the experience felt to me, and why it felt that way.

"I've included information that doesn't really support my point. For instance, how I paid for my plane ticket isn't important here, and the mess in his room isn't either. And I think I spend too much time talking about getting to the visit itself. I want to get more quickly to the point where I arrived at Josh's room.

"Maybe I should try putting in some conversation, too. That might show people how this whole thing felt to me, and how it seemed like there was this wall between my brother and me."

Mark used two strategies—the self-critique, above, and questioning—to generate material. He created an outline, then revised his paragraph until he produced the version that appears on page 145.

WRITING A NARRATIVE PARAGRAPH

How to Write a Narrative Paragraph

1) Think of an event or experience that seems meaningful to you. Such an experience will probably have caused you to change, learn something, or grow in some way.

2) Prewrite to pile up details of your experience. Do not be concerned if you do not immediately find an easy-to-state single point.

3) After your initial prewriting, look for a *conflict*, some moment when your actions or expectations met with something unforeseen, causing you to change direction. This is probably your "moment of enlightenment," your focus for your paragraph. Try to state what you learned at this moment, or try to name your dominant emotion: this will become the topic, the point of your paragraph.

4) Write out your point as a topic sentence and create an outline for your narrative. *Organize* your details in time sequence as they occurred. *Select* details from your prewriting that (1) cover only a limited amount of time, and (2) truly support your point.

5) Draft and revise your paragraph with one aim: to *recreate* emotions, actions, and speech as vividly as possible. "Show" readers your experience, and achieve accuracy in your writing by doing so.

• • • • •   **Writing Assignment 1**

Write a paragraph about an experience in which a certain emotion was predominant. The emotion might be fear, pride, satisfaction, embarrassment, or any of the following:

Frustration	Sympathy	Shyness
Love	Bitterness	Disappointment
Sadness	Violence	Happiness
Terror	Surprise	Jealousy
Shock	Nostalgia	Anger
Relief	Loss	Hate
Envy	Silliness	Nervousness

The experience should be *limited in time.* Note that the two paragraphs presented in this chapter detail experiences that occurred within relatively short periods. One writer describes the anger he felt at his brother's dishonesty during a brief visit; another describes the disappointing loss of a prize.

A good way to recreate an event is to *include some dialogue,* as the writers of the two paragraphs in this chapter have done. Repeating what you have said or what you have heard someone else say helps make the situation come alive. First, though, be sure to check Chapter 33, on quotation marks.

Prewriting

a Begin by prewriting. Think of an experience or event in your life in which you felt a certain emotion strongly. Then spend ten minutes freewriting about the experience. Do not worry at this point about such matters as spelling or grammar or putting things in the right order; instead, just try to get down all the details you can think of that seem related to the experience.

b This preliminary writing will help you decide whether your topic is promising enough to develop further. If it is not, choose another emotion. If it is, do three things:

- First, write your topic sentence, underlining the emotion you will focus on. For example, "My first day in kindergarten was one of the *scariest* days of my life."
- Second, make up a list of all the details involved in the experience. Then arrange these details in time order.
- Third, write an outline or detailed plan for your paragraph.

c Using the list and outline as guides, prepare a rough draft of your paper. Use time signals such as *first, then, next, after, while, during,* and *finally* to help connect details as you move from the beginning to the middle to the end of your narrative. Be sure to include not only what happened but also how you felt about what was going on.

Revising

Put your first draft away for a day or so. When you return to it, read it over, asking yourself these questions:

- Does my topic sentence clearly state what emotion the experience made me feel?
- If it is appropriate to my paragraph, have I included some dialogue to make the experience come alive?
- Have I explained how I felt as the experience occurred?
- Have I used time order to narrate the experience from beginning to end?
- Have I used time signals to connect one detail to the next?
- Have I checked my paper for sentence skills, including spelling, as listed on the inside front cover of this book?

Continue revising your work until you can answer yes to all these questions.

● ● ● ● ● **Writing Assignment 2**

Narrate a real-life event you know about or have witnessed. Listed below are some incidents that you may have observed or participated in. You may need to make notes to help recall the details in the event.

A winter-driving mishap
The final goal in an exciting sporting championship
The lineup waiting to buy tickets to a popular concert as it is announced that the event is sold out
Children at a birthday party
An irate defendant in a traffic court or small claims court
A performance review for a new employee
An audition or tryout for a performance or sports event

Prewriting

a Decide what point you will make about the incident. What one word or phrase characterizes the scene you witnessed? Your narration of the incident will emphasize and use that characteristic to focus its details. This word or phrase is the "keynote" or dominant emotion that will tie your paragraph together.

b Write your topic sentence. The topic sentence should state where the incident happened as well as your point about it. Notice the keynote word or phrase in these possible topic sentences:

> Slippery roads contributed to a freak accident during a heavy snowstorm in Calgary's downtown.
> The children at Hui's seventh birthday party were out of control.

c Use the questioning technique to remind yourself of details that will make your narrative come alive. Ask yourself questions like these and write down your answers:

> Whom was I observing?
> How were they dressed?

What were their facial expressions?
What tones of voice did they use?
What did I hear them say?

d Using the Paragraph Outline Form on page 33, create an outline that begins with your topic sentence, in which you have underlined or italicized your keynote word or phrase. Be sure that your subtopics and supporting details all explain and illustrate that main emotion or descriptive phrase.

e Drawing details from your notes and your outline, write the first draft of your paragraph. Remember to use time signals such as *then, after that, during, meanwhile,* and *finally* to connect your details and sentences together.

Revising

After you have put your paragraph away for a day, read it to a friend or fellow student who will give you honest feedback. Both of you should consider these questions:

- Does the topic sentence make a general point about the incident and state the "keynote" word or phrase?
- Do descriptions of the appearance, tone of voice, and expressions of the people involved paint a clear picture that illustrates the keynote word or phrase?
- Is the sequence of events made clear by transitional words such as at *first, later,* and *then?*

Continue revising your work until you and your reader can answer yes to all these questions. Then check to make sure your paragraph is free of sentence-skills mistakes, including spelling errors. Use the list on the inside front cover of this book.

● ● ● ● **Writing Assignment 3**

Write a paragraph that shows, through some experience you have had, the truth *or* falsity of a popular belief. You might write about any one of the following statements or some other popular saying.

Haste makes waste.
Don't count your chickens before they're hatched.
It isn't what you know, it's who you know.
Borrowing can get you into trouble.
What you don't know won't hurt you.
You never really know people until you see them in an emergency.
If you don't help yourself, nobody will.
Hope for the best but expect the worst.
You get what you pay for.
There is an exception to every rule.

Begin your narrative paragraph with a topic sentence that expresses your attitude, your agreement or disagreement, with a popular saying. For example, "My sister learned recently that 'keeping a promise is easier said than done.'" Or

"'Never give advice to a friend' is not always good advice, as I learned after helping a friend reunite with her boyfriend."

Refer to the suggestions for prewriting, outlining, and revising on pages 153–154. Remember that the purpose of your story is to *support* your topic sentence. Feel free to select carefully from your experience and even add to it so that the details truly support the point of your story.

• • • • Writing Assignment 4

Write an account of a memorable personal experience where you gained insight into yourself or of human nature. Make sure that your story has a point, expressed in the first sentence of the paragraph. If necessary, tailor your narrative to fit your purpose. Use *time order* to organize your details (*first* this happened; *then* this; *after* that, this; *next,* this; and so on). Concentrate on providing as many specific details as possible so that the reader can really "see" and share your experience. Try to make it as vivid for the reader as it was for you when you first experienced it.

You might want to use one of the topics below, or a topic of your own choosing. Regardless, remember that every sentence of your story must illustrate or support a point stated in the first sentence of your paragraph.

The first time you felt like an adult
A major decision
A moment you knew you were happy
Your best or worst date
A foolish risk
An argument you will never forget
An incident that changed your life
A time when you did or did not do the right thing
Your best or worst holiday or birthday
A triumph in sports or some other event

You may want to refer to the suggestions on prewriting and revising in Writing Assignment 1.

• • • • Writing Assignment 5

In many programs of study, potential graduates must complete a practicum or internship to demonstrate that they can apply the skills and concepts they have learned in an authentic situation. Recall or imagine such a situation in any appropriate field (human services; theatre or arts production; business management; medical or scientific research or technology; and so on). Identify the exact job title, and then write a paragraph in the form of an objective narrative report about that practical experience. You may collect your information from your own experience, but you should write it in the third person, putting the emphasis on the events of the narrative rather than on yourself.

You may wish to use a form of prewriting such as listing to discover a main idea about the practicum as well as the three reasons that will support that idea.

Do not write a summary, but focus on a lesson learned. Write a topic sentence that identifies both the work and the idea, such as "Children's recreation coordinators require unlimited energy." From there construct an outline that includes the main idea, and supporting reasons in time order. Continue by sketching in explanatory details as well as at least one specific example (if not more) for each supporting reason.

After you write your first draft, review it with special attention to the factual details that you record, and to the way you use transitions to move your central idea through the time frame of your narrative. Once you are satisfied with the structure and content of your paragraph, edit carefully to make sure that the sentences are clear and error-free.

REVIEWING THE LEARNING OUTCOMES FOR NARRATIVE WRITING

When you complete any of the writing assignments in this chapter, review your work to decide how well you have met the learning outcomes for narrative writing. Decide how well your paragraph meets each of these requirements.

✓ Does your paragraph open with a clear statement of its point about the emotion, experience, or lesson that is its subject?

✓ Does each detail of your storyline contribute specifically to clarifying your point or lesson?

✓ Are your details arranged in time order, with transitional words and phrases to show the relationships between events?

✓ Are your details specific and vividly described: do they recreate your experience?

✓ Do you conclude with a return to your point, rather than with the last event in your story?

Chapter 8

Describing a Scene or Person

L E A R N I N G   O U T C O M E S

By working through the activities and writing tasks in this chapter, you will create a descriptive paper that

- opens with a dominant impression of its subject in its topic sentence;

- offers a rich, focused, careful selection of sense-oriented details to confirm and strengthen aspects of your dominant impression;

- guides your readers with a clear point of view and a consistent method of tracking observations about your subject; and

- concludes with a thought that fixes your dominant impression in the reader's mind.

Descriptive writing gives readers pictures in words. Describing is a basic communication activity that serves all forms of writing. Narration succeeds because of the power of its descriptive details; readers' thoughts and emotions are touched directly by description that provokes reactions or that persuades. Locations, technical processes, or situations are explained and re-created in words by accurate description.

Descriptive "word-pictures" may have many purposes, but to be effective, they must be as vivid and real as possible. You perceive the subject you describe through your senses, so you must, in turn, record your subject in specific details to appeal to your readers' senses: sight, hearing, taste, smell, and touch. More than any other type of writing, a descriptive paragraph needs sharp, colourful details.

Here is a description in which only the sense of sight is used:

A rug covers the living-room floor.

In contrast, here is a description rich in sense impressions:

A thick, forest green, plush broadloom rug stretches wall to wall across the living-room floor. The deep and densely woven fibres of the carpet hush your steps as you walk through them in your bare feet, and as your feet relax into the cushiony pile, the soft wool pushes back at you with a spongy resilience. How many senses do the writer's details speak to?

- Sight: *thick, forest green, plush broadloom rug; stretches wall to wall; walk through them in your bare feet; cushiony pile*
- Hearing: *hush*
- Touch: *bare feet, deep and densely woven fibres, pushes back, spongy resilience*

Sharp, vivid images provided by the sensory details create a clear picture of the rug: we are able to share in the writer's experience.

Descriptive writing skills and techniques are essential to any college assignment where an event, procedure, human behaviour pattern, or strategy must be carefully tracked and re-created. Advertising and sales rely on description; training manuals require careful description of objects, gestures, and processes; in fact, every form of career writing demands the accuracy, precision, and careful detail selection of effective descriptive writing. Reviews of restaurants, movies, theatre productions, and other cultural events rely heavily upon vivid and detailed description.

In this section, you will be asked to describe a person, place, or thing for your readers by using words rich in sensory details. To help you prepare for the assignment, read the next two paragraphs and answer the questions that follow.

PARAGRAPHS TO CONSIDER

An Athlete's Room

[1]As I entered the bright, cheerful space, with its beige walls and practical, flat-pile carpet, I noticed a closet to my right with the door open. [2]On the shelf above the bunched-together clothes were a red baseball cap, a fielder's glove, and a battered brown gym bag. [3]Turning from the closet, I noticed a single bed with its wooden headboard against the far wall. [4]The bedspread was a brown, orange, and beige print of basketball, football, and baseball scenes. [5]A lamp shaped like a baseball and a copy of Sports Illustrated were on the top of a nightstand to the left of the bed. [6]A sports schedule and several yellowing newspaper clippings were tacked to the cork bulletin board on the wall above the nightstand. [7]A desk with a bookcase top stood against the left wall. [8]I walked toward it to examine it more closely. [9]As I ran my fingers over the items on the dusty shelves, I noticed some tarnished medals and faded ribbons for track accomplishments. [10]These lay next to a heavy gold trophy inscribed "MVP: Windsor Varsity Basketball." [11]I accidentally tipped an autograph-covered, slightly deflated basketball off one shelf, and the ball bounced with dull thuds across the width of the room. [12]Next to the desk was a window with brightly printed curtains that matched the bedspread. [13]Between the window and the left corner stood a dresser with one drawer half open, revealing a tangle of odd sweat socks and a few stretched-out T-shirts emblazoned with team insignias. [14]As I turned to leave the room, I carefully picked my way around scattered pairs of worn-out athletic shoes.

A Depressing Place

¹The pet shop in the mall is a depressing place. ²A display window attracts passersby who stare at the prisoners penned inside. ³In the right-hand side of the window, two puppies press their forepaws against the glass and attempt to lick the human hands that press from the outside. ⁴A cardboard barrier separates the dogs from several black-and-white kittens piled together in the opposite end of the window. ⁵Inside the shop, rows of wire cages line one wall from top to bottom. ⁶At first, it is hard to tell whether a bird, hamster, gerbil, cat, or dog is locked inside each cage. ⁷Only an occasional movement or clawing, shuffling sound tells visitors that living creatures are inside. ⁸Running down the centre of the store is a line of large wooden perches that look like coat racks. ⁹When customers pass by, the parrots and mynahs chained to these perches flutter their clipped wings in a useless attempt to escape. ¹⁰At the end of this centre aisle is a large plastic tub of dirty, stagnant-looking water containing a few motionless turtles. ¹¹The shelves against the left-hand wall are packed with all kinds of pet-related items. ¹²The smell inside the entire shop is an unpleasant mixture of strong chemical deodorizers, urine-soaked newspapers, and musty sawdust. ¹³Because so many animals are crammed together, the normally pleasant, slightly milky smell of the puppies and kittens is sour and strong. ¹⁴The droppings inside the uncleaned birdcages give off a dry, stinging odour. ¹⁵Visitors hurry out of the shop, anxious to feel fresh air and sunlight. ¹⁶The animals remain there.

Questions

About Unity

1. Which paragraph lacks a topic sentence?

_____

2. Which sentence in the paragraph in "A Depressing Place" should be omitted in the interest of paragraph unity? (*Write the sentence number here.*) _____

About Support

3. Label as *sight, touch, hearing,* or *smell* all the sensory details in the following sentences taken from the three paragraphs. The first one is done for you as an example.

            touch   *sight*   *sight*

  a. I accidentally tipped an autograph-covered, slightly deflated basketball off

                  sight   *hearing*   *sight*

    one shelf, and the ball bounced with dull thuds across the width of the room.

  b. Because so many animals are crammed together, the normally pleasant,

    slightly milky smell of the puppies and kittens is sour and strong.

c. As I ran my fingers over the items on the dusty shelves, I noticed some

tarnished medals and faded ribbons for track accomplishments.

4.   After which sentence in "A Depressing Place" are specific details needed?

_____

About Coherence

5.   Space signals (*above, next to, to the right,* and so on) are often used to help organize details in descriptive paragraphs. List four space signals that appear in "An Athlete's Room":

_____

_____

_____

_____

FORMS OF DESCRIPTIVE WRITING

All effective description records its subject by using a consistent and clear method of tracking or viewing that subject and by using the most accurate and vivid details appropriate for its purpose. While subjectively focused description relies on the writer's impressions of a subject, objective description seeks to present an impersonal and accurate word-picture recorded by a camera-like "invisible writer."

Subjective Descriptions

- This chapter shows primarily personally based subjective descriptions. The writer's response to a subject is the essence of a subjective descriptive paragraph. The writer's dominant impression of some place, object, or person derives from and is coloured by his or her involvement with that subject. Descriptive paragraphs based on such personal response rely on details that consistently convey the writer's attitude toward the subject.
- The focus of a personal or subjective description may be subtly shifted by the writer's use of third-person point of view. An example of this difference in focus is the paragraph "A Depressing Place"; it focuses on the pet shop itself, not on the writer's feelings as she walks through it. Many details included could be considered objective details; anyone entering the pet shop would observe the sights, sounds, and smells. This choice of third-person focus often makes the paragraph more persuasive.

Objective Descriptions

- Some college and career writing requires more objectivity—less personal involvement in description. Objective descriptions are always written in the third-person point of view; the writer's aim is to record his or her subject with the impersonal accuracy of a camera.

- The focus of objective description is totally on its subject and on offering the reader an obvious and clear path to follow as he or she reads the description. The dominant impression in objective description is simply an overview of the object or situation to be described; it does not include any indication of the writer's presence.

Further Insight—More strategies for effective description

Some circumstances allow for more creative or imaginative forms of description. When writing about literature, for example, or when reviewing something that itself is sensory—such as a restaurant or a theatre production—writers frequently use *similes* and *metaphors* to draw *analogies* between the subject of the description and other scenes that would be familiar to the audience.

A **simile** draws a comparison to an image that is (in the author's mind) *similar*, and uses the words "like" or "as" to link the two images. Many common sayings use *similes* by pairing an adjective with a noun to form a new description: *I have been working like a dog. His mind is as slow as molasses. It feels as smooth as a baby's bottom.*

A simile will often be preceded by an active or sensory verb.

A risk of using these phrases is that they are so well known that they are easily considered to be overworked phrases, or *clichés*. A good descriptive writer "invents" unique *similes*, as such phrases will often interest, and even delight, their readers. Practise devising your own *similes* by using *like* or *as* to describe these images:

- a newborn baby
- a blanket
- a sandy beach
- an aroma
- a derelict building
- a fruit

A **metaphor** is much like a *simile*, except that it draws a more direct analogy. Instead of suggesting that one thing is *like* another, a *metaphor* states that it *is* something else, even though it clearly is not. An exasperated parent may claim that an adolescent's room "is a cesspool"; using a strong *metaphor* to get the teen's attention. A nice home may be described as "a palace"; a person as "a gem"; a busy highway "a nightmare"; and so on.

An effective descriptive piece may construct an *extended metaphor*, which not only states an alternate image for the subject, but also continues to draw upon that analogy in many details. A paragraph giving an *extended metaphor* would state the image in the topic sentence, and then continue to describe it in parts that show more ways in which the comparison would apply. It may also include appropriate *similes*, as well as other descriptive terms. What is the *extended metaphor* describing in the following passage?

> The computer was a dinosaur; so old, and slow, and dangerous, it should have been extinct long ago. The case was chipped and battered, and discoloured like mottled reptilian scales. The monitor was like a, dark, odd-shaped little head, hanging brainlessly

(continued)

to one side. Worst of all, when it was finally turned on, the sound was like a growl-ing tyrannosaurus that had been woken from its sleep. It wheezed, and whined, and finally growled in increasing anger as the primeval processor screeched in fury. Small animals must have run in fear of its horrible terror.

Metahpors can be very effective in giving an audience a unique image with a lasting impact. When using *extended metaphors,* though, be careful that the image retains consistency, and stays on track. The danger is in losing the image and transforming it to another, or creating a *mixed metaphor.* For example, when a student wrote, "My car was the fastest bird who ever flew, purring happily along at 150 kilometres an hour. . . ." the instructor pointed out that cats, not birds, purr.

Give metaphors for the following subjects:

- a crowded nightclub
- a nasty person
- an old tree
- a sailboat
- an aquarium
- a mood or feeling

Note: When approaching a writing task that requires effective description, you must first decide whether the purpose of that writing is to provide a personal response to the subject or to record that subject as accurately and impersonally as possible.

DEVELOPING A DESCRIPTIVE PARAGRAPH

Development through Prewriting

When Mariana was assigned a descriptive paragraph, she thought at first of describing her cubicle at work. She started by listing the details she noticed while looking around a place she knew inside out.

But Mariana quickly became bored with the very idea of putting together a paragraph. She said later, "As I wrote down what I saw in my cubicle, I was thinking, 'What a drag this assignment is.' I gave up and did some filing. Later that evening, I told my friend Nestor that I was going to write a boring paragraph about my boring office. He started laughing at me. I asked what was so funny, and he said, 'You're so sure that an English assignment has to be boring that you deliberately picked a subject that bores you. Why don't you write about some-thing you care about?' At first I was annoyed, but then I realized he was right. When I hear the words *writing* and *assignment* I automatically think 'boring pain in the neck' and just want to get it over with."

Mariana's attitude is anything but uncommon. Many students who are hes-istant or inexperienced writers don't take the time to find a topic that interests them. They tend to leave facing their assignment until the last moment, then grab the first topic at hand and force themselves to write about it just for the sake of handing in the assignment. Like Mariana, they ensure that they (and probably their instructors, too) will be bored with the task.

Mariana decided that this assignment would be different. She remembered a recent experience. Her mother was looking for a new collar and some toys for

Sebastian, the family spaniel, so they went to a pet store. Mariana found the pet store a horrible place. "As I remembered the store, a lot of nasty details came back to me—sounds, smells, and sights. I didn't really want to recall them, but they made an impact on me," Mariana said. "I realized not only that it would be a lot easier to describe a place like that than my bland office cubicle, but that I might find it an interesting challenge to make a reader see it through my words. For me to realize writing could be enjoyable was a shock!"

Now that Mariana had her subject, she began to make a list of details about the pet shop.

Sawdust, animal droppings on floors of cages
Unhappy-looking puppies and kittens
Screech of birds
Chained parrots
Tanks with green dirty water
No place for animals to play
Bored-looking clerks
Animals scratching cages for attention
Strong urine smell

As she looked over her list of details, the word that came to mind was *depressing*. She decided this was the strongest feeling she'd had and that her topic sentence would be "The pet store in the mall is depressing." She then outlined her paragraph.

Topic Sentence: The pet store in the mall is depressing.

Subtopic 1: Puppies and kittens look miserable
Supporting Details:
a. scratching
b. trapped in small cages

Subtopic 2: Parrots and turtles
Supporting Details:
a. parrots are chained and wings are clipped
b. turtles in filthy tubs

Subtopic 3: Nasty smells
Supporting Details:
a. cleaning stuff, droppings, musty
b. should smell nice, like young animals

Mariana quickly tried to recapture her impressions in a first draft.

The pet store in the mall is depressing. There is sawdust and animal droppings all over the floor. Sad-looking puppies and kittens scratch on their cages for attention. In too many cages stacked up. Dead fish and motionless turtles float in tanks of greenish water. The loud screeching of birds is everywhere, and parrots with clipped wings try to fly off when customers get too near. Everywhere there is the smell of animal urine that has soaked through the sawdust and newspapers. The clerks, who should be cleaning the cages or patting the animals, stand around talking to each other and ignoring the animals.

Development through Revising

After class the next day, Mariana's instructor went over the students' first drafts. The instructor's notes to Mariana suggested that she had made a good beginning in her paragraph, especially by using strong details that appealed to a reader's senses of smell, hearing, and sight. He then suggested that she should organize her work using "spatial order," or by following a logical path through the scene she was describing. In that way, she would be able to lead her readers through the pet store as if they were actually there. He also suggested that she use more specific details. The instructor noted that it would be helpful to know in what way the puppies and kittens seemed sad, and suggested that she use sharp descriptive words to construct a vivid picture of the scene.

Mariana rewrote the paragraph, beginning with the display window that attracts visitors, then going on to the store's right-hand wall, the centre aisle, and the left-hand wall. She ended the paragraph by taking the reader back outside the shop. Thinking about the store this way helped Mariana to remember and add a number of new specific details as well. She then wrote the second draft of "A Depressing Place" that appears on page 159.

WRITING A DESCRIPTIVE PARAGRAPH

Further Insight—Using specific descriptors (describing words)

The impact of good descriptive writing depends upon the accuracy and impact of the words being used. As you revise a descriptive paragraph, think critically about the vocabulary you are using, and assess that your choices reflect the characteristics of the image you are describing. For example, while it would be accurate to say, "The baby walked to the next room," it would have more impact if the baby "waddled," giving a better image of the back-and-forth movement of a baby's walk.

Keep notes of descriptive words or phrases as you prewrite and draft your work. Then, scan your draft for sections where you should use specific and vivid descriptors. You should also use a dictionary and thesaurus to help determine which are the most accurate, descriptive, and satisfying terms you can use.

Many descriptors naturally fit with specific subjects, such as the verb *waddle* with the subject *baby*, above. Depending upon your comfort with the language you choose, you may also wish to experiment with other combinations that become uniquely yours. Just remember to always assess your choices to see if they are vivd and accurate to the scenes you wish to draw. How can you use these words as interesting descriptors?

- plummeting
- fuchsia
- expansive
- acrid
- grizzled
- sultry
- chattering
- sumptuous

What descriptors could you use for these items? You may use single words, lists, or phrases.

- meringue
- athlete
- mountain
- graffiti
- chickadee
- smile
- pizza
- class

How to Write a Descriptive Paragraph

1) Use all of your senses as you remember or observe your subject. In your prewriting, accumulate as many kinds of details as you can come up with. Try questioning yourself: "What do I feel when I touch this?" "What do I see when I look at it from this angle?"

2) When you have recorded as many details as possible, decide on the best way to track your progress as you describe your subject. If you describe a place, how will you take your reader along with you? If you describe a person or an object, where will you begin, and what path will you follow as you show your subject to your reader?

3) Decide on your main impression of or feeling about your subject, and write this down as a trial topic sentence.

4) Begin your formal outline with this topic sentence, and order your details in the outline according to the way your reader will view your subject along with you.

5) As you begin to draft your paragraph, revise and select only those details that contribute to your dominant impression. Try to use the most precise and accurate descriptive words possible for your details.

6) Conclude with a sentence that reminds the reader of your opening dominant impression.

Writing Assignment 1

Write a paragraph about a particular place that you can observe carefully or that you already know well. It might be one of the following or some other place:

Student lounge area   Hair salon
Car showroom   Doctor's or dentist's office
Gymnasium   Classroom

Fast-food restaurant   Bank
Inside of a car   Dressing room
Ladies' or men's washroom   Attic
Movie theatre   Street market
Auto repair garage   Place where you work
Music store   Porch

Prewriting

a **Consider the dominant impression you want to create.** Remember that, like all paragraphs, a descriptive paper must have an opening point. This point, or topic sentence, should state a dominant impression about the place you are describing. State the place you want to describe and the dominant impression you want to make in a single short sentence. The sentence can be refined later. For now, you just want to find and express a workable topic, an overview to guide your readers. You might write, for example, a sentence like one of the following:

The student lounge was hectic.
The music store was noisy.
The car's interior was very clean.
The dressing room in the department store was stifling.
The dentist's office was soothing.
The movie theatre was freezing.
The gymnasium was tense.
The attic was gloomy.
The restaurant was elegant.
The office where I work was strangely quiet.

b **Accumulate supporting details.** Now make a list of all the details you can think of that support the general impression. Refer back to page 163 to see the list that Mariana made after she visited the pet store.

c **Make your details specific and appealing to the senses.** Use as many senses as possible in describing a scene. Chiefly you will use sight, but to some extent you may be able to use touch, hearing, smell, and perhaps even taste as well. Remember that it is through the richness of your sense impressions that the reader will gain a picture of the scene.

d **Choose a method of organization to track your subject.** Organize your paper by using a spatial method of organization. For instance, the writer of "A Depressing Place" organizes the paper in terms of physical order (from one side of the pet shop to the centre to the other side).

Revising

As you are working on the drafts of your paper, refer to the checklist on the inside front cover. Make sure you can answer yes to the questions about unity, support, coherence, and sentence skills.

● ● ● ● ● **Writing Assignment 2**

Write a paragraph describing a person. Here are some examples of people you might want to write about.

TV or movie personality	Co-worker
Instructor	Clergyperson
Employer	Police officer
Child	Store owner or manager
Older person	Bartender
Close friend	Joker
Enemy	Neighbour

Prewriting

a Begin by thinking of one thing, one characteristic that makes your subject most like himself or herself. That one characteristic is your dominant impression, your guiding focus for your paragraph; it can be an aspect of that person's personality, appearance, or behaviour.

Once you have chosen the person you will write about and the impression you plan to portray, put that information into a topic sentence.

Here are some possible topic sentences that mention a particular person and the dominant impression of that person. Your instructor may let you develop one of these or may require you to write your own.

Brendan gives the impression of being permanently nervous.
The old man was as faded and brittle as a dying leaf.
The child was an angelic little figure.
Our high-school principal resembled a cartoon drawing.
The young woman seemed to belong to another era.
The rock singer seemed to be plugged in to some special kind of energy source.
The drug addict looked as lifeless as a corpse.
The owner of that grocery store seems burdened with troubles.

b Make a list of the person's qualities that support or illustrate your topic sentence. Write quickly; don't worry if you find yourself writing down something that doesn't quite fit. You can always edit the list later. For now, just write down all the details that occur to you that support the dominant impression you want to convey. Include details that involve as many senses as possible (sight, sound, hearing, touch, smell). For instance, here's a list one writer jotted down to support the topic sentence "The child was an angelic little figure."

soft black ringlets of hair
pink cheeks
wide shining eyes
shrieking laugh
joyful smile
starched white dress
white flowers in hair

c Edit your list, striking out details that don't support your topic sentence and adding others that do. The author of the paragraph on the angelic child crossed out one detail from the original list and added a new one.

> soft black ringlets of hair
> pink cheeks
> wide shining eyes
> ~~shrieking laugh~~
> joyful smile
> starched white dress
> white flowers in hair
> *sweet singing voice*

d Decide on a spatial order of organization. In the example above, the writer ultimately decided to describe the child from head to toe.

e Write an outline for your paragraph, based on the organization you have chosen.

f Then write the first draft of your paragraph.

Revising

Put your paragraph away for a day or so if at all possible. When you read it and your later drafts, ask yourself these questions:

- Does my topic sentence clearly state my dominant impression of my subject?
- If I left out the keywords in my topic sentence, the words that state my dominant impression, would a reader know what idea fits there?
- Does every detail support my topic sentence?
- Are the details I have used specific rather than vague and general?
- Have I used a logical spatial organization that helps my reader follow my description?
- Have I checked my paper for sentence skills, as listed on the inside front cover of this book?

Continue revising until you can answer yes to all these questions.

● ● ● ● **Writing Assignment 3**

Write a paragraph that would describe to visitors the best place in Canada to visit. You may think about the types of destinations that have been included as UNESCO World Heritage Sites, such as Quebec City, or Lunenburg, Nova Scotia, as examples. Or you may be interested in a place with strong natural, cultural, or sports associations, such as Banff National Park; a major city that presents jazz, theatre, or comedy festivals; or places such as Calgary or Montreal that have hosted the Olympics. You may also choose a location that is special to you. Assume that you are a representative of that destination, appealing to national and international audiences.

Follow the writing process by first prewriting in order to identify the place that you would describe, as well as the specific details that make your choice such a great place. Compose a working topic sentence that tells where your potential visitors should come, and for what specific purpose; these create the dominant impression you wish to promote. As you organize, draft, and revise your paragraph, fine-tune the topic sentence so that it makes a distinct point.

Throughout the process, collect descriptive words and phrases to use to describe each supporting reason and the specific details of your paragraph. Remember to appeal to your audience's senses by describing the sights, sounds, and other sensations that are most appropriate. Use an appropriate spatial order to "tour" your potential visitors through the area. Try to strike a balance in tone between sincere objectivity—reassuring your audience with specific factual evidence—and the enthusiasm of a promoter who is keenly committed to offering an invitation to a favourite destination. Consider that your audience might be interested, but somewhat skeptical, until you are able to give a vivid and convincing description of the place you consider the best to visit in Canada.

Writing Assignment 4

Option A: Imagine that you are an interior designer. A new residence is going to be built on your college campus, and you have been asked to create a model residence room for two students. Write a paragraph describing your design of the room, specifying what it would include and how it would be arranged. In your prewriting for this assignment, you might list all the relevant student needs you can think of, such as a good study space, storage space, and appropriate lighting and colours. Then put all the parts together so that they work well as a whole. Use a spatial order in your paragraph to help readers "see" your room. If you are short on ideas, look up a few colleges and universities on a search engine and see if there is information on residence facilities on their websites.

Begin with the following topic sentence or something like it:

An ideal design for a residence room offers both efficiency and comfort for two students.

Feel free to use a less than serious tone.

Option B: Alternatively, write a paragraph describing your ideal design of another type of room, including any of the following:

Classroom	Kitchen
Porch	Restaurant
Game room	Bakery

REVIEWING THE LEARNING OUTCOMES FOR DESCRIPTIVE WRITING

When you complete any of the writing assignments in this chapter, review your work to decide how well it meets the following tests.

✓ Does your paragraph begin with a well-focused statement of your dominant impression of your subject? Is this dominant impression supported by each idea and supporting detail in your paragraph?

✓ Are all your details specific and vivid? Are your descriptive words as precise as they can be? Do your details appeal to several different senses?

✓ Can your reader follow your descriptive path as you move through or around your subject? Have you provided transitional words and phrases to help the reader and to reinforce your tracking of your subject?

✓ Does your concluding sentence return to and reinforce your dominant impression?

Visit the *English Skills with Readings: Examining Paragraphs* Online Learning Centre at www.mcgrawhill.ca/olc/langan to access self-quizzes, internet-based questions and research skills, web resources, and other learning and study tools.

Chapter 9

Providing Examples

LEARNING OUTCOMES

By completing the activities and writing tasks in this chapter, you will write a paragraph that explains its point with examples and effectively

- opens with a topic sentence or controlling idea that makes a specific and clear point about a subject;

- offers three subtopics that are primary examples to support your point;

- supplies supporting details (which may themselves be secondary examples) for each subtopic; and

- ends with a conclusion that returns to your main point and sums up what your examples have clarified or explained.

Examples in exposition provide readers with clarifications or explanations of the writer's ideas. If narration offers sharing of experience, and description offers sharing of impressions, exposition with examples offers a chance to share knowledge or understanding of a subject. Each time an idea is supported with apt, specific, and sharply written examples, the reader's ability to grasp that idea is increased; examples help readers to see fully what the writer means.

Our daily conversations are full of *examples*—that is, details, particulars, specific instances—to *explain or make clear* statements that we make.

Statement	*Example*
Registration for this semester was frustrating.	Just as I was about to log in, the system crashed, and then when I finally got through, three of the courses I wanted to take were full and closed.

Examples sometimes provide *reasons why* we make a particular point and may help to prove to readers the truth of that statement.

Statement	**Example**
The corduroy shirt I bought is badly made.	The first time I washed it, the colour began to fade, one button cracked and another fell off, and the sleeves shrank almost five centimetres.

Examples offer *specifics,* or hooks, for readers to grasp and remember.

The cat can be very annoying.	She howls for fifteen minutes at a time and uses her claws to climb the curtains, only to get stuck at the top and howl some more.

In each case, the examples help us *see for ourselves* the truth of the statement that has been made. In paragraphs, too, explanatory examples help the audience fully understand and perhaps be persuaded by a point. Lively, specific examples also add interest to a paragraph. Consider the sentences you have just read; they are *examples* used to support the point that examples are essential to effective writing. Instructors and textbooks teach by constantly using examples.

All forms of expository and persuasive writing required during college and careers make use of examples; explaining by example is a basic and essential skill that is practised throughout life.

In this chapter, you will be asked to provide a series of examples to support a topic sentence. First read the next two paragraphs; they both use examples to develop their points. Then answer the questions that follow.

PARAGRAPHS TO CONSIDER

The Cruelty of Children

[1]Children can be very cruel. [2]For one thing, they start very early to use words that wound. [3]Three-year-olds in nursery school, for example, call each other "dum-dum" or "weirdo," and slightly older children use nicknames like "fatty" or "four-eyes" to tease their schoolmates. [4]Children who are just a bit older learn facts about other kids from their parents and use those facts to make someone break down and cry. [5]Perhaps even more harmful, children attack one another physically. [6]For instance, whenever a group of elementary-school children come home from school, there is a lot of pushing, tripping, punching, and pinching. [7]An argument may end in shoving and hair-pulling. [8]But far worse than harsh words or physical violence is the emotional hurt that children can cause their classmates by their cruelty. [9]By junior high school days, for example, young teenagers start to shut out the people they do not like. [10]They ignore the kids whose looks, clothes, interests, or finances differ from their own. [11]Popular kids form groups, and the unpopular ones are left to face social isolation, loneliness, and depression. [12]Many adults think that childhood is an ideal time, but terribly cruel things can happen at this stage in life.

Office Politics

^{1}Office politics may be Canada's real national sport, a destructive game played everywhere by several kinds of people. ^{2}A part-time worker often has a clearer view of these goings-on. ^{3}For instance, two supervisors may get into a conflict over how to do a certain job. ^{4}Instead of working out an agreement like adults, they carry on a power struggle that turns the poor employees working under them into human hockey pucks being shot back and forth between two angry players. ^{5}Another common example of office politics is the ambitious worker who takes credit for other people's ideas. ^{6}He or she will chat in a friendly fashion with new or less experienced employees, getting their ideas about how to run things more smoothly. ^{7}These people seem so pleasant at first. ^{8}Next thing anyone knows, Mr. or Ms. Idea-Stealer is having a private meeting with the boss and getting promotion points for his or her creativity. ^{9}Yet another star player in office politics is the spy. ^{10}This employee acts very chummy with other workers, often dropping little comments about things he or she doesn't like in the workplace. ^{11}The spy encourages people to talk about their problems at work, how they don't like their boss, the pay, and the working conditions. ^{12}Then the spy goes straight back and repeats all he or she has heard to the management, and the employees get blamed for their "poor attitude." ^{13}A final example of office politics is people who gossip. ^{14}Too often the players on the office politics team can turn a perfectly fine work situation into a stressful one.

Questions

About Unity

1. Which two sentences in "Office Politics" are irrelevant to the point about people's office behaviour? *(Write the sentence numbers here.)* _____

About Support

2. In "The Cruelty of Children," how many examples are given of children's cruelty?
   _____ one _____ two _____ three _____ four

3. After which sentence in "Office Politics" are specific details needed? _____

About Coherence

4. What are the three main transition words used in "The Cruelty of Children"?
   a. _____
   b. _____
   c. _____

5. What are two of the transition words in "Office Politics"?
   a. _____
   b. _____

6. Which paragraph clearly uses emphatic order to organize its details, saving for last what the writer regards as the most important example?

_____

_____

DEVELOPING AN EXAMPLES PARAGRAPH

Development through Prewriting

Backing up your statements with clear, specific illustrations is the key to a successful examples paragraph. Follow Vince, the author of "Office Politics" through the writing process he used from the beginning to the final version of his paragraph.

When Vince was assigned an examples paragraph, he at first did not know what to write about. Then his instructor made a suggestion. "Imagine yourself having lunch with friends," he said. "You're telling them *how* you feel about something and *why*. You would not just make a general statement, as your friends may not be convinced. To explain your idea, you would make a general point and back it up with examples. That's what you need to do in this paper."

Later, Vince was on the phone with his brother. He was complaining about the office where he worked. "Suddenly I realized what I was doing," he said. "I was making a statement—I hate the game-playing at work—and giving examples of those political moves people make. I knew what I could write about."

That realization inspired Vince to freewrite for ten or fifteen minutes, and this is what he came up with.

> Of all the places I've worked since I was in high school this one is the worst that way. Can't trust anybody there—everybody's playing some kind of game and hoping to score. Maybe they think I can't see them doing stuff because I'm only part-time there. Worst of all is Mr. Simchuck and the way he pretends to be friendly with people. Gets them to complain about Ms. Wyland and Mr. Martinez and then runs back to them and reports everything. He ought to realize that people are catching on to his game and figuring out what a jerk he is. Melissa steals people's ideas and then takes credit for them. Anything to get brownie points. She's always out for herself first, you can tell. Then there's the gossip that goes on. You think you're in a soap opera or something and it's kind of fun in a way but it's also very distracting people always talking about each other and worrying about what they say about you. And people always talk about our bosses a lot. Nobody knows why Ms. Wyland and Mr. Martinez hate each other so much but they each want the workers on their side. You do something one boss's way, but then the other boss appears and is angry you're not doing it another way. You don't know what to do sometimes to keep people happy.

Vince read over his freewriting and still felt a little confused about what he was trying to say. He then spent some time asking questions about his paragraph.

(You may find a second stage of prewriting, one in which you try another technique, to be very effective.) "Exactly what do I want my point to be?" he asked. "And exactly how am I going to support that point?" Keeping those questions in mind, he tried a few different outlines and wound up with the following short-form outline.

Office politics are ruining the office:
1. Simchuk reports people's complaints
    —his weaselly "chats"
2. Melissa steals ideas
    —"Oh, how would you do this?"
3. People gossip
4. Ms. Wyland and Mr. Martinez make workers pick sides
    —nobody feels safe or knows what to do

Working from his sketch outline, Vince then tried the following first draft.

My office is being ruined by office politics. Maybe they think I don't see things because I only work half-time. It seems like everybody is trying to play some kind of game to get ahead and don't care what it does to anybody else. One example is Simchuk. Although he pretends to be friendly with people, he isn't sincere. What he is trying to do is get them to complain about their bosses. Once they do, he goes back to the bosses and tells them what's been said and gets the worker in trouble. I've seen the same kind of thing happen at one or two other places I've worked. Melissa is another example of someone who plays office politics games. She steals other people's ideas and takes the credit for them. I had a good idea once to save paper. I told her we ought to use mostly e-mail for office memos instead of printing them all out. She went to Ms. Wyland and pretended the idea was her own. I guess I was partly to blame for not acting on the idea myself. And Ms. Wyland and Mr. Martinez hate each other and try to get us to take sides in their conflict. Then there is all the gossip that goes on. People do a lot of backbiting and you have to be very careful about your behaviour or people will start talking about you. All in all, office politics is a real problem where I work.

Development through Revising

After completing his first draft, Vince put it aside until the next day. When he reread it, he realized that he had a topic that was more universal than he thought. He decided to write about office politics in general, rather than just his own situation. He realized that this would also help him to write a third-person piece, as his instructor had encouraged. Finally, he saw how using transitions would help him move the piece from its point through the examples he wished to use as illustrations.

With these thoughts in mind, Vince started revising his paper, and after several drafts he produced the paragraph that appears on page 173.

WRITING AN EXAMPLES PARAGRAPH

How to Write a Paragraph That Explains with Examples

1) Begin by prewriting to accumulate details about your subject. Questioning, list making, and clustering are good methods for generating examples. Visualizing a place, person, or situation helps you discover your ideas.

2) Write a few trial topic sentences, then decide which one best states a clear point of view or controlling attitude about your subject. Examples paragraphs sometimes begin by specifying how many subtopic examples the paragraph will provide: for example, "Three situations that occurred last week show how stubborn my friend Javier can be."

3) Begin your paragraph outline with your best topic sentence, and select three primary examples as subtopics to explain, clarify, or prove your topic's point. Write these as subtopic sentences (subtopic + attitude). Next, note in point form under each subtopic any supporting details or secondary examples that further illustrate your subtopics.

4) As you draft and revise, ask yourself if your major or primary examples and details or secondary examples truly support your point. Eliminate non-supporting material and add any clarifying details that may occur to you.

5) In your concluding sentence, sum up the way in which your examples have demonstrated your point.

Extended Examples

At times examples are used to *extend* the paragraph's supporting details in an organized manner, rather than just to supplement them. When using examples as the paragraph organizer, the examples illustrate the point, or topic as well as the supporting reasons. Some of the ways examples are used to organize a paragraph include giving an anecdote, using analogies, and suggesting hypothetical suggestions.

Giving an Anecdote—or repeating a story. An anecdote is often (but not always) a first-person recollection of a scene or event that has a specific point or "lesson." For example, at the presentation of an award, the introductory speaker may make a point such as, "From the first moment that I saw WeiWei present a case in class in her halting but exact English, I knew she was a woman determined to succeed." The supporting reasons and specific details that follow would then retell the incident by focussing on the actions and events that proved the speaker's assessment of WeiWei's determined character.

Using Analogies—or illustrating the point by drawing a comparison between it and an object or concept. In the famous line from the movie *Forrest Gump,* "Life is like a box of chocolates," the explanation that, "You never know what you're gonna get" sets the analogy. It could be continued by using specific types of chocolate found in the box to represent particular aspects of life. Someone might use an example that sometimes all that can be found are nuts, to describe the crazy times in life; perhaps the chocolates that melt in the mouth represent the sense of satisfaction; and so on.

Suggesting Hypothetical Situations—or examples that *could* be possible, even if unlikely. A hypothetical statement speculates on an answer to "What if . . . ?" The details would be the examples that are used to further extend the point. Discussions around public policy often use examples based in hypothetical situations, such as, "If the voting age were lowered, there would be significant consequences." The examples used would depend upon whether the author was for or against the proposal. They could range from the positive such as, "Youth might start to care about their political representatives" and include the appropriate details, to the extremes of outrage such as, "The highways would be clogged with skateboards!"

When using such techniques as described above, be careful to stay fair and reasonable in your ideas. Do not make a point that is too outlandish, or use examples that are inappropriate and unbelievable. Remember that your audience must feel included—and not insulted—in order to follow the examples that you use to develop your paragraph.

• • • • Writing Assignment 1

The assignment here is to complete an unfinished paragraph outline that has as its topic sentence "My husband Sean is a selfish person." Provide the supporting details needed to fill out the subtopic examples of Sean's selfishness. The first subtopic example out of four has been supplied for you.

How to Proceed

For this assignment, you will provide secondary examples, examples that support the main subtopic examples provided on the outline form on the following page. Note that this paragraph outline will show two types of examples: primary or subtopic examples (refusal to move, Sean's constant choice of vacations, selfish spending habits, and ignoring child care) and secondary supporting examples for each subtopic.

Point

Topic Sentence: <u>My husband Sean is a selfish person</u>

Support

Subtopic 1: <u>For one thing, he refuses to move out of the city, even</u> <u>though it is a bad place to raise the children.</u>

Supporting Details (examples, explanations):

a. <u>We inherited some money when my parents died, and it might be</u> <u>enough for a down payment on a small house in a nearby town. But</u> <u>Sean says he would miss his buddies in the neighbourhood.</u>

---

b. _____

c. _____

Subtopic 2: <u>Also, when we go on vacation, we always go where Sean</u>
<u>wants to go.</u>

Supporting Details (examples, explanations):

a. _____

b. _____

c. _____

Subtopic 3: <u>Another example of Sean's selfishness is that he always</u>
<u>spends any budget money that is left over.</u>

Supporting Details (examples, explanations):

a. _____

b. _____

c. _____

Subtopic 4: <u>Finally, Sean leaves all the work of caring for the children</u>
<u>to me.</u>

Supporting Details (examples, explanations):

a. _____

b. _____

c. _____

Prewriting

a As you prewrite consider answers for questions such as:

- What specific vacations did the family go on because Sean wanted to go? Give places, length of stay, time of year. What vacations has the family never gone on (for example, to visit the wife's relatives), even though the wife wanted to?
- What specific items has Sean bought for himself (rather than for the whole family's use) with leftover budget money?
- What chores and duties involved in the everyday caring for the children has Sean never done?

Your instructor may ask you to work with one or two other students in generating the details needed to develop the three examples in the paragraph. Someone from each group may then be asked to read the group's details aloud, with the class deciding which details are the most effective for each example.

Here and in general in your writing, try to generate *more* supporting material than you need. You are then in a position to choose the *most convincing details* for your paper.

b Read over the details you have generated and decide which sound most effective. Jot down additional details as they occur to you.

c Take your best details, reshape them as needed, and use them to complete the paragraph about Sean.

Revising

Read over your paragraph. Ask yourself these questions or discuss them in your group:

- Do the examples really support the idea that Sean is selfish?
- Are there enough examples to make each subtopic or primary example clear?
- Are there enough examples to make the overall point about Sean and have people agree with it?
- Are any of the examples too similar to one another?
- Have I or we checked the paragraph for spelling and other sentence skills, as listed on the inside front cover of this book?

Continue revising until you can answer yes to all these questions.

● ● ● ● Writing Assignment 2

Write a paragraph providing examples that clarify and explain one quality of a person you know well. The person might be a member of your family, a friend, a roommate, a boss or supervisor, a neighbour, an instructor, or someone else. Following are some descriptive words that can be applied to people. They are only suggestions; you can write about any other specific quality.

Honest	Hard-working	Jealous
Ambitious	Suspicious	Sarcastic
Bigoted	Open-minded	Self-centred
Considerate	Lazy	Spineless
Argumentative	Independent	Good-humoured
Energetic	Flirtatious	Disciplined
Patient	Irresponsible	Sentimental
Reliable	Stingy	Defensive
Generous	Trustworthy	Dishonest
Persistent	Aggressive	Insensitive
Sloppy	Compulsive	Tidy

Prewriting

a Select the individual you will write about and the quality of this person that you will focus on.

b Make a list of examples that will support and clearly explain the point of your topic sentence. For example, if you decide to write about your brother's irresponsibility, jot down several examples of times when he showed this quality.

Another way to get started, or a second way of prewriting, is to ask yourself the journalists' questions about your topic and write down the answers. Again, if you were writing about your brother's irresponsibility, you might ask yourself questions such as these.

> *How* has he been irresponsible?
> *What* are examples of times he's shown this quality?
> *What* happened on these occasions?
> *Who* was involved?
> *What were the results* of his actions?

The answers to these questions should serve as an excellent source of details for the paragraph.

   c Think about categories or subtopics. Read over your list or your answers to the questions and see how you might group the items into categories. The list above, for example, could be broken into three categories that might make good subtopics: apartment, home, and college.

Apartment
> Lost rent money
>
> Left dog alone in the apartment for two days

Home
> Didn't show up for family dinner
>
> Left my bike out in the rain

College
> Forgot to return borrowed textbooks
>
> Missed conference with instructor

Another way of categorizing these details might be to consider who the irresponsibility affects most—the brother himself and other people.

   d **Make an outline showing subtopics and support.** Your outline should be made up of the strongest examples from the prewriting material you have generated. The grid, above, shows how the prewriting may lead to a logical outline. As you make this outline, group related details together according to the catagories you chose, creating subtopics or subheadings. For example, the items in the list about the irresponsible brother can be categorized into subtopics.

   e **Write the topic sentence containing your subject and overall attitude toward it.** This first sentence should tell the name of the person you are writing about, your relationship to the person, and the specific quality you are focusing on. For example, you might write, "Linda is a flirtatious girl I know at school," or "Stubbornness is Uncle Carl's outstanding characteristic."

Do not begin with more than one quality ("I have a cousin named Jamal who is soft-hearted and generous") or with a vague general quality ("My boss is a good person"). Focus on *one specific quality.*

f Develop enough specific and typical examples. Remember that you don't want to *tell* readers about the person; rather, you want to *show* the person by detailing words, actions, or both. Provide *enough* specific details so that you solidly support your point.

g Write a concluding sentence that sums up your examples and reinforces your point.

Revising

It is very hard to criticize your own work honestly, especially right after you've done it and it's still "warm" from your efforts. If it is at all possible, put your paragraph away for a day or so and return to it with fresh eyes. Better yet, wait a day and read it aloud to someone whose judgment you trust.

You can also refer back to the "Peer Review" format discussed in Chapter 2. Ask your peer to read the paragraph to check that you have made a specific point and supported it with explanatory examples. You may also emphasize some specific questions such as:

- Does my topic sentence clearly state whom I am writing about, what that person's relationship is to me, and what quality of that person I am going to focus on?
- Do the examples I provide truly show that my subject has the quality I'm writing about?

Continue revising your work until you and your reader can answer yes to these questions.

● ● ● ● ● **Writing Assignment 3**

Write a paragraph that uses examples to develop one of the following statements or a related statement of your own.

1. _____ is a distracting place to try to study.
2. The daily life of a student is filled with conflicts.
3. Life in Canada [*or* your city or town] is faster-paced than ever before.
4. Violence on television [*or* video games] is widespread.
5. Some students here at _____ do not care about learning [*or* are overly concerned about marks].

Be sure to choose specific and related examples that truly support your point. They should be relevant facts, statistics, personal experiences, or incidents you have heard or read about. Organize your paragraph by grouping several examples that support your point. Save the most vivid, most convincing, or most important example for last.

• • • • Writing Assignment 4

Write a paragraph with this topic sentence: "The diet of the average Canadian is unhealthy." Using strategies described in "Research Skills" on the Online Learning Centre, find three strong pieces of support for this point. Be sure to give credit for paraphrased material and to cite any quoted phrases correctly.

• • • • Writing Assignment 5

Write a paragraph that discusses a positive or negative aspect of social networking Internet sites by introducing your topic with an *anecdote,* an *analogy,* or a *hypothetical situation.* You could start with a topic sentence such as:

- Having a MyBlob site was like the time I left my personal diary in the gym washroom.
- A MyBlob site is much like hosting a never-ending party.
- Imagine that a potential employer could screen your suitability for a job merely by viewing your social networking site.

As you develop your supporting reasons, assess that your examples show the point that you are making by providing more and specific details. If you choose to write an anecdote, you may rely on your memories and impressions of the event you wish to recall. On the other hand, an analogy or hypothetical situation may require some research to inform yourself, and your audience, of valid information that will support your point. To move from one set of examples to the next, use adequate transitions so that your audience can easily follow the flow of your ideas. Finally, end with a concluding thought that recalls your original anecdote, analogy, or hypothetical situation.

REVIEWING THE LEARNING OUTCOMES FOR PROVIDING EXAMPLES

After completing any of the writing assignments in this chapter, review your work, using the following questions, to see how well it meets the learning outcomes for this chapter.

✓ Do you open with a topic sentence that makes a specific and clear point about your subject?

✓ Is your main point supported by three subtopics that are your primary examples?

✓ For each subtopic or primary example, are there enough specific details or secondary examples to explain or clarify your subtopics and add to your main point?

✓ Do you conclude with a statement that returns to your main point and sums up the meaning of your paper?

Visit the *English Skills with Readings: Examining Paragraphs* Online Learning Centre at www.mcgrawhill.ca/olc/langan to access self-quizzes, internet-based questions and research skills, web resources, and other learning and study tools.

Chapter 10

Explaining a Process

The goal of any process writing is for its readers to be able to successfully complete the procedure it sets out. By completing this chapter's activities and carefully following the instructions for writing assignments, you will write a process paragraph that

- is appropriate to the knowledge level and ability of its readers;

- opens with a clear statement of the value and purpose of the process to be followed and of its approximate degree of difficulty;

- tells readers exactly what they will need (equipment, time, space, tools, and so on) to complete the process successfully;

- offers complete, carefully ordered steps and explanations for each stage of the process;

- mentions both possible problems and potential difficulties that may occur; and

- concludes with a reassurance of the value of the process for the reader.

Process writing explains how to do something or describes how something occurred. The most common and useful form of process writing is *instructive;* its purpose is to explain *how to* do something and *why* following its instructions will achieve the desired result. Process writing always sets out its goal or end product and offers a time-sequenced series of steps for reaching that goal.

Everyone performs activities that are processes, or series of steps carried out in a definite order. Many of these processes are familiar and automatic: tying shoelaces, using a vending machine, and starting a car. Similarly, everyone routinely follows written instructions every day: working through textbook exercises or even following the commands in any word-processing program. In other cases, when we are asked for directions to a particular place or when we try to read and follow the directions for some new piece of technology, we are painfully conscious of the whole series of steps involved in the process. Process writing requires us to become aware of the steps in a procedure and of the stages into which we group these steps for ease of following them.

Process writing skills and techniques are used constantly in college and career writing. Students in business, human services, and technology programs must frequently write both instructions and step-by-step descriptions of procedures and changes in situations.

In this chapter, you will be asked to write a process paragraph—one that explains clearly how to do or make something. To prepare for this assignment, you should first read the student process paragraphs and respond to the questions that follow.

Note: In process writing, where you are often giving instructions, the pronoun *you* can appropriately be used. One of the model paragraphs here uses *you*. Indeed, much of this book, which gives instruction on how to write effectively, uses *you*, a style known as direct address.

PARAGRAPHS TO CONSIDER

Sneaking into the House at Night

[1]Your first step is bringing your key along with you. [2]Obviously, you don't want to have to knock on the door at 1:30 in the morning and rouse your parents out of bed. [3]Second, make it a point to stay out past midnight. [4]If you come in before then, your father might still be up. [5]You would find it hard to face his disapproving look after a night out. [6]All you need in your life right now is for him to make you feel guilty. [7]Trying to make it as a college student is as much as most people are ready to handle. [8]Next, be careful to be very quiet upon entering the house. [9]This involves lifting the front door up slightly as you open it, so that it does not creak. [10]It also means treating the floor and steps like a minefield, stepping carefully over the spots that squeak. [11]Finally, stop briefly in the bathroom without turning on the light and then tiptoe to your room, put your clothes in a pile on a chair, and slip quietly into bed. [12]With this careful method of sneaking into the house at night, you can avoid some major hassles with your parents.

How Shareen Broke the D Barrier

[1]Shareen decided she wanted to excel when she returned to college at twenty-nine, but she just was not sure how. [2]Her first-semester transcripts were a long list of Bs, with a glaring D in English. [3]First, she acknowledged the biggest problem she had to tackle: the D, with the writing problems it represented. [4]The fact that she couldn't seem to write clearly was dragging down her marks on written assignments in business courses as well. [5]So after avoiding the campus tutorial centre for three months, she decided her second move would be to gather up her red-ink-scarred essays and register for weekly sessions with a tutor. [6]At the same time, Shareen realized she had to face another potential problem:

time. [7]As a next step, she would either have to cut back on hours at her part-time job or keep her daughter in daycare for several more hours a day. [8]Shareen decided the best decision was to stop working Wednesday evenings. [9]A stroke of luck followed her decision: her aunt Bharati offered to loan Shareen her computer and printer, so she could work at home instead of waiting to use the college computers. [10]Now she could work more conveniently, without paying for extra daycare; she was motivated to follow her tutor's advice and not try to write every essay in a single draft. [11]The computer allowed Shareen to take the final step toward improving her writing. [12]She started to spend twice as long revising a paper as she had spent writing her first draft. [13]Because Shareen no longer felt the need to try to write a "perfect" first draft, she actually started to enjoy writing, seeing it as a puzzle to solve. [14]The final step was pure lucky coincidence, because Shareen was a born problem solver. [15]The result of her decision, her follow-up, and her revising efforts began to arrive when three English papers came back to her with Bs and encouraging comments on them, instead of Ds. [16]And the final, most satisfying moment arrived in the last week of classes, when Shareen received an A on both a business report and an English research paper. [17]She had broken both the B and the D barriers and was on the way to excelling at college.

Note: The first paragraph gives a process by directing the audience *how to* follow a series of steps in order to fulfill a goal. You might find a similar type of process intended to teach how to repair a household item, play a game, or any other activity that proceeds in a specific order and requires attention to the process.

The second paragraph *describes* a process or a transitional series of stages that has already occurred. The writer is analyzing a situation or result and tracing the steps by which his or her subject arrived at that result. *Descriptive process writing* does not show "how to"; it analyzes a result and describes each stage that led to it. Students in technological and science-based programs will find descriptive process writing skills extremely useful.

Questions

About Unity

1. Which paragraph lacks a topic sentence?

   _____

2. Which two sentences in "Sneaking into the House at Night" should be eliminated in the interest of paragraph unity? (*Write the sentence numbers here.*) _____ _____

About Support

3. After which sentence in "How Shareen Broke the D Barrier" are supporting details needed? _____

4. Summarize the four steps in the process of breaking the D barrier.

    a. _____

    b. _____

    c. _____

    d. _____

About Coherence

5. Do these paragraphs use time order or emphatic order?

    _____

6. List the four main transition words in "Sneaking into the House at Night."

    a. _____   c. _____

    b. _____   d. _____

DEVELOPING A PROCESS PARAGRAPH

Development through Prewriting

To be successful, a process paragraph or essay must explain clearly each step in an activity or sequence of events. The key to preparing to write such an assignment is thinking through the activity or sequence as though you are doing it or experiencing it for the first time. Shareen is the author of "How Shareen Broke the D Barrier." As her paragraph relates, she had done poorly in her English classes before she put her mind to doing better. She debated possible topics for her paragraph, then realized that her previous semester's improvement in writing skills involved a process worth describing.

She started by doing something she never used to do: she did some prewriting, making a list of the realizations and steps she went through on the path to writing better papers.

Borrowed Auntie's computer
Couldn't work at college on computers there
No time because of looking after Kerima
Went for weekly tutoring
Spent a lot of time on tutorial work
Too many work hours every week
Learned to take writing "one step at a time"
Not trying to fix everything at once
Daycare was expensive
Could work at home and not use daycare

Next, she numbered the steps she had gone through in the order in which she'd experienced them. She crossed out some items she realized weren't parts of the process of becoming a better writer and added some revisions and new items that seemed necessary.

> *6* Borrowed Auntie's computer
> *4* Couldn't work at college on computers there—used a lot of time waiting
> ~~No time because of looking after Kerima~~
> *2* Went for weekly tutoring
> ~~Spent a lot of time on tutorial work~~
> *3* Too many work hours every week—cut down on nights
> *7* Started to work on essays on computer at night—it was not hard
> ~~Learned to take writing "one step at a time"~~
> *8* Not trying to fix everything at once
> *9* Fixing and changing more important than just writing—getting it right takes time ~~Daycare was expensive~~
> *5* Could work at home and not use daycare
> *1* Admitted I needed some outside help

Then Shareen grouped her items into four stages: (1) admitting she had to face her problem and doing something about it; (2) realizing she needed more time to work on her writing and figuring out what to do; (3) giving up work one evening and being loaned a computer, which made it easier to work at home; (4) starting to follow her tutor's advice and take writing "one step at a time," leaving lots of time for revision.

Shareen was ready to write her first draft now.

> I was always a perfectionist. So returning to college as a mature student offered me a lot of challenges, the worst of which was English. At the end of my first semester, it was my only D. So, if you are facing problems with English and writing, you may want to find out how I faced this challenge. I didn't want to admit that I needed help (after all, I'm an adult), but my grade point average was getting pulled down by that D, and I wanted to stay in International Business. Finally, I went to the tutoring centre—they were really nice there. But I had another problem to cope with. I didn't have enough extra time to devote to writing drafts and going over them because I worked three nights a week. So I knew I'd either have to keep Kerima in daycare longer or give up one of those evenings of work. Plus the computer rooms at college are always full, and I felt pressured trying to work there and too tired to think after waiting for my chance. My next stage was a lucky break—my auntie Bharati lent me her computer and printer! So now, after I got Kerima to sleep, I could sit comfortably in my sweatpants and follow the steps my tutor showed me. At first I didn't want to keep going back to the same page of writing. But really it was like I stopped trying to be perfect, and somehow got better—weird. In fact, the most amazing part of this process is that I get at least Bs now, and sometimes As on both my business and English papers.

Development through Revision

After Shareen wrote her first draft, she showed it to a classmate for her comments. Here are the notes her classmate made.

> *In order to make this a good process paragraph, I think you need to do a couple of things.*
>
> *First, although this paper is based on what you went through, I think it's a little too much about your own experience, so perhaps other people will not relate to it Don't take yourself out of it completely, as some of your personal details are inspiring. But I think that this paragraph needs to be more about the process you went through, so someone could realistically try some of these things if they needed to. Do you see what I mean?*
>
> *Second, you need a good topic sentence that explains what process you're going to describe.*
>
> *Third, you've used some transitions, so I have a rough idea of what happened when, but you need some more. And I think the stages themselves could be clearer. Maybe you could sort out some of those details into neater "packages."*
>
> *But don't be discouraged, because I think this is a great inspiration to people—just tell them how you did it, and then step into the background a bit.*

When Shareen read her classmate's comments, she agreed with most of them. Because she enjoyed a challenge, she decided to try for a "descriptive process" paragraph, rather than a "how-to" paragraph. She then wrote the version of "How Shareen Broke the D Barrier" that appears on pages 184–185.

WRITING A PROCESS PARAGRAPH

How to Write a Process Paragraph

1) Decide how much your readers are likely to know about the process you will describe. Ask yourself what information they would need to understand and follow your instructions successfully.

2) Prewrite until you have listed details, pieces of equipment, possible problems, and steps: any ideas about your process that occur to you.

3) Note considerations such as time involved, equipment, ingredients, or other items at the top of another page. Under these notes, begin to number and order the steps in your process in point form.

4) Group the steps in your process into approximately three general stages, using time order.

5) Transfer your stages and steps to an outline form. The stages in your process paragraph are your three subtopics. Leaving space for additional details or examples that may be needed, add the necessary number of steps involved in each stage.

6) Write a topic sentence that gives the purpose, value, and relative level of difficulty of your process; then draft your paragraph from your outline.

7) Revise your paragraph to ensure
   • that you have mentioned any possible warnings needed or problems that might occur, and have not omitted any details; and
   • that you have used transitional words and phrases to assist understanding of your process.

8) Conclude by refocusing on the value or importance of having performed the actions described.

Writing Assignment 1

Choose one of the topics below to write about in a process paragraph.

How to change a car or bike tire
How to get make a home energy efficient
How to devlop an exercise program
How to choose the right college for you
How to live on a limited budget
How to plant an organic garden
How to fix a leaky faucet, a clogged drain, or the like
How to enjoy a Canadian winter
How to study for an important exam
How to undertake a specific hobby or recreational activity

Prewriting

a Begin by freewriting for ten minutes on the topic you have chosen. Do not worry about spelling, grammar, or organization. Just write whatever comes into your head regarding the topic.

   Write for more than ten minutes if added details about the topic occur to you. This freewriting will give you a base of raw material that you can draw on in the next phase of your work on the paragraph. After freewriting, you should have a sense of whether there is enough material available for you to write a process paragraph about the topic. If so, continue as explained below. If not, choose another topic and freewrite about *it* for ten minutes.

b Identify a controlling idea to focus on in your paragraph. You should keep the nature of your audience in mind. Write a clear, direct topic sentence stating the process you are going to describe or give directions for as well as the attitude you will be presenting. For instance, if you are going to describe a way to study for major exams, your topic sentence might be "Students need focus and organization in order to study for a major exam." In this topic sentence, you can count on an audience of other students who recognize the value of your topic. A very good type of topic sentence tells its readers the topic and the number of steps involved: "Even if you have never tried to grow anything, before, you can succeed as an organic gardener by following four important steps."

c List all the steps you can think of that may be part of the process. Don't worry, at this point, about how each step fits or whether certain steps overlap.

d Number your items in time order and revise for completeness. Strike out items that do not fit in the list; add others that come to mind.

~~Quiet on stairs~~
2 Come in after Dad's asleep
~~House is freezing at night~~
1 Bring key
5 Know which steps to avoid
3 Lift up front door
~~Late dances on Saturday night~~
6 Don't turn on bathroom light
4 Avoid squeaky spots on floor
8 Get into bed quietly
7 *Undress quietly*

e Refer to your list as a guide to write the outline and first rough draft of your paper. As you write, try to think of additional details that will support your opening sentence. Group the details of your process into three or more stages, or subtopics. Make sure each stage is complete and clearly explained, and is illustrated with specific examples. You should be ready to write a series of lists and drafts as you work toward the goals of unity, support, and coherence.

Revising

After you have written your first draft, set it aside for a while. Then read it out loud, perferably to a trusted peer editor. Process writing requires you to be especially aware of your readers because your purpose is to either teach them how to do something or describe exactly how something is done.

- Consider how much your reader knows about your topic. A reader cannot follow a process or do so with much interest if he or she does not have any idea about the general nature of your subject. For example, if you are writing about how to install a particular piece of software, you may need to explain some terms to readers who are unfamiliar with either computers or your particular software. Have you included any necessary background information about equipment, ingredients, or terms?

- Be sure that the pronoun point of view in your paragraph is consistent. For instance, if you open with "How I got rid of mice" (first person), do not switch to "*You* must buy the right kind of traps" (second person). Have you written your paragraph consistently in the first person (*I, we*), or as an address to your reader in the second person (*you*), or in the third person as Shareen did in her descriptive process paragraph?

- The goal of all process writing is to be clear and easy to follow. Are the steps in your paragraph described in a clear, logical way? Is your sequence correct?

Have you omitted any steps or stages that would keep readers from following your process? Have you informed your readers about any difficulties with your process?

- Transitions are essential in a process paragraph or essay. Have you used transitions to reassure readers of the order in which your steps or stages are presented, while making sure that your paragraph moves smoothly from one step to another?
- Use appropriate terminology to identify all items and processes. To be sure that your audience will be able to identify all materials, use commonly accepted vocabulary with appropriate identification or descriptors as necessary. Avoid slang, jargon, abbreviations, acronyms, and other language that may confuse or exclude your audience. Explain specific terms wherever necessary.
- Look at your topic sentence again. There are three very effective ways to open an effective process paragraph. Your challenge is to engage your readers' interest or to get them to try your process. Your choice of topic sentence pattern will depend on three things: (1) your reading audience, (2) the level of difficulty involved in the process involved, and (3) your readers' knowledge, likely understanding, or interest in your topic.

    One effective type of topic sentence states the importance of your subject to your readers ("Knowing how to study effectively for a major exam can mean the difference between passing and failing a course"). Another method offers your opinion of the value of your process ("My technique for building a charcoal barbecue fire is almost foolproof"). A third opener presents the results of the process to give readers an idea of the goal ("A delicious plate of crispy samosas awaits anyone who follows my formula").

    Does your topic sentence reflect the interests and knowledge of your reading audience? Have you used an appropriate version of one of the types of topic sentence suggested above?
- Return to your closing sentences. Have you taken your process beyond its final step? Have you summed up your process, reassured readers of its value or results, or encouraged readers to see the wider value of your process?
- Have you corrected any sentence-skills errors that you noticed while reading your paper out loud? Have you checked the paper carefully for sentence skills, including spelling, as listed on the inside front cover of this book?

Continue revising until you and your reader can answer yes to all these questions.

Transitions for Process Paragraphs

first	next, then	finally
as you begin	while this is happening	to finish
first of all	during this step	at last
to start out	the second (third, fourth) step	as a last step
the first step	after you have	to complete

● ● ● ● **Writing Assignment 2**

Write a paragraph about one of the following processes. For this assignment, you will be working with more general topics than those in Writing Assignment 1. In fact, many of the topics are so broad that entire self-help books have been written about them. A big part of your task, then, will be to narrow the topic down enough so that it can be covered in one paragraph.

You will find, in many cases, that you must invent your own steps in a particular process. You will also have to make decisions about how many steps to include, the order in which to present them, and the number of stages or subtopics in your process.

How to break a bad habit such as smoking, overeating, or excessive drinking
How to meet people
How to improve the place where you work
How to show appreciation to others
How to get over a broken relationship
How to enjoy a day off
How to maintain a vehicle

Prewriting

a Choose a topic that appeals to you. Then ask yourself, "How can I make this general topic narrow enough to be covered in one paragraph?" One way is to focus on an aspect of the process, that you believe is most important. Another way to proceed is to think of a particular time you have gone through this process. For example, if the general topic is "how to decorate economically," you might think about a time when you decorated your own apartment.

b Write a topic sentence about the process you are going to describe. Your topic sentence should clearly reflect the narrowed-down topic you have chosen. If you chose the topic mentioned in step *a*, for example, your topic sentence could be "I made my first apartment look nice without spending a fortune."

c Make a list of as many different items as you can think of that concern your topic. Don't worry about repeating yourself, about putting them in order, about whether details are major or minor, or about spelling. Simply make a list of everything about your topic that occurs to you.

d Next, decide what order you will present your items in and number them. (As in the example of decorating an apartment, there may not be an order that the steps *must* be done in. If that is the case, you should decide on a sequence that makes sense or that you followed yourself.) If you think of any potential problems or setbacks that you or others might experience, list those as well and put them into your sequence. As you number your items, strike out any that do not fit in the list and add others you think of, like this:

6   Bought fabric ends and used them as wall hangings
~~Trimmed overgrown bushes in the yard~~
7   Used old jars and bottles as vases for flowers from the yard

> *4*   Found an oriental rug at a warehouse sale
> *2*   Painted unmatched kitchen chairs in bright yellow
> ~~Kept dishes washed and put away~~
> *1*   Bought a slipcover for a ratty couch
> *8*   Used pink light bulbs
> *5*   Hung sheets over the windows
> *3*   *Built bookcases out of bricks and boards*

   e Write an outline for your paragraph. Begin by putting down your topic sentence. Then try to group your steps or stages into related items. Think about details that might fill out any stage or step or might explain it better.

   f Referring to your outline and list, write the first draft of your paragraph. Add any additional steps or details as they occur to you.

Revising

If you can, put away your first draft for at least a day and then return to it. Read it out loud to yourself or to a friend who will give you honest feedback.

Here are the questions to ask yourself as you read over your first draft and the drafts to follow:

- Have I included a clear topic sentence that tells the limits of the process I will be describing? Should I give an idea of the value of my process in my topic sentence?
- Have I included all the essential information so that anyone reading my paper could follow the same process? Did I mention any potential problems that could occur and what to do about them?
- Have I grouped any steps that naturally belong together?
- Have I made the sequence of steps easy to follow by using transitions like *first, second, then, next, during,* and *finally?*
- Have I used clear and appropriate terminology?
- Have I written a closing sentence or two to sum up the process and reassure readers of its value or relative easiness?
- Can I answer yes to other questions about unity, support, and coherence found on the inside cover of the book?
- Have I corrected sentence-skills mistakes, including spelling errors?

Continue revising your work until you can answer yes to all these questions.

• • • • • Writing Assignment 3

Everyone is an expert at something. Write a *descriptive* process paragraph that explains some skill that you can perform very well. The skill might be, for example, playing goalie, putting up a tent, making an ice cream soda, becoming a long distance runner, or fine-tuning a car engine. Write from the point of view that "this is how _____ should be done." Be sure that your paragraph *describes* and *explains* how your process occurs. *Descriptive* process writing does *not* give instructions.

Writing Assignment 4

Write a process paragraph on how to succeed at a job interview. Using strategies described on the Online Learning Centre, do some research on the topic. Take a look at job search websites like Monster.ca, for instance. Such research will help you think about how to proceed with this assignment.

Condense the material you have found into three, four, or five basic steps. Choose the steps, tips, and pointers that seem most important to you or that recur most often in the material you examine. Remember that you are doing research only to obtain background information for your paragraph. Do not copy material or repeat someone else's words or phrases in your own work.

Writing Assignment 5

Write an explanation of a new process that you have mastered for your program of study for a friend at college who is *not in your program*. Examples might include explaining how a particular piece of software is used, how to do some special activity in a lab, how to make an audio demo, or another specialized activity unique to your program. Explain each step of the task in a way that a friend would understand.

REVIEWING THE LEARNING OUTCOMES FOR PROCESS WRITING

After completing any of the writing assignments in this chapter, answer the following questions to decide how well your paragraph meets the learning outcomes for process writing.

✓ Overall, have you supplied enough information or background material to make your process understandable to your readers? Have you explained any technical or specialized points you have included?

✓ Do you open with a topic sentence that states the value of your process and perhaps its approximate level of difficulty?

✓ Have you mentioned any necessary equipment or supplies? Have you indicated the amount of time needed for your process and its stages?

✓ Are your steps grouped into logical stages?

✓ Is each step completely and carefully described with enough details or examples to make it clear and easy to follow? Have you mentioned any possible problems that may occur while following your instructions?

✓ Do you conclude with a reassurance of the value of the process to the reader?

 **Online LearningCentre** Visit the *English Skills with Readings: Examining Paragraphs* Online Learning Centre at www.mcgrawhill.ca/olc/langan to access self-quizzes, internet-based questions and research skills, web resources, and other learning and study tools.

Chapter 11

Examining Cause and Effect

By carefully working through this chapter's activities and successfully completing one or more of its writing assignments, you will write a cause and effect paragraph that

- opens with a topic sentence that states your point of view on your subject and indicates whether you will examine causes or effects;

- shows a selection of causes and/or effects focused on proving the point of the paragraph;

- uses true and logical causes and/or effects to support its point;

- presents its subtopic causes and/or effects in order of importance;

- supports its subtopic causes and/or effects with sufficient and specific details; and

- concludes with a reassurance that its point is effectively supported.

Cause and effect writing examines the *reasons why* things happen (cause) and the *results* of those things happening (effects). It explains causal or resultant relationships between events.

Writing a paragraph that discusses causes and/or effects demands clear thinking and observation, or *analysis*. To analyze is to break a subject down into its component parts. An event or situation may appear to have many causes and many effects, but not all these may be true causes or effects; they may simply have happened before or after the event or situation. So to write about causes or effects, a writer must first analyze whether they are truly causes or effects.

Every day we ask questions about why things happen; this is a normal response to our environment. We seek to understand why someone seems unhappy or why our car stopped working, and we look for the causes as answers. We also ask what will happen as the result of an action, or the effects.

We realize that many actions do not occur without causes, and we also realize that a given action can have a series of effects—good or bad.

Both career and college writing and speaking often focus on cause and effect. Why does a product not sell? Why is a specific piece of software inefficient? What will happen if a new initiative is introduced? The skills and techniques in analyzing and communicating cause and effect are in constant use in any number of communications formats.

In this section, you will be asked to examine the causes or the effects of something. First read the two paragraphs that follow and answer the questions about them. Both paragraphs support their opening points by explaining a series of causes or a series of effects.

Further Insight—A quick guide to *effect* and *affect*

Effect as a noun can mean that which happens as a result of an action or something that acts upon something else:

> The townspeople are worried about the effect the big mall will have on the town's commercial area.
>
> An effect of globalization has been an increased gap between the very richest and the very poorest.

Effect as a verb is to produce a result:

> To effect personal growth, people must start with open minds.

Affect as a verb means to influence.

> How does the new puppy affect your cat?

Affect as a noun is an emotional state.

> A Canadian winter can produce depressed affects in sun lovers.

When needing a verb, the most likely word to choose is *affect*.
When needing a noun, the most likely word to choose is *effect*.

PARAGRAPHS TO CONSIDER

New Puppy in the House

[1]Buying a new puppy can have drastic effects on a quiet household. [2]For one thing, the puppy keeps the entire family awake for at least two solid weeks. [3]Every night when the puppy is placed in its box, it begins to howl, yip, and whine. [4]Even after the lights go out and the house quiets down, the puppy continues to moan. [5]Since it is impossible to sleep while listening to a heartbroken, trembling "Woo-woooo," the family soon begins to suffer the effects of loss of sleep. [6]Soon people become hostile, short-tempered, depressed, and

irritable. ⁷A second effect is that the puppy tortures the family by destroying its material possessions. ⁸Every day something different is damaged. ⁹Family members find chewed belts and shoes, gnawed table legs, and leaking sofa cushions. ¹⁰In addition, the puppy usually ruins the wall-to-wall carpeting and makes the house smell like a public washroom at a big-city bus station. ¹¹Worst of all, though, the puppy causes family disagreements. ¹²Parents argue with children about who is supposed to feed and walk the dog. ¹³Children argue among themselves about whose turn it is to play with the puppy. ¹⁴Everyone argues about whose idea it was to get the puppy in the first place. ¹⁵These continual arguments, along with the effects of sleeplessness and the loss of valued possessions, seriously disrupt a household. ¹⁶Only when the puppy gets a bit older will the house become peaceful again.

My Ghost Town

¹My hometown near Lake Erie is drying up and disappearing. ²First, there are an increasing number of problems for employees of the company that used to be the biggest employer in town. ³The huge car-parts factory supported hundreds of families, but there have been three strikes in five years, and the workers' complaints never seem to be addressed. ⁴Also, more workers are being laid off because more and more parts are made in Mexico or Asia. ⁵Then this week the U.S. parent company admitted the plant is unprofitable and said it will close the factory completely. ⁶Another reason the town looks unhappy and deserted is that one of our largest stores closed down and relocated last year. ⁷The other chain store was sold to Wal-Mart, an American company. ⁸The Wal-Mart store brought in management and employees from other locations, so one-third of the old discount store's workers were out of a job and either looked for a new job, moved away, or both. ⁹There are very few new jobs available, and there are no new companies opening near here. ¹⁰But the most visibly depressing cause of all for my town's empty streets is a half-hour's drive away: a big new mall built last year. ¹¹People drive there for entertainment as they do their shopping and banking. ¹²No one wants to use the little family owned businesses on the main street any more. ¹³So more Queen Street stores sit empty every week and the two banks are closing their branches, which means fewer jobs for even fewer people. ¹⁴All these changes leave my town looking and feeling as lonely and sad as a frontier ghost town.

Questions

About Unity

1. Which sentences in "New Puppy in the House" repeat an idea already stated and so should be omitted? (*Write the sentence numbers here.*) _____

2. Which sentence in "My Ghost Town" does not directly support the paragraph's point? (*Write the sentence number.*) _____

About Support

3. How many causes are given to support the opening idea in "My Ghost Town"?

    _____ one   _____ two   _____ three   _____ four

4. How many effects of bringing a new puppy into the home are given in "New Puppy in the House"?

    _____ one   _____ two   _____ three   _____ four

About Coherence

5. What are the five major transition words used in "My Ghost Town"?

    a. _____   c. _____   e. _____

    b. _____   d. _____

6. Which words signal the most important effect in "New Puppy in the House"?

    _____

● ● ● ● ● **Activity 1**

A. Give three causes for each of the following:

    1. _____, _____, and _____ have caused me to learn respect for _____ [a friend or relative].

    2. _____, _____, and _____ caused my car to fail a safety inspection.

    3. _____, _____, and _____ have contributed to climate change.

    4. _____, _____, and _____ are necessary to achieve success in college.

    5. The most important factors toward enjoying a long and satisfying life are _____, _____, and _____.

B. Give three consequences of the following:

    1. Since I started college, I have _____, _____, and _____.

    2. Rishma was frustrated with her job, so she _____, _____ and _____.

    3. The car was too hot for groceries so finally we decided to _____, _____ and, _____.

    4. Wherever humans have explored in the world, _____, _____, and _____ have occurred.

    5. As a result of the intense need for labour in Alberta, there have been changes in _____, _____, and _____.

DEVELOPING A CAUSE AND EFFECT PARAGRAPH

Development through Prewriting

Cause and effect writing requires an extra step in logical thinking that can be done effectively during your prewriting and information-gathering stages. In order to write a good cause and effect paragraph, you must clearly define an effect (*what* happened) and the contributing causes (*why* it happened)—or, you will define some cause and its resulting effects. In addition, you will need to provide details that support and explain the causes and effects you're writing about. In many formal or complex cause and effect pieces, your reasons and explanations must be supported through adequate research so that valid information is presented logically.

Terry, the student author of "My Ghost Town," was given an assignment to write a paragraph about some change that he had experienced. Chapter 2 shows Terry's initial freewriting, during which he discovered his focus—how his hometown had changed. Through focused freewriting; he took the known *effect* that his hometown was losing people and businesses, until he came up with more details. To clarify his thinking, he made a list based on his focused freewriting of *causes* (reasons for the town's problems). This is what he came up with.

> Car-parts plant in trouble
> Plant will close now
> Big store closed and moved
> No new jobs
> The Westland Mall—everybody goes there
> Stores and banks shut down

He found it hard to think of his causes clearly, so he labelled the causes, then listed the details in point form under each one.

> Cause #1 <u>Car-parts plant is biggest employer & it's in trouble</u>
> —three strikes
> —layoffs—cause? Lower production
> —plant will close down
> Cause #2 <u>Big stores closing and changing hands</u>
> —one store closed completely—new one near Simcoe
> —big discount store turned into Wal-Mart—brought in outside people
> —No new jobs
> —People moved away, on unemployment
> Cause #3 <u>Westland Mall opened up</u>
> —no one shops in town any more
> —the movie house closed
> —banks closing

Terry now had his effect and three causes with details, and he knew he had most of a good outline done, as well. He then wrote a first draft.

My hometown is drying up and shutting down. That's one of the reasons why I'm here in London at college. The car-parts plant has always been where most people worked, including my father. Now they don't even try to settle with workers after three strikes. They're making the same parts cheaper in Mexico or Asia now, so they keep laying people off. And the last straw was last week when the American parent company decided to close it down completely. I don't know what my dad is going to do. The big chain stores where everybody shopped, even people from the other places around here, are either closed or have new owners, too. Sears closed and it only has a little catalogue office now, so that put a lot of people out of work. The big discount store turned into a Wal-Mart, and all its managers and a lot of staff are from other places, nearly a third of its employees lost their jobs. Also the new Westland Mall is just killing the local stores and businesses. Even the Festival Theatre closed, and the banks will only have machines or branches in the mall. Nobody goes downtown any more, and my town looks as empty as a ghost town.

Development through Revising

In his next class, Terry traded papers with his classmate Roger. This is what Roger wrote about Terry's first draft.

> You have really good facts, but it feels a bit bumpy. I suggest that you add transitions to tie your sentences together.
>
> I also wonder if one of these reasons is more important than the others. Which of these really is the biggest reason your town's hurting? If you know, it would be good if you told people that by using an emphatic order to organize your paragraph.
>
> You could add some more details in some places, too. Why is the mall hurting your town so much? Why do people go there so much? And the other thing I notice is that sometimes you're telling a story about yourself, and sometimes this is about the town. You should keep your subject clear.

As Terry read over his own paper, the first thing he realized was that he'd run out of steam toward the end. He realized that while he had been careful with his outline, he had hurried with the draft, especially the last part. He saw that he hadn't explained how big an effect the mall was having on the town's main street. So, he wrote more about Queen Street by freewriting for more details about how empty it was. He also realized that to make this a proper cause and effect paragraph, his own story didn't belong.

Using Roger's comments and his own thoughts, Terry rewrote his first draft, fixing the point of view and producing the paragraph that appears on page 197.

● ● ● ● ● **Activity 2**

In this exercise you will create a cause and effect outline that will help you tell the difference between *reasons* that back up a point and the supporting *details* that go with each of the reasons or subtopics. The scrambled list below contains both reasons (subtopics) and supporting details. Complete the outline following

Further Insight—Using adverbs and adverb clauses as conjunctions and transitions in a cause and effect paragraph

Adverb clauses describe where, when, or why something happened; the causes or purposes of an action or event; or the condition under which something occurred. Adverb clauses are always dependent and serve as subordinating conjunctions; accordingly, they are often used to join cause and effect. They answer the adverbial forms of the journalists' questions:

Question	Type	Subordinating Conjunction	Sample
When?	Time	After, before, until, while	I will work out at the gym daily until I lose some weight.
Where?	Place	Where, wherever	The puppy follows wherever Sam goes.
Why?	Cause or Purpose	Accordingly, because, consequently, in order that, so that, therefore	Social services must be enhanced in order that inner-city youth may escape grinding poverty.
How?	Condition	Also, although, even though, however, if, otherwise, similarly, since, unless, whether, though	Students must register early; otherwise, classes may be filled.

You may often start a sentence with an adverb or adverb clause, but you must take care not to write *sentence fragments* (see Chapter 21). Note: *who* and *what* are pronoun forms. Adverbs are also introduced in Chapter 27.

the list by writing the reasons in the numbered blanks (*1, 2, 3*) and the appropriate supporting details in the lettered blanks (*a, b, c, d*). Arrange the reasons in their order of importance, as you see them. Summarize the reasons and details in a few words rather than writing them out completely.

Point: There are a number of reasons why college students find first semesters difficult.

There are so many kinds of expensive supplies to buy, like drafting materials and zip disks.

Reading, doing assignments, and attending labs take up many hours.

Assignments are often more difficult than previous school tasks.

Most students work several hours a week at part-time jobs.

Travelling to and from college is costly, whether the student pays for a car, gas, and parking or whether the student must buy monthly public transit passes.

College classes and coursework are demanding and unfamiliar to many students.

Classes usually take up at least twenty hours a week.

Students find time management to be a problem.

It is hard for a student who lives away from home to pay for tuition, rent, and food.

Lectures are often an intimidating experience for students used to informal classes.

Attending college is frequently financially draining.

Managing assignments for four or more courses, attending required lab hours, and attempting extracurricular interests can be a major worry.

Textbooks for several courses may cost hundreds of dollars.

Almost all the course material is totally new to students and may be quite difficult to grasp.

Students often find there is no time left for families, friends, or children.

Outline

1. _____

   a. _____

   b. _____

   c. _____

   d. _____

2. _____

   a. _____

   b. _____

   c. _____

   d. _____

3. _____

   a. _____

   b. _____

   c. _____

   d. _____

A Note about Causes, Effects, and Logic

Some problems may occur in cause and effect writing. Be careful not to make an error in logic by confusing time order with causality; similarly, do not assume that there is only a single cause or effect in any situation.

- Sometimes facts or events appear to be causes or effects when they merely *precede* or *follow* something *in time.* For instance, if a dog crossed the road just before your car stalled, the dog was not the cause of the breakdown. The dog's crossing the road simply occurred before your car stalled, but the two events have no causal relationship.

- There are also often multiple or underlying causes and effects. If a writer states that catching frequent colds is caused by being in constant contact with people with colds, he or she could be ignoring other less apparent causes, such as low resistance due to fatigue or persistent conditions like asthma.

- When writing about causal relationships, keep a clear sight upon whether you are analyzing the causes of a single effect, or the multiple effects of a given action.

- A good way to keep your ideas straight without confusing causes and effects, and to eliminate false causal relationships, is to use a graphic organizer as you sort your material. This method will help you to identify the factors that cause an effect more readily than with a simple list. Some organizers, such as the following, can be altered in order to illustrate a series of causes or the consequences of an effect.

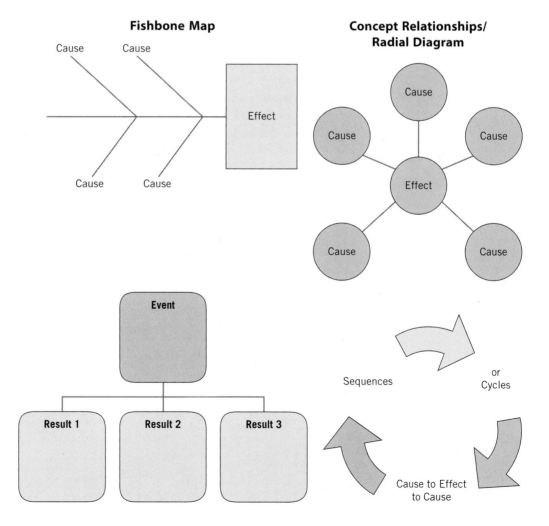

Activity 3

A. Use a graphic organizer to help you arrange the causes or effects that contribute to the following ideas. Note that you may need to decide whether the event was the effect or result of multiple causes, or whether it was an action with multiple consequences.

-A big power failure
-A cat jumped on a laptop computer
-Rising fuel prices
-A missed flight

-Personal bankruptcy
-An effective résumé
-A fender-bender
-Receiving an award

Determine whether you are discussing causes toward an effect, or the multiple effects of an act. For example, you could chart that you missed an airline flight (the effect) because you overslept, could not find a cab, and had trouble with airport security. Notice that while the date is Friday the 13th, that fact does not logically become a cause for the missed flight. You could also analyze the effects of missing a flight to explain that because of it, you had to wait eight hours for the next flight, sit next to an annoying passenger on the airplane, and land in a distant airport because the flight you eventually took was diverted due to bad weather.

B. Choose one of the above suggestions and then write a cause and effect paragraph about it. Use the information from the graphic organizer to construct an outline that will identify your point, and then support it in a logical order. As you draft your paragraph, add as many details and descriptions as necessary to explain the importance of each subtopic. Revise to ensure that your causes and effects are consistent and clearly illustrated with specific examples. Finally, edit for clear transitions, including conjunctive adverbs as described in the Further Insight box in this section.

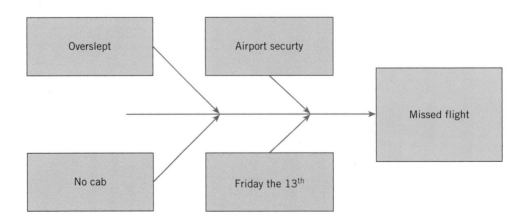

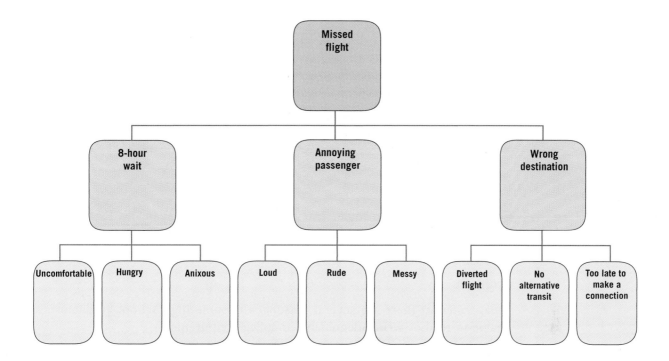

WRITING A CAUSE AND EFFECT PARAGRAPH

How to Write a Cause and Effect Paragraph

1) Look at your topic. Does it require a paragraph on causes only or effects only, or could it be treated either way? After deciding on either a causes or an effects paragraph, begin to prewrite.

2) Use listing, questioning, or diagramming to create either causes or effects for your topic. Examine your notes to be sure that your points are true and logical causes or effects; are there other or deeper causes or effects that you may have missed in your prewriting? Should others be omitted?

3) Number and try to group points or details that are related or similar. Check to be sure that similar points are not merely repetitions of each other. If you have several points that are related, group them under a common subheading as a possible subtopic cause or effect. (See Writing Assignment 1 below for an example.)

4) Use your outline to list your major or subtopic causes or effects and the details that support each. Write a topic sentence that both states your point of view on your subject and indicates whether your paragraph is about causes or about effects.

5) As you work on drafts based on your outline, use an order that is most effective for your subtopics and supporting details: is one cause or effect
(*continued*)

> more important than the others? Is the order in time in which your causes or effects occur important to your point?
>
> **6)** Be sure to use transitional words and phrases appropriate to cause and effect writing to help readers to follow your thoughts.
>
> **7)** Conclude by reinforcing your main point with a reference to the evidence you have presented.

Writing Assignment 1

Choose one of the two topic sentences and brief outlines below. Each is made up of three subtopics (causes or effects). Your task is to turn the topic sentence and outline into a causes or an effects paragraph.

Option A

Topic sentence: There are several reasons why some high school graduates are unable to read or write adequately for college requirements.

1) Failure of parents (*cause*)
2) Failure of schools (*cause*)
3) Failure of students themselves (*cause*)

Option B

Topic sentence: Attending college may change students' characters in positive ways.

1) More confident (*effect*)
2) More knowledgeable (*effect*)
3) More assertive (*effect*)

Prewriting

a After you have chosen the option that appeals to you most, jot down all the details you can think of that might go under each of the subtopics. Use separate files for each list. Don't worry yet about whether you can use all the items—your goal is to generate more material than you need.

b Edit, order, and select details. Look for possible subtopics. Decide which details you will use to develop the paragraph. Also, number the details in the order in which you will present them. Here is how the writer of "New Puppy in the House" made decisions about the details that were the *effects* of having a puppy.

2	Whines and moans
6	Arguments about walking dog
6	Arguments about feeding dog
	~~Purchase collar, leash, food~~

> *4* Chewed belts and shoes
> *6* Arguments about playing with dog
> *1* Loss of sleep
>   ~~Visits to vet~~
> *3* Short tempers
> *5* Accidents on carpet
> *4* Chewed cushions and tables

Notice that the writer has found possible subtopics and put the same number in front of certain details that go together. For example, there is a "*4*" in front of "Chewed belts and shoes" and also in front of "Chewed cushions and tables."

  c Organize your subtopics and details. Group details that are related (as indicated by numbers), and arrange them in a rough trial outline or diagram form under subtopic headings. At this stage, causes and effects may still be scrambled. This may be a good opportunity to use one of the graphic organizers discussed previously to help you decide which are the main supporting reasons, and which are details to illustrate them.

  d Revise your outline, taking care to cover only causes or effects and to supply sufficient details to support each cause or effect. Here is the final outline for the "New Puppy in the House" paragraph on pages 196–197.

Topic Sentence: Having a new puppy disrupts the household.

1. Keeps family awake
   a. Whines at night
   b. Howls
   c. Loss of sleep
2. Destroys possessions
   a. Chews belts & shoes
   b. Chews furniture
   c. Has accidents on couch & carpet
3. Causes arguments
   a. Arguments about walking dog
   b. Arguments about feeding dog
   c. Arguments about who gets to play with dog

---

  e Now you are ready to write your paragraph. With cause and effect paragraphs and essays, *outlining is essential* because of the need to sort out causes from effects, as well as the need (as with any paper) to supply sufficient supporting details. Be sure to develop each of the subtopics from your outline into a complete sentence, and then back it up with the best of the details you have generated.

Revising

Revise your paragraph with these questions in mind:

- Have I begun the paragraph with the topic sentence provided?
- Is each subtopic stated in a complete sentence?
- Have I provided effective details, and enough of them, to back up each subtopic?
- Have I used transitions such as in *addition, another thing,* and *also* to make relationships between the sentences clear?
- Have I proofread the paragraph for sentence-skills errors, including spelling mistakes?

Revise your paragraph until you are sure the answer to each question is yes.

• • • •   **Writing Assignment 2**

Most of us criticize others readily, but we find it more difficult to give compliments. For this assignment, write a paragraph praising someone. The paragraph may be about a person you know (parent, relative, friend); a public figure (actor, politician, musician, sports star, and so on); or a product, company, or organization (for example, about a recent purchase, the service given by a company, or the activities of an organization).

Prewriting

a Writing this paragraph indicates that its subject (person, group, or object) has had an *effect* on you because you like, admire, or appreciate the person or product. Your job will be to put into words the *causes,* or reasons, for this good feeling. Begin by making a list of reasons for your admiration. Here, for example, are a few reasons why a person might praise a car manufacturer.

> My car is dependable.
> There was prompt action on a complaint.
> The car is well designed.
> The price was reasonable.
> The car dealer was honest and fair.
> The car has needed little maintenance.

Reasons for admiring a co-worker might include these.

> He [or she, according to your choice] is patient with me.
> S/he always listens to me.
> S/he has a great sense of humour.
> S/he encourages me in several ways.
> I know s/he has covered for me.

Develop your own list of reasons for admiring the person or organization you have chosen.

b Now that you have a list of reasons, you need details to back up each reason. Jot down as many examples or supporting details as you can for each reason. Turn your list of reasons and details into an outline, using the order you think best.

c Next, select from your outline list the three or four reasons that you can best support with effective details. These will make up the body of your paragraph.

d For your topic sentence, make the positive statement you wish to support. For example, the writer of the paragraph about the car manufacturer might begin like this: "I am the very satisfied owner of a 2004 Toyota."

e Now combine your topic sentence, reasons, and supporting details, and write a draft of your paragraph.

Revising

If possible, put your paragraph aside for a day. Then read it aloud to a friend. As you both listen to your words, keep these questions in mind:

- Is my topic sentence a positive statement that is supported by all my details?
- Do I clearly state several different reasons why I like or admire the person or organization I'm writing about?
- Do I support each of those reasons with specific evidence?
- Have I linked my sentences together with transitional words and phrases?
- Is my letter free of sentence-skills errors, including spelling mistakes?

Continue revising until you and your friend can answer yes to all these questions.

Writing Assignment 3

Investigate the reasons behind a current news event. For example, you may want to discover the causes behind one of the following events.

A labour strike or other protest
A tax increase
Changes in education
A traffic accident, fire, or other disastrous event
A military action by a government

Research the reasons for the event by reading current newspapers (especially the national papers, which may cover a story in detail), reading a newsmagazine such as *Maclean's*, watching the television news, or checking various news websites. Try to find sources you consider trustworthy.

Decide on the major cause or causes of the event and their specific effects. Then write a paragraph explaining in detail the causes and effects. Below is a sample topic sentence for this assignment.

Recent charges of racial profiling by Toronto police have set off a variety of angry reactions.

Note how this topic sentence uses general descriptive words (*angry reactions*) that can summarize specific supporting details. Support for the words *angry reactions,* for example, might include specific ways in which police, city officials, and the public have responded to these allegations.

REVIEWING THE LEARNING OUTCOMES FOR CAUSE AND EFFECT WRITING

After completing any of the writing assignments in this chapter, review your work to decide how well it meets the following tests.

✓ Does your paragraph open with a topic sentence that states your point of view on your subject and indicates whether your paragraph deals with causes or effects?

✓ Is each cause or effect in your paragraph truly a cause or effect? Does each clearly support the point you make?

✓ Are your causes or effects presented in an effective order, with appropriate transitions to guide your reader and reinforce your point?

✓ Are your subtopics adequately supported by adequate and specific details?

✓ Do you conclude with a reinforcement of your point that sums up your paragraph?

Visit the *English Skills with Readings: Examining Paragraphs* Online Learning Centre at www.mcgrawhill.ca/olc/langan to access self-quizzes, internet-based questions and research skills, web resources, and other learning and study tools.

Chapter 12

Comparing or Contrasting

LEARNING OUTCOMES

By working through this chapter's activities, practising the skills used in both types of comparison or contrast patterns of development, and completing one or more of its writing assignments, you will write a comparison or contrast paragraph that

- compares or contrasts limited aspects of two subjects that have a logical reason to be considered together;

- begins with a focused, clear topic sentence stating (1) both its subjects, (2) its intention either to compare or to contrast, and (3) your point in comparing or contrasting these subjects;

- uses either the one-side-at-a-time or the point-by-point method to state and develop its comparison or contrast;

- carefully compares or contrasts each subject within one of these structures according to several major points or bases for comparing or contrasting; and

- concludes with a summing-up of the results of comparing or contrasting your two subjects and a confirmation of your point of view or judgment on these results.

Papers that *compare* two things show *similarities;* papers that *contrast* two things show *differences.* Comparison papers may *inform* readers by showing them similarities between familiar concepts and unknown or seemingly dissimilar concepts. Contrast papers may *persuade* readers by allowing them to examine the differences between two points, then align their views with one side or the other. Both types of paper involve *analysis,* or thinking that breaks down concepts into their component ideas. Both types of papers begin with a judgment (or viewpoint) on the part of the writer and lead to a judgment on the part of the reader.

Finally, both types of papers analyze the qualities of only two concepts (for three or more, see Chapter 14: Dividing and Classifying)

Comparing and contrasting are two thought processes we constantly perform in everyday life. We compare or contrast products—Fila versus Reeboks shoes—two television shows, two instructors, two friends, or two possible courses of action in a situation. As we compare or contrast, we understand each of the two things more clearly and become able to make judgments about them. Comparison and contrast writing structures simply imitate and extend our thinking habits.

Comparing and contrasting occur constantly in college and career writing. Why is digital reproduction superior to photographic processing? How does one accounting software package compare with another? How does one advertising campaign's use of media coverage differ from another's? Responding to any such question requires competence in the techniques of comparing or contrasting to structure your thinking and to achieve the response you desire from readers.

In this chapter, you will be asked to write a paragraph of comparison or contrast. First, however, you must learn the two common methods of developing a comparison or contrast paragraph. Read the two paragraphs that follow and try to explain the difference in the two methods of development.

PARAGRAPHS TO CONSIDER

Last Dance

[1]My graduation dance was nothing like I had expected it to be. [2]From the start of grade twelve, I had pictured getting dressed in a blue gown that my aunt would make and that would cost five hundred dollars in any store. [3]No one else would have a gown as attractive as mine. [4]I imagined my boyfriend coming to the door with a lovely blue corsage, and I pictured myself happily inhaling its perfume all evening long. [5]I saw us setting off for the evening in his brother's Audi. [6]We would make a flourish as we swept in and out of a series of parties before the dance. [7]Our evening would be capped by a delicious steak dinner and by dancing close together into the early morning hours. [8]The formal was held on a May day, at the Riding Club on the Pembina Highway. [9]However, because of sickness in her family, my aunt had no time to finish my gown and I had to buy an ugly pink one at the last minute for eighty dollars. [10]My corsage of yellow carnations looked terrible on my pink gown, and I do not remember its having any scent. [11]My boyfriend's brother was out of town, and I stepped outside to the stripped-down Chevy that he used at races on weekends. [12]We went to one party where I drank a glass of wine that made me sleepy and upset my stomach. [13]After we arrived at the dance, I nibbled on a roll and some celery sticks. [14]Worst of all, we left early without dancing because my boyfriend and I had had a fight several days before, and at the time, we did not really want to be with each other.

Day versus Evening Students

[1]As a part-time college student who has taken both day and evening courses, I have observed notable differences between day and evening students. [2]First of all, the students in my daytime classes are all about the same age, with similar clothing styles and similar interests. [3]Most are in their late teens to early twenties, and whether male or female, they pretty much dress alike. [4]Their uniform consists of jeans, T-shirts, running shoes, baseball caps, and maybe a gold earring or two. [5]They use the same popular slang, talk about the same movies and TV shows, and know the same musical artists. [6]But students in my evening courses are much more diverse. [7]Some are in their late teens, but most range from young married people in their twenties and thirties to people my grandparents' age. [8]Generally, their clothing is more formal than the day students'. [9]They are dressed for the workplace, not for a typical college classroom. [10]Many of the women wear suits, while the men often wear dress shirts or sweaters. [11]As well, they are more comfortable talking about their mortgages or work schedules or child care than about what was on TV last night. [12]Second, for day students, college is generally their only major responsibility. [13]They have plenty of time to study and get assignments done. [14]However, evening students lead much more complicated lives than most day students. [15]They may come to campus after putting in a nine-to-five day at work. [16]Most have children to raise or grandchildren to babysit. [17]When they miss a class or hand in an assignment late, it's usually because of a real problem, such as a sick child or an important deadline at work. [18]Finally, day and evening students definitely have different attitudes toward school. [19]Day students often seem more interested in the view out the window or the attractive classmate in the next row than in what the instructor is saying. [20]They doze, draw cartoons, whisper, and write notes instead of paying attention. [21]Evening students sit up straight, listen hard, and ask the instructor lots of questions. [22]They obviously are there to learn, and they don't want their time wasted. [23]In short, day students and night students are as different as . . . day and night.

Complete this comment: The difference in the methods of contrast in the two paragraphs is _____

_____

_____

_____

_____

Compare your answer with the following explanation of the two methods of development used in comparison or contrast paragraphs.

METHODS OF DEVELOPMENT

There are two common methods, or formats, of development in a comparison or contrast paper. Details can be presented *one side at a time* or *point by point*. Each format is illustrated below.

One Side at a Time

Look at the outline of "Last Dance":

Topic sentence: My senior prom was nothing like I had expected it to be.

1) Expectations (*first half of paper*)
    a. Gown (expensive, blue)
    b. Corsage (lovely, fragrant, blue)
    c. Car (Audi)
    d. Partying (much)
    e. Dinner (steak)
    f. Dancing (all night)
2) Reality (*second half of paper*)
    a. Gown (cheap, pink)
    b. Corsage (wrong colour, no scent)
    c. Car (stripped-down Chevy)
    d. Partying (little)
    e. Dinner (roll and celery sticks)
    f. Dancing (didn't because of quarrel)

When you use the one-side-at-a-time method, follow the same order of points of contrast or comparison for each side, as in the outline above. For example, both the first half of the paper and the second half begin with the subtopic of what dress would be worn. Then both sides go on to the corsage, the car, and so on.

Point by Point

Now look at the outline of "Day versus Evening Students":

Topic sentence: There are notable differences between day and evening students.

1) Age and related tastes in clothing and interests
    a. Youthful nature of day students
    b. Older nature of evening students
2) Amount of responsibility
    a. Lighter responsibilities of day students
    b. Heavier responsibilities of evening students
3) Attitude toward school
    a. Casual attitude of day students
    b. Serious attitude of evening students

The outline shows how the two kinds of students are contrasted point by point under three subtopics, or bases of comparison. First, the writer compares the ages, clothing styles, and interests of the young daytime students and the older evening students. Next, the writer compares the limited amount of responsibility of the daytime students with the heavier responsibilities of the evening students. Finally, the writer compares the casual attitudes toward school of the daytime students with the serious attitudes of the evening students.

When you begin a comparison or contrast paper, you should decide immediately whether you are going to use the one-side-at-a-time format or the point-by-point format. Your subject matter will often help you determine which format is preferable. Following are some of the advantages and disadvantages of each format.

One-side-at-a-time format (also called *block* format) is most effective when you wish to explore each idea in great depth. When you present one side of your subject in an uninterrupted way, you are able to examine any complexities at length or build a detailed or dramatic argument or description. *But,* if you present one side at a time, be sure to carefully remind readers of each point of comparison or contrast as you present the other side of your subject.

Point-by-point format works best with brief, specific points of comparison or contrast for two subjects or two aspects of the same subject. The reader sees both sides one after the other; he or she is constantly reminded of the comparing or contrasting activity and is less likely to forget points being examined. Point-by-point format is also best for a subject with numerous bases of comparison or contrast for this reason.

An outline is an essential step in helping you decide which format will be more workable for your topic.

Activity

Complete the partial outlines provided for the two paragraphs that follow.

How My Parents' Divorce Changed Me

In the three years since my parents' divorce, I have changed from a spoiled brat to a reasonably normal college student. Before the divorce, I expected my mother to wait on me. She did my laundry, cooked and cleaned up after meals, and even straightened up my room. My only response was to complain if the meat was too well done or if the sweater I wanted to wear was not clean. In addition, I expected money for anything I wanted. Whether it was an expensive ski trip or my own cellphone, I expected Mom to hand over the money. If she refused, I would get it from Dad. However, he left when I was fifteen, and things changed. When Mom got a full-time job to support us, I was the one with the free time to do housework. I did the laundry, started the dinner, and cleaned not only my own room but the whole house. Also, I no longer asked her for money since I knew there was none to spare. Instead, I got a part-time job on weekends to earn my own spending money. Today I have my own car that I am paying for, and I am putting myself through college. Things have been hard sometimes, but I am glad not to be that spoiled kid any more.

Topic sentence: In the three years since my parents' divorce, I have changed from a spoiled brat to a reasonably normal college student.

1. Before the divorce

   a. _____

   b. _____

2. After the divorce

   a. _____

   b. _____

Complete the following statement: This paragraph uses a _____ method of development.

Good and Bad Horror Movies

A good horror movie is easily distinguished from a bad one. A good horror movie, first of all, has both male and female victims. Both sexes suffer terrible fates at the hands of monsters and maniacs. Therefore, everyone in the audience has a chance to identify with the victim. Bad horror movies, on the other hand, tend to concentrate on women, especially half-dressed or seemingly sluttish ones. These movies are obviously prejudiced against half the human race. Second, a good horror movie inspires compassion for its characters. For example, the audience will feel sympathy for the victims of Freddy or Dracula, and also for Freddy or Dracula, who are themselves shown to be sad victims of fate. In contrast, a bad horror movie encourages feelings of aggression and violence in viewers. For instance, in the <u>Halloween</u> or <u>Scream</u> films, the murder scenes use the murderer's point of view. The effect is that the audience stalks the victims along with the killer and feels the same thrill he does. Finally, every good horror movie has a sense of humour. In <u>Dracula</u>, the Count says meaningfully at dinner, "I don't drink wine," as he stares at Jonathan Harker's juicy neck. Humour provides relief from the horror and makes the characters more human. A bad horror movie, though, is humourless and boring. One murder is piled on top of another, and the characters are just cardboard figures. Bad horror movies may provide cheap thrills, but the good ones touch people's emotions and lives forever.

Topic sentence: A good horror movie is easily distinguished from a bad one.

1. Kinds of victims

   a. _____

   b. _____

2. Effect on audience

   a. _____

   b. _____

3. Tone

a. _____

b. _____

Complete the following statement: This paragraph uses a _____ method of development.

ADDITIONAL PARAGRAPHS TO CONSIDER

Read these additional paragraphs of comparison or contrast, and then answer the questions that follow.

My Broken Dream

[1]When I became a police officer in Hamilton, the job was not as I had dreamed it would be. [2]I began to dream about being a police officer at about age ten. [3]I could picture myself wearing a handsome blue uniform and having an impressive-looking badge. [4]I could also picture myself driving a powerful patrol car through town and seeing everyone stare at me with envy. [5]But most of all, I dreamed of working on a SWAT team using all the equipment that "TV cops" use. [6]I just knew everyone would be proud of me. [7]I could almost hear the guys on the block saying, [8]"Boy, Devon made it big. Did you hear he's a cop?" [9]I dreamed of leading an exciting life, solving big crimes, and meeting lots of people. [10]I just knew that if I became a cop everyone in town would look up to me. [11]However, when I actually did become a police officer, I soon found out that the reality was different. [12]My first disappointment came when I was sworn in and handed a well-used, baggy uniform. [13]My disappointment continued when I was given a badge that looked like something pulled out of a cereal box. [14]I was assigned bicycle patrol duty and given a used bike. [15]I got to wear navy Bermuda shorts and knee socks while dodging traffic. [16]Disappointment seemed to continue. [17]I soon found out that I was not the envy of all my friends. [18]When I cycled through town, they acted as if they had not seen me. [19]I was told I was crazy doing this kind of job, by people I thought would look up to me. [20]My job was not as exciting as I had dreamed it would be either. [21]Instead of solving robberies and murders every day, I found that I spent a great deal of time comforting a local resident because a neighbourhood dog had watered his favourite bush.

Two Views on Toys

[1]There is a vast difference between children and adults where presents are concerned. [2]First, there is the matter of taste. [3]Adults pride themselves on taste, while children ignore the matter of taste in favour of things that are fun. [4]Adults, especially grandparents, pick out educational and tasteful toys that go unused,

while children love the trendy playthings advertised on television. ⁵Then, of course, there is the matter of money. ⁶The new games on the market today are a case in point. ⁷Have you ever tried to lure a child away from some expensive game in order to get him or her to play with an old-fashioned game or toy? ⁸Finally, there is a difference between an adult's and a child's idea of what is educational. ⁹Adults, filled with memories of their own childhoods, tend to be fond of the written word. ¹⁰Today's children, on the other hand, concentrate on anything electronic. ¹¹These things mean much more to them than to adults. ¹²Next holiday season, examine the toys that adults choose for children. ¹³Then look at the toys the children prefer. ¹⁴You will see the difference.

Questions

About Unity

1. Which sentence in "My Broken Dream" does not directly add to the support for its topic? (*Write the sentence number.*)

    _____

2. Which paragraph has a topic sentence that is too broad?

    _____

About Support

3. Which paragraph contains virtually no specific details?

    _____

4. Which paragraph do you feel offers the most effective details?

    _____

About Coherence

5. What method of development (one side at a time or point by point) is used in "My Broken Dream"?

    _____

6. What transitional words are used in "Two Views on Toys"?

    _____

DEVELOPING A COMPARISON OR CONTRAST PARAGRAPH

Development through Prewriting

Randi, the author of "Last Dance," had no trouble thinking of a topic for her comparison or contrast paragraph.

"My communications instructor said, 'You might compare or contrast two individuals, jobs you've had, or places you've lived,'" Randi said. "Then he added,

'Or you might compare or contrast your expectations of a situation with the reality.' My friends and I had just been talking about high-school dances, and no one could remember a good experience. My expectations for my grade twelve formal were so different from the reality! I thought it would be the high point of my last year, but instead it was a total disaster."

Because she likes to think visually, Randi started her preparations for her paragraph by clustering. She found this a helpful way to "see" the relationships between the points she was developing. Her diagram looked like this:

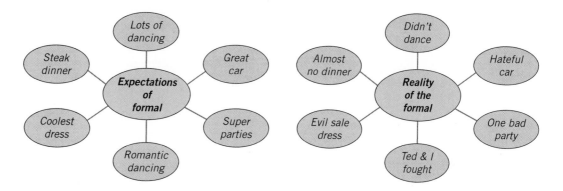

Taking a detail first from the "Expectations" part of the diagram, then from the "Reality" part of the diagram, then another from "Expectations," and so on, Randi began to write her paragraph using the point-by-point format.

> My graduation dance was nothing like I expected. First of all, I expected to be wearing a beautiful dress that my aunt would make for me. But because she couldn't finish it in time, I had to buy a cheesy one on sale at the last minute. Second, I thought I'd have a wonderful romantic evening with my boyfriend. But we'd been fighting a few days earlier and by the time the formal came around we were barely speaking. I thought we'd have a great time stopping in at lots of parties before the dance, too, but we went to only one—a really dull one—and I left with an upset stomach.

Randi stopped there, because she wasn't satisfied with the way the paragraph was developing. "I wanted the reader to really picture the way I had imagined that last dance, and I didn't like interrupting that picture with the nasty reality of the evening. I wanted to show the dream, then the reality. So I decided to try the one side-at-a-time approach instead." Here is Randi's first draft.

> My graduation dance was nothing like I expected. I imagined myself wearing a beautiful, expensive-looking dress that my aunt would make. I thought my boyfriend and I would have a wonderful romantic evening together. We'd dance all through the night and we would cruise around in Ted's brother's

> hot new Audi. We would stop in at a lot of the best of the pre-dance parties, I thought, and we'd have an excellent steak dinner at the club. But instead my uncle Pete had a gallbladder attack that they thought might be a heart attack, and my aunt went to the hospital with him instead of finishing my dress. I had to run to the mall at the last minute and buy the most pathetic dress that nobody else had wanted off the sale rack. Ted and I had been fighting for days. Because he played minor-league hockey and they were in playoffs and he had a part-time job, too, we didn't have much time together and he still wanted to go out weekends with the boys. So by the night of the dance we were hardly speaking to each other. We went to only one really dull party before the dance and I left it feeling sick. And the room at the club where the dance was held was so crowded that I hardly got anything to eat and it was only a buffet anyway. Because we were angry at each other, we didn't dance at all. And instead of his brother's luxury car, we ended up in Ted's friend Lou's stripped-down stock car.

Development through Revising

Randi's instructor reviewed the in-class first drafts of students who wanted his feedback. Here are his comments on Randi's work.

> *All this is very promising and full of details, but some of those details are out of order—you mention the pre-dance parties after the dance itself. Be sure to follow the evening's sequence of events.*
>
> *You need more descriptive details of some of the important issues. For instance, what was that "beautiful" dress supposed to look like, and why was the one you ended up with "pathetic"?*
>
> *You've got some unnecessary information in here: for example, the details of your uncle's illness. Everything in your paragraph should support your topic sentence.*

Taking her instructor's suggestions (and remembering a few more details she wanted to include), Randi wrote the version of her paragraph that appears on page 212.

WRITING A COMPARISON OR CONTRAST PARAGRAPH

How to Write a Comparison or Contrast Paragraph

1) An effective comparison or contrast paragraph examines two subjects that have some relationship to each other and examines the same specific aspects of each subject. Do your two subjects share a common quality or category so you can find points or bases on which to compare or contrast them? Can you focus your two-part topic enough to create a *limited* comparison or contrast paper that addresses specific points about both your subjects?

2) When prewriting for a comparison or contrast paper, divide your document into two columns: one for each side of your comparison or contrast. List or freewrite for one side (or for one of your subjects) in one column, and for your other side in the other column.

3) Decide whether your paragraph will compare or contrast either both sides of your subject or both of your subjects. Prewrite, using the two column method, to accumulate enough details for both sides of your paper. Then revise your prewriting to be sure one side's points of comparison or contrast have "matching" points for the other side. Eliminate any details or points that cannot apply to both sides.

4) Decide which method of development best suits your subject: one side at a time, or point by point. Set up your outline to reflect the format you choose. (See the outlines for the two paragraphs on page 214 for examples of both.) Begin your outline by stating your reason for making a comparison or contrast, and state this point, as well as whether you will compare or contrast your two sides, in a trial topic sentence. In the body of your outline, create subtopics or groupings for your major points of comparison or contrast. Under each subtopic (base for comparison or contrast), list details for each side.

5) As you create drafts based on your outline, be sure to use transitional words and phrases (see page 224) appropriate to comparing or contrasting to assist your readers and to clarify the point your paragraph will make.

6) Be sure to write a conclusion that reaffirms the point of your comparison or contrast, based on the information your paragraph has presented.

- - - - - **Writing Assignment 1**

Write a comparison or contrast paragraph on one of the topics below.

Two holidays	Two jobs
Two instructors	Two characters in the same TV show
Two children	Two homes
Two kinds of eaters	Two neighbourhoods
Two drivers	Two computer games
Two PDAs (Personal Digital Assistants)	Two cars
Two members of a team	Two friends
Two singers or groups	Two crises
Two pets	Two bosses or supervisors
Two parties	Two magazines

Prewriting

a Choose your topic, the two subjects you will write about.

b Decide whether your paragraph will *compare* the two subjects—discuss their similarities—or *contrast* them—discuss their differences. Students most often choose to write about differences. For example, you might write about how a musical group you enjoy differs from a musical group you dislike. You might discuss important differences between two employers you have had or between two neighbourhoods you have lived in. You might contrast a job you have had in a factory with a job you've had as a receptionist.

c Write a direct topic sentence for your paragraph. Here's an example: "My job in a car-parts factory was very different from my job as a receptionist."

d Come up with at least three strong subtopics to support your topic sentence. If you are contrasting two jobs, for example, your points might be that they differed greatly (1) in their physical settings, (2) in the skills they required, and (3) in the people they brought you into contact with.

e Use your topic sentence and subtopics to create a basic outline for your paragraph. Leave lots of space under each point you list. For the jobs paragraph, the outline might start out like this.

Topic sentence: My job in a car-parts factory was very different from my job as a receptionist.

1. The jobs differed in physical setting.
2. The jobs differed in the skills required.
3. The jobs differed in the people they brought me into contact with.

---

f Under each of your subtopics, jot down as many details as occur to you. Don't worry yet about whether the details all fit perfectly or whether you will be able to use them all. Your goal is to generate a wealth of material to draw on. An example:

Topic Sentence: My job in a car-parts factory was very different from my job as a receptionist.

1. The jobs differed in physical setting
   Factory loud and dirty
   Office clean and quiet
   Factory full of machines, hunks of metal, tools
   Office full of desks, computers, files
   Factory smelled like oil
   Office smelled like new carpet
   Windows in factory too high and dirty to look out of
   Office had big windows along walls

> 2. The jobs differed in the skills and behaviour they required
>   Factory required physical strength and speed
>   Office needed mental activity
>   Didn't need to be polite in factory
>   Had to be polite in office
>   Didn't need to think much for myself in factory
>   Constantly had to make decisions in the office
> 3. The jobs differed in the people they brought me into contact with
>   In factory, worked with same crew every day
>   In office, saw a constant stream of new customers
>   Most co-workers in factory had high school or less
>   Many co-workers and clients in office well educated
>   Co-workers in factory spoke a lot of different languages
>   Heard mostly English in the office

g Decide which format you will use to develop your paragraph: one side at a time or point by point. Either is acceptable; it is up to you to decide which you prefer and which suits your subject better. The important thing is to be consistent: whichever format you choose, be sure to use it throughout the entire paragraph.

h Write the first draft of your paragraph.

Revising

Put your writing away for a day or so. You will return to it with a fresh perspective and a better ability to critique what you have done.

Reread your work with these questions in mind:

- Does my topic sentence make it clear what two things I am comparing or contrasting?
- Have I compared or contrasted the subjects in at least three important ways?
- Have I provided specific details that effectively back up my subtopics?
- If I have chosen the point-by-point format, have I consistently discussed a point about one subject, then immediately discussed the same point about the other subject before moving on to the next point?
- If I have chosen the one-side-at-a-time format, have I discussed every point about one of my subjects, then discussed the same points in the same order about the second subject?
- Have I used appropriate transitions, such as *first, in addition, also,* and *another way* or any reasonable choices from the box below, to help readers follow my train of thought?
- Have I carefully proofread my paragraph, using the list on the inside front cover of this book, and corrected all sentence-skills mistakes, including spelling errors?

Continue revising your work until you can answer yes to all these questions.

Transitions for Comparison or Contrast Papers	
Comparison Transitions	**Contrast Transitions**
just as, just like	on the other hand
like, likewise	in contrast to, contrasting
similarly, in a similar way, similar to	as opposed to, in opposition to
also, too, again	although, even though
moreover, further, furthermore	whereas, while but, still, nonetheless, nevertheless, yet

● ● ● ● **Writing Assignment 2**

Write a paragraph in which you compare or contrast your life in the real world with your life in an imagined "perfect world." Your paragraph may be humorous or serious.

Prewriting

a Because your "real life" and "perfect world" are too broad for a paragraph, decide on three specific areas to focus on. Select any of the areas below, or think of others yourself.

Work	Physical location	Possessions
Money	Personal appearance	Housing
Romance	Friends	Talents

b Write the name of one of your three areas (for example, "Work") across the top of a page. Divide the page into two columns. Label one column "Real Life" and the other column "Perfect World." Under "Real Life," write down as many details as you can think of that describe your real-life work situation. Under "Perfect World," write down details that describe what your perfect work life would be like. Repeat the process on separate pages for your other two major areas.

c Write a topic sentence for your paragraph. Here is an example: "In my perfect world, my life would be quite different in the areas of work, money, and housing."

d Decide which approach you will take: one side at a time or point by point.

e Write a quick outline that reflects the format you have selected. The outline for a point-by-point format would look like this.

Topic sentence: In my perfect world, my life would be quite different in the areas of work, money, and housing.

1. Work
   a. Real-life work
   b. Perfect-world work

> 2. Money
>   a. Real-life money
>   b. Perfect-world money
> 3. Housing
>   a. Real-life housing
>   b. Perfect-world housing

The outline for a one-side-at-a-time format would look like this.

> Topic sentence: In my perfect world, my life would be quite different in the areas of work, money, and housing.
>
> 1. Real life
>   a. Work
>   b. Money
>   c. Housing
> 2. Perfect world
>   a. Work
>   b. Money
>   c. Housing

f Drawing from the three pages of details you generated in step *b*, complete your outline by jotting down your strongest supporting details for each point. Also provide specific examples.

g Write the first draft of your paragraph.

Revising

Reread your paragraph, then show it to a friend who will give you fair feedback. You should both review it with these questions in mind:

- Does the topic sentence make it clear what three areas of your life are being compared or contrasted?
- Does the paragraph follow a consistent format: point by point or one side at a time?
- Does the paragraph provide specific details that describe both the "real life" and the "perfect world"?
- Does the paragraph include transitional words and phrases that make it easy to follow?
- Have all the sentence-skills mistakes, including spelling errors, been corrected?

Continue revising your work until you and your reader can answer yes to all these questions.

Writing Assignment 3

Write a contrast paragraph on one of the topics below.

Neighbourhood stores versus a shopping mall
Driving on an expressway versus driving on side roads
Shift versus *Wired* (or any other two popular magazines)
Working parents versus stay-at-home parents
Last year's fashions versus this year's
Shopping in stores versus shopping online
Hip hop versus R&B, electronica, or another music style
News in a newspaper versus news on television or online
Yesterday's toys versus today's
One Canadian TV series versus a similar U.S. network series
"Winning" locker room after a game versus "losing" locker room
Ad on television versus ad (for the same product) in a magazine
Your values versus those of your parents and their generation
Your experience in one country versus your experience in Canada.

Follow the directions for prewriting and revising in Writing Assignment 2.

Writing Assignment 4

You have volunteered to contribute a monthly column to the students' section of your college's website. You are asked to post on articles giving helpful advice and information about various issues of interest to your peers. This month's column is dedicated to first-semester students.

Write a column comparing or contrasting *specific aspects* of two sides of one of the following subjects:

- life as a first-semester college student versus life as a working person (*or* a high-school student or other option)
- issues faced by the "mature student" versus those faced by the "just-out-of-high-school student"

Writing Assignment 5

Television talk shows share certain features, but they also differ in significant ways. Write a paragraph contrasting two talk shows. In preparation, watch two different talk shows, taking some notes on various aspects of the shows. Then arrange the details of your notes into a few categories, such as the performance of the hosts, the types of guests, and the behaviour of their audiences. Use your notes to help you decide on a point of view to take in your topic sentence, which might be similar to this one.

While _____ (*name of show*) aims to help its viewers,

_____ (*name of other show*) is more interested in satisfying viewers'

desire for dramatic conflict.

Once you decide on your topic sentence, use only those details that support it. Then decide which method of organization you will use, and prepare your outline. Since readers will focus mainly on your subjects and contrasts, write in the third person. Be sure to use transition words and to edit your next-to-final draft carefully.

REVIEWING THE LEARNING OUTCOMES FOR COMPARISON OR CONTRAST WRITING

After completing one of the writing assignments in this chapter, review your work to see how well it meets the following tests.

✓ Does your paragraph compare or contrast two sides of an idea or two subjects that have a logical reason to be considered together? Does a worthwhile point emerge from the activity of comparing or contrasting the two parts of your topic?

✓ Do you open with a topic sentence that states (1) both parts of your subject, (2) your intention to either compare or contrast, and (3) the point your paragraph makes by comparing or contrasting your two subjects?

✓ Have you carefully and consistently used the method most appropriate to your subject

matter? If you have many specific details on each side, have you used the point-by-point format? If you wished to pursue each side in some depth, have you used the one-side-at-a-time format?

✓ Within either format, are your points of comparison or contrast and your supporting details for each relatively equal and balanced for both sides or both subjects?

✓ Do you conclude with a summing-up of the points you have made in your paragraph and an indication of how these points reaffirm and strengthen your main point?

Visit the *English Skills with Readings: Examining Paragraphs* Online Learning Centre at www.mcgrawhill.ca/olc/langan to access self-quizzes, internet-based questions and research skills, web resources, and other learning and study tools.

Chapter 13

Defining a Term

By working through this chapter's activities and completing one or more of its writing assignments, you will write a definition paragraph that

- sets its subject in an appropriately focused category of similar subjects and then sets its subject apart from other members of that category with adequate explanations of how the subject differs from them;

- begins with a topic sentence placing the subject in its category, setting out the subject as somehow unique, and indicating the relative degree of formality or objectivity involved in the definition to follow;

- offers at least three subtopics (or one extended subtopic) to clarify and limit the meaning of its subject; such points may be examples, brief anecdotes, or comparisons or contrasts with other closely related concepts;

- offers meanings appropriate both to the subject and to the needs of the reader for either an objective or a personal and subjective definition; and

- concludes with a summary of the meaning of the term and its significance, based on what has been stated in the paragraph.

Defining is essential to clear communication. Unless people agree on what a speaker or writer means by a given term, misunderstandings occur, and communication may fail. Definition paragraphs explain the meaning of some term or concept; they are forms of extended definitions—extended beyond the limited definitions found in dictionaries. Although a paragraph defining some concrete or abstract term may initially use elements of a dictionary definition, such a paragraph's purpose is to state fully the writer's sense of that term's meaning. The writer's task, in defining, is to do three things: (1) to *classify* the subject appropriately in terms of other items of its type, (2) to *make specific* his or her explanation of the subject's meaning by limiting that meaning, and (3) to offer meanings *relevant to the needs of the readers* of the paragraph.

Every day we offer informal definitions to explain what we mean by a particular term. We may say, "Mario is an anxious person." Then, without pausing, we try to be more exact about what we mean by *anxious*. We expand on our definition by giving *examples:* "He's always worrying about the future. Yesterday he was talking about how many bills he'll have this year." Or we offer a *story* to show Mario's anxiety in a specific circumstance. Or perhaps we may *compare or contrast* Mario's anxiety with what we feel in similar situations. We even describe the stages in the *process* by which Mario became so anxious. Our aim is to *set limits* around exactly what we mean by *anxious* in the *context of our conversation,* as opposed to what a dictionary may mean by *anxious* or what a psychologist may mean by the term. Even in ordinary conversations, we use the same assortment of methods for defining that we use in writing definition papers.

The word *definition,* as derived from its Latin origin, refers to putting "fines," or limits, around a subject. This boundary-setting happens every time you define any subject. You will work with and create definitions for many purposes in your life; as language and situations change, so does the way words are used. Misunderstandings may be remedied quickly in conversation, but there is little tolerance for misunderstanding or not knowing a term in career contexts. The growth of technology has obviously increased the need for definitions of new words and of existing words with new meanings; business constantly creates its own terminologies, and careers in human and social services rely on precise definitions for terms in reports and studies.

In this section, you will be asked to write a paragraph in which you define a term. The two student paragraphs below are examples of definition writing. Read them, and then answer the questions that follow.

PARAGRAPHS TO CONSIDER

Luck

[1]Luck is putting $1.75 into a vending machine and getting the money back with your snacks. [2]It is an instructor's decision to give a retest on a test where you first scored thirty. [3]Luck refers to moments of good fortune that happen in everyday life. [4]It is not going to the dentist for two years and then going and finding out that you do not have any cavities. [5]It is calling up a plumber to fix a leak on a day when the plumber has no other work to do. [6]Luck is finding a used car for sale at a good price at exactly the time when your car rolls its last kilometre. [7]It is driving into a traffic bottleneck and choosing the lane that winds up moving most rapidly. [8]Luck is being late for work on a day when your boss arrives later than you do. [9]It is having a new checkout aisle at the supermarket open up just as your cart arrives. [10]The best kind of luck is winning a new TV set with a raffle ticket for which you paid only a quarter.

Disillusionment

[1]Disillusionment is the feeling of having one of our most cherished beliefs stolen from us. [2]I learned about disillusionment first-hand the day Mr. Khalid, our grade eight teacher, handed out the marks on our class biology projects. [3]I had worked hard to assemble what I thought was the best insect collection any school had ever seen. [4]For weeks, I had set up homemade traps around our house, in the woods, and in vacant lots. [5]At night, I would stretch a white sheet between two trees, shine a lantern on it, and collect the night-flying insects that gathered there. [6]With my own money, I had bought killing jars, insect pins, gummed labels, and display boxes. [7]I carefully arranged related insects together, with labels listing each scientific name and the place and date of capture. [8]Slowly and painfully, I processed and printed the report that accompanied my project at the Moose Jaw school science fair. [9]In contrast, my friend Michael did almost nothing for his project. [10]He had his father, a doctor, build an impressive maze complete with live rats and a sign that read, "You are the trainer." [11]A person could lift a little plastic door, send a rat running through the maze, and then hit a button to release a pellet of rat food as a reward. [12]This exhibit turned out to be the most popular one at the fair. [13]I felt sure that our teacher would know that Michael could not have built it, and I was certain that my hard work would be recognized and rewarded. [14]Then the marks were finally handed out, and I was crushed. [15]Michael had an A+, but my mark was a B. [16]I suddenly realized that honesty and hard work don't always pay off in the end. [17]The idea that life is not fair hit me with such force that I felt sick. [18]I will never forget that moment.

Questions

About Unity

1. Which paragraph places its topic sentence within the paragraph rather than, more appropriately, at the beginning?

    _____

2. Which sentence in "Disillusionment" is somewhat repetitive and might be revised for paragraph unity? (*Write the sentence number here.*) _____

About Support

3. Which paragraph develops its definition through a series of short examples?

    _____

4. Which paragraph develops its definition through a single extended example?

    _____

About Coherence

5.   Which paragraph uses emphatic order, saving its best detail for last?

_____

6.   Which paragraph uses time order to organize its details?

_____

Further Insight—Concrete or abstract

A definition paragraph generally extends an explanation of a *thing*, or *noun*. How that noun will be defined and described, though, depends upon whether it *concrete* or *abstract*.

Concrete terms will be perceived through the senses. List the different kinds of concrete examples you can find for each of these:

Sight	**Hearing**	**Touch**	**Taste**	**Smell**
Niagara Falls	Buzzing	Sandpaper	Pizza	Burnt toast

Abstract terms are ideas and concepts, but have no physical properties. We may understand them well in specific contexts, but their meanings may be relative to a particular use. Consider the following *abstract* concepts, and what specific acts or attitudes may be indicated for each situation.

	A Family	**A Classroom**	**A Workplace**	**A Country**	**Commitment**
Love	Saving up to buy my brother a hockey helmet	Helping your best friend to study for a programming exam	Staying late to finish the decorations for the retirement banquet	Attending Canada Day activities	Continuing to coach girl's soccer even when her daughter went away to college
Neglect					
Equality					
Creativity					
Persistence					

Note: Both of the paragraphs to consider—"Luck" and "Disillusionment"—define abstract concepts.

Another Definition Paragraph

The following is a definition paragraph written by a student, to explain the traditional concept of the word *awesome*.

> Awesome, in its traditional sense, means "to fill a person with a sense of incredible wonder," or awe. Despite popular usage, awesome does not mean "cool"; in fact, the meaning could more correctly be considered as hot. This

awesome is like the coursing of your blood through your veins as you watch the incredible fury of the tides rushing through the Bay of Fundy. You can almost feel the tides roiling as much water as all the rivers in the world through a tiny cragged straight, to form the highest tides in the world. Awesome means inspiring, just as the endless peaks of the Rocky Mountains, one after the other, each nodding a white-tonsured cap, urge you onward to the crystal skies. Awesome means deep, unfathomable, or more meaningful than humans can expect to understand. It can describe the sheets of ice slipping from the polar fields, melting soundlessly into the churning oceans. Awesome means so much when it invokes the power it deserves. So, if you use this little word with all its strength, well, that's awesome.

DEVELOPING A DEFINITION PARAGRAPH

Development through Prewriting

When Thuyen, a biochemistry student and the author of "Disillusionment," started working on her assignment, she did not know what she wanted to write about. Not sure of a topic, she looked over her notes from that day's class. Her instructor had listed some terms, saying, "Maybe you could focus on what one of these words has meant in your own life." Thuyen scanned the words she had copied down: *honesty, faith, betrayal, disillusionment* . . . "When I got to the word *disillusionment*, my grade eight science fair flashed into my mind," Thuyen said. "That was a bitter experience that definitely taught me what disillusionment was all about."

Because the science fair had occurred years before, Thuyen had to work to remember it clearly. She decided to try questioning herself to come up with the details of what really had happened. Here are the questions Thuyen asked herself and the answers she wrote.

When did I learn about disillusionment?
When I was in grade eight

Where did it happen?
At the school science fair

Who was involved?
Me, Michael Schmidt and his father, and Mr. Khalid

What happened?
I had worked really hard on my insect collection. Michael had done almost nothing but he had a rat maze that his father had built. I got a B on my project while Michael got an A.

Why was the experience so disillusioning?
I thought my hard work and my interest would be rewarded. I was sure Mr. Khalid would know that I had put far more effort into my project than Michael had. When he won, I learned that cheating can pay off and honest work isn't always recognized.

> <u>How did I react?</u>
> I felt sick to my stomach. I wanted to confront Mr. Khalid and Michael and make them see how unfair the grades were. But I knew I'd just look like a whiner, so I didn't do anything.
>
> <u>Based on this experience, how would I define disillusionment?</u>
> It's finding out that something you really believed in isn't true.

Drawing from the ideas she came up with in her self-questioning, Thuyen wrote an outline, then the following first draft.

> Disillusionment is finding out that one of your most important beliefs isn't true. I used to want to be an entomologist, and science was always my favourite subject. In my grade eight science fair, I learned all about disillusionment. I had worked very hard on my project, an insect collection. I was sure it would get an A. I had worked so hard on it, even spending nights outside making sure it was very good. My friend Michael also did a project, but he barely worked on his at all. Instead, he had his father build a maze for a rat to run through. The trainer lifted a little plastic door to let the rat into the maze, and if it completed the maze, the trainer could release a food pellet for it to eat. It was a nice project, but the point is that Michael hadn't made it. He just made things like the banner that hung over it. Mr. Khalid was our science teacher. He gave Michael an A+ and me just a B. So that really taught me about disillusionment.

Development through Revising

Thuyen's instructor divided the class up into groups of three. The groups reviewed each member's paragraph. Thuyen was grouped with Stefanie and Trevor. After reading through Thuyen's paragraph, the group had a discussion.

"My first reaction is that I want to know more about your project," said Stefanie. "You say a lot about Michael's, but not much about your own. What was so good about it? Is an entomologist somebody who studies bugs? You should define any specific terminology you use that some people won't know. You also need to *show* us why your project was so incredible, not just *tell* us. Also, you say how hard you worked, but you don't show us how hard."

"Yeah, you're right," said Thuyen. "I remember my project clearly, but somebody reading this has to know what it was like and how much effort went into it."

Trevor said, "I like your topic sentence, but when I finished the paragraph, I wasn't sure what 'important belief' you'd learned wasn't true. What was it that you believed in so much?"

Thuyen thought a minute. "I was brought up to believe that honest hard work would always be rewarded. I found out it doesn't always happen that way, and that cheaters can actually win."

Trevor nodded. "So put that in your paper."

Stefanie added, "I know I'd have been really angry if I got that mark. So I think you should say how you felt after you saw your mark. If you don't explain that a bit, your paragraph ends abruptly."

Thuyen agreed with her classmates' suggestions. After she had gone through several revisions, she produced the paragraph that appears on page 230.

WRITING A DEFINITION PARAGRAPH

How to Write a Definition Paragraph

1) Looking at the subject for your paragraph, first ask yourself this question: Is your subject a *concrete* thing or an *abstract* concept? Concrete objects, like dogs or computers, have precise basic (denotative) definitions, to which personal experience-based shadings (connotative descriptions) may be added. Abstract ideas like honour or ambition are defined almost completely according to personal interpretations and understandings of their meaning. Some terms occupy a "middle space" between the concrete and the abstract, like "an ideal employee."

2) Next, consider the degree of objectivity most suitable to defining your subject. Is your paragraph a personal definition of some abstract subject or quality best explained by your own experience with that quality, or is it an extended definition of some concrete subject where more objective details, even scientific or factual ones, are required? Although the methods for writing a definition are the same for both types of subjects, the tones, points of view, types of details, and needs of readers differ.

3) Prewrite to accumulate as many details as possible of any sort about your subject. As you prepare to create an outline for your paragraph, consider the methods that will best define your subject: examples, comparing or contrasting with other subjects of its type, brief anecdotes, or a description of how your subject works. Decide on a method of development for your definition and create an outline based on that method. Determine a logical order through which to draw your audience so that your message is coherent.

4) Write a topic sentence that places your subject in a logical category and includes at least one specific detail that distinguishes your subject. Include an indication of the nature and tone of your definition: subjective and personal, or objective and factual.

5) Be sure that the body of your definition truly clarifies the meaning of your subject and does not merely repeat itself or offer unclear synonyms as alternative definitions. Make sure that your examples or distinguishing details are vivid and logically connected. The details or support for your definition may also state what your subject is by setting out what it is not.

6) Conclude with a summation of your understanding of your term, and its significance.

● ● ● ● ● **Writing Assignment 1**

Write a paragraph that defines the term *Internet addict*. Base your paragraph on the topic sentence and three subtopics below.

Topic sentence: Internet addicts are people who will surf the Internet for as long as they can, rather than do anything else.

1) Internet addicts, first of all, will click on anything on the Internet, no matter how bad it is . . .

2) In addition, addicts surf the Internet more hours than normal people do . . .

3) Finally, addicts feel that the Internet is more important than other people or any other activities or events that might be going on . . .

Prewriting

a Generate as many examples as you can for each of the three qualities of an Internet addict. You can do this by asking yourself the following questions:

- What are some of the truly awful sites that I (or Internet addicts I know) browse through just because they are logged on to the Internet?
- What are some examples of the large amounts of time that I (or Internet addicts I know) spend surfing?
- What are some examples of ways that I (or Internet addicts I know) neglect people or give up activities in order to stay online?

Write down every answer you can think of for each question. At this point, don't think about writing full sentences or about grammar or spelling. Just get your answers down.

b Look over the list of examples you have accumulated. Select the strongest examples you have thought of. You should have at least two or three for each quality. If not, ask yourself the questions in step *a* again.

c Write out the examples you will use, this time expressing them in full, grammatically correct sentences. Look for possible comparisons or contrasts within your examples—these can be useful ways to limit and clarify a point. For example, how much time does an Internet addict spend online, compared with someone else?

d Start with the topic sentence and the three subtopics provided in the assignment. Fill in the examples you've generated to support each subtopic. You now have a very complete sentence-form outline, and you are ready to write a first draft of your paragraph.

Revising

Put your first draft away for as long as possible. When you come back to it, reread it critically, asking yourself these questions:

- Have I used the topic sentence and the three subtopics that were provided?
- Have I backed up each subtopic with at least two examples?
- Does each of my examples truly illustrate the point it backs up?

- Have I used appropriate transitional language (*another, in addition, for example, in contrast to*) to tie my thoughts together?
- Have I proofread my paragraph and corrected any sentence-skills errors, including spelling mistakes?

Keep revising your paragraph until you can answer yes to each question.

Writing Assignment 2

Our conversations are full of labels for people. These labels are a convenient kind of verbal shorthand, but how often do people know exactly what we mean by our terms? Write a paragraph that states your definition of what is meant by one of these labels. Each term refers to a certain kind of person.

Big-mouth	Clown	Pessimist
Charmer	Jellyfish	Hypocrite
Loser	Leader	Perfectionist
Lazybones	Nerd	Pack rat
Con artist	Good neighbour	Hard worker
Fair-weather friend	Optimist	Team player

Prewriting

a Write a topic sentence for your definition paragraph. This is a two-part process:

- First, place the term in a class, or category. For example, if you are writing about a certain kind of person, the general category is *person*. If you are describing a type of friend, the general category is *friend*.
- Second, describe what you consider the special feature or features that set your term apart from other members of its class. For instance, say what *kind* of person you are writing about or what *type* of friend.

In the following topic sentence, try to identify three things: the term being defined, the class it belongs to, and the special feature that sets the term apart from other members of its class.

A chocoholic is a person who craves chocolate.

The term being defined is *chocoholic*. The category it belongs to is *person*. The words that set *chocoholic* apart from any other person are *craves chocolate*.

Below is another example of a topic sentence for this assignment. It is a definition of a *whiner*. The class, or category, is underlined: a whiner is a type of person. The words that set the term *whiner* apart from other members of the class are double-underlined.

A whiner is a person who feels wronged by life.

In the following sample topic sentences, underline the class and double-underline the special features.

A clotheshorse is a person who needs new clothes to be happy.
The class clown is a student who gets attention through silly behaviour.
A worrywart is a person who sees danger everywhere.

b Develop your definition by using one of the following methods.
Example: Give several examples that support your topic sentence.
Extended example: Use one longer example to support your topic sentence.
Contrast: Support your topic sentence by showing what your term is *not*.
For instance, you may want to define a *fair-weather friend* by contrasting his or her actions with those of a true friend.

c Write an outline. Once you have created a topic sentence and decided how to develop your paragraph, write an outline. This step is especially important if you are using a contrast method of development.

d Write a first draft of your paragraph.

Revising

As you revise your paragraph, keep these questions in mind:

- Does my topic sentence (1) place my term in a class and (2) name some special features that set it apart from its class?
- Have I made a clear choice to develop my topic sentence through several examples, one extended example, or contrast?
- If I have chosen to illustrate my topic through contrast, have I consistently followed either a point-by-point or a one-side-at-a-time format?
- Have I used appropriate transitions (*another, in addition, in contrast, for example*) to tie my thoughts together?
- Is my paragraph free of sentence-skills errors, including spelling mistakes?

Continue revising until you can answer yes to all these questions.

● ● ● ● **Writing Assignment 3**

Write a paragraph that defines one of the abstract terms below.

Persistence	Responsibility	Fear
Rebellion	Insecurity	Arrogance
Sense of humour	Assertiveness	Conscience
Escape	Jealousy	Class
Danger	Nostalgia	Innocence
Curiosity	Gentleness	Freedom
Common sense	Depression	Violence
Family	Obsession	Shyness
Practicality	Self-control	

As a guide in writing your paper, use the suggestions for prewriting and revising in Writing Assignment

Defining an abstract term or concept requires you to select certain specific examples or circumstances that make your view of that term's meaning clear to your reader. Definition papers make use of many methods of paragraph development.

Here are several approaches to writing such a paper.

- Begin with an objective definition of your concept, then compare or contrast that meaning with your own specific experiences with or knowledge of that concept.
- Consider explaining what your concept or term means by using *negation;* explain what something is by stating clearly what it is *not* or need not be.
- Sometimes using an anecdote, or brief story, can vividly show an abstract quality in action.
- Dividing your abstract quality into different aspects or categories, with examples for each, often makes a broad concept clearer to readers.

Writing Assignment 4

Many issues are important, but complex, so need clear definition. A serious contemporary concern is *sustainability,* or living in a way that does not harm the environment. Write a paragraph about an aspect of *sustainability* by first defining the term, and then elaborating on three elements needed to acquire it. Organize your paragraph in one of these ways:

- Use a series of examples (see Chapter 9) of sustainable practices.
- Use comparison and contrast (see Chapter 7) to show differences between present unsustainable activities and preferable sustainable ones.
- Create a hypothetical home, business, or community and show how it emulates sustainable principles.

Using strategies described on the Online Learning Centre, research the topic of sustainability. Narrow down your findings to support the person or examples you have decided on.

Note: Do not simply write a series of general, abstract sentences that repeat and reword your definition. If you concentrate on your topic sentence and on providing specific support for it, you will avoid the common trap of getting lost in a maze of generalities.

Writing Assignment 5

At the place where you work, one employee has just quit, creating a new job opening. Since you have been working there for a while, your boss has asked you to write a job description of the position. That description, which is really a detailed definition of the job, will be sent to employment agencies. These agencies will be responsible for interviewing candidates. Choose any position you know about, and write a job description for it. First, give the purpose of the job, and then list its duties and responsibilities. Finally, give the qualifications for the position.

Here is a sample topic sentence for this assignment.

Purchasing department clerk is a <u>position</u> in which someone <u>provides a variety of services</u> to the purchasing-department managers.

In a paragraph with this topic sentence, the writer would go on to list and explain the various services the clerk must provide.

REVIEWING THE LEARNING OUTCOMES FOR DEFINITION WRITING

After completing any of the writing assignments in this chapter, review your work to see how well it meets the following tests.

✓ Does your paragraph open with a topic sentence that both places your subject to be defined in an appropriate category and sets it off from other members of that category?

✓ Does your topic sentence indicate your paper's tone and the degree of objectivity or subjectivity with which you will define your subject?

✓ Do you offer at least three subtopics and details for your definition of your subject? Are your points and details specific, and does each directly support your topic sentence's point about your subject?

✓ Have you used a method of development for your supporting material that is appropriate to the subject you define: examples, comparison or contrast, negation, or anecdote?

✓ Does your paper conclude with a summary of your meanings, a reminder of your topic sentence's point, and a suggestion of the significance of your definition?

Visit the *English Skills with Readings: Examining Paragraphs* Online Learning Centre at <u>www.mcgrawhill.ca/olc/langan</u> to access self-quizzes, internet-based questions and research skills, web resources, and other learning and study tools.

Chapter 14

Dividing and Classifying

By working through this chapter's activities and completing at least one of its writing assignments, you will write a classification and division paragraph that

- divides its subject according to a consistent classifying principle logically related to your purpose in analyzing that subject;

- arranges its categories or subject divisions in a sequence that best supports the point and purpose of the paper;

- begins with a topic sentence that states the paper's subject, the divisions of its subject, and your point in making those divisions;

- offers a balanced number of specific and adequate details for each subtopic or subject division; and

- concludes with a return to your subject as a whole and offers a closing thought based on your paragraph's examination of your subject divisions.

Dividing a subject into classes or categories occurs constantly in everyday life. People break groups of things or ideas into subgroups, based on some purpose or need, hoping to manage situations or understand ideas more easily. The process of dividing and classifying seeks to create order out of apparent confusion and often leads to decision making. Division and classification paragraphs imitate a natural human tendency to divide up a subject or to open it up and examine its parts according to some logical pattern.

If you were doing the laundry, you would probably separate the clothing into piles. If your purpose was to decide when to use bleach, you would sort all the whites into one pile and all the colours into another. If your purpose was to see how many types of washing cycles were needed, you might put all cottons in one pile, polyesters in another, silks in a third, and so on. Such ordinary processes of sorting according to various principles demonstrate how we organize and order our environment in order to make decisions.

Classifying and dividing are two separate and different processes. *Classifying* is the process of taking many things and separating them into categories or kinds. We generally classify to better manage or understand many things. Music stores classify CDs into many different genres such as hip hop, dance, electronica, and so on, so that customers can find the artists they enjoy. Librarians classify books into groups (novels, travel, health, etc.) to make them easier to find. Each category is defined through its adherence to specific characteristics, or *attributes*. The writing models and activities in this text are classified according to the type, or *mode*. *Dividing,* in contrast, is taking one thing and breaking it down into parts, or *components*. We often divide, or analyze, to better understand, teach, or evaluate something. For example, a botanist divides a tree into its parts to explain their functions. A music reviewer may analyze the elements of a band's performance—for example, the skill of the lead guitarist, rapport with the audience, songs chosen, and so on. Each paragraph that you write is divided into its component parts, such as the topic sentence, the supporting reasons, and the explanatory details.

In short, if you are classifying, you are sorting *numbers of things* into categories. If you are dividing, you are breaking *one thing* into several parts. It all depends on your purpose—you might classify flowers into various types or divide a single flower into its parts. Take note, though, that you must classify or divide according to three or more factors, as discussions of only two parts are considered to be *comparison* and *contrast*.

Division and classification activities are ongoing parts of your college and career communications tasks. Sorting a mass of consumers into demographic groups to examine and report on buying patterns; dividing components of a software program into categories to analyze their effectiveness: these involve the same set of structuring and analyzing skills.

In this chapter, you will be asked to write a paragraph in which you divide or classify a subject according to a single principle. To prepare for this assignment, first read the division and classification paragraphs below and then work through the questions and the activity that follow.

PARAGRAPHS TO CONSIDER

Studying for a Test

[1]Phase 1, often called the "no problem" phase, runs from the day the test is announced to approximately forty-eight hours before the dreaded exam is passed out. [2]During phase 1, the student is carefree, smiling, and kind to helpless animals and small children. [3]When asked by classmates if he or she has studied for the test yet, the reply will be an assured "No problem." [4]During phase 1, no actual studying takes place. [5]Phase 2 is entered two days before the test. [6]For example, if the test is scheduled for 9 a.m. Friday, phase 2 begins at 9 a.m. Wednesday.

[7]During phase 2, again, no actual studying takes place. [8]Phase 3, the final phase, is entered twelve hours before "zero hour." [9]This is the acute phase, characterized by sweaty palms, nervous twitches, and confused mental patterns. [10]For a test at nine o'clock on Friday morning, a student begins exhibiting these symptoms at approximately nine o'clock on Thursday night. [11]Phase 3 is also termed the "shock" phase, since the student is shocked to discover the imminent nature of the exam and the amount of material to be studied. [12]During this phase, the student will probably be unable to sleep and will mumble meaningless phrases like "$a^2 + c^2$." [13]This phase will not end until the exam is over. [14]If the cram session has worked, the student will fall gratefully asleep. [15]On waking up, he or she will be ready to go through the whole cycle again with the next test.

Three Kinds of Dogs

[1]A city walker will notice that most dogs fall into one of three categories. [2]First there are the big dogs, which are generally harmless and often downright friendly. [3]They walk along peacefully with their owners, their tongues hanging out and big goofy grins on their faces. [4]Apparently, they know they're too big to have anything to worry about, so why not be nice? [5]Second are the spunky medium-sized dogs. [6]When they see a stranger approaching, they go on alert status. [7]They prick up their ears, they raise their hackles, and they may growl a little, deep in their throats. [8]"I don't know you," they seem to be saying, "so be careful what you do." [9]Unless the walker confronts their owners, these dogs usually won't do anything more than threaten. [10]The third category is made up of the shivering, neurotic little yappy dogs whose shrill barks could shatter glass and whose needle-like little teeth are ready to sink into a friendly outstretched hand. [11]Strollers always wonder about these dogs: don't they know that anyone who really wanted to could pick them up in one hand and growl right back at them? [12]Apparently they do not, because of all the dogs a walker meets, these are the most irritating. [13]Such dogs are only one of the potential hazards a city walker meets.

Questions

About Unity

1. Which paragraph lacks a topic sentence?

_____

2. Which sentence in "Three Kinds of Dogs" should be eliminated in the interest of paragraph unity? (*Write the sentence number here.*) _____

About Support

3. Which of the three phases in "Studying for a Test" lacks specific details?

_____

About Coherence

4. Which paragraph uses time order to organize its details?

    _____

5. Which paragraph uses emphatic order to organize its details?

    _____

6. What words in the emphatic-order paragraph signal the most important
    detail?

    _____

● ● ● ● ● **Activity**

This activity will sharpen your sense of the classifying process.

Classification *always* divides items in a group according to some criterion,
or *principle of classification*. This principle is used both for *dividing* a
group into its members and for maintaining *unity* of the classifications. In
each of the following ten groups, cross out the one item that has not been
classified on the same basis as the other three. Also, indicate in the space
provided the single *principle of classification* used for the three items. Note
the examples.

Examples

Water
a. Cold
b. ~~Lake~~
c. Hot
d. Lukewarm
Unifying principle:
temperature

Household pests
a. ~~Mice~~
b. Ants
c. Roaches
d. Flies
Unifying principle:
insects

1. Eyes
    a. Blue
    b. Nearsighted
    c. Brown
    d. Hazel
    Unifying principle:

    _____

2. Mattresses
    a. Double
    b. Twin
    c. Queen
    d. Firm
    Unifying principle:

    _____

3. Zoo animals
    a. Flamingo
    b. Peacock
    c. Polar bear
    d. Ostrich
    Unifying principle:

    _____

4. Vacation
    a. Summer
    b. Holiday
    c. Seashore
    d. Weekend
    Unifying principle:

    _____

5. College classes
    a. Enjoy
    b. Dislike
    c. Tolerate
    d. Morning
    Unifying principle:

    _____

6. Wallets
    a. Leather
    b. Plastic
    c. Stolen
    d. Fabric
    Unifying principle:

    _____

7. Newspaper
    a. Wrapping garbage
    b. Editorials
    c. Making paper planes
    d. Covering floor while painting
    Unifying principle:

    _____

8. Music
    a. Metal
    b. Country
    c. Melodic
    d. R & B
    Unifying principle:

    _____

9. Exercise
    a. Running
    b. Swimming
    c. Gymnastics
    d. Fatigue
    Unifying principle:

    _____

10. Leftovers
    a. Cold chicken
    b. Feed to dog
    c. Reheat
    d. Use in a stew
    Unifying principle:

    _____

DEVELOPING A DIVISION AND CLASSIFICATION PARAGRAPH

Development through Prewriting

Adam walked home from his bus stop, thinking about the assignment to write a division and classification paragraph. As he strolled along his familiar route, his observations made him think of a few possibilities. "First I thought of writing about the businesses in my neighbourhood, dividing them into the kinds of customers they attract," he said. "When I stopped in at my favourite coffee place, I thought about dividing the people who hang out there. There is a group of men who sit with cups of espresso and play cards, and there are some students like me, but there didn't seem to be a clear third category and I wasn't sure two would be enough. As I continued walking home, I saw a dog walker with four dogs on a joined leash. Then I saw Mr. Kobielski with his big golden Lab and a lady with two nervous little dogs that acted as if they wanted to eat me, and I thought, 'Dogs! I can classify different kinds of dogs.'"

But how would he classify them? Thinking further, Adam realized that he thought of dogs as having certain personalities depending on their sizes. "I know there are exceptions, of course, but since this was going to be a comical paragraph, I thought it would be all right if I exaggerated a bit." He wrote down his three categories.

Big dogs
Medium-sized dogs
Small dogs

Under each division, he wrote down as many characteristics as he could think of.

<u>Big dogs</u>
    calm
    friendly
    good-natured
    lazy
    slow-moving
<u>Medium-sized dogs</u>
    spunky
    energetic
    ready for a challenge
    protective
    friendly if they know you
<u>Small dogs</u>
    nervous
    trembling
    noisy
    yappy
    snappy
    annoying

Adam then wrote a topic sentence: "Dogs seem to fall into three categories." Using that topic sentence and the rough outline he'd just produced, he wrote the following first draft.

Most dogs seem to fall into one of three categories. First there are the big slow-moving friendly dogs. They give the impression of being sweet and your best friend in the world. One example of this kind of dog is Lucy. She's a golden Lab belonging to a man in my neighbourhood. Lucy goes everywhere with Mr. Kobielski. She doesn't even need a leash but just follows him. Dogs like Lucy never bother you. She just lies at Mr. K's feet when he stops to talk to anyone. The guy who runs every day near here has a spunky medium-sized dog. Once the dog knows you he's friendly and even playful. But he's always on the lookout for a stranger who might mean trouble. For a dog who's not very big he can make himself look pretty fierce if he wants to. Then there are my least favourite kind of dogs. Little nervous yappy ones. My aunt used to have a Pomeranian like that. It smelled, too. It knew me for nine years and still went crazy shaking and yipping at me every time we met. She loved that dog but I can't imagine why. If I had a dog it would definitely come from category 1 or 2.

Development through Revising

Adam traded his first draft with a fellow student, Rachel, and asked her to give him feedback. Here are the comments Rachel wrote on his paper.

This is a change in point of view —you weren't using "you" before.

Is this a new category? That's not clear.

Not a sentence

You've gone from third person to "you" to "me."
Adam—I think you need to make your three categories clearer. Your first one is OK—"big dogs," which you say are friendly—but categories 2 & 3 aren't stated as clearly.

It's distracting to have your point of view change from third person to "you" to "we" and "me."

Since you're trying to divide and classify all dogs, I'm not sure it's a good thing to talk only about three individual dogs. This way it sounds like you're just describing those three dogs instead of putting them into groups.

Most dogs seem to fall into one of three categories. First there are the big slow-moving friendly dogs. They give the impression of being sweet and your best friend in the world. One example of this kind of dog is Lucy. She's a golden Lab belonging to a man in my neighbourhood. Lucy goes everywhere with Mr. Kobielski. She doesn't even need a leash but just follows him. Dogs like Lucy never bother you. She just lies at Mr. K's feet when he stops to talk to anyone. The guy who runs every day near here has a spunky medium-sized dog. Once the dog knows you he's friendly and even playful. But he's always on the lookout for a stranger who might mean trouble. For a dog who's not very big he can make himself look pretty fierce if he wants to. Then there are my least favourite kind of dogs. Little nervous yappy ones. My aunt used to have a Pomeranian like that. It smelled, too. It knew me for nine years and still went crazy shaking and yipping at me every time we met. She loved that dog but I can't imagine why. If I had a dog it would definitely come from category 1 or 2.

When Adam thought about Rachel's comments and reread his own paragraph, he agreed with what she'd written. "I realized it was too much about three particular dogs and not enough about the categories of dogs," he said. "I decided to revise it and focus on the three classes of dogs."

Adam then wrote the version that appears on page 242.

Further Insight—Division and classification in action

Division and classification are more than just methods to organize college papers. In fact, they are fundamental to the organization of almost any scientific, commercial, or professional concept. Before any task or study can be undertaken, it must be classified into its proper categories, or *domains*, and divided into its component parts.

Below are some areas where division and classification appear in authentic situations. Choose at least one to identify and describe according to its classification, or *category*, by describing its important features, or *attributes*. You will find that some are further divided into subcategories, with each becoming more specific than the previous.

- Canada is divided into twenty *ecozones*. To understand ecozones and identify your own, as well as any other of interest, see: http://www.ccea.org/ecozones/index.html
- How do you know if you are maintaining a healthy diet? Check your eating habits against the Canada Food Guide: http://www.hc-sc.gc.ca/fn-an/food-guide-aliment/order-commander/index-eng.php
- *Service Canada* identifies occupations by nine categories, or *sectors*. What can you find out about the employment prospects of the occupation that interests you? http://www.jobfutures.ca/noc/browse-occupations-noc.shtml

You may wish to investigate your own field of study to see how division and classification are used in its professional context.

WRITING A DIVISION AND CLASSIFICATION PARAGRAPH

How to Write a Division and Classification Paragraph

1) As you begin your prewriting, think about your reason or purpose for dividing up your subject. Consider your audience: who are your readers, and what would they want to know about your subject? What do you know about your subject, and how will that help you to divide and classify your subject into interesting and appropriate categories? Write down your purpose and subject in a trial topic sentence at the top of your prewriting page.

2) Divide your subject into at least three groups and set up your prewriting as three columns, one for each of your groups. Be sure that your groups all follow a single principle for classification. List, freewrite, or question until you have fairly equal numbers of details for each of your categories.

3) Read over and revise your prewriting to discover the clear *point* that emerges from your divisions and details: what are you saying about your subject? Edit any details that do not directly support your point as well as your purpose for dividing and classifying your subject. State your point about your subject, your purpose for dividing it as you do, and your divisions or categories in a topic sentence. Proceed to create a detailed outline, showing each division and its supporting details.

4) As you write your drafts based on your outline, be sure that each point and its support (each division or category and details) relate clearly to your subject as a whole and the point you make about your subject.

5) Conclude by refocusing your reader on your subject as a whole and on the significance of what your dividing and classifying has shown about your subject.

● ● ● ● **Writing Assignment 1**

Below are three possible division and classification writing assignments, along with possible divisions or subtopics. Choose *one* of them to develop into a paragraph.

Option A

Supermarket shoppers
1. Slow, careful
2. Average
3. Rushed, hurried

Option B

Eaters
1. Super-conservative
2. Typical
3. Adventurous

Option C

Attitudes toward money
1. Tight-fisted
2. Sometimes splurge
3. Spendthrift

Prewriting

a Begin by doing some prewriting on the topic you have chosen. For ten minutes, simply write down everything that comes into your head when you think about "types of shoppers," "attitudes toward money," or whichever option you choose. Don't worry about grammar, spelling, or organization—just write.

b Now that you've loosened up your brain a little, try some second-stage prewriting. Try asking yourself questions about the topic and writing down your answers. If you are writing about supermarket shoppers, for instance, you might ask questions like these.

How do the three kinds of shoppers pick out the items they want?
How many aisles will each type of shopper visit?
Which shoppers bring lists, calculators, coupons, cellphones, and so on?
How much time does it take each type of shopper to finish shopping?

Decide on an appropriate order for your details.

c Start a new document. Divide your page or screen into three columns (use the tables tool to do so on your computer). Label each column with one of your categories and fill in each column with appropriate items from your prewriting and questioning.

d Reread the material in your three columns. If some of the details you have written make you think of even better ones, add them. Select the details that best support your three points.

e Make decisions about the exact information you will use to support each point. Number the details within each classification *1, 2, 3*, and so on, in the order you will present them. To ensure a balanced paragraph, try to have roughly the same number of supporting details for each of your three classifications. Keep track of any sources you have used if you are using researched information.

f Restate your topic as a grammatically correct sentence. For example, if you are writing about eaters, your topic sentence might be "Eaters can be divided into three categories." Turn each of your three subtopics at the tops of your columns into a full sentence as well.

g Using your topic sentence and three supporting subtopic sentences and adding the details you have generated, write the first draft of your paragraph.

Revising

Put away your work for a day or so. Reread it with a critical eye, asking yourself these questions:

- Does my paragraph include a complete topic sentence and three subtopics?
- Have I backed up each subtopic or category with strong, specific details?
- Does my paragraph hold together in terms of unity, support, and coherence?
- Have I edited my paragraph and corrected sentence-skills mistakes, including spelling errors?

Continue revising your work until you can answer yes to all these questions.

Writing Assignment 2

Write a division and classification paragraph on one of the following topics.

Instructors	Drivers
Sports fans	Mothers or fathers
Eating places	College programs
Attitudes toward life	Presents
Commercials	Neighbours
Employers	Rock, pop, hip hop, or country singers
Jobs	Amusement parks or rides
Bars	Guests or company
Family get-togethers	Ways to get an A (or an F) in a course
Geography	On-line games

Prewriting

a Choose a single logical principle for dividing your subject. The first step in writing a division and classification paragraph is to divide your tentative topic into three reasonably complete parts. *Always use a single principle of division* when you form your three parts. For example, if your topic was "automobile drivers" and you divided them into slow, moderate, and fast drivers, your single basis for division would be "rate of speed." It would be illogical, then, to have as a fourth type "teenage drivers" (the basis of such a division would be "age") or "female drivers" (the basis of such a division would be "sex"). You could probably classify automobile drivers on the basis of age or sex or another division, for almost any subject can be analyzed in more than one way. What is important, however, is that *in any single paper you choose only one basis for division and stick to it.* Be consistent.

In "Studying for a Test," the writer divides the process of studying into three time phases: from the time the test is announced to forty-eight hours before the test; the two days before the test; and the final twelve hours before the test.

b Decide on your purpose for making such a decision. Remember that your topic sentence and your paragraph must *make a point*. It is not enough simply to *announce,* "There are three categories of shoes." *What point* do you wish to make by dividing up your topic? Do you wish to *explain* more about your topic, to *describe* each classification in greater detail? As part of your prewriting, aim at discovering your point. After prewriting about commercials, for example, you might decide that they mainly they are *annoying* in three distinct ways.

c Freewrite to accumulate details about your subtopics or divisions. Divide your page into three columns, each headed by the name of one of your divisions. List details for each division under your headings for ten minutes.

d Expand your topic into a fully stated topic sentence.

e At this point, you have all three elements of your paragraph: the topic sentence, the three main points or categories, and the details needed to support each point. You are ready to outline your paragraph.

To ensure a clear three-part division in your own paragraph, fill in the outline below before starting to write and make sure you can answer yes to the questions that follow. You should expect to do a fair amount of thinking before coming up with a logical plan.

Topic (subject, point, and divisions): _____

Three-part division of the topic and purpose: _____

1. _____

2. _____

3. _____

Is there a single basis of division for the three parts? _____

Is the division reasonably complete? _____

f Now expand your outline to include all your supporting details and write your first draft.

Revising

Do not attempt to revise your paragraph right away. Put it away for a while; if possible, leave it until the next day. When you reread it, try to be as critical of it as you would be if someone else had written it. As you go over the work, ask yourself these questions:

- Have I divided my topic into three distinct parts?
- Is each of those parts based on the same principle of division?
- Have I given each of those parts approximately equal weight? In other words, have I spent about the same amount of time discussing each part?

- Have I provided effective details to back up each of my three points?
- Does my paragraph satisfy the requirements of unity, coherence, and support?
- Have I edited my paragraph for sentence-skills mistakes, including spelling errors?

Continue revising until you are sure the answer to each question is yes.

Writing Assignment 3

Along with students from other colleges and universities in your area, you have been invited to be part of a panel speaking to graduating students at local high schools. You are to give your audience an overview of student life at your college, or at your campus of your college.

Write a script for a brief presentation that discusses aspects of "Life at _____ College." Divide the college experience into three categories you feel would be of use and interest to your audience. Be sure to (1) indicate your purpose in having chosen each aspect of college life you include in your presentation, and (2) include enough specifics about each aspect to help and inform students who have not yet had any experience of post-secondary education.

Writing Assignment 4

Write a review of a restaurant by analyzing its (1) food, (2) service, and (3) atmosphere. For this assignment, try to do some field research by visiting a restaurant. You may also wish to read restaurant reviews in a city newspaper. Take a notebook with you and write down observations about such elements as:

Type of food	Quantity of food you receive
Attitude of servers	Taste of the food
Efficiency of servers	Temperature of the food
Décor	Freshness of the ingredients
Level of cleanliness	How the food is presented (garnishes,
Noise level and music, if any	dishes, and so on)

Feel free to write about details other than those listed above. Just be sure each detail fits into one of your three categories: food, service, or atmosphere.

For your topic sentence, rate the restaurant by giving it from one to five stars, on the basis of your overall impression. Include the restaurant's name and location in your topic sentence. Here are some examples.

Borsalino, an Italian restaurant in North Vancouver, deserves three stars.
The Tim Hortons near Winston Churchill and Dundas barely merits two stars.
Frank's Noodle Parlour and Internet Café is a five-star favourite with downtown students.

REVIEWING THE LEARNING OUTCOMES FOR CLASSIFICATION AND DIVISION WRITING

After completing any of the writing assignments in this chapter, review your work to see how well it meets the following tests.

✓ Do the divisions in your paragraph's subject follow a consistent principle? Is this dividing principle logically related to your purpose in examining your subject? Does it lead to new and interesting information about your subject?

✓ Does your paragraph open with a topic sentence that states your purpose for dividing and classifying your subject, your point about doing so, and your categories or divisions?

✓ Do your divisions and supporting details appear in an order that makes your point most strongly?

✓ Do you have a balanced number of supporting details for each subject division, and is each detail closely related to your point about your subject?

✓ Does your conclusion remind readers of your opening point about your subject and reinforce whatever has been shown in examining your divisions of your subject?

LearningCentre Visit the *English Skills with Readings: Examining Paragraphs* Online Learning Centre at www.mcgrawhill.ca/olc/langan to access self-quizzes, internet-based questions and research skills, web resources, and other learning and study tools.

Chapter 15

Arguing a Position

By completing this chapter's activities and at least one of its writing assignments, you will write an argumentation paragraph that

• opens with a clear, definite, and well-crafted statement of the point to be argued or action to be undertaken through persuasion;

• shows in its opening section, based on some knowledge of its audience, possible counter-arguments and responses to them;

• uses a method of development most appropriately suited to stating logical and well-reasoned points and details to support the point to be argued;

• shows logic and knowledge of the specifics of its subject in its subtopics and details;

• argues its point and support cleanly, without slanting its point with emotional appeals, insulting its audience, or committing other logical fallacies; and

• concludes by reaffirming its point, as justified by the evidence presented in the paragraph.

An argument is a statement whose main purpose is to argue a point—to influence or persuade the thoughts of a reader, to encourage a change in opinion, or even to promote an action. Even though responding to persuasion or to an argument usually involves some degree of emotion, a paragraph arguing a position must, itself, be presented in a rational and controlled way. Logic, reason, valid evidence, knowing the interests of the audience, and being able to rebut other arguments, are the most potent tactics for effectively arguing a point.

Every day, on the basis of feelings, we make general statements of opinion. Occasionally, someone will greet one of our statements with the question "Why do you say that?" or "What are your reasons for saying that?" We can hope that our questioner then listens carefully as we work to muster our reasons, and wait to see if we really do have solid evidence to support our point of view. We may also feel grateful to the author for helping us think through our opinions. At times, the questioner may also present ideas with which we may not agree. We must then refute that position by constructing a logical counter-argument that makes the opposing one less valid.

The ability to advance sound and compelling arguments is an important skill in everyday life. We may use persuasion to get an extension on a term paper or convince an employer that we are the right person for a job. Understanding persuasion based on clear, logical reasoning can also help develop critical awareness of arguments advanced by advertisers, artists, editors, and politicians. The ability to assess and possibly oppose those views will help us to develop more critical views of the issues that confront us regularly. Argumentation skills are essential to college and career communications needs. Oral and written presentations are generally persuasive in nature, and proposals and reports often require competent use of the skills and techniques of argumentation and persuasion.

In this chapter, you will be asked to argue a position, persuade for a thought or action, and defend your argument with a series of solid reasons. You are in a general way doing the same thing—making a point and then supporting it—with all the paragraphs in this book. The difference is that here, in a more direct and formal manner, you will advance a point about which you feel strongly and seek to persuade others to agree with you.

PARAGRAPHS TO CONSIDER

"Teensploitation" Insults Teenagers

[1]Some people my age never question all the "teensploitation" movies and TV shows these days, but I believe they are insulting to the audiences they are made for. [2]One reason is that the creators of these movies and programs present unrealistic main characters, teenagers who are all good-looking, well off, and basically idle, self-centred consumers. [3]Teen watchers are separated into "the ones who idolize the characters" and "the ones who feel inadequate because they're not Britney or Paris Hilton." [4]Being either of those types of watchers can cause any sensitive young person to feel dissatisfied and unhappy with himself or herself after a while. [5]Another problem is that these movies and shows suggest that high school is the most important stage in life, an unreal stage that never ends. [6]Many Canadian teenagers cope with very real financial pressures and demanding family and home situations every day; to them, endless worries about a dance or riding around in a friend's Humvee seem as unrealistic as Paris Hilton's rural adventures. [7]These shows and movies are candy-coloured dreams that leave many young people feeling lied to and miserable when they consider their own lives by comparison. [8]Perhaps the main reason "teensploitation" entertainment is so insulting is that it assumes that teenagers are empty-headed, waiting to be told what is good or bad. [9]Also, teens are assumed to be so dull and gullible that they want only sequels or copies of the last ten successful teen movies or TV shows. [10]Creators of these repetitive "copycat"

products insult their teen audiences by boring them to death. ¹¹Teens and college-age audiences are not so stupid that new or interesting ideas must be sugar-coated with new titles, flashy settings, and renamed characters played by Ashton Kutcher or the Olsen twins. ¹²In fact, teens often end up watching the shows and movies they do simply because there don't seem to be any other choices available. ¹³Moreover, teenagers and young people are no different from other consumers: they buy what is advertised—every teen mag and every entertainment TV show and magazine promotes "teensploitation" stars, shows, and movies. ¹⁴No one can resist forever, especially teens who already feel pressure to conform to the tastes of their peers and the media. ¹⁵For all these reasons, creators of entertainment for young people should stop insulting and maybe damaging their target audiences.

Living Alone

¹Living alone is quite an experience. ²People who live alone, for one thing, have to learn to do all kinds of tasks by themselves. ³They must learn—even if they have had no experience—to reset circuit breakers, put up curtains and shades, temporarily dam an overflowing toilet, cook a meal, and defrost a refrigerator. ⁴When there are no fathers, husbands, mothers, or wives to depend on, a person can't fall back on the excuse "I don't know how to do that." ⁵Those who live alone also need the strength to deal with people. ⁶Alone, singles must face noisy neighbours, unresponsive property managers, and dishonest repair people. ⁷Because there are no buffers between themselves and the outside world, people living alone have to handle every visitor—friendly or unfriendly—alone. ⁸Finally, singles need a large dose of courage to cope with occasional panic and unavoidable loneliness. ⁹That weird thump in the night is even more terrifying when there is no one in the next bed or the next room. ¹⁰Frightening weather or unexpected bad news is doubly bad when the worry can't be shared. ¹¹Even when life is going well, little moments of sudden loneliness can send shivers through the heart. ¹²Struggling through such bad times taps into reserves of courage that people may not have known they possessed. ¹³Facing everyday tasks, confronting all types of people, and handling panic and loneliness can shape singles into brave, resourceful, and more independent people.

Questions

About Unity

1. The topic sentence in "Living Alone" is too broad. Circle the letter of the topic sentence below that states accurately what the paragraph is about.
   a. Living alone takes courage.
   b. Living alone can create feelings of loneliness.
   c. Living alone should be avoided.

2. Which sentence in "Teensploitation Insults Teens" should be eliminated in the interest of paragraph unity? (*Write the sentence number here.*) _____

About Support

3. How many reasons are given to support the topic sentence in each paragraph?

a. In "Teensploitation Insults Teens":

_____ one _____ two _____ three _____ four

b. In "Living Alone":

_____ one _____ two _____ three _____ four

4. After which sentence in "Teensploitation Insults Teens" are more specific details needed?

About Coherence

5. Why is emphatic order the most logical choice for both paragraphs?

_____

6. What are the three main transition words in "Living Alone"?

a. _____ b. _____ c. _____

About Point of View

7. These selections are written in the third-person objective point of view. How does that strengthen the tone of the arguments?

Further Insight—Using objective pronouns

Chapter 26, Pronoun Types, gives instruction in using pronoun references correctly. To assess your ability, practise with a short passage, now. How would you rewrite the following passage using third-person pronouns to retain objectivity?

As I consider the negative effects that global warming is having on our world, I invite you to join me and my friends by living your lives in a more sustainable fashion. I hope you will modify your lifestyles by reducing the waste that you create, reusing the many containers that you purchase every time you shop, and sending your waste products to the appropriate recycling depots every time you are finished with them.

Hint: Objective writing is often very efficient, making many of the first- and second-person pronouns unnecessary.

● ● ● ● **Activity 1**

Complete the outline below of a paragraph about "a terrible vacation." Summarize in a few words the primary and secondary supporting material that fits under the topic sentence. Two items have been done for you as examples.

Topic sentence: Despite much advertising to the contrary, taking a cruise is a terrible way to spend a vacation.

1. _____
   a. _____
   b. _____
2. _____
   a. _____
   b. *Little room for jogging* _____
3. _____
   a. _____
   b. *Dull conversations with other passengers* _____
   c. _____

Conclusion: _____

Developing An Argument Paragraph

Development through Prewriting

Amanda is the student author of "Teensploitation Insults Teenagers." When she was assigned an argument essay in English class, she recalled an evening of movie watching that she had recently undertaken with friends, but had not particularly enjoyed. Amanda realized that something about the movies was the problem. She did some freewriting from this idea. She looked back into the freewriting and picked out some main ideas that she identified through her earlier writing. Then, she constructed a working outline as follows:

Am I talking about TV or movies, or videos?

1. Characters—least important?
   —Britney and Paris Hilton—they come across as mindless
   —other TV shows—nobody I know has that much time or money
   —these aren't supposed to be "fantasy" people, like in <u>LotR</u>—supposed to be real, so people my age feel bad compared with them and their lives
   —in fact, nobody is like teens in TV and movies—who has that many clothes? Would we watch them if they were like us? Another argument? (<u>Joan of Arcadia</u>—Joan is sort of "idealistic")
2. Settings—unrealistic
   —high school lasted forever on most shows—actors look too old, look at <u>Smallville</u>, unbelievable—don't look like college students either, when they go to college
   —the characters all have these great jobs, <u>if</u> they work—isn't anybody a cashier?—look at <u>The O.C.</u>

—the problems and situations are stupid, teens are not that dumb
—shows insult teens, with fairy-tale lives, cars, and situations that never change or get worse
3. TS is just about all we're offered—there's not much choice
—movies and shows are advertised everywhere—end up watching
—sequels and copies—how many Jasons will there be?—don't young people want something new or different?
—if friends watch something, we'll eventually want to—peer pressure & media uses this
—dumbed-down versions of Shakespeare and novels—candy coated (not <u>O</u>, though—it was good)
What order do I put these details in?

Even though she still felt her thoughts were a bit muddled, Amanda was running out of time, so she wrote the following first draft of her paragraph.

A lot of people my age never question the movies and TV shows they watch. Maybe they don't realize how different they are from the characters they like so much. Not one of my friends has as many clothes as Britney, Hilary Duff, or Paris Hilton. These are supposed to be realistic characters, not fantasies like Bilbo in <u>Lord of the Rings</u> or Luke Skywalker. If young people compare themselves with TV and movie characters, they could feel bad about themselves and their lives. The settings and situations are unrealistic, too. High school seems to go on forever, and the actors look too old even when they're supposed to be in college. If they have to work, then they get jobs that are glamorous. Nobody is ever a cashier in a discount store. Again, if somebody knows they're supposed to think Stiffler is realistic, how can they not be insulted? The biggest problem is that the media uses the thing we're supposed to ignore against us—peer pressure. Because we rent a lot of movies and watch TV, movies and shows targeted at us are advertised everywhere. We end up watching just because we see so many ads in the magazines we read and even on the sides of buses. And over half the time, movies are just sequels, too. Young people are victims of our own power, and we're being insulted because of it.

Development through Revising

Amanda's instructor reviewed her first draft and made these comments.

It's obvious you feel very strongly about your point, and it is an interesting one. The first thing I notice is that you're working on offering balanced supporting details for each point. You may want to add a few more illustrations and examples, especially for your third subtopic.

Although you make good use of emphatic order by ending with "The biggest problem is . . . ," you need more transitions to make your argument's buildup stronger and your paragraph clearer.

With these comments in mind, Amanda revised her paragraph until she produced the version that appears on pages 254–255.

Challenge—The element of persuasion

Amanda's paragraph articulates her argument that "teensploitation movies" insult teens by presenting youth with unrealistic and banal entertainment. She could have taken that argument further by attempting to persuade her audience to boycott such movies, or to spend their money on more enlightening fare. The element of persuasion is closely tied to the principles of argument, but calls on an audience not only to agree with an opinion, but also to alter previous attitudes. This may even include acting upon the appeal in a tangible way. Persuasion often draws upon a direct and possibly more personal response than formal argument and may include elements of controlled emotion as well as logic.

Activity

Refer to the choices in Writing Assignment 2 (page 265). Choose one of those to develop as a persuasive appeal to a public audience in a blog or webpage. You might consider starting a hypothetical newsletter or online petition, for example. Be sure to identify the audience you are likely to reach online. Start by developing your argument as instructed, but then proceed to make your point one that persuades your audience to respond with a particular action. As you write, keep in mind the kinds of situations in which you might actually use persuasion in such a manner.

Fact versus Opinion

We often mix fact and opinion as we describe, judge, or otherwise discuss experiences or ideas. Facts apply to everyone, can be observed, duplicated, or proven, are historically accurate, and are always true. Opinions are points of view, beliefs, judgments, or preferences, but may not be absolutely true. Facts are often used to support opinions, but opinions do not support facts (in which case they can be used as propaganda or the manipulation of facts to promote an opinion). When we use facts and opinions together, it is important that we clearly identify which is which.

An example of the use of fact and opinion together is when we judge or review a place or activity. Read the following informal restaurant review written online for a site about local restaurants. Then, list the facts and opinions—and whether positive in the activity that follows.

> My husband and I decided to try out a new restaurant, Lindsay's, on Evans St., and we enjoyed it so much, we just want to tell everyone to try out this marvellous little place. Lindsay's is close to our downtown condo, and it was a pleasant fall evening, so we walked there. When we arrived around 7:00 on a Wednesday, it was packed; obviously people loved it. We were taken to a seat under an outdoor heater on the patio as we waited for a table, and it was incredibly pleasant as we sipped a light and surprisingly good local Riesling. We continued to be treated

courteously as we were seated inside about 20 minutes later, and a basket of warm sourdough rolls was brought immediately. I ordered the starter special, mussels in a Cajun sauce. The appetizers are an indication of the quality of the dining to come, and they were so delicious that we eagerly looked forward to our meal. My plate of lamb with a rosemary-mint glaze was every bit as sumptious as I had anticipated. My husband's plate of Steak Pizzaiola, was richly flavoured with fresh organic heirloom tomatoes, garlic, mushrooms, and colourfully garnished with strips of red and yellow peppers. I tasted a bit and found it rich and deep. We sipped on a carafe of the Riesling and finished with a light plate of European-inspired fruit and cheese, both produced in the Okanagan Valley. My husband and I think that Lindsay's is the best new restaurant in town. We hope it stays open because we already reserved a place for a special dinner to celebrate my graduation in May.

Activity

The point of persuasion in this informal review is simply to encourage others to try out a new locale. Identify the facts and opinions in this online restaurant review. Space has been provided for five of each, although there may be more.

A. List five elements of this review that are based upon *facts* (the first one is done for you):

    1. Lindsay's is a new restaurant on Evans St.

    2. _____

    3. _____

    4. _____

    5. _____

B. Now list five qualities that are *opinion* (again, the first is done for you):

    1. a pleasant fall evening

    2. _____

    3. _____

    4. _____

    5. _____

Challenge—Analyze an online review

One of the biggest benefits of the Internet is that a vast array of information can be found on just about anything. Unfortunately, one of the drawbacks is that often the information is not reliable. If ever the old adage "Don't believe everything you read!" has been true, it is a most important caution now. In order to gain good material from the Internet, you must be able to discern verifiable fact from personal opinion in almost everything you find.

You can develop a sense through practice. Start by finding an online review of an event, piece of music or other entertainment, or place that you know well. Assess the information by listing its content of fact and opinion as you did in the activity above. Finally, determine whether you think that the review you found was a fair representation, or whether the author may hold a view that is overly negative—or positive—shows bias, a grudge, or a hidden motive other than to be helpfully informative.

Using Logic and Identifying Logical Fallacies

The principles of logical reasoning in argument evolved from the same purposes as those used for modern scientific inquiry. Just as modern science expects researchers to propose, experiment, and prove a hypothesis, writers must invent an argument—in the form of a topic or thesis—support those ideas with evidence, and present those ideas logically. Where an error in method could result in a failed experiment in a lab, poor reasoning will result in a faulty logic in a paper.

Faulty logic, or "logical fallacies" as errors are often called, present themselves when the author does not think through the absolute meaning of his or her statements. We encounter this poor reasoning frequently, but may not be aware of it without analyzing statements critically. Fallacies are often offered by mistake, but may sometimes be consciously set as traps in order to manipulate an audience. These flaws happen so often that many have been identified and named, and can be pointed out in counterargument. By familiarizing yourself with some of the most common logical fallacies, you will not only be able to write stronger argument or persuasive papers of your own, you will also gain an upper hand in showing the weaknesses of arguments used by others. In general, these flaws in reasoning put heavy emphasis on a cause and effect, but without properly taking other factors into account. The table below lists the most prevalent errors of logic.

Fallacy	Description	Example	
Ad hominem	Attack of the person rather than the idea or issue.	*What could a soccer mom know about fiscal policy?*	Identifying a person demographically in a negative way. Also *ad hominem abusive*. An online news comments section about social funding may have someone claiming that, "You bleeding-hearts liberals all think that money just grows on trees." Name calling.
Begging the Claim	The intended conclusion is stated without evidence.	*Organic foods are healthy foods.*	While that is a general impression, the claim needs more specific evidence.

(continued)

Appeal to Authority	Calling upon the belief of someone who is not an authority on the specific issue.	*A beautiful actor says, "Feel younger in just ten days."*	The actor may be highly respected in his or her field, but is not an authority on health or beauty products. Obviously, advertising bases many of its campaigns on faulty claims to authority.
Appeal to Emotion	Associating positive or negative emotions with a corresponding claim.	*If you care about the future for your children, you will support this national security bill.*	Often used to manipulate for commercial or political gain. These can also be appeals to fear, pity, tradition, popularity, or other strong emotions.
Either/Or	Oversimplification by allowing only two possible choices.	*We must ban cars or never see blue skies, again.*	This fails to discuss other alternatives.
Genetic Fallacy	Basing the quality of an idea upon its supposed historical origins.	*Living off the power grid is just an old hippie idea.*	While some early experiments with self-sustaining living arrangements may have been initiated by the youth of the 1960s, subsequent energy concerns may provide different rationale for such innovation.
Hasty Generalization	Jumping to a conclusion.	*That won't be a good movie. I saw the first one that actor did, and it was awful.*	This person made an assessment based upon a prior experience, without considering other factors.
Red Herring/ Digression	Diverting the actual topic of discussion by inserting an unrelated topic.	*Students must tighten their belts and not expect more assistance. We need funding for public transportation.*	The speaker obviously does not want to discuss student funding, so switches the topic to another with perhaps broader public appeal.
Slippery Slope	The suggestion that allowing one action will lead, inevitably, to other and more extreme ones.	*If the voting age is lowered now, then soon even babies will be allowed to vote.*	It is often tempting to believe that if one action occurs, then it will lead incrementally to other, and disturbing—but unlikely—outcomes.
Straw Man	The distortion of an original position.	*A safe injection site means that we are inviting our youth to try out drugs of all kinds.*	This distorts the intended medical purpose of the facility and stretches the concept wrongly to include all street drugs for all people.

• • • • **Activity**

How would you respond to a call for a uniform dress code in your former high school or present college? Develop your own reasoned argument for or against such a code, paying careful attention to the use of logic and provable evidence as you make your case. Note that you may need to define the form of dress code that you will be arguing for or against so that your argument does not start with an ambiguous premise. State your side of the argument, and develop your defence of that argument through three logical reasons. Before you revise your final draft, ask a peer to scrutinize the logic you have used to help you avoid committing any logical fallacies.

Writing an Argument Paragraph

How to Write an Argument Paragraph

1) If your topic is one with which you are not very familiar, or one for which you will need more facts to support your viewpoint, take some time to look up some information on your topic at the library or on the Internet. Assess your source material to make sure that all of it is credible, accurate, and current. Try to read both supporting and opposing views of your topic so that you can anticipate likely counter-arguments and your own responses. Be sure you are firm in your point of view on your subject.

2) Prewrite, using as many methods as needed to accumulate as many facts as possible to support your viewpoint on your topic. Add any points you may have found during research. Keep track of all sources you use.

3) Begin your outline by looking for the main points to support your viewpoint. Rank your main points (subtopics) in order of increasing importance, or emphatic order. Under each point, note any examples, details, facts or statistics, or anecdotes to support that point. Compose a trial topic sentence that states your topic and moves your audience to accept your viewpoint; many such topic sentences use the words *should, must,* and *ought*.

4) Look over your outline and think about your audience. How much does your reader know about your subject? If you feel that your reader will be more ready to accept your views if you supply some information, do so. What will be your reader's attitude toward your topic? Think of any possible objections your reader might have, and counter these with appropriate facts as part of the first section of your paper.

5) Review your outline and draft looking at the logic you have used. Is it reasonable and valid, or are there logical fallacies to be corrected?

6) Be prepared to work on your drafts until you are satisfied that your audience will see your viewpoint as clearly as you do. Make sure all the facts and details that support your argument follow logically from one another.

7) Conclude with a statement that both reinforces your viewpoint and is justified by the facts you have presented.

● ● ● ● **Writing Assignment 1**

Write a paragraph in which you take a stand on one of the controversial subjects below. As a lead-in to this writing project, your instructor might give the class a chance to "stand up for what they believe in." One side of the front of the room should be designated *strong agreement* and the other side *strong disagreement*, with the space between for intermediate degrees of agreement or disagreement. As the class stands in front of the room, the instructor will read one value statement at a time from the list below, and students will move to the appropriate spot, depending on their degree of agreement or disagreement. Some time will be allowed for students to discuss with those near them the reasons they are standing where they are and to state to those at the other end of the scale the reasons for their position.

1) Students should not be required to attend high school.

2) Prostitution should be legalized.

3) Recreational drugs should be legalized.

4) Casinos and legalized gambling benefit provincial economies.

5) Gay couples should receive the same benefits and legal status as heterosexual couples.

6) Federal prisons should be co-ed, and prisoners should be allowed to marry.

7) Parents of girls under eighteen should be informed if their daughters receive birth control aids.

8) The government should legalize euthanasia.

9) Canada should have one official language only, and all signs and publications should be in this language.

10) Parents should never hit their children.

Prewriting

a Begin your paragraph by writing a sentence that expresses your attitude toward one of these value statements. For example, "Prostitution should be legalized." Notice that this can be stated objectively by avoiding words such as, "I think."

b Outline the reason or reasons you hold the opinion that you do. Your support may be based on your own experience, the experience of someone you know, logic, or research. Start with a statement such as the following:

Prostitution should be legalized for the following reasons:

c Use your outline as the basis for writing a paragraph, providing specific details to back up each point in your outline.

Revising

Put your paragraph away for a while, ideally at least a day. Ask a friend whose judgment you trust to read and critique it. Your friend should consider each of these questions as he or she reads:

- Does the topic sentence clearly state the writer's opinion on a controversial subject?
- Does the paragraph include at least three separate and distinct reasons that support the author's argument?
- Is each of the three reasons or subtopics backed up by specific, relevant evidence?
- Is the logic free of fallacies?
- Has the author saved the most powerful reason for last?
- Is the paragraph free of spelling errors and other sentence-skills mistakes listed on the inside front cover of this book?

Continue revising your work until you and your reader can answer yes to all these questions.

Writing Assignment 2

Write a paper in which you use research findings to help support one of the following statements.

Many people do not need vitamin supplements.
Disposable cans and bottles should be banned.
Everyone should own a pet.
Mandatory retirement ages should be abolished.
Advertising should not be permitted on Saturday-morning cartoon shows.

Using strategies described on the Online Learning Centre, research the topic you have chosen. Reading material on your topic will help you think about that topic. See if you can then organize your paper in the form of three reasons that support the topic. Put these reasons into a short-form outline, and use it as a guide in writing your paragraph. Here is an example.

> Many people do not need vitamin supplements.
> 1. Some vitamins, taken in high dosages, are actually harmful.
> 2. Other vitamins do not clearly improve health in any specific way.
> 3. Most Canadians' diets provide enough of daily vitamin requirements.

Note that statistics could support these reasons. Do not hesitate to cite studies and other data in a limited way; they make your argument more objective and compelling.

REVIEWING THE LEARNING OUTCOMES FOR ARGUING A POSITION

After completing any of the writing assignments in this chapter, review your work to see how well it meets the following tests.

✓ Does your paragraph open with a clear statement of your viewpoint on the topic to be argued?

✓ Does your paragraph acknowledge and counter any opposing viewpoints close to its beginning?

✓ Do you use a method of development appropriate to the type of argument you have chosen (facts and statistics for a logical argument, anecdotes or examples for an experience-based argument)?

✓ Does each subtopic and detail clearly support your expressed viewpoint in a logical way?

✓ Is your reasoning sound and your argument free of fallacies?

✓ Is your concluding statement justified by the evidence you have presented in the body of your paragraph?

Online **Learning Centre**

Visit the *English Skills with Readings: Examining Paragraphs* Online Learning Centre at www.mcgrawhill.ca/olc/langan to access self-quizzes, internet-based questions and research skills, web resources, and other learning and study tools.

Section 3

Essay Development

Preview

Section Three moves from the single-paragraph paper to the multiple-paragraph essay. The differences between a paragraph and an essay are explained and then illustrated with a paragraph that has been expanded into an essay. Please review the rhetorical modes discussed previously in the book, and use the same principles, expanding them to construct a full essay. You are shown how to begin an essay, how to tie its supporting paragraphs together, and how to conclude it. Two student essays are presented, along with questions to increase your understanding of the essay form. Finally, directions on how to plan an essay are followed by a series of essay writing assignments.

Chapter 16

Writing the Essay

After working through this chapter's activities, you will be ready to write an effective essay that

- contains an opening paragraph that attracts a reader's interest and presents a clear point in a solid thesis statement;

- is *unified* because it the focused thesis in the introduction is reinforced with each following paragraph's topic sentences, subtopics, and supporting details;

- shows *adequate and specific support* for the viewpoint of the thesis in the body paragraphs, with each one offering distinct and sufficient explanatory information and supporting details to clarify or explain the thesis point made in its topic sentence;

- demonstrates *coherence* because (1) you have chosen a definite, clear method of organization appropriate to the subject matter, and (2) you have used transitional sentences and phrases to link paragraphs and help readers follow your ideas;

- uses consistent and appropriate rhetorical modes, expanded as necessary for an essay format;

- finishes with a conclusion that sums up the overall point of your thesis and then offers a parting thought to round off the essay and signal completion; and

- communicates ideas easily and smoothly because of *effective use of sentence skills*.

WHAT IS AN ESSAY?

Differences between an Essay and a Paragraph

An essay is an expanded, more detailed form of the paragraph that you have learned to write in the preceding chapters. In an essay, the main idea—the point of view and subject that you will develop—is called the *thesis statement* and the idea is developed and explored in the supporting paragraphs that follow. Your essay ends with a brief concluding paragraph. Just as the paragraph modes are basic models of paragraph structure, the essay structure presented in this text is a model of a standard and accepted formula. Following this formula will help you to express your ideas clearly and will allow your audience to follow your reasoning.

Paragraph	*Essay*
Made of several related sentences	Made of several related paragraphs
Each sentence supports the point in a topic sentence	Each paragraph supports the point in the thesis statement
The topic sentence is generally at the beginning of the paragraph	The thesis statement is generally at the end of the introductory paragraph.
There are generally three supporting reasons in a paragraph	There are generally three supporting reasons in an essay
Of limited scope	Explores an issue more fully than a paragraph
Ends with a concluding sentence	Ends with a concluding paragraph

You will now use the skills you have acquired and practised in creating effective paragraphs as you learn to organize, outline, and write a successful essay. You will discover and state your main idea: your viewpoint on some subject.

Begin your approach to essay writing by looking at the form of an essay, below. Compare this structure with the Paragraph Outline Form in Chapter 2, on page 33. Note that the supporting paragraphs all echo the format for paragraph construction you have already learned. You will be expanding on skills here rather than acquiring totally new ones.

The Form of an Essay

Introductory Paragraph

Introduction
Thesis statement
Plan of development:
Supporting points 1, 2, 3

The *introduction* attracts the reader's interest.

The *thesis statement* states the main idea advanced in the paper.

The *plan of development* is a list of points that support the thesis. The supporting points are presented in the order in which they will be developed in the essay, and often included in a single sentence with the thesis statement.

First Supporting Paragraph

> Topic sentence (point 1)
> Subtopics
> Supporting details

The topic sentence advances the first supporting point for the thesis. The subtopics, specific examples, and supporting details explain or defend that first thesis point, as presented in the topic sentence.

Second Supporting Paragraph

> Topic sentence (point 2)
> Subtopics
> Supporting details

The topic sentence advances the second supporting point for the thesis. The subtopics, specific examples, and supporting details explain or defend that second thesis point, as presented in the topic sentence.

Third Supporting Paragraph

> Topic sentence (point 3)
> Subtopics
> Supporting details

The topic sentence advances the third supporting point for the thesis. The subtopics, specific examples, and supporting details explain or defend that third thesis point, as presented in the topic sentence.

Concluding Paragraph

> Summary, conclusion, or both

A *summary* is a brief restatement of the thesis and its main points. A *conclusion* is a final thought or two stemming from the subject of the paper, perhaps placing those thoughts in a wider context.

A Model Essay

Alexa, the writer whose paragraph "Torture by Telephone" described her nightly ritual of working as a telemarketer (page 80), later decided to develop her subject more fully and change her method of organization. Here is the essay that resulted.

Tele-Torture

INTRODUCTORY PARAGRAPH

¹When I left high school in grade eleven, I became an expert in the field of awful short-term jobs. ²I have worked nine-hour holiday shifts as a sales clerk—a job where counting inventory in freezing stockrooms feels like a relief from picky customers. ³I have also pushed the limits of my patience babysitting a four-month-old boy and his three-year-old sister—she called me "the bad lady" and liked to bite me. ⁴I have been a fairground fry cook, making chips and Beaver Tails, with oil-burn scars on both arms that kept me in bandages all summer. ⁵But none of these jobs came close to the torture of my only office job, telemarketing. ⁶The hours messed up my life; the office and the equipment were miserable; and, worst of all, the people I worked with were scary robots.

Thesis statement and plan of development

**FIRST
SUPPORTING
PARAGRAPH**

[7]First, I did not work day shifts; I worked late hours that taught me how to really waste my life. [8]My workday started at five in the evening and ended at eleven o'clock at night. [9]This schedule turned me into a slug. [10]Because I was getting home after midnight, I started sleeping in until after noon, waking up feeling anxious about the coming shift. [11]Then I would start worrying about what to wear, fiddling with my school clothes, making an effort not to look like a seventeen-year-old who is "just in it for the money." [12]I never caught up on the things I intended to do during the day, like seeing my friends or registering for correspondence courses—all I had the energy for was watching soap operas and reading magazines. [13]My routine felt like sleepwalking: any skills I'd had disappeared, now that I was programmed only to sell credit cards over the phone. [14]I gave up all my habits and plans, just to make "easy money."

**SECOND
SUPPORTING
PARAGRAPH**

[15]Although I might have got used to the late shift eventually, the equipment I used and the office itself made every hour misery. [16]I sat under glaring lights in a little cubicle. [17]The lights made my eyes water as I strained to read my sales script from the computer screen, and the chairs were the wrong height, so my back stiffened up from hours of hunching over. [18]The phone headset burst out in static every time I moved my head, and I often couldn't hear the person I'd called. [19]To make matters worse, the program that guided me through each call was slow, and I would start babbling nervously at the person I'd called while waiting for my next screen to appear. [20]Babblers don't make sales, and I grew frustrated and nervous.

**THIRD
SUPPORTING
PARAGRAPH**

[21]But more than the physical discomfort, what upset me most about the job was the supervisors. [22]I felt they were there to judge my every call. [23]Their real job was to motivate the telemarketers and to help us when we had problems. [24]In fact, they behaved like robots who had scripts like our computer programs. [25]Over and over they told me to "sound positive," to beware of "not living up to my potential," and to always "smile and dial." [26]They thought women should "act perky" and flirt with male customers. [27]As a result, I became so upset that I started speed-talking, and that was usually the moment when supervisors would monitor my calls. [28]I could not "calm down, slow down," and be "perky" when these robots were whispering in one ear and a customer was hanging up in my other ear. [29]I never felt so pressured in my life.

**CONCLUDING
PARAGRAPH**
Restatement of
the thesis

[30]I lasted for two months as a telemarketer—the hours, the office, and the supervisors made it the hardest money I ever earned. [31]By the time I quit, I questioned my sanity, my decision to leave school, and my urge for an office job with "easy money."

IMPORTANT POINTS ABOUT THE ESSAY

The essay is a longer writing format than the paragraph. On a page, an essay appears as a piece of text with distinct breaks in it. The "breaks" are the spatial divisions between paragraphs; a line of text ends and a new line begins with an indentation, as you see here in what you are reading. These breaks serve to reinforce the coherence of each supporting idea. The trick with an essay or any longer piece of writing is to transform those "breaks" into "pauses," while keeping the reader following the path you create as a writer.

Essays give you the opportunity to pursue your ideas at greater length and in more detail in separate paragraphs. Because these separate paragraphs take readers more deeply into your paths of thought, essays also present some challenges. Your first challenge is maintaining *unity*—keeping a strong, clear relationship from paragraph to paragraph through to your conclusion.

A way to maintain unity in an essay is to state or imply in your introduction which method of development—or the rhetorical mode identified in previous chapters—you will be using. This will provide structure for you to use and your readers to follow throughout the essay. As you plan and write your own essay, keep in mind the type of essay you are writing, and construct an outline according to that method. You may wish to review the chapters in the book that deal with each form, to remind yourself of the tips and techniques for each type.

An example of extending a paragraph form into an entire essay can be seen in the student essay "An Interpretation of *Lord of the Flies*." The author writes, " . . . William Golding describes a group of schoolboys shipwrecked on an island with no authority figures to control their behaviour." This indicates that the essay will use description as an essay method, and in the subsequent paragraphs the author describes each of his points in detail. You should note, also, that literature is discussed in the present tense, which indicates that the author unfolds the details as the piece is read.

You can begin to create a unified essay by following tested, straightforward methods, beginning with your first paragraph.

Introductory Paragraph

An introductory paragraph has certain purposes or functions and can be constructed using various methods.

Purposes of the Introduction

An introductory paragraph should do four things:

1) Attract the reader's *interest*. Use one of the suggested methods of introduction described below to help draw the reader into your paper.

2) Present a *thesis statement*—a clear, direct statement of the central idea that you will develop in your paper. The thesis statement, like a topic sentence, should have a keyword or key phrase reflecting your attitude about the subject. For example, in the essay on the telemarketing job, the keyword is *torture*.

3) Indicate a *plan of development,* a list or *preview* of the *major points* that will support your thesis statement, listed *in the order in which they will be presented.* A more specific way to indicate your method of development— the rhetorical modes—for the paragraphs to follow is to use keywords identifying that method: for example, *a description, a comparison* (or *contrast), the causes* (or *effects), the advantages* (or *disadvantages), a definition, or an analysis* or *examination.* It is often expected that the thesis statement and the plan of development may appear in the same sentence. In other

cases, the plan of development may be omitted, modified, or shown sepa-rately. It may be advisable to secure approval from your instructor for such a construction.

4) Draw the reader's attention from a general idea—the point of interest used at the beginning of the introduction—to the most specific, which is indicated in the thesis statement.

● ● ● ● ● **Activity 1**

1. In "Tele-Torture," which sentences are used to attract the reader's interest?

_____ sentences 1 to 3 _____ 1 to 5 _____ 1 to 6

2. The thesis in "Tele-Torture" is presented in

_____ sentence 4 _____ sentence 5 _____ sentence 6

3. The thesis is followed by a plan of development.

_____ Yes _____ No

4. Which words in the plan of development announce the three major sup-porting points in the essay? Write them below.

a. _____

b. _____

c. _____

Common Methods of Introduction

Here are some common methods of introduction. Use any one method or a combination of methods to introduce your subject in an interesting way.

- **Broad statement.** Begin with a broad, general statement of your topic and narrow it down to your thesis statement. Broad, general statements ease the reader into your thesis statement by providing a background for it. In "Tele-Torture," Alexa opens with a general statement on the topic of unpleas-ant jobs and then narrows her focus to a specific job that was the worst of them all. Most effective introductions will follow this construction to some degree.

- **Background information or context.** In many college and career writing tasks, you will write about subjects unfamiliar to general readers. You will need to offer some background information to make your meaning clear to readers. Opening with a few sentences to "set up" or explain your subject or situation is a useful method of introduction. Whenever you write about a subject that is not considered common knowledge, use this approach. If you must explain some technical process or a complicated situation, always give enough background information to make your thesis and supporting state-ments clear and understandable to readers. Here is an introductory para-graph that presents background information.

> Canadians usually think of DVDs as something they rent instead of videotapes. Well, DVDs have certainly replaced analog tapes for movies, but they are much more than a new kind of shiny disk. DVD now means "digital versatile disk," and it really lives up to its name. A DVD is a CD-size disk that can hold up to 17 GB of visual and sound information; it works with computers or players; in fact, it is the fastest-growing electronics format available today. DVD-ROMs are replacing CD-ROMs; they hold games that are more realistic and interesting to play—games that can run on the computer rather than only on consoles like the Xbox. DVD Audio is becoming popular with music fans because it can offer surround sound with visuals of bands and performers. Now there are recordable DVDs, too, for use as higher-capacity backup disks for computer data and as alternatives to videotapes for recording TV programs. DVDs truly are versatile items—as small and convenient as CDs, but with much larger capacities and more diversified uses.

Note: When giving background information, provide only enough to allow your audience to identify your general topic. More elaborate information may need to be provided in the essay body where it will not confuse your point or divert the audience's attention. For example, in the excerpt above, if the author felt it necessary to explain how DVDs are manufactured, it would be best to put that information into a paragraph that deals with a related concept, or, if the information is extensive, possibly even into one of its own.

- **Contrast.** Start with an idea or situation that is the opposite of the one you will develop. This approach works because your readers will be surprised, and then intrigued, by the contrast between the opening idea and the thesis that follows it. Here is an example of a "contrast" introduction.

> When I was a girl, I never argued with my parents about differences between their attitudes and mine. My father would deliver his judgment on an issue, and that was usually the end of the matter. Discussion seldom changed his mind, and disagreement was not tolerated. But the situation is different with today's parents and children. My husband and I have to contend with radical differences between what our children think about a given situation and what we think about it.

A contrast introduction may logically precede an essay that deals with comparison and contrast, as it sets up that method in advance.

- **Relevance.** Explain the importance of your topic. If you can convince your readers that the subject applies to them in some way, or is something they should know more about, they will want to continue reading. The introductory paragraph of "Consuming Canadians" (pages 281–282) provides an example of a "relevance" introduction.

- **Anecdote.** Use an incident or brief story. Stories are naturally interesting. They appeal to a reader's curiosity. In your introduction, an anecdote will grab the reader's attention right away. The story should be brief and should be related to your central idea. The incident in the story can be something that happened to you, something that you may have heard about, or something that you have read about in a newspaper or magazine. This is most acceptable in informal essays in the first person, such as narration or description essays. Here is an example of a paragraph that begins with a story.

> Down in the basement lived a monster. He squatted right in the centre of his dark, cement-walled cave and stretched his huge metal arms right up into the ceiling. The big metal monster was old; he had once eaten coal, we were told, and was probably mean from surviving through decades of northern Ontario winters. Now the monster was tamed and attached to the oil tank that leaned against the side of the house, so at least we knew he could not mysteriously move and come creaking after us. But he was still a monster; this we knew from his grated mouth, right in the middle of his steely face—behind those grates blazed infernal fires, day and night. This monster, the furnace, was part of a story invented by our father, and such stories are typical of "real" fairy tales, told not so much to scare children as to teach some important lessons needed for survival.

- **Questions.** Ask your readers one or more questions. These questions catch the readers' interest and make them want to read on; they serve as a lead-in to the thesis. Here is an example of a paragraph that begins with questions. This device is also most appropriate for informal essays, and is often used in journalistic and human interest writing.

> What would happen if we were totally honest with ourselves? Would we be able to stand the pain of giving up self-deception? Would the complete truth be too much for us to bear? Such questions will probably never be answered, for in everyday life we protect ourselves from too much reality. All of us cultivate defence mechanisms that prevent us from seeing, hearing, or feeling too much. Included among such defence mechanisms are rationalization, reaction formation, and substitution.

Note: Remember that the thesis must not be a question. In an essay you must maintain your authority (see Chapter 1). As the author, you state a definite idea; your authority will be weakened if you query your own idea, because it suggests that you are unsure of your own point.

- **Quotation.** A quotation can be something you have read in a book or an article. It can also be something that you have heard: a popular saying or proverb ("Never give advice to a friend"); a current or recent advertising slogan ("Reach out and touch someone"); a favourite expression used by your friends or family ("My father always says . . ."). Using a quotation in your introductory paragraph lets you add someone else's voice to your own. Remember that all quotes must be referenced accurately, and even proverbs must be attributed with a reasonable context. Here is an example of a paragraph that begins with a quotation.

> "Evil," wrote Martin Buber, "is lack of direction." In my school days as a fatherless boy, with a mother too confused by her own life to really care for me, I strayed down a number of paths. Before my eighteenth birthday, I had been thrown out of school, fired from jobs, and put into a group home.

The Thesis Statement

An essay's thesis statement is like a paragraph's topic sentence: it contains two elements, the essay's subject and your position or viewpoint on that subject. As a topic sentence does with a paragraph, a thesis statement previews the essay's content. The thesis guides readers on what to expect from the paragraphs that follow. To write a strong thesis statement, follow these steps.

1) To develop an effective thesis, begin by working out a focus on your subject. Narrow a general subject to find your focus.

Refer back to pages 51–58 on writing an effective topic sentence for additional help with writing your thesis statement, since a thesis and a topic sentence are the same in principle: they should not be announcements, and they should be neither too broad nor too narrow.

A focused subject for an essay will help you write a good thesis statement. Your goal is to find a focused view of your subject that is (1) clear, (2) specific, and (3) a suitable size to develop in three supporting paragraphs. (Three paragraphs—or supporting sections—are the generally accepted number for a standard essay. Some essays will have only two supporting paragraphs or sections; others, four or more, depending upon the depth and complexity of the essay.)

Alexa, the student who wrote about telemarketing, was assigned the general subject of "part-time jobs." She did some prewriting and, in doing so, came up with details about four or five part-time jobs she had worked at. No single focus appeared right away. Rereading her material, she found herself returning to the idea of job routines, so that became the focus of the paragraph on page 80. When she returned to her subject weeks later, it was because she had been assigned the task of turning her paragraph into an essay. She changed her focus and considered some other possibilities before deciding to write about one particularly awful job.

An unclear focus: part-time jobs are awful
A non-specific focus: students and part-time jobs
A focus that is too broad for an essay: profiles of students in telemarketing
A clearly focused subject: telemarketing, and why it was so awful

One good way to find a focus is to brainstorm or prewrite on the one aspect of your general subject to which you relate most easily. Write about what you know.

2) Write a sentence about your narrowed, focused subject that expresses a single viewpoint or position. The viewpoint you express in your thesis is your attitude toward your subject—the limits you place around your coverage of it. As with writing a topic sentence, use keywords to express your attitude or position (page 54). Do not offer more than one viewpoint on your subject in your thesis. In an essay, promote only one point of view, and be sure that it is defensible. Avoid these common pitfalls:

  A thesis that offers more than one viewpoint or attitude: Telemarketing is depressing work, but it pays well.

  A thesis that is too general: Telemarketing is the kind of job that students all across Canada take.

  A thesis that is too narrow and a dead-end statement: Telemarketing is a typical part-time job.

Contrast the above ineffective thesis statements with the following effective one:

  Telemarketing was the worst job I have ever had.

Write a thesis statement that is general enough to cover each of your supporting points, but not so general that it uses wordings or ideas such as "All over the world" or refers to what "everyone" knows, thinks, or does. Specify your focus on your subject.

3) Suggest or list your supporting points as part of your thesis statement. The attitude or viewpoint stated in your thesis may be enough to imply the nature of your supporting evidence, but most effective thesis statements offer or preview these points as well.

  A thesis that presents its supporting points: Three types of people end up working in telemarketing include starving students, out-of-work actors, and social misfits.

Note: Sometimes writing full thesis statements can feel long and unwieldy. You may wish to review some of the Sentence Skills sections, particularly the chapters on "Fragments" and "Run-Ons and Comma Splices" to help you write complicated sentences more effectively.

4) If you are writing an essay using a specific method of development, your thesis should suggest that method with related keywords.

  A thesis for a division and classification essay: First-semester students can be divided into three groups: the eager beavers, the frankly frightened, and the "too cool for school."

  A thesis for a definition essay: Urban renewal is the revitalization of rundown cities through the development of sustainable and efficient systems, and by making them aesthetically pleasing.

• • • • **Activity 2**

Following is one general subject and a list of narrowed or focused subjects that fit under that general term. Write a thesis statement for one of each group of narrowed subjects. Ask yourself what point you wish to make about the narrowed subject you choose in each case, so that your thesis statements show a clear, single attitude. Include the plan of development in the same sentence if possible.

1. *General subject:* School clothes
   - Showing too much skin
   - Suits and career wear
   - Comfort clothes
   - Personalities of wearers
   - Good taste

   Your thesis statement: _____

2. *General subject:* Music today
   - Downloading songs
   - Rap videos
   - Indie bands
   - Songs on the radio
   - Concert behaviour

   Your thesis statement: _____

3. *General subject:* Food
   - Fast food
   - Vegetarianism
   - Comfort foods
   - Healthy eating
   - Eating on a budget

   Your thesis statement: _____

• • • • **Activity 3**

Construct thesis statements for the given topics that also reflect the essay methods indicated:

1. Considerations when downloading mp3s—Process
2. Taking care of your health—Cause and Effect
3. How being a college student changes your life—Compare and Contrast
4. Environmental considerations when buying a car—Divide and Classify
5. The use of genetically modified goods—Argue for or against

Placement of a Thesis Statement

Technically a thesis statement can be placed anywhere in an introduction, but it is often preferred at the end of the first paragraph. The advantages of this are that:

- it is easily visible
- it is predictable, which helps the reader to follow the rest of the essay

- it follows logically from the set-up of the introduction and forms a transition to the essay body

It may be helpful to view an introduction graphically as an upside-down triangle, with a broad opening statement at the top, and the narrow, specific thesis statement as the point leading to the essay body.

Supporting Paragraphs

Most college essays have three supporting points, developed in three separate paragraphs. Each of the supporting paragraphs should begin with a topic sentence that states the point to be detailed in that paragraph. Just as the thesis provides a focus or controlling idea for the entire essay, the topic sentence provides a focus for each supporting paragraph.

Activity 4

1. What is the topic sentence for the first supporting paragraph of "Tele-Torture"?

   (*Write the sentence number here.*) _____

2. What is the topic sentence for the second supporting paragraph? _____

3. What is the topic sentence for the third supporting paragraph? _____

As you compose each supporting paragraph, you will find it helpful to review Chapters 3 and 4 in this book. Your topic sentences focus each paragraph and help unify your essay by referring to your thesis and continuing its train of thought. Now, as you work on the body of your essay, keep in mind the guiding principle of providing *adequate and specific support.* Be certain that every supporting paragraph explains or proves the point stated in its topic sentence thoroughly, illustrating its meaning with specific ideas and phrases. Your supporting paragraphs should be roughly equal in length, so that your essay is balanced in content and appearance.

Activity 5

1. What details explain the topic sentence in the first supporting paragraph of "Tele-Torture"? Which seem most effective to you, and why? Are there details that might be more specific?
2. How many subtopics are there in the second supporting paragraph?
3. Which details in the third supporting paragraph explain the idea that the supervisors were like "robots"?

Structuring Supporting Paragraphs

In a simple essay, each supporting point for the thesis becomes the topic of one of the essay's body paragraphs—each supporting paragraph's topic sentence presents one of the points of the thesis. The supporting paragraphs
(continued)

> then follow the structure you have learned in earlier chapters of this book. Writers do not always need three subtopics for every supporting paragraph of every essay, however. Sometimes a supporting point may be best explained with one extended discussion containing strong specific details or examples. Two natural subtopics may be a realistic number for other essays; your content will guide you as you create an internal structure for your supporting paragraphs.

Transitions and Transitional Sentences

In Chapter 4, you learned to use a clear method of organization and transitional words and devices within your paragraphs to achieve the goal of *coherence,* to help readers follow your thinking. You should organize your supporting paragraphs according to a definite method and provide transitional words and cues to link your sentences and show their relationship to one another.

● ● ● ● **Activity 6**

1. In the first supporting paragraph of "Tele-Torture," how many transitional words or phrases are used? What type of transition is each one?
2. Where is the transitional phrase within the second supporting paragraph? Could another transitional word be used in this paragraph? If so, what kind of transition, and where would it appear?
3. What types of transitions are used in the third supporting paragraph?

These transitions and other connective devices (pages 86–87) help to create smoothly flowing paragraphs that are *coherent* to readers.

Similarly, in an essay, *transitional sentences* are used to help tie the supporting paragraphs together. Such transitional sentences usually occur near the end of one paragraph or the beginning of the next.

In "Tele-Torture," the first transitional sentence is:

> Although I might have got used to the late shift eventually, the equipment I used and the office itself made every hour misery.

In this sentence, the keywords *late shift* remind us of the point of the first supporting paragraph, while the words *equipment, office,* and *misery* tell us the point to be developed in the second supporting paragraph.

Here is the other transitional sentence in "Tele-Torture":

> But more than the physical discomfort, what upset me most about the job was the supervisors.

Note: Notice that the dependent or subordinate first part of the sentence refers to the previous paragraph, and the independent (or main) part of the sentence takes the reader into the paragraph to follow.

Concluding Paragraph

The concluding paragraph often summarizes the essay by briefly restating the thesis and the main supporting points of the essay. The conclusion also brings the paper to a natural and graceful end, and usually leaves the reader with a final thought on the subject.

Consider the conclusion of the essay by Martha Brooks, "Surviving the Journey: Literature Meets Life," on page 475 of the Reading Selections. How does she manage to link her conclusion to the body of her story? What lingering thought does she present?

A concluding paragraph should be balanced against the introductory paragraph. Think of it as inverted from the introduction, starting with the specific—readdressing the thesis but in new wording—and leading out toward a general concluding idea. When writing a conclusion, reflect the style used in the introduction. Be sure to tie up the ideas you have discussed in your essay so that you and your audience end with a satisfying sense of completion. An effective conclusion will usually end with an idea that will point to a general or future thought; however, it must not introduce a new idea or controversy that must be explained.

● ● ● ● **Activity 7**

1. Which sentence in the concluding paragraph of "Tele-Torture" restates the thesis and supporting points of the essay? _____

2. Which sentence contains the concluding thought of the essay? _____

ESSAYS TO CONSIDER

Read the two student essays below and then answer the questions that follow.

Consuming Canadians

[1]Canadians are consumed by consuming. [2]They shop all the time for just about anything. [3]They shop instead of doing just about anything else. [4]Shopping is a pretty innocent, ordinary activity—everyone needs things, and people enjoy buying something new. [5]But Canadians, especially those who live in cities, now spend far too much of their daily lives being consumers, as they think about shopping every day; they spend weekends at the mall, and then they go online and shop some more.

[6]Constant advertising everywhere makes Canadians believe that they need to buy or consume something every single day. [7]What they need is not just

something, but a brand-name something that they saw on TV, on a website banner, at the movies, on a billboard, in a magazine, in the paper, on a bus-shelter wall, or even on a taxicab's hubcap covers. [8]If people want their daily cups of coffee, they go to Timothy's, Second Cup, or Starbucks for some frothy, flavoured four-dollar beverage in a trademarked cup. [9]When Canadians want some exercise, do they just step out the door for a walk? [10]No, they go to a well-advertised sportswear store to buy a brand-name outfit and shoes. [11]Or they remember that fitness club they liked the ad for, and spend a few hundred on a membership and workout clothes they may not make much use of. [12]People would rather buy things than actually do things.

[13]Shopping has also replaced socializing, hobbies, and other weekend activities. In fact, going to the mall is now considered a "weekend activity." [14]Canadians claim they prefer going to malls because of the convenience or because they can avoid bad weather. [15]But the fact is that families don't spend weekend time mowing the lawn, washing the windows, hiking, playing games, or going to the museum—they go to the mall. [16]Teenagers don't just spend weekends shopping at malls; malls are their social centres, where they meet friends, eat, go to movies, and generally hang out in groups like mall rats, not leaving until they're forced to.

[17]Just how good Canadians are at consuming shows most of all when they go online. [18]The Internet is a huge international communications medium, but ads, banners, and pop-ups have turned it into an advertising and shopping system. [19]When people go home in the evening and open up their personal email, their in-boxes are full of advertising—promotional posts from Bell or Rogers or e-mail "coupons" from stores like Staples or Shoppers Drug Mart, and of course spam advertisements. [20]Canadians respond so well that major U.S. online retailers like Ebay and Amazon have opened Canadian sites. [21]Every major Canadian store chain, like the Bay, Chapters, and Canadian Tire, is open for business 24/7 to catch every possible customer. [22]In fact, people must be too busy even to shop for food in person, because Canadians lead the world in online use of sites like Grocery Gateway. [23]Shopping by computer supposedly saves time, but what are Canadians saving that time for? [24]Probably more "real-time" shopping.

[25]Canadians really do seem to live to consume. [26]Perhaps they really believe all the advertising they're surrounded by. [27]Perhaps twenty-first-century life will be just a cycle of working and shopping. [28]Whatever the reason, Canadians do "shop 'til they drop."

An Interpretation of <u>Lord of the Flies</u>

[1]Modern history has shown us the evil that exists in human beings. [2]Assassinations are common, governments use torture to discourage dissent, and six million Jews were exterminated during World War II. [3]In <u>Lord of the Flies</u>, William Golding describes a group of schoolboys shipwrecked on an island with no authority figures to control their behaviour. [4]One of the boys soon yields to dark forces within himself, and his corruption symbolizes the evil in all of us. [5]First, Jack Merridew kills a living creature; then, he rebels

against the group leader; and finally, he seizes power and sets up his own murderous society.

[6]The first stage in Jack's downfall is his killing of a living creature. [7]In Chapter 1, Jack aims at a pig but is unable to kill. [8]His upraised arm pauses "because of the enormity of the knife descending and cutting into living flesh, because of the unbearable blood," and the pig escapes. [9]Three chapters later, however, Jack leads some boys on a successful hunt. [10]He returns triumphantly with a freshly killed pig and reports excitedly to the others, "I cut the pig's throat." [11]Yet Jack twitches as he says this, and he wipes his bloody hands on his shorts as if eager to remove the stains. [12]There is still some civilization left in him.

[13]After the initial act of killing the pig, Jack's refusal to cooperate with Ralph shows us that this civilized part is rapidly disappearing. [14]With no adults around, Ralph has made some rules. [15]One is that a signal fire must be kept burning. [16]But Jack tempts the boys watching the fire to go hunting, and the fire goes out. [17]Another rule is that at a meeting, only the person holding a special seashell has the right to speak. [18]In Chapter 5, another boy is speaking when Jack rudely tells him to shut up. [19]Ralph accuses Jack of breaking the rules. [20]Jack shouts: "Bollocks to the rules! We're strong—we hunt! If there's a beast, we'll hunt it down! We'll close in and beat and beat and beat—!" [21]He gives a "wild whoop" and leaps off the platform, throwing the meeting into chaos. [22]Jack is now much more savage than civilized.

[23]The most obvious proof of Jack's corruption comes in Chapter 8, when he establishes his own murderous society. [24]Insisting that Ralph is not a "proper chief" because he does not hunt, Jack asks for a new election. [25]After he again loses, Jack announces, "I'm going off by myself. . . . Anyone who wants to hunt when I do can come too." [26]Eventually, nearly all the boys join Jack's "tribe." [27]Following his example, they paint their faces like savages, sacrifice to "the beast," brutally murder two of their schoolmates, and nearly succeed in killing Ralph as well. [28]Jack has now become completely savage—and so have the others.

[29]Through Jack Merridew, then, Golding shows how easily moral laws can be forgotten. [30]Freed from grown-ups and their rules, Jack learns to kill living things, defy authority, and lead a tribe of murdering savages. [31]Jack's example is a frightening reminder of humanity's potential for evil. [32]The "beast" the boys try to hunt and kill is actually within every human being.

Questions

1. In which essay does the thesis statement appear in the last sentence of the introductory paragraph?

_____

2. In the essay on *Lord of the Flies*, which sentence of the introductory paragraph contains the plan of development? _____

3. Which method of introduction is used in "Consuming Canadians"?
   a. Broad statement   c. Anecdote
   b. Relevance   d. Questions

4. Complete the following brief outline of "An Interpretation of *Lord of the Flies*." Jack Merridew's evil became evident as he:

   a. _____

   b. _____

   c. _____

5. Which essay uses a transitional sentence between the first and second supporting paragraphs?

   _____

   _____

6. Complete the following statement: Emphatic order is shown in the last supporting paragraph of "Consuming Canadians" with the words _____; and in the last supporting paragraph of "An Interpretation of *Lord of the Flies*" with the words _____.

7. List four major transitions used in the supporting paragraphs of "An Interpretation of *Lord of the Flies*."

   a. _____   c. _____

   b. _____   d. _____

8. Which essay includes a sentence in the concluding paragraph that summarizes the three supporting points?

   _____

   _____

9. Which essay includes two final thoughts in its concluding paragraph?

   _____

Further Insight—Writing extended essays

A simple or straightforward essay will probably stick to a single mode; however, more complex essays may need to use multiple modes within its body to define, provide extensive examples, or otherwise provide complete information. As you write and revise, take note of any time that you or a peer needs to ask clarifying questions; these may indicate moments when paragraphs should be added so that enough information is given before such questions could arise. For example, if you were writing an essay about the role of carbon taxes in reducing greenhouse gases, you may need specific paragraphs to explain terminology or provide examples as required to reinforce clarity. Ask yourself the Journalists' Questions (Chapter 2) as you review your work. If a response requires a lot of explanation, there is a good chance it should be dealt with in a paragraph of its own. As you develop more sophisticated writing skills, you will learn to judge where and how such paragraphs should be included.

PLANNING THE ESSAY

As you prepare to write an essay, first refer to the four-step sequence for effective writing in Chapter 2.

Begin by prewriting to discover the point you wish to make about your subject. As you are considering your thesis, remember that each supporting point for the view expressed in your thesis will now be explained in an entire paragraph.

You will find that the prewriting stage will take more time now—after all, an essay has many paragraphs. Be sure to allow yourself enough prewriting time to discover (1) strong supporting points for your thesis and (2) enough specific details to explain or prove those supporting points.

Outlining the Essay

Because an essay's structure and content are more complex than those of a single paragraph, planning is essential for success, and outlining is absolutely crucial to creating a solid essay. You should plan your essay by outlining in two ways:

1) Prepare a brief outline. This should consist of a short statement of the thesis followed by the main supporting points for the thesis. Here is Alexa's outline for her essay on the telemarketing job:

Telemarketing was an awful job.
1. Night shifts
2. Office and equipment
3. Supervisors

Do not underestimate the value of this initial outline—or the work involved in achieving it. Be prepared to do a good deal of plain hard thinking at this first and most important stage of your writing.

2) Prepare a more detailed outline. The Essay Outline Form that follows will serve as a guide. Your instructor may ask you to submit a copy of this form either before you write an essay or along with your finished essay.

Essay Outline Form

Photocopy this outline form, or create your own on disk by setting it up and saving it as a blank document. Each time you are ready to outline, just paste your outline document onto a new document page.

Introductory Paragraph

Introduction: _____

Thesis Statement: _____

Plan of Development: _____

    Supporting Point 1: _____

    Supporting Point 2: _____

    Supporting Point 3: _____

First Supporting Paragraph

Topic Sentence: _____

Subtopic 1: _____

    Supporting Details:

        a. _____

        b. _____

        c. specific example _____

Subtopic 2: _____

    Supporting Details:

        a. _____

        b. _____

        c. specific example _____

Subtopic 3: _____

    Supporting Details:

        a. _____

        b. _____

        c. specific example _____

Paragraph Conclusion: _____

Second Supporting Paragraph

Topic Sentence: _____

Subtopic 1: _____

    Supporting Details:

        a. _____

        b. _____

        c. specific example _____

Subtopic 2: _____

    Supporting Details:

        a. _____

        b. _____

        c. specific example _____

Subtopic 3: _____

    Supporting Details:

        a. _____

        b. _____

        c. specific example _____

Paragraph Conclusion: _____

Third Supporting Paragraph

Topic Sentence: _____

Subtopic 1: _____

    Supporting Details:

        a. _____

        b. _____

        c. specific example _____

Subtopic 2: _____

    Supporting Details:

        a. _____

        b. _____

        c. specific example _____

Subtopic 3: _____

    Supporting Details:

        a. _____

        b. _____

        c. specific example _____

Paragraph Conclusion: _____

Concluding Paragraph

Summary, conclusion, or both _____

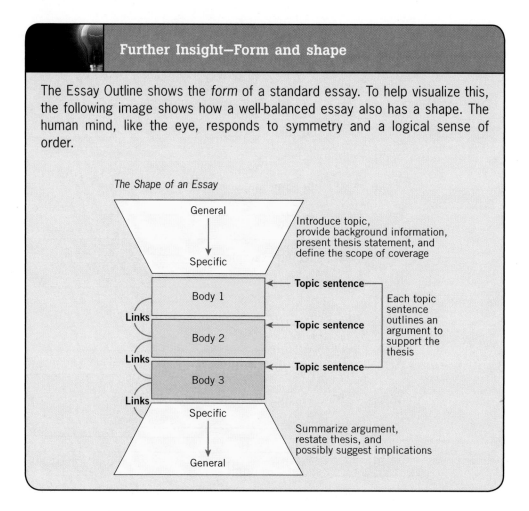

Further Insight—Form and shape

The Essay Outline shows the *form* of a standard essay. To help visualize this, the following image shows how a well-balanced essay also has a shape. The human mind, like the eye, responds to symmetry and a logical sense of order.

The Shape of an Essay

General → Specific: Introduce topic, provide background information, present thesis statement, and define the scope of coverage

Body 1 ← Topic sentence
Links
Body 2 ← Topic sentence
Links
Body 3 ← Topic sentence
Links

Each topic sentence outlines an argument to support the thesis

Specific → General: Summarize argument, restate thesis, and possibly suggest implications

ESSAY WRITING ASSIGNMENTS

Hints: Keep the following points in mind when writing an essay on any of the topics below.

1) As you prewrite to develop your thesis and support, remember that your essay will be longer and more detailed than a single paragraph. Allow yourself more time or perhaps more sessions for the prewriting stage.

2) After leaving your prewriting for a day, or at least a few hours, prepare to plan your essay. Begin with a brief outline of its thesis and main supporting points; then create a more detailed outline using the Essay Outline Form above.

3) While writing your essay, use the checklist that follows to make sure your essay touches all four bases of effective writing. Compare these with the checklist on the inside cover of your textbook, and on page 123.

Base 1: Unity

_____ Clearly stated thesis in the introductory paragraph of your paper

_____ All the supporting paragraphs on target in backing up your thesis

Base 2: Support

_____ Three separate supporting points for your thesis

_____ *Specific* evidence for each of the three supporting points

_____ *Plenty* of specific evidence for each supporting point

Base 3: Coherence

_____ Clear method of organization

_____ Transitions, other connecting words, or transitional sentences

_____ Effective introduction and conclusion

Base 4: Sentence Skills

_____ Clear, error-free sentences (use the checklist on the inside front cover of this book)

1 Your House or Apartment

Write a description essay on the advantages *or* disadvantages (not both) of the house, apartment, or residence room where you live. In your introductory paragraph, briefly describe the place you plan to write about. End the paragraph with your thesis statement and a plan of development. Here are some suggestions for thesis statements.

> The best features of my apartment are its large windows, roomy closets, and great location.
>
> The drawbacks of my house are its unreliable oil furnace, tiny kitchen, and old-fashioned bathroom.
>
> An inquisitive property manager, sloppy neighbours, and troops of mice came along with our rented house.
>
> My apartment has several advantages, including friendly neighbours, lots of storage space, and a good security system.

2 Considerations in Purchasing a Valued Possession

Write an essay about a purchasing a valued material possession. Write it in the third person, in the form of advice to consumers, so that your essay is informative and helpful. You may wish to use a mode such as those studied in the paragraph sections of "Explaining a Process," "Examining Cause and Effect,"

"Comparing and Contrasting," or "Dividing and Classifying." Here are some suggestions.

Car	Book
TV set	Photograph album
Piece of furniture	Piece of clothing
Piece of jewellery	Sound system (car or home)
Camera	Piece of hobby equipment

In your introductory paragraph, describe the item to be purchased: tell what it is, where people may acquire it, and any important details that should be considered. Your thesis statement should centre on the idea that there are several reasons this possession will be valued. In each of your supporting paragraphs, provide details to back up one of the reasons.

For example, here are the three supporting points of an essay written about purchasing a leather jacket:

1) It must be comfortable.

2) It should be durable.

3) It should make the person look and feel good.

3   An Essay Based on a Reading Selection

Write an essay based on the selection "Website Design" on pages 498–500. Read the selection through several times, noting its main points about designing an effective website. You may wish to write this essay from the third-person point of view, as in the sample introductory paragraph below.

Choose three topics for your supporting paragraphs from among the article's suggested study skills. Select the three suggestions that relate best to your own experience as a student. Do not simply copy words or phrases from the selection—that would be plagiarism. (Refer to Chapters 17 and 18 for more information on using sources effectively.) Express your own responses to the article's ideas in your own words.

One possible introductory paragraph and possible topic sentences for the supporting paragraphs are provided below. In addition to developing the supporting paragraphs, you should write a brief conclusion for the essay.

Introductory Paragraph

Using Study Skills

Why do some students in a college class receive As, while others get Ds and Fs? Are some people just naturally smarter? Are other students doomed to failure? Motivation—willingness to do the work—is a factor in good grades. But the main difference between successful and unsuccessful students is that the ones who do well have mastered the specific skills needed to handle college work. Fortunately, these skills can be learned by anyone. Doing well in college depends on knowing how to . . . *(Complete this sentence with the three study skills you decide to write about.)*

Possible Topic Sentences for Three Supporting Paragraphs

Time control is one aid to success as a student.
Another aid is the use of memory techniques.
Knowing how to concentrate is another essential skill.
Studying a textbook effectively is another key to success.
Perhaps the most crucial step of all is effective classroom note-taking.

5   Single Life

Write an essay using the third-person point of view discussing either the advantages or drawbacks of single life. (See the model essay "Consuming Canadians" for an example of third-person point of view, pages 281–282.) This might be a good essay topic for comparing and contrasting single life with lives in couples or families. To get started, make a list of all the advantages and drawbacks you can think of. Advantages might include:

Fewer expenses
Fewer responsibilities
More personal freedom
More opportunities to move or travel

Drawbacks might include:

Parental disapproval
Being alone at social events
No companion for shopping, movies, and so on
Sadness at holiday time

After you make up two lists, select the thesis for which you feel you have more supporting material. Then organize your material into a brief outline. Be sure to include an introduction, a clear topic sentence for each supporting paragraph, and a conclusion.

Alternatively, write an essay on the advantages or drawbacks of married life. Follow the directions given above.

6   A Major Decision

All of us come to various crossroads in our lives, times when we must make an important decision about which course of action to follow. Think about a major decision you had to make (or one you are planning to make). Then write an essay on the reasons for your decision. In your introduction, describe the decision you have reached or are contemplating. Each of the supporting paragraphs that follow should fully explain one of the reasons for your decision. Here are some examples of major decisions that often confront people.

Enrolling in or dropping out of college
Accepting or quitting a job
Breaking up with a boyfriend or girlfriend
Having a baby
Moving away from home

7   Reviewing a TV Show or Movie

Write an essay about a television show or movie you have seen very recently. The thesis of your essay will be that the show (or movie) has both good and bad features. (If you are writing about a TV series, be sure that you evaluate only one episode. Remember also to see pages 423–424 for correct formatting of titles of movies, TV shows, and episodes.) You may wish to use division and classification in this essay, so that you can group positive or negative aspects in an organized way.

In your first supporting paragraph, briefly summarize the episode of the show or the movie. Don't get bogged down in small details here; just give an overview, describe briefly the major characters and give the highlights of the action.

In your second supporting paragraph, explain what you feel are the best features of the show or movie. Listed below are some examples of good features you might write about.

Suspenseful, ingenious, or realistic plot
Good acting
Good scenery or special effects
Surprise ending
Good music
Believable characters

In your third supporting paragraph, explain what you feel are the worst features of the show or movie. Here are some possibilities.

Far-fetched, confusing, or dull plot
Poor special effects
Bad acting
One-dimensional characters
Unrealistic dialogue

Remember to cover only a few features in each paragraph; do not try to include everything. However, if further information is needed—such as background about a specific genre, for example—you may wish to insert a paragraph that defines or explains. In that case, be sure that the information is located within the first supporting reason or within the supporting section that seems most logical in the essay.

Use your concluding paragraph to sum up your overall positive or negative view of the show or movie, based on your three previous paragraphs.

REVIEWING THE LEARNING OUTCOMES FOR ESSAY WRITING

After working through this chapter's activities and completing one of its essay assignments, review your final draft to see how well your essay responds to the following questions.

✓ Does your essay attract the reader's interest with its introduction? Does your introduction clearly relate to your thesis? Is the rhetorical mode you will use clearly indicated?

✓ Does your introductory paragraph contain a clear thesis statement and some indication of the method of organization, or plan of development, you will use?

✓ Does each supporting paragraph open with a topic sentence that relates to one of the supporting points for your thesis?

✓ Does each supporting paragraph contain enough specific and separate explanatory and supporting details to clarify that paragraph's point, answer potential questions in advance, and thus reinforce your thesis? Is the essay consistent in its form or mode?

✓ Are your supporting paragraphs linked smoothly to one another by transitional devices or transitional sentences? Do the sentences within each supporting paragraph show effective use of transitional words where needed?

✓ Does your conclusion return the reader to the point of your thesis? Does it sum up the meaning and evidence supplied in the body of your essay? Do you leave the reader with a parting thought to signal completion or suggest wider meaning? Does it more-or-less balance the introduction?

✓ Have you revised your essay carefully to avoid errors in spelling and other mechanics?

Visit the *English Skills with Readings: Examining Paragraphs* Online Learning Centre at www.mcgrawhill.ca/olc/langan to access self-quizzes, internet-based questions and research skills, web resources, and other learning and study tools.

Chapter 17

Research Skills

When you have studied this chapter, you will:

- work through two linked activities to create an effective research essay;

- focus your research topic and create a trial outline;

- work successfully through the stages of the research process;

- find appropriate and credible sources of research information;

- judge your sources of information according to suitable criteria;

- evaluate information for quality and usefulness; and

- use your research material suitably and correctly in research assignments.

You have been the main source of information for many of the writing assignments in the textbook. However, for many assignments in college, for communications-related programs and in other courses, you will need to supplement and extend your own views with material from other sources. Here you will find a brief introduction to the process, purposes, and methods of doing college-level research.

THE RESEARCH PROCESS

Conducting research, like writing, is a process, and like writing, effective researching includes sets of skills that can be mastered if you are willing and determined to learn. Research can be interesting and enjoyable, *if* you allow yourself enough time and learn how to do it. When you learn to manage and use your research, you are actually acquiring the important life skill of learning to educate yourself. This is an essential skill you will need in almost every area of your life, from renting an apartment or purchasing a new home, car, or other major investment, to participating in civic events such as organizing community activities or following elections.

Dividing the research process into five steps gives you a clear strategy, like a map to follow. If you work through these stages carefully, allowing yourself enough time to complete each one, you will be prepared to write a solid research essay. Each time you follow this strategy, you will find research less demanding and confusing, and more rewarding. Each time you undertake a college research task, your goals will be the same.

Goals for Research

In college-level research your goals are:

1) The discovery of:
   a. your own thoughts about your subject, and
   b. appropriate externally derived support for your ideas; and
2) The **blending** of your own points with support and extension from research sources to create a clear and correctly documented essay.

With a strategy to follow and clear goals in mind, take each research assignment a step at a time, and the task will be less intimidating.

Five Steps for Preparing to Write an Effective Research Essay

Step 1   Find your topic focus and create a trial outline.

Step 2   Discover what you will need from your research.

Step 3   Find information using the library and the Internet.

Step 4   Evaluate and select appropriate information.

Step 5   Absorb your research findings and take notes.

Begin by discovering what you know and think about your topic. Doing so will show you where you need more information, and where you need to begin the research process for your essay.

Step 1: Find Your Topic Focus and Create a Trial Outline

The first stage of writing a research essay for most subjects follows the same methods you have learned for paragraph and essay writing. You begin by discovering your own responses to a topic, and then developing a main point with some general supporting reasons. Keep in mind that allowing adequate time to consider the subject area or areas of the assignment is essential to developing a clear guideline as you search for information.

Read through your assignment carefully to understand the assigned topic If you have a choice of subjects or topics, select the one that interests you most. Then, carefully consider any requirements for the length of your essay—the length of your text will determine how you should narrow and focus your working thesis, based on the topic you have chosen.

Activity 1

Consider a topic you have wished to learn about for which you have not had adequate information. Some suggestions are provided, but you may choose one that interests you:

- Sustainable housing
- Designing a commercial website
- Best practices in office management
- Gun violence in Canada

Once you choose a topic, try to apply each of the following Research Tip techniques to find out as much as you can about your chosen subject before you write a model research essay.

Research Tip: Limit your topic by asking research questions College-level research essays should *thoroughly* develop a *limited topic*. This means that once you have selected an appropriate topic, you must work out one line of discovery or one line of argument that you will follow in your essay. A good way to discover this line (which will ultimately help you create a working, or trial, thesis) is to ask yourself a series of *research questions,* such as those in the box on the next page. These are based on the "Journalists' Questions," introduced in Chapter 2.

Typical Research Questions
What do I want to discover about _____?
Who are the relevant people (or characters) I should find out about?
When do things occur in _____?
Where does _____ happen?
Why or *how* does _____ occur, or *why* is _____ so _____?

Answering one or more of these questions will lead you to a point that you will be able to prove, and this will help you to formulate a trial thesis. Each of these questions helps to narrow a general subject area or refine a topic so that you discover the point for your research. Strive for an answer that suggests an idea such as: "It is important to show why _____ led to _____," or "It is necessary to explain what _____ is," then you are ready to proceed to writing a trial thesis.

Your trial thesis may be as simple as "Three considerations make sustainable housing desirable _____." This is a guide to help you move on to a working outline. Moreover, you may, as with any prewriting, change your working thesis as you progress. But once you have a thesis, you know the general direction and the line of development your essay may take. Follow the outline pattern on pages 285–287 of the textbook as you consider possible supporting points. You will find that you have gaps in your supporting information, and those are ideal places to do some research later. But you must always shape your essay with your own ideas as its structure. Writing a research essay never entails simply finding information and piecing it together into a patchwork of others' ideas. It is essential to first discover your viewpoint, the focus for your topic, and how much you already know about your subject area.

When you have a clear focus and a satisfying trial outline, you are ready to begin the next stage in the research process: finding information related to your focused thesis and trial supporting points.

Activity 2

Apply the Journalists' Questions to the research topic you have chosen. For example, if you wished to find out about sustainable housing, you might search for answers to questions such as:

"What do I need to discover about sustainable housing?"
"Who develops sustainable housing?"
"When was the concept of sustainable housing introduced?"
"Where have there been good models of sustainable housing developed?"
"Why be concerned about sustainable housing?"
"How could sustainable housing be incorporated into the community?"

You may need to modify the W5 questions to suit your specific research area. Then, arrange your material into a working outline to organize your search efforts.

Step 2: Discover What You Will Need from Your Research

Your instructor may have included suggestions or requirements about the types of research material that are expected for your assignment. Even if this is the case, discovering precisely what information you will need from these resources can be a challenge. Your working outline is the ideal place to tackle that challenge.

Examine your outline with the following questions in mind:

- In general, what do I need to know more about in order to add supporting details?
- Where are the gaps in my outline?
- Where do I need more facts to expand my support and make it specific?
- What kinds of information—facts, statistics, details, quotations, technical data—are relevant to this course or subject area and will make parts of my essay stronger?
- Where can I find some reliable information in the areas I've noted above?

Begin a document called "Research Notes," or something similar, in which you keep the answers you gave to the questions above. Keep your trial outline with these notes, so you can use them for reference when you go to the library or go online for information.

Research Tip: Distinguish between primary and secondary sources   There are two main types of information available to you: primary and secondary sources.

- **Primary sources** are original, first-hand sources that are the subject itself or inform you directly about the subject. Primary sources do not comment on, explain, or analyze the subject. Primary sources would be a story or article you are writing about for a research essay, a fact-finding interview with a person on the subject of your research, or an event or experiment you are observing as the basis for your essay—these are direct sources of information.
- **Secondary sources** are any works in any media that refer to, comment on, or analyze your subject area. They are second-hand information, material that has been published on the subject of your research—in other words, the viewpoints of others. Secondary sources include encyclopedia articles, reference books, journal, newspaper, and magazine articles, TV programs, and websites.

As you begin college-level research work, you will probably use mostly secondary sources for your essays. After you have explored the primary source for your topic—be it a short story, a business report, or an experiment—and created a working outline, you are ready to start your search for good-quality, relevant secondary sources of information.

In the box below are questions to guide you in the third and fourth steps of your research process, when you will be locating and evaluating information. Generally, your two main resources will be the library and the Internet.

Basic Research Questions

What are you looking for?

Information that:

- is clearly relevant to the points you make;
- is clearly understandable to you;
- you can paraphrase or incorporate reasonably;
- comes from reputable, reliable sources.

Why are you performing this research?

To find information that:

- supports the views that you hold;
- expands on and strengthens points you make;
- lends authority to your viewpoints.

Step 3: Find Information Using the Library and the Internet

Library Resources

Your college or local library contains many resources for your research, in the forms of printed and computerized material. This material is stored systematically.

- **Discover** how the library's storage systems work: this is essential to finding useful information. Learn what is available from your library's cataloguing system and technological resources; they make starting your research much easier.
- **Don't forget librarians and help-desk staff:** they are information experts, and they are there to help you. Developing effective research techniques and habits is one of your main tasks in college.

Library Catalogues

The library catalogue is your first key to available information. The catalogue is usually a computerized listing of two types of holdings: those in your library, and those available on loan from affiliated library collections.

- **Library collections** consist of information in a variety of media: books, periodicals, encyclopedias, films, CDs, and so on.
- **College libraries' online resources** can extend your research resources. If your college's library or learning centre is online as part of the college website, it may use a system like BIBCAT, which allows you to look up all kinds of reference materials in different media.
- **Library databases** are specially purchased tools that hold carefully selected sources of information related to programs offered by your college. The catalogue and databases will be accessible to you on the terminals in your library, but how will you decide whether some book, journal, or magazine article you see listed onscreen is a good choice? To learn how to locate and understand information from your library's systems, ask for help the first time you start any research work.

Research Tip: Learn the value of author, title, *and* subject *searches* Computerized and online library catalogues allow you to search by *author, title,* or *subject,* or even by keywords. Author and title screens contain much useful information including the call number, which helps you to locate the item, and the current availability of additional items you want to see. Obviously, though, to use *author* or *title* searches, you will need to know the authors or titles of items you are looking for.

Most often, as you begin your research, searching by *subject* will be most productive for you. If you have worked out a focused topic for your research, then your task is to find the most effective search words to define your topic area. Trying out search words to use in a library catalogue is like using an online search engine: the quality of your keywords or search words determines the quality of the results you will receive.

The *subject* section of the catalogue performs three valuable functions:

1) It will give you a list of books, articles, and other publications on a given topic.
2) It will often provide related topics that may yield information on your subject.

3) It will lead you to more limited topics, helping you to further narrow your topic.

As you look at *subject* section screens, you see a traditional source of information listed: books. But you also see listings for other sources, such as articles from special-interest and professional journals and other periodicals. Libraries and resource centres have bound volumes and computerized versions of periodicals as well as indexes for them. You will also find a wide range of material on your college's databases. Much of this information is specialized and not available from online sites, or available only through your college library's subscriptions.

Each type of library resource is appropriate for various research needs, depending on your subject and the length and demands of a particular assignment. Details about these resources follow.

Criteria for College Research Findings

When you are trying to decide the value of a particular source of information, consider the following questions.

Focus: How focused is this material on my subject area and topic? Is the information I need a small part of the material or its main content?

Depth of Information: How deeply does this material treat my area of interest? Does it offer a good quantity of information that is new to me?

Currency of Information: How recently was this material published? For this course and for my topic, how important is recent information?

Quality of Information: Is this material at a level of expertise that my instructor expects for this assignment?

Authorship: This is often considered the most important of all criteria. Is the author a reputable source, a specialist in this field? Is the author known to have a particular agenda—or motive—to promote through the writing of this work?

Books

Traditionally, books have been the most trusted starting point for research. This is often still the case, especially in some subject areas, but locating just the right books and finding the time to read them can be problematic. To locate books you find in the library catalogue, ask a librarian to explain the call-number system by which your library arranges books on the shelves. Once you find the book you saw in the catalogue, try the following tips to help you judge its usefulness.

- Look at the front and back pages and the cover text of the book. Check the date of publication and look for information on the author's credentials.
- Check the table of contents for material related to your topic. If many chapters relate to it, the book may be a good resource.

- Look through the index of the book (at the back) for words and phrases related to your topic. If there are many pages for each such reference, consider using the book.
- Scan the introduction or preface for the author's statement of intentions, the author's viewpoint, and a summary of the book's contents.
- To find related books on the same subject, look for a bibliography in any book you find useful.

Depending on the time you have, examine at least two books on your topic so that you have two viewpoints on the same material. Practise critical thinking with any source of information: weigh one author's views against another's and against your own ideas, so you can make informed decisions about the quality of any information.

Further Insight—The Library of Congress classification system for books

Over the years, libraries have developed systems to classify books according to their subject matter. One of the most commonly used systems is the Library of Congress system, which has organized subjects into sets indicated by initial letters for its call numbers. Each letter is further subdivided by subsequent letters and numbers. This is a partial list as used by most college libraries:

A. General Works (includes encyclopedias)
B. Philosophy, Psychology, Religion
C.D.E. History
F. Canadian History
G. Geography
H. Social Sciences
J. Politics
K. Law
L. Education
M. Music
N. Fine Arts
P. Language and Literature
Q. Science
R. Medicine
S. Agriculture
T. Technology
U. Military Science
V. Naval Science
Z. Library Science

● ● ● ● **Activity**

Identify the most likely initial call letter of the book listing for each of the following topics:

Canadian Confederation	Water birds	Early childhood education
Youth crime	Medical emergencies	Weather phenomena
Digital photography	Canadian literature	Climate change Business organization

Choose three of these topics and find at least three books for each. Record the call numbers, and note how they conform to the Library of Congress system.

Research Databases and Online Search Services

Learn how to use the electronic research databases and online search services available through your college's library site. These databases are vital assets in college research. College research tasks require specialized or academic information, known as the deep Internet, which you will not find online at general access sites or through search engines. In fact, over 70 percent of this high-quality information exists only on pages protected by firewalls and pages inaccessible to search engines. Colleges purchase library portals and databases to give you entry to these essential online resources, which are available in three forms:

- controlled websites to which your college has purchased access rights;
- online databases to which your college provides access;
- CD-ROM databases owned by your college's library.

Your college user ID and password or other student codes give you access to database publications ranging from trade and technological publications to encyclopedias and online collections like *Research Library* and *Bluebook of Canadian Business.*

Databases include Dialog, *Proquest,* and *ERIC* (Educational Resources Information Centre). EBSCOhost and Infotrac house online computer search services. Dialog and CPI.Q (the Canadian Periodical Index search service) give you access to thousands of magazine articles listed by subject. Listings often have summaries or abstracts, and sometimes whole articles. Using the EBSCOhost service, you can perform keyword searches through hundreds of periodicals for articles on your topic. You can then e-mail these to yourself at home or print them in the college library.

Internet Resources

Doing research online allows you to do much of your work from any place with Internet access. But while college resources are selected specifically for student and faculty needs, Internet resources are limitless, and therefore risk being without focus.

Therefore, it is necessary to learn some of these basic guidelines for sorting through the Internet's vast content and mix of commercial and non-commercial material.

Research Tip: Open a "Favourites" folder for the sites you find relevant to your topic As you work with search engines, keep track of the sites that may be of use to you. Keep these sites separate from your other favourites by creating a new folder for your topic, perhaps with subfolders for specific supporting points. This will save you time, as well as the frustration of scrolling through screens to locate exactly which sections are relevant.

Search Engines

Search engines use automated software called bots, spiders, or crawlers. When you trigger a search by typing in keywords, these "crawl" through the Internet seeking content. Search engines vary in the quality and extent of their findings; it is worth experimenting to find an engine that best meets your needs. One specialized type of search engine is the directory search engine. Directory engines contain information assembled and categorized by people who collect that material from various databases. Findings on directory engines are presented under a set of progressively more specific headings based on your keywords. Several engines today combine robot and directory functions. Metasearch engines, such as Google, search other engines as well as their own databases, and then compile the results.

To find useful information about various engines and tips for using them more effectively, go to http://www.lib.berkeley.edu/TeachingLib/Guides/Internet/SearchEngines.html. For general purposes, many search engines work well, but they demand time to review results. Google is excellent; it is a "smart search" engine, a type that not only accumulates findings but also rates them by appropriateness of content.

Google, unlike many engines, checks the context or words surrounding your keywords to see if they are related to the topic you are searching for. Google Scholar has been developed specifically to search for the types of results appropriate for college research, and includes links to online periodicals (although access to them may still be limited). Google (and some other engines) can also search for results in newsgroups and different media as well—they can return findings as text files, image files, and sound files. Directory engine searches open with a display of categories under which to explore your topic; these can save you time and offer more results in a limited category. If you are still working on your focus, or know that you wish to confine your search to a specific area, you will find a directory engine search useful.

All search engines deliver results quickly (with some variations, according to your speed and type of Internet connection), but there are three important reasons to allow yourself some time to work with search engines. First, even if you have done preliminary work on focusing your research topic, you will need time for some trial attempts with your search words. If your results are not satisfying, try playing with similar words and concepts until you become familiar with the types of words that give good returns, or "hits."

Next, you need time to sift through and scan the sites and links that your searches bring up. Be sure to save any useful-looking sites. Finally, you need time to read the material you have saved and to decide which sites and which passages will be most useful—your preliminary work of outlining and discovering directions for your essay pays off here, because you will spot relevant material more quickly.

Activating a search engine is a simple matter of telling that engine's database what to look for by entering keywords. But to search with any speed and success, carefully targeted keywords are essential. Use words from your subject area or discipline, try synonyms, and try placing your words in order of importance—allow time for some trial and error. Learn to increase the power of your search words and phrases from search engines' help pages: combining words with Boolean operators (a system of logical thinking) such as *and* and *not,* using plus and minus symbols, and sub-searching are skills that maximize the effectiveness of your online research time. A simple guide to Boolean methods and symbols can be found at http://www.lib.berkeley.edu/TeachingLib/Guides/Internet/Boolean.pdf.

Newsgroups and RSS Feeds

Your Internet software gives you access to other information sources for research: newsgroups and RSS feeds. You may find them useful, although reading hundreds of postings takes time and requires you to decide how useful or credible those posts are. As such technology advances, though, these types of posts are becoming more manageable, allowing students to choose which information they wish to receive on a regular basis.

Because lists and groups are "communities" of people linked by a common interest, they do not represent an accepted authority on your topic, so use careful judgment in choosing information from these sources.

Note: Be aware, especially, that you do not accept blogs (weblogs) as valid editorial content, as they are usually highly subjective and unmoderated. Similarly, while the large community of *wiki-* sites, or user-generated information sites, may return quickly on Internet searches, their popularity and promise of oversight do not mean that the information is accurate or commonly accepted. In order to be suitable sources of information, only groups or sites with appropriate standards of focus, depth, currency, quality, and authorship meet criteria for valid research.

Periodicals

Periodicals (magazines, journals, and newspapers) are essential resources for your college tasks. You need specific, focused information devoted to your research area, not the general sorts of information found in encyclopedias. Instead, look for articles that provide current and focused information.

To use periodical articles, you must learn to locate the various types of information available to you, and then judge them for quality and currency. Here you will find an introduction to locating and using these resources. For information on evaluation, see Step 4 later in this chapter.

To find periodical articles, discover which periodicals your library carries, how these are indexed, and how you will access the articles contained in the indexes. If this is the first time you are working with periodicals, ask a librarian to help you. You will find there are both printed and online indexes of every kind of periodical, from daily newspapers to highly specialized professional and scientific journals.

Periodical Indexes

Librarians can direct you to the large bound indexes of various magazines and periodicals and help you to use them. *The Readers' Guide to Periodical Literature* and *The Canadian Periodical Index* are good places to begin; these are printed each year. Articles are listed by author and subject, with cross-references to related articles. The *CPI* indexes articles from Canadian specialized and academic publications as well as popular magazines. Other bound volumes of more specialized periodical indexes will be shelved near these volumes, so check for any indexes related to your topic or subject area.

Indexes to these and other periodical groups are also available online and on CDs in most libraries. You may find these versions easier to use. Search by subject or author, as you would with the library catalogue.

Once you have found articles whose titles sound promising or whose listings offer summaries that seem relevant to your topic, you must locate the full text of the article itself. If your library stocks a specific periodical, ask the librarian to help you locate the issue you need. If you are using an online index, you may find an option onscreen to take you to the full text of the article. Alternatively, your library may have databases where you can find such articles.

Note: Using the various periodical indexes and databases in your library is a vital skill you will need for successful college research. If research tutorials are offered to you, be sure to take advantage of them.

Step 4: Evaluate and Select Appropriate Information

Now is the time to go back to your reference notes and add to them. Begin a reference list—a set of notes about your sources—to keep track of possible research sources for your essay. Each time you find suitable information from library and online sources, list the names and locations of books, articles, and database information you found useful. Print your bookmarks as well, to include in your reference list.

For each source, write down the author's name, the title of the book, article, or website, and some point-form notes of the main useful points you found. You should have more items than you will eventually need, because you will eliminate some during the step of evaluating each source of information for its quality and relevance.

With your list at hand, review your assignment's requirements for clues as to how many sources will be appropriate. If it is a fairly brief essay, you should select only the best pieces of information from your list; if a minimum or specified number of sources is stipulated, then use that as a guideline. Research *supports* and *extends* your own points and support; it is *not* the backbone of your essay.

Determining how useful your sources are and deciding how much information to use from each source are skills you will refine throughout college, but the following guidelines will help you evaluate sources. Three criteria will guide you as you examine any source of information: relevance to your topic, reliability of content, and timeliness.

Relevance

- Use sources that are primarily devoted to your topic. If a source's main focus is your topic area, its information will be less superficial and more specialized.
- Check that a source's treatment of topic-related information is suited to your understanding and needs. Is it too technical, or too general?
- Consider the source type of the publication: is it a general interest magazine or a specialized journal? Journals, notable for their lack of advertising, offer superior, peer-reviewed research. The quality of the information is ensured through a process of rigorous scrutiny by acknowledged scholars. In contrast, general-interest magazines and newspapers are designed to appeal to readers' senses—using glossy pages or stimulating visuals—and may have goals other than that of providing unbiased information. These distinctions apply to both print and online versions.
- Rank the source in terms of its importance to your essay's focus on your topic to make your final selection easier.

Authorship and Reliability

- Use sources whose author is recognized in the field. Look for the author's biography, scan for other material by the same author, or ask your instructor or a librarian for help.
- Check for authors whose books and articles contain bibliographies and reference lists.
- Check that the links on a website are active and reliable.
- Learn all you can about the author's overall view of or bias on your topic. Check biographical material, the introduction or preface to the work, or other writers' views of the author. Website authors should include identifying biographical information and an e-mail address.
- Check for references within the source to other material and authors on the subject. If other sources are not named, the information may be one-sided or biased.
- Look for well-supported arguments, clear logic, and ample solid proof for points made in your source. (Use the same criteria you have learned in the textbook.)
- Always verify important pieces of information in at least three sources. If some information reappears frequently, then it is probably reliable.
- Check for website sponsorship. Does it represent commercial interests? Check the three-letter sequence at the end of its URL: *org* generally refers to non-commercial organizations; *ca* is used throughout Canada, and is not exclusive to educational or governmental organizations; *edu* indicates an educational institution in the United States. Personal websites need careful evaluation.

Timeliness and Currency

- Check for recent publication dates of books and periodical articles.
- On websites, look for the most recent updating—this information often appears on the homepage or final page of a site.

Decide on a reasonable number of reference sources for your purpose, based on your assignment's requirements and these three criteria, and you will be prepared to absorb the content of your chosen resources and make notes of material to use in your assignment.

Step 5: Absorb Your Research Findings and Take Notes

Set a few sessions aside during which you will be able to concentrate on the sources of information you have selected. Using the source notes in your reference list, read each book section, article, and webpage you have listed carefully; look for similarities and differences among them. You are digesting and absorbing ideas while you read.

Do not try to review your reference choices in one sitting; your understanding of the material deepens when you use several unhurried sessions. You will make connections and find new ideas of your own as you go along.

Keep your working outline nearby, as well as extra paper or readily-available documents, on which to make notes of ideas, connections, and additional sources. Keep referring to your essay's outline to maintain your focus and help you make decisions on what to record for which part of your outline. Here are some tips for note-taking for research purposes.

- Use a computer file, paper, or note cards to keep notes.
- Take notes on one source at a time, and note the author, title, location or URL, and page numbers at the top of each note.
- Keep all notes from a single source together.
- Put a topic-related or supporting-point heading at the start of each of your notes.
- Distinguish with colour or quotation marks between your own words and direct quotations from any source. Note the page number or URL for any material.
- Do not simply copy long quotations or copy material directly without quotation marks. Long quotations (over five lines) are rarely suitable for college research essays. Instead, note in point form the essential ideas from a long passage, and record the page numbers where you found the information.

As you make your research notes, think about *why* you are doing so. Information from sources other than your own ideas and outline has three functions:

- to expand on facts with examples, statistics, or data that clarify and strengthen your points and ideas;
- to present another explanation or view of some point that strengthens your points and ideas;
- to support with some recognized authority a point or claim you make.

The purpose of taking notes is not to replace your own ideas or to save yourself writing solid support. In Chapter 18, you will learn how to blend the information you have absorbed with your own ideas, give credit for the material you have found, and thus create an effective research essay.

• • • • **Activity 3**

Using the techniques discussed in this chapter, search for information about the research topic you have chosen. Check that you have taken adequate notes and that you have full reference data for each piece of information your find. This may be an ongoing process that takes several days, so take time to organize your search efforts so that you will be able to use them once you begin to write.

Be sure to look for gaps or discrepancies in any information you find. Remember that you may need to find more than one source to verify any information, to make sure that you are discovering the most accurate and current data available.

REVIEWING THE LEARNING OUTCOMES FOR RESEARCH SKILLS

Now that you have studied this chapter, answer the following questions:

✓ What are your overall goals when you write a college-level research essay?

✓ What are two distinguishing characteristics of a college-level research essay?

✓ What is one method for focusing and limiting a research topic?

✓ What are the next four steps in the research process?

✓ What criteria should you use to help you decide if an information source is an appropriate one?

✓ What is the difference between using a college library database and using a search engine to find relevant information?

✓ What are the three guidelines for evaluating a reference source?

✓ What are three functions of externally derived information in a research essay?

Visit the *English Skills with Readings: Examining Paragraphs* Online Learning Centre at www.mcgrawhill.ca/olc/langan to access self-quizzes, internet-based questions and research skills, web resources, and other learning and study tools.

Chapter 18

Preparing a Research Essay

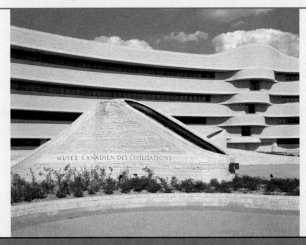

MUSÉE CANADIEN DES CIVILISATIONS

LEARNING OUTCOMES

When you have worked through this chapter, you will:

- prepare revised research notes with all necessary information;
- coordinate your research notes with your trial outline;
- prepare and use quotations effectively and correctly;
- paraphrase information accurately and use paraphrasing appropriately;
- summarize information succinctly;

- incorporate and credit quotations, paraphrases, and summaries in a research essay;
- use MLA or APA citation styles appropriately;
- understand elements that form plagiarism, how to avoid them; and
- assemble, write, and reference an effective college research essay.

After completing the steps in the research process covered in Chapter 17, you face the challenges of combining your research with your own ideas in order to proceed to the actual writing of your essay. This chapter will take you step by step through assembling and writing an effective college research essay.

Your first general goal for research assignments, as discussed in Chapter 17, was the *discovery* of your own ideas about your topic and of research material to strengthen, support, or lend authority to those ideas. Now you are ready to take your outline and research notes and work on the second overall goal in creating a research essay: *blending* your own structure and ideas with suitable support from your research.

To blend your ideas with support from outside sources, you must:

- have a firm enough grasp of the quality of your own points and support that you do not substitute ideas from outside sources simply because they seem preferable or impressive;
- review and absorb your research material so that you can select material of relevance and appropriate length;
- combine your words with those of others into smooth sentences, introducing your quotations correctly into your text; and
- give credit to your sources each time you use them as quotations or paraphrases, employing an appropriate style of citation.

No one accomplishes these tasks all at once. Assemble your essay one step at a time, and you will acquire a solid working strategy for college research assignments. This chapter breaks the preparation of a research essay into six steps. Allow yourself at least three days to work through them.

Six Steps in Preparing a Research Essay

Step 1   Revise your working outline.

Step 2   Review and prepare your research material.

Step 3   Write your first draft.

Step 4   Revise your first draft, inserting and citing your sources.

Step 5   Document your research and prepare a works-cited or reference list.

Step 6   Write your final draft.

STEP 1: REVISE YOUR WORKING OUTLINE

Now that you have read a number of different sources relating to your topic and support, it is time to revise your outline. Your aim is to create a strong, clear, detailed outline to guide you and allow you to mesh your own supporting details with appropriate items from your research.

Begin a new document; you may find this the ideal time to use the computer so that you can easily change words and phrases and leave blank spaces. Review the assignment you were given. Are there clues to the type or purpose of the essay you must submit? Before you begin revising your outline, reconsider your purpose. The requirements for your assignment may present a purpose. If you are choosing your own, choose between the two main purposes of research essays—to inform or to persuade.

Look at the research questions in Step 1 of the research process in Chapter 17. Do you wish to answer a *what* or *who* question? In that case, your purpose may be to inform, to supply a detailed, logical answer to your research question. Was a *why* or *how* question most useful to you? Then you may have looked for research to support your viewpoint on *why* or *how* something is as it is: you may want to persuade your reader. Use the questions you found most relevant, along with your assignment's requirements, to help you decide on your purpose. Making this decision helps you reformulate your working thesis into a stronger thesis statement that guides your choices of supporting details. Reread the section of Chapter 16 (pages 276–277) on writing thesis statements, if necessary.

If your main purpose is to inform your reader of *what* something is, or *what has led* to something, then your thesis should state this clearly, while presenting the point you will prove. Your supporting points and details will provide examples, explanations, descriptions, facts, or statistics to demonstrate the soundness of your thesis to readers.

Informative Thesis Statements

1) "Four trends in urban development have led to 'box store' retail groupings."

Not

"'Box store' retail groupings are appearing everywhere in Canadian cities."

2) "Kate Chopin's use of characters under pressure adds drama to three of her most famous short stories."

Not

"Kate Chopin writes about characters under pressure."

If your main purpose is to persuade your reader of *why* you hold some position on your topic, then your thesis should state this clearly, suggesting strong reasons why your viewpoint is valid. Your supporting points and details will offer solid evidence and authoritative backup—specifics carefully targeted at convincing the reader of the truth of your thesis.

Persuasive Thesis Statements

1) "Attempts to obstruct music downloading by the recording industry are pointless, expensive, and ultimately harmful to artists."

Not

"The recording industry will never stop people downloading music."

2) "Student financial aid in Ontario is insufficient for students' needs, confusing to navigate, and often humiliating to applicants."

Not

"Students find it difficult to get financial aid in Ontario."

Once you have revised your thesis to your satisfaction, review your supporting points. Be sure that each one is truly distinct from the others, and that each one clearly proves, supports, and clarifies one aspect of your thesis.

As you set up your revised outline document, leave plenty of blank space under each supporting-point heading so that you can note your own supporting details as well as the quotations and paraphrases you wish to include from your research. Often, instructors require an outline to be handed in along with a research essay, or even beforehand, so revising your outline to finalize your points and support and incorporate your research will take care of such a requirement. The partial outline below shows how to start modifying an essay outline so that you can add quotations and paraphrases from your research sources in the appropriate places. Notice that, for a short research essay, only a few well-chosen pieces of research support are needed—your ideas, developed on your own and during your research, are the backbone of the essay.

Introductory Paragraph

Introduction: _____

Thesis Statement: _____

Plan of Development: _____

Supporting Point 1: _____

Supporting Point 2: _____

Supporting Point 3: _____

First Supporting Paragraph

Topic Sentence: _____

Subtopic 1: _____

Supporting Details:

a. _____

b. _____

c. _____

Concluding Statement: _____

Subtopic 2: _____

Supporting Details:

a. _____

b. _____

c. _____

Concluding Statement: _____

Subtopic 3: _____

Supporting Details:

a. _____

b. _____

c. _____

Concluding Statement: _____

This partial outline should also include the page numbers for the quotations and paraphrases you intend to use. Transfer the author's name and the page numbers from your research notes each time you make a note of material from a research source. The next step will show you how to prepare your research notes correctly so that you can properly credit quotations, paraphrases, and summaries.

• • • • **Activity 1**

Gather the information you have collected from the previous chapter and assess what kind of research question you wish to answer. Follow the directions above to develop a working thesis statement that will express the point you wish to make. Once you have developed your thesis statement, continue by following the essay outline. Pay particular attention to places where you think you might need more information or clarification. Later, you will include sources in your outline to guide your research and documentation processes.

STEP 2: REVIEW AND PREPARE YOUR RESEARCH MATERIAL

Preparing your research material means, first, recording the words of others correctly, as:

- **quotations:** the exact words of another writer, enclosed by double quotation marks;

Add quotation from _____: "........." (page #)

Add paraphrase from _____ (page #) about this idea

Add quotation from _____: "........." (page #)

- **paraphrases:** restatements of another writer's words in your own wording; or
- **summaries:** condensed versions of another writer's ideas in your own words.

Preparing the material you have drawn from another source also means correctly and fully recording all the necessary information from that source.

Choose one method for setting up your revised research notes, and use it consistently. Use a computer document, a small notebook, or three-by-five-inch cards. Begin each research note with a phrase or keyword that refers to the point or idea that the note applies to.

This step will necessitate a trip back to the library, and perhaps the help of a librarian, because you will need to record certain information for each research note.

For a book
- The author of the book
- The title of the book
- The page numbers you have referred to or quoted or paraphrased from

- The publisher of the book
- The city where the book was published
- The year the book was published (and the edition of the book, if applicable)
- Locating information: the call number on the cover or spine of the book

For a periodical article (whether in print or on a database)
- The author of the article
- The title of the article
- The title of the magazine, journal, or newspaper where the article appeared
- For journals, the volume (and issue number, if any) in which the article appeared
- The date the article appeared
- The page numbers of the whole article or of the quote referred to
- Locating information: where and how you accessed the article

For a website
- The author of the website or of an article on the website
- The title of any section or article that you refer to
- The title of the website
- The date listed for the website or the section of the site that you refer to
- Locating information: the URL of the website
- The date or dates when you accessed the website

Following are sample research notes showing first a reference to the particular point the student wishes to support, then the correct citation (in MLA style) of the required items. The required elements listed above are indicated with arrows. In Step 5 of this chapter, you will learn more about setting out these items correctly according to accepted styles of documentation.

Sample Research Note for a Book Used as a Source

Author of book

Title of book

Internet-connected communities and changes in social networks
—how networked communities behaved differently from neighbourhoods where people met only physically

Publisher of book

Year of publication

Hoffert, Paul. All Together Now: Connected Communities. Toronto: Stoddart, 2000.

Locating information

Call Number: 842.91

City where book was published

"Residents also shared information about reliable auto-repair shops and neighbourhood retail stores that were having sales. They shared information about baby-sitters, garbage pick-ups, and used ice skates that their kids had outgrown."

Page number referred to

Page 85

Sample Research Note for a Periodical Article Used as a Source

Gender Identity Disorder

—argument in favour of adjusting a child's gender tendencies

—authority: Dr. Kenneth Zucker, head of Child and

Author of article —— Adolescent GID Clinic at CAMH, Toronto —— *Title of article*

Bauer, Gabrielle. "If Your Little Boy Wants to Be a Little Girl." Saturday Night Nov. 2002: 61.

Locating ——→ Location: InfoTrac —— *Date of article*

information

Title of periodical

Paraphrase with quotation: Dr. Zucker feels that children, particularly boys, with GID suffer from bullying and loneliness. He believes that helping them to "be happy with the gender they were born with" prevents later unhappiness in life.

Sample Research Note for a Website Used as a Source

Author of article on website ——

Beginning of electric blues in Chicago that led to rock music—when musicians moved, and how blues music changed

→ Baker, Robert M. "A Brief History of the Blues." The Blue Highway. 1996.

Title of website

Date of article or website ——

"During the decades of the thirties and forties, the blues spread northward with the migration of many blacks from the South and entered into the repertoire of big-band jazz."

Title of article on website

http://thebluehighway.com/history.html

Locating information ——

Date of access: May 12, 2003

Date of access ——

Be sure that your final research notes are as complete as these samples. Make a note of when you are paraphrasing, or putting into your own words the ideas of another, as you see in the sample note for a periodical article above. By keeping complete and correct research notes, you will find that inserting your source material into drafts of your essay will be much easier, as will be creating the works-cited or reference list that appears as the final page of your research essay.

Quotations, Paraphrases, and Summaries

What Is a Quotation?

Each time you use the exact words of another writer, you must identify these words as a *direct quotation*—with double quotation marks. Quoting means using phrases or sentences word for word, with punctuation exactly as it appears in the original. Here is a direct quotation.

"Conversely, the category of boredom implies a set of expectations of the external world that apparently did not afflict our remote predecessors" (Spacks 11).

The parentheses at the end of the quotation contain the author's last name and the page number in the source on which the words quoted appear. You will learn more about giving credit to your research sources in Step 4.

You may omit words from a quotation, so long as you do not change its meaning by doing so. To signal omission, you must use *ellipsis,* or three dots. Here is a direct quotation with missing words replaced by ellipsis.

"During the decades of the thirties and forties, the blues spread northward . . . and entered into the repertoire of big-band jazz" (Baker).

This example is from a website. The author of the article on the *Blue Highway* website is given in the parentheses. Because websites are not paginated, there is no page reference. The full quotation appears in the third sample research note above.

When Should You Use a Quotation?

Use quotations sparingly and only when they truly extend, explain, or lend authority to your own points. You may also wish to use a striking or particularly apt quotation to strengthen your introduction or conclusion. Quotations are accepted and expected in research and academic writing, but they are only enrichments to research assignments; they should not make up most of the body of the work.

In a short (1,000 words) research essay, five short quotations would be sufficient. A short quotation is no longer than four lines of text. Quotations can add strength and authority to research essays when used correctly and sparingly; they dilute the power of any piece of writing when overused. Essays created out of chunks of quotations strung together are annoying and confusing to read—the effect of reading such essays is like overhearing a babble of voices. The message is obscured; the writer's intention is lost under all those other voices, and the essay loses the force of one person's solid argument.

If you must use a quotation of more than four lines of text, do so cautiously and correctly. In short essays, such long quotations give the impression of filling space to replace your own thoughts. If your subject requires you to insert a long quotation, set it up as follows.

Campbell presents a clarification of the common view of early peoples' weather, healing, and seasonal rituals.

> It has been customary to describe the seasonal festivals of so-called native peoples as efforts to control nature. This is a misrepresentation. There is much of the will to control in every act of man, and particularly in those magical ceremonies that are thought to bring rain clouds, cure sickness, or stay the flood; nevertheless, the dominant motive in all truly religious . . . ceremonial is that of submission to the inevitables of destiny. . . . (384)

Long quotations (1) start on a new line, (2) are not enclosed by quotation marks, and (3) are indented from the left margin for their full length. A long quotation is double-spaced, as is the rest of the essay, and concludes with the page number of the source in parentheses (or, if the author is not named in the text before the quote, the author's name and the page number). Notice that the quotation above contains two ellipses: the first indicates that words are omitted (without changing the meaning or altering the grammatical flow of the quotation), and the second ellipsis shows that the sentence in the original does not end there.

What Is a Paraphrase?

When you paraphrase the words of another writer, you put that writer's ideas *completely* into your own words. Paraphrasing requires care and some skill for three reasons.

- You must understand the meaning of the words you paraphrase so clearly that you can restate that meaning in your own words.
- You must not simply change a few words in the original; you must use synonyms, modify the grammatical structure, and present the original source's idea as you understand it.
- You must not borrow even two-word or three-word phrases from your original; if you include these in a paraphrase, put quotation marks around them.

Because your paraphrase of someone else's idea is simply a rewording of the work of someone else, you are borrowing that idea. To avoid plagiarism (which will be discussed later in this section) you must credit anything you paraphrase just as you would a quotation—with the page number in parentheses at the end of the sentence that contains the paraphrase.

When Should You Paraphrase a Passage?

Paraphrasing is essential to the process of *blending* or synthesizing your research with your own ideas on your topic. Never present paraphrased passages as your own. Paraphrases make reading your essay a smooth process for readers because paraphrases do not interrupt the flow of your words as much as quotations. Correctly paraphrased ideas also demonstrate your understanding of your research sources and your ability to use these intelligently. Good paraphrases (1) shorten lengthy passages, (2) eliminate or explain unnecessary technical language, and (3) make the ideas in the source material clear in the context of your essay.

This example shows how to avoid plagiarism and paraphrase correctly. Here, a student wishes to use the ideas in a passage from page 35 of *A History of Reading* by Alberto Manguel.

Original Source

By the time the first scribe scratched and uttered the first letters, the human body was already capable of the acts of writing and reading that still lay in the future; that is to say, the body was able to store, recall, and decipher all manner of sensations, including the arbitrary signs of written language yet to be invented.

If the student writes this sentence or the version that appears below without crediting the source, he or she is plagiarizing, because the student has borrowed Manguel's wording without acknowledging him as the author. Even though the author of the version below has changed the general form of the passage and shortened it, sections of the phrasing belong to the original.

Plagiarism

As soon as people had figured out alphabets, the human body was already capable of writing and reading letters. The body could store, recall, and decipher feelings and letters that had yet to be invented.

The student could, however, use these sentences if he or she introduces them correctly and cites the page number of the source.

Acceptable Use of Paraphrasing

Alberto Manguel suggests in The History of Reading that once people had figured out alphabets, the human body was ready to read and write letters. He contends that the body could store, recall, and decipher feelings and letters that had yet to be invented (35).

In this case, the student has indicated the source of the ideas (Manguel and the book's title) and used the correct MLA style of inserting the page reference in parentheses at the end of the sentence. Here, and in the following example, paraphrasing is sometimes referred to as *indirect quotation*. Indirect quotation means that the words that follow the author's name contain the gist of the original but have been restated.

A better method of writing a paraphrase that contains some exact wording of an original source is to put in quotation marks any words directly quoted within a paraphrase.

Better Use of Paraphrasing

Alberto Manguel suggests in The History of Reading that once people had figured out alphabets, the human body was ready to read and write letters. He contends that the body could "store, recall, and decipher" feelings and letters that had "yet to be invented" (35).

Methods of introducing paraphrases appropriately will be covered in Step 4.

Summaries

Occasionally you will need to condense the meaning of a longer passage from a source text; this is the time to summarize. Summaries range in length from a sentence or two to several paragraphs, depending on the length and density of ideas in the original. When you summarize a piece of text, your aim is to reduce it to its essential ideas and to re-express its main points in your own words.

Summarizing is a skill you will practise and refine in several college English courses; this section introduces you to the basics. Writing a summary requires good understanding of the original text, so that you do not distort or change the meaning of it. These steps will get you started on writing good summaries.

1) Read the passage you will summarize several times, looking up any words or phrases you do not understand.

2) Note the author's main points and support in the order in which these appear in the original.

3) Write your summary from the third-person point of view.

4) Do not comment or make judgments on the original in your summary; simply write down, as economically as possible, its main ideas.

5) Put any technical or subject-specific terms into your own words.

6) Do not include quotations from the original in your summary, and omit examples, unless these are essential to the point of the passage.

7) Begin your summary by stating, in your first sentence, the name of the author and title of the work which you are summarizing, correctly cited. Do so as you would when introducing a quotation or paraphrase.

A summary in a brief research essay might consist of only a few sentences, so you may write several drafts of your first few summaries before you are able to reduce the original without losing its essence.

Plagiarism

Plagiarism means presenting someone else's ideas, words, or images as your own. Any uncredited borrowing—a phrase or two without credit information—amounts to plagiarism as much as does an entire essay that is not of your own creation. Plagiarism is considered theft, and universities and colleges impose strong academic penalties for plagiarism.

During their first semesters at college, students are sometimes not aware of how easy it is to "unconsciously plagiarize" material. Instructors generally understand that students must learn to write in their own voices and styles, and develop necessary awareness and skills to avoid plagiarism. Instructors usually have a fair idea when an error has occurred, and have tools at their disposal, including software programs especially designed for the purpose, to detect plagiarized material. Students can continue to develop quoting, paraphrasing and summarizing skills by exercising their language abilities and carefully documenting all sources, with the intents to avoid conscious or unconscious plagiarism.

Ideas and knowledge are free and available to everyone, but students must always incorporate others' ideas according to the assigned system of documentation. This is not only as a sign of integrity, but also enhances students' own development. It may require time and assistance, but with effort, students can learn the skills needed to express and support their ideas in scholastically-acceptable ways.

If a student fears that he or she has unconsciously and unknowingly copied words or phrases, the best course of action is to explain the situation immediately to the instructor. If, on the other hand, a student knowingly decides to use someone else's work, then he or she has made a conscious decision to defraud the instructor. This sort of dishonesty is taken very seriously by all institutions, and usually there are severe academic penalties for such actions.

Activity 2

As you gathered information for your research essay, you probably found material that seemed extremely important, interesting, or well-written. The temptation is to transfer such text directly into your own essay; however, to do so would be to commit plagiarism. To avoid plagiarism, you must incorporate the skills of quoting, summarizing, and paraphrasing as shown, above.

These are skills that you will develop over the course of your formal education, and perhaps beyond. They take time and practice, so it is advisable to try them out as often as possible. For now, select a passage from your research which has information you know you will want to include. Use that passage to answer the following questions; answer each in only a few key words or short phrases:

a. What is the main idea of the passage you have selected?
b. What attracted you to that selection?
c. Is the author credible?
d. How does that information compare or contrast with other information you have gained?
e. Is there a phrase you wish to repeat, or can the information be rewritten in another way?

From this information, write a short and unique sentence that describes what you wish to express from the research material. Continue with this sort of analysis and rewording for any other important material you have researched. Be sure to maintain documentation notes each time you write similar summaries of your research material.

STEP 3: WRITE YOUR FIRST DRAFT

Proceeding as you would for a regular essay, write the first draft of your research essay. Use your revised outline as a guide for this first full draft. Do not worry about spelling or mechanical errors; just concentrate on writing clear sentences that get your ideas across. At each point where you would like to add some support from your research, make a note to yourself in your draft of the research note you would like to use there. Do not worry about documenting or including quotations or paraphrases at this stage; just write in reminders of where you would like to include them.

When you are satisfied with your first draft, put it away for at least one day. You may wish to read your draft aloud to yourself or to someone else, to help you find any potential weak spots, repetitions, or problems with logic. Make notes of any areas you would like to change in your revised draft.

Note: Research essays are nearly always written from the third-person point of view. The emphasis in a research essay is on your ideas, your proof, and the quality of your research, rather than on you as a person. Therefore, using "I" could distract readers from the content and argument in your essay, and should be avoided. Let your facts speak for themselves.

Activity 3

Proceed with Step 3, above, incorporating your research notes as you go. As you review, be alert for any parts that seem out-of-place either in the information they project or in the way they are written. Be sure that the phrases you use are uniquely yours and that all ideas or words that are not have reference notes to accompany them.

STEP 4: REVISE YOUR FIRST DRAFT, INSERTING AND CITING YOUR SOURCES

Revise your first draft in two stages. In the first stage of your revision, focus only on inserting quotations or paraphrases of material from your sources. Before beginning any of this revision work, arrange your research notes in the order in which you will refer to them. When you write your draft, leave blank spaces, insert research material, and move words around.

Your goals with this first stage of your revision are to work your quotations and paraphrases smoothly into your sentences and to give essential credit information as you do so. Remember to use quotation marks where needed and to insert page references for all quotations and paraphrases according to the citation style your instructor prefers. You will find information on the two main documentation styles in Step 5; but first, it is necessary to understand *why* correct documentation is so important.

Documentation: A Contract between Writer and Reader

You must always signal when you are writing the words of another writer, even when you have paraphrased or summarized those words. Giving credit or citing your sources correctly sends immediate signals to your readers. It tells them you have taken the time to do your research and incorporate it carefully into your work; and it tells them you recognize that your audience needs to see the same signals to be aware of when you are borrowing ideas. The contract of trust between reader and writer, between instructor and student, is maintained and the writer is seen as trustworthy and careful.

Setting Up and Integrating Material from Another Source

There are three requirements for integrating each item of research material into the overall flow of your essay.

1) Write the idea for which you are adding a supporting quotation or paraphrase in clear sentences so that the source material makes sense in the context of that aspect of your essay. You must create a background for, explain, or set up the ideas to which you are adding support from outside sources so that this support makes sense to readers and adds to the quality of your own thoughts.

2) Set up your borrowed research material by identifying the author, either before or immediately after your quotation, paraphrase, or summary.

3) Complete the context or surroundings for your quotation or paraphrase by explaining it further, adding your own ideas to it, or arguing against it.

To set up a direct quotation according to MLA style, follow one of the methods shown in the examples below.

- **Identify your source before you quote:** E. A. Thompson, in *The Huns,* argues that Rome did not fall because of the force of one powerful leader: "[T]here is not much evidence to show that Attila was a genius. It is only in terms of the development of their society that we can explain why the Huns attacked Rome at all . . ." (46).

This student will go on to explain why she agrees or disagrees with Thompson's point, thus completing the context for the quotation with her own ideas. The page number in parentheses appears before the period that ends the student's sentence. Note the use of the colon after the independent clause that precedes the quotation (see page 434).

- **Identify your source following your quotation:** "[T]here is not much evidence to show that Attila was a genius. It is only in terms of the development of their society that we can explain why the Huns attacked Rome at all . . . ," writes E.A. Thompson in *The Huns* (46).

Notice, in this example, that the quotation flows grammatically into the remainder of the sentence, following the comma after the ellipsis.

To introduce a paraphrase or indirect quotation, follow the same methods, as shown in the examples below.

- **Identify your source before your paraphrase:** In *The Prospect before Her,* Olwen Huften gives examples of early forms of daycare used by working mothers in the 1700s in England and France whose jobs prevented them from raising children at home (197).

This student then explains the relationship of this paraphrase to the point he is making in his essay, to be certain that the context for this paraphrase is clear to readers.

- **Identify your source after your paraphrase:** Working mothers' use of daycare for infants and children is not a recent development. In fact, there are recorded examples of women in the silk industry and in mills in France and England in the 1700s whose jobs required them to arrange daycare for their children, as Olwen Huften writes in *The Prospect before Her* (197).

Integrate short summaries of passages from other authors in the same ways as you would paraphrases. Identify the source of the summary, and give the page number(s) of the original material you are summarizing at the end of the final sentence of your summary.

When you have carefully set up the research material you wish to include in your essay, you are ready to work on the second goal for revising your essay: editing and proofreading for clear expression of your meaning and for sentence-skills errors. Follow the same methods you learned in Chapter 5: revise your sentences for clarity and variety of structure, then proofread your essay for sentence-skills and mechanical errors, referring to Section Four of the textbook and to your dictionary for help.

Activity 4

As before, continue developing your essay according to the directions in Step 4. As you continue with this section, pay attention to the way you use researched material, how you introduce it in your sentences, and how you identify your sources. You must now incorporate what you have learned from Chapter 16— Writing the Essay—with the skills you have learned in Chapter 17. As always, be sure that your essay has a clear point and adequate supporting details. You will have learned these details from your research; now be sure that they are carefully explained and attributed throughout. Once you are satisfied with the content and structure of your essay, proceed to check for sentence structure and to fix any technical errors. Before you finish the final copy, review the notes on citation style that follow.

STEP 5: DOCUMENT YOUR RESEARCH AND PREPARE A WORKS-CITED OR REFERENCE LIST

Citation Styles: MLA and APA

Two of the most used styles of documentation and citation are MLA (Modern Language Association) style, used for English and humanities subjects, and APA (American Psychological Association) style, used for social-sciences subjects such as psychology, sociology, journalism, and public health studies. Always ask which style your instructor wishes you to follow. No matter which you use, correct documentation gives your reader two important pieces of information: that the material cited is from an outside source, and where to find information about that original source. This chapter uses MLA style and presents MLA citation first, but brief coverage of some aspects of APA style is offered in this section as well.

MLA-Style Documentation

MLA style is in the *MLA Handbook for Writers of Research Papers*. You have already seen MLA-style documentation in the examples above. Citations appear in two locations in your research essay: in the identification of author and page number within your text (in-text citations in parentheses) and in the list of works cited at the end of your essay.

In-Text Citations

In-text citations are the signals you place directly in your text to give credit information for any source you are using. In the examples you have seen of research notes, quotations, and paraphrases, the in-text citations give the page numbers and sometimes the author's name in parentheses at the end of a sentence containing a quotation or paraphrase, or at the end of a quotation or paraphrase itself. In MLA style, in-text citation is always used, rather than footnotes or endnotes.

In-text citation is preferable because it does not distract the reader's attention from the flow of your essay's ideas. In-text citation is a "clue," a signal to readers that they will find full information about the source used on the works-cited page at the end of the research essay.

First, here are several points to note about citations within your essay:

- When the author's name is given in your introduction to the material quoted, only the page number or numbers are given in parentheses after the quotation.
- If the author's name is not given before or after the cited material, then the author's last name only is placed within the parentheses before the page number, with no punctuation between the name and the page number: (Atkins 328).
- If you are using more than one work by the same author, include a short-ened version of the title of that work within the parenthetical citation. For example, if you were using two books by Freda Marshall, your in-text cita-tion after a quotation from her book *Marketing Trends in Canadian Retail Development* would be: (Marshall, *Marketing Trends* 122). Note that a comma separates the author's last name from the abbreviated title and the page number.
- When the borrowed material is in the body of your text, the parenthetical citation is placed after the borrowed material but before the period at the end of the sentence containing it. When a long quotation starts on a new line and is indented, the citation is placed after the final punctuation of the quotation.

In order for readers to follow the clue provided by your in-text citations, create a page of works cited.

Works Cited

The final page of your essay is a list of "works cited," which are all the sources you actually quoted or paraphrased in the essay. Do not list any other sources, no matter how many you may have read.

To set up your works-cited page, follow the instructions below.

1) Centre the title "Works Cited," in regular typeface (no quotation marks), approximately 2.5 cm (one inch) from the top of page.
2) Double-space before the first entry at the top of your page.
3) Begin each entry at the left margin. When the entry runs for more than one line of text, indent each additional line by five spaces, using the indent tab on your keyboard or the "hanging indent" feature of your word-processing application.
4) Organize your list alphabetically according to the authors' last names. If no author is given, the entry is alphabetized by title, ignoring *A, An,* and *The.*
5) Do not number entries.
6) Double-space entries, with no extra space between entries. Follow the pat-terns shown in the model entries below for the reference works you list.

In general, the goals for documentation in any research essay are (1) to ensure that the reader can follow your path and find the same sources as you have used; and (2) to give credit to the original author or source of an idea. If you keep those goals in mind, you will see the rationale behind the seemingly rigid organization of either MLA or APA documentation styles.

The essential information you must give for references at the end of an essay includes:

- The name of the author; these are listed in alphabetical order using the last name, and then the first name
- The title of the publication—this is underlined (MLA) or *italicized* (APA);
- The place the work was published;
- The name of the publisher or agent responsible for the publication;
- The date of publication; and
- The date the work was accessed if it is an online source.

Consider these examples:

Book by One Author

> Schwarcz, Joe. An Apple a Day: The Myths, Misconceptions and Outright Exaggerations about Diet, Nutrition, and the Food We Eat. Toronto: Harper Collins, 2007.

Authors' names are reversed, with the last name first and separated from the first name or initials by a comma. If there is more than one author, only reverse the first name; if there are more than three authors, use only the first name and follow it with the term *et al* (Latin for "and others").

After the title (underlined) comes the publication information: city of publication, publisher, and year of publication appear at the front of any book, often on the reverse side of the title page.

The second line of the entry is indented by five spaces.

Note: Titles of books, periodicals, films, websites, TV series, and CDs are underlined; *MLA style allows italics* for these types of titles but prefers underlining. Titles of articles or chapters within books, magazines, or journals or on websites appear in double quotation marks.

Two or More Entries by the Same Author

If you list two or more books by the same author, do not repeat the author's name. Instead, begin the second entry with a line made of three hyphens followed by a period. Arrange the works by the same author in alphabetical order by title. The words *A, An,* and *The* are ignored in alphabetizing by title.

> ... The Mysteries Within: A Surgeon Reflects on Medical Myths. New York: Simon, 2000.

Second or Later Edition of a Book

> Myers, David G. Social Psychology. 6th ed. New York: McGraw-Hill, 1999.

Magazine Article

> Callwood, June. "A Date with AIDS." Saturday Night March 1995: 52–3.

After the name of the magazine, the month and year of the issue are listed, followed by a colon and then the pages on which the article appeared.

Article in a Scholarly Journal

> Maynard, Charles. "Coding Correlations." Computers and the Humanities 33 (1999): 675–90.

This example shows an entry from a scholarly journal whose pages run consecutively for an entire year. The *33* after the title of the journal is the annual volume number for the year 1999. The year of publication is placed within parentheses for journal articles.

Newspaper Article

> Goddard, Peter. "The New Crime Photography." Toronto Star Jan. 17, 2004: J1+.

When citing newspaper articles, omit *The* if it is part of the newspaper's name.

Article in a Reference Book

> Meredith, Elaine. "Fibre Optics." The New Encyclopedia Britannica: Macropedia. 15th ed. 1987.

Editorial

> "Trade Wars Laughable." Editorial. Winnipeg Free Press Mar. 15, 1995: A10.

Editorials are often unsigned, so no author's name appears in this entry. Indicate the nature of the article by adding the word *Editorial* in plain type after the article's title.

Selection in an Edited Collection or Anthology of Readings

> MacKenzie, Judith. "Letter." English Skills with Readings. Ed. John Langan. Toronto: McGraw-Hill. 4th Can. Ed. 2009. 457–58.

Pamphlet

> Your Guide to Hazardous Waste in the Home. Toronto: Metro Works Planning, Control and Development Division, 1995.

Website

> "Waves of Warning." EnviroZine. August 21, 2008. Environment Canada. November 30, 2008 <http://www.ec.gc.ca/EnviroZine/english/issues/84/feature3_e.cfm>.

The first item in this citation is the title of the article on the website that the student has used as a reference. The second item is the site's title, which is underlined. Next comes the date of publication of the article "Waves of Warning," followed by the site's authoring agency, *Environment Canada*. The next date is the date on which the student accessed the site. The URL comes last.

When you cite a website, include first the date that the site itself or the section or article you have used was published or last updated, then the date(s) on which you accessed the site, just before the URL.

Online Source in a Reference Database

> "Heredity." Britannica Online. Sept. 1999. *Encyclopaedia Britannica.* Mar. 2, 2004 <http://www.britannica.com/bcom/eb/article/4/0,5716,120934,00. html#Article>.

Online Article

> Ehrenreich, Barbara. "Will Women Still Need Men? *Time Online* Feb. 21, 2000. Apr. 15, 2004 <http://www.time.com/time/reports/v21/live/men_ mag.html>.

These model entries do not show all possible sources you may consult for your college research. If you are uncertain of how to document a source, ask a reference librarian to help you, and check your college library's website under "MLA citation" for more information.

APA-Style Documentation

APA style is in the *Publication Manual of the American Psychological Association.* This style is used by students and professionals in the social sciences such as psychology, sociology, political science, and journalism. Like MLA style, APA style requires in-text citation in parentheses of sources each time one is used, and a list of sources at the end of the research essay. Basic coverage of some aspects of APA style follows; for more information, check your college library's website or ask your instructor.

Once you learn one style of documentation, adapting to the requirements of another is not difficult. MLA and APA styles differ in a number of areas. One significant difference between MLA and APA styles is based on the importance of dates of publication in the social sciences: current information is often essential. Therefore, the date is always included in in-text citations. APA style also uses a different title for the list of references. Always check with your instructor early in the semester to see which style is expected in assignments.

In-Text or Parenthetical Citation

Whether you are introducing a paraphrase or quotation, or placing the documentation within parentheses at the end of borrowed material, APA style requires you to always include both the author's name and the date of publication.

Integrating a Paraphrase into a Sentence

> Developments in satellite carrier digital transmission have sped up the progress of convergence among different media, according to Miller's 2003 article.

If you do not mention the author's name or the publication date at the beginning or end of a sentence containing a paraphrase, then these items must be included in parentheses at an appropriate place in the sentence, as in the example below.

As noted in a pivotal article (Miller, 2003), developments in satellite carrier digital transmission have sped up the progress of convergence among different media.

Both citations above refer readers to the reference list at the end of an essay that follows APA style.

Integrating a Quotation into a Sentence

More students than ever are "suffering financially through years, even decades of their careers because of enormous loans incurred to pay tuition fees" (LaRose, 2002, p. 310).

In the example above, the student is quoting a specific sentence from the source. In APA style, the page number on which the quoted material appears is placed after the publication date and is preceded by the abbreviation *p.* for page.

Other abbreviations used in APA parenthetical citations include *pp.* for *pages* and *chap.* for *chapter*.

Citing a Work with Two or More Authors

In APA style, every author of a given work (up to five authors) is mentioned in a citation in the body of a essay:

Changes in patient behaviour are rapid and long lasting during intensive therapies (Annis, McLellan, Stuart, & Main, 2001, chap. 6).

APA Reference List

The APA-style reference list is the equivalent of an MLA works-cited page. The main differences in page and item formatting are noted in this section.

To set up your reference list, follow the steps below.

1) Place your page number (as for your other pages) in the upper right corner of the page, within the header area.
2) Centre the title "References" (or "Reference") in regular type, approximately 2.5 cm (one inch) from the top of page. Double-space before the first entry.
3) Start each entry at the left margin. Second and further lines of an entry are indented five spaces from the left margin.
4) Each entry is listed alphabetically by the last name of the author, or if no author is given, by the first main word in the title.
5) Do not number entries.
6) Double-space between lines.

One notable difference between MLA and APA styles of documentation lies in the citation of titles and use of capitalization in the APA references list. In an MLA style works-cited list, a book's title is underlined and its main words are capitalized: <u>The Common Writer</u>. In an APA-style reference list, only the first word of a book's title, the first word of a subtitle, and any names are capitalized: *The common writer*. In APA style, titles of books, journals, magazines, websites, films, and so on are italicized rather than underlined.

The placement of information in APA documentation style follows this basic order:

- The name of the author; each entry is listed in alphabetical order using the last name, and then the first name;
- The date of publication;
- The title of the publication—this is italicized;
- The place the work was published;
- The name of the publisher or agent responsible for the publication; and
- The date the work was accessed if it is an online source.

Consider these examples:

Book by One Author

Stanley, R. (2003). *Making sense of movies: Filmmaking in the Hollywood style*. New York: McGraw-Hill.

Book by Two or More Authors

Marriott, L., & Lennard, P. (1997). *Heralding the new age*. Vancouver: Raincoast Press.

Chapter from a Book

Wellinski, J. (2000). Variable audience demographics. In *Media patterns* (pp. 134–156). Toronto: Sigma.

Article in a Magazine

Silberman, S. (2001, December). The geek syndrome. *Wired, 9*(12), 174–183.

Article in a Scholarly Journal

Zylberberg, M. (2002). Online consumer trends. *Journal of Marketing, 32*, 210–216.

. . . . . **Activity 5**

Convert the information in each of the following reference-list items into the correct form for a MLA works-cited list. Use the appropriate model from pages 325–327 as a guide.

- An article by Alex Yannis titled "In New League, Women Get Payoff and Payday" on page D5 of the April 13, 2001, issue of the *New York Times*
- An article by Marni Jackson titled "Our Bodies, Our Suits" on pages 71–72 of the March 2003 issue of *Saturday Night* magazine

- A book: by Francis McInerney and Sean White called *Futurewealth: Investing in the Second Great Wave of Technology* and published in New York by St. Martin's in 2000
- A book by Ellen N. Junn and Chris Boyatzis titled *Child Growth and Development* and published in a seventh edition by McGraw-Hill in New York in 2000
- An article called "Get a Grip" by Al Rosen in *Canadian Business Online*, dated September 29, 8, at the URL http://www.canadianbusiness.com/columnists/al_rosen/articlejsp?content=20080929_198719_198719. The site was accessed on December 12, 2008.

Now, using pages 327–329 as a guide, convert each of the above items into the correct format for an APA Reference list.

STEP 6: WRITE YOUR FINAL DRAFT

Revise, then proofread your second draft, following the revision instructions in Chapter 6. Revise first for content, using the checklist below to be sure that your essay meets the writing goals of *unity, support,* and *coherence.* Leave yourself enough time to rewrite anything that seems unclear, and to check your documentation of quotations, paraphrases, or summarized material in your work.

This second revision is essential for two reasons: research essays usually have a significant mark value, and instructors may make significant deductions for errors in documentation, language, usage, and mechanics. Be especially careful with proofreading your revision. Use Section Four of the textbook to help you correct sentence-skill and mechanical errors; use your dictionary as well as your computer's spell checker to catch spelling errors, and follow the guidelines outlined below.

Guidelines for Checking Research Essays
- Does your essay meet all the requirements on your assignment sheet?
- Does your first paragraph introduce your essay's focus on your topic?
- Does your first paragraph begin with an interesting opening that is appropriate to your topic and purpose?

Checking for Unity
- Do your thesis statement and supporting points clearly relate to both your topic and the assignment's requirements?
- Does each supporting paragraph open with a topic sentence that clearly relates to one of your supporting points?
- Does your concluding paragraph return to your thesis and sum up the points your essay has proved?

Checking for Support
- Is your support well organized? Do your supporting points appear in the order in which you stated them in your first paragraph?
- Is each of your supporting points distinct from the others? Is each supporting point clearly tied to your thesis?

- Is each supporting point adequately explained by your own ideas and, if needed, by appropriate material from your research?

Checking for Coherence
- Do transitional words and phrases clearly connect each paragraph to the next one?
- Within your paragraphs, do you use sequencing and logical transition words and phrases to show relationships between your ideas and your sentences?

Checking for Use of Research Materials and Correct Documentation
- Are your research materials from reputable, acknowledged sources in your essay's subject area?
- Have you used an appropriate amount of externally derived research material relative to the length of your essay?
- Do the items derived from your research truly explain, extend, or lend further authority to your own ideas in the essay?
- Are your quotations, paraphrases, and summaries correctly introduced and cited, according to the required style of documentation?
- Does your list of works cited or references correctly cite each type of research material you have used?

Checking for Sentence Skills
- Have you checked for sentence-skills problems noted by your instructor on previous assignments and corrected them?
- Have you checked your spellings of common homonym errors, such as *its* and *it's*, and for commonly confused words? (Misspellings of both of these are not caught by computer spell checkers and must be checked with a dictionary.)
- Have you checked for possible punctuation errors, not only in your sentences but in your introductions to and integrations of quotations?

Checking Manuscript Form
- Have you created a title page, according to your instructor's requirements?
- Are your pages numbered correctly?
- Have you used headers, if these are required?
- Does your essay have a title, expressed as a phrase, that suggests your overall focus on your topic?
- Have you included an outline, if one is required?

Always leave yourself at least one day between your revising and proofreading and writing your final draft. You will see your content with clearer eyes, and you may spot errors that previously eluded you.

You now have the fundamentals for conducting research, assembling an essay, and documenting your sources. You will learn more in various college courses about conducting and reporting on research in different disciplines, but you are now ready to meet such challenges with confidence.

Activity 6

Near the end of your essay, finish by comparing your work with the checklist above. Most importantly, check that you have:

- followed the assignment carefully;
- constructed a main idea in your thesis statement;
- supported your thesis with adequate details;
- drawn these details from research using sufficient and reliable sources;
- revised for clear, error-free sentences; and
- documented your sources using in-text citations and a complete Works Cited list.

REVIEWING THE LEARNING OUTCOMES FOR PREPARING A RESEARCH ESSAY

Now that you have worked through this chapter, answer the following questions.

✓ What changes will you make to your trial outline when you revise it?

✓ What must you record for any book you will use as a resource for your research essay?

✓ What are the reasons for including quotations, paraphrases, or summaries of material in a research essay?

✓ What information must appear with a quotation in the body of your essay?

✓ Why is it sometimes preferable to paraphrase an author's words, rather than quoting them directly?

✓ What information must be included when you integrate a paraphrase or summary into the body of your essay?

✓ What is the goal of summarizing, and what is never included in a summary?

✓ According to either MLA or APA style, how is the title of a book shown in your essay? How is the title of a chapter within a book shown?

✓ What is plagiarism? What is the difference between "unintentional plagiarism" and "intentional plagiarism"?

✓ How many drafts of a research essay should you prepare? Why?

Visit the *English Skills with Readings: Examining Paragraphs* Online Learning Centre at www.mcgrawhill.ca/olc/langan to access self-quizzes, internet-based questions and research skills, web resources, and other learning and study tools.

Section 4

Handbook of Sentence Skills

Preview

You can refer to Section Four of this book at any time when you need help with grammar or sentence skills.

In Section One, you first encountered the four steps to, or bases for, effective writing. Section Four is a handbook that focuses on the *fourth step: writing clear, error-free sentences.* Turn to Section Four whenever you are uncertain about a point of grammar or punctuation, or when a sentence "seems wrong." Most of all, turn to this handbook when you are revising and proofreading your work.

To help you make the best use of Section Four, first consult the Online Learning Centre at www. mcgrawhill.ca/olc/langan for a diagnostic test. This test will reveal to you how well you currently handle and understand sentence skills, and teach you to identify and name the areas of grammar and sentence skills that challenge you. Knowing the usual labels for important sentence-skills concepts helps you find the relevant chapters within Section Four.

After you've made your way through the lessons in Section Four on grammar, mechanics, punctuation, and word use, again take advantage of the additional material available on the Online Learning Centre. Mastery tests and editing tests reinforce basic writing skills and give you practice in editing and proofreading, and an achievement test helps you measure your improvement in important sentence skills. When you've completed Section Four, try the achievement test online and compare your new results with the results you obtained for the initial diagnostic test.

Chapter 19

Subjects and Verbs

The building blocks of English sentences are subjects and verbs. Understanding them is an important first step toward mastering many sentence skills.

Every sentence has a subject and a verb. Who or what the sentence speaks about is called the subject; what the sentence says about the subject is called the verb.

The children laughed.

Several branches fell.

Most students passed the test.

That man is a crook.

A SIMPLE WAY TO FIND A SUBJECT

To find a subject, ask *who* or *what* the sentence is about. As shown below, your answer is the subject.

Who is the first sentence about? Children

What is the second sentence about? Several branches

Who is the third sentence about? Most students

Who is the fourth sentence about? That man

A SIMPLE WAY TO FIND A VERB

To find a verb, ask what the sentence *says about* the subject. As shown below, your answer is the verb.

What does the first sentence *say about* the children? They laughed.

What does the second sentence *say about* the branches? They fell.

What does the third sentence *say about* the students? They passed.

What does the fourth sentence *say about* that man? He is (a crook).

A second way to find the verb is to put *I, you, we, he, she, it,* or *they* (whichever form is appropriate) in front of the word you think is a verb. If the result makes sense, you have a verb. For example, you could put *they* in front of *laughed* in the first sentence above, with the result—*they laughed*—making sense. Therefore you know that *laughed* is a verb. You could use *they* or *he,* for instance, to test the other verbs as well.

Verbs of Action and Linking Verbs

It helps to remember that most verbs show action. In the sentences already considered, the three action verbs are *laughed, fell,* and *passed*. Certain other verbs, known as *linking verbs,* or *verbs of appearance or perception,* do not show action. They do, however, give information about the subject. In "That man is a crook," the linking verb *is* tells us that the man is a crook. Other common linking verbs include *am, are, was,* and *were*. Verbs indicating appearance or perception include *feel, appear, look, become,* and *seem*.

• • • • **Activity**

In each of the following sentences, draw one line under the subject and two lines under the verb.

1. The heavy backpack cut into my shoulders.
2. Small stones pinged onto the windshield.
3. The test directions confused the students.
4. Cotton shirts feel softer than polyester ones.
5. The fog rolled into the cemetery.
6. Sparrows live in the eaves of my porch.
7. A green fly stung her on the ankle.
8. Every other night, garbage trucks rumble down my street on their way to the dump.
9. The family played badminton and volleyball, in addition to a game of softball, at the picnic.
10. With their fingers, the children drew pictures on the steamed window.

MORE ABOUT SUBJECTS AND VERBS

1) A noun is often the subject of a sentence. The words in the four examples on page 334, *children, branches, students,* and *man,* are called *nouns*. The word *noun* comes from the Latin word *nomen,* meaning "name." Nouns *name* an object, a place, a person, or another living thing. *Proper nouns* are those which are used for people's names or for place names, such as *Mr. Khan* or *Windsor. Abstract nouns* identify an idea, condition, or state of being: *truth, beauty,* or *honesty,* for instance.

Note: Avoid repeating subjects. In English, a particular subject must be used only once in each clause, or word group with a subject and verb. Do not repeat a subject in the same clause by following a noun with a pronoun.

Incorrect: The *manager he* asked Devon to lock up tonight.
Correct: The **manager** asked Devon to lock up tonight.
Correct: **He** asked Devon to lock up tonight.

Even when the subject and verb are separated by a long word group, the subject should not be repeated in the same clause.

Incorrect: The *girl* that danced with you *she is* my cousin.
Correct: The **girl** that danced with you **is** my cousin.

2) A pronoun (a word like *he, she, it, we, you,* or *they* used in place of a noun) can serve as the subject of a sentence.

> He seems like a lonely person.
> They both like to gamble.

Without a surrounding context (so that we know who *he* or *they* refers to), such sentences may not seem clear, but they *are* complete.

3) A sentence may have more than one verb, more than one subject, or several subjects and verbs.

> My heart skipped and pounded.
> The radio and CD player were stolen from the car.
> Minh and Elsa prepared the report together and presented it to the class.

4) Articles often come before nouns in English. Many other languages do not use articles the same way, so learning how to use them correctly in English may take some time.

There are two kinds of articles: indefinite and definite.

A. **Indefinite Articles: *a* and *an***   Generally, an indefinite article does not specify a particular item.

  - Use *a* before a word that begins with a consonant sound.

    a carrot, *a* pig, *a* uniform (An *a* is used before *uniform* because the *u* in that word sounds like the consonant *y* plus *u*, not the vowel sound of the letter *u*.)

  - Use *an* before a word beginning with a vowel sound.

    an answer, *an* excuse, *an* onion, *an* umbrella, *an* honour (The word *honour* sounds as if it begins with a vowel because the *h* is silent.)

B. **The Definite Article: *the***   The definite article specifies one item or particular items.

> *the* fan, *the* lemons

C. **Placement of Articles**   An article may come directly before a noun.

> *a* circle, *the* summer

Or an article may be separated from the noun by adjectives (words that describe the noun).

> *a* large *circle, the* hot, humid summer

D. **Articles with Count and Non-Count Nouns**   To know whether to use an article with a noun and which article to use, you must learn to recognize count and non-count nouns. A *noun* names a person, place, thing, or concept.

> *Count* nouns name people, places, things, or ideas that can be counted. Therefore, count nouns can be made into plurals: *window (one window,*

three windows); table (a table, some tables); principal (one principal, four principals).

Non-count nouns name things or ideas that cannot be counted and thus cannot be made into plurals, such as *weather, anger, flour,* and *happiness.* The box below lists common types of non-count nouns.

Common Non-Count Nouns

Abstractions and emotions: anger, bravery, health, humour, pride, truth

Activities: baseball, jogging, reading, teaching, travel

Foods: bread, broccoli, chocolate, cheese, flour, rice

Gases and vapours: air, helium, oxygen, smoke, steam

Languages and areas of study: Korean, Spanish, algebra, history, physics

Liquids: blood, gasoline, lemonade, tea, water

Materials that come in bulk form: aluminum, cloth, dust, sand, soap

Natural occurrences: magnetism, moonlight, rain, snow, thunder

Other things that cannot be counted: clothing, furniture, homework, machinery, money, news, transportation, vocabulary, work

---

The quantity of a non-count noun (or a count noun) can be expressed with a word or words called a **quantifier**, such as *some, a lot of, a unit of,* and so on. (In the following two examples, the quantifiers are shown in *italic* type, and the non-count nouns are shown in **boldface** type.)

Please have *some* **patience**.
We need to buy *two bags of* **flour** today.

Some words can be either count or non-count nouns depending on whether they refer to one or more individual items or to something in general.

Certain *cheeses* give some people headaches. (This sentence refers to individual cheeses; *cheese* in this case is a count noun.)
The yearly *rains* in India are called monsoons. (This sentence refers to specific, individual rains; *rains* in this case is a count noun.)
Cheese is made in almost every country where milk is produced. (This sentence refers to cheese in general; in this case, *cheese* is a non-count noun.)
Rain is something farmers cannot do without. (This sentence refers to rain in general; in this case, *rain* is a non-count noun.)

E. **Using *a* or *an* with Non-Specific Singular Count Nouns** Use *a* or *an* with singular nouns that are non-specific. A noun is *non-specific* when the reader doesn't know its specific identity.

A left-handed person faces special challenges with right-handed tools. (The sentence refers to any left-handed person, not a specific one.)
Today, our cat proudly brought *a* baby bird into the house. (The reader isn't familiar with the bird. This is the first time it is mentioned.)

F. **Using *the* with Specific Nouns** In general, use *the* with all specific nouns—specific singular, plural, and non-count nouns.

A noun is specific—and therefore requires the article *the*—in the following cases:

- When it has already been mentioned once
  Today, our cat proudly brought a baby bird into the house. Luckily, *the* bird was still alive.
  The is used with the second mention of *bird*.

- When it is identified by a word or phrase in the sentence
  The pockets in the boy's pants are often filled with sand and dirt.
  Pockets is identified by the words *in the boy's pants*.

- When its identity is suggested by the context
  At Willy's Diner last night, *the* service was terrible and *the* food was worse.
  Service and *food* are identified as belonging to the context of Willy's Diner.

- When it is unique
  Scientists are concerned about the growing hole in *the* ozone layer.
  Earth has only one ozone layer.

- When it is preceded by a superlative adjective (*best, biggest, wisest*)
  The best way to store broccoli is to refrigerate it in an open plastic bag.

G. **Omitting Articles** Omit articles with non-specific plurals and non-count nouns. Plurals and non-count nouns are non-specific when they refer to something in general.

> *Pockets* didn't exist until the end of the 1700s.
> *Service* is as important as *food* to a restaurant's success.
> Iris serves her children homemade *lemonade*.

H. **Using *the* with Proper Nouns** Proper nouns name particular people, places, things, or ideas and are always capitalized. Most proper nouns do not require articles; those that do, however, require *the*. Following are general guidelines about when and when not to use *the*.

Do not use *the* for most singular proper nouns, including names of the following:

- *People and animals* (Paul Martin, Fido)
- *Continents, provinces or states, cities, streets,* and *parks* (North America, Canada, Alberta, Lethbridge, Portage Street, Banff National Park)
- *Most countries* (France, Mexico, Russia)
- Individual bodies of water, islands, and mountains (Lake Erie, Prince Edward Island, Mount Everest)

Use *the* for the following types of proper nouns:

- *Plural proper nouns* (the Turners, the United States, the Great Lakes, the Rocky Mountains)
- *Names of large geographic areas, deserts, oceans, seas,* and *rivers* (the South, the Gobi Desert, the Atlantic Ocean, the Black Sea, the Don River)
- *Names with the format* the _____ of _____ (the People's Republic of China, the University of Manitoba)

• • • • **Activity**

Underline the correct form of the noun in parentheses.

1. (*A library, Library*) is a valuable addition to a neighbourhood.
2. This morning, the mail carrier brought me (*a letter, the letter*) from my cousin.
3. As I read (*a letter, the letter*), I began to laugh at what my cousin wrote.
4. Every night we have to do lots of (*homework, home works*).
5. We are going to visit our friends in (*the British Columbia, British Columbia*) next week.
6. Cats are known for having a great deal of (*curiosity, the curiosity*).
7. The soldiers in battle showed a great deal of (*courage, courages*).
8. A famous park in Toronto is (*High Park, the High Park*).
9. My son would like to eat (*the spaghetti, spaghetti*) at every meal.
10. It is dangerous to stare directly at (*the sun, sun*).

5) The subject of a sentence never appears within a prepositional phrase. A *prepositional phrase* is simply a group of words that begins with a preposition. Nouns and pronouns *follow* prepositions in prepositional phrases. Because nouns and pronouns appear as the subjects of sentences, confusion may arise when they also appear in a prepositional phrase at the beginning of a sentence. A noun or a pronoun following a preposition is the *object* of a preposition; it completes the "positioning" thought begun by the preposition.

The use of prepositions in English is often idiomatic, not based on their usual meanings, and exceptions to general rules are common. Therefore, correct preposition use must be learned gradually through experience. The box shows how three of the most common prepositions are used in some customary references to time and place.

The Use of on, in, *and* at *to Refer to Time and Place*

Time

On *a specific day:* on Monday, on January 1, on your anniversary

In *a part of a day:* in the morning, in the daytime (but *at* night)

In a month or a year: in December, in 1867

In *a period of time:* in an hour, in a few days, in a while

At *a specific time:* at 10:00 a.m., at midnight, at sunset, at dinnertime

Place

On *a surface:* on the desk, on the counter, on a ceiling

In *a place that is enclosed:* in my room, in the office, in the box

At *a specific location:* at the mall, at his house, at the ballpark

Note: The word *preposition* contains the word *position;* many prepositions indicate positions in time or space. Below is a list of common prepositions.

about	before	by	inside	over
above	behind	during	into	through
across	below	except	of	to
among	beneath	for	off	toward
around	beside	from	on	under
at	between	in	onto	with

Cross out prepositional phrases when looking for the subject of a sentence.

~~Under my pillow~~ I found a quarter left by the tooth fairy.
One ~~of the yellow lights at the school crossing~~ began flashing.
The comics section ~~of the newspaper~~ disappeared.
~~In spite of my efforts,~~ Derek dropped out of school.
~~During a rainstorm,~~ I sat in my car reading magazines.

● ● ● ● **Activity**

Underline the correct preposition in parentheses.

1. Can you baby-sit for my children (*on, at*) Thursday?
2. Please come to my office (*on, at*) 3:00 p.m.
3. You will find some computer disks (*in, on*) the desk drawer.
4. Miguel will begin his new job (*in, at*) two weeks.
5. People like to feed the ducks (*on, at*) the park.

6) Many verb forms consist of more than one word. Here, for example, are some of the many forms of the verb *smile.*

to smile	smiled	should smile
smiles	were smiling	will be smiling
does smile	have smiled	can smile
is smiling	had smiled	could be smiling
are smiling	had been smiling	must have smiled

Notes:

1) Words like *not, just, never, only,* and *always* are not part of the verb, although they may appear between parts of the verb.

Larry did not finish the paper before class.
The road was just completed last week.

2) No verb preceded by *to*—the infinitive form of a verb—is ever the verb of a sentence. The infinitive form (for example, *to do, to make*) is the beginning point for all other forms of a verb. The infinitive form never changes but is used in combination with other verb forms, as in the following examples.

My car suddenly began to sputter on the highway.
I swerved to avoid a squirrel on the road.

3) No *-ing* word *by itself* is ever the verb of a sentence. (It may be part of the verb, but it must have a helping verb in front of it.)

They leaving early for the game. (This is not a sentence, because the verb is not complete.)
They are leaving early for the game. (This is a sentence.)

Avoid the progressive (or continuous) tenses of certain verbs. The progressive (or continuous) tenses are made up of forms of *be* plus the *-ing* form of the main verb (the present participle). They express actions or conditions that have a definite beginning and a definite end.

George **will be taking** classes this summer.

However, verbs for mental states, the senses, possession, and inclusion are generally not used in the progressive tense.

Incorrect: Luisa is seeming to be ill.
Correct: Luisa **seems** to be ill.
Incorrect: That box *is containing* a surprise for Paulo.
Correct: That box **contains** a surprise for Paulo.

Activity

Draw a single line under the subjects and a double line under the verbs in the following sentences. Be sure to include all parts of the verb.

1. A burning odour from the wood saw filled the room.
2. At first, sticks of gum always feel powdery on your tongue.
3. Vampires and werewolves are repelled by garlic.
4. Three people in the long bank lineup looked impatiently at their watches.
5. The driving rain had pasted wet leaves all over the car.
6. She has decided to buy a condominium.
7. The trees in the mall were glittering with tiny white lights.
8. The puppies slipped and tumbled on the vinyl kitchen floor.
9. Tanya and Luis ate at Swiss Chalet and then went to a movie.
10. We have not met our new neighbours in the apartment building.

Visit the *English Skills with Readings: Examining Paragraphs* Online Learning Centre at www.mcgrawhill.ca/olc/langan to access self-quizzes, internet-based questions and research skills, web resources, and other learning and study tools.

Chapter 20

Sentence Sense

WHAT IS SENTENCE SENSE?

You already possess a very valuable writing and revising skill. As someone who speaks English all or some of the time in your everyday life, you often communicate effectively, and often in complete sentences. Canadian college students come from many cultures and many linguistic backgrounds, but you all have a gift you learned "by ear." You have *sentence sense*—an instinctive feel for where a sentence begins, where it ends, and how it can be developed. You learned sentence sense automatically and naturally, as part of learning the English language, and you have practised it through however many years you have been speaking English. It is as much a part of you as your ability to speak and understand English is a part of you.

Sentence sense can help you recognize and avoid fragments and run-ons, two of the most common and serious sentence-skills mistakes in written English. Sentence sense will also help you to place commas, spot awkward and unclear phrasings, and add variety to your sentences.

You may ask, "If I already have this 'sentence sense,' why do I still make mistakes in punctuating sentences?" One answer could be that your past school experiences in writing were unrewarding or unpleasant. English may have been a series of dry writing topics and heavy doses of "correct" grammar and usage, or it may have devoted no time at all to sentence skills. Or perhaps you studied English primarily as a written language and had little opportunity to practise speaking English every day before coming to Canada. For any of these reasons, or perhaps for other reasons, the instinctive sentence skills you practise while *speaking* may turn off when you start *writing*. The very act of picking up a pen or touching a keyboard may shut down your whole natural system of language abilities and skills.

TURNING ON YOUR SENTENCE SENSE

Chances are you don't read a paper aloud after you write it, or you don't do the next best thing: read it "aloud" in your head. But reading aloud is essential to turn on the natural language system within you. By reading aloud, you will be able to hear the points where your sentences begin and end. In addition, you will be able to pick up any trouble spots where your thoughts are not communicated clearly and well.

The activities that follow will help you turn on and rediscover the enormous language power within you. You will be able to see how your built-in sentence sense can guide your writing just as it does your speaking.

● ● ● ● ● **Activity**

Each item that follows lacks basic sentence punctuation. There is no period to mark the end of one sentence and no capital letter to mark the start of the next. Read each item aloud (or in your head) so that you hear where each sentence begins and ends. Your voice will tend to drop and pause at the point of each sentence break.

Put a light slash mark (/) at every point where you hear a break. Then go back and read over the item a second time. If you are now sure of each place where a split occurs, insert a period and change the first small letter after it to a capital. Minor pauses are often marked in English by commas; these are already inserted. Part of item 1 is done for you as an example.

1. I take my dog for a walk on Saturdays in the big park by the lake I do this very early in the morning before children come to the park that way I can let my dog run freely he jumps out the minute I open the car door and soon sees the first innocent squirrel then he is off like a shot and doesn't stop running for at least half an hour.

2. Anna hates huge tractor-trailers that sometimes tailgate her Honda the enormous smoke-belching machines seem ready to swallow her small car she shakes her fist at the drivers, and she lets fly a lot of angry words recently she had a very satisfying dream she broke into a party supply store and stole fireworks she then became the first person in history to illuminate a truck

3. When I sit down to write, my mind is blank all I can think of is my name, which seems to me the most boring name in the world often I get sleepy and tell myself I should take a short nap other times I start daydreaming about things I want to buy sometimes I decide I should make a telephone call to someone I know the piece of paper in front of me is usually still blank when I leave to watch my favourite television show

4. One of the biggest regrets of my life is that I never told my father I loved him I resented the fact that he had never been able to say the words "I love you" to his children even during the long period of my father's illness, I remained silent and unforgiving then one morning he was dead, with my words left unspoken a guilt I shall never forget tore a hole in my heart I determined not to hold in my feelings with my daughters they know they are loved, because I both show and tell them this all people, no matter who they are, want to be told that they are loved

5. Two days ago, Greg killed several flying ants in his bedroom he also sprayed a column of ants forming a colony along the kitchen baseboard yesterday, he picked the evening newspaper off the porch and two black army ants scurried onto his hand this morning, he found an ant crawling

on a lollipop he had left in his shirt pocket if any more insects appear, he is going to call an exterminator he feels like the victim in a horror movie called *The Ants* he is half afraid to sleep tonight he imagines the darkness will be full of tiny squirming things waiting to crawl all over him

SUMMARY: USING SENTENCE SENSE

You probably did well in locating the end stops in these selections, proving to yourself that you *do* have sentence sense. This instinctive sense will help you deal with sentence fragments and run-ons, perhaps the two most common sentence-skills mistakes.

Remember the importance of *reading your paper aloud*. By doing so, you turn on the natural language skills that come from all your experience of speaking English. The same sentence sense that helps you communicate effectively in speaking will help you communicate effectively in writing.

Visit the *English Skills with Readings: Examining Paragraphs* Online Learning Centre at www.mcgrawhill.ca/olc/langan to access self-quizzes, internet-based questions and research skills, web resources, and other learning and study tools.

Chapter 21

Fragments

Introductory Project

Every sentence must have a subject and a verb and must express a complete thought. A word group that lacks a subject or a verb and that does not express a complete thought is a *fragment*. Underline the statement in each numbered item that you think is *not* a complete sentence.

1. Because I could not sleep. I turned on my light and read.
2. Calling his dog's name. Todd walked up and down the street.
3. My little sister will eat anything. Except meat, vegetables, and fruit.
4. The reporter turned on her laptop computer. Then began to type quickly.

Understanding the answers: Read and complete each explanation.

1. *Because I could not sleep* is an incomplete sentence. The writer does not complete the _____ by telling us what happened because he could not sleep. Correct the fragment by joining it to the sentence that follows it:

   Because I could not sleep, I turned on my light and read.

2. *Calling his dog's name* is not a complete sentence. The word group lacks both a _____ and a verb, and it does not express a complete thought. Correct the fragment by adding it to the sentence that follows it:

   Calling his dog's name, Todd walked up and down the street.

3. *Except meat, vegetables, and fruit* is not a complete sentence. Again, the word group lacks a subject and a _____, and it does not express a complete thought. Correct the fragment by adding it to the sentence that comes before it:

   My little sister will eat anything except meat, vegetables, and fruit.

4. *Then began to type quickly* is not a complete sentence. The word group lacks a _____. One way to correct the fragment is to add the subject *she:*

   Then she began to type quickly.

Answers are provided on the Online Learning Centre.

345

WHAT ARE FRAGMENTS?

Every sentence must have a subject and a verb and must express a complete thought. A word group that lacks a subject or a verb and that does not express a complete thought is a *fragment.* The most common types of fragments are:

1) Dependent-word fragments

2) *-ing* and *to* fragments (participial and infinitive fragments)

3) Added-detail fragments

4) Missing-subject fragments

Once you understand the specific kind or kinds of fragments that you may write, you should be able to eliminate them from your writing. The following pages explain all four types of fragments.

1   Dependent-Word Fragments

Some word groups that begin with a dependent word are fragments. Here is a list of common dependent words.

Dependent Words		
after	if, even if	when, whenever
although, though	in order that	where, wherever
as	since	whether
because	that, so that	which, whichever
before	unless	while
even though	until	who, whoever
how	what, whatever	whose

Whenever you start a sentence with one of these words, you must be careful that a fragment does not result.

The word group beginning with the dependent word *after* in the example below is a fragment.

After I learned the price of new cars. I decided to keep my old Toyota.

A *dependent statement*—one starting with a dependent word like *after*—cannot stand alone. It *depends on* another statement to complete the thought. "After I learned the price of new cars" is a dependent statement. It leaves us hanging.We expect in the same sentence to find out *what happened after* the writer learned the price of new cars. When a writer does not follow through and complete a thought, a fragment results.

To correct the fragment, follow through and complete the thought.

After I learned the price of new cars, I decided to keep my old Toyota.

Remember, then, that dependent statements *by themselves* are fragments. They must be *attached* to a statement that makes sense standing alone.

Here are two other examples of dependent-word fragments.

My daughter refused to stop smoking. Unless I quit also.
Bill asked for a loan. Which he promised to pay back in two weeks.

"Unless I quit also" is a fragment; it does not make sense standing by itself. We want to know—in the same statement—*what would not happen unless* the writer quit also. The writer must complete the thought. Likewise, "Which he promised to pay back in two weeks" is not in itself a complete thought. We want to know in the same statement what *which* refers to.

Correcting a Dependent-Word Fragment

In most cases you can correct a dependent-word fragment by attaching it to the sentence that comes after it or the sentence that comes before it.

After I learned the price of new cars, I decided to keep my old Toyota. (The fragment has been attached to the sentence that comes after it.)
My daughter refused to quit smoking unless I quit also. (The fragment has been attached to the sentence that comes before it.)
Bill asked for a loan which he promised to pay back in two weeks. (The fragment has been attached to the sentence that comes before it.)

Another way of correcting a dependent-word fragment is simply to eliminate the dependent word by rewriting the sentence.

I learned the price of new cars and decided to keep my old Toyota.
She wanted me to quit also.
He promised to pay it back in two weeks.

Do not use any method of correction too frequently, however, for it may cut down on interest and variety in your writing style.

Notes:

1) Use a comma if a dependent-word group comes at the beginning of a sentence (also see page 428).

After I learned the price of new cars, I decided to keep my old Toyota.

However, do not generally use a comma if the dependent-word group comes at the end of a sentence.

My daughter refused to stop smoking unless I quit also.
Bill asked for a loan which he promised to pay back in two weeks.

2) Sometimes the dependent words *who, that, which,* and *where* are not at the very start of a word group but are near the start. A fragment often results.

The city council decided to put more lights on South Street. A place where several people have been harassed.

"A place where several people have been harassed" is not in itself a complete thought. We want to know in the same statement *where the place was* where several people were harassed. The fragment can be corrected by attaching it to the sentence that comes before it.

> The city council decided to put more lights on South Street, a place where several people have been harassed.

Activity 1

Turn each of the following dependent-word groups into a sentence by adding a complete thought. Put a comma after the dependent-word group if a dependent word starts the sentence.

Examples   Although I arrived in class late

Although I arrived in class late, I still did well on the test.

The little boy who plays with our daughter

The little boy who plays with our daughter just came down with measles.

1. Because the weather is bad

_____

_____

2. If I lend you twenty dollars

_____

_____

3. The car that we bought

_____

_____

4. Since I was tired

_____

_____

5. Before the instructor entered the room

_____

_____

Activity 2

Underline the dependent-word fragment or fragments in each item. Then correct each fragment by attaching it to the sentence that comes before or the sentence that comes after, whichever sounds more natural. Put a comma after the dependent-word group if it starts the sentence.

1. Whenever our front and back doors are open. The air current causes the back door to slam shut. The noise makes everyone in the house jump.

   _____

   _____

   _____

2. Chris always watches *Breakfast Television* in the morning to see the traffic reports. He wants to see how driving conditions are on Highway 400. Before he gets on with his day.

   _____

   _____

   _____

3. Since the line at the driver's licence office crawls at a snail's pace. Eng waited two hours there. When there was only one person left in front of him. The office closed for the day.

   _____

   _____

   _____

4. My dog ran in joyous circles on the wide beach. Until she found a dead fish. Before I had a chance to drag her away. She began sniffing and nudging the smelly remains.

   _____

   _____

   _____

5. When the air conditioner broke down. The temperature was over thirty degrees. I then found an old fan. Which turned out to be broken also.

   _____

   _____

   _____

2   *-ing* and *to* Fragments

When an *-ing* word (the present participle form of a verb) appears at or near the start of a word group, a fragment may result. Such fragments often lack a subject and part of the verb. Underline the word groups in the examples below that contain *-ing* words. Each is a fragment.

Example 1

I spent almost two hours on the phone yesterday. Trying to find a garage to repair my car. Eventually I had to have it towed to a garage across the city.

Example 2

Anita was at first happy with the blue hatchback she had bought for only five hundred dollars. Not realizing until a week later that the car averaged twenty litres of gas per hundred kilometres.

Example 3

He looked forward to the study period at school. It being the only time he could sit unbothered and dream about his future. He imagined himself as a lawyer with lots of money, a huge office, and great clothes.

People sometimes write *-ing* fragments because they think the subject in one sentence will work for the next word group as well. Thus, in the first example, the writer thinks that the subject *I* in the opening sentence will also serve as the subject for "Trying to find a garage to repair my car." But the subject must actually be *in* the sentence.

Correcting *-ing* Fragments (Participial Fragments)

1) Attach the *-ing* fragment to the sentence that comes before it or the sentence that comes after it, whichever makes sense. Example 1 could read: "I spent two hours on the phone yesterday, trying to find a garage to repair my car."

2) Add a subject and change the *-ing* verb part to the correct form of the verb. Example 2 could read: "She realized only a week later that the car averaged twenty litres of gas per hundred kilometres."

3) Change *being* to the correct form of the verb *be (am, are, is, was, were)*. Example 3 could read: "It was the only time he could sit unbothered and dream about his future."

Correcting *to* Fragments (Infinitive Fragments)

When *to* appears at or near the start of a word group, a fragment sometimes results.

> I plan on working overtime. To get this job finished. Otherwise, my boss may get angry with me.

The second word group is a fragment and can be corrected by adding it to the preceding sentence.

> I plan on working overtime to get this job finished.

Activity 1

Underline the *-ing* fragment in each of the items that follow. Then make it a sentence by rewriting it, using the method described in parentheses.

Example   A thunderstorm was brewing. A sudden breeze shot through the windows. Driving the stuffiness out of the room. (*Add the fragment to the preceding sentence.*)

A sudden breeze shot through the windows, driving the stuffiness out of the room.

(In the example, a comma is used to set off "driving the stuffiness out of the room," which is extra material placed at the end of the sentence.)

1. Sweating under his heavy load. Brian staggered up the stairs to his apartment. He felt as though his legs were crumbling beneath him. (*Add the fragment to the sentence that comes after it.*)

2. He works ten hours a day. Then going to class for three hours. It is no wonder he writes sentence fragments. (*Correct the fragment by adding the subject* he *and changing* going *to the proper form of the verb,* goes.)

3. Jennifer loved the movie *The Red Violin*, but Mark hated it. His chief objection being that it had no action sequences. (*Correct the fragment by changing* being *to the proper verb form,* was.)

Activity 2

Underline the *-ing* or *to* fragment or fragments in each item. Then rewrite each item, correcting the fragments by using one of the three methods of correction described on page 350.

1. A mysterious disk appeared in my backpack yesterday. Having no label on it. I was too worried about viruses to open it.

2. Jeff bundled up and went outside on the bitterly cold day. To saw wood for his fireplace. He returned half frozen with only two logs.

3. Looking tired and drawn. The little girl's parents sat in the waiting room. The operation would be over in a few minutes.

_____

_____

4. Sighing with resignation. Teresa switched on her television. She suspected there would be no picture. Her cable being off at that time.

_____

_____

_____

_____

5. Jabbing the ice with a screwdriver. Luis attempted to speed up the defrosting process in his freezer. However, he used too much force. The result being a freezer compartment riddled with holes.

_____

_____

_____

_____

3 Added-Detail Fragments

Added-detail fragments lack a subject and a verb. They often begin with one of the following words.

also	except	including
especially	for example	such as

See if you can locate and underline the one added-detail fragment in each of these examples.

Example 1

I love to cook and eat Italian food. Especially spaghetti and lasagna. I make everything from scratch.

Example 2

The class often starts late. For example, yesterday at a quarter after nine instead of at nine sharp. Today the class started at five after nine.

Example 3

He failed a number of courses before he earned his diploma. Among them English I, Economics, and Introductory Marketing.

People often write added-detail fragments for much the same reason they write *-ing* fragments. They think the subject and verb in one sentence will serve for the next word group as well. But the subject and verb must be in *each* word group.

Correcting Added-Detail Fragments

1) Attach the fragment to the complete thought that precedes it. Example 1 could read, "I love to cook and eat Italian food, especially spaghetti and lasagna."

2) Add a subject and a verb to the fragment to make it a complete sentence. Example 2 could read, "The class often starts late. For example, yesterday it began at a quarter after nine instead of at nine sharp."

3) Change words as necessary to make the fragment part of the preceding sentence. Example 3 could read, "Among the courses he failed before he earned his diploma were English I, Economics, and Introductory Marketing."

Activity 1

Underline the fragment in each of the items below. Then make it a sentence by rewriting it, using the method described in parentheses.

Example   I am always short of pocket money. Especially for everyday items like magazines and pop. Luckily my friends often have change. (*Add the fragment to the preceding sentence.*)

I am always short of pocket money, especially for everyday items like magazines and pop.

1. Nina is trying hard for a promotion. For example, taking night classes and a public speaking course. She is also working overtime for no pay. (*Correct the fragment by adding the subject and verb* she is.)

2. I could feel Sean's anger building. Like a land mine ready to explode. I was silent because I didn't want to be the one to set it off. (*Add the fragment to the preceding sentence.*)

3. We went on vacation without several essential items. Among other things, our running shoes and fleece jackets. (*Correct the fragment by adding the subject and verb we forgot.*)

_____

_____

• • • • **Activity 2**

Underline the added-detail fragment in each item. Then rewrite part of the item to correct the fragment. Use one of the three methods of correction described above.

1. It's always hard for me to get up for work. Especially on Mondays after a holiday weekend. However, I always wake up early on days with no classes and no work.

_____

_____

2. Tony has enormous endurance. For example, the ability to run seven kilometres in the morning and then play basketball all afternoon.

_____

_____

3. A counsellor gives you a chance to talk about your problems. With your family or the boss at work. You learn how to cope better with life.

_____

_____

4. Phil and Maria do most of their shopping at online sites. Especially the Grocery Gateway and Chapters sites.

_____

_____

5. One of my greatest joys in life is eating desserts. Such as cherry cheesecake and vanilla cream puffs. Almond fudge cake makes me want to dance.

_____

_____

4 Missing-Subject Fragments

In each example below, underline the word group in which the subject is missing.

Example 1

The truck skidded on the rain-slick highway. But missed a telephone pole on the side of the road.

Example 2

Michelle tried each of the appetizers on the table. And then found that, when the dinner arrived, her appetite was gone.

People write missing-subject fragments because they think the subject in one sentence will apply to the next word group as well. But the subject, as well as the verb, must be in each word group to make it a sentence.

Correcting Missing-Subject Fragments

1) Attach the fragment to the preceding sentence. Example 1 could read, "The truck skidded on the rain-slick highway but missed a telephone pole on the side of the road."

2) Add a subject (which can often be a pronoun standing for the subject in the preceding sentence). Example 2 could read, "She then found that, when the dinner arrived, her appetite was gone."

Activity

Underline the missing-subject fragment in each item. Then rewrite that part of the item as needed to correct the fragment. Use one of the two methods of correction described above.

1. I tried on an old suit hanging in our basement closet. Then discovered, to my surprise, that it was too tight to button.

_____

_____

_____

_____

2. When Tina had a sore throat, friends told her to gargle with salt water. Or suck on an ice cube. The worst advice she got was to avoid swallowing.

_____

_____

_____

_____

3. One of my elementary-school teachers embarrassed us with her sarcasm. Also, seated us in rows from the brightest students to the dumbest. I can imagine the pain the student in the last seat must have felt.

_____

_____

_____

_____

A REVIEW: HOW TO CHECK FOR FRAGMENTS

✓ Read your paper aloud from the *last* sentence to the *first*. You will be better able to see and hear whether each word group you read is a complete thought.

✓ If you think a word group is a fragment, ask yourself: Does this contain a subject and a verb and express a complete thought?

✓ More specifically, be on the lookout for the most common fragments:

- Dependent-word fragments (starting with words like *after, because, since, when,* and *before*)

- *-ing* and *to* fragments (*-ing* or *to* at or near the start of a word group)

- Added-detail fragments (starting with words like *for example, such as, also,* and *especially*)

- Missing-subject fragments (a verb is present but not the subject)

Visit the *English Skills with Readings: Examining Paragraphs* Online Learning Centre at www.mcgrawhill.ca/olc/langan to access self-quizzes, internet-based questions and research skills, web resources, and other learning and study tools.

Chapter 22

Run-ons and Comma Splices

A run-on (or fused sentence) occurs when two sentences are run together with no punctuation to mark the break between them. A comma splice occurs when two sentences are joined together with only a comma, which is insufficient punctuation. Shown below are four examples of runons or comma splices and four correctly punctuated sentences. See if you can complete the statement that explains how each sentence error is corrected.

1. He is the meanest little kid on his block he eats only the heads of animals crackers. (*Run-on or fused sentence*)

    He is the meanest little kid on his block. He eats only the heads of animal crackers. (*Correct*)

    The run-on or fused sentence has been corrected by using a _____ and a capital letter to separate the two complete thoughts.

2. Josh Evans likes to gossip about other people, he doesn't like them to gossip about him. (*Comma splice*)

    Josh Evans likes to gossip about other people, but he doesn't like them to gossip about him. (*Correct*)

    The comma splice has been corrected by using a joining word, _____, to connect the two complete thoughts.

3. The chain on my bike likes to chew up my pants, it leaves grease marks on my ankle as well. (*Comma splice*)

    The chain on my bike likes to chew up my pants; it leaves grease marks on my ankle as well. (*Correct*)

    The comma splice has been corrected by using a _____ to connect the two closely related thoughts.

4. The window shade snapped up like a gunshot, her cat leaped a metre off the floor. (*Comma splice*)

    When the window shade snapped up like a gunshot, her cat leaped a metre off the floor. (*Correct*)

    (continued)

> The run-on has been corrected by using the subordinating word
> _____ to connect the two closely related
> thoughts.
>
> Answers are provided on the Online Learning Centre.

WHAT ARE RUN-ONS AND COMMA SPLICES?

A *run-on* is two complete thoughts that are run together with no punctuation to mark the break between them. They are also known as *fused sentences:* they are fused or joined together as if they were only one thought.

Note: Some instructors refer to each complete thought in a run-on as an independent clause. A clause is simply a group of words having a subject and a verb. A clause may be independent (expressing a complete thought and able to stand alone) or dependent (not expressing a complete thought and not able to stand alone). A run-on is two independent clauses that are run together with no punctuation to mark the break between them.

Run-ons or Fused Sentences

My grades are very good this semester my social life rates only a C.
Our father was a madman in his youth he would do anything on a dare.

In *comma splices,* a comma is used to connect or "splice" together the two complete thoughts. However, a comma alone is *not enough* to connect two complete thoughts. Some stronger connection than a comma alone is needed.

Comma Splices

My grades are very good this semester, my social life rates only a C.
Our father was a madman in his youth, he would do anything on a dare.

Comma splices are common mistakes. Students sense that some kind of connection is needed between two thoughts, and so they put a comma at the dividing point. But the comma alone is not sufficient, and a stronger, clearer mark between the two thoughts is needed.

Words That Can Lead to Run-ons and Comma Splices: People often write run-ons when the second complete thought begins with one of the following words.

I	we	there	now
you	they	this	then
he, she, it		that	next

Remember to be on the alert for run-ons whenever you use one of these words in a series of sentences.

CORRECTING RUN-ONS AND COMMA SPLICES

Here are four common methods of correcting a run-on or a comma splice.

1) Use a period and a capital letter to break the two complete thoughts into separate sentences.

> My grades are very good this semester. My social life rates only a C.
> Our father was a madman in his youth. He would do anything on a dare.

2) Use a comma plus a joining word (*and, but, for, or, nor, so, yet*) to connect the two complete thoughts.

> My grades are very good this semester, but my social life rates only a C.
> Our father was a madman in his youth, for he would do anything on a dare.

3) Use a semicolon to connect the two complete thoughts.

> My grades are very good this semester; my social life rates only a C.
> Our father was a madman in his youth; he would do anything on a dare.

4) Use subordination.

> Although my grades are very good this semester, my social life rates only a C. Because my father was a madman in his youth, he would do anything on a dare.

The following pages will give you practice in all four methods of correcting a run-on or a comma splice. The use of subordination is explained further on page 365, in the section about sentence variety.

Method 1: Period and a Capital Letter

One way of correcting a run-on or a comma splice is to use a period and a capital letter at the break between the two complete thoughts. Use this method especially if the thoughts are not closely related or if another method would make the sentence too long.

Activity 1

Locate the split in each of the following word groups. Each is a *run-on* or *fused sentence*; that is, each consists of two sentences that are fused or joined together with no punctuation between them. Reading each fused sentence aloud will help you "hear" where a major break or split in the thought occurs. At such a point, your voice will probably drop and pause.

Correct the run-on by putting a period at the end of the first thought and a capital letter at the start of the next thought.

Example   Marta shuffled around the apartment in her slippers. her husband couldn't stand their slapping sound on the floor.

1. The goose down jacket was not well made little feathers leaked out of the seams.

2. Liam cringed at the sound of the dentist's drill it buzzed like a twenty-kilogram mosquito.

3. Last summer no one swam in the lake a little boy had dropped his pet piranhas into the water.

4. A horse's teeth never stop growing they will eventually grow outside the horse's mouth.

5. Sue's doctor told her he was an astrology nut she did not feel good about learning that.

6. Ice water is the best remedy for a burn using butter is like adding fat to a flame.

7. In the apartment the air was so dry that her skin felt parched the heat was up to thirty degrees.

8. My parents bought me an ant farm it's going to be hard to find tractors that small.

9. Lobsters are cannibalistic this is one reason they are hard to raise in captivity.

10. Julia placed an egg timer next to the phone she did not want to talk more than three minutes on her long-distance calls.

● ● ● ● **Activity 2**

Locate the split in each of the following word groups. Some of these word groups are *run-ons,* and some of them are *comma splices,* independent clauses spliced or joined together with only a comma. Correct each item by putting a period at the end of the first thought and a capital letter at the start of the next thought.

1. A bird got into the house through the chimney we had to catch it before our cat did.

2. Some so-called health foods are not so healthy, many are made with oils that raise cholesterol levels.

3. We sat only a few metres from the magician, we still couldn't see where all the birds came from.

4. Mohammed needs only five hours of sleep each night his wife needs at least seven.

5. Our image of dentistry will soon change dentists will use lasers instead of drills.

6. Halina entered her apartment and jumped with fright someone was leaving through her bedroom window.

7. There were several unusual hair styles at the party one woman had bright green braids.

8. Jeremy saves all of his magazines, once a month, he takes them to a nearby nursing home.

9. The doctor seemed to be in a rush, I still took time to ask all the questions that were on my mind.

10. When I was little, my brother tried to feed me flies, he told me they were raisins.

● ● ● ● **Activity**

Write a second sentence to go with each of the sentences that follow. Start the second sentence with the word given in the margin. Your sentences can be serious or playful.

Example   *she*   Jackie works for the phone company. She climbs telephone poles in all kinds of weather.

it   1. The alarm clock is unreliable. _____

_____

he   2. My uncle has a peculiar habit. _____

_____

then   3. Tatiana studied for the math test for two hours. _____

_____

it   4. I could not understand why the car would not start. _____

_____

there   5. We saw all kinds of litter on the highway. _____

_____

Method 2: Comma and a Joining Word

A second way of correcting a run-on or a comma-splice error is to use a comma *plus* a joining word to connect the two complete thoughts. Joining words (also called *conjunctions*) include *and, but, for, or, nor, so,* and *yet.* Here is what the four most common joining words mean.

and   in addition to, along with

His feet hurt from the long hike, and his stomach was growling.

(*And* means "in addition": His feet hurt from the long hike; *in addition,* his stomach was growling.)

but   however, except, on the other hand, just the opposite

I remembered to get the cocoa, but I forgot the marshmallows.

(*But* means "however": I remembered to get the cocoa; *however,* I forgot the marshmallows.)

for   because, the reason why, the cause of something

She was afraid of not doing well in the course, for she had always struggled with English before.

(*For* means "because" or "the reason why": She was afraid of not doing well in the course; *the reason why* was that she had always struggled with English before.)

Note: If you are not comfortable using *for*, you may want to use *because* instead of *for* in the activities that follow.

so   as a result, therefore

The windshield wiper was broken, so she was in trouble when the rain started.

(*So* means "as a result": The windshield wiper was broken; *as a result,* she was in trouble when the rain started.)

Activity 1

Insert the joining word (*and, but, for, so*) that logically connects the two thoughts in each sentence.

1. The couple wanted desperately to buy the house, _____ they did not qualify for a mortgage.

2. A lot of men today get their hair streaked, _____ they use cologne and other cosmetics as well.

3. Winston asked his wife if she had any bandages, _____ he had just sliced his finger with a paring knife.

4. He failed the vision part of his driver's test, _____ he did not get his driver's licence that day.

5. The restaurant was beautiful, _____ the food was overpriced.

Activity 2

Add a complete and closely related thought to go with each of the following statements. Use a comma plus the joining word in the margin when you write the second thought.

    Example   *for*   Ayesha spent the day walking barefoot, *for the heel of one of her shoes had come off.*

but   1. She wanted to go to the party _____

_____

and   2. Terry washed his car in the morning _____

_____

so   3. The day was dark and rainy _____

_____

for   4. I'm not going to eat in the school cafeteria any more _____

_____

but   5. I asked my brother to get off the telephone _____

_____

Method 3: Semicolon

A third method of correcting a run-on or a comma splice is to use a semicolon to mark the break between two thoughts. A *semicolon* (;) is made up of a period above a comma. The semicolon signals more of a pause than a comma alone but not quite the full pause of a period.

Semicolon Alone: Here are some earlier sentences that were connected with a comma plus a joining word. Notice that a semicolon, unlike the comma alone, can be used to connect the two complete thoughts in each sentence.

> A lot of men today get their hair streaked; they use cologne and other cosmetics as well.
> She was afraid of not doing well in the course; she had always struggled with English before.
> The restaurant was beautiful; the food was overpriced.

The semicolon can add to sentence variety. For some people, however, the semicolon is a confusing mark of punctuation. Keep in mind that if you are not comfortable using it, you can and should use one of the first two methods of correcting a run-on or comma splice.

• • • • **Activity**

Insert a semicolon where the break occurs between the two complete thoughts in each of the following run-ons.

Example   I missed the bus by seconds; there would not be another for half an hour.

1. I spend eight hours a day in a windowless office it's a relief to get out into the open air after work.
2. The audience howled with laughter the comedian enjoyed a moment of triumph.
3. It rained all week parts of the highway were flooded.
4. Tony never goes to a certain gas station any more he found out that the service manager overcharged him for a valve job.
5. The washer shook and banged with its unbalanced load then it began to walk across the floor.

Semicolon with a Transitional Word: A semicolon is sometimes used with a transitional word and a comma to join two complete thoughts.

> We were short of money; therefore, we decided not to eat out that weekend.
> The roots of a geranium have to be crowded into a small pot; otherwise, the plant may not flower.
> I had a paper to write; however, my brain had stopped working for the night.

Following is a list of common transitional words (also known as *adverbial conjunctions*). Brief meanings are given for the words.

Transitional Word	Meaning
however	but
nevertheless	but
on the other hand	but
instead	as a substitute
meanwhile	in the intervening time
otherwise	under other conditions
indeed	in fact
in addition	and
also	and
moreover	and
furthermore	and
as a result	in consequence
thus	as a result
consequently	as a result
therefore	as a result

• • • • • **Activity 1**

Choose a logical transitional word from the list in the box above and write it in the space provided. Put a semicolon *before* the connector and a comma *after* it.

Example   Exams are over; *however,* I still feel tense and nervous.

1. I did not understand her point _____ I asked her to repeat it.

2. With his thumbnail, Jason tried to split open the cellophane covering on the new video game _____ the cellophane refused to tear.

3. Post offices are closed for today's holiday _____ no mail will be delivered.

4. They decided not to go to the movie _____ they went to play miniature golf.

5. I had to skip lunch _____ I would have been late for class.

● ● ● ● **Activity 2**

Punctuate each sentence by using a semicolon and a comma.

Example My brother's asthma was worsening; as a result, he tried a new medication.

1. Manny ate an entire pizza for supper in addition he had a big chunk of pound cake for dessert.
2. The man leaned against the building in obvious pain however no one stopped to help him.
3. Our instructor was absent therefore the test was postponed.
4. Incandescent lights take too much energy instead you should buy compact fluorescent bulbs.
5. Benita loves the velvety texture of mango pudding moreover she loves to squish it between her teeth.

Method 4: Subordination

A fourth method of joining related thoughts is to use subordination. *Subordination* is a way of showing that one thought in a sentence is not as important as another thought or depends on it.

Here are three earlier sentences that have been recast so that one idea is subordinated to (made less important than) the other idea.

When the window shade snapped up like a gunshot, her cat leaped a metre off the floor.
Because it rained all week, parts of the highway were flooded.
Although my grades are very good this semester, my social life rates only a C.

Notice that when we subordinate, we use dependent words like *when, because,* and *although.* Here is a brief list of common dependent words.

Common Dependent Words		
after	before	unless
although	even though	until
as	if	when
because	since	while

Subordination is explained further on pages 107–108.

○ ○ ○ ● **Activity**

Choose a logical dependent word from the box on page 365 and write it in the space provided.

Example   *Because* I had so much to do, I did not even turned on the TV last night.

1. _____ we emerged from the darkened theatre, it took several minutes for our eyes to adjust to the light.

2. _____ "All Natural" was printed in large letters on the yogourt container, the fine print listing the ingredients told a different story.

3. I can't study for the test this weekend _____ my boss wants me to work overtime.

4. _____ the vampire movie was over, my children were afraid to go to bed.

5. _____ you have a driver's licence and two major credit cards, that store will not accept your cheque.

A REVIEW: HOW TO CHECK FOR RUN-ONS AND COMMA SPLICES

✓ To see if a sentence is a run-on or a comma splice, read it aloud and listen for a break between two complete thoughts. Your voice will probably drop and pause at the break.

✓ To check an entire paper, read it aloud from the *last* sentence to the *first*.

Doing so will help you hear and see each complete thought.

✓ Be on the lookout for words that can lead to run-on sentences and comma splices:

| I | he, she, it | they | this | then |
| you | we | there | that | next |

✓ Correct run-on sentences and comma splices by using one of the following methods:

• Period and capital letter

• Comma and joining word (*and, but, for, or, nor, so, yet*)

• Semicolon

• Subordination

Visit the *English Skills with Readings: Examining Paragraphs* Online Learning Centre at <u>www.mcgrawhill.ca/olc/langan</u> to access self-quizzes, internet-based questions and research skills, web resources, and other learning and study tools.

Chapter 23

Irregular Verbs

Introductory Project

You may already have a sense of which common English verbs are regular and which are not. To test yourself, fill in the past tense and past participle of the verbs below. Five are regular verbs and so take *-d* or *-ed* in the past tense and past participle. Five are irregular verbs and will probably not sound right when you try to add *-d* or *-ed*. Write *I* for *irregular* in front of these verbs. Also, see if you can write in their irregular verb forms. (The item at the top is an example.)

Present	Past	Past Participle
shout	*shouted*	*shouted*
1. crawl		
2. bring		
3. use		
4. do		
5. give		
6. laugh		
7. go		
8. scare		
9. dress		
10. see		

Answers are provided on the Online Learning Centre.

A BRIEF REVIEW OF REGULAR VERBS

Every verb has four principal parts: present, past, past participle, and present participle. These parts can be used to build all the verb tenses (the times shown by a verb).

The past and past participle of a regular verb are formed by adding *-d* or *-ed* to the present. The *past participle* is the form of the verb used with the helping verbs *have, has,* and *had* (or some form of *be* with passive verbs). The *present* *participle* is formed by adding *-ing* to the present. Here are the principal forms of some regular verbs.

Present	Past	Past Participle	Present Participle
crash	crashed	crashed	crashing
shiver	shivered	shivered	shivering
kiss	kissed	kissed	Kissing
apologize	apologized	apologized	apologizing
tease	teased	teased	teasing

Most verbs in English are regular.

FORMS OF IRREGULAR VERBS

Irregular verbs have irregular forms in the past tense and past participle. For example, the past tense of the irregular verb *know* is *knew;* the past participle is *known.*

   Almost everyone has some degree of trouble with irregular verbs. When you are unsure about the form of a verb, you can check the following list of irregular verbs. (The present participle is not shown on this list because it is formed simply by adding *-ing* to the base form of the verb.) Or you can check a dictionary, which gives the principal parts of irregular verbs.

Present	Past	Past Participle
arise	arose	arisen
awake	awoke	awoken
be (am, are, is)	was (were)	been
become	became	become
begin	began	begun
bend	bent	bent
bite	bit	bitten
blow	blew	blown
break	broke	broken
bring	brought	brought

Note: The base form of a verb is its present-tense form. If this form of the verb ends in *e*, the *e* is removed before adding *-ing*, the present participle ending.

Present	Past	Past Participle
build	built	built
burst	burst	burst
buy	bought	bought
catch	caught	caught
choose	chose	chosen

come	came	come
cost	cost	cost
cut	cut	cut
do (does)	did	done
draw	drew	drawn
drink	drank	drunk
drive	drove	driven
eat	ate	eaten
fall	fell	fallen
feed	fed	fed
feel	felt	felt
fight	fought	fought
find	found	found
fly	flew	flown
freeze	froze	frozen
get	got	got *or* gotten
give	gave	given
go (goes)	went	gone
grow	grew	grown
have (has)	had	had
hear	heard	heard
hide	hid	hidden
hold	held	held
hurt	hurt	hurt
keep	kept	kept
know	knew	known
lay	laid	laid
lead	led	led
leave	left	left
lend	lent	lent
let	let	let
lie	lay	lain
lose	lost	lost
make	made	made
meet	met	met
pay	paid	paid
ride	rode	ridden
ring	rang	rung
run	ran	run
say	said	said
see	saw	seen
sell	sold	sold
send	sent	sent
shake	shook	shaken
shrink	shrank *or* shrunk	shrunk
shut	shut	shut
sing	sang	sung

sit	sat	sat
sleep	slept	slept
speak	spoke	spoken
spend	spent	spent
stand	stood	stood
steal	stole	stolen
stick	stuck	stuck
sting	stung	stung
swear	swore	sworn
swim	swam	swum
take	took	taken
teach	taught	taught
tear	tore	torn
tell	told	told
think	thought	thought
wake	woke *or* waked	woken *or* waked
wear	wore	worn
win	won	won
write	wrote	written

• • • • **Activity 1**

Cross out the incorrect verb form in each of the following sentences. Then write the correct form of the verb in the space provided.

Example   ___drew___ The little boy ~~drawed~~ on the marble table with permanent ink.

_____ 1. Tomatoes were once thought to be poisonous, and they were growed only as ornamental shrubs.

_____ 2. Julio has rode the bus to school for two years while saving for a car.

_____ 3. My cats have tore little holes in all my good wool sweaters.

_____ 4. The pipes in the bathroom freezed last winter, and they burst when they thawed.

_____ 5. Every time my telephone has rang today, there has been bad news on the line.

_____ 6. Only seven people have ever knowed the formula for Coca-Cola.

_____ 7. Amy blowed up animal-shaped balloons for her son's birthday party.

_____ 8. I shaked the bottle angrily until the ketchup began to flow.

_____ 9. While waiting for the doctor to arrive, I sitted in a plastic chair for over two hours.

_____ 10. The pile of bones on the plate showed how much chicken the family had ate.

• • • • Activity 2

For each of the italicized verbs, fill in the three missing forms in the following order:

a. Present tense, which takes an -s ending when the subject is *he, she, it,* or any *one person* or *thing*
b. Past tense
c. Past participle—the form that goes with the helping verb *have, has,* or *had*

Example   My uncle likes to *give* away certain things. He (a) _____gives_____ old, thread-bare clothes to the Salvation Army. Last year he (b) _____gives_____ me a worthless television set in which the picture tube was burned out. He has (c) _____given_____ away stuff that a junk dealer would reject.

1. I like to *freeze* chocolate bars. A chocolate bar (a) _____ in half an hour. Once I (b) _____ a bottle of cola. I put it in the freezer to chill and then forgot about it. Later I opened the freezer and discovered it had (c) _____ and exploded.

2. Sue knows how to *speak* French. She (a) _____ Vietnamese too. Her late grandmother (b) _____ both languages and taught them to her. Since she was a child, Sue has (c) _____ them both as well as she speaks English.

3. I *know* the route from Mississauga to the Lake Erie shore better than Theo does. He (a) _____ the main roads. But I drove him down to Port Stanley, and he soon realized that I (b) _____ all the backroads and shortcuts. I have (c) _____ these shortcuts for at least ten years.

4. I *go* to parties a lot. Often Camille (a) _____ with me. She (b) _____ with me just last week. I have (c) _____ to parties every Friday for the past month.

5. My brother likes to *throw* things. Sometimes he (a) _____ socks into his bureau drawer. In high school years ago he (b) _____ footballs while quarterbacking the team. And he has (c) _____ Frisbees in our backyard for as long as I can remember.

6. I *see* her every weekend. She (a) _____ her other friends during the week. We first (b) _____ each other on a cold Saturday night last winter, when we went for supper at an Indian restaurant. Since then we have (c) _____ each other every weekend except when my car was broken down.

7. I often *lie* down for a few minutes after a hard day's work. Sometimes my cat (*a*) _____ down near me. Yesterday was Saturday, so I (*b*) _____ in bed all morning. I probably would have (*c*) _____ in bed all afternoon, but I wanted to get some planting done in my vegetable garden.

8. I *do* not understand the assignment. It simply (*a*) _____ not make sense to me. I was surprised to learn that Shareen (*b*) _____ understand it. In fact, she had already (*c*) _____ the assignment.

9. I often find it hard to *begin* writing a paper. The assignment that I must do (*a*) _____ to worry me while I'm watching television, but I seldom turn off the set. Once I waited until the late movie had ended before I (*b*) _____ to write. If I had (*c*) _____ earlier, I would have had a decent night's sleep.

10. Alissa likes to *eat*. She (*a*) _____ all day long. Once she (*b*) _____ a large pack of cookies in half an hour. Even if she has (*c*) _____ a heavy meal, she often starts munching snacks right afterwards.

Online Learning Centre   Visit the *English Skills with Readings: Examining Paragraphs* Online Learning Centre at www.mcgrawhill.ca/olc/langan to access self-quizzes, internet-based questions and research skills, web resources, and other learning and study tools.

Chapter 24

Subject–Verb Agreement

Introductory Project

As you read each pair of sentences below, make a check mark beside the sentence that you think uses the underlined word correctly.

There <u>was</u> too many people talking at once. _____

There <u>were</u> too many people talking at once. _____

The green peppers on that pizza <u>gives</u> me indigestion. _____

The green peppers on that pizza <u>give</u> me indigestion. _____

The mayor and her husband <u>attends</u> neighbourhood meetings. _____

The mayor and her husband <u>attend</u> neighbourhood meetings. _____

Everything <u>seem</u> to slow me down when I'm in a hurry. _____

Everything <u>seems</u> to slow me down when I'm in a hurry. _____

Answers are provided on the Online Learning Centre.

Nouns and pronouns are generally the subjects of sentences; as words standing for single or multiple objects or beings, they may be *singular* (a single unit of something) or *plural* (more than one of something). Verbs, which show the actions or perceptions of their subjects, have corresponding singular and plural forms.

A verb must agree with its subject in number. A *singular subject* (one person or thing) takes a singular verb. A *plural subject* (more than one person or thing) takes a plural verb. Mistakes in subject–verb agreement are sometimes made in the following situations (each situation is explained on the following pages):

1) When words come between the subject and the verb
2) When a verb comes before the subject
3) With compound subjects
4) With indefinite pronouns

1 WORDS BETWEEN SUBJECT AND VERB

Words that come between the subject and the verb do not change—agreement. Such word groups are often prepositional phrases. In the sentence

The tomatoes in this salad are pale pink and mushy.

the subject (tomatoes) is plural, and so the verb (are) is plural. The words *in this salad,* which come between the subject and the verb, do not affect subject–verb agreement.

To help find the subject of certain sentences, you should cross out prepositional phrases (see page 340):

Nell, ~~with her three dogs close behind~~, runs around the park every day.
The seams ~~in my new coat~~ have split after only two wearings.

● ● ● ● **Activity**

Underline the correct verb form in the parentheses.

1) The decisions of the judge (*seem, seems*) questionable.
2) The flakes in this cereal (*taste, tastes*) like sawdust.
3) The woman in the dark sunglasses (*is, are*) our mayor.
4) Many people in Europe (*speak, speaks*) several languages.
5) A salad and a small yogourt (*is, are*) my usual lunch.
6) That silk flower by the candles (*look, looks*) real.
7) One of my son's worst habits (*is, are*) leaving an assortment of dirty plates on the kitchen counter.
8) The rust spots on the back of Emma's car (*need, needs*) to be cleaned with a special polish.
9) The collection of shampoo bottles in my bathroom (*overflow, overflows*) the cabinet shelves.
10) A tired-looking student in my class often (*sleep, sleeps*) through most of the lectures.

2 VERB BEFORE SUBJECT

A verb agrees with its subject even when the verb comes *before* the subject. Words that may precede the subject include *there, here,* and, in questions, *who, which, what,* and *where.*

On Glen's doorstep were two police officers.
There are many pizza places in our town.
Here is your receipt.
Where are they going to sleep?

If you are unsure about the subject, look at the verb and ask *who* or *what*. With the first example above, you might ask, "*Who* were on the doorstep?" The answer, *police officers,* is the subject.

● ● ● ● **Activity**

Write the correct form of the verb in the space provided.

is, are	1. What _____ your middle name?
was, were	2. Among the guests _____ a private detective.
do, does	3. Where _____ you go when you want to be alone?
is, are	4. There _____ many hungry people in Canadian cities.
rest, rests	5. In that grave _____ the bones of my great-grandfather.
was, were	6. There _____ too many people in the room for me to feel comfortable.
is, are	7. Why _____ the lights turned off?
stand, stands	8. Across the street _____ the post office.
is, are	9. Here _____ the tickets for tonight's game.
was, were	10. Stuffed into the mailbox _____ ten pieces of junk mail and three ripped magazines.

3 COMPOUND SUBJECTS

Subjects joined by *and* generally take a plural verb. These are called compound subjects.

Maple syrup and sweet butter taste delicious on pancakes.
Fear and ignorance have a lot to do with hatred.

When subjects are joined by *either . . . or, neither . . . nor, not only . . . but also,* the verb agrees with the subject closer to the verb.

Either cross-country skis or a sled make a great Christmas present.

The nearer subject, *a sled,* is singular, and so the verb is singular.

● ● ● ● **Activity**

Write the correct form of the verb in the space provided.

stays, stay	1. Our cats and dog _____ at a neighbour's house when we go on vacation.
is, are	2. _____ the birthday cake and ice cream ready to be served?
holds, hold	3. Staples and sticky tape _____ all our old photo albums together.
was, were	4. Rent and car insurance _____ my biggest expenses last month.

wants, want   5. Neither the students nor the instructor _____ to postpone the final exam till after the holidays.

is, are   6. An egg and a banana _____ required for the recipe.

was, were   7. Owning a car and having money in my pocket _____ the chief ambitions of my adolescence.

visits, visit   8. My aunt and uncle from Poland _____ us every other summer.

was, were   9. Before they saw a marriage therapist, Peter and Sylvia _____ planning to get divorced.

acts, act   10. Not only the property owner but also her children _____ unfriendly to us.

Using Only Transitive Verbs for the Passive Voice

Only *transitive* verbs—verbs that need direct objects to complete their meaning—can have a passive form (one in which the subject receives the action instead of performing it). Intransitive verbs cannot be used in the passive voice.

Incorrect: If you don't fix those brakes, an accident *may be happened.*

Happen is an intransitive verb—no object is needed to complete its meaning.

Correct: If you don't fix those brakes, an accident **may happen.**

If you are not sure whether a verb is transitive or intransitive, check your dictionary. Transitive verbs are indicated with an abbreviation such as *v.tr.* or *v.t.* Intransitive verbs are indicated with an abbreviation such as *v.intr.* or *v.i.*

Using Gerunds and Infinitives after Verbs (Idiomatic Verb Structures)

A gerund is the -*ing* form of a verb that is used as a noun.
Complaining is Ian's favorite activity. (*Complaining* is the subject of the sentence.)
An *infinitive* is *to* plus the basic form of the verb (the form in which the verb is listed in the dictionary); for example, *to eat, to stand, to revise.* The infinitive can function as an adverb, an adjective, or a noun.
We decided **to eat** dinner on the porch. (*To eat dinner on the porch* functions as an adverb that describes the verb *decided.*)
Aaron built a shelf **to hold** his DVD collection. (*To hold his DVD collection* functions as an adjective describing or modifying the noun *shelf.*)
To have a good time is the best we can expect. (*To have a good time* functions as a noun: the subject of the verb *is.*)
Some verbs can be followed by only a gerund or only an infinitive; other verbs can be followed by either. Examples are given in the following lists. You will encounter many others in your reading.

Verb + *gerund* (admit + stealing)
Verb + *preposition* + *gerund* (apologize + for + yelling)

Some verbs can be followed by a gerund but not by an infinitive. In many cases, there is a preposition (such as *for, in,* or *of*) between the verb and the gerund. Here are some verbs and verb/preposition combinations that can be followed by gerunds but not by infinitives.

admit	deny	look forward to
apologize for	discuss	postpone
appreciate	dislike	practise
approve of	enjoy	suspect of
avoid	feel like	talk about
be used to	finish	thank for
believe in	insist on	think about

> *Incorrect:* He must *avoid to jog* until his knee heals.
> *Correct:* He must **avoid jogging** until his knee heals.
> *Incorrect:* The instructor apologized for to be late to class.
> *Correct:* The instructor **apologized for** being late to class.

Verb + infinitive (agree + to leave)

These common verbs can be followed by an infinitive but not by a gerund.

agree	expect	plan
arrange	have	refuse
claim	manage	wait
decide		

> Incorrect: The students refuse staying after class.
> *Correct:* The students **refuse to stay** after class.

Verb + noun or pronoun + infinitive (cause + them + to flee)

These common verbs are followed first by a noun or pronoun and then by an infinitive (not a gerund).

cause	force	remind
command	persuade	warn

> Incorrect: The coach persuaded Mario studying harder.
> *Correct:* The coach **persuaded Mario to study** harder.

Here are common verbs that can be followed either by an infinitive alone or by a noun or pronoun and an infinitive.

ask	need	want
expect	promise	would like

Dena **asked to have a day** off next week.
Her boss **asked her to work** on Saturday.

Verb + gerund or infinitive (*begin + packing or begin + to pack*)

These verbs can be followed by either a gerund or an infinitive.

begin	hate	prefer
continue	love	start

The meaning of each of the above verbs remains the same or almost the same whether a gerund or an infinitive is used.

Zoë **hates being** late.
Zoë **hates to be** late.

With the verbs below, the gerunds and the infinitives have very different meanings.

forget	remember	stop

Esta **stopped to call** home. (*Meaning:* She interrupted something to call home.)
Esta **stopped calling** home. (*Meaning:* She discontinued calling home.)

● ● ● ● ● **Activity**

Underline the correct form in parentheses.

1. The doctor (*asked me, she asked me*) if I smoked.
2. The coffee is very fresh. (*Is, It is*) strong and delicious.
3. (*Are mice, There are mice*) living in our kitchen.
4. The box (*is containing, contains*) a beautiful necklace.
5. Unless you take your foot off the brake, the car will not (*be going, go*).
6. Most basketball players (*very tall, are very tall*).
7. Many people (*enjoy to spend, enjoy spending*) a day in the city.
8. The teacher (*plans taking, plans to take*) us on a field trip tomorrow.

9. Some old men in my neighbourhood (*play cards, they play cards*) every afternoon.
10. When I am happy, I feel like (*to sing, singing*).

4 PRONOUNS

Including Pronoun Subjects and Verbs

Some languages may omit a pronoun as a subject, but in English, every clause and every sentence other than a command must have a subject. (In a command, the subject *you* is understood: [**You**] Hand in your papers now.)

> *Incorrect:* The Yellow head Highway is in central Alberta. Runs across the province.
> *Correct:* The Yellow head Highway is in central Alberta. **It** runs across the province.

Every English clause and sentence must also have a verb, even when the meaning of the clause or sentence is clear without the verb.

> *Incorrect:* Angelita's piano teacher very patient.
> *Correct:* Angelita's piano teacher **is** very patient.

Indefinite Pronouns

The following words, known as *indefinite pronouns,* always take singular verbs.

(-one words)	(-body words)	(-thing words)	
one	nobody	nothing	each
anyone	anybody	anything	either
everyone	everybody	everything	neither
someone	somebody	something	

Note: *Both* always takes a plural verb.

● ● ● ● **Activity**

Write the correct form of the verb in the space provided.

is, are   1. Everybody in my marketing class _____ friendly.

feel, feels   2. Neither of those mattresses _____ comfortable.

knows, know   3. Nobody in my family _____ how to swim.

needs, need   4. Each of the children _____ some attention.

sounds, sound 5. Something about Robbie's story _____ suspicious.

pitches, pitch 6. If each of us _____ in, we can finish this job in an hour.

was, were   7. Everybody in the theatre _____ getting up and leaving before the movie ended.

provides, provide   8. Neither of the restaurants _____ facilities for physically challenged customers.

likes, like   9. No one in our family _____ housecleaning, but we all take a turn at it.

steals, steal   10. Someone in our neighbourhood _____ vegetables from people's gardens.

Visit the *English Skills with Readings: Examining Paragraphs* Online Learning Centre at www.mcgrawhill.ca/olc/langan to access self-quizzes, internet-based questions and research skills, web resources, and other learning and study tools.

Chapter 25

Pronoun Agreement and Reference

Introductory Project

Read each pair of sentences below. Then write a check mark beside the sentence that you think uses the underlined word or words correctly.

Someone in my neighbourhood lets their dog run loose. _____

Someone in my neighbourhood lets his or her dog run loose. _____

After Kieran reviewed his notes with Scott, he passed the exam with ease. _____

After reviewing his notes Scott, Kieran passed the exam with ease. _____

Answers are provided on the Online Learning Centre.

Pronouns are words that take the place of nouns (persons, places, or things). In fact, the word *pronoun* means "for a noun." Pronouns are shortcuts that keep you from unnecessarily repeating words in writing. Here are some examples of pronouns.

> Ivana had not finished *her* paper. (*Her* is a pronoun that takes the place of *Ivana's*.)
> Brendan swung so heavily on the tree branch that *it* snapped. (*It* replaces *branch*.)
> When the three little pigs saw the wolf, *they* pulled out cans of pepper spray. (*They* is a pronoun that takes the place of *pigs*.)

This section presents rules that will help you avoid two common mistakes people make with pronouns. The rules are:

1) A pronoun must agree in number with the word or words it replaces.
2) A pronoun must refer clearly to the word it replaces.

PRONOUN AGREEMENT

A pronoun must agree in number with the word or words it replaces. If the word a pronoun refers to is singular, the pronoun must be singular; if that word is plural, the pronoun must be plural.

> Jacquie agreed to lend me her Nickelback CDs.
> People walking the trail must watch their step because of snakes.

In the first example, the pronoun *her* refers to the singular word *Jacquie;* in the second example, the pronoun *their* refers to the plural word *people*.

Note: The word a pronoun refers to is also known as the *antecedent. Antecedent* means "going before" in Latin.

● ● ● ● **Activity**

Write the appropriate pronoun (*their, they, them, it*) in the blank space in each of the following sentences.

Example   I lifted the pot of rice and boiling water carefully, but _____ *it* slipped out of my hand.

1. The value that people receive for _____ dollars these days is rapidly diminishing.

2. Rick never misses his daily workout; he believes _____ keeps him healthy.

3. Sometimes, in marriage, partners expect too much from _____ mates.

4. For some students, college is their first experience with a less structured learning situation, and _____ are not always ready to accept the responsibility.

5. Our new neighbours moved in three months ago, but I have yet to meet _____.

Indefinite Pronouns

The following words, known as *indefinite pronouns,* are always singular.

(**-one** *words*)	(**-body** *words*)	
one	nobody	each
anyone	anybody	either
everyone	everybody	neither
someone	somebody	

If a pronoun in a sentence refers to one of the singular words above, the pronoun should be singular.

Each father felt that (his) child should have won the contest.

One of the women could not find (her) purse.

Everyone must be in (his) seat before the instructor takes attendance.

In each example, the circled possessive pronoun is singular because it refers to one of these special singular words.

Note: The last example is correct *if* everyone in the class is a man. If everyone in the class is a woman, the pronoun would be *her.* If the class has both women and men, the pronoun form would be *his or her.*

Everyone must be in his or her seat before the instructor takes attendance.

Some writers follow the traditional practice of using *his* to refer to both women and men. Many now use *his or her* to avoid an implied gender bias. To avoid using *his* or the somewhat awkward *his or her,* a sentence can often be rewritten in the plural.

Students must be in their seats before the instructor takes attendance.

● ● ● ● **Activity**

Underline the correct pronoun.

1. Someone has blocked the parking-lot exit with (*his or her, their*) car.
2. Everyone in the women's group has volunteered some of (*her, their*) time for the voting drive.
3. Neither of the men interviewed for the job was willing to relocate (*his, their*) family.
4. Not one of the women coaches will be returning to (*her, their*) job next year.
5. Each of the CEO's advisers offered (*his or her, their*) opinion about the rail strike.

PRONOUN REFERENCE

A sentence may be confusing and unclear:

- if a pronoun appears to refer to more than one word, or
- if the pronoun does not refer to any specific word.

Look at this sentence:

Jeremy almost dropped out of high school, for he felt *they* emphasized discipline too much.

Who emphasized discipline too much? There is no specific word that *they* refers to. Be clear:

Jeremy almost dropped out of high school, for he felt *the teachers* emphasized discipline too much.

Here are sentences with other kinds of faulty pronoun references. Read the explanations of why they are faulty and look carefully at how they are corrected.

Faulty	*Clear*
Jade told Marisa that *she* lacked self-confidence.	Jade told Marisa, "You lack self-confidence."
	(continued)

(*Who* lacked self-confidence: Jade or Marisa? Be clear.)	(Quotation marks, which can sometimes be used to correct an unclear reference, are explained in Chapter 33.)
Nazima's mother is a hairdresser, but Nazima is not interested in *it*. (There is no specific word that *it* refers to. It would not make sense say, "Nazima is not interested in hairdresser.")	Nazima's mother is a hairdresser, but Nazima is not interested in becoming one.
Ron blamed the police officer for the ticket, *which* was foolish. (Does *which* mean that the officer's giving the ticket was foolish, or that Ron's blaming the officer was foolish? Be clear.)	Foolishly, Ron blamed the police officer for the ticket.

● ● ● ● ● **Activity**

Rewrite each of the following sentences to make clear the vague pronoun reference. Add, change, or omit words as necessary.

Example   Our cat was friends with our hamster until he bit him.

Until the cat bit the hamster, the two were friends.

1. Maria's mother let her wear her new earrings to school.

_____

2. When I asked why I failed my driver's test, he said I drove too slowly.

_____

3. Dad ordered my brother to paint the garage because he didn't want to do it.

_____

4. Julian dropped his psychology courses because he thought they assigned too much reading.

_____

5. I love mozzarella cheese on veal, but it does not always agree with me.

_____

Chapter 26

Pronoun Types

This chapter describes some common types of pronouns: subject-case and object-case pronouns, possessive pronouns, and demonstrative pronouns.

SUBJECT AND OBJECT CASES OF PRONOUNS

The form of a pronoun is called its case. *Case* means the form of a pronoun that shows its grammatical function in a sentence. Pronouns appear in the subject case, the object case, or the possessive case. Because pronouns change form, they pose challenges to speakers and writers of English.

Here is a list of subject-case and object-case pronouns.

Subject-Case Pronouns	*Object-Case Pronouns*
I	me
you	you (*no change*)
he	him
she	her
it	it (*no change*)
we	us
they	them

SUBJECT-CASE PRONOUNS

Subject-case pronouns are subjects of verbs.

She is wearing blue nail polish on her toes. (*She* is the subject of the verb *is wearing*.)

They ran up three flights of steps. (*They* is the subject of the verb *ran*.)

We children should have some privacy too. (*We* is the subject of the verb *should have*.)

Rules for using subject-case pronouns and several kinds of mistakes people sometimes make with them are explained below.

1) Use the subject case of a pronoun where you have a compound (more than one) subject.

Incorrect	Correct
Eliza and *me* are exactly the same size.	Eliza and *I* are exactly the same size.
Her and *me* share our wardrobes with each other.	*She* and *I* share our wardrobes with each other.

Hint: If you are not sure which pronoun case to use, try each pronoun by itself in the sentence. The correct pronoun will be the one that sounds right. For example, "Her shares her wardrobe" does not sound right; "She shares her wardrobe" does.

2) Use the subject case of a pronoun after forms of the verb *be*. Forms of *be* include *am, are, is, was, were, has been,* and *have been.*

> It was *I* who called you a minute ago and then hung up.
> It may be *they* entering the coffee shop.
> It was *he* who put the white tablecloth into the washing machine with a red sock.

The sentences above may sound strange and stilted to you because they are seldom used in conversation. When we speak with one another, forms such as "It was me," "It may be them," and "It's her" are widely accepted. In formal writing, however, the grammatically correct forms are still preferred.

Hint: To avoid having to use the subject-case pronoun after *be*, you can reword a sentence. Here is how the examples above could be reworded.

> I was the one who called you a minute ago and then hung up.
> They may be the people entering the coffee shop.
> He put the white tablecloth into the washing machine with a red sock.

3) Use subject-case pronouns after *than* or *as*. The subject case is used because a verb is understood after the pronoun.

> Mark can hold his breath longer than *I* (can). (The verb *can* is understood after *I*.)
> Her thirteen-year-old daughter is as tall as *she* (is). (The verb *is* is understood after *she*.)
> You drive much better than *he* (drives). (The verb *drives* is understood after *he*.)

Hint: Avoid mistakes by mentally adding the "missing" verb at the end of the sentence.

OBJECT-CASE PRONOUNS

The object-case of pronouns (*me, him, her, us, them*) is used for the objects of verbs or prepositions. (*Prepositions* are connecting words like *for, at, about, to, before, with,* and *of.* See also page 340.) An object, in grammatical terms, receives the action of a verb or completes a prepositional phrase.

> Lee pushed *me.* (*Me* is the object of the verb *pushed.*)
> We dragged *them* all the way home. (*Them* is the object of the verb *dragged.*)
> She wrote all about *us* in her diary. (*Us* is the object of the preposition *about.*)
> Vera passed a note to *him* as she walked to the pencil sharpener. (*Him* is the object of the preposition *to.*)

People are sometimes uncertain about which pronoun to use when two objects follow the verb.

Incorrect	Correct
I argued with his sister and *he.*	I argued with his sister and *him.*
The cashier cheated Connor and *I.*	The cashier cheated Connor and *me.*

Hint: If you are not sure which pronoun to use, try each pronoun by itself in the sentence. The correct pronoun will be the one that sounds right. For example, "I argued with he" does not sound right; "I argued with him" does.

● ● ● ● **Activity**

Underline the correct subject-case or object-case pronoun in each of the following sentences. Then show whether your answer is a subject-case or an object-case pronoun by circling S or O in the margin. The first one is done for you as an example.

Ⓢ O   1. (*She, Her*) and Darcy kept dancing even after the band stopped playing.

S O   2. The letters Mom writes to Stella and (*I, me*) are always printed in red.

S O   3. Pilar drove to Thunder Bay but her sister, who took the bus, got there faster than (*she, her*).

S O   4. Their relay team won because they practised more than (*we, us*).

S O   5. (*We, Us*) choir members get to perform for the premier of the province.

S O   6. The rest of (*they, them*) came to the wedding by train.

S O   7. (*She, Her*) and Sammy got divorced and then remarried.

S O   8. Since we were both taking a tough statistics course, it was a long, hard semester for my best friend and (*me, I*).

S O   9. (*He, Him*) and Terrell look a lot alike, but they're not even related.

S O   10. Our neighbours asked Rosa and (*I, me*) to help with their parents' surprise party.

POSSESSIVE PRONOUNS

Pronouns in the possessive case—possessive pronouns—show ownership or possession.

> Using a small branch, Siu wrote *his* initials in the wet cement.
> The furniture is *mine*, but the car is hers.

Here is a list of possessive pronouns.

my, mine	our, ours
your, yours	your, yours
his	their, theirs
her, hers	
its	

Note: A possessive pronoun *never* uses an apostrophe. (Also see pages 415–416.)

Incorrect	*Correct*
That earring is *hers'* (or *her's*).	That earring is *hers*.
The orange cat is *theirs'* (or *their's*).	The orange cat is *theirs*.

• • • • • **Activity**

Cross out the incorrect possessive pronoun form in each of the sentences below. Write the correct form in the space at the left.

Example   ___hers___   Those gloves are ~~hers'~~.

_____   1. A porcupine has no quills on it's belly.

_____   2. The Power Book on that table is theirs'.

_____   3. You can easily tell which team is our's by when we cheer.

_____   4. The car with the leather seats is hers'.

_____   5. My experience with the flu was nothing compared with your's.

DEMONSTRATIVE PRONOUNS

Demonstrative pronouns point to or single out a person or thing. Demonstrative pronouns do not have cases, but they do change in singular and plural forms. There are four demonstrative pronouns.

this	these
that	those

Generally speaking, *this* and *these* refer to things close at hand; *that* and *those* refer to things farther away.

> *This* is the milk that has gone sour.
> *These* are the computer magazines that my son insists on saving.
> *That* is the roller skate that I almost tripped on at the bottom of the stairs.
> *Those* are the plants in the corner that don't get enough light.

These four pronouns are commonly used as demonstrative adjectives as well.

> *This* milk has gone sour.
> My son insists on saving all *these* computer magazines.
> I almost tripped on *that* roller skate at the bottom of the steps.
> *Those* plants in the corner don't get enough light.

Online **Learning**Centre

Visit the *English Skills with Readings: Examining Paragraphs* Online Learning Centre at www.mcgrawhill.ca/olc/langan to access self-quizzes, internet-based questions and research skills, web resources, and other learning and study tools.

Chapter 27

Adjectives and Adverbs

ADJECTIVES

What are Adjectives?

Adjectives describe nouns (names of persons, places, or things) or pronouns.

Emil is a *rich* man. (The adjective *rich* describes the noun *man.*)
He is also *generous.* (The adjective *generous* describes the pronoun *he.*)
Our *grey* cat sleeps a lot. (The adjective *grey* describes the noun *cat.*)
She is *old.* (The adjective *old* describes the pronoun *she.*)

Adjectives usually come before the words they describe (as in *rich man* and *grey cat*). But they also come after forms of the verb *be* (*is, are, was, were,* and so on). They also follow verbs of appearance or perception such as *look, appear, seem, become, sound, taste,* and *smell.*

That speaker was *boring.* (The adjective *boring* describes the speaker.)
The Petersons are *homeless.* (The adjective *homeless* describes the Petersons.)
The soup looked *good.* (The adjective *good* describes the soup.)
But it tasted *salty.* (The adjective *salty* describes the pronoun *it.*)

USING ADJECTIVES TO COMPARE

For all one-syllable adjectives and some two-syllable adjectives, add *-er* when comparing two things and *-est* when comparing three or more things.

My sister's handwriting is *neater* than mine, but Mother's is the *neatest.*
Canned or boxed juice is sometimes *cheaper* than fresh juice, but frozen juice is often the *cheapest.*

For some two-syllable adjectives and all longer adjectives, add *more* when comparing two things and *most* when comparing three or more things.

The first novel in the series is *more interesting* than the second, but the latest is the *most interesting* of them all.
Jeans are generally *more comfortable* than slacks, but sweat pants are the *most comfortable* of all.

You can usually tell when to use *more* and *most* by the sound of a word. For example, you can probably tell by its sound that "carefuller" would be too awkward to say and that *more careful* is thus correct. But there are many words for which both *-er* or *-est* and *more* or *most* are equally correct. For instance, either "a more fair rule" or "a fairer rule" is correct.

To form negative comparisons, use *less* and *least*.

When I slipped on the black ice, I tried to look *less* hurt than I felt.
Many people say men gossip *less* than women do, but I don't believe it.
Suzanne is the most self-centred, *least* thoughtful person I know.

Points to Remember about Comparing

1) Use only one form of comparison at a time. In other words, do not use both an *-er* ending and *more* or both an *-est* ending and *most*.

Incorrect	*Correct*
My Newfoundland accent is always *more stronger* after I visit my family in Bonavista.	My Newfoundland accent is always *stronger* after I visit my family in Bonavista.
My *most luckiest* day was the day I met my wife.	My *luckiest* day was the day I met my wife.

2) Learn the irregular forms of the words shown below.

	Comparative (for Comparing Two Things)	*Superlative (for Comparing Three or More Things)*
bad	worse	worst
good, well	better	best
little (in amount)	less	least
much, many	more	most

Do not use both *more* and an irregular comparative or *most* and an irregular superlative.

Incorrect	*Correct*
It is *more better* to stay healthy than to have to get healthy.	It is *better* to stay healthy than to have to get healthy.
Yesterday I went on the *most best* date of my life—and all we did was go on a picnic.	Yesterday I went on the *best* date of my life—and all we did was go on a picnic.

● ● ● ● **Activity**

Add to each sentence the correct form of the word in the margin.

bad   ***Examples***   The ___*worst*___ scare I ever had was when I thought my son was on an airplane that crashed.

wonderful   The day of my divorce was even ___*more wonderful*___ than the day of my wedding.

good   1. The Juno awards are given to the _____ Canadian recording artists of each year.

popular   2. Vanilla ice cream is even _____ than chocolate ice cream.

bad   3. One of the _____ things you can do to people is ignore them.

light   4. A kilogram of feathers is no _____ than a kilogram of stones.

less   5. The _____ expensive way to accumulate a wardrobe is by buying used clothing whenever possible.

Following the Order of Adjectives in English

Adjectives modify nouns and pronouns. In English, an adjective usually comes directly before the word it describes or after a linking verb (a form of *be* or a verb of appearance or perception such as *look*, *seem*, or *taste*), in which case it modifies the subject. In each of the following two sentences, the adjective is **boldfaced** and the noun it describes is *italicized*.

> That is a **false** *story*.
> The *story* is **false**.

When more than one adjective modifies the same noun, the adjectives are usually stated in a certain order, though there are often exceptions. The box shows the typical order of English adjectives.

Typical Order of Adjectives in a Series

1) An article or other determiner*: a, an, the, Lee's, your, some, this, three, another

2) Opinion adjective: dull, handsome, unfair, useful

3) Size: big, huge, little, tiny

4) Shape: long, short, round, square

5) Age: ancient, medieval, old, new, young

6) Colour: blue, green, scarlet, white

7) Nationality: Italian, Korean, Mexican, Vietnamese

8) Religion: Buddhist, Catholic, Jewish, Muslim

9) Material: cardboard, gold, marble, silk

10) Noun used as an adjective: house (as in *house call*), tea (as in *tea bag*), wall (as in *wall hanging*), or participle **as an adjective:** rocking (as in *rocking chair*), watering (as in *watering can*)

---

*These are the categories of *determiners,* with examples of each:

- *Possessive forms of nouns:* Karen's, the college's
- *Possessive pronouns:* my, your, our
- *Quantifiers:* some, several, many, a few of, a lot of
- *Demonstrative adjectives:* this, these
- *Numbers:* one, ten, 120
- *Indefinite pronouns:* another, both, few

Here are some examples of the order of adjectives.

a long cotton scarf
the beautiful little silver cup
your new lavender evening gown
Anna's sweet Italian grandmother

In general, use no more than *two or three* adjectives after the article or other determiner. Numerous adjectives in a series can be awkward: **the beautiful big new blue cotton** sweater.

Using the Present and Past Participles as Adjectives

The present participle ends in *-ing*. Past participles of regular verbs end in *-ed* or *-d*; a list of the past participles of many common irregular verbs begins on page 368. Both types of participles may be used as adjectives. A participle used as an adjective may come before the word it describes.

It was a **boring** *program*.

A participle used as an adjective may also follow a linking verb and describe the subject of the sentence.

The *program* was **boring.**

While both present and past participles of a particular verb may be used as adjectives, their meanings differ. Use the *present participle* to describe whoever or whatever *causes* a feeling.

a **surprising** *conversation* (The conversation *caused* the surprise.)

Use the *past participle* to describe whoever or whatever *experiences* the feeling.

a **surprised** cashier (The cashier *is* surprised.)

Here are two more sentences that illustrate the differing meanings of present and past participles.

The horror movie was **frightening;** the audience was **frightened**. (The movie *caused* the fear; the audience *experienced* the fear.)

Following are pairs of present and past participles with similar distinctions.

annoying/annoyed	exhausting/exhausted
boring/bored	fascinating/fascinated
confusing/confused	frightening/frightened
depressing/depressed	surprising/surprised
exciting/excited	

• • • • • Activity

Underline the correct form in parentheses.

1. The Johnsons live in a (*stone big, big stone*) house.
2. Mr. Kim runs a (*popular Korean, Korean popular*) restaurant.

3. For her party, the little girl asked if her mother would buy her a (*beautiful long velvet, beautiful velvet long*) dress.

4. When their son didn't come home by bedtime, Mr. and Mrs. Singh became (*worried, worrying*).

5. The constant humming of the laboratory equipment is very (*annoyed, annoying*).

ADVERBS

What Are Adverbs?

Adverbs describe verbs, adjectives, or other adverbs. They usually end in *-ly*.

The referee *suddenly* stopped the fight. (The adverb *suddenly* describes the verb *stopped.*)

Her yellow rosebushes are *absolutely* beautiful. (The adverb *absolutely* describes the adjective *beautiful.*)

The auctioneer spoke so *extremely* fast that I couldn't understand him. (The adverb *extremely* describes the adverb *fast.*)

A Common Mistake with Adverbs and Adjectives

People often mistakenly use an adjective instead of an adverb after a verb.

Incorrect	*Correct*
I jog *slow.*	I jog *slowly.*
The nervous witness spoke *quiet.*	The nervous witness spoke *quietly.*
The first night after I left home, I wanted to call *bad.*	The first night after I left home, I wanted to call *badly.*
Reid is *real* sneaky.	Reid is *really* sneaky.

● ● ● ● **Activity**

Underline the adjective or adverb needed. (Remember that adjectives describe nouns, and adverbs describe verbs or other adverbs.)

1. During a quiet moment in class, my stomach rumbled (*loud, loudly*).

2. I'm a (*slow, slowly*) reader, so I have to put aside more time to study than some of my friends.

3. Thinking no one was looking, the young man (*quick, quickly*) emptied his car's ashtray onto the parking lot.

4. The cottage mice wait (*patient, patiently*) in the shadows; at night they'll have the place to themselves.

5. I hang up the phone (*immediate, immediately*) whenever the speaker is a recorded message.

Comparative and Superlative Forms of Adverbs

Adverbs, like adjectives, have comparative and superlative forms. Comparative or superlative forms of adverbs, except for common irregular adverbs such as *well*, are formed by adding *more* or *most* before the adverb. Examples are *more slowly, most carefully*, and so on.

Well and *Good*

Two words that are often confused are *well* and *good*. *Good* is an adjective; it describes nouns. *Well* is usually an adverb, but it is also used as an adjective when referring to a person's health. The opposite of *well* in this sense is *unwell* (not *bad* or *badly*).

• • • • Activity

Write *well* or *good* in each of the sentences that follow.

1. I could tell by the broad grin on Delia's face that the news was _____.

2. They say he sang so _____ that even the wind stopped to listen.

3. The food at the salad bar must have been too heavy because I didn't sleep _____ that night.

4. When I want to do a really _____ job of washing the floor, I do it on my hands and knees.

5. The best way to get along _____ with our boss is to stay out of his way.

Including *there* and *here* at the Beginning of Clauses

Some English sentences begin with *there* or *here* plus a linking verb (usually a form of *be: is, are*, and so on). In such sentences, the verb comes before the subject.

There are masks in every culture on earth. (The subject is the plural noun *masks*, so the plural verb *are* is used.)

Here is your driver's license. (The subject is the singular noun *license*, so the singular verb *is* is used.)

In sentences like the ones above, remember not to omit *there* or *here*.

Incorrect: Are several chickens in the Bensons' yard.
Correct: **There are** several chickens in the Bensons' yard.

Chapter 28

Misplaced Modifiers

Introductory Project

Because of misplaced words, each of the sentences below has more than one possible meaning. In each case, see if you can explain the intended meaning and the unintended meaning. Also, circle the words that you think create the confusion because they are misplaced.

1. The sign in the restaurant window reads, "Wanted: Young Man—To Open Oysters with References."

    Intended meaning: _____

    Unintended meaning: _____

2. Carlo and Charlotte decided to have two children on their wedding day.

    Intended meaning: _____

    Unintended meaning: _____

3. Marissa eats only chocolates with hazelnut filling.

    Intended meaning: _____

    Unintended meaning: _____

Answers are provided on the Online Learning Centre.

WHAT MISPLACED MODIFIERS ARE AND HOW TO CORRECT THEM

Modifiers are descriptive words. *Misplaced modifiers* are words or groups of words that, because of awkward placement, do not describe the words the writer intended them to describe. Misplaced modifiers often obscure the meaning of a sentence. To avoid them, place words as close as possible to what they describe.

Misplaced Words	Correctly Placed Words
Alex bought an old car from a crooked dealer *with a faulty transmission.* (The dealer had a faulty transmission?)	Alex bought an old car with a faulty transmission from a crooked dealer. (The words describing the old car are now placed next to *car*.)
I *nearly* earned a hundred dollars last week. (You just missed earning a hundred dollars, but in fact earned nothing?)	I earned nearly a hundred dollars last week. (The meaning—that you earned a little under a hundred dollars—is now clear.)
We could see the football stadium *driving across the bridge.* (The stadium was driving?)	Driving across the bridge, we could see the football stadium. (The words describing us are placed next to *we*.)

Activity

Underline the misplaced word or words in each sentence. Then rewrite the sentence, placing related words together and thereby making the meaning clear.

Example   The suburbs <u>nearly</u> had ten centimetres of rain.
The suburbs had nearly ten centimetres of rain.

1. During the city workers' strike, I saw mountains of uncollected garbage walking along the streets.

   _____

2. I almost had a dozen job interviews after I sent out my résumé.

   _____

3. Clark swatted the wasp that stung him with a newspaper.

   _____

4. Joanne decided to live with her grandparents when she attended college to save money.

   _____

5. Paula returned the yogourt to the supermarket with mould on top.

   _____

6. Roger visited the old house still weak with the flu.

   _____

7. The phone almost rang fifteen times last night.

   _____

8. My uncle saw a kangaroo at the window under the influence of whisky.

   _____

9. We decided to send our daughter to college on the day she was born.

   _____

10. Farid always opens the bills that arrive in the mailbox with a sigh.

   _____

 **Online LearningCentre**

Visit the *English Skills with Readings: Examining Paragraphs* Online Learning Centre at <u>www.mcgrawhill.ca/olc/langan</u> to access self-quizzes, internet-based questions and research skills, web resources, and other learning and study tools.

Chapter 29

Dangling Modifiers

Introductory Project

Because of dangling words, each of the sentences below has more than one possible meaning. In each case, see if you can explain the intended meaning and the unintended meaning.

1. While smoking a pipe, my dog sat with me by the crackling fire.

   Intended meaning: _____

   Unintended meaning: _____

2. Looking at the traffic accident, his sports car went through a red light.

   Intended meaning: _____

   Unintended meaning: _____

3. After baking for several hours, Dad removed the moussaka from the oven.

   Intended meaning: _____

   Unintended meaning: _____

Answers are provided on the Online Learning Centre.

WHAT DANGLING MODIFIERS ARE AND HOW TO CORRECT THEM

Dangling modifiers are words, phrases, or clauses that modify, describe, or refer to (1) something not present in the sentence or (2) something these modifiers are not intended to describe. Often, dangling modifiers appear at the beginnings of sentences.

A modifier that opens a sentence must be *followed immediately* by the word it is meant to describe. Otherwise, the modifier will be *dangling,* and the sentence takes on an unintended meaning. For example, in the sentence

While smoking a pipe, my dog sat with me by the crackling fire, the unintended meaning is that the *dog* was smoking the pipe. What the writer meant, of course, was that *he,* the writer, was smoking the pipe. The dangling modifier could be corrected by placing *I,* the word being described, directly after the opening modifier.

While smoking a pipe, *I* sat with my dog by the crackling fire.

The dangling modifier could also be corrected by placing the subject within the opening word group.

While *I* was smoking my pipe, my dog sat with me by the crackling fire.

Here are other sentences with dangling modifiers. Read the explanations of why they are dangling, and look carefully at how they are corrected.

Dangling	*Correct*
Swimming at the lake, a rock cut Samantha's foot. (*Who* was swimming at the lake? The answer is not *rock* but *Samantha*. The subject *Samantha* must be added.)	Swimming at the lake, *Samantha* cut her foot on a rock. *Or:* When *Samantha* was swimming at the lake, she cut her foot on a rock.
While eating my sandwich, five mosquitoes bit me. (*Who* is eating the sandwich? The answer is not *five mosquitoes,* as it unintentionally seems to be, but *I*. The subject *I* must be added.)	While *I* was eating my sandwich, five mosquitoes bit me. *Or:* While eating my sandwich, *I* was bitten by five mosquitoes.
Getting out of bed, the tile floor was so cold that Yoko shivered all over. (*Who* got out of bed? The answer is not *tile floor* but *Yoko*. The subject *Yoko* must be added.)	Getting out of bed, *Yoko* found the tile floor so cold that she shivered all over. *Or:* When *Yoko* got out of bed, the tile floor was so cold that she shivered all over.
To join the team, a C average or better is necessary. (*Who* is to join the team? The answer is not *C average* but *you*. The subject *you* must be added.)	To join the team, *you* must have a C average or better. *Or:* For *you* to join the team, a C average or better is necessary.

The preceding examples make clear the two ways of correcting a dangling modifier. Decide on a logical subject and do one of the following:

1) Place the subject *within* the opening word group.

When Samantha was swimming at the lake, she cut her foot on a rock.

In some cases an appropriate subordinating word such as *when* must be added, and the verb may have to be changed slightly as well.

2) Place the subject right *after* the opening word group.

Swimming at the lake, Samantha cut her foot on a rock.

● ● ● ● **Activity**

Ask "Who?" as you look at the opening words in each sentence. The subject that answers the question should be nearby in the sentence. If it is not, provide the logical subject by using either method of correction described above.

Example   While sleeping at the campsite, a Frisbee hit Derek on the head.

While Derek was sleeping at the campsite, a Frisbee hit him on the head.

or   *While sleeping at the campsite, Derek was hit on the head by a Frisbee.*

1. Watching the horror movie, goosebumps came up all over me.

_____

_____

2. After putting on a corduroy shirt, the room didn't seem so cold.

_____

_____

3. Flunking out of school, my parents demanded that I get a job.

_____

_____

4. Covered with food stains, my brother decided to wash the tablecloth.

_____

_____

5. Joining several college clubs, Anton's social life became more active.

_____

_____

6. While visiting the African Lion Safari, a baboon scrambled onto the hood of their car.

_____

_____

7. Under attack by beetles, Nina sprayed her roses with insecticide.

_____

_____

8. Standing at the ocean's edge, the wind coated my glasses with a salty film.

_____

_____

9. Braking the car suddenly, my shopping bags tumbled off the seat.

_____

_____

10. Using binoculars, the hawk was clearly seen following its prey.

_____

_____

Chapter 30

Capital Letters

Introductory Project

Items 1 to 13: You probably know a good deal about the uses of capital letters. Answering the questions below will help you check your knowledge.

1. Write the full name of a person you know: _____

2. In what city and province or in what country were you born? _____

3. What is your present street address? _____

4. Name a country where you would like to travel: _____

5. Name a school that you attended: _____

6. Give the name of a store where you buy food: _____

7. Name a company where someone you know works: _____

8. Which day of the week gives you the best chance to relax? _____

9. Which holiday is your favourite? _____

10. Which brand of toothpaste do you use? _____

11. Give the brand name of a candy or gum you like: _____

12. Name a top song of the year: _____

13. Give the title of a book or textbook: _____

Items 14 to 16: Three capital letters are needed in the lines below. Underline the words that you think should be capitalized. Then write them, capitalized, in the spaces provided.

the caped man started his sleek black car, waved goodbye, and roared out of town. My heart thrilled when i heard someone say, "that was Batman. You don't see superheroes much any more."

14. _____   15. _____   16. _____

Answers are provided on the Online Learning Centre.

MAIN USES OF CAPITAL LETTERS

Capital letters are used with:

1) The first word in a sentence or direct quotation

2) Names of persons and the word *I*

3) Names of particular places
4) Names of days of the week, months, and holidays
5) Names of commercial products
6) Names of organizations such as religious and political groups, associations, companies, unions, and clubs
7) Titles of books, magazines, newspapers, articles, stories, poems, films, television shows, songs, papers that you write, and the like

Each use is illustrated on the pages that follow.

1 First Word in a Sentence or Direct Quotation

The street person touched me and asked, "Do you have any change?"

↑ (Capitalize the first word in the sentence.)

↑ (Capitalize the first word in the direct quotation.)

"If you want a ride," said Tammy, "get ready now. Otherwise, I'm going alone." (*If* and *otherwise* are capitalized because they are the first words of sentences within a direct quotation. But *get* is not capitalized because it is part of the first sentence within the quotation.)

2 Names of Persons and the Word *I*

Last night I ran into Terry Kowalski and Liane Morrison.

3 Names of Particular Places

Candi graduated from St. Boniface High School in Winnipeg, Manitoba. She then moved with her parents to Red Deer, Alberta, and worked there for a time at Freda's Gift Shop. Eventually she married and moved with her husband to a Canadian Forces Base in Norfolk County, Ontario. She takes courses two nights a week at Fanshawe College. On weekends, she and her family drive to Point Pelee National Park and go birdwatching and swimming in Lake Erie. She does volunteer work at the Simcoe Hospital in connection with Holy Trinity Church. In addition, she works during the summer as a host at the Eva Brook Donly Museum and the Holiday Inn.

But: Use small letters if the specific name of a place is not given.

Candi sometimes remembers her unhappy days in high school and at the gift shop where she worked after graduation. She did not imagine then that she would one day be going to college and doing volunteer work for a church and a hospital in the community where she and her husband live.

4 Names of Days of the Week, Months, and Holidays

I was angry at myself for forgetting that Sunday was Mother's Day.

During July and August, Franco's company works a four-day week, and he has Mondays off.

Aaron still has a scar on his ankle from a firecracker that exploded near him on Victoria Day and a scar on his arm where he stabbed himself with a fishhook on Labour Day weekend.

But: Use small letters for the seasons—summer, fall, winter, spring.

5 Names of Commercial Products

Louis uses Scope mouthwash, Certs mints, and Dentyne gum to drive away the taste of the Export cigarettes and Monte Cristo cigars that he always smokes.

My sister likes to play Monopoly and Trivial Pursuit; I like chess and poker; my brother likes Scrabble, baseball, and table tennis.

But: Use small letters for the *type* of product (mouthwash, mints, gum, cigarettes, and so on).

6 Names of Organizations Such as Religious and Political Groups, Associations, Companies, Unions, and Clubs

Tom Wilcox attended the United Church for many years but converted to Catholicism when he married. Both he and his wife, Louise, are members of the Liberal Party. Both belong to the Canadian Automobile Association. Louise works part-time as a service representative at Sears. Tom is an ambulance driver and belongs to the Canadian Union of Public Employees.

Enzo met Carla when he was a Boy Scout and she was a Girl Guide; she claimed he needed some guidance.

7 Titles of Books, Magazines, Newspapers, Articles, Stories, Poems, Films, Television Shows, Songs, Papers That You Write, and Other Literature

The reqirements for this course, Canadian Literature in Society, include extensive independent reading. In addition to the textbook, students will be required to read "The LRC 100: Canada's Most Important Books", by Margaret Atwood, in *The Literary Review of Canada*. Students will choose two related selections to compare and contrast; for example, *Dry Lips Oughta Move to Kapuskasing* by Tomson Highway may be chosen alongside Thomas King's *Green Grass, Running Water*. In addition, students must regularly scan issues of *MacLean's* magazine, and newspapers such as the *Globe and Mail*.

• • • • Activity

Cross out the words that need capitals in the following sentences. Then write the capitalized forms of the words in the spaces provided. The number of spaces tells you how many corrections to make in each case.

Example   I brush with ~~crest~~ toothpaste but get cavities all the time. _____*Crest*_____

1. A spokesperson for general motors announced that the prices of all chevrolets will rise next year.

   _____

2. Steve graduated from Bishop Maroccco/thomas merton secondary in june 2008.

   _____

3. The mild-mannered reporter named clark kent said to the Wolfman, "you'd better think twice before you mess with me, buddy."

   _____

4. While watching television, Spencer drank four pepsis, ate an entire package of ritz crackers, and finished up a bag of oreo cookies.

   _____

5. A voyageur bus almost ran over Tony as he was riding his yamaha to a friend's home in quebec.

   _____

6. Before I lent my canon digital camera to Janette, I warned her, "be sure to return it by friday."

   _____

7. Before christmas George took his entire paycheque, went to zellers, and bought a twenty-inch zenith television.

   _____

8. On their first trip to Toronto, Sam and Mattias visited the CN tower and Nathan Phillips square. They also saw the Toronto Blue jays at the roger's centre.

   _____

9. Rob was listening to the Trews' song "Confessions," Erica was reading an article in *Chatelaine* titled "Wedding bell blues," and their son was watching *Robson arms* on TV.

   _____

10. When a sign for a tim hortons rest stop appeared on the highway, anita said, "let's stop here and stretch our legs for a bit."

    _____

OTHER USES OF CAPITAL LETTERS

Capital letters are also used with:

1) Names that show family relationships
2) Titles of persons when used with their names
3) Specific school courses
4) Languages
5) Geographic locations
6) Names of ships, aircraft, spacecraft, and trains
7) Historical periods and events
8) Races, nations, and nationalities
9) Openings and closings of letters

Each use is illustrated on the pages that follow.

1   Names That Show Family Relationships

I got Mother to babysit for me.
I went with Grandfather to the church service.
Uncle Carlo and Aunt Rachel always enclose five dollars with birthday cards.

But: Do not capitalize words like *mother, father, grandmother, aunt,* and so on when they are preceded by a possessive word (*my, your, his, her, our, their*).

I got my mother to babysit for me.
I went with my grandfather to the church service.
My uncle and aunt always enclose five dollars with birthday cards.

2   Titles of Persons When Used with Their Names

I wrote to Premier Laurent and Mayor Miller.
Professor Snorrel sent me to Chair Ruck, who sent me to Dean Guzzi.
He drove to Dr. Jolanda Thompson's office after the cat bit him.

But: Use small letters when titles appear by themselves, without specific names.

I wrote to the premier and the mayor.
The professor sent me to the chair, who sent me to the dean.
He drove to the doctor's office after the cat bit him.

3   Specific School Courses

I got an A in both Accounting I and Small Business Management, but I got a C in Human Behaviour.

But: Use small letters for general subject areas.

I enjoyed my business courses but not my psychology or language courses.

4   Languages

She knows German and Portuguese, but she speaks mostly Canadian slang.

5   Geographic Locations

I grew up in the Maritimes. I worked in the East for a number of years and then moved to the West Coast.

But: Use small letters in directions.

A new high school is being built at the south end of town.

Because I have a compass in my car, I know that I won't be going east or west when I want to go north.

6   Names of Ships, Aircraft, Spacecraft, and Trains

Roberta Bondar flew aboard the space shuttle *Discovery*; she was the second Canadian astronaut.

The name of the *Discovery* appears in italics; names of individual ships, aircraft, spacecraft, and trains are italicized as well as capitalized.

7   Historical Periods and Events

Mario did well answering an essay question about the Second World War, but he lost points on a question about the Great Depression.

8   Races, Nations, and Nationalities

The research study centred on Native Canadians and Québécois.

They have German knives and Danish glassware in the kitchen, an Indian wood carving in the bedroom, Mexican sculptures in the study, and a Persian rug in the living room.

9   Openings and Closings of Letters

Dear Sir:

Dear Madam:

Sincerely yours,

Truly yours,

Note: Capitalize only the first word in a closing.

● ● ● ● **Activity**

Cross out the words that need capitals in the following sentences. Then write the capitalized forms of the words in the spaces provided. The number of spaces tells you how many corrections to make in each case.

1. Although my grandfather spoke german and polish, my mother never learned either language.

   _____   _____

2. The chain letter began, "dear friend—You must mail twenty copies of this letter if you want good luck."

   _____   _____

3. Tomorrow in our cultural studies class, Dr. connalley will start lecturing on the war of 1812.

   _____   _____   _____   _____

4. aunt Catherine and uncle Hank, who are mennonites, took us to their church services when we visited them on the prairies.

   _____   _____   _____   _____

5. My sister has signed up for a course titled eastern religions; she'll be studying buddhism and hinduism.

   _____   _____   _____   _____

UNNECESSARY USE OF CAPITALS

Many errors in capitalization are caused by using capitals where they are not needed.

● ● ● ● **Activity**

Cross out the incorrectly capitalized words in the following sentences. Then write the correct forms of the words in the spaces provided. The number of spaces tells you how many corrections to make in each sentence.

1. Although the Commercials say that Things go better with Coke, I prefer Root Beer.

   _____   _____   _____   _____

2. The old man told the Cabdriver, "I want to go out to the Airport and don't try to cheat me."

   _____   _____

3. A front-page Newspaper story about the crash of a commercial Jet has made me nervous about my Overseas trip.

   _____   _____   _____

4. During Hurricane Hazel in the 1950s, People's Houses were flooded in the Northern Suburbs of Toronto.

   _____ _____ _____ _____

5. I asked the Bank Officer at Scotiabank, "How do I get a bank Card to use the automatic teller machines?"

   _____ _____ _____

Visit the *English Skills with Readings: Examining Paragraphs* Online Learning Centre at www.mcgrawhill.ca/olc/langan to access self-quizzes, internet-based questions and research skills, web resources, and other learning and study tools.

Chapter 31

Numbers and Abbreviations

NUMBERS

1) Spell out numbers that can be expressed in one or two words. Otherwise, use numerals—the numbers themselves.

> During the past five years, over five hundred lampreys have been caught in the lake.
> The parking fine was twenty dollars.
> In my grandmother's attic are eighty-four pairs of old shoes.

But:

> Each year about 250 baby trout are added to the lake.
> My costs after contesting a parking fine in court were $135.
> Grandmother has 110 old copies of the Eaton's catalogue in her attic.

2) Be consistent when you use a series of numbers. If some numbers in a sentence or paragraph require more than two words, then use numerals throughout the selection.

> During his election campaign, Premier Lou Stanley went to 3 local fairs, 16 parades, 45 cookouts, and 112 club dinners and delivered the same speech 176 times.

3) Use numerals for dates, times, addresses, percentages, and parts of a book.

> The letter was dated April 3, 1872.
> My appointment was at 6:15. (*But:* Spell out numbers before *o'clock*. For example: "The doctor didn't see me until seven o'clock.")
> He lives at 212 West 19th Street.
> About 20 percent of our class has dropped out of school.
> Turn to page 179 in Chapter 8 and answer questions 1 to 10.

● ● ● ● ● **Activity**

Cross out the mistakes in numbers and write the corrections in the spaces provided.

1. Roy was born on February fifteen, nineteen eighty.

_____

_____

2. When the 2 children failed to return from school, over 50 people volunteered to search for them.

_____

_____

3. At 1 o'clock in the afternoon last Thursday, an earthquake destroyed at least 20 buildings in the town.

_____

_____

ABBREVIATIONS

While abbreviations are a helpful time-saver in note-taking, you should avoid most abbreviations in formal writing. Listed below are some of the few abbreviations that can acceptably be used in compositions. Note that a period is used after most of these abbreviations.

1) Mr., Mrs., Ms., Jr., Sr., Dr. when used with proper names:

    Mr. Tibble   Dr. Stein   Ms. O'Reilly

2) Time references:

    a.m.   p.m.   B.C. and A.D., or B.C.E. and C.E.

3) First or middle name in a signature:

    Pierre E. Trudeau   Otis T. Redding   J. Alfred Prufrock

4) Organizations and common terms known primarily by their initials:

    RCMP   UN   CBC   FM   ISP

● ● ● ● **Activity**

Cross out the words that should not be abbreviated and correct them in the spaces provided.

1. On a Sat. morning I will never forget, Dec. 5, 1998, at ten min. after eight o'clock, I came downstairs and discovered that I had been robbed.

    _____   _____   _____

2. For six years I lived close to Thorncliff Pk., near Misericordia Hosp., in W. Edm., AB.

    _____   _____   _____   _____   _____

3. Before her biol. and Eng. exams, Linda was so nervous that her doc. gave her a tranq.

_____   _____   _____   _____   _____

Visit the *English Skills with Readings: Examining Paragraphs* Online Learning Centre at www.mcgrawhill.ca/olc/langan to access self-quizzes, internet-based questions and research skills, web resources, and other learning and study tools.

Chapter 32

Apostrophe

The three main uses of the apostrophe are:

1) To show the omission of one or more letters in a contraction

2) To show ownership or possession

3) To form the plural of letters, numbers as numerals, and words used as special terms

Each of these uses of the apostrophe is explained on the pages that follow.

1 APOSTROPHE IN CONTRACTIONS

A contraction is formed when two words (often a pronoun and a verb) are combined to make one word. An apostrophe is used to show where letters are omitted in forming the contraction. Here are two contractions.

> have + not = haven't (o in not has been omitted)
> I + will = I'll (*wi* in *will* has been omitted)

These are some other common contractions.

I +	am = I'm		it +	is = it's
I + have = I've			it +	has = it's
I + had = I'd			is +	not = isn't
who +	is = who's		could +	not = couldn't
do +	not = don't		I +	would = I'd
did +	not = didn't		they +	are = they're

Note: Will + not has an unusual contraction: won't.

Activity 1

Combine the following words into contractions. One is done for you.

1. we + are = ___we're___
2. are + not = _____
3. you + are = _____
4. they + have = _____
5. would + not = _____

6. you + have = _____
7. has + not = _____
8. who + is = _____
9. does + not = _____
10. there + is = _____

Activity 2

Write the contractions for the words in parentheses. One is done for you.

1. (*Are not*) ___Aren't___ you coming with us to the concert?

2. (*I am*) _____ going to take the car if (*it is*) _____ all right with you.

3. (*There is*) _____ an extra bed upstairs if (*you would*) _____ like to stay here for the night.

4. (*I will*) _____ give you the name of the human resources director, but there (*is not*) _____ much chance that (*he will*) _____ speak to you.

5. Denise (*should not*) _____ complain about the cost of vegetables if (*she is*) _____ not willing to grow her own by planting a backyard garden.

Note: Even though contractions are common in everyday speech and in written dialogue, it is usually best to avoid them in formal writing.

2 APOSTROPHE TO SHOW OWNERSHIP OR POSSESSION

To show ownership or possession, we can use such words as *belongs to, possessed by, owned by,* or (most commonly) *of.*

the jacket that *belongs to* Terrell
the marks *possessed by* James
the gas station *owned by* our cousin
the footprints *of* the animal

But the apostrophe plus *s* (if the word is singular or a plural that does not end in *-s*) is often the quickest and easiest way to show possession. Thus we can say:

Terrell's jacket
James's marks
our cousin's gas station
the animal's footprints

Points to Remember

1) The *'s* ending goes with the owner or possessor (in the examples given, *Terrell, James, cousin, animal*). What follows is the person or thing possessed (in the examples given, *the jacket, marks, gas station, footprints*).

2) When *'s* is handwritten, there should always be a break between the word and the *'s.*

Terrell 's   not   *Terrell's*

Correct   **Incorrect**

3) A singular word ending in *-s* (such as *James* in the earlier example) also shows possession by adding an apostrophe plus *s* (*James's*).

● ● ● ● ● **Activity 1**

Rewrite the italicized part of each of the sentences below, using *'s* to show possession. Remember that *'s* goes with the owner or possessor.

Example   *The toys belonging to the children filled an entire room.*
              The children's toys

1. *The Rollerblades owned by Dawn* have been stolen.

2. *The visit of my cousin* lasted longer than I wanted it to.

3. *The fenders belonging to the car* are badly rusted.

_____

4. *The prescription of a doctor* is needed for the pills.

_____

5. *The Jeep owned by Doris* was recalled because of an engine defect.

_____

6. Is this *the hat of somebody?*

_____

7. The broken saddle produced a sore on *the back of the horse.*

_____

8. *The cords coming from the computer* were so tangled that they looked like spaghetti.

_____

9. *The skates belonging to Salé and Pelletier* are on display in the museum.

_____

10. *The foundation of the house* is crumbling.

_____

● ● ● ● **Activity 2**

Add *'s* to each of the following words to make them the possessors or owners of something. Then write sentences using the words. Your sentences can be serious or playful. One is done for you.

1. dog _____*dog's*_____   _____*That dog's bite is worse than his bark.*_____

2. instructor _____   _____

   _____

3. Avril _____   _____

   _____

4. store _____   _____

   _____

5. mother _____   _____

Apostrophe and Possessive Forms of Pronouns

Do not use an apostrophe with possessive forms of pronouns. They already show ownership. Possessive forms of pronouns include *his, hers, its, yours, ours,* and *theirs.*

Incorrect	*Correct*
The bookstore lost its' lease.	The bookstore lost its lease.
The racing bikes were theirs'.	The racing bikes were theirs.
The change is yours'.	The change is yours.
His' problems are ours', too.	His problems are ours, too.
His' skin is more sunburned than hers'.	His skin is more sunburned than hers.

Apostrophe and Plurals

Do not add an apostrophe to make a word plural (except in three specific instances explained on page 417). For example, the plural of the word movie is *movies,* not *movie's* or *movies'.* Look at this sentence:

Ina admires Martin's broad shoulders, rippling muscles, and warm eyes.

The words *shoulders, muscles,* and *eyes* are simple plurals, meaning "more than one shoulder," "more than one muscle," "more than one eye." The plural is shown by adding *-s* only. On the other hand, *'s* after *Martin* shows possession—that Martin owns the shoulders, muscles, and eyes.

● ● ● ●   **Activity**

In the space provided under each sentence, add the one apostrophe needed and explain why the other word or words ending in *-s* are plurals.

Example   Karens tomato plants are almost as tall as her two-year-old.

Karens: *Karen's, meaning "belonging to Karen"*

plants: *plural meaning "more than one plant"*

1. My fathers influence on his brothers has been enormous.

   fathers: _____

   brothers: _____

2. Ben Mulroneys job—interviewing celebrities—makes him a celebrity, too.

   Mulroneys: _____

   celebrities: _____

3. As Tinas skill at studying increased, her grades improved.

   Tinas: _____

   grades: _____

4. When I walked into my doctors office, there were six people waiting who also had appointments.

   doctors: _____

   appointments: _____

5. For the presentation, they uploaded three spreadsheets as well as the groups slide presentation.

   sheets: _____

   groups: _____

6. After six weeks without rain, the nearby streams started drying up, and the lakes water level fell sharply.

   weeks: _____

   streams: _____

   lakes: _____

7. Everyone wanted to enroll in Dr. Bodors class, but all the sections were closed.

   Bodors: _____

   sections: _____

8. When the brakes failed on Eriks truck, he narrowly avoided hitting several parked cars and two trees.

   brakes: _____

   Eriks: _____

   cars: _____

   trees: _____

9. My familys favourite breakfast is bacon, eggs, and home-fried potatoes.

   familys: _____

   eggs: _____

   potatoes: _____

10. We like British Columbias winters, but we prefer to spend the summers in Nova Scotia.

   British Columbias: _____

   winters: _____

   summers: _____

Apostrophe with Possessive of Plural Words

Plurals that end in -s show possession simply by adding the apostrophe (rather than an apostrophe plus s):

My *parents'* van is ten years old.
The many *students'* complaints were ignored by the high-school principal.
All the *Boy Scouts'* tents were damaged by the hailstorm.

Plurals that do not end in -s (*women*, *men*, *mice*, *geese*, and so on) show possession by adding an apostrophe plus *s*.

The *women's* files are in the library.
We were woken up by the *geese's* honking.

● ● ● ● **Activity**

In each sentence, cross out the one plural word that needs an apostrophe. Then write the word correctly, with the apostrophe, in the space provided.

Example   _soldiers'_   All the ~~soldiers~~ boots were polished for inspection.

1. My parents car was stolen last night.

   _____

2. The transit workers strike has just ended.

   _____

3. Two of our neighbours homes are up for sale.

   _____

4. The door to the ladies room is locked.

   _____

5. When students complaints about the cafeteria were ignored, many started to bring their own lunches.

   _____

3 APOSTROPHE TO FORM THE PLURALS OF LETTERS, NUMERALS, AND SPECIAL TERMS

Plural forms of small (lower-case) letters or characters, numerals, and words used as specialized terms or phrases are formed by adding an apostrophe plus *s*.

Dotting the *i's* and crossing the *t's* in a handwritten assignment is important.
Two *6's* were scribbled on the Post-it note.
Mike had two *Incomplete's* and three *Unsat's* on his transcript.

Do not use italics for these plurals; in the examples above, the italics are used only for emphasis.

Note: Do not use apostrophes to form the plurals of dates, capital letters, abbreviations that end in capital letters, or abbreviations that end in numerals.

1990s   CDs   MP3s   VCRs   MAs   PhDs

● ● ● ● **Activity**

In each sentence, supply the correct plural form of the word shown in italics.

1. Mark typed in four bold (*X*) _____ at the end of the page.

2. During the _____ (*1970*), platform shoes were popular.

3. Remove all the _____ (*and*) from that sentence.

4. Now that I download _____ (*MP3*), I do not buy as many _____ (*CD*).

5. Fanny received two _____ (*Satisfactory*) on the last set of assignments.

Chapter 33

Quotation Marks

Introductory Project

Read the following scene and underline all the words enclosed within quotation marks. Your instructor may also have you dramatize the scene, with one person reading the narration and two persons acting the two speaking parts, Mike and Derrick. The two speakers should imagine the scene as part of a stage play and try to make their words seem as real and true-to-life as possible.

Mike and Derrick were sitting in the library working on a research assignment. After deciding on a list of twenty good keywords, they each took ten. "So, are you going to use Google or some other engine?" asked Mike. As Derrick stared at his screen and typed busily, he hesitated before answering. "Oh, I'm trying out a few," he finally replied. Fifteen minutes passed and Mike became curious about how Derrick was doing. "Oh, I'm doing," Derrick said. Finally, Mike's impatience got the best of him. "Come on. Tell me what you've got!"

"Five new music sites with great downloads," said his classmate with a smile. "This is my lucky day."

1. What is the purpose of quotation marks?

   _____

2. Do commas and periods that come at the end of a quotation go inside or outside the quotation marks?

   _____

Answers are provided on the Online Learning Centre.

The two main uses of quotation marks are:

1) To set off the exact words of a speaker or a writer

2) To set off the titles of short works

Each use is explained on the pages that follow.

1 QUOTATION MARKS TO SET OFF EXACT WORDS OF A SPEAKER OR A WRITER

Use quotation marks when you want to show the exact words of a speaker or a writer.

"Say something tender to me," whispered Rachel to André. (Quotation marks set off the exact words that Rachel spoke to André.)

Leonard Cohen once wrote, "I want history to jump on Canada's spine with sharp skates." (Quotation marks set off the exact words that Leonard Cohen wrote.)

"The only dumb question," the instructor said, "is the one you don't ask." (Two pairs of quotation marks are used to enclose the instructor's exact words.)

Koji complained, "I worked so hard on this paper. I spent two days getting information in the library and two days writing it. Guess what mark I got on it." (Note that the end quotation marks do not come until the end of Koji's speech. Place quotation marks before the first quoted word of a speech and after the last quoted word. As long as no interruption occurs in the speech, do not use quotation marks for each new sentence.)

Elaine exclaimed, "You're stepping on the cat's tail!" (Quotation marks set off Elaine's exclamation.)

Adam asked, "Why is this test necessary?" (Quotation marks set off Adam's question.)

Punctuation with Quotations

- A comma is used to set off a quotation from the rest of a sentence.

- Commas and periods go *inside* the quotation marks.

- Semicolons and colons appear *outside* the quotation marks in a sentence.

> I just heard about the provincial government's proposal to charge a "health premium"; which is just another a tax, is it not?
>
> Here is "the truth, the whole truth, and nothing but the truth": I don't know the answer.

- Exclamation marks and question marks that belong to the quotations go inside the quotation marks. But these marks go outside the quotation marks when they belong to the sentence, not the quotation.

> She begged for a clear answer, but all he said was, "Maybe"!
> Can you believe Mom said, "Do whatever you want"?

Complete the following statements explaining how capital letters, commas, and periods are used in quotations. Refer to the examples as guides.

1. Every quotation begins with a _____ letter.

2. When a quotation is split (as in the sentence about dumb questions), the second part does not begin with a capital letter unless it is a _____ sentence and follows a period.

3. _____ are used to separate the quoted part of a sentence from the rest of the sentence.

4. Commas and periods that come at the end of a quotation should go _____ the quotation marks.

The answers are *capital, new, Commas,* and *inside.*

● ● ● ● **Activity 1**

Place quotation marks around the exact words of a speaker or writer in the sentences that follow.

1. Try zinc lozenges and vitamin C for your cold, Anna told Dylan.
2. How are you doing in school? my uncle always asks me.
3. An epitaph on a tombstone in Key West reads, I told you I was sick!
4. Dave said, Let's walk faster. I think the game has already started.
5. Marshall McLuhan wrote, The medium is the message.
6. Cheryl said, My brother is so lazy that if opportunity knocked, he'd resent the noise.
7. Wayne Gretzky may be the best Canadian hockey player to your generation, the coach said. Still, I don't think we should forget Maurice Richard.
8. Ice-cold drinks! shouted the vendor selling lukewarm drinks.
9. Be careful not to touch the fence, the guard warned. It's electrified.
10. Just because I'm deaf, Lin said, many people treat me as if I were stupid.

● ● ● ● **Activity 2**

1. Write a sentence in which you quote a favourite expression of someone you know. Identify the relationship of the person to you.

    Example   One of my father's favourite expressions is, "Don't sweat the small stuff."

2. Write a quotation that contains the words *Dylan asked Anna*. Write a second quotation that includes the words *Anna replied*.

3. Copy a sentence or two that interests you from a book or magazine article. Identify the title and author of the work.

    Example   In "Hockey and Culture," Gary Genosko writes, "Hockey was, in fact, the last North American sport to have black athletes enter its ranks."

Indirect Quotations

An indirect quotation is a rewording of someone else's statement, rather than a word-for-word direct quotation. The word *that* often signals an indirect quotation. Quotation marks are *not* used with indirect quotations.

Direct Quotation	*Indirect Quotation*
Sean said, "The distributor cap on my car is cracked." (Sean's exact spoken words are given, so quotation marks are used.)	Sean said that the distributor cap on his car was cracked. (We learn Sean's words indirectly, so no quotation marks are used.)
Alexandra's note to Jay read, "I'll be working late. Don't wait up for me." (The exact words that Alexandra wrote in the note are given, so quotation marks are used.)	Alexandra left a note for Jay saying she would be working late and he should not wait up for her. (We learn Alexandra's words indirectly, so no quotation marks are used.)

● ● ● ● **Activity**

Rewrite the following sentences, changing words as necessary to convert the sentences into direct quotations. The first one is done for you as an example.

1. Matt asked Luisa if she had tickets to the Sum 41 concert.

   Matt asked Luisa, "Do you have tickets to the Sum 41 concert?"

2. Luisa said she did not think there were any left.

3. Matt replied that a whole new block of tickets was on sale on Ticketmaster.

4. Luisa said that as long as she could use her mother's credit card, she would order two tickets.

5. Matt said that he hoped she would be able to go to the concert.

2 QUOTATION MARKS TO SET OFF TITLES OF SHORT WORKS

When referred to in sentences, titles of short works are usually set off by quotation marks, while titles of long works are underlined. Use quotation marks to set off the titles of such short works as articles in books, newspapers, or magazines; chapters in a book; short stories; poems; and songs.

On the other hand, you should underline or italicize the titles of books, newspapers, magazines, plays, movies, music albums, and television shows.

Quotation Marks	Underlines or Italics
the article "Yes, There Are Canadian Comics"	in the book *Canuck Comics*
the article "A Day at the Beach"	in the newspaper The Vancouver Sun
the article "Biters' Banquet"	in the magazine *Canadian Geographic*
the chapter "Mila, the Movie"	in the book More Than a Rose
the story "Blossom"	in the book *Sans Souci*
the poem "Suzanne"	in the book The Spice-Box of Earth
the song "Closing Time"	on the CD *The Future*
the episode "Life Is Messy"	from the TV series Train 48

Note: In printed works, titles of books, newspapers, and so on are set off by italics—slanted type that looks *like this*—instead of being underlined.

● ● ● ● **Activity**

Use quotation marks or underlines as needed.

1. Spending Smart is the title of the fourth chapter of Dian Cohen's book Money.
2. No advertising is permitted in Consumer Reports, a non-profit consumer magazine.
3. I cut out an article from Maclean's called Canadian Universities: Rankings for 2008 to use in my sociology report.
4. Vince's favourite television show is Angel, and his favourite movie is The Ring.
5. Our instructor gave us a week to buy the textbook titled Personal Finance and to read the first chapter, Work and Income.
6. Every holiday season, our family watches the movie A Christmas Carol on television.
7. Allen bought Chatelaine because he wanted to read the cover article, titled Secrets Men Never Tell You.
8. Edgar Allan Poe's short story The Murders in the Rue Morgue and his poem The Raven are in a paperback titled Great Tales and Poems of Edgar Allan Poe.
9. When Victoria got her Starweek TV Magazine, she read an article titled The New Comedians and then thumbed through the listings to see when Pop-Up Video would be on that week.
10. The night before his exam, he discovered with horror that the chapter Becoming Mature was missing from Childhood and Adolescence, the psychology text that he had bought second-hand.

OTHER USES OF QUOTATION MARKS

1) Quotation marks are used to set off special words or phrases from the rest of a sentence.

> Many people spell the words "a lot" as *one* word, "alot," instead of correctly spelling them as two words.
>
> I have trouble telling the difference between "their" and "there."

Note: In printed works, *italics* are often used to set off special words or phrases. That is usually done in this book, for example.

2) Single quotation marks are used to mark off a quotation within a quotation.

> The instructor said, "Know the chapter titled 'Status Symbols' in *Adolescent Development* if you expect to pass the test."
>
> Kyra said, "One of my favourite Mae West lines is, 'I used to be Snow White, but I drifted.'"

Visit the *English Skills with Readings: Examining Paragarphs* Online Learning Centre at www.mcgrawhill.ca/olc/langan to access self-quizzes, internet-based questions and research skills, web resources, and other learning and study tools.

Chapter 34

Comma

SIX MAIN USES OF THE COMMA

Commas are used mainly:

1) To separate items in a series
2) To set off introductory material

3) Before and after words that interrupt the flow of thought in a sentence
4) Between two complete thoughts connected by *and, but, for, or, nor, so, yet*
5) To set off a direct quotation from the rest of a sentence
6) For certain everyday material

Each use is explained on the pages that follow.

You may find it helpful to remember that the comma often marks a slight pause or break in a sentence. Read aloud the sentence examples given for each rule, and listen for the minor pauses or breaks that are signalled by commas.

1 Comma between Items in a Series

Use commas to separate items in a series.

Do you drink tea with milk, lemon, or honey?
Today the dishwasher stopped working, the garbage bag split, and the oven door fell off.
The television talk shows enraged him so much he did not know whether to laugh, cry, or scream.
Reiko awoke from a restless, nightmare-filled sleep.

Notes:

a The final comma in a series of three or more items is optional, but it is generally used.

b A comma is used between two adjectives (descriptive words) in a series only if *and* inserted between the words sounds natural. You could say:
Reiko awoke from a restless *and* nightmare-filled sleep.

But notice in the following sentence that the descriptive words do not sound natural when *and* is inserted between them. In such cases, no comma is used.

Barbara drove a shiny blue Saturn. (A shiny *and* blue Saturn doesn't sound right, so no comma is used.)

● ● ● ● **Activity**

Place commas between items in a series.

1. Godzilla lives for revenge violence and destruction.
2. My father taught me to swim by talking to me in a calm manner holding my hand firmly and throwing me into the pool.
3. Enzo added white wine mushrooms salt pepper and oregano to his spaghetti sauce.
4. Baggy threadbare jeans feel more comfortable than pyjamas to me.
5. Carmen grabbed a tiny towel bolted out of the bathroom and ran toward the ringing phone.

2 Comma after Introductory Material

Use a comma to set off introductory material. *Introductory material* may be clauses, phrases, or words.

> After punching the alarm clock with his fist, Bill turned over and went back to sleep.
> Looking up at the sky, I saw a man who was flying faster than a speeding bullet.
> Holding a baited trap, Jesse cautiously approached the gigantic mouse hole.
> In addition, he held a broom in his hand.
> Also, he wore a football helmet in case a creature should leap out at his head.

Notes:

a If the introductory material is brief, the comma is sometimes omitted. In the activities here, you should use the comma.

b A comma is also used to set off extra material at the end of a sentence. Here are two sentences where this comma rule applies.

> A sudden breeze shot through the windows, driving the stuffiness out of the room.
> I love to cook and eat Italian food, especially penne and lasagna.

• • • • **Activity**

Place commas after introductory material.

1. When the movie started the theatre quieted down.
2. Feeling brave and silly at the same time Bernie volunteered to go on stage and help the magician.
3. While I was eating my tuna sandwich the cats circled my chair like hungry sharks.
4. Because my parents died when I was young I have learned to look after myself. Even though I am now independent I still carry a special loneliness within me.
5. At first putting extra hot pepper flakes on the pizza seemed like a good idea. However I felt otherwise when flames seemed about to shoot out of my mouth.

3 Comma around Words Interrupting the Flow of Thought

Use commas before and after words or phrases that interrupt the flow of thought in a sentence.

> My brother, a sports nut, owns over five thousand hockey cards.
> That game show, at long last, has been cancelled.
> The children used the old Buick, rusted from disuse, as a backyard clubhouse.

Phrases and clauses that interrupt a sentence's flow or rhythm are called *non-essential* (or non-restrictive). Such phrases or clauses are not essential to the sentence, which means that they are not needed for its meaning to be clear.

Usually you can "hear" words that interrupt the flow of thought in a sentence. However, if you are not sure that certain words are interrupters, remove them from the sentence. If it still makes sense without the words, you know that the words are interrupters and the information they give is non-essential. Such non-essential information is set off with commas. In the sentence

Doris Thompson, who lives next door, won the javelin-throwing competition.

the words *who lives next door* are extra information, not needed to understand the subject of the sentence, *Doris Thompson.* Put commas around such non-essential information.

On the other hand, some phrases and clauses are *essential* in order for the reader to grasp the meaning of a sentence. In the sentence

The woman who lives next door won the javelin-throwing competition.

the words *who lives next door* supply essential information—information needed for us to identify the woman being spoken of. If the words were removed from the sentence, we would no longer know who won the competition. Commas are *not* used around such essential information.

Here is another example, this time of a non-essential clause.

Wilson Hall, which the hurricane destroyed, was ninety years old.

Here the words *which the hurricane destroyed* are extra information, not needed to identify the subject of the sentence, *Wilson Hall.* Commas go around such nonessential information. On the other hand, in the sentence

The building that the hurricane destroyed was ninety years old.

the words *that the hurricane destroyed* are needed to identify the building. Commas are *not* used around such essential information. The word *that* is generally used to introduce an essential clause, as in the example above. In the preceding example about Wilson Hall, the word *which* is used; *which* is generally used to introduce non-essential clauses. Clauses beginning with *who,* however, may be either essential or non-essential.

As noted above, however, most of the time you will be able to "hear" words that interrupt the flow of thought in a sentence and will not have to think about whether the words are essential or non-essential.

● ● ● ● ● Activity

Use commas to set off interrupting words.

1. On Friday my day off I went to get a haircut.
2. Dracula who had a way with women is Lyle's favourite movie hero. He feels that the Wolfman on the other hand showed no class in handling women.
3. Many people forget that Mackenzie King one of our most effective prime ministers also talked to his dead mother.

4. Mowing the grass especially when it is three centimetres high is my least favourite job.
5. A jar of chicken noodle soup which was all there was in the refrigerator did not make a very satisfying meal.

4 Comma between Complete Thoughts

Use a comma between two complete thoughts or independent clauses connected by coordinating conjunctions: *and, but, for, or, nor, so, yet.*

The wedding was scheduled for four o'clock, but the bride changed her mind at two.
We could always tell when our instructor felt disorganized, for his shirt would not be tucked in.
Amelia has to work some nights, so she tapes the hockey games on her DVR.

Notes:

a The comma is optional when the complete thoughts are short.

Grace's skin tans and Mark's skin freckles.
Her pop was flat but she drank it anyway.
The day was overcast so they didn't go swimming.

b Be careful not to use a comma in sentences having *one* subject and a *double* verb. The comma is used only in sentences made up of two complete thoughts (two subjects and two verbs). In the following sentence, there is only one subject (*Kevin*) with a double verb (*will go* and *forget*). Therefore, no comma is needed.

Kevin will go partying tonight and forget all about tomorrow's exam.

Likewise, the following sentence has only one subject (*Rita*) and a double verb (*was* and *will work*); therefore, no comma is needed.

Rita was a server at the Banff Hotel last summer and probably will work there this summer.

● ● ● ● ● **Activity**

Place a comma before a joining word that connects two complete thoughts (two subjects and two verbs). Remember, do *not* place a comma within sentences that have only one subject and a double verb.

1. The oranges in the refrigerator were covered with blue mould and the potatoes in the cupboard felt like sponges.
2. All the jeans in the shop were on sale but not a single pair was my size.
3. Phil often window shops in the malls for hours and comes home without buying anything.
4. Zeeshan left the dentist's office with his mouth still numb from Novocaine and he talked with a lisp for two hours.

5. I covered the walls with three coats of white paint but the purple underneath still showed through.
6. The car squealed up the on-ramp and sped recklessly out onto the Gardiner Expressway.
7. Winters in Vancouver are much milder than winters in Winnipeg and snow rarely sits long on the ground.
8. The singer in the group kept jumping into the audience but they kept throwing him back up on stage.
9. I felt that I did not belong in the statistics course but did not dare to admit it.
10. Emil claims he wants to succeed in college but he has missed classes all semester.

5 Comma with Direct Quotations

Use a comma to set off a direct quotation from the rest of a sentence.

His father shouted, "Why don't you go out and get a job?"
"Our modern world has lost a sense of the sacredness of life," the speaker said.
"No," said Celia to Jerry. "I won't go to the bingo hall with you."
"Money," wrote Marshall McLuhan, "is the poor people's credit card."

Note: Commas and periods at the end of a quotation go inside quotation marks. See also page 421.

● ● ● ● **Activity**

Use commas to set off quotations from the rest of the sentence.

1. Hassan appeared at the door and called out "Welcome to my home!"
2. My partner on the dance floor said "Don't be so stiff. You look as if you'd swallowed an umbrella."
3. The question on the anatomy test read "What human organ grows faster than any other, never stops growing, and always remains the same size?"
4. The student behind me whispered "The skin."
5. "My stomach hurts" Bruce said "and I don't know whether it was the hamburger or the math test."

6 Comma with Everyday Material

Use a comma with certain everyday material.

Persons Spoken To, or Direct Address

Tina, go to bed if you're not feeling well.
Aaron, where did you put my shoes?
Are you coming with us, Omar?

When a sentence is directly addressed to someone, separate the name or identifying noun from the rest of the sentence with a comma.

Dates

July 1, 1867, is the date of Confederation.

Addresses

Tony's grandparents live at 183 Roxborough Avenue, Toronto, Ontario M4S 1V3.

Note: No comma is used to mark off the postal code (Canada) or Zip code (U.S.).

Openings and Closings of Letters

Dear Santa,
Dear Larry,
Sincerely yours,
With regards,

Note: In formal letters, a colon is used after the opening: Dear Sir: *or* Dear Madam:

Numbers

Place a comma before each group of three digits.

The dishonest dealer turned the used car's odometer from 98,170 kilometres to 39,170 kilometres.

• • • • Activity

Place commas where needed.

1. I expected you to set a better example for the others Michel.
2. Janet with your help I passed the test.
3. Andre DaCosta and Jason Peters started college on September 2 2003 and shared an apartment at 346 Pembina Highway Winnipeg Manitoba for two semesters.
4. The winner of the first *Canadian Idol* competition Ryan Malcolm received over 50000 fan letters during the first few weeks after he took the title.
5. The new computers for the software design program were purchased on March 12 2003 and cost the college $15000.

Chapter 35

Other Punctuation Marks

Introductory Project

Each of the sentences below needs one of these punctuation marks:

; — - ( ) :

See if you can insert the correct mark in each sentence. Each mark should be used once.

1. The following holiday plants are poisonous and should be kept away from children and pets holly, mistletoe, and poinsettias.

2. The freeze dried soups and casseroles sealed in plastic bags that we took to Algonquin Park tasted worse than they looked.

3. William Shakespeare 1564–1616 married a woman eight years his senior when he was eighteen.

4. Grooming in space is more difficult than on Earth no matter how much Marc Garneau combed his hair, for instance, it still tended to float loosely around his head.

5. I opened the front door, and our cat walked in proudly with a live mouse hanging from his mouth.

Answers are provided on the Online Learning Centre.

COLON (:)

A colon in a sentence signals two things: a distinct pause and a pause that precedes the introduction of something. Colons also have numeric and mathematical significance; they are used when writing numerals indicating time and ratios.

Colons Used with Numerals

Use a colon between the numbers used to show the hour and the numbers used to show minutes (and seconds, if necessary) when writing times of day.

9:30 a.m.   11:05 p.m.   8:27:35

Use a colon between numerals indicating a ratio of one thing to another.

The ratio of students to tutors in the lab is 1:7.

Colons Used in Sentence Punctuation

A colon functions like an equal sign in arithmetic; it appears between an introductory independent clause (a complete statement) and a list, explanation, or long quotation. The colon signals that the material following it is equivalent to or explains the content of the independent clause preceding it.

Be sure that an independent clause appears before a colon within a sentence. These examples show correct and incorrect uses of the colon.

Colon Introducing a List

Incorrect	*Correct*
Marino's favourite things are: sleeping late, noisy parties, and extensions on deadlines.	Marino's favourite things are easy to name: sleeping late, noisy parties, and extensions on deadlines.
("Marino's favourite things are" is not a complete statement.)	

A colon should not appear between a linking verb and the words that describe the subject.

Incorrect	*Correct*
Kathy's shopping list for the party includes: dip, bottled water, and paper towels.	Kathy's shopping list for the party includes dip, bottled water, and paper towels.
("Kathy's shopping list for the party includes" is not a complete statement.)	

A colon should not appear between a verb and its object.

Colon Introducing an Explanation

Incorrect	*Correct*
Brent based his research report on: the effect of federal and provincial sales taxes on fast-food sales.	Brent based his research report on one idea: the effect of federal and provincial sales taxes on fast-food sales.
("Brent based his research report on" is not a complete statement.)	

A colon should not appear between a verb and its object.

Colon Introducing a Long Quotation

Incorrect	*Correct*
In his essay "The Role of New Media in Social Change," Marshall McLuhan wrote: "The average	In his essay "The Role of New Media in Social Change," Marshall McLuhan discusses the effects of television

distance from the page of children in the first three grades is . . . 6 1/2 inches. The children seem to be striving to do a version of their relation to the TV image."

watching on children's reading habits: "The average distance from the page of children in the first three grades . . . is 6 1/2 inches. The children seem to be striving to do a version of their relation to the TV image."

The introductory statement before the colon must be complete and independent.

● ● ● ● **Activity**

Place colons where needed.

1. Foods that are high in cholesterol include the following eggs, butter, milk, cheese, shrimp, and well-marbled meats.
2. All the signs of the flu were present hot and cold spells, heavy drainage from the sinuses, a bad cough, and an ache through the entire body.
3. A new study published online, *Canadian College Student Finance,* makes college students' money problems sound tolerable "Over three-quarters of college students report spending less than $5,000 on education-related expenses (tuition, fees, books and supplies) for one year."

SEMICOLON (;)

A semicolon signals more of a break in a sentence than a comma but less of an interruption than a colon. Its main function is to join independent clauses or to mark a break between them, as explained on page 363. Another use of the semicolon is to mark off items in a series when the items themselves contain commas. Here are some examples.

Winning prizes at the national flower show were Roberta Collins, British Columbia, azaleas; Sally Hunt, Alberta, roses; and James Weber, Ontario, shasta daisies.

The following books must be read for the course: *The Handmaid's Tale*, by Margaret Atwood; *The English Patient,* by Michael Ondaatje; and *Man's Search for Meaning,* by Viktor Frankl.

● ● ● ● **Activity**

Place semicolons where needed.

1. The specials at the restaurant today are eggplant Parmesan, for $5.95 black beans and rice, for $4.95 and chicken burritos, for $6.95.
2. The top of the hill in France offered an awesome view of the Canadian soldiers' cemetery thousands of headstones were arranged in perfect rows.
3. Curtis's favourite older movies are *Psycho,* starring Anthony Perkins and Janet Leigh *Alien,* the first movie in the *Alien* series and *Fast Times at Ridgemont High,* with Sean Penn.

DASH (—)

A dash signals a pause longer than a comma but not as complete as a period. Use a dash to set off words for dramatic effect.

> I didn't go out with him a second time—once was more than enough.
> Some of you—I won't mention you by name—cheated on the test.
> It was so windy that the Mini passed him on the highway—overhead.

Notes:

a The dash is formed on a keyboard by striking the hyphen twice (--). In handwriting, the dash is as long as two letters would be.

b Be careful not to overuse dashes.

● ● ● ● **Activity**

Place dashes where needed.

1. Riding my bike, I get plenty of exercise especially when dogs chase me.
2. I'm advising you in fact, I'm telling you not to bother me again.
3. The package finally arrived badly damaged.

HYPHEN (-)

A hyphen is created with a single strike of the hyphen key. Hyphens are used when joining two words to create a descriptive phrase, when forming compound words, when joining letters and words, and when dividing words at the end of a line of text.

1) Use a hyphen with two or more words that act as a single unit describing a noun.

> The fast-talking journalist was so ambitious that she went into local politics.
> (*Fast* and *talking* combine to describe the journalist.)
> Vince was a little naive and starry-eyed when he began his internship at CTV.
> When Neo removed his narrow black-tinted sunglasses, he looked a lot less mysterious and sort of good-natured.

2) Use a hyphen to form some familiar compound words.

> Marisa's great-great-grandmother celebrated her ninetieth birthday with a helicopter ride.
> Sam's father-in-law was adamant about his son-in-law carrying on the family restaurant business.
> The best buy at the flea market was a ten-year-old portable stereo that was still in its box.

3) Use a hyphen to form words that are combinations of letters and words.

> The T-shirts at the Smashmouth concert were overpriced.

Rose was so anxious that she made a U-turn on a one-way street in downtown Hamilton.

The V-shaped tear in the convertible top would be expensive to repair.

4) Use a hyphen to divide a word at the end of a line of writing or keyed text. When you need to divide a word at the end of a line, divide it between syllables. Use a dictionary to be sure of correct syllable divisions.

When Tom lifted up the hood of his Toyota, he realized that one of the radiator hoses had broken.

Notes:
a Do not divide words of one syllable.
b Do not divide a word if you can avoid doing so.

● ● ● ● ● **Activity**

Place hyphens where needed.

1. High flying jets and gear grinding trucks are constant sources of noise pollution in our neighbourhood, and consequently we are going to move.
2. When Linda turned on the porch light, ten legged creatures scurried everywhere over the crumb filled floor.
3. Scott had ninety two dollars in his pocket when he left for the supermarket, and he had twenty two dollars when he got back.

PARENTHESES ( )

Parentheses are used to set off extra or incidental information from the rest of a sentence.

The section of that book on the dangers of eating disorders (pages 35 to 72) is outdated.

Yesterday at Pizza Nova (my favourite pizza place), the guy behind the counter asked me to go out with him.

Note: Do not use parentheses too often in your writing.

● ● ● ● ● **Activity**

Add parentheses where needed.

1. Certain sections of the novel especially Chapter 5 made my heart race with suspense.
2. Did you hear that George Linda's first husband just remarried?
3. Sigmund Freud 1856–1939 was the founder of psychoanalysis.

Visit the *English Skills with Readings: Examining Paragraphs* Online Learning Centre at www.mcgrawhill.ca/olc/langan to access self-quizzes, internet-based questions and research skills, web resources, and other learning and study tools.

Chapter 36

Commonly Confused Words

Homonyms

The commonly confused words on the following pages have the same sounds but different meanings and spellings; such words are known as *homonyms*. Complete the activity for each set of homonyms, and check off and study the words that give you trouble.

a lot   a fair quantity
allot   give a share or portion to

    I wish the person who schedules our timetables would *allot* more than one period in the middle of the day for lunch; I need *a lot* more time than just one hour.

Fill in the blanks: Fahrid needs _____ more webspace for his site than the college will _____ each student.

Note: "alot" is not a word.

all ready   completely prepared
already   previously; before

    We were *all ready* to start the play, but the audience was still being seated. I have *already* called the police.

Fill in the blanks: I am _____ for the economics examination because I have _____ studied the chapter three times.

| **brake** | stop; *the* stopping device in a vehicle |
| **break** | come *apart* |

His car bumper has a sticker reading, "I *brake* for animals."
"I am going to *break* up with Bill if he keeps seeing other women," said Rita.

Fill in the blanks: When my car's emergency _____ slipped, the car rolled back and demolished my neighbour's rose garden, causing a _____ in our good relations with each other.

| **coarse** | rough |
| **course** | part of a meal; a school subject; direction; certainly (in *of course*) |

By the time the server offered the customers the second *course* of the meal, she was aware of their *coarse* eating habits.

Fill in the blanks: Theo felt that the fitness instructor's humour was too _____ for his taste and was glad when he finished the _____.

| **complement** | add to, fill out, go well with |
| **compliment** | praise |

Van's navy sweater *complemented* his khaki pants and pea jacket; he received several *compliments* on his outfit.

Fill in the blanks: The coconut rice _____ the curried chicken that you plan to serve for dinner; you will probably get some _____ on your cooking.

| **hear** | perceive with the ear |
| **here** | in this place |

"The salespeople act as though they don't see or *hear* me, even though I've been standing *here* for fifteen minutes," the woman complained.

Fill in the blanks: "Did you _____ about the distinguished visitor who just came into town and is staying _____ at this very hotel?"

| **hole** | an empty spot |
| **whole** | entire |

"I can't believe I ate the *whole* pizza," moaned Raphael. "I think it's going to make a *hole* in my stomach lining."

Fill in the blanks: The _____ time I was at the party I tried to conceal the _____ I had in my sweater.

| **its** | belonging to it |
| **it's** | shortened form of *it is* or *it has* |

The car blew *its* transmission (the transmission belonging to it, the car).
It's (it has) been raining all week and *it's* (it is) raining now.

Fill in the blanks: _____ hot and unsanitary in the restaurant kitchen I work in, and I don't think the restaurant deserves _____ good reputation.

knew   past form of *know*
new   not old

"I had *new* wallpaper put up," said Sarah.
"I *knew* there was some reason the place looked better," said Bill.

Fill in the blanks: Lisa _____ that getting her hair cut would give her face a _____ look.

know   understand
no   a negative

"I don't *know* why my dog Fang likes to attack certain people," said Kerry.
"There's *no* one thing the people have in common."

Fill in the blanks: I _____ of _____ way of telling whether the politician is honest.

pair   set of two
pear   fruit

"What a great *pair* of shorts Tim bought," said Keesha to Nora. Tim didn't
    hear her, for he was feeling very sick after munching on an unripe *pear*.

Fill in the blanks: In his lunch box was a _____ of _____ s.

passed   went by; succeeded in; handed to
past   time before the present; beyond, as in "We worked past closing
             time"

Someone *passed* him a wine bottle; it was the way he chose to forget his
    unhappy *past*.

Fill in the blanks: I walked _____ the instructor's office but was afraid to
ask her whether I had _____ the test.

peace   calm
piece   part

Nations often risk world *peace* by fighting over a *piece* of land.

Fill in the blanks: Helen did not have any _____ until she gave her dog a
_____ of her meat loaf.

plain   simple; flat area
plane   aircraft

The small, *plain* snacks and meals that airlines serve on *planes* these days
    are not worth eating.

Fill in the blanks: The game-show contestant opened the small box wrapped in
_____ brown paper and found inside the keys to his own jet _____.

| *pore* | opening in skin or other surface; look at intently |
| *pour* | flow; cause something to flow |

> *Pour* boiling water into a bowl; put a towel over your head, then lean over the bowl. The steam will open your *pores*.

Fill in the blanks: The soup _____ all over the counter because of the tiny _____ in the strainer that Willie ignored as he _____ over the recipe book.

| *principal* | main; a person in charge of a school |
| *principle* | law, standard, or rule |

> Pete's high school *principal* had one *principal* problem: Pete. This was because there were only two *principles* in Pete's life: rest and relaxation.

Fill in the blanks: The _____ reason she dropped out of school was that she believed in the _____ of complete freedom of choice.

Note: It might help to remember that the *e* in *principle* is also in *rule*—the meaning of *principle*.

right	correct; opposite of left
write	convey thoughts in words in print
wright	a builder or craftsperson, a maker of something

> "You are *right* to watch while I *write* this," said the play*wright*.

Fill in the blanks: Dimitri thinks I am strange because I make a check mark in the air every time I am _____ when I _____ an answer that I am not sure about.

| *stationary* | still or not moveable |
| *stationery* | paper and envelopes |

> Denise spent ten minutes in a *stationary* position in the lineup while she waited to buy printer paper and other *stationery*.

Fill in the blanks: Put the _____ that you have chosen for your wedding invitations into the box carefully so that it remains _____ while it is being shipped.

| *than* | used in comparisons |
| *then* | at that time |

> When we were kids, my friend Shannon had prettier clothes *than* I did. I really envied her *then*.

Fill in the blanks: Carol thought she was better _____ the rest of us, but _____ she got the lowest grade on the accounting test.

Note: It might help to remember that then (with an *e*) is also a tim*e* signal.

their	belonging to them
there	at that place; neutral word used with verbs like *is, are, was, were, have,* and *had*
they're	shortened form of they are

> Two people own that van over *there* (at that place). *They're* (they are) going to move out of *their* apartment (the apartment belonging to them) and into the van, in order to save money.

Fill in the blanks: _____ not going to invite us to _____ table because _____ is no room for us to sit down.

| *threw* | past form of *throw* |
| *through* | from one side to the other; finished |

> The fans *threw* so much litter onto the field that the teams could not go *through* with the game.

Fill in the blanks: When Shereen was _____ with her juice bottle, she _____ it in the recycling bin.

to	verb part, as in *to smile;* toward, as in "I'm going *to* Montreal"
too	overly, as in "The pizza was *too* hot"; also or as well, as in "The coffee was hot, *too*"
two	number 2

> Kyle drove *to* the park *to* be alone with Cheryl. (The first *to* means "toward"; the second *to* is a verb part that goes with *be.*)
> Kyle's shirt is *too* tight; his pants are tight, *too.* (The first *too* means "overly"; the second *too* means "also.")
> You need *two* hands (2 hands) to handle a floor sander.

Fill in the blanks: _____ times tonight, you have been _____ ready _____ make assumptions without asking questions first.

| *wear* | to have on |
| *where* | on what place |

> Tino wanted to *wear* his light jacket on the hot day, but he didn't know *where* he had put it.

Fill in the blanks: Exactly _____ on my leg should I _____ this elastic bandage?

| *weather* | atmospheric conditions |
| *whether* | if it happens that; in case; if |

> Some people go on vacations *whether* or not the *weather* is good.

Fill in the blanks: I always ask Bill _____ we're going to have a storm, for his bad knee can feel rainy _____ approaching.

| *whose* | belonging to whom |
| *who's* | shortened form of *who is* and *who has* |

Who's the instructor *whose* students are complaining?

Fill in the blanks: _____ ready to leave, and _____ car is closest to the exit?

your	belonging to you
you're	shortened form of *you are*

You're (meaning "you are") not going to the fair unless *your* brother (the brother belonging to you) goes with you.

Fill in the blanks: _____ going to have to put aside individual differences and play together for the sake of _____ team.

Other Words Frequently Confused

Following is a list of other words that people frequently confuse. Complete the activities for each set of words, and check off and study the words that give you trouble.

a, an	Both *a* and *an* are used before other words to mean, approximately, "one."

Generally you should use *an* before words starting with the sound of a vowel (*a, e, i, o, u*).

an ache   an experiment   an elephant   an idiot   an ox

Generally you should use *a* before words starting with the sound of a consonant (all other letters).

a card   a brain   a cheat   a television   a gambler

Fill in the blanks: The girls had _____ argument over _____ former boyfriend.

accept (ăk sĕpt′)	receive; agree to
except (ĕk sĕpt′)	exclude; but

"I would *accept* your loan," said Nga to the his uncle, "*except* that I'm not ready to pay 25 percent interest."

Fill in the blanks: _____ for the fact that she can't _____ any criticism, Lori is a good friend.

advice (ăd vīs′)	noun meaning "an opinion"
advise (ăd vīz′)	verb meaning "to counsel, to give advice"

I *advise* you to take the *advice* of your friends and stop working so hard.

Fill in the blanks: I _____ you to listen carefully to any _____ you get from your boss.

affect (uh fĕkt′)	verb meaning "to influence"
effect (i fĕkt′)	verb meaning "to bring about something"; noun meaning "result"

The full *effects* of marijuana and alcohol on the body are only partly known; however, both drugs clearly *affect* the brain in various ways.

Fill in the blanks: The new tax laws go into _____ next month, and they are going to _____ your income tax deductions.

| **among** | implies three or more |
| **between** | implies only two |

We had to choose from *among* 125 shades of paint but *between* only two fabrics.

Fill in the blanks: The layoff notices distributed _____ the unhappy workers gave them a choice _____ working for another month at full pay and leaving immediately with two weeks' pay.

| **anyone** | some item or person out of a number; not a particular one |
| **any one** | any person, or other single choice of a selection |

Any one of the computer stations is ready for *anyone* who wants to work.

Fill in the blanks: Is _____ available for tutorial help? I have more assignments due than _____ student can handle.

| **beside** | along the side of |
| **besides** | in addition to |

I was lucky I wasn't standing *beside* the car when it was hit.
Besides being unattractive, these uniforms are impractical.

Fill in the blanks: _____ the colour printer Jeff bought recently, he also has a scanner _____ his computer.

| **conscience** | sense of right and wrong |
| **conscious** | aware or awake |

Once Brian was *conscious* of where he was, his *conscience* told him he should not be there.

Fill in the blanks: Your _____ may be ready to guide you, but you must be of what it is saying to you.

| **desert** (děz′ ert) | stretch of dry land; (di zûrt′) to abandon one's post or duty |
| **dessert** (dǐ zûrt′) | last part of a meal |

Sweltering in the *desert,* I was tormented by the thought of an icy *dessert.*

Fill in the blanks: At the buffet, André said, "Now is not the time to _____ me, just when I'm lining up for!"

| **disinterested** | impartial or unbiased |
| **uninterested** | not interested |

Sam was *uninterested* in participating in the student survey, but he did think that a *disinterested* committee should examine the results.

Fill in the blanks: Try appointing a _____ third party to judge the contest, even if everyone seems _____.

fewer	used with things that can be counted
less	refers to amount, value, or degree

There were *fewer* than seven people in all my classes today.
I seem to feel *less* tired when I exercise regularly.

Fill in the blanks: With _____ people driving large cars, Canadians are using _____ gas than they used to.

loose (lōōs)	not fastened; not tight-fitting
lose (lōōz)	misplace; fail to win

Phil's belt is so *loose* that he always looks ready to *lose* his pants.

Fill in the blanks: At least once a week our neighbours _____ their dog because they let him run _____.

precede	come before, go before
proceed	go ahead, move on

Rajiv *preceded* Kim out of the room, after the fire-drill announcement told people to *proceed* to the closest exit doors.

Fill in the blanks: "The *i* _____ the *j* in my name," said Alicija, and she _____ to write her name on the board to demonstrate.

quiet (kwī′ĭt)	peaceful
quite (kwīt)	entirely; really; rather

After a busy day, the children are now *quiet,* and their parents are *quite* tired.

Fill in the blanks: The _____ halls of the church become _____ lively during swing dance evenings.

though (thō)	despite the fact that
thought (thôt)	past form of *think*

Even *though* she worked, she *thought* she would have time to go to school.

Fill in the blanks: Yoshiko _____ she would like her job, but even _____ the pay was good, she hated the travelling involved.

Visit the *English Skills with Readings: Examining Paragraphs* Online Learning Centre at www.mcgrawhill.ca/olc/langan to access self-quizzes, internet-based questions and research skills, web resources, and other learning and study tools.

Chapter 37

Effective Word Choice

Introductory Project

Put a check beside the sentence in each pair that you feel makes more effective use of words.

1. I'm totally bummed that I missed the concert. _____

   I'm really disappointed that I missed the concert. _____

2. Doctors as dedicated as Dr. Khan are few and far between. _____

   Doctors as dedicated as Dr. Khan are rare. _____

3. Yesterday I ascertained that Elena and Wes broke up. _____

   Yesterday I found out that Elena and Wes broke up. _____

Now see if you can circle the correct number in each case:

   Pair (1, 2, 3) contains a sentence with slang.
   Pair (1, 2, 3) contains a sentence with a cliché.
   Pair (1, 2, 3) contains a sentence with a pretentious word.

Answers are provided on the Online Learning Centre.

Choose your words carefully when you write. Once you are revising your work, take the time to think about your word choices, rather than simply using the first words that come to mind. Give your ideas the settings they deserve—the words and phrases that truly express what you mean.

Always keep two criteria in mind when you revise the wording of any piece of writing:

- Your purpose: what are you trying to say, and why? Which words best carry the meaning you intend so that your writing fulfills your goals for it?
- Your audience: to whom are you writing, and what word choices will best carry your meaning most accurately to him or her?

Your main writing goal is always clarity; your writing should explain your ideas as exactly as possible. One concrete first step to making your words work effectively for you and your readers is to avoid slang, clichés, and pretentious words.

Slang

We often use slang expressions when we talk because they are so vivid and colourful. However, slang is usually out of place in formal writing. Here are some examples of slang expressions.

My friend in the statistics class *gave me the 411* on the assignments.
The atmosphere in the club was *way cool;* everybody was *just chillin'*.
His skateboard was *totally rad*.

Slang works against clear expression of meaning for three reasons:

- Slang depends on its trendiness, on being current. As a result, it goes out of date quickly and can cause confusion for readers.
- Slang expressions arise from some group's desire to have a "private code" or language not understood by the general public. Therefore, using slang runs counter to communicating clearly to most audiences.
- Slang is habit-forming in speech; current expressions become overused very quickly, and then they are annoying. In print, the risk of annoyance to reading audiences from frequent use of slang is significantly higher.

But, most important, using slang is generally an evasion, a way of avoiding specific, careful details that are often needed to make one's meaning clear in writing. For example, in "The tires on the SUV make the car look like something else," the writer has not provided the specific details about the tires necessary for us to understand the statement clearly. In general, then, you should avoid slang in your writing. If you are in doubt about whether an expression is slang, it may help to check a recently published dictionary.

Activity

Rewrite the following sentences, replacing the italicized slang words with more standard ones.

Example   The movie was the *bomb,* so we *hit replay.*

The movie was excellent, *so we* watched it again.

1. My roommate told me he was going to Vancouver for study week, but later he admitted he was just *messing with my head.*

_____

_____

2. Once Mikela and her friends *scoped the place out,* they decided to stay.

_____

_____

3. If the instructor stops *hassling* me, I am going to *get my act together* in the course.

_____

_____

Clichés

A cliché is an expression that has been worn out through constant use. Some typical clichés are listed in the box.

Clichés	
all work and no play	saw the light
at a loss for words	short but sweet
better late than never	sigh of relief
drop in the bucket	singing the blues
easier said than done	taking a big chance
had a hard time of it	time and time again
in the nick of time	too close for comfort
in this day and age	too little, too late
it dawned on me	took a turn for the worse
it goes without saying	under the weather
last but not least	where he (she) is
make ends meet	coming from
on top of the world	word to the wise
sad but true	work like a dog

Clichés are common in speech but make your writing seem tired and stale. Also, clichés—like slang—are often a way of evading the specific details that you must work to provide in your writing. You should avoid clichés and try to express your meaning in fresh, original ways.

● ● ● ● **Activity**

Underline the cliché in each of the following sentences. Then substitute specific, fresh words for the trite expression.

Example   I passed the test <u>by the skin of my teeth</u>.

I barely passed the test.

1. Anyone turning in a paper late is throwing caution to the winds.

   _____

2. Yolanda doesn't make any bones about her ambition.

   _____

3. I met with my instructor to try to iron out the problems in my paper.

   _____

Pretentious Words

Some people feel they can improve their writing by using fancy and elevated words rather than simple and natural words. They use artificial and stilted language that more often obscures their meaning than communicates it clearly.

Here are some unnatural-sounding sentences.

I comprehended her statement.
While partaking of our morning meal, we engaged in an animated conversation.
I am a stranger to excessive financial sums.
Law enforcement officers directed traffic when the lights malfunctioned.

The same thoughts can be expressed more clearly and effectively by using plain, natural language.

I understood what she said.
While eating breakfast, we had a lively talk.
I have never had much money.
Police officers directed traffic when the lights stopped working.

● ● ● ● Activity

Cross out the artificial words in each sentence. Then substitute clear, simple language for the artificial words.

Example   The manager ~~reproached~~ me for my ~~tardiness~~.

The manager criticized me for being late.

1. One of Irina's objectives in life is to accomplish a large family.

   _____

   _____

2. Upon entering our residence, we detected smoke in the atmosphere.

   _____

   _____

3. I am not apprehensive about the test, which encompasses five chapters of the book.

   _____

   _____

Visit the *English Skills with Readings: Examining Paragraphs* Online Learning Centre at www.mcgrawhill.ca/olc/langan to access self-quizzes, internet-based questions and research skills, web resources, and other learning and study tools.

Section 5

Twelve Reading Selections

Preview

This book assumes that writing and reading are closely connected skills, so that practising one helps the other and neglecting one hurts the other. Section Five will enable you to work on becoming a better reader as well as a stronger writer. Following an introductory section that offers a series of tips on effective reading, there are twelve reading selections. Each selection begins with a preview that supplies background information about the piece. After the selection are ten questions to give you practice in key reading comprehension skills. A set of discussion questions is also provided, both to deepen your understanding of the selection and to point out basic writing techniques used in the essay. Then come several writing assignments, along with guidelines to help you think about the assignments and get started working on them.

Chapter 38

Introduction to the Readings

You will find twelve readings in Section Five; they are presented for you to enjoy and to help you find topics for writing. These selections deal in various ways with interesting, often thought-provoking concerns or experiences of contemporary life. Subjects of the essays and articles include attitudes of Canadians toward their food; the need for care in using language to prepare websites, communicate, or even search for a job; how people reach out to others in their communities; and the challenge of managing anxiety. Readings about our values offer a compassionate view of depression and youth violence; one writer's thoughts about charity; and a thoughtful look at the otherwise thoughtless way we may consume food products. Selections on the subject of education present how to decide on a career; how to use language clearly; and how diverse skills should be respected. The final set of readings look outward at various Canadian communities and interests: Tony Wong's consideration of his lack of mathematical ability offers a humorous touch; while Anna Baum's recollection of a special moment after a war-torn, World War II winter gives warmth to a bleak moment in history. The selections are current and most are Canadian. All should inspire lively class discussions as well as some individual thought. The selections should also provide interesting material for a wide range of writing assignments.

The selections serve another purpose as well. They will help develop reading skills, with direct benefits to you as a writer. First, through analytic reading, you will learn how to recognize the thesis or point of a selection and how to identify and evaluate the supporting material that develops the thesis. In your writing, you will aim to achieve the same essential structure: an overall thesis followed by detailed and valid support for that point. Second, careful reading will help you explore a selection and its possibilities thoroughly. The more you understand about what is said in a piece, the more ideas and feelings you may have about writing on an assigned topic or a related topic of your own. A third benefit of such reading is in becoming more aware of authors' stylistic devices—for example, their introductions and conclusions, their ways of presenting and developing a point, their use of transitions, and their choice of language to achieve a particular tone. Recognizing these devices in other people's writing will help you enlarge your own range of writing techniques.

The Format of Each Selection

Each selection begins with a short overview that gives helpful background information as well as a brief idea of the topic of the reading. The selection is then followed by two sets of questions.

- First, there are ten reading comprehension questions to help you measure your understanding of the material. These questions involve several important reading skills: recognizing a subject or topic, determining the thesis or main idea, identifying key supporting points, making inferences, and understanding vocabulary in context. Answering the questions will enable you and your instructor to check your basic understanding of a selection quickly. More significantly, as you move from one selection to the next, you will sharpen your reading skills as well as strengthening your thinking skills—two key factors in making you a better writer.
- Following the comprehension questions are several discussion questions. In addition to dealing with issues of content, these questions focus on matters of structure, style, and tone. *Structure* refers to the ways in which the author has given shape to the work; *style* refers to word choice and the technical skills used by the writer; and *tone* is the "feeling" of a piece of work: whether it is serious, light, or comic.

The assignments range from personal narratives to expository and persuasive essays about issues in Canada and the world at large. Many assignments provide detailed guidelines on how to proceed, including suggestions for prewriting and appropriate methods of development. A number of new essay assignments require the use of Internet research. When writing your paragraph and essay responses to the readings, you will have opportunities to apply all the methods of development presented in Section Two as well.

How to Read Well: Four General Steps

Skilful reading is an important part of becoming a skilful writer. Following are four steps that will make you a better reader—both of the selections here and in your reading at large.

1   Concentrate as You Read

To improve your concentration, follow these tips.

- First, read in a place where you can be quiet and alone. Don't choose a spot where a TV or stereo is on or where friends or family are talking nearby.
- Next, sit in an upright position when you read. If your body is in a completely relaxed position, sprawled across a bed or nestled in an easy chair,

your mind is also going to be completely relaxed. The light muscular tension that comes from sitting in an upright chair promotes concentration and keeps your mind ready to work.

- Finally, consider using your index finger (or a pen) as a pacer while you read. Lightly underline each line of print with your index finger as you read down a page. Hold your hand slightly above the page and move your finger at a speed that is a little too fast for comfort. This pacing with your index finger, like sitting upright on a chair, creates a slight physical tension that will keep your body and mind focused and alert.

2   Skim Material Before You Read

It In skimming, you spend about two minutes rapidly surveying a selection, looking for important points and skipping secondary material. Follow this sequence when skimming:

- Begin by reading the overview that precedes the selection.
- Then study the title of the selection for a few moments. A good title is the shortest possible summary of a selection; it often tells you in several words what a selection is about. For example, the title "The Many Forms of Literacy" suggests that you're going to read about some form of learning because of its use of the concept "literacy."
- Next, form a basic question (or questions) out of the title. For instance, for the selection titled "The Many Forms of Literacy" you might ask, "What exactly does the author mean by 'literacy'? Is he referring to reading and writing? If so, what could he be offering in addition to the literacy that we know as reading and writing? Is the idea he is writing about the same as the literacy we learn in school?" Forming questions out of the title is often a key to locating a writer's main idea—your next concern in skimming.
- Read the first two or three paragraphs and the last two or three paragraphs in the selection. Very often a writer's main idea, *if* it is directly stated, will appear in one of these paragraphs and will relate to the title. For instance, in "Why Should We Hire You?" the author states in the final paragraph, "You need to work hard in order to find the work you desire. That means knowing the reasons you should be hired and taking the steps needed to prepare a solidly based answer before you are asked The Question."
- Finally, look quickly at the rest of the selection for other clues to important points. Are there any subheadings you can relate in some way to the title? Are there any words the author has decided to emphasize by setting them off in *italic* or **boldface** type? Are there any major lists of items signalled by words such as *first, second, also, another,* and so on?

3   Read the Selection Straight Through with a Pen Nearby

Read the selection without slowing down or turning back; just aim to understand as much as you can the first time through. Place a check or star beside answers to basic questions you formed from the title and beside other ideas that seem important. Number the important points *1, 2, 3,* and so on. Circle words you don't understand. Put question marks in the margin next to passages that are unclear and that you will want to reread.

4 Work with the Material

Now go back and reread passages that were not clear the first time through. Look up words that block your understanding of ideas and write their meanings in the margin. Also, reread carefully the areas you identified as most important; doing so will enlarge your understanding of the material. Now that you have a sense of the whole, prepare a short outline of the selection by answering the following questions on a sheet of paper:

- What is the thesis?
- What key points support the thesis?
- What seem to be other important points in the selection?

By working with the material in this way, you will significantly increase your understanding of a selection. *Effective reading, just like effective writing, does not happen all at once.* Rather, it is a *process.* Often you begin with a general impression of what something means, and then, by working at it, you move to a deeper level of understanding of the material.

How to Answer the Comprehension Questions: Specific Hints

Several important reading skills are involved in the ten reading comprehension questions that follow each selection. The skills are:

- Summarizing the selection by providing a title for it
- Determining the main idea
- Recognizing key supporting details
- Making inferences
- Understanding vocabulary in context

The following hints will help you apply each of these reading skills:

- ***Subject or title.*** Remember that the title should accurately describe the *entire* selection. It should be neither too broad nor too narrow for the material in the selection. It should answer the question "What is this about?" as specifically as possible. Note that you may at times find it easier to answer the "title" question *after* the "main idea" question.
- ***Main idea.*** Choose the statement that you think best expresses the main idea or thesis of the entire selection. Remember that the title will often help you focus on the main idea. Then ask yourself, "Does most of the material in the selection support this statement?" If you can answer yes to this question, you have found the thesis.
- ***Key details.*** If you were asked to give a two-minute summary of a selection, the major details would be the ones you would include in that summary. To determine the key details, ask yourself, "What are the major supporting points for the thesis?"

- ***Inferences.*** Answer these questions by drawing on the evidence presented in the selection and on your own common sense. Ask yourself, "What reasonable judgments can I make on the basis of the information in the selection?"
- ***Vocabulary in context.*** To decide on the meaning of an unfamiliar word, consider its context. Ask yourself, "Are there any clues in the sentence that suggest what this word means?"

A chart is provided on the Online Learning Centre to help you keep track of your performance as you answer the ten questions for each selection. Using this chart will also help you to identify reading skills you may need to strengthen.

Knowing Ourselves and Our Values

LETTER

Judith MacKenzie

In all of our lives, there have been times when we survived some difficult situation not because of our own efforts or toughness but because of the kindness, grace, or generosity of others. There are also times in our lives when we are privileged to be able to help others. Both giving and receiving such generosity are our finest moments as humans: the "gift" gives to both giver and receiver endlessly. This "mystery" that is "charity" is the essence of human goodness. Sometimes highly publicized, it also occurs unnoted every day; in fact, it is often overlooked or dismissed by those too cynical to believe in it, or by those who see only the arithmetic of "give something; get something in return." In "Letter," Judith MacKenzie contemplates two intertwined personal experiences with the mysterious and life-enriching nature of charity in action.

When I was eight years old, my father, a union organizer in the forties and fifties, was blacklisted, accused of communist activities. It meant no work—with a vengeance. My mother, then in her forties, had twin boys that spring—premature, and in premedicare times you can imagine the devastating costs for their care. I was hungry that year, hungry when I got up, hungry when I went to school, hungry when I went to sleep. In November I was asked to leave school because I only had boys' clothes to wear—hand-me-downs from a neighbour. I could come back, they said, when I dressed like a young lady.

The week before Christmas, the power and gas were disconnected. We ate soup made from carrots, potatoes, cabbage and grain meant to feed chickens, cooked on our wood garbage burner. Even as an eight-year-old, I knew the kind of hunger we had was nothing compared to people in India and Africa. I don't think we could have died in our middle-class Vancouver suburb. But I do know that the pain of hunger is intensified and brutal when you live in the midst of plenty. As Christmas preparations increased, I felt more and more isolated, excluded, set apart. I felt a deep, abiding hunger for more than food. Christmas

1

2

Eve day came, grey and full of the bleak sleety rain of a west-coast winter. Two women, strangers, struggled up our driveway, loaded down with bags. They left before my mother answered the door. The porch was full of groceries—milk, butter, bread, cheese and Christmas oranges. We never knew who they were, and after that day, pride being what it was, we never spoke of them again. But I'm forty-five years old, and I remember them well.

3   Since then I've crafted a life of joy and independence, if not of financial security. Several years ago, living in Victoria, my son and I were walking up the street, once more in west-coast sleet and rain. It was just before Christmas and we were, as usual, counting our pennies to see if we'd have enough for all our festive treats, juggling these against the necessities. A young man stepped in front of me, very pale and carrying an old sleeping bag, and asked for spare change—not unusual in downtown Victoria. No, I said, and walked on. Something hit me like a physical blow about a block later. I left my son and walked back to find the young man. I gave him some of our Christmas luxury money—folded into a small square and tucked into his hand. It wasn't much, only ten dollars, but as I turned away, I saw the look of hopelessness turn into amazement and then joy. Well, said the rational part of my mind, Judith, you are a fool, you know he's just going up the street to the King's Hotel and spend it on drink or drugs. You've taken what belongs to your family and spent it on a frivolous romantic impulse. As I was lecturing myself on gullibility and sensible charity, I noticed the young man with the sleeping bag walking quickly up the opposite side of the street, heading straight for the King's. Well, let this be a lesson, said the rational Judith. To really rub it in, I decided to follow him. Just before the King's, he turned into a corner grocery store. I watched through the window, through the poinsettias and the stand-up Santas. I watched him buy milk, butter, bread, cheese and Christmas oranges.

4   Now, I have no idea how that young man arrived on the street in Victoria, nor will I ever have any real grasp of the events that had led my family to a dark and hungry December. But I do know that charity cannot be treated as an RRSP. There is no best-investment way to give, no way to insure value for our dollar. Like the Magi, these three, the two older women struggling up the driveway and the young man with the sleeping bag, gave me, and continue to give me, wonderful gifts—the reminder that love and charity come most truly and abundantly from an open and unjudgemental heart.

● ● ● ● **Reading Comprehension Questions**

1. Which of the following would be the best alternative title for the selection?
   a. Christmas Gifts
   b. Giving Is the Best Gift of All
   c. Charity Begins at Home
   d. Lessons in Life

2. Which sentence best expresses the main idea of the selection?
   a. Learning to give is a lifelong process.
   b. People never really know the suffering of others.

c. Memories of generosity can make us generous.

d. Giving freely rewards both giver and receiver.

3. At age eight the author felt her family's situation most acutely when
   a. she was constantly hungry and was not allowed to go to school.
   b. she realized there would be no Christmas gifts.
   c. her family was so poor they had to take handouts.
   d. she was embarrassed by the women bringing food.

4. *True or false?* The author and her son were no better off than her family

   was during her childhood. _____

5. The author argues with herself about giving the young street person money because
   a. she resented people begging on the street.
   b. her past had made her prone to giving in to foolish impulses.
   c. she wanted to be logical and sensible, but remembered her own past.
   d. she was ashamed of looking stingy in front of her son.

6. The author implies that
   a. she was ashamed of wearing boys' clothes to school.
   b. school regulations of the time were cruel and unreasonable.
   c. wearing used "charity" clothes was painful to her.
   d. she enjoyed dressing like a "tomboy."

7. The author implies that the worst part of being hungry was
   a. the awfulness of eating food cooked on a garbage burner.
   b. her shame at starving like people in Third World countries.
   c. that the family's health was at risk because of their poor diet.
   d. feeling set apart by their deprivation in the midst of a comfortable society.

8. From the selection, we can infer that the author feels that
   a. sometimes our best actions are impulsive, rather than rational.
   b. we never understand the situations in which we find ourselves.
   c. the best gifts are those we give away.
   d. we should do without to learn the true meaning of charity.

9. The word *abiding* in "I felt a deep, abiding hunger for more than food" (paragraph 2) means
   a. gnawing.
   b. annoying.
   c. enduring.
   d. grinding.

10. The word *gullibility* in "As I was lecturing myself on gullibility and sensible charity" (paragraph 3) means
    a. stupidity.
    b. naïveté.
    c. practicality.
    d. generosity.

● ● ● ● **Discussion Questions**

About Content

1. What were the reasons for the author's family's poverty during her childhood? Why was there "no work—with a vengeance" (paragraph 1) for her father?

2. Why, as Christmas approached, did the author feel a "hunger for more than food" (paragraph 2)?

3. What specific elements of the setting, the characters, and their actions make the visit of the women to the family so magical and unexpected?

4. What are the author's reasons for saying to herself in paragraph 3, "Judith, you are a fool," and what is she "rub[bing] in" as she follows the young man?

About Structure

5. "Letter" is primarily a narrative selection, and generally a brief narrative covers only a single event. However, two situations are narrated in "Letter" rather than one. Why might MacKenzie have decided to include two events?

6. Where in the selection do you find the best statement of the author's thesis? Write the sentence(s) in the space below:

   _____

   _____

   Why has MacKenzie chosen this position for her thesis?

7. Narratives are mostly structured in *time order*. "Letter" uses transitional words and phrases to "set the stage" for each paragraph. List words and phrases that show readers when each paragraph occurs:

   a. _____

   b. _____

   c. _____

   d. _____

About Style and Tone

8. The author offers several parallel elements, as well as some elements that differ, in the two major "scenes" of her narrative. Which elements are similar in the two situations, and which are different? What is achieved by the parallels and differences?

9. "Letter" is perhaps an odd title for an essay. Why do you think MacKenzie chose this title? One element common to good personal letters and this selection is the inclusion of finely drawn details, probably aimed at evoking an emotional response. Which two of the selection's details do you find most effective, and why?

● ● ● ● **Writing Assignments**

Assignment 1: Writing a Paragraph

Consider what the author has to say about generosity and its rewards. Using the concept of charity (or generosity) as your topic, and basing your work on your own experience, write a paragraph that divides charity into different types or forms according to the classifying principle of the rewards involved.

To get started, think carefully about two things: the forms of generosity or charity you have offered to others and those you have received from others. Start your prewriting with whichever form of charity you find easiest to write about. Write only and specifically about your own experience; do not generalize. Focus on one specific situation and the rewards that arose from it, and look for headings under which to classify those rewards: possibilities might be "personal rewards," "material rewards," "unexpected rewards," and so on. As in the reading selection, look for an overall "lesson" or summarizing statement about your experience and its meaning with which to conclude your paragraph.

Assignment 2: Writing a Paragraph

Some ancient cultures believed that beggars must always be treated kindly because they might be gods in disguise. Judith MacKenzie's reaction to the street person in Victoria is probably typical of most people in today's cities: she feels torn between reason, cynicism, and sympathy. What is your reaction to being approached by one of the growing number of homeless people in Canadian cities? What would you say to someone like the young man in "Letter"?

Write a paragraph in the form of a letter, either to the person in MacKenzie's essay or to a real person who has approached you for a handout. What would you give such a person, either as advice or as direct help, or as both? Why?

Assignment 3: Writing an Essay

Charity, or unselfish, active love for fellow humans, is held as the highest good by most of the world's cultures and religions. Indeed, in classical Judaism, the best form of charity is that where the receiver never knows the giver. Not all charity is public or even acknowledged by others. In our society, there are many types of charity, from well-publicized corporate, tax-deductible donations to the personal gift of one's time and energy to help another person.

What, to you, is the finest form of charity, and why? In an essay that explains its point with examples, discuss why one specific type of generosity is most beneficial. Think of people who exemplify human generosity or charity, or of several instances of a single person's generosity; think of situations where someone or some group of people acted unselfishly for another's good; such self-questioning will lead you to the specific and well-explained examples you need to argue your point of view.

ANXIETY: CHALLENGE BY ANOTHER NAME

James Lincoln Collier

> What is your basis for making personal decisions? Do you aim to rock the boat as little as possible, choosing the easy, familiar path? There is comfort in sticking with what is safe and well-known, just as there is comfort in eating mashed potatoes. But James Lincoln Collier, author of numerous articles and books, decided soon after leaving college not to live a mashed-potato sort of life. In this essay, first published in *Reader's Digest*, he tells how he learned to recognize the marks of a potentially exciting, growth-inducing experience, to set aside his anxiety, and to dive in.

1   Between my sophomore and junior years at college, a chance came up for me to spend the summer vacation working on a ranch in Argentina. My roommate's father was in the cattle business, and he wanted Ted to see something of it. Ted said he would go if he could take a friend, and he chose me.

2   The idea of spending two months on the fabled Argentine pampas* was exciting. Then I began having second thoughts. I had never been very far from New England, and I had been homesick my first weeks at college. What would it be like in a strange country? What about the language? And besides, I had promised to teach my younger brother to sail that summer. The more I thought about it, the more the prospect daunted me. I began waking up nights in a sweat.

3   In the end I turned down the proposition. As soon as Ted asked somebody else to go, I began kicking myself. A couple of weeks later I went home to my old summer job, unpacking cartons at the local supermarket, feeling very low. I had turned down something I wanted to do because I was scared, and I had ended up feeling depressed. I stayed that way for a long time. And it didn't help when I went back to college in the fall to discover that Ted and his friend had had a terrific time.

4   In the long run that unhappy summer taught me a valuable lesson out of which I developed a rule for myself: *do what makes you anxious, don't do what makes you depressed.*

5   I am not, of course, talking about severe states of anxiety or depression, which require medical attention. What I mean is that kind of anxiety we call stage fright, butterflies in the stomach, a case of nerves—the feelings we have at a job interview, when we're giving a big party, when we have to make an important presentation at the office. And the kind of depression I am referring to is that downhearted feeling of the blues, when we don't seem to be interested in anything, when we can't get going and seem to have no energy.

6   I was confronted by this sort of situation toward the end of my senior year. As graduation approached, I began to think about taking a crack at making my living as a writer. But one of my professors was urging me to apply to graduate school and aim at a teaching career.

---

*A vast plain in south-central South America.

I wavered. The idea of trying to live by writing was scary—a lot more scary **7** than spending a summer on the pampas, I thought. Back and forth I went, making my decision, unmaking it. Suddenly, I realized that every time I gave up the idea of writing, that sinking feeling went through me; it gave me the blues.

The thought of graduate school wasn't what depressed me. It was giving up **8** on what deep in my gut I really wanted to do. Right then I learned another lesson. To avoid that kind of depression meant, inevitably, having to endure a certain amount of worry and concern.

The great Danish philosopher Søren Kierkegaard believed that anxiety always **9** arises when we confront the possibility of our own development. It seems to be a rule of life that you can't advance without getting that old, familiar, jittery feeling.

Even as children we discover this when we try to expand ourselves by, say, **10** learning to ride a bike or going out for the school play. Later in life we get butterflies when we think about having that first child, or uprooting the family from the old hometown to find a better opportunity halfway across the country. Any time, it seems, that we set out aggressively to get something we want, we meet up with anxiety. And it's going to be our traveling companion, at least part of the way, in any new venture.

When I first began writing magazine articles, I was frequently required to **11** interview big names—people like Richard Burton, Joan Rivers, sex authority William Masters, baseball great Dizzy Dean. Before each interview I would get butterflies and my hands would shake.

At the time, I was doing some writing about music. And one person I particularly admired was the great composer Duke Ellington. On stage and on television, he seemed the very model of the confident, sophisticated man of the world. Then I learned that Ellington still got stage fright. If the highly honored Duke Ellington, who had appeared on the bandstand some ten thousand times over thirty years, had anxiety attacks, who was I to think I could avoid them? **12**

I went on doing those frightening interviews, and one day, as I was getting **13** onto a plane for Washington to interview columnist Joseph Alsop, I suddenly realized to my astonishment that I was looking forward to the meeting. What had happened to those butterflies?

Well, in truth, they were still there, but there were fewer of them. I had **14** benefited, I discovered, from a process psychologists call "extinction." If you put an individual in an anxiety-provoking situation often enough, he will eventually learn that there isn't anything to be worried about.

Which brings us to a corollary to my basic rule: *you'll never eliminate anxiety* **15** *by avoiding the things that caused it.* I remember how my son Jeff was when I first began to teach him to swim at the lake cottage where we spent our summer vacations. He resisted, and when I got him into the water he sank and sputtered and wanted to quit. But I was insistent. And by summer's end he was splashing around like a puppy. He had "extinguished" his anxiety the only way he could—by confronting it.

The problem, of course, is that it is one thing to urge somebody else to take on **16** those anxiety-producing challenges; it is quite another to get ourselves to do it.

Some years ago I was offered a writing assignment that would require three **17** months of travel through Europe. I had been abroad a couple of times on the usual "If it's Tuesday this must be Belgium"* trips, but I hardly could claim to know my way around the continent. Moreover, my knowledge of foreign languages was limited to a little college French.

18   I hesitated. How would I, unable to speak the language, totally unfamiliar with local geography or transportation systems, set up interviews and do research? It seemed impossible, and with considerable regret I sat down to write a letter begging off. Halfway through, a thought—which I subsequently made into another corollary to my basic rule—ran through my mind: *you can't learn if you don't try.* So I accepted the assignment.

19   There were some bad moments. But by the time I had finished the trip I was an experienced traveler. And ever since, I have never hesitated to head for even the most exotic of places, without guides or even advance bookings, confident that somehow I will manage.

20   The point is that the new, the different, is almost by definition scary. But each time you try something, you learn, and as the learning piles up, the world opens to you.

21   I've made parachute jumps, learned to ski at forty, flown up the Rhine in a balloon. And I know I'm going to go on doing such things. It's not because I'm braver or more daring than others. I'm not. But I don't let the butterflies stop me from doing what I want. Accept anxiety as another name for challenge, and you can accomplish wonders.

● ● ● ● ● **Reading Comprehension Questions**

1. The word *daunted* in "The more I thought about [going to Argentina], the more the prospect daunted me. I began waking up nights in a sweat" (paragraph 2) means
   a. encouraged.
   b. interested.
   c. discouraged.
   d. amused.

2. The word *corollary* in "Which brings us to a corollary to my basic rule: *you'll never eliminate anxiety by avoiding the things that caused it*" (paragraph 15) means
   a. an idea that follows from another idea.
   b. an idea based on a falsehood.
   c. an idea that creates anxiety.
   d. an idea passed on from one generation to another.

3. Which of the following would be the best alternative title for this selection?
   a. A Poor Decision
   b. Don't Let Anxiety Stop You
   c. Becoming a Writer
   d. The Courage to Travel

---

*Reference to a film comedy about a group of American tourists who visited too many European cities in too little time.

4. Which sentence best expresses the main idea of the selection?
   a. The butterflies-in-the-stomach type of anxiety differs greatly from severe states of anxiety or depression.
   b. Taking on a job assignment that required traveling helped the author get over his anxiety.
   c. People learn and grow by confronting, not backing away from, situations that make them anxious.
   d. Anxiety is a predictable part of life that can be dealt with in positive ways.

5. When a college friend invited the writer to go with him to Argentina, the writer
   a. turned down the invitation.
   b. accepted eagerly.
   c. was very anxious about the idea but went anyway.
   d. did not believe his friend was serious.

6. *True or false?* As graduation approached, Collier's professor urged him to try to make his living as a writer. _____

7. *True or false?* The philosopher Søren Kierkegaard believed that anxiety occurs when we face the possibility of our own development. _____

8. "Extinction" is the term psychologists use for
   a. the inborn tendency to avoid situations that make one feel very anxious.
   b. a person's gradual loss of confidence.
   c. the natural development of a child's abilities.
   d. the process of losing one's fear by continuing to face the anxiety-inspiring situation.

9. The author implies that
   a. it was lucky he didn't take the summer job in Argentina.
   b. his son never got over his fear of the water.
   c. Duke Ellington's facing stage fright inspired him.
   d. one has to be more daring than most people to overcome anxiety.

10. The author implies that
    a. anxiety may be a signal that one has an opportunity to grow.
    b. he considers his three-month trip to Europe a failure.
    c. facing what makes him anxious has eliminated all depression from his life.
    d. he no longer has anxiety about new experiences.

● ● ● ● **Discussion Questions**

About Content

1. Collier developed the rule "Do what makes you anxious; don't do what makes you depressed." How does he distinguish between feeling anxious and feeling depressed?

2. In what way does Collier believe that anxiety is positive? How, according to him, can we eventually overcome our fears? Have you ever gone ahead and done something that made you anxious? How did it turn out?

About Structure

3. Collier provides a rule and two corollary rules that describe his attitude toward challenge and anxiety. Below, write the location of that rule and its corollaries.

   Collier's rule: paragraph _____
   First corollary: paragraph _____
   Second corollary: paragraph _____

   How does Collier emphasize the rule and its corollaries?

4. Collier uses several personal examples in his essay. Find three instances of these examples and explain how each helps Collier develop his main point.

About Style and Tone

5. In paragraph 3, Collier describes the aftermath of his decision not to go to Argentina. He could have just written, "I worked that summer." Instead he writes, "I went home to my old summer job, unpacking cartons at the local supermarket." Why do you think he provides that bit of detail about his job? What is the effect on the reader?

6. Authors often use testimony by authorities to support their points. Where in Collier's essay does he use such support? What do you think it adds to his piece?

7. In the last sentence of paragraph 10, Collier refers to anxiety as a "traveling companion." Why do you think he uses that image? What does it convey about his view of anxiety?

8. Is Collier just telling about a lesson he has learned for himself, or is he encouraging his readers to do something? How can you tell?

● ● ● ● **Writing Assignments**

Assignment 1: Writing a Paragraph

Collier explains how his life experiences made him view the term *anxiety* in a new way. Write a paragraph in which you explain how a personal experience of yours has given new meaning to a particular term. Following are some terms you might wish to consider for this assignment.

Failure
Friendship
Goals
Homesickness
Maturity
Success

Here are two sample topic sentences for this assignment.

I used to think of failure as something terrible, but thanks to a helpful boss, I now think of it as an opportunity to learn.
The word *creativity* has taken on a new meaning for me ever since I became interested in dancing.

Assignment 2: Writing a Paragraph

The second corollary to Collier's rule is "You can't learn if you don't try." Write a paragraph using this idea as your main idea. Support it with your own experience, someone else's experience, or both. One way of developing this point is to compare two approaches to a challenge: one person may have backed away from a frightening opportunity while another person decided to take on the challenge. Or you could write about a time when you learned something useful by daring to give a new experience a try. In that case, you might discuss your reluctance to take on the new experience, the difficulties you encountered, and your eventual success. In your conclusion, include a final thought about the value of what was learned.

Listing a few skills you have learned will help you decide on the experience you wish to write about. To get you started, below is a list of things adults often need to go to some trouble to learn.

Driving with a stick shift
Taking useful lecture notes
Knowing how to do well on a job interview
Asking someone out on a date
Making a speech
Standing up for your rights

Assignment 3: Writing an Essay

Collier describes three rules he follows when facing anxiety. In an essay, write about one or more rules, or guidelines, that you have developed for yourself through experience. If you decide to discuss two or three such guidelines, mention or refer to them in your introductory paragraph. Then go on to discuss each in one or more paragraphs of its own. Include at least one experience that led you to develop a given guideline, and tell how it has helped you at other times in your life. You might end with a brief summary and an explanation of how the guidelines as a group have helped. If you decide to focus on one rule, include at least two or three experiences that help to illustrate your point.

To prepare for this assignment, spend some time freewriting about the rules or guidelines you have set up for yourself. Continue writing until you feel you have a central idea for which you have plenty of interesting support. Then organize that support into a rough outline, such as this one:

<u>Thesis:</u> I have one rule that keeps me from staying in a rut: Don't let the size of a challenge deter you; instead, aim for it by making plans and taking steps.

<u>Topic sentence 1:</u> I began to think about my rule one summer in high school when a friend got the type of summer job that I had only been thinking about.

<u>Topic sentence 2:</u> After high school, I began to live up to my rule when I aimed for a business career and entered college.

<u>Topic sentence 3:</u> My rule is also responsible for my having the wonderful boyfriend [*or* girlfriend *or* job] I now have.

BEING TRUE TO OUR HOME AND NATIVE LAND

Joe Fiorito

> How is the food you consume produced? Do you know where it comes from, who has grown or processed it, or even when it was harvested? Does it even matter? Should the government take a more active role in overseeing and promoting the food that is produced in Canada and even in guaranteeing that Canadian food will be used in Canadian institutions? Joe Fiorito and increasing numbers of Canadians think so. In this selection, Fiorito describes a lunch he shares with well-known advocate, Donald Ziraldo, and the observations they share about the lack of official Canadian oversight in the food we consume every day.

1   Donald Ziraldo and I were having lunch downtown the other day. He ordered the salad; me, too. When the waiter brought our plates, Donald was curious about the lettuce. He poked at his plate with an interrogatory fork.

2   The waiter said it was a California mix. Donald wondered why it could not have been a Niagara mix. That is precisely the question which occupies me of late: Why, when Toronto is surrounded by farmland and greenhouses, do we rely on others for food we could grow here?

3   The waiter was unsure how to answer, or if he should even try. When Donald explained that we had been talking about local food, the waiter smiled discreetly, filled our glasses with water and returned to his post.

4   The water was sparkling and European, and there's that question again: Is it so hard to add bubbles to our own water and market it as stylishly as others do?

5   Our water is at least as good as, and it costs a lot less than, the waters of Italy, France, Portugal, Poland.

6   I suppose under other circumstances, we would have been drinking wine—Donald is the co-founder of the Inniskillin Winery—but he said these days he only drinks professionally, and I get sleepy if I drink at noon.

7   I had wanted to have lunch with him because he has strong opinions on the importance of local produce. He is not just a pioneering vintner, he rubs shoulders with the big chefs and calls them Greg and Jamie.

8   He consults with governments, and he has travelled the province, the country and the world on the strength of his palate and the depth of his agricultural acumen.

9   As it happens, Cadbury Schweppes had just announced it was pulling out of the grape juice business in the Niagara peninsula, and the farmers who grow juice grapes are clearly worried about their livelihoods.

10   Nobody knows more about grapes than Donald Ziraldo. He said there was a neat solution. "The government could buy the plant from Cadbury, and mandate that fresh grape juice be served in all the schools in the region." Is it really that simple?

He said, "I know a guy in Niagara who would love to have grape juice in the schools instead of pop. He's got kids in school, and he also knows a bit about business." **11**

Yep, it is that simple. **12**

Me? I'd have nationalized Cadbury as soon as they said they were leaving. But Donald is a practical man, and much more temperate than am I. **13**

He said we could also encourage our national and regional air carriers to serve Canadian juices on their flights. This would be unusual—us, doing as other nations do—and it would be good for producers and consumers alike. **14**

We grow excellent cherries, cranberries, blueberries, apples, peaches and pears. Why shouldn't we serve ourselves? It's good business. It keeps farmers on the land. And it keeps the land in production. **15**

On the subject of which, Donald noted that there is rising pressure in the greenbelt from developers. He talked about the creation of agricultural easements, whereby farmers could get tax relief when the value of their land rises, in return for which their asset would remain in use as farmland. **16**

Yesss! **17**

The discussion then got back to my pet peeve, which is the importing of food from far away. You recall my earlier surprise at finding organic Egyptian cucumbers in my supermarket. **18**

Turns out the problem is more pervasive than I thought. Donald said, "The food we grow in the Niagara region is picked locally and shipped to a warehouse in Toronto, and then it gets shipped back to us." **19**

Gee, what a great way to ensure that the food we eat in season is not as fresh as it ought to be. **20**

As for organics, he said, "New York hands out $300 million to farmers to keep the watershed around the city clean. There is a real incentive to keep local agriculture green." **21**

I hope government is listening. **22**

Donald, perhaps sensing that I was about to spin out of control, turned the talk to other matters. He said he was fond of travelling in Italy because there you could take some pleasure in looking at the fields. **23**

We don't do that here. **24**

We put up concrete walls, as if our fields were not worth looking at. Oh, I understand about the use of walls as noise baffles. That we do not at least cover these walls with vines baffles me. **25**

I asked Donald how he was keeping busy now that he's out of the wine business. He talked about the research station at Vineland; he sits on the advisory panel. **26**

He wants to see more local research devoted to the production of flowers, soft fruit, and cold-climate crops. **27**

The advisory panel recently submitted an extensive research proposal along these lines and asked the Ontario government to contribute $25 million. **28**

The Vineland Station was awarded a grant for half that much the other day. Oh, well, it's better than nothing, and a man's reach should exceed his grasp. **29**

I reached for a piece of bread. At least it was made locally. **30**

● ● ● ● **Reading Comprehension Questions**

1. Which of the following would be the best alternative title for the selection?
   a. Importing Food
   b. Nationalizing Food Production
   c. The Importance of Local Food Production
   d. California Mix

2. Which sentence best expresses the main idea of the selection?
   a. Canadians can and must support the sale of local produce.
   b. Niagara wines have become increasingly popular.
   c. Developers need to use urban green belts to support urban growth.
   d. We should eat more fruits and vegetables.

3. The author wanted to have lunch with Donald Ziraldo because
   a. Ziraldo is a famous chef.
   b. the author wanted to taste some new wine.
   c. Ziraldo was selling his winery for development.
   d. Ziraldo is well informed about Canada's agricultural industries.

4. *True or false?* Ziraldo is in favour of a plan which allows farmers to maintain their land as farmland, rather than forcing them to sell it for development?

   _____

5. What is the first mention of the problem that the author and his guest have with the way food is distributed in Canada?
   a. When Ziraldo decided he did not want a salad.
   b. When the waiter described the salad as California mix.
   c. When the Belgian water was not sparkly.
   d. When the author mentions the threat to the local grape juice industry.

6. The author implies that
   a. Canada does not produce enough food to support its people.
   b. Food produced in Canada is of inferior quality.
   c. Canadians have not paid enough attention to the way in which their food is distributed.
   d. Canadians wish to import more food.

7. Ziraldo says that he appreciates travelling in Italy where the fields are openly visible, rather than behind sound baffles, which implies that
   a. Canadians choose to ignore their agricultural regions, but Italians show them off proudly.
   b. Canadian roads are too dangerous to go through agricultural regions.
   c. Canadian farms are poorly managed and unsightly.
   d. Italian farms are better than Canadian farms.

8. From this reading, the audience can infer that
   a. Canadian food production is well managed.
   b. Canadians enjoy the best quality for the best prices.
   c. Canadians promote their food industries well.
   d. Canadians do not support their food industries well.

9. In the sentence, "He poked at his plate with an interrogatory fork" (paragraph 1), the word *interrogatory* means
   a. disgusting.
   b. questioning.
   c. sharp.
   d. decorated.

10. The author reports that, "there is rising pressure in the greenbelt from developers" (paragraph 16). The word *greenbelt* refers to
    a. an agricultural region.
    b. an area around cities that is not developed for housing or commercial purposes.
    c. the warmest area of the country.
    d. where money is made.

● ● ● ● **Discussion Questions**

About Content

1. Why did the author wish to meet with Donald Ziraldo?
2. Why does the author feel that this is an important topic?
3. What is significant about the two men meeting at a restaurant?
4. What sort of temperament does the author display?

About Structure

5. In this reading, the author uses elements of more than one mode of writing to promote a single argument. What is the main argument of his piece? Where does he use
   a. narrating a story?
   b. describing a scene or person?
   c. Explaining a process?
6. Where in the selection does the author state his thesis?
7. How does the author indicate transitions from one idea to the next?

About Style and Tone

8. How does the author use the attitudes about food found in other countries to compare or contrast to those he discusses in Canada?
9. Why would the author used the phrase, "Our home and native land" in the title?

● ● ● ● **Writing Assignments**

Assignment 1: Writing a Paragraph

Food is one of our primary comforts. When we look forward to a specific meal, we may do so with specific tastes, aromas, images, and settings in mind. What to you is an ideal meal? Write a description paragraph that illustrates a perfect meal; decide upon the overall feature that describes that meal, and then support that description with three distinct elements. For example, you might consider a meal that depicts a special day, such as a Canadian Thanksgiving Dinner, or one that you enjoy during a certain activity, such as a hot dog at a game or a lobster boil on a beach. Try to describe your meal so that your audience can see, smell, taste, or even hear the features that you are describing. Conclude your paragraph with a reference back to the point that you made in your topic sentence.

Assignment 2: Writing a Paragraph

There have been many recent trends in food preparation or acquisition, which encourage people to understand and enjoy their food, rather than to merely accept mass-produced food whose origins and ingredients cannot be identified. Some people wish to buy only organic foods, for example, or encourage preparing their meals according to "slow-food" principles, in opposition to the 'fast food' that has been so prevalent for a generation. Whole towns have stated their intention to embrace "fair trade" goods, and some families are starting to develop menus based on food that is produces within one hundred kilometres from their homes. Which, if any, of these, makes sense for a Canadian family?

Identify a recent food trend, and compare and contrast it to standard fare. Identify three factors to describe, and compare them using either the one-side-at-a-time or the point-by-point method as explained in Chapter 12. Be sure to explain each with details that give a complete overview of the point and by providing specific examples. Write in an objective, third-person, point of view, so that your emphasis lies in the comparisons and contrast you are explaining, rather than in your personal preferences. In your conclusion, remind your audience of the value of the food trend you have just discussed.

Assignment 3: Writing an Essay

The author in this selection is concerned about food security, quality, and availability in the Canadian market. He and his guest are displeased with the trends they identify, and feel that the Canadian attitude to food production could be greatly enhanced. The author even suggests—partly in jest—that he would nationalize a chocolate company. Is the nationalization of food production a viable response to the types of problems that the author discusses? Or, perhaps, rather than outright nationalization, would Canadians at least be better served if the industry was held more accountable to Canadians?

Choose an element of food production from anywhere in Canada that you think should be supported, enhanced, or otherwise more carefully considered, and argue for a particular action regarding that industry. You may select a particular food industry, such as the meat industry, or produce, or even a specific item, such as chocolate. Investigate the industry through basic research to find out how the product reaches the Canadian table; then, determine whether this provides the best result for Canadian consumers. Through prewriting, discover a topic to write about, and then identify your particular issue in a thesis statement, and provide three supporting reasons. You may state your thesis in a sentence such as, "Meat production in Canada should be supported by more government investment, oversight, and promotion in order that Canadians continue to enjoy the best of meat products in their homes."

As you argue your point, provide sufficient details so that your audience can understand exactly the situation you are discussing, and the factors that have led you to your point of view. Describe the processes as necessary, and provide specific examples throughout to illustrate your supporting reasons. Conclude with a paragraph that refers to your thesis statement, and leaves your audience thinking about the food that Canadians eat.

(*Note:* Keep track of the reference material you use. You may be required to document your sources according to the MLA or APA styles of documentation, as your instructor indicates.)

SURVIVING THE JOURNEY: LITERATURE MEETS LIFE

Martha Brooks

> In this address given by the author in a panel discussion entitled "Compassionate Teenagers Making Choices," author Martha Brooks discusses the factors that cause some young people to become so disturbed that they drop out of society or even commit acts of violence. Yet, Brooks does not blame youth for their acting out, and instead points to the way in which they may have been let down by the adults in their lives. This speech gives a compassionate voice to troubled youth, as Brooks explains how she has come to understand youth through her own interaction and care.

Lethbridge, Alberta—When he was six, schoolmates doused him with lighter fluid **1**
and threatened to torch him. By 14, he wouldn't leave his house for months because he was frequently kicked and punched by peers who considered him a squeaky voiced geek, a pimply-faced loser. One attack left a hole in his lower lip so large he could put his tongue through it. For a lark, a girl took pictures of the beating. When he finally got up the nerve to register an assault complaint with police, his file got lost. Nothing was done for months. At 14, say psychologists and psychiatrists, he had become so lost and explosive, he took a sawed-off semi-automatic rifle into W.R. Myers high school in Taber, Alberta, and opened fire at the first students he saw. He didn't know Jason Lang, 17, who was fatally shot, nor did he know the student he seriously wounded. Details of his life, revealed at recent court hearings, were held under a publication ban that was lifted with the boy's guilty pleas yesterday.

18 November 2000, Canadian Press.

This is the opening of a disturbing piece that appeared in Canadian newspapers **2**
as I was preparing to leave for Milwaukee. It is particularly poignant in its resonance with the fact that every adult associated with this boy had failed him.

We can never assume anything when we look at a young person. We may **3**
be looking at someone whose support systems have all the outward appearance of solidity, whose family we may think we know intimately. *But young people who are in the process of falling off the rails don't always give off signals that*

anything is wrong. They become masters of the social mask and they can keep their secrets, whatever they may be, or, in some cases, whomever they may be protecting from everyone, even from close family members.

4   Kids do not go wrong or fall into despair for no good reason. There could be legitimate medical causes such as undiagnosed emotional or mental illness. There could be issues of physical or emotional or sexual abuse, either inside or outside the family. There could be certain extremely challenging issues arising in adolescence which revolve around sexual identity. There could be the slow erosion, for whatever reason, of the family unit. Poverty has no corner on any of this. And we all know that bad things happen to good people no matter what their life circumstances. And so we have the young alcoholic from the upper-middle-class neighbourhood who, unbeknownst to his parents has some very unpleasant memories, from between the ages of four and six, involving his trusted baby-sitter. Or the young woman who can't quite seem to make a decision, who seems forever immature and flailing and stalled in her journey to adulthood, whose uncle or older brother or cousin or family friend regularly abused her, stole her childhood, and uttered threats that he would kill her if she told anyone—and indeed she hasn't. She loves her parents. How could she tell them anything so awful? Or maybe it's the 17-year-old girl whose doctor father is distracted and rarely available, and whose sad and harried mother is the anxious and frustrated caregiver not only of three teenage daughters, but also of an elderly mother, recently diagnosed with Alzheimer's disease.

5   This 17-year-old has known most of her life that she prefers girls to boys; she also knows that her parents will not, under any circumstances, tolerate her choice. And that may or may not be true. In any event she opts not to tell them that she is a lesbian, and the growing estrangement and its repercussions are deeply wounding and mystifying to everyone around her. To everyone except, of course, her latest girlfriend. We expect a great deal from our children. We fill their lives, where we can, with lessons and sports and incredible stimulation. We spend time with them. Give to them. Love them. Most children grow up just fine in this sometimes scary world, filled as it is with the odd dragon behind the cupboard door. We are safe and they are safe and the world as we perceive it, as it translates to our own corner of Milwaukee, or Fargo, or Winnipeg, Manitoba, is safe. Safe to us and to our beloved children.

6   But when adults who are supposed to be protecting young people are not paying attention, or are avoiding certain untenable truths within their own lives, things can go wrong very fast. Patterns of family dysfunction may be involved, as well as the eroding stress of simply trying to keep life going. Balance, or harmony, is synonymous with beauty to the Navajo way of thinking; they even have a word for it: *horzho.* But we all know that finding balance within a modern world with its reeling and often completely unrealistic demands is a trick that many of us find out of reach.

7   For a few years our house had a revolving door for disenfranchised young people. They are all grown up now. Some still call me Ma, or Mum, or Mommy, or simply Martha where the image of "mother" does not carry with it the standard warm fuzzy memories. These young people have taught me a great deal about patience and compassion and trust. Of the three that I remain closest to,

one was born into a life of privilege, the other two into a life of poverty. Their shared experience is that the adults around them either let them down, or could not protect them, or a combination of the two. The other things they have in common are intelligence, awareness, creativity, warmth, pride, courage, considerable charm, amazing resilience, a marvellous sense of humour, and a daily struggle with personal demons. Life is not easy when you have suffered early sorrow and have learned that the world can be unimaginably unsafe.

The young people who survive this place of unsafety, I have found, have an **8** innate ability to recognize nurturers, making the conscious choice that is involved in seeking them out, basking in their often unwitting warmth, looking for their advice, a smile, a pat on the back, a shred of hope. These nurturers can be a teacher, the woman next door, a minister, a music teacher, somebody else's dad, the family of a girlfriend, a librarian, or as one young man who is close to me remarked, when I asked him, with affection, "How did you turn out so good?" "It was girls," he responded with a quick smile. "Girls kept me out of trouble and saved me."

When you see street kids, it's easy to think, okay, they fell onto hard times **9** because of extreme social issues. But when I walk around in my own upper-middle-class neighbourhood and I see a young person who stands out, whose personal aura sends forth the message: screw-up, I don't blame the kid, I say to myself, "What the hell happened here?"

Despite the truth I am speaking we are all inculturated to certain areas of **10** social blindness and denial. And the function of all good literature is to break though that. Just as I took those children into my home, I take readers into my books in an attempt to unmask and show inner realities. In my work I want to explore the fact that life throws us curves, things we don't expect or deserve. I want to present the reality that *good people do bad things and can survive and grow from the experience*. I also want to present the fact that there is not only for young adults but for adults, as well, a sense of passage in everything we do. We are continually moving. Reconstructing. Re-examining. Refocusing. And for each of us there are those private unheralded moments of utter courage. And many of us live those moments daily.

A few years ago, when I was writing my book, *Bone Dance*, my own daugh- **11** ter guided me through the intricacies of spiritual awakening. We had had a hard time, she and I. Now we were both healing. On the day of summer solstice she invited me out to a sweat lodge for a naming ceremony, her own. I will briefly explain here that she is a published poet, a playwright, and more recently, partly because her association with her spiritual teacher, an Ojibway elder and healer, is in her pre-master's year of anthropology, cross-examining Ojibway and Icelandic cultures. The actual event was stunning. Stars shot up the prairie sky. All good prayers and songs were offered to the Creator and influencing sacred forces. In the mist and flames and scent of cedar, and in the presence of many good and humble people, my daughter received her new name and found a different kind of family and a different sense of belonging. As for myself, I came away thinking in a more profound way about the Lakota phrase: All my relations.

We are bound together on this planet. We are all related whether or not we **12** choose to believe it or to accept it. And it's often the young who show us the way. In them we can see ourselves—alive, imperfect, and everlastingly hopeful.

● ● ● ● **Reading Comprehension Questions**

1. Which of the following would be the best alternative title for the selection?
   a. The Trouble with Kids
   b. Problem Parents
   c. A Sense of Passage
   d. Navajo Customs

2. Which sentence best expresses the main idea of the selection?
   a. Some people may never have a chance in life.
   b. Adults must take responsibility for their own lives in order to provide stability and care to youth.
   c. Young people have problems.
   d. The young show us the way.

3. The author came to an understanding of young people because
   a. she had many children.
   b. they taught her to consider their unique situations.
   c. she trained extensively to work with youth.
   d. her daughter fought with her.

4. *True or false?* The author had a difficult childhood. _____

5. The author explains that the role of literature is
   a. to provide relief from tension.
   b. a source of income that she can use to spend her time with youth.
   c. is irrelevant to youth.
   d. is necessary in its ability to reflect society, and help people connect with each other.

6. The author implies that
   a. young people who show psychological problems may have been neglected or abused when they were young.
   b. girls become lesbians if they are sexually abused when they are young.
   c. boys become alcoholics if they are sexually abused when they are young.
   d. troubled youth only claim to have been abused as an excuse for antisocial behaviour.

7. The author implies that
   a. her daughter used to bring home many troubled friends.
   b. she has had difficult relationships with many young people.
   c. she is a natural nurturer.
   d. her daughter was a street kid.

8. After reading this selection, we can infer that the author feels that
   a. adults need to understand the complexities that many young people face within their families.
   b. youth crime should be dealt with severely.
   c. abused children will become school killers.
   d. she wishes she had been a better mother.

9. The word *poignant* in the sentence "It is particularly poignant in its resonance with the fact that every adult associated with this boy had failed him" (paragraph 2) means
   a. annoying.
   b. frightening.
   c. frustrating.
   d. touching.

10. The word *disenfranchised* in the sentence "For a few years our house had a revolving door for disenfranchised young people" (paragraph 7) means
    a. disturbed.
    b. worried.
    c. deprived.
    d. creative.

● ● ● ● ● **Discussion Questions**

About Content

1. What is the main reason the author reports for the emotional imbalances that young people experience?
2. Why does the author feel that she has learned from the youth who have lived in her house?
3. What is the role of literature, according to the author?
4. What does the author ask readers to consider when they encounter troubled young people?

About Structure

5. "Surviving the Journey" is written in the first-person, but unlike a simple narrative the author, Brooks, does not relate a single event. Instead, this essay talks about an idea, and presents an argument. What is her central argument, and how does she support it?
6. Where in the selection do you find the best statement of the author's thesis? Why has Brooks chosen this location to state her primary argument?
7. Brooks wrote this speech to give in a panel discussion called, "Compassionate Teenagers Making Choices." What kind of logical order does she use to organize her speech? Are her transitions equally as effective in a piece of writing as they might be in a speech for a panel?

About Style and Tone

8. The reading starts with an excerpt from a news report about an infamous event, the school shooting in a small town, Taber, Alberta. Is using such a sensational event as a hook effective, or even necessary? How does it influence the audience as it reads the rest of the work?

   The sense of violence does not persist throughout the reading. What other tone does the author use in the reading, and how does the author shift her tone? Why do you think she chose not to focus on other youth violence?

9. The full title of this reading is, "Surviving the Journey: Literature Meets Life." How does that title reflect the author's conviction of the role of the author, and of all literature? Is literature as vital to the good of society as the author insists?

● ● ● ● **Writing Assignments**

Assignment 1: Writing a Paragraph

You may know of incidents where a young person has deteriorated emotionally because of neglect or bullying at home, school, or elsewhere. Identify such a situation (though you do not have to identify the specific person if it is a private case) and write a paragraph that explains what happened and why, the consequences, and any suggestions you have so that people avoid such trauma in their own lives.

Assignment 2: Writing a Paragraph

In the reading, Brooks draws upon the wisdoms of some Native cultures—highlighting the need for care and balance—to show contrast to the sense of alienation young people may feel in the twenty-first century. How much is modern life to blame for youth alienation, and in what ways?

Identify a single aspect of your idea, and develop it as a point for the topic sentence. Express your opinion with this point; however, do so without using the first person point of view. Instead of writing a topic sentence that states, "I believe that young people are harmed by . . . " phrase your idea objectively. For example, you might write, "The extreme competitive pressures to succeed in the twenty-first century may be a core cause of youth alienation."

By structuring and supporting your paragraph in the third person, your audience will consider your point of view more thoughtfully. Your readers will understand that you are supporting *your* own idea, but accept it as more reasoned and objective than if you had identified yourself, rather than your idea, as the subject of the paragraph.

Assignment 3: Writing an Essay

Often young people claim that having little say in the direction of their own lives is a major sense of personal frustration. When this becomes too great, the result can be so serious that they may be driven to antisocial, addictive, or even violent reaction. How could society address this initial frustration—through policy or action—so that adolescents and young adults could take more control over their lives? For example, should youth have a direct vote at the local, provincial or federal levels? Is it possible to construct institutions or programs in a way that youth are officially included at the decision-making level? Alternately, can more youth outreach programs be established, involving agencies such as police services, social agencies, or even cultural organizations? Do examples of such programs or policies already exist, anywhere, and are they effective?

Identify a single constructive initiative, stating whether it is one that has been implemented, or is mainly an ideal. Express this as your thesis statement, arguing for the ideal or persuading your audience to consider accepting a novel approach to developing youth policy. (Conversely, you could argue against a specific initiative.) Include a plan of action that will analyze three vital aspects— three supporting reasons—of your suggestion. Support your reasons with adequate details, explanations, and specific examples. Conclude your essay so that you refer, again, to your thesis and encourage your audience to consider the argument you have just presented.

This will require research in order to find accurate information that explains why, where and how such has been established, and whether it has been effective. Be sure to retain all of your sources, and to document them according to the style your instructor expects. For further information with research and documentation, consult Chapters 16 and 17, and apply the methods given as you write your essay.

Education and Self-Improvement

Jim Maloney

> The workplace of the third millennium is a new place: perhaps a not-so-pleasant prospect for the college student and a place of decreasing possibilities for the already-employed individual. Neither "a job for a lifetime" nor the chance of steady advancement in a field of personal expertise can be expected, much less taken for granted by anyone. A diploma, a degree, and a snappy résumé are no guarantees of a lifetime's steady employment. Instead, a sense of direction, steady and careful academic preparation, and active job research during the college years are needed to face the realities of the twenty-first-century job market. Jim Maloney, coordinator of the Technical Communication program at Seneca College in Toronto and a long-time expert in career-based areas of writing, poses student readers "The Question"—a question he faced, and a question most companies' human resources personnel will ask any student reading this essay: "Why should we hire you?"

I

1   "Why should we hire you for this position?"

2   I remember the first time I was asked that question. I remember it the same way I remember the first time a police officer asked to see my driver's licence and registration. I was no more prepared to be caught speeding than I was prepared to explain why I should be permanently employed teaching English at a community college. In both cases, I experienced a sinking feeling in my stomach, and a quickening of my pulse: the sensations that come with being caught.

3   I got a speeding ticket, but I didn't get the job.

4   Looking back at the difficulty I had with that basic question, I can't believe that I approached the interview so badly prepared. If I had been as prepared for the job interview as I was for doing the job, I would have felt no surprise. I had had a number of previous jobs where I was hired only for my ability to perform physical tasks, so the interviews for these jobs were far less crucial than was the simple ability to do the work. However, just as exceeding the speed limit will, when traffic police are performing properly, lead to a speeding ticket, so being

interviewed for an attractive career-entry position will, when the interviewer knows what to look for, lead directly or indirectly to the question "Why should we hire you?"

The question is a significant one, not just because you will encounter it, in some form, as part of a job interview, along with other "open-ended" queries designed to uncover your understanding of the position and of the suitability of your qualifications. The question is also important to consider in preparing your resume and application letter—documents crucial to creating possible interviews. Moreover, the question is relevant to you, who haven't yet finished your postsecondary career preparation and, therefore, won't be immediately facing interviews for positions in your chosen field. For you at this stage, the question "Why should we hire you?" may seem pointless, premature, or irrelevant. Try turning the question around: "Why should *I* be hired?" Now the question may have more meaning to you. Indeed, considered in this form, the question can guide you towards preparing for a career. So, thinking about how you will answer such a question will help you not only to understand the significance of the question but also to back up your answers with the right credentials, skills, and experiences. **5**

II

Too frequently, students seem to take for granted their right, or even their access, to interviews and to jobs needed to begin their careers. Such optimism can no longer be justified. Ten years ago, graduating students were warned that continued employment in one field for one company for one's entire working life was increasingly becoming a thing of the past. Students could expect three or four career shifts. Today, many college or university graduates will never have the chance even to begin careers in their chosen fields. Others may find only part-time or contract work. The last decade has produced enormous changes in the way business and industry operate in North America, and in the ways in which people are employed. **6**

Corporate downsizing—reductions in the workforce needed by a company for operating purposes—has been a fact in business life for some time now. Global competition is usually given as the reason for smaller workforce requirements, while, it is claimed, technological developments, especially computerization, have led to massive employee lay-offs with no loss to productivity. Of course, there is an alternative view of downsizing: that remaining employees are expected to be more productive—to work longer and harder—to pick up the slack. A consequence of downsizing and technological change is a reduced full-time workforce, many of whom either handle more tasks or perform more specialized technological activities. In some companies, another consequence of a smaller workforce is the replacement of permanent full-time employees who receive higher salaries and significant benefit packages with part-time or contract workers who are offered lower salaries and few, if any, benefits. Some companies have virtually nothing to offer but these limited, rather unpromising positions. **7**

These changes are not limited to the private sector. Recently, the governments of Alberta and Ontario initiated large-scale downsizing projects in their civil services. Many job lay-offs in health care, education, and local governments have resulted from such funding cuts. For someone wishing to begin a new **8** career, the prospects are starting to look nasty and brutish, and the immediate picture is distinctly short of jobs, hours, and rewards for new employees. Quite simply, there may not be jobs for college and university graduates who don't know how they fit into this brave new workworld.

9   Consequently, it is now more important than ever for you to consider and act on The Question while there is still time for you to learn the needs of employers and to make yourself capable of meeting those needs.

III

10   There are numerous reasons why students may not be seriously addressing The Question. Many students place so much trust in the educational system that they fail to look onward to life beyond graduation. Often, the very fact that students are attending college or university may be the reason they don't take advantage of their school years to prepare themselves effectively for the next step. Some students make the error of seeing an employment ad's requirement of a post-secondary diploma or degree as a guarantee of entry into that career. These students may be so impressed by their status as college or university students that they are complacent about their futures. Unfortunately, being a student is not a career and, with few exceptions, is not very profitable. Other students may find their academic work difficult and demanding enough without adding the headache of anticipating yet more demands. Still others may trust their chosen vocationally based academic program to put them on the correct job track. The problem is that they may not actually know where it is that they are going. I am amazed every semester by the number of students in specialized programs who are utterly unaware of jobs that may be available to them, of skills needed and of the actual nature of duties they may be expected to perform. Clueless in an academic fool's paradise, all of these students are caught in wishful rather than realistic thinking.

11   But what *actual* difference will it make to familiarize yourself with job specifications and employment prospects during your education instead of when you graduate? Preparing yourself to be desirable to prospective employers can have clear advantages during your college or university years. Even if there were no other consequences, a sense of the ultimate purpose of your studies should make your efforts more significant, less abstract—less academic. Being aware of the competition you face in your chosen field could certainly make the pursuit of good grades more meaningful. If you are in a program with a variety of optional courses, your knowledge of the job market's demands will help you to make more informed decisions. Should you be registered in a more rigidly structured program, knowing that the real requirements of the job you want differ from your program's offerings could indicate that you should supplement your education with additional courses beyond your curriculum. Reading job descriptions during your school years will teach you that certain types of work experience are desired, even for entry-level positions. Therefore, choosing summer or part-time work in an area related to your chosen career, even if the pay is less attractive, may ultimately be more rewarding. Most career-advice agencies now recommend volunteer work, and many students volunteer their time to organizations connected to their career paths. In

the cases of both occasional and volunteer work, the contacts made and the experience gained can be very valuable. Finally, you may never need a total personality make-over, but you should think about personal characteristics of successful people in your chosen field.

IV

With all these advantages to be gained from planning ahead for employment, how do you go about finding out what employers want? **12**

One place to start is within your school. Many vocationally based programs have a faculty member responsible for student employment. Some of your instructors may be actively involved in their fields; others may have informal but vital contacts with employers or former students in business and technology. You may discover that it is quite easy to gain insight into your field of interest just by sounding out your teachers. Yet another source of information is your school's student employment office. As well as placing graduating students, this facility usually offers a range of services including personality testing, career counselling, information resources on companies, and job profiles. Graduation is too late to find out what your school has to offer. **13**

Don't feel limited to these paths as you try to discover a career direction. Find out requirements for actual jobs in order to become the candidate you want to be. Even though you are not applying for a permanent position now, make a habit of following not only jobs listed in your school's employment office but also those advertised in newspapers, professional journals, or occupational periodicals. Best of all, visit human resources offices of major employers in your field; check job requirements for current or future positions; meet personnel officers, and read any information available about their companies. The time spent will pay off in your career. **14**

At this point, you may be ready to get in touch with someone already working in your chosen field to gain first-hand knowledge of positions you would like. You don't need to know personally someone who fits this description; one of your teachers or friends may know someone you can contact. Alternatively, speaking with or writing to an employer in your field may help you to find a person suitably placed to answer your questions about qualifications, duties, and responsibilities. You would be surprised by how easy it is to get information, even from a stranger. If you try some of these approaches, you are on your way to a personal network. **15**

Today, you need to work hard to find the work you desire. That means knowing the reasons you should be hired and taking the steps needed to prepare a solidly based answer before you are asked The Question. **16**

● ● ● ● ● **Reading Comprehension Questions**

1. Which of the following would be the best alternative title for this selection?
   a. Diplomas and Dim Prospects
   b. Prepare to Work to Find Work
   c. Career Confusion
   d. The Best Degree Is No Guarantee

2. Which sentence best expresses the main idea of the selection?
    a. Intelligent choices of the right courses give students fair chances of getting work on graduation.
    b. The workplace is a crowded "buyer's market," and students must work to prepare themselves to be the "right product."
    c. Today's students must expect several changes in career paths, and several different employers in their professional futures.
    d. Technological developments have eliminated many traditional job opportunities.

3. Maloney believes that
    a. students should concentrate on the employer's viewpoint as they acquire education, skills, and experience.
    b. concentrating on writing good résumés and cover letters will ensure job interviews.
    c. students can focus on career goals from the beginning of their college experience.
    d. due to changes in business and industry, finding a job in the next few years is a hopeless task.

4. Corporate downsizing has led to
    a. a need for more highly trained technological workers.
    b. a mixture of highly versatile and very specialized workers.
    c. companies consisting only of part-time workers.
    d. changes only in the private sector.

5. *True or false?* Maloney believes that choice of a diploma program in a developing area of industry and careful attention to course work can

    maximize chances for full-time future employment. _____

6. The author implies that
    a. looking toward the employment market involves looking at all aspects of oneself.
    b. looking forward to job interviews is pointless and terrifying.
    c. it is never too early to start preparing a good resumé and cover letter.
    d. looking for work in the public sector is a waste of time.

7. The essay suggests that
    a. being in focused vocational training is a demanding occupation and gives students enough of an advantage in the job search.
    b. a sense of future job needs may motivate students toward better performance, better course choices, and the acquisition of suitable experience.
    c. knowing which skills will be needed and what jobs may be available will lead to success.
    d. becoming "the ideal lab technician" or "the perfect accountant" while in college is the only way to ensure job interviews.

8. *True or false?* Professional contacts, college student employment offices, "go-see" interviews, and daily reading of employment ads are enough to

    guarantee a shot at the ideal job. _____

9. The word *crucial* in "documents crucial to creating possible interviews" (paragraph 5) means
   a. special.
   b. justifiable.
   c. reasonable.
   d. important.

10. The word *anticipating* in "without adding the headache of anticipating yet more demands" (paragraph 10) means
   a. awaiting.
   b. worrying about.
   c. denying.
   d. looking ahead to.

● ● ● ● **Discussion Questions**

About Content

1. Why does Professor Maloney recall so vividly the first time he heard the question "Why should we hire you?"

2. The essay's proposed strategy for early focusing on future work is opposed to some traditional thinking which saw college years as a time for discovering yourself and your goals. Do you agree with Maloney's suggestions? What do you think of such "one-track" end-directed approaches to your college experience?

3. What are the early advantages the author sees for the student who is aware of future job needs and possibilities?

4. What resources are available to students within their own colleges?

About Structure

5. The thesis of many essays is found near the beginning or the end. Locate the thesis statement of "Why Should We Hire You?" and write it here.

6. Which method(s) of introduction does the author use in this selection?
   a. Broad statement
   b. Relevance
   c. Anecdote
   d. Contrast

7. What methods of achieving transitions between paragraphs does Maloney use more than once in this selection?
   a. Repetition of keywords
   b. Transitional phrases
   c. Questions followed by explanations
   Find examples of at least three of these, and note them below, with the appropriate paragraph numbers.

   _____ (paragraph _____)
   _____ (paragraph _____)
   _____ (paragraph _____)

About Style and Tone

8. Maloney begins his essay with a highly personal and directly voiced confession containing a comparison between two apparently dissimilar events.

   How does the tone of the opening three paragraphs compare with that of the rest of the essay? What do you learn about the author, and how does what you discover affect your connection with him as a writer? Does it make the information in the essay more or less credible? Why?

9. After the introductory paragraphs, the essay is divided into three sections. How would you subtitle each of these sections?

   1. _____

   2. _____

   3. _____

   What general method of organization do your subtitles seem to suggest?

● ● ● ● Writing Assignments

Assignment 1: Writing a Paragraph

Jim Maloney describes three types of attitudes prevalent among students. Choose the attitude that most closely resembles your own and write a paragraph that defends your position.

Assignment 2: Writing a Paragraph

Put yourself in Jim Maloney's position as he begins his essay. Imagine you have successfully graduated from your current program, have your résumé in hand, and are sitting in a job interview. Now answer "The Question" posed by the essay's title. Start with a specific job you may have in mind or may have read about in the paper. Now, list what you think the employer may be looking for in skills, academic training, and part-time experience. Your paragraph should answer "The Question." You may want to begin with a topic sentence like "Working in fire protection has been a lifelong goal of mine, and I've done a lot of academic and practical preparation to get ready to enter the field." Make use of the groups of details you have listed under the headings above to build up your paragraph.

Assignment 3: Writing an Essay

You are an employer in the year 2009. *You* ask "The Question." You are a human resources officer in a company, and *you* must write the job description to be read by all those eager college graduates.

Write an essay that follows the format of a job description for a position for which your diploma is preparing you. To see examples of these, go to your student services office or look at some periodicals special to your area of study for employers' advertisements. Your mission is to find and persuade that "ideal candidate" that this job is what that person is after. Be as specific in your details as possible. You can't offer "the world on a string"; you have limited salary and promotion possibilities in this uncertain economy. But you are going to be facing hundreds of applicants.

Make an outline similar to the following:

Thesis/Introduction: Omnitech Incorporated is looking for an energetic and ambitious entry-level _____. The successful candidate will have three main qualifications: _____, _____ and especially _____. [Also include a brief company description and approximate salary range, as well as any special requirements, such as a willingness to travel.]

Topic Sentence 1: Your background and education will include

a. _____

b. _____

c. _____

Topic Sentence 2: The skills we are looking for are

a. _____

b. _____

c. _____

Topic Sentence 3: The types of experience we prefer are

a. _____

b. _____

c. _____

Conclude by summarizing your needs, emphasizing that the successful applicant will come close to or exceed all the requirements listed, and stating that only resumés received within a certain time frame will be considered.

LANGUAGE OUT, STYLE IN

Jerry Amernic

A recent television commercial for a major car company had a text screen that read, "First in it's class." Do you see a problem in that sentence? If not, you are not alone. Thousands of North Americans, like the Canadian students Jerry Amernic discusses in this selection, seem oblivious to spelling and grammatical errors. Why did no one at the advertising agency that created the car commercial catch the error? Are literacy skills lower than ever, now that communication technology is more pervasive than ever? Consider what Amernic, who teaches corporate communications at a college, has to say.

1   We all know the most famous line in movies when Rhett Butler said to Scarlett O'Hara, "Frankly, my dear, I don't give a damn," but another Butlerian comment to that same southern belle carries a lot more meaning. "What most people don't seem to realize is that there is just as much money to be made out of the wreckage of a civilization as from the upbuilding of one . . . I'm making my fortune out of the wreckage."

2   Today, as we close out the millennium in a time of prosperity, it's clear that the wreckage of society is coming in many forms, among them the continual erosion of language. Indeed, language skills are at their lowest ebb ever. For the past 30 years, educators have come up with every reason why *not* to teach spelling, grammar, and punctuation in favour of a "holistic" approach to learning. The result is an entire generation of people who aren't up to snuff on basics. Item. Earlier this year, an American TV news announcer—whose name I didn't catch—was commenting on the Senate impeachment hearings, and what she said still boggles my mind. "It's just getting interesting-er and interesting-er."

3   Now she was young and pretty and if those were the only requirements for a TV news announcer in the '90s, terrific, but it would be nice if they knew something about words too. With her hair neatly coiffed and her colours perfectly coordinated for the camera, she had the temerity to coin a comparative right up there with *fascinatinger, remarkabler,* and *tremendouser* and if we made these words superlatives, we'd have *fascinatingest, remarkablest,* and *tremendousest.*

4   She's not alone. Spelling errors and bad grammar are increasingly common in ads and newspapers, never mind the Internet, which is the best place to learn how *not* to spell. Author Tom Wolfe calls the Internet a "great time waster," but he's 68 and what does he know? Maybe more than we think. His colleague, Gore Vidal, once said: "Fewer and fewer young people are addicted to reading. If they don't get into it from the time they are ten or 12 years old, they'll never enjoy reading, and if you don't enjoy reading, there goes literature. Literature is still the most profound of arts, but its prognosis is very bad." Vidal said this five years ago when the Internet was just coming out of the embryo and now that it's a child, our young read even less than they did back in '94, opting to surf instead.

5   In the middle of the last century, Alexis de Tocqueville wrote in **Democracy in America** that the future would result in an egalitarian dismissal of excellence. Well, guess what? The future is here! While companies like Microsoft and IBM keep telling us about the benefits of the Internet, who stops to think that maybe no one is really benefiting—except Microsoft and IBM?

6   Any parent with kids in high school knows that standards aren't what they used to be. I teach writing to public relations students in college, some of them with university degrees and many from other countries. Without fail, the ones with the worst proficiency in English are those who were educated in Canada. Not Jamaica, Algeria or Russia. Canada. A Canadian-educated student up on grammar is a diamond in the rough; it's usually due to a grade 9 English teacher who went against the grain and stressed what the curriculum abandoned.

7   What do you do with 20-year-olds who are just learning the basics? I give them some standard punctuation and the parts of speech, tell them to toss "spellcheck" and "grammarcheck" out the window, and take a look at George Orwell's

"Six Rules of Good Writing." (Some of them have actually heard of Orwell.) Come to think of it, professionals could use these rules too.

1. *'Never use a figure of speech which you are used to seeing in print.'* This brings to mind techies who use "connectivity," "multi-tasking," and "design methodology" when they should just try to speak plain English. **8**

2. *'Never use a long word where a short one will do.'* A popular phrase like "home sweet home" would never have lasted if the original was "residence sweet residence." **9**

3. *'If it's possible to cut out a word, always cut it out.'* Lawyers are especially guilty of breaking this rule. Example. "If the company revises this policy form with respect to policy revisions, endorsements or rules by which the insurance hereunder could be extended or broadened without additional premium charge, such insurance as is afforded hereunder shall be so extended or broadened effective immediately upon approval or acceptance of such revision during the policy by the appropriate insurance supervisory authority." Doesn't it work better this way? "We will automatically give you the benefits of any extension of this policy if the change doesn't require additional cost." By the way, the word count dropped from 59 to 20, so a pox on all those history and English majors who think it's better to use more words. **10**

4. *'Never use the passive where you can use the active.'* This is any politician's pet peeve; be vague and don't take responsibility for anything (and your writing will be as exciting as a Hansard debate). **11**

5. *'Never use a foreign phrase, a scientific word or a jargon word if you can think of an everyday English equivalent.'* (See lawyer example in No. 3). **12**

6. *'Break any of these rules sooner than say anything outright barbarous.'* In other words, a good lead with 18 words is still better than a bad one with 15, but we should still strive to say more with less. **13**

Rules aside, it is also a good idea to study both good and bad communicators. Former U.S. Secretary of State Alexander Haig ("a dialectic fashion at one end of the spectrum"), aspiring presidential candidate Dan Quayle ("We Republicans understand the importance of bondage between a mother and child"), and many of our leaders in Canada (anything Jean Chrétien says) are all poor communicators. Winston Churchill and Martin Luther King, on the other hand, were wonderful. Unfortunately, male cadavers are unyielding of testimony. Huh? Sorry. I mean, "Dead men don't talk." But that's not really true. Their speeches survive. Why not have a look? **14**

● ● ● ● **Reading Comprehension Questions**

1. Which of the following would make the best alternative title for the selection?
   a. Education Neglects Literacy
   b. The End of Excellence
   c. The Internet and Illiteracy
   d. Reading, Writing, and Miscommunication

2. Which sentence best expresses the selection's main point?
   a. Media are responsible for careless language use.
   b. The decline in language skills is symptomatic of wider social disintegration.
   c. The Canadian educational system has left students weak in literacy skills.
   d. Corporate interests work against literacy.

3. Why does Amernic find fault with the American news announcer he mentions in paragraphs 2 and 3?
   a. She is commenting on serious news but is unable to speak correctly.
   b. She is too attractive to be a news commentator.
   c. She is too young to know any better.
   d. She reflects network hiring practices.

4. *True or false?* The Internet, which forces people to read text screens, encourages literacy, according to the author. _____

5. A Canadian student who has a good grasp of grammar probably
   a. learned from students from other countries.
   b. worked hard in English classes.
   c. had a teacher who ignored the standard curriculum.
   d. uses spell-checking and grammar-checking tools regularly.

6. *True or false?* Rules for good writing apply to everyone, not just students. _____

7. We learn from this article that
   a. the author recommends staying up to date on new word uses.
   b. the author recommends breaking grammatical rules occasionally.
   c. the author dislikes those with English degrees.
   d. the author values clear, straightforward writing.

8. We can conclude from this article that Amernic believes that
   a. politicians and public figures are poor communicators.
   b. people can learn from poor and effective communicators.
   c. the only good politician or public figure is a dead one.
   d. Canadian politicians are especially poor communicators.

9. The word *prognosis* in "Literature is still the most profound of the arts, but its prognosis is very bad" (paragraph 4) means
   a. effectiveness.
   b. market share.
   c. history or track record.
   d. future or predictable outlook.

10. The word *cadavers* in "Unfortunately, male cadavers are unyielding of testimony" (paragraph 14) means
    a. corpses.
    b. politicians.
    c. celebrities.
    d. communicators.

● ● ● ● **Discussion Questions**

About Content

1. What does the author mean by a "'holistic' approach to learning" (paragraph 2)? Which subject areas has such an approach affected most? How does your own educational experience compare with what Amernic describes?

2. Why does the author call the Internet "the best place to learn how *not* to spell"? Where, in online communication, do you see proof of this statement?

3. What is the risk if children are not strong readers by a certain age, according to author Gore Vidal? What is potentially lost if this possibility becomes the norm?

4. Who does Amernic see as making their "fortune out of the wreckage" (paragraph 1) of today's society? Why does he say so? Do you agree or not, and why?

5. What are the author's methods for teaching language and writing skills to his students? How do these differ from the way you are learning to write?

About Structure

6. What purposes are served by Amernic's introduction?

7. Where in the selection do you find the clearest statement of the author's thesis? Why does it appear in this position?

8. How many paragraphs does the author use to provide supporting evidence for his first point about the decline in language-use standards? How many examples does he provide in these paragraphs? Which are most effective, and why?

About Style and Tone

9. Amernic includes George Orwell's "Six Rules of Good Writing" in their entirety, with his own commentary added beneath each rule. What is the effect of including the full text of Orwell's rules in a short selection? Should Amernic have paraphrased the rules? Does the author's commentary on each rule lessen the effectiveness of the rules or explain their meaning more fully?

10. Does the author's use of a slightly comic tone strengthen or weaken his point? Why?

● ● ● ● **Writing Assignments**

Assignment 1: Writing a Paragraph

In 2003, Bruce Sterling wrote an article called "10 Technologies That Deserve to Die," about pieces of technology that are annoying or ineffective. Try your own, language-based version of this topic: "Three [or some other number] Words That Deserve to Disappear."

To begin, make a list of words that particularly annoy you. Then consider the *reasons why* these words should disappear. Come up with three words that fit into a single category, such as "words that are impossible to spell," "words that don't mean anything," "trendy words I don't understand," or "words that always upset me." Explain, with examples, why that word really fits the category into which you have placed it. Your topic sentence could be something like one of these.

When people are dating, they use words that should disappear forever from the English language because of the arguments these words cause.

There are three words that never mean what they say in advertisements: "new," "free," and "improved."

Assignment 2: Writing a Paragraph

"Internetspeak" or "chat language" is an English teacher's nightmare. Is there a place in the development of English for Internet-based usages such as "IMO" or "BTW," or for "chat code" spellings like "u r the best—c u b4 tuesday" that ignore case and spelling rules completely?

Write a paragraph in which you argue that certain specific Internet spelling and language changes should or should not be considered acceptable written English. If you argue for these new spellings and word patterns, in which situations would they be appropriate, and why? Would everyone who reads text written this way understand it? Why is it preferable to current standard English?

Assignment 3: Writing an Essay

Writing well is the subject of this book as well as of Amernic's article. All of us, at one time or another, in some language, and for some reason, have written something that we feel is very good. This piece of writing could be a note on a birthday card to a friend or parent, a story you wrote as a child, or a letter of application for college or a job.

Write a narrative-style essay in which you relate the story of one piece of writing of which you are proud. Your thesis statement could involve what you learned from writing it, what it means to you, or what the effect of your writing was on the person who read it. In your opening paragraph, set up the background or context needed for readers to understand your point. Your body paragraphs could describe the circumstances prompting you to create your piece of writing, the process of writing it, or the significance of doing so. Here is one student's partly completed outline.

Thesis Statement: My first résumé might be the best thing I have ever written.

Topic Sentence 1: I wanted to get a good summer job, so I knew my résumé needed to be impressive.
—never had jobs where I needed one before
—wanted a job where I wasn't doing physical labour

Topic Sentence 2: I had no idea how to lay out or write a résumé, so it took a lot of work.
—I nearly paid for a résumé service to write one for me
—I wanted to prove to myself I could do it
—Learned a lot about formatting documents

Topic Sentence 3: It worked—I got a job at my local cable station.
—the interviewer complimented me on my résumé
—have to write memos sometimes, so the practice was good?

Assignment 4: Writing an Essay Using Internet Research

The Internet is actually a source of some good information about writing well. Use Google or another search engine to look up a few webpages about good writing. Try keywords such as *rules for good writing, writing well,* and other combinations, until you find at least five pages whose main content is how to write effectively. Good sites include http://www.uniquecritique.net/AspiringWriters.html and http://palc.sd40.bc.ca/palc/StudentWriting/tipsforgood.htm, and there are many others, including some sponsored by colleges and universities.

Choose two sites about writing well and write an essay that compares them, based on their usefulness to you. In your prewriting, begin with two columns, one for each site. List the items you found most or least helpful on the sites. In a second stage of prewriting, add notes that explain why you chose your helpful or unhelpful list items. Next, for your outline, select three comparable items for each site, so that the body of your essay is balanced.

THE MANY FORMS OF LITERACY

Silver Donald Cameron

> We often think of the term "literacy" to mean the ability to read and write well enough to cope with modern life. In this piece, author and sailor Silver Donald Cameron, extends the word to include the knowledge of any useful skill. To Cameron, the ability to understand anything from sail-making to music-making are worthy of our respect, and he shows through examples he has encountered. As you read this selection, consider the many other skills, and particularly traditional ones, that people learn and maintain from one generation to the next.

This year, I want to learn to use a sewing machine. A man named John Tompkins, who lives—well, he lives somewhere in the world—has posted the plans for a small Chinese junk sail on an Internet discussion group. I'd like to make the sail and try it out on a dinghy.   **1**

The junk rig has many advantages. It carries no jib, so there's no casting off and hauling in when the boat tacks. It has no shrouds or stays, so the sail can swing freely in any direction. Because part of the sail is ahead of the mast, a junk sail doesn't slam around as a normal mainsail does.   **2**

3   The sail is ridged with full-length "battens," strips of wood that make the sail look like a fat ladder. To reduce sail you simply lower it until the second batten rests on the first.

4   Joshua Slocum considered this "the most convenient boat rig in the whole world."

5   You can lay out a junk sail using stakes driven in to your lawn. No fancy cambered shapes are needed, and because no part of the sail is particularly heavily stressed, it can be made of almost anything—plastic tarp, woven matting, cheap canvas, whatever. Chinese sailors sometimes cruised along with great holes in the sails. It didn't seem to matter much.

6   But to make even a simple sail, I have to learn sewing. That's fine; any sailor should be able to sew. Actually, almost anyone should be able to sew. It's a basic competency, like driving a nail, driving a car, doing arithmetic or reading. I've come to think of it as a form of literacy, part of an impossible lifelong project to become fully literate.

7   I don't want to empty the word "literacy" of meaning, but it's a wonderful word. It doesn't suggest an ability to use language brilliantly, but only to use it capably, to understand language well enough that it becomes a useful tool. Numeracy is the ability to use mathematics in the same basic way.

8   But what do we call the ability to manage money competently—to make a budget, do household bookkeeping, understand percentages and the basic principles of investment? We have no word for that essential life skill. I'd call it financial literacy.

9   What about a citizen's understanding of government and politics—how laws come into being, how various forces influence government, how parties function and whose interests they serve? Is there a better term than "political literacy?"

10   Cape Bretoners place a high value on musical literacy—the ability to listen to music intelligently, to know scales and chords, to play a few tunes on an instrument or two, to hear the stories that music tells. A deeper musical literacy includes the ability to read music—not just to know that the note in one space is A and the one in the next space is C, but to read the page and hear the music. I've seen David MacIsaac pick up a book of jigs and reels, lift it close to his good eye and read his way down the page, humming the tune as he goes. He reads music as easily as you read these words.

11   Small communities often suffer greatly from a lack of organizational literacy—knowing how an organization is structured, what a board does, what an executive does, how to ensure that the organization does what it's designed for. An effective organization is a powerful tool. A badly run organization is a swamp into which good ideas sink without a trace, not unlike a royal commission.

12   Most of us are woefully short of scientific literacy, an understanding of how the world is put together—from atoms to acid, from tectonics to transistors, from psoriasis to psychosis. The forms of literacy make a list that never ends. The literacy of the household, the ability to change a fuse or a furnace filter, defrost a fridge, prime a water pump. Visual literacy, gustatory literacy, media literacy, the literacy of the garden, the literacy of the forest.

I seek the literacy of the sea and the sky, too—an ability to read the waves and **13** the wind and the clouds, grasping both what has created them and what they can tell about the future. And the literacy of seamanship, knowing how to navigate, handle a vessel in a seaway, tie a knot that won't let go.

Literacy is not mastery. It is simply competence—an understanding of the **14** subject and the tools that allows a person to function adequately. A diligent person can achieve mastery in one or two fields during a lifetime. But literacy is a lifetime undertaking—and nothing in the world is more stimulating and absorbing.

• • • • • Reading Comprehension Questions

1. Which of the following would be the best alternative title for the selection?
   a. What We Need to Know
   b. Give Knowledge Its Due Respect
   c. About Sailing
   d. How to Sew

2. Which sentence best expresses the main idea of the reading selection?
   a. The ability to be competent in any basic skill should be given the same importance as verbal literacy.
   b. Everyone must know how to sew.
   c. Sailors must know how to read.
   d. Everyone should know how to read music.

3. The author wishes to know how to sew because
   a. he needs new clothes.
   b. he lives in Cape Breton.
   c. sewing is a necessary skill in sailing.
   d. he admires people who sew.

4. *True or false?* The author argues that as a society we do not value the acquisition of the variety of skills that we need throughout life. _____

5. The author feels that people generally consider literacy as
   a. only the ability to read and write.
   b. only important for education.
   c. the ability to calculate mathematical problems.
   d. unimportant for sailors, musicians, and homemakers.

6. The author admires people who
   a. can produce works of art or music.
   b. can sew their own sails.
   c. understand business and organizational structure.
   d. are competent in diverse skills and understandings.

7. The author implies that
   a. our education fails us in many important ways.
   b. he is a friend of Joshua Slocum.
   c. he is going to build a Chinese junk.
   d. most people are self-sufficient.

8. The author suggests that
   a. small towns run better than cities.
   b. girls should be required to take home economics in schools.
   c. people do not need to be expert in everything, but should become competent at all life skills.
   d. there is too much focus on science and technology in schools.

9. From this writing, we can infer that the author
   a. is a sailor.
   b. is a musician.
   c. is a teacher.
   d. is a business manager.

10. Even if you are not familiar with Cape Breton society, you can infer that "jigs and reels" (paragraph 10) refer to
    a. types of fish.
    b. types of music.
    c. local delicacies.
    d. types of sails.

11. The word *woefully* in the sentence "Most of us are woefully short of. . . ." (paragraph 12) means
    a. adequately.
    b. dependently.
    c. wilfully.
    d. sorrowfully.

● ● ● ● **Discussion Questions**

About Content

1. What were the reasons that the author started to think about the basic skills that people do or do not have?
2. What does the author admire about other people? Why?
3. What worries the author about the limited competencies, or "literacies" that he observes throughout society?
4. When, according to the author, should people learn the various skills and abilities that they need?

About Structure

5. The author introduces his selection by focusing on sewing. Sewing serves as
   a. a representation of all necessary skills.
   b. a lost skill.
   c. a skill that is respected only as a women's skill.
   d. an example of a skill that is no longer needed.

6. Where does the author state his definition of "literacy"? Is that an effective technique, or should it be introduced elsewhere?

About Style and Tone

7. How does the author draw the audience from the specific skill of learning to sew, to his broader interpretations of the *literacies*?

8. Why does the author go into so much detail about the form and purpose of the Chinese junk sail?

● ● ● ● **Writing Assignments**

Assignment 1: Writing a Paragraph

Most of us appreciate learning how to do something that isn't absolutely required of us. Children, for example, generally feel special if they are included in a process that is significant to an elder in their lives. This ranges from cooking, to fishing, to sports, to music, to almost any specialized activity. Consider a skill or ability that you gained—at any age—through the direction of someone special to you. Write a paragraph that explains the process by which you became interested in, developed the basic skills for, and ultimately mastered that "literacy." Use a topic sentence that describes the specific skill, and the meaning it holds for you. Describe a single aspect of the process of that skill development that you followed in each of your supporting reasons. Give adequate details and specific examples for each of those subtopics, so that your audience can follow and "see" the process, as well as your reaction to it, along with your description. Conclude with a sentence that restates the original topic sentence, emphasizing the value of this special ability.

Assignment 2: Writing a Paragraph

Is there an ability or skill which you feel has been neglected in your education or upbringing but in which you would like to become at least "literate"? Identify not only the ability, but also the process through which you could start to acquire a new ability. For example, you could perhaps learn to sew by asking a friend or relative who is known for his or her sewing skills. Or, perhaps you wish to take a class in photography or scuba diving, or even prefer learning 'on the job' by working in a vineyard, as suggestions.

Write a paragraph where you define an art, skill or type of ability you wish to learn, and then describe the process anyone could use to acquire it. Construct this paragraph with attention to the way in which someone can attain mastery, rather than by simply describing the skill, itself. Start with a topic sentence that states the skill, its importance, and a general direction a person would need to take to pursue it. For example, an appropriate topic sentence might be, "Taking a community education program in digital photography is an easy and fun way to learn how to get the most out of your camera." Then, divide the learning process into logical steps.

The steps for this topic might include the way to access such a program, the subject matter of the course, and the ways in which someone would benefit aside from the learning of photography. Ensure that these steps follow an order that leads your audience to understand both the process and your point. Support each with the appropriate details and specific examples to make the entire process clear. Conclude with a statement that restates the topic, and perhaps gives your audience some encouragement to follow through with your idea.

Assignment 3: Writing an Essay Using Research

Cameron has identified that people—and even communities—do not always learn how to manage the aspects of their lives that they need the most. This could be because education systems determine what seems necessary, for us, according to the time, place, and philosophies that these systems represent (or must be accountable to). For example, public education systems, now, may emphasize "literacies" in communication, finance, and technology, but perhaps neglect others in general "life skills," the arts, physical development, ethics, or a host of other areas. While boards of education probably do not wish to eliminate so many types of learning, they may not be supported in any attempts to provide more than the "bare bones" of education as determined by significant agents of power. Write an essay that identifies a necessary type of education which you feel is not adequately addressed in the systems you know. You may need to limit your topic to a specific age range or form of institution.

Determine where present institutions may lack focus, and choose three disciplines—in addition to traditional literacy and numeracy—which should be included in a standard educational program. The focus you state will be a part of the thesis statement and the three areas to be included will each define a supporting reason. In order to make your idea clear, be sure to explain each reason fully; each should include a rationale, a method, and discussion of particular aspects that must be taken into consideration. Research to find information about effective programs, elsewhere, being careful to save all reference information. Illustrate each with specific details and examples—from research where possible—to avoid confusion and to heighten interest in your plan. Finally, conclude your essay by referring back to the type of education that you have promoted, while finishing with an idea for your audience to consider.

WEBSITE DESIGN: KEEP YOUR REAL AUDIENCE IN MIND

Wayne MacPhail

As you have been reading this text, you have learned the principle that a writer must write with the audience in mind, and provide the specific details that the audience needs and wants. Wayne MacPhail extends this principle to website design, and shows how any successful website must use the same ideals. Too often, MacPhail reports, website designers become preoccupied by organizational details that do not matter to an audience; or, they may clutter their sites without thinking what the audience will even notice. MacPhail cleverly uses a hypothetical audience, elements of research, and his own experience, to help young website developers remember the most important principle of website design.

1   Any time I start an online project I imagine a very specific user: the single mother. She's busy, distracted, multi-tasking, goal oriented and short on time. So, she's like most of us, but with more pressure and baby food stains. Let's call her Wendy.

One of the biggest mistakes organizations make when creating online content is imagining that users like Wendy will give their content their undivided attention. In fact, Wendy has precious little, if any, time to spend online. So, let's pretend you were designing a single mom site for Wendy. Here are some things to understand.   **2**

First, you can't give Wendy any more time and certainly can't give her any more time to spend online. That means that if Wendy is already spending some fraction of her online time looking at single parent sites, you'll need to rob time from those sites. If you're no different from those other sites, chances are slim that Wendy will be making repeat visits.   **3**

Second, Wendy's goal-oriented and on a mission. If you can't show her that your site is mission critical, she will bail. *Eye-scan studies* carried out by the Poynter Institute show that users like Wendy rapidly scan the text of a webpage in search of words and phrases that match their goal. If they don't find them within seconds, they move on.   **4**

Third, Wendy's distracted. She's not giving your page all her attention. She may be worrying about her bank balance, is probably sleep-deprived and is wondering when the baby will wake up or if the repairman will show. So, if your site's not clearly laid out with words that are familiar to her, she will feel lost and frustrated.   **5**

Many years ago I saw a button in the MIT bookstore that read: "Know thy users, for they are not you." This remains great advice. Wendy doesn't work for your non-profit, doesn't use the jargon you do, and could care less about what your org chart looks like, what your stretch goals are or which sub-department is responsible for which deliverables. That's all noise to her.   **6**

And the committee meetings where you all fight over what Wendy would like to see on your homepage? That's all noise too. Here's an insider secret. Web designers call those "make it more blue" sessions. As in, "Jeez, I really like that page, but could you make it more blue, my husband loves blue." Unless your husband is Wendy, who cares what he thinks? Nobody but the thousands of companies that make web content decisions on the say-so of a bad focus group of one.   **7**

All of this is common sense. But, over the past 20 years I've seen client after client act like they're maladroit lumberjacks designing feminine hygiene products. They're not interested in talking to anyone and can't imagine the world through anything but their inwardly focused lens. As a result the sites they produce are ham-handed and as off-target as a birchbark tampon.   **8**

The reality is, we're all Wendys. We want clear, concise websites that let us achieve our goals, are resonant with our tasks and let us get in and get out quickly, the way a well-designed convenience store does. Well, that's what we want until we get into a committee room to design a site, then all that practically and common sense gets tossed in the blue box and politics, egos and dumbassed thinking trumps good user-centric design.   **9**

Let me give you an example. A few years back I was redesigning the International microsite (with a focus on Chinese students) for a college in Toronto. Before we began the process I invited a dozen Chinese students in for pizza and we talked about how they made the decision to pick the college. We expected we would hear about how they wanted to know about marks, the college's reputation, the visa application process, etc. Instead we made two important discoveries.   **10**

11   First, it was the students' parents, not the students, who made the real decisions. Second, those parents, who often had weak English skills, didn't care as much about reputation and marks as they did about one main worry: "Will my child be safe?"

12   That learning made us completely rethink the way we designed the site.

13   We had been completely wrong about who the audience was and what they cared about. The only way we discovered that was by talking to the target audience. In the time it took, the committee would have only managed to decide on takeout and would have been halfway through an argument about what shade of blue the site should be.

14   Listening to folks inside your organization who think they know how to design sites because they browse them makes about as much sense as letting someone operate on you because they're big *Scrubs* fans. Instead, pay attention to your Wendys.

● ● ● ● ●   **Reading Comprehension Questions**

1. Which of the following would be the best alternative title for the selection?
   a. Website Design: The Audience is Always Right
   b. Wendy's Website Design Tips
   c. How to Become a Website Designer
   d. Website Design: Always Use Blue

2. Which sentence best expresses the main idea of the selection?
   a. Single mothers have too much to do.
   b. It takes intensive training to be a good website designer.
   c. Most successful websites are designed by committees.
   d. A website must appeal to the audience it intends to attract.

3. Why has the audience used the imaginary profile of a single mother, Wendy, to illustrate his point?

4. *True or false?* The principles of good website design parallel the principles of good college writing? _____

5. According to the author, what is the most serious mistake that organizations and their designers make when designing a website?

6. The author implies that the average person who accesses a website is
   a. very busy.
   b. a single mother.
   c. happy to browse through many pages on a site.
   d. interested in understanding all aspects of the organization which hosts the site.

7. In this selection, the author suggests that his experience shows that many website designers
   a. understand which details are important to include in their sites.
   b. may neglect the audience's point of view in their enthusiasm to impress.
   c. should work with a committee.
   d. use the colour blue too much.

8. This selection is directed to an audience of
   a. single mothers.
   b. committees.
   c. students.
   d. website designers.

9. In the phrase, "over the past 20 years I've seen client after client act like they're maladroit lumberjacks" (paragraph 8), the word *maladroit* means
   a. rude.
   b. burly.
   c. clumsy.
   d. dirty.

10. By "user-centric design" (paragraph 9), the author means
    a. content that is created so for the user's ease.
    b. content that is created to attract new users.
    c. content that is created to generate advertising.
    d. content that is blue.

● ● ● ● **Discussion Questions**

About Content

1. What is the main reason that MacPhail has written this piece of advice?
2. Why does the author use the character of Wendy to illustrate his point?
3. In what ways are the author's guidelines for good website design similar to the guidelines for good paragraph writing?
4. What does the author feel preoccupies many new website designers?

About Structure

5. This reading deals with the process a good website designer should use to consider the purpose and audience for which a site is to be designed. He does this by revealing issues that cause websites to be poorly designed. Where and how does the author make this clear?
6. Which sentence best identifies the main idea of the reading?
   a. With a little practice, anyone can be a great website designer.
   b. A committee is necessary in order to produce a great website.
   c. Website designers often lose site of the purpose and audience to which they are directing their sites.
   d. Blue is the best colour to use in a website background.
7. Where and how does the author clarify his ideas by using a clear logical order? Which transition words or phrases does he use?

About Style and Tone

8. The tone of this piece is that of an instructor advising a group of new students. In what ways does MacPhail show his authority to instruct?
9. How is the title a clear example of the principles that the author presents?

• • • ● Writing Assignments

Assignment 1: Writing a Paragraph

Have you ever designed a website? If not, have you ever discovered a website that particularly interested you for its design or style? Describe such a site (or, conversely, one that you thought was particularly poor), by identifying the overall characteristic of the site that impressed you most. State this feature as your topic sentence, and then describe it further with three reasons that support your point. Illustrate your reasons with vivid and distinct details, using specific examples for each. Conclude by stating, again, what was remarkable—positively or negatively—about that website.

Assignment 2: Writing a Paragraph

This article focuses on the principles of good website design; however, these principles may also apply to other processes. Consider another act or activity where you could instruct a specific audience, as the author has, not only in how to follow a process, but also in how to avoid poor results. Use an objective tone in the third person so that your paragraph will be respected as carefully reasoned and credible. You may wish to make your point, as the author does, by developing a typical scenario that depicts your process. For example, you may start a paragraph about digital photography with a line such as, "The first mistake that new photographers make, is to expect the camera to 'see' with the same eyes as they do." You would then support your paragraph with three ways in which the camera's sights differ from the user's expectations. Supply complete details to explain exactly what you mean, and use specific examples to further clarify your ideas. Finish your paragraph by reminding your audience of the importance of your overall point.

Assignment 3: Writing an Essay

The article reviews the importance of website design in an organization's aim to attract and audience and to promote its message. What, though, is the role of the Internet, in promoting any message in the twenty-first century? According to the Canadian scholar, Marshal McLuhan, "The medium is the message." McLuhan's principle is that people will learn, not according to what they want to learn, but according to how it is presented to them. In that case, does the Internet alter the type of learning that is available to Canadians, and in any way enhance, or taint, it?

Write a standard essay that discusses the role of the Internet in the dissemination of information and the way in which people understand the world, today. You may choose to write an essay that describes the process of sending or receiving information—from emails to websites—or the process of controlling information. Alternately, you could write an essay that compares and contrasts the way in which people expect to find information now, as opposed to how it would be done if no Internet was available. In either case, construct a thesis that states the value—or hazards—of the role of the Internet, and then support your thesis with three clear reasons. Be sure to follow a logical order that will maintain the clarity of your discussion, and illustrate the exact meanings you intend. Use specific examples from authentic Internet sources, where possible, and maintain a list of sources that you use. (You may document these according to your instructor's wishes, but even if you are not required to write in a research format, you should always be able to refer to the sites you have used.) Conclude by referring back to your thesis, and by reminding your audience of your main reaction to the role of the Internet, today.

Human Groups and Society

HAVE YOU SEEN MY MISSING MATH GENE?

Tony Wong

> One of Canada's favourite stereotypes is that of the Asian math and computer whiz. As high-school and college students, we automatically assume that the Asian student next to us will get an A in Accounting and can probably program our PC to do everything but cook dinner. All nations and peoples are prone to stereotyping; it's one of the ways in which our brains learn to classify and sort information. However, when we apply these categorizing principles to people, the results can range from silly social mistakes to deep-seated and harmful prejudices that lead to movements such as neo-Nazism and apartheid. Tony Wong, a reporter for *The Toronto Star*, takes a light-hearted look at the Canadian perception of the typical Asian: its origins in economic necessity and its effects on him and his non-typical brother and cousin.

1   It seems every year I am asked to speak to Asian kids about alternate careers.

2   An alternate career for an Asian child being defined as anything but a doctor, dentist, pharmacist, accountant or any vocation requiring addition.

3   I am uniquely qualified to give these seminars, it seems, because I must be one of the few Asians, according to programs like *60 Minutes* (which once did a segment on why so many Asians are taking over the medical schools of America), who cannot add. Or subtract or multiply.

4   I also stink at chess and have trouble turning on my computer.

5   To this day I have not figured out how to properly program my VCR, although I have cleverly got rid of the flashing 12 o'clock sign by pasting electrical tape over it. So you see, I am not bereft of resources.

6   If there is a math gene for Chinese folk, I have somehow missed out.

7   Philippe Rushton would have a field day with me, and I have not even got into the issue of Asian versus Black versus Caucasian penis size, which has been—for goodness sake—the topic of the good professor's latest research. I already have enough of a complex, thank you.

8   But do not despair for me, for I have been living a fulfilling life despite my handicap, although my job has been made more difficult with China's win this summer at, what else, the International Math Olympiad, where, to top things off, Canada's top-gun was Chinese Canadian.

This leaves folks like me in a precarious situation, burdened with trying to lead Asian youth out of their computer and slide rule-induced stupor.   **9**

I remember one year where Metro Councillor Olivia Chow and I were dragged out as mathematically challenged role models for a workshop on alternate career skills for teens.   **10**

Olivia, who can actually add but faked it for my benefit, seemed doubly qualified for this job as she started life as an artist before becoming a high-powered politician.   **11**

For the occasion, I wrote a skit to demonstrate the pressures faced by Asian kids at home. Olivia kindly agreed to play my mom, while I played a bratty kid who wants to be an artist. I gave Olivia all the good lines.   **12**

Olivia: "Jimmy Li got into pharmacy. His mother said he got scholarship, too."   **13**

Me: "That's nice, Mom. I think I'll continue practising my Spider-Man doodle. You never know when Marvel will call."   **14**

Actually my own segue into the writing life wasn't so difficult. My brother Victor inadvertently paved the way when he decided to be an artist.   **15**

When my mother got a look at his work, which included the influences of Matisse and Rubens with a little *Playboy* thrown in, she was not amused.   **16**

She seemed relieved when I told her I just wanted to be a starving writer.   **17**

She changed her tune, though, after a visit to the Barnes exhibition at the Art Gallery of Ontario.   **18**

"That looks like something your brother would draw," she would exclaim seeing Matisse's dance of life which consists of a bunch of fat nudes frolicking. It was then she figured that my poor brother had not been "marketed" properly, especially after seeing that a bunch of naked people dancing in a park by a dead guy could fetch so much money. Moreover, my brother is alive to boot.   **19**

It reminded me of the time my cousin Walter, a photographer who had shot covers for all the top international fashion magazines, including *Vogue, Elle* and *Cosmopolitan,* was told by his mother that he shouldn't have a studio upstairs where no one could see him.   **20**

After all, suppose someone wanted to get a passport picture? He would lose business. It was the ever-pragmatic Asian philosophy at work. Don't forget the walk-by traffic. At that time, national media profiles pegged his daily fee at $50,000. But, as my aunt would say, you never know when another $9.95 might come in handy.   **21**

So you see, there can be life after math. Diversity is the name of the game. And stereotypes, like bad clichés, just won't hold any water—at least if you don't subscribe to them.   **22**

● ● ● ● Reading Comprehension Questions

1. Which of the following would be the best alternative title for this article?
   a. Adding Up Those Accurate Asians
   b. A Writer of a Different Colour
   c. Asians and the Arts
   d. Sticky Stereotypes and Tricky Truisms

2. Which sentence best expresses the main idea of the selection?
   a. Asian students are driven by their families into science-based careers.
   b. Tony Wong comes from an artistically gifted family.
   c. People of any racial group are prone to vary in their gifts and abilities.
   d. Asians are basically practical in their view of valuable life skills.

3. The stereotype of Asians as gifted only in areas of technical expertise
   a. is part of our social fabric and further exploited by media and academics.
   b. is probably true because of Chinese students' abilities in math and medicine.
   c. is a product of the Western drive for economic success.
   d. makes life almost impossible for Chinese young people gifted in other areas.

4. The author found that starting a career as a writer was less difficult because
   a. he was mathematically challenged anyway.
   b. his brother had already become an artist.
   c. his mother thought it was better than being a cartoonist.
   d. there wasn't much Asian competition in the field.

5. Wong's aunt believed that his cousin should have a street-level office
   a. because her own view of economics suggested that he might miss out on daily customers.
   b. because she wanted him to take passport pictures.
   c. because she didn't know what he really did for a living.
   d. because upstairs offices are bad for business.

6. The author implies that
   a. he feels threatened by Chinese abilities in technical fields.
   b. Asian students are perhaps not encouraged toward less practical careers.
   c. he is so inept that he had to become a writer to explain himself.
   d. a sense of humour is not appreciated in Asian cultures.

7. *True or false?* Wong's mother's main objection to Victor Wong's career as an artist was that he painted mostly naked women. _____

8. Paragraphs 19 to 21 imply that Tony Wong
   a. finds the Asian culture too money-conscious.
   b. thinks his mother's values are out of touch with reality.
   c. respects the survival instinct in his culture but sees the irony in it.
   d. envies those more successful than he is.

9. The word *precarious* in "This leaves folks like me in a precarious situation, burdened with trying to lead Asian youth out of their computer and slide rule-induced stupor" (paragraph 9) means
   a. uncertain.
   b. scary.
   c. impossible.
   d. overworked.

10. The word *pragmatic* in "It was the ever-pragmatic Asian philosophy at work" (paragraph 21) means
    a. changing.
    b. working.
    c. stubborn.
    d. realistic.

● ● ● ● ● **Discussion Questions**

About Content

1. What careers does Tony Wong give as those expected of Asian students? Why?

2. What reasons does the author offer for being "uniquely qualified" to give seminars on "alternate careers" for Asian students? How serious is he, do you think? Why?

3. What made Wong's mother decide that his brother's choice of career was not so stupid? What did she decide was the problem with his being an artist?

About Structure

4. Wong's article has three sections, as well as an introductory and a concluding paragraph. What subtitles would you give each of these sections? Identify each section with your choice of appropriate subtitles.

   Paragraphs 2 to ＿＿＿＿＿＿
   Paragraphs ＿＿＿＿＿＿ to 14
   Paragraphs 15 to ＿＿＿＿＿＿

   Why have you chosen your subtitles? What is the subject of each of these sections? How does each section advance Wong's main idea?

5. In which paragraph do you find the author's thesis? Why has he chosen this position for his thesis?

6. What is the keyword in the author's thesis statement? What examples in the essay support this keyword? Which examples seem to contradict the idea implied by this word?

About Style and Tone

7. Tony Wong is evidently a writer with a sense of humour. Some techniques natural to the comic writer or comedian include the following: exaggeration, understatement or deflation, unlikely comparisons, shifts in vocabulary levels, and the use of surprising punch lines.

   Find examples of four of these comic techniques in the article, and list the phrases after the paragraph number in which you find the example required.

   Exaggeration ＿＿＿＿＿＿＿＿＿＿＿＿＿＿＿＿ (paragraph ＿＿＿＿)

   Understatement ＿＿＿＿＿＿＿＿＿＿＿＿＿＿＿ (paragraph ＿＿＿＿)

   Shift in vocabulary level ＿＿＿＿＿＿＿＿＿＿ (paragraph ＿＿＿＿)

   Unexpected punch line ＿＿＿＿＿＿＿＿＿＿＿ (paragraph ＿＿＿＿)

8. What type of publication would you expect to find this selection in: a weekly magazine or daily newspaper, a scholarly journal on sociology, or a text on race relations in Canada?

What do the word choices, subject matter, and tone suggest about the audience Wong is writing for?

● ● ● ● **Writing Assignments**

Assignment 1: Writing a Paragraph

Tony Wong feels he is missing a math gene. Write a descriptive paragraph about some aspect of *you* that seems to be missing, dormant, or undiscovered. Your paragraph may be humorous or straightforward in approach.

Assignment 2: Writing a Paragraph

People often surprise us because they don't always conform to the stereotypes or judgments we have developed about them on the basis of appearances. Either their behaviour or their reasons for their actions do not follow our preconceived notions. Tony Wong's mother and his aunt are examples of apparent adherence to the Asian stereotype of practicality, but both manage to adapt to their offspring's radical career choices. Wong himself, his brother, his cousin Victor, and the politician Olivia Chow are contradictions to the stereotypical Asian.

Write a paragraph about a person whose appearance completely misled you (or someone else) at first. Describe the person's appearance and characteristics in some detail, and contrast them with what you found to be the person's underlying character. Be sure to be precise in your choice of details and to contrast them with details that relate to your first impressions, so that the reader will follow your discovery of the difference between appearance and reality.

You might want to begin with a topic sentence like this one, which gives a remembered first or dominant impression of the subject, based solely on what the writer first observed.

> Jim's three earrings, Metallica T-shirt, ripped black jeans, and shaved head had him marked as one mean punk in my mind, and the silver skull on his belt buckle did nothing to change my opinion.

Conclude your paragraph with a summary of what you learned and a statement of your current feelings about this person.

Assignment 3: Writing an Essay

Tony Wong mentions in his seventh paragraph a controversial professor from an Ontario university, Philippe Rushton. Rushton studies racial and genetic patterns in human beings. His findings about human intelligence have prompted criticism of his supposed racist views. When carried to an extreme, or when misapplied, judgments or findings based on race, religion, or culture are always questionable and have led to horrendous social problems, persecution, and such atrocities as Nazism and terrorist activities around the world.

Although stereotyping or classifying is indeed a standard part of the process by which humans learn to distinguish one thing from another and to group similar ideas, it is very dangerous when applied to people. Most Canadian students attend colleges and universities where diversity in the classroom is the rule, not the exception. Moreover, our laws and college charters guarantee the rights of all Canadians. A fast glance at any major Canadian city's newspaper will, unfortunately, disabuse us of the notion that we have created the "perfect egalitarian society"; various racial groups continue to labour under stereotypes, and factions that support racist views continue to form.

Write an essay that tackles an experience of your own with stereotyping, whether on your part or as applied to you by someone else. Make use of the cause-and-effect format for your essay. What caused you or someone else to make a premature judgment, and what were the consequences? You may choose a light-hearted approach, as Tony Wong did, or you may treat the subject seriously.

Opening sentences in the paragraph that includes your thesis statement could be like these.

> Because I am a female student of Italian descent, people sometimes assume I must be a good cook, interested in babies, and intensely religious. Are they in for some surprises!
>
> When I registered in my first course in chemical engineering and answered to the name "Littlefeather, Jim" on the attendance list, the student in the next chair raised his hand to me and said, "How." I said, "I don't know; do you?"
>
> Arriving from Beijing was difficult enough, but registering in a new school system, dealing with an unfamiliar language, and trying to understand the other students' behaviour all seemed just too much.

THE IMPORTANCE OF COOKING DINNER

Nancy Eng

> Do you remember the first time you tried to cook a meal? Cooking is never as easy as recipes or relatives make it seem. Food, its preparation, and the rituals of the table are important parts of our daily social and family lives. In the twenty-first century, it seems that everyone is interested in food, if not in cooking. But despite the advances of feminist advice, statistics show that most cooking is still done by women and is regarded (other than in the elevated realm of the great chefs) as part of essential female knowledge and skills. Nancy Eng, an English student at the University of British Columbia, takes issue with the idea that the honourable womanly place in the kitchen is somehow genetically inherited.

This was not to be just any dinner. This meal was to be a part of my rites of passage, another step into womanhood. Like the first pair of pantyhose, the first teetering steps on high heels, and the first taste of lipstick, an entire dinner prepared on   1 one's own has always been an initiation into the adult female ranks. Despite all the advances women have made in this male-dominated world, despite the inspiration of the Sandra Day O'Connors, the Pat Carneys, and the Sally Rides, woman continues to carry certain limiting connotations. When one thinks of women, terms like *gentle, maternal,* and *domestic* still spring even to some of the most liberal minds. No matter how capable a woman is in the work world, it is still difficult to shake the time-honoured tradition of Mom baking cookies for her family, or Grandma fixing turkey for the clan. So, as I entered the kitchen that fateful day of my fifteenth year, armed with *The Joy of Cooking* and enshrouded in a "Kiss the Cook" apron, I was ready to tackle green salad, roast chicken, and chocolate mousse. I rolled up my sleeves, took a deep breath, and went to work.

2   The salad was easy enough. For that, I didn't even need to consult the cooking bible. I managed to wash and tear up a quantity of lettuce, and I threw in a variety of appropriately coloured vegetables so that my bowl more or less resembled green salad. This accomplished, I moved on with an air of confidence to the next course.

3   The chicken sat in all its slimy glory on a roasting pan, awaiting an expert touch. Cold and slippery in my hands, it was placid and cooperative as I dangled it awkwardly from one of its slick little limbs, trying to decide which end was up. I viewed my fowl friend from several angles, puzzled as to where exactly its head had been during its previous life. The directions called for stuffing the animal, so I located my box of Stouffer's Stovetop and contemplated where it belonged. Flipping the chicken around a few more times, I finally discovered an opening. I peered into its damp darkness, feeling slightly perverse about my actions, and hoping the chicken didn't mind this kind of intrusion. I couldn't see how I was going to hold that small hole open wide enough to fill the creature up, until I spied a funnel hanging invitingly from its hook in the cupboard. Inserting the funnel's tip into the bird, I poured in the contents of the box of stuffing, not realizing the dry, crumbly mess I was forcing in was meant to be cooked first. The chicken soon bulged slightly with uncooked stuffing and the innards, which I had not bothered to remove. Pleased with its bumpy plumpness, I went on to basting.

4   "Butter outer chicken generously," the book directed. I partially unwrapped a cold block of margarine, hoping such a substitution wouldn't offend anyone too much, and proceeded to rub the block over the surface of the equally cold, nubbly chicken skin with as much generosity as I could muster toward raw poultry. Large clots of yellow stuck here and there on the uneven epidermis, along with some bits of gold foil from the margarine wrapper. Good enough, I thought as I flicked off some of the larger, more conspicuous pieces of foil, time for seasoning. Nothing warms the heart of an inexperienced cook more than a spice rack chock full of multicoloured substances that one can sprinkle and toss with a certain chef-like finesse. I sprinkled and tossed to my heart's content until, inspecting my masterpiece, I discovered that I had liberally covered my poor chicken with cinnamon, garlic powder, and sugar. Quickly, I snapped out of my Julia Child act and remedied my mistake by attempting to wipe off my wrongs with a paper towel. Shreds of tissue now decorated the main course, alongside the already present foil. As dinnertime was nearing, I tried to hurry myself along and ended up dusting the bird with allspice, something that sounded like a good general spice to me, but which I later discovered to be the chief flavouring for

gingerbread and apple and pumpkin pies. Being behind schedule, I didn't bother with any more fancy stuff; I popped the chicken into the oven and cranked the temperature up to 500° to speed up the cooking time.

Finally, it was time to prepare the dessert. A cinch, I said: no problem. Setting   **5** a large pot on the burner, I began to throw in haphazardly whatever the recipe called for: squares of semisweet chocolate, cream, butter, three separated eggs. Separated from what? I wondered; from their shells, I guess. Happy with my conclusion, I continued, smashing the eggs along the rim of the pot, and watching the bright yellow yolks float on top of the chocolate with only a few bits of shell mixing in with them. I stirred the concoction vigorously, but it failed to resemble the light, fluffy delicacy from the glossy picture in the cookbook. Since the recipe said that this dessert was supposed to set awhile before serving, I left it on the stove, assuming it would magically take on the appearance of the cookbook picture by the time I spooned it out. Satisfied with my efforts, I left my dinner roasting and setting while I wandered off to watch *Donahue*.

In the middle of "Bisexual Men and Voodoo Priestesses—Compatible   **6** Marriages?" a crescendo of domestic noise swelled in my ears. The smoke alarm wailed, the oven bell clanged, and the stove crackled and sputtered. Something had gone terribly wrong. Sprinting into the kitchen, I leaped up toward the smoke alarm, waving my arms frantically in an attempt to clear the smoke and shut off the ear-piercing screech. A sharp rap with a broom handle finally silenced that contraption and allowed me to attend to what was left of dinner. The chicken was charred beyond recognition, with the bits of paper towel burning brightly and the foil glinting mockingly at me. The mousse had not transformed itself into a dessert delight that would elicit praise from my family; instead, it had melded itself to the bottom of the pot, hardening to the point where it had become an immovable part of the metal. Even my previously trouble-free salad had succumbed to the disaster surrounding it. Left sitting on the stove, the lettuce had wilted and turned an unsightly brown around its edges. As I stood in the midst of this catastrophe, in came my mother, two aunts, and my grandmother. They shook their heads sadly, and I think I actually saw tears welling up in the eyes of my grandmother. I had failed the initiation; I would never be a traditional female. No one would savour my cookies or ask for second helpings at supper. Somehow, I'd proven myself incomplete.

Suddenly, in the midst of this horrible, laughable affair, it dawned on me   **7** that I didn't really mind. I didn't care. This was not the be-all and end-all; I would be a woman yet. Culinary skills or not, I would amount to something. I would be one of the new breed of women who throw aside tradition to be themselves. My heart lightened. I threw off my baking mitts, untied the apron, tossed them to my grandmother, and yelled, "Call Pizza Pizza."

• • • • Reading Comprehension Questions

1. Which of the following would be the best alternative title for the selection?
   a. Dinner, Denial, and Disaster
   b. Chicken à la Nancy
   c. The Importance of Poisoning Your Family
   d. Cooking Means Caring

2. Which sentence best expresses the main idea of the selection?
    a. Cooking, like caring and cleaning, is seemingly inseparable from the idea of womanhood.
    b. Cooking dinner for the family is a time-honoured coming-of-age ritual for all women.
    c. With the right cookbook, equipment, and ingredients, anyone can prepare a dinner.
    d. Failing at cooking dinner for the author meant failure in the traditional arts of womanhood.

3. The concept of womanhood, according to Nancy Eng,
    a. has changed radically because of a female judge, a female politician, and a female astronaut.
    b. is still narrowed by expectations of nurturing, gentleness, and domesticity.
    c. carries a double burden: workplace success and kitchen miracles.
    d. necessitates the wearing of high heels, lipstick, and an apron.

4. *True or false?* The author messed up the initial preparation of every course in her meal. _____

5. Eng's main problem with preparing the chicken was
    a. not knowing which end to stuff.
    b. not removing the heart, liver, and gizzards prior to stuffing the bird.
    c. leaving foil and paper towel on its skin.
    d. all of the above, and more.

6. The author implies that
    a. she had at least read the recipes before trying to cook dinner.
    b. she had watched female relatives cook enough to know the basics.
    c. she had looked at the cookbook and examined her materials in advance.
    d. she mistook dressing for the event and grabbing a book for cooking.

7. Eng implies that she believed
    a. that the rules and techniques for cooking weren't that important.
    b. that all good women take time for a TV break during meal preparation.
    c. she would never be a real woman.
    d. dinner would somehow be edible, if not praiseworthy.

8. *True or false?* The author implies that her attempt at cooking has been a real life crisis, as well as a rite of passage (paragraph 1) for her. _____

9. The word *enshrouded* in "So, as I entered the kitchen that fateful day of my fifteenth year, armed with *The Joy of Cooking* and enshrouded in a 'Kiss the Cook' apron" (paragraph 1) means
    a. dressed.
    b. disguised.
    c. wrapped up.
    d. trapped.

10. The word *crescendo* in "a crescendo of domestic noise swelled in my ears" (paragraph 6) means
    a. rumblings.
    b. buildup.
    c. shriek.
    d. cacophony.

● ● ● ● **Discussion Questions**

About Content

1. What characteristics of womanhood does Eng list as persisting into modern times? Do you agree with her? Are these innate aspects of all women?

2. Why does the author feel "slightly perverse" (paragraph 3) about what she was doing with the stuffing mix?

3. Do you agree with Nancy Eng that "nothing warms the heart of an inexperienced cook more than a spice rack chock full of multicoloured substances" (paragraph 4)? Why do people feel this way? What's the problem with this feeling?

4. What happened to each of the author's dishes? Why, in each case?

About Structure

5. How does the author link her title with the content of her essay in the opening paragraph? Which sentences support and expand on the meaning of the title? List the number of the sentence, note the appropriate phrase, and briefly explain how each connects to the title.

   Sentence _____ Phrase _____

   Sentence _____ Phrase _____

   Sentence _____ Phrase _____

6. This is a comic version of a process essay. Generally, such essays contain transitional words and phrases to direct and assist the reader in following the process. Do you think that Nancy Eng wants you to follow her process?

   There are, in fact, *two* types of process essays: prescriptive (how-to), and descriptive (telling how by describing). Which type of process essay is "The Importance of Cooking Dinner"? Why?

7. The transitions in this essay are unusually placed. They are more like "time marker" phrases, which indicate the progress of an event or process.

   Where do you find such phrases in paragraphs 2 to 5? What are the phrases, and what do they have in common?

About Style and Tone

8. The chicken is clearly an object for the author to contend with. Which of the rhetorical comic devices listed below does Eng use to make her description in paragraph 3 of her struggles with the bird so funny?

   a. Personification (giving an object human qualities) _____

   b. Alliteration (beginning closely placed words with the same letter)

      _____

   c. Exaggeration _____

   d. Puns or wordplay _____

   List examples of any of these comic devices which you find, and suggest why they are amusing in the context of the essay.

9. For what type of publication (and its reading audience) would such an article be likely to be written? Why?
   a. a feminist magazine
   b. a cookbook or cooking magazine
   c. a general-interest monthly magazine
   d. a sociology text

● ● ● ● **Writing Assignments**

Assignment 1: Writing a Paragraph

There are "rites of passage" for every person: special (although sometimes quite mundane) activities, which, when first performed, have time-marking significance for all of us. These actions or events signal some change or turning point in our lives. Some are gender-specific, such as shaving the face (as opposed to shaving the legs, which would be a female "rite of passage"), and some transcend gender boundaries, such as learning to drive.

Write a paragraph about "the importance of. . . . " Describe a particular "first" coming-of-age ritual which you experienced. Why was it important to you? What was its importance to that stage in your life? Consider the first time you played a game of pool, your first date, the first time you changed the oil or a tire, or some such turning point.

As Eng does, begin with some background information about yourself and the importance of the event. Then describe the stages in the process you went through in your personal "rite of passage." Be sure to use very specific details so that readers may re-experience the event along with you. Conclude with a statement of the significance, or lack thereof, that this "rite" had for you.

Assignment 2: Writing a Paragraph

We have all tried to cook something. Our first attempts may not have been as disastrous as Nancy Eng's; in fact, some of us are natural cooks, and those first scrambled eggs may have been quite edible. Write a paragraph in which you describe your first try at cooking for other people. If your first meal was suitable only for a decent burial, give the causes for the awful results; on the other hand, if you succeeded in not making your family or guests ill, make sure your paragraph tells clearly *why* you managed to cook reasonably well.

Follow the cause-and-effect format on pages 205–208 as you structure your paragraph. Begin with what you achieved; then explain the reasons for the meal that resulted, whether it was good or bad.

Assignment 3: Writing an Essay

Will you, like Nancy Eng, be among the "new breed" of men or women who have left behind the expectations and stereotypes of previous generations? Is this possible, or are certain characteristics innate within each gender? Do we want to disturb all fundamental male and female qualities as we know them?

Write a prescriptive (how-to) process essay about *your* views on "the new man" or "the new woman." Does each really exist? Do you know any examples of either? What elements would make up such creatures? Would there be changes in personality, in behaviour, in appearance? How much do we really want men and women to change, and why?

Here is your chance to play Dr. Frankenstein: Construct a new being. Tell your readers how to become "the new man" or "the new woman" in the traditional "three easy steps." Because this is a direct-advice process essay, address your reader directly as "you." If there are things you would rather not change about the gender in question, say so, but tell the reader how and why he or she should retain an existing quality you value.

Before beginning your outline, review the chapter on process writing (pages 183–194). Decide on your viewpoint first of all. You may take a reverse or comic view, and give instructions on how to become "a traditional gentleman" (which may, in fact, be a new creature) or "a real lady" (perhaps equally mythic). Consider what ingredients may be needed. In either case, list your steps, then group them into logical stages that become your three body paragraphs, and flesh out your instructions with careful details about becoming the "gender-perfect creature." Watch out for potential pitfalls or problems in your stages, and give lots of transitional help. Remember, you may be creating a new being.

THE UNEXPECTED MATZO

Anna Baum

> In this gentle and touching story, Anna Baum reaches back into her memory to relate a significant moment she experienced. This was during World War II, and Baum was living a life of hunger, hard work, and deprivation during one of the coldest winters in memory. Yet, in contrast to this stark scene, Baum's story tells of a heart-warming gesture by members of her extended community, that not only helped her and her family through this dark time, but still resonates with her many years later.

The winter of 'forty-two–'forty-three was the coldest in living memory in war-stricken Europe: farther east, beyond the Ural Mountains, the cold was of extreme

1

severity, and the temperature kept steadily at about minus forty degrees Celsius. The abundant snows buried the long communal dwellings and log cabins almost to the top of their windows, keeping the interior dark but warm and cozy. The streets and narrow lanes seemed devoid of any life except at shift-change time, when tens of thousands of gray-faced, haggard, and bent people, wrapped in everything they could tie around themselves, all at once hurried to their bare rooms and dormitories in complete silence.

2   The Germans, though with considerable difficulty, were still pushing into the Russian hinterland, annihilating everything in their path. As if the cold was not enough, the food rations were unbearably meager and of the poorest quality. There were no trains to bring anything in. Everything was needed for the front, which was understandable enough, but then how was one to survive?

3   We relied on potatoes, which were our main food staple, but after that rainy summer, not much was left, and the potatoes turned black very quickly. Every day Mother boiled a few of them and prayed that they would last a bit longer. For a while we had a substantial supply of dried and pickled mushrooms which Mother had picked in the fall in the *taiga*. Cooked with a few potatoes, they made a nourishing meal. But now our stock was diminishing at a frightening speed, and the future seemed grim, almost hopeless.

4   Mother desperately tried to get some flour instead of a bread ration, or exchange some pieces of clothing we still possessed for a cup of cereal or flour, but neither was possible. Those luxuries could only be obtained on the black market, where the going currency was alcohol or bread.

5   One evening, after school, I had to go back to the office to complete some urgent work. I worked through the night and returned home around nine o'clock the next morning, tired and worn out. Mother, as usual, was busy. I hastily swallowed my potatoes and fell asleep instantly.

6   As if in a dream, I heard a muffled knock at the door, and then somebody coming in. Half asleep, I made out some strange whisperings. I tried to wake up. But suddenly, some half-forgotten words shook me out of my torpor. I woke with a start, in the belief that something of importance was happening, and that I should not miss it.

7   Sitting at the table were two young women. They were simply though decently dressed, and spoke Yiddish: a soft, melodious Yiddish which I had not heard for a very long time; not in this part of the world, anyway. At first I could not make out anything, but gradually everything fell into place.

8   Our guests were two Chassidic women from the vicinity of Ekaterinburg. Their grandparents and parents had been resettled at the end of the last century by the Czar, and, since then, had lived, worked, and practised their religion there. The Chassidic community was, and always had been, a closed one, but counted among its members many highly educated people working in very specialised fields, including the government. They had undergone much suffering during the Civil War. But always, they kept mostly to themselves. Because they were so far removed from any large centre, not many outsiders knew about them, and thus they quietly managed to survive so far, and, God willing, they would continue to do so in the future.

9   I heard the women say that members of their community were aware that there were some Jewish families scattered throughout this vast province, and that

the community would like to let them know that they were not forgotten. They were used to coping with food shortages. Since the outbreak of war, food supplies had been more limited than ever, and that year was a particularly bad one, and they could store up only a minimum of grain and flour. Soon it would be Pesach and they had nevertheless managed, as usual, to bake some matzot, and wanted to share it with the less fortunate.

They asked to be forgiven for having brought so little: they had travelled more   **10** than five hundred miles by train, and had done their best. Everything had to be hidden and be done in secret. One of the women opened her canvas bag and took out a small package of round matzo sewn up in grayish linen: the other took out from her muff a little bag, also sewn up in linen, containing matzo meal.

Mother was searching for words appropriate for the occasion, but the women   **11** would not accept any thanks. Finally, Mother offered some tea, murmuring quietly that she only had "kipiatok," boiling water, but no tea and no sugar. "We know," the women answered, "and you should not be ashamed of it." Asked how they had known about us, they smiled radiantly. "We know about a lot of people, but have to be careful. We visit only one family at a time, and carry only one single package. The name and address? They are in our heads."

We helped them with their coats and embraced three times, Russian style.   **12** "May I know your names?" Mother asked. "Malka and Esphira," said one after the other. "And may you have a healthy and happy Pesach."

● ● ● ● **Reading Comprehension Questions**

1. Which of the following would be the best alternative title for the selection?
   a. Hard Times
   b. The Horrors of War
   c. The Compassionate Guests
   d. Mother Makes Do

2. Which sentence best expresses the main idea of the reading selection?
   a. even during the most desperate times, people can help each other.
   b. young people should not be forced to work through the nights.
   c. nobody is safe during a war.
   d. humans cause each other to suffer.

3. The author suggests that
   a. modern societies will never again face shortages of basic necessities.
   b. the visiting women should have brought more supplies.
   c. her mother should have provided for her family more carefully.
   d. humans can endure much as long as they feel connected to their communities.

4. The author implies that
   a. all Jews had been deported from Russia.
   b. only German Jews lived in great danger.
   c. they lived in a forced-labour camp.
   d. everyone in the community was forced to contribute to the war effort.

5. *True or false?* The main reason the family was suffering was because the mother had not prepared for a harsh winter. _____

6. The two women who visited came to the author's family because
   a. they were lost in a storm.
   b. they knew of the family's straightened circumstances.
   c. they were spies.
   d. they had been displaced and needed a new home.

7. The author implies that
   a. Chassidic Jews lived safely in Russia.
   b. the two young women looked down on the author's family.
   c. people will help others even at great risk to themselves.
   d. Yiddish was her only language.

8. From this story, the audience can infer that
   a. understanding history is unimportant.
   b. the gift of matzo at Pesach still holds great significance to the author.
   c. cultural and religious symbols do not matter during times of starvation.
   d. the family would have been better served if the women had brought a nutritious meal.

9. The phrase *devoid of* in the sentence "The streets and narrow lanes seemed devoid of any life except at shift-change time . . . " (paragraph 1) means
   a. empty of.
   b. full of.
   c. strange with.
   d. limited to.

10. The word *meager* in the phrase "the food rations were unbearably meager" (paragraph 2) means
    a. disgusting.
    b. delicious.
    c. limited.
    d. expensive.

● ● ● ● **Discussion Questions**

About Content

1. According to the information that the author provides, what are at least three reasons for the family's poverty?
2. Why does the author explain is the only source for food during this story? Why does the family not use that source?
3. What Jewish elements does the author use? Does she explain what they mean? Why, or why not?
4. What is the author's role in the events of this story? Why does she present herself this way?

About Structure

5. In which paragraph does Baum switch from setting the scene of the story, to telling the actual events? How does a description of the scene enhance the details that follow?

6. Is the main idea of the story clearly stated? Why has the author chosen this structure?

7. How does the story progress from one idea to the next? Does the author use clear transitional terms to indicate changes in the events?

About Style and Tone

8. How does the author's description of the setting contribute to the tone of the entire story?

9. The setting and subject matter of this story are bleak; however, the message contains some optimism. How do the sombre details of the story compare or contrast to the positive message of the story?

● ● ● ● ● **Writing Assignments**

Assignment 1: Writing a Paragraph

Small acts of kindness can often be as important as large or official actions. Have you ever been a part of, or witnessed, a situation where a simple gesture of kindness has had a profound effect on the recipient? Think of an experience that happened in a limited time and place—over the course of a day, perhaps, and in a setting such as a school, home, or community—and relate that in a paragraph. Identify the importance of the act of kindness in your topic sentence, and provide three supporting reasons for your point. Explain each with adequate details and provide specific examples for each. Conclude with a thought that emphasizes your original point.

Assignment 2: Writing a Paragraph

Anna Baum's story describes the conditions of Eastern Europe in World War II. She shows the depth of the winter, the living conditions, and the deprivation that all of her town, along with the entire region, endured. Her simple but vivid descriptions help her audience to understand not only the events, but also the sombre mood of the times.

Consider a location that is an important element in the description of an activity. For example, the way a hockey arena looks or feels could contribute to the sensations of a paragraph about a hockey game; the physical presence of a school, college, or workplace may help to depict an activity held there.

Write a paragraph about an activity or event with a specific setting. Determine how the setting depicts a sense of the point of your paragraph. Support your point with three reasons that also depend upon the physical description. As you explain and provide details, pay special detail to those elements which help your audience "see" the scene you are describing. Conclude with a sentence that refers your audience, again, to the image you depicted in your topic sentence.

Assignment 3: Writing an Essay

In Anna Baum's story, the act of charity given by the two Chassidic women, serves not so much to improve the family's immediate standard of living, but to reassure the individual members of their connection to the larger community. Yet, has the role of community in twenty-first century Canada shifted beyond such a quaint idea? What does "community" mean, in Canada, and how can people who may be increasingly alienated from the traditional communities in which they were born, still consider themselves connected to others?

Write an essay that defines the concept of "community" and explains how it is or could be maintained in the Canadian context. You may choose a specific initiative with goals toward community development, in which case you should research to find out exactly what and where that initiative is, how it is enacted, and any other pertinent information that your audience should know. It would be most interesting to choose a model that is important to you or to a specific group with known needs. However, to provide information, rather than just personal impression, write the essay in the third-person, objective, point of view. This will encourage your audience to see the merits of your ideas, rather than simply to share your personal experiences.

Identify the particular community you will discuss in your thesis statement. Include three supporting reasons that contribute to your thesis, and explain each of those with information from the research you undertake. Be sure to keep track of the sources you use. Use examples to illustrate how these initiatives function, and analyze how they fit the community you have defined. Conclude by returning to your thesis to remind your audience of the initial point you have made.

THE OLDEST PROFESSION: SHOPPING

Candace Fertile

> Most people think of shopping as a modern activity; after all, where were the malls in the Middle Ages? Candace Fertile maintains that there is nothing current about going out to bring things home. She believes that shopping, in fact, can be traced back to the earliest stages of human behaviour, to our most primitive survival instincts. Is it possible that we are simply imitating the hunting and gathering behaviours of our distant ancestors when we go to the store? Read on and decide for yourself.

1   My shopping career began in earnest when I was seven. My currency was time and deceit. My boutiques were the garbage cans in the alley behind our apartment house in Edmonton.

2   I could not believe that people threw out such wonderful stuff. What a deal—something for nothing. Perhaps like the first-time gambler who wins and is forever hooked on that adrenaline rush, my love of shopping began with that first

magical exposure, on a day when I was wandering home from school, taking my usual route through back alleys. To my extreme delight, I saw peeking out of a galvanized-steel garbage pail what looked like a blue three-ring binder. Acquisition grabbed my seven-year-old soul, and to this day it hasn't let go, fuelled no doubt by relentless advertising and the creation of more and more stuff that announces to the world who we are. Or perhaps who we want to be.

In that alley, my paper-loving self honed in on that blue binder like a cat **3** streaking up from the basement at the sound of a can opener, and I started to understand the power of objects. As a second-grader, I was (unjustly, I thought) required to use despised scribblers. The covers were barely more substantial than the rather nasty paper within them. The booklets had three staples in the middle holding the whole ugly mess together. I hated these scribblers, and I hated their name. And I particularly hated the fact that the teacher would stalk around the room, checking to see if we were properly holding our pencils (another affront— I longed to use a pen). Periodically she would sneak up and grab our yellow HBs to make sure that we were not gripping them too tightly. Her actions made me clutch my pencil as if it were keeping my heart pumping. And the choke-hold I had on my pencil meant that I frequently made holes in the flimsy paper of the scribbler. With grim regularity the teacher and I would get into a tug-of-war over my pencil.

It was after such a dismal war (I always had to lose) that the bright blue **4** plastic corner of the binder caught my eye. I debated for some time about whether or not I was allowed to look in the can, or if taking something from a garbage can was stealing. I should mention: not only was I polite, but I was also Catholic. I knew God was watching my every move, and should I be so vile as to commit a mortal sin, lightning bolts would descend and incinerate my evil little soul, so that all that would be transported to Hell would be something the size of a barbecue briquette. The possibility of owning a binder seemed worth the risk.

I inched closer, then looked up and down the alley to make sure no one was **5** watching me. I carefully removed the lid, which was already precariously perched to one side, and laid it on the ground. A perfect, blue, three-ring binder glowed at me. I was in Heaven. I picked it up and with disbelief discovered an unopened packet of three-hole paper inside. The narrow blue (not even the more babyish wide) lines on the stark white paper with the margins marked with a thin pink line were everything my crummy scribbler wasn't. This paper and binder were for grownups, not little kids.

I could hardly wait to write in my new binder. With a pen. I felt instantly **6** grown-up, more important, more substantial, the tug-of-war over my pencil forgotten. I had gained a new status. And this emotional boost into the stratosphere was accomplished by the simplest of means: I had acquired a new object. And it was free. No drug would ever reproduce the rush I felt as my concept of myself and the world tilted.

On subsequent shopping expeditions down the back alleys I never found **7** anything as great as the binder and paper, but sometimes I found stuff for my little brother. At two, he would play with just about anything. I enjoyed his delight, and finding free stuff meant saving my allowance. I now suspect my kid-sized version of dumpster-diving sparked my career as a bargain shopper.

8   Once I found a scarf—a sophisticated, almost sheer, leopard-spotted scarf. It spoke of glamour, beauty, and fashion, with just an edge of wildness. It was a scarf worn by elegant and capable women on television. It was perfect for my mother, who set off for work each morning with her matching high heels and handbag.

9   Maybe the scarf wasn't even supposed to have been thrown out, but there it was, dangling from a garbage can a few blocks away from home. (In the space of a few weeks, I had increased my territory substantially.) My mother would love this scarf, I thought, but I had no idea how I would explain the acquisition of such a treasure. I didn't have that kind of money. I had finally revealed the binder to her, as it was too difficult trying to write in it without being found out. Even that was hard, as I'd had to commit what I hoped was a venial sin by lying that a friend's older sister had given me the stuff. I knew that wouldn't work again with a scarf. And I still felt a bit singed around the edges from the lie. For a week I had imagined everyone thought I smelled like a campfire. And while I knew what the wrath of God entailed, I was absolutely sure that the wrath of my mother was worse.

10   I decided to come clean. I took the scarf home, and when my mother got home from work, I presented it to her. She was astonished, and then asked where I got it. I told her. To my bafflement, she burst into gales of laughter, nearly hic-cupping herself into a coma while trying to catch her breath.

11   When she regained control, she announced that my garbage-looting days were over. Nice girls didn't do such things. And there could be dangerous things in the garbage. Like what, I wanted to know, but she wouldn't tell me. These events happened decades ago—I'm sure my mother was worried I'd cut myself on a tin can or broken bottle, not get jabbed by some hypodermic needle. Garbage was safer then, but not safe enough for my mother's daughter to play in it.

12   But what sticks indelibly in my mind is that my mother carefully washed and ironed the scarf and wore it faithfully, even proudly, a splash of jungle against her ever-so-fashionable green wool coat with the fur around the sleeves. She would fling one end over her shoulder as she headed out the door in the morning, as if to announce her formidable presence in the universe.

13   Scavenging no longer an option, I had to find another way to satisfy the desire for acquisition now flowing through my veins. Little did I know that I was turning into a good little twentieth-century consumer. According to Lauren Langman, an academic who studies human development:

14   In the contemporary world, the signifying and celebrating edifice of consumer culture has become the shopping mall which exists in [a] pseudo-democratic twilight zone between reality and a commercially produced fantasy world of com-modified goods, images, and leisure activities that gratify transformed desire and provide packaged self-images to a distinctive form of subjectivity. (40)

15   Langman's thesis certainly helps to explain not only the label consciousness of shoppers but also the desire of many shoppers to become apparent walking billboards for name-brand products. How much difference, if any, is there between my girlish desire for white go-go boots and the current stampede to wear T-shirts emblazoned with "Roots" or "Nike"?

I prefer to think the difference is significant. I could be wrong, in which case,   **16**
Langman's argument is unassailable. But another academic offers me some hope.
In an article in *Vogue* titled "The Professor Wore Prada," Elaine Showalter, professor of English at Princeton and recently president of the Modern Language
Association, comments on her love of fashion and shopping. She does so in a
humorous way, defending her intellectualism, femininity, and feminism. As she
says, "For years I have been trying to make the life of the mind coexist with the
day at the mall, and to sneak the *femme* back into feminist" (80). Showalter
delineates the various ways female academics (herself included) have dressed in
an effort to be taken seriously, and ends her essay by saying, "if you want to
deconstruct my feminist criticism, go right ahead. But you'd better not sneer at
my angel backpack or step on my blue suede shoes. I've paid my dues dressing
'feminist,' and now I'm going to wear what I like" (92). Showalter's essay is full
of the pleasure one can gain from shopping, both the activity of looking and
actual purchase. Throughout history and likely before, human beings have been
drawn to objects of beauty (although certainly the concepts of beauty change).

The acquisition of objects, beautiful or otherwise, is usually an economic   **17**
transaction. As a child prevented from plundering garbage bins, I needed a new
way to get the stuff I wanted. So from time and deceit as currency, I turned to
the more usual one: money. Getting that required work. My first job was ironing
for my mother. I had seen a T-shirt in Sears, and my mother refused to buy it
for me because, as she said, "You don't need it." It's no wonder that nowadays
when I buy yet another object I don't need I think of King Lear's "Oh, reason
not the need." The other object that captured my fancy was a particular lava
lamp. I loved that lava lamp, but it was out of the realm of financial possibility.
And my mother was right about the T-shirt. I didn't need it. I wore a uniform
to school, and I had sufficient play clothes. Incessant pestering of my mother
resulted in the ironing agreement. I ironed like a demon, encouraging my belea-
guered mother to change clothes frequently so I could have something to iron.
Eventually I saved enough to buy the T-shirt, and I wore it to shreds. It was the
first thing I bought for myself with my own money, and I remember it in every
detail. Still. It had short white sleeves, a white back, and a front in four coloured
squares of red, yellow, blue, and green. If I had had white go-go boots to match,
life would have achieved its pinnacle. (Elaine Showalter, by the way, wore white
go-go boots to her Ph.D. defence.)

Since those very early days, my shopping has expanded in terms of money,   **18**
objects, and range. Like many middle-class Canadians, I have more material
goods than some small nations, and I am constantly acquiring more. What is
interesting is that none of us needs all these things, but lemming-like we hurl
ourselves at the nearest mall, which has acquired the status of a cathedral for
some. Or else we seek out independent and unique shops in downtowns and
other shopping areas. We go to outlets and discount centres. We are the consumer society of which much has been written. Thorstein Veblen's *The Theory of
the Leisure Class* (1934), Christopher Lasch's *The Culture of Narcissism* (1979),
and Hilary Radner's *Shopping Around: Feminine Culture and the Pursuit of Pleasure* (1995) are just three of the many works written to explore humans' need to
shop even when we are way beyond buying what is necessary for our survival.

Veblen's term "conspicuous consumption" indicates that the purchase of many unnecessary items is a performance. It's interesting to imagine what the performance means. If we examine advertising, which certainly fuels consumer desire, we see that Langman's view of buying an identity is accurate. To wear a certain brand (a "Roots" or "Nike" T-shirt is infinitely more desirable to certain groups than, say, a "K-Mart" T-shirt) or to drive a certain car or to drink a certain beer is presumably a statement of who we are. Or is it?

19   In his essay "The Individual, Consumption Cultures and the Fate of Community," Rob Shields attends to the performative aspect of purchasing and gives consumers some credit: "Many consumers are now ironic, knowing shoppers, conscious of the inequalities of exchange and the arbitrary nature of exchange value. As social actors, they attempt to consume the symbolic values of objects and the mall environment while avoiding the inequalities of exchange" (100). Shields's essay notes that public spaces have changed and that the mall serves as a gathering place. Thus, the activity of shopping (whether or not a purchase is made) plays a significant social role. Shields argues: "It is necessary to recognize that consumption itself is partly determined by the non-rational, cultural element of society. Shopping is not just a functional activity. Consumption has become a communal activity, even a form of solidarity" (110). It appears to me that shopping plays a number of roles, and one of these is certainly a communal one, as Shields argues. But it can also be said that in addition to having a connective importance, shopping—and more specifically the purchased goods—can fulfill people's desires both to join a group and to differentiate themselves from one another. For example, clothing choices are laden with meaning, even if the message is inaccurate.

20   Shoppers, as Shields notes, are becoming more sophisticated and particular, if the growth in thrift stores is any indication. A CBC newscast in July 1998 noted that the thrift store business is so popular that charities depending on donations have to be much more competitive. We are still conspicuously consuming, but we want a bargain. Certain sections of the population have always needed to shop for sale goods, but the practice is now losing any stigma it might have had. In fact, getting a bargain, or a "steal," marks one as a consummate shopper. Getting a deal has become a selling point for much commercial activity. I'd like to mention sales, for example. Anyone in western Canada familiar with Woodward's $1.49 Day will remember the thrust and parry of grabbing for the goodies on this once-a-month sale extravaganza. The deals were often extraordinary, and people didn't want to miss this opportunity. Encountering sharp elbows was common. In contrast, the former frenzy of Bay Day has abated now that the sale lasts for ages and has lost any special air. No need to dive in a scrum for the merchandise. No, it's all there in stacks, and then we stand in line to pay. Infrequent sales events such as Boxing Day sales create line-ups hours before the stores open. The sale must appear to be an unusual event or it garners little excitement. I once worked at Harrods, and the annual sale was marked by the sound of crashing crockery as maniacal shoppers stormed the aisles.

21   But what are we doing when we shop, and why do I refer to it as the oldest profession? The answer is simple. Well, sort of. In *Shopping Around: Feminine Culture and the Pursuit of Pleasure*, Hilary Radner argues the following: "Feminine culture

emphasizes a process of investment and return, of negotiation, in which the given articulation of pleasure is always measured against its costs, the inevitable price of an invitation that is never extended freely, never absolutely, the terms of which change from day to day, from place to place" (178). While the terms and values change, it is surely the case that a shopper considers the relative costs (whether in time, effort, or money) and the benefits of the object gained. And these judgments will differ from person to person even within the same socio-economic group.

Shopping is our contemporary form of hunting and gathering. Men may have **22** hunted, and women may have gathered, but both processes resulted in maintaining life. And if the effort expended exceeded what was gained—the result was death. Such an obvious relationship between acquisition (shopping in a sense) and survival is still evident in the world today. But in rich countries like Canada, hunting and gathering is largely done at the mall, and our survival is not in question. In "Dressed to Kill," Don Gillmor makes fun of men at a clothing sale, and he uses the metaphor of the hunt:

> The big game is on the suit rack, though. Some of the men simply drape a dozen **23** business suits over one arm and then try to find a little room in which to sort and sniff them, like lions defending their kill. But to bring down a threebutton, blue wool crepe 42R Donna Karan (reg. $2,295, now $395) in open country requires keen eyesight, stealth, and a burst of cheetah-like speed. . . . [Men] are taking home cashmere and silk and cotton that feels like whipped butter. They have hunted well and they are filled with the self-knowledge that comes with risk and death and loss and dramatic savings. (75)

Whether the hunting is done in an exclusive boutique or a thrift store, it's **24** the thrill of the chase that drives shoppers. It could be the lure of low prices, or exclusive merchandise, or the media-created buzz about something completely useless like Cabbage Patch Dolls or Beanie Babies that gets everyone out there, roaming, foraging, stalking, pouncing, occasionally even wrestling another shopper for the item.

Then we bag our prize and take it back to our cave, er, home. I bet those **25** cave-people never stopped and said to each other, "Listen, honey, I think we have too many acorns or dried fish or fur blankets." I think they were out there scooping up whatever they thought might come in handy for survival.

And so while many of us shop for a variety of reasons, including pleasure, **26** but rarely need (even grocery stores are full of stuff no one needs to survive; in fact, some of that junk probably shortens lives), perhaps somewhere at the heart of the endeavour is a genetic link to our past, when tracking and locating food was essential for survival. Now different needs drive our shopping expeditions. And survival is perceived in ways beyond the merely physical.

REFERENCES

Gillmor, Don. "Dressed to Kill: What Really Happens When Men Go Hunting for Deep Discounts." *Saturday Night* 113, no. 5 (June 1998): 75.

Langman, Lauren. "Neon Cages: Shopping for Subjectivity." In *Lifestyle Shopping: The Subject of Consumption,* ed. Rob Shields, 40–82. London: Routledge, 1992.

Radner, Hilary. *Shopping Around: Feminine Culture and the Pursuit of Pleasure.* New York: Routledge, 1995.

Shields, Rob. "The Individual, Consumption Cultures and the Fate of Community." In *Lifestyle Shopping: The Subject of Consumption*, ed. Rob Shields, 99–113. London: Routledge, 1992.
Showalter, Elaine. "The Professor Wore Prada." *Vogue*, December 1997: 80, 86, 92.

• • • • Reading Comprehension Questions

1. Which of the following would make the best alternative title for the selection?
   a. Addicted to Acquiring Things
   b. Canadian Consumer Patterns
   c. Shopping and Survival Instincts
   d. Feminism and Fashion

2. Which sentence best expresses the selection's main point?
   a. Shopping is a way of defining who we are and who we dream of being.
   b. Shopping may be a remnant of primitive instinctual drives.
   c. Shopping is a way of showing off, of performing or acting a role.
   d. Shopping is all about the thrill of finding that special item.

3. The author and her grade two teacher were in conflict because
   a. the author tore holes in her notebook.
   b. the teacher terrorized students.
   c. the author would not let go of her pencil.
   d. the author held her pencil too tightly.

4. *True or false?* The author never told her mother how she acquired the blue binder. _____

5. We can conclude that the author's mother
   a. prized the scarf her daughter fished out of the garbage.
   b. was disgusted by her daughter's garbage picking.
   c. thought that taking things from the garbage was a sin.
   d. felt ill at the thought of her daughter picking through garbage.

6. *True or false?* Brand-name and logo-printed clothing and accessories are just "wearable advertising." _____

7. According to Rob Shields, shopping
   a. is an irrational activity.
   b. is an unfair activity.
   c. is a social activity.
   d. is a necessity.

8. We can conclude that the author believes
   a. we shop even though we don't need to do so.
   b. we shop because we hope to find a bargain.
   c. we shop because we are driven to search for things.
   d. all of the above.

9. The word *precariously* in "the lid, which was already precariously perched to one side" (paragraph 5) means
   a. definitely.
   b. uncertainly.

c. wildly.

d. specially.

10. The word *incessant* in "Incessant pestering of my mother resulted in the ironing agreement" (paragraph 17) means

a. rude.

b. noisy.

c. whiny.

d. constant.

● ● ● ● **Discussion Questions**

About Content

1. What were the reasons why the author was so excited about the blue binder that she found?

2. What did the author's garbage picking lead to in adulthood? Does this make sense to you? Why or why not?

3. What two seemingly opposite things does Professor Showalter wish to reconcile within herself, according to the quotation from her article in *Vogue?* Why might it be hard for these opposites to coexist?

4. How did the desire for a particular object change the author's behaviour after she was forbidden to root through garbage cans?

About Structure

5. Where in this selection do you find the clearest statement of the author's thesis? Why, judging by the article's content, do you believe Fertile chose this position?

6. How many paragraphs of "The Oldest Profession: Shopping" use narrative as their main method of development? Which paragraphs are these?

7. Where in this selection does the author refer to her title? Why might she have chosen this particular location to do so? To what does the title refer, and how does Fertile connect this idea to shopping?

About Style and Tone

8. This selection contains, as well as narrative sections, paragraphs with a distinctly scholarly flavour. Which paragraphs demonstrate the author's research into her subject? What stylistic aspects and forms of support used in these paragraphs make their tone different from the narrative sections of the article?

9. Candace Fertile uses figures of speech in this selection. She uses metaphors such as "My currency was time and deceit." What does she mean by this metaphor? She also uses similes such as this one from paragraph 2: "like the first-time gambler who wins and is forever hooked on that adrenaline rush." Find another such simile and explain its meaning.

10. There are many effective descriptive passages in "The Oldest Profession: Shopping." Choose one such passage and explain why it is effective. One aspect of good writing, and of good descriptive writing in particular, is the writer's choice of interesting and appropriate verbs. In this selection, examples are "stalk," "sneak up," and "clutch" in paragraph 3. Find three examples of striking verb use and explain their effect on you as a reader.

● ● ● ● Writing Assignments

Assignment 1: Writing a Paragraph

Childhood memories can be funny or painful, and they may often be tied to a particular object, like the scribbler that Candace Fertile describes. Generally, we learn something from memories that cluster around such objects. Choose an object you remember from childhood and write a descriptive paragraph about it.

Remember that your topic sentence should give some idea of why this object is significant and should also begin the "picture in words" that your paragraph will create of this object. Sample topic sentences could be similar to these:

A grubby one-eared plush bunny that still sits on my dresser takes me back to the day my family arrived in Canada.

A little box containing curly-edged brown pieces of fabric—my Brownie badges—turned out to be a box of bad memories.

Assignment 2: Writing a Paragraph

Do you shop to live or live to shop? Do you even enjoy shopping? Write a third-person paragraph in which you take a definite position on shopping. Such a position stated as a topic sentence could be like one of the following: "Shopping is one of life's great pleasures" or "Shopping is an expensive waste of time."

As well as arguing your position, use a cause or effect method to develop your paragraph. In other words, if you choose to write about the reasons why shopping is such a pleasure, you have chosen to write a "causes" paragraph that looks at what causes shopping to be so pleasant for you. If, on the other hand, you choose to discuss the negative results of shopping, you are writing an "effects" paragraph, one that explains effects only.

Assignment 3: Writing an Essay

Sociologists, psychologists, and advertisers use the concept of "social validation" to describe the persuasive power behind clothing and accessories that display their brand names or logos prominently. Social validation involves people's need to do or wear what they hope will get approval from some chosen group, rather than thinking for themselves.

Look around your classroom. How many people are wearing ball caps with logos; how many T-shirts have a band's name on them; how many hoodies or pairs of sweatpants have designers' names or brands displayed on them? What do all these signatures, these pieces of "free advertising," say about us? From whom are people looking for approval? Whose "world" or fantasy do the logos associate the wearers with?

Choose one such type of apparel, or one such brand name or logo, and write an essay that explains what this type of garment or brand identification says about the wearers—their interests, the ideas they wish to be identified with, and the sort of person they hope to appeal to.

Here is a thesis statement for such an essay: "Phat Pharm and other hip-hop-style clothing say that the wearer dreams of being an urban character, a tough dude of either gender, and very, very edgy."

Photo Credits

Chapter 1
p. 1: Image Source/Getty Images
p. 14: (left) The McGraw-Hill Companies, Inc./Christopher Kerrigan; (middle) Digital Vision/Getty Images; (right) The McGraw-Hill Companies, Inc./Christopher Kerrigan.

Chapter 3
p. 49: Geostock/Getty Images.

Chapter 5
p. 97: BananaStock/PunchStock.

Chapter 9
p. 171: Creatas/PunchStock.

Chapter 10
p. 183: Pando Hall/Getty Images.

Chapter 11
p. 195: Brand X Pictures/PunchStock.

Chapter 12
p. 211: PhotoLink/Getty Images.

Chapter 14
p. 240: Corbis.

Chapter 16
p. 267: Comstock Images/JupiterImages.

Chapter 17
p. 294: The McGraw-Hill Companies, Inc./Christopher Kerrigan, photographer.

Chapter 18
p. 309: Perry Mastrovito/Creatas/PictureQuest.

Index